CH

D0933932

LUCKY
LADY

LUCKY LADY

THE WORLD WAR II HEROICS OF THE
USS *SANTA FE* AND *FRANKLIN*

STEVE JACKSON

CARROLL & GRAF PUBLISHERS
NEW YORK

LUCKY LADY
THE WORLD WAR II HEROICS OF THE USS SANTA FE AND FRANKLIN

Carroll & Graf Publishers
An imprint of Avalon Publishing Group Inc.
161 William Street, 16th Floor
New York, NY 10038

Copyright @ 2003 by Steve Jackson

First Carroll & Graf edition 2003

Library of Congress Cataloging-in-Publication Data is available.

ISBN: 0-7867-1061-6

Printed in the United States of America
Distributed by Publishers Group West

To those who have made the supreme sacrifice
upon this country's altar . . . from Lexington
to Kabul . . . the beaches of Normandy
and of Iwo Jima . . . from the North Atlantic
to the Philippine Sea . . . soldiers, sailors,
Marines, aviators . . . and on September 11, 2001,
firefighters, police officers, flight crews, and
those Americans for whom "Let's Roll" became
a battle cry we will always remember

Contents

The Lock of Hair

March 2000
Colorado Springs, Colorado

T he old box smelled like time. There was nothing particularly special about its appearance though. It was just another one of thousands of brown packing boxes familiar to any Navy brat, even several decades after my childhood. But the heady aroma of old newspapers and letters, of photographs yellowed by age, was intoxicating as I pulled back the flaps and looked inside for the first time.

I was at my parents' home, sitting in my father's office, which is where I always head when I have a few minutes alone in their house. On his desk were photographs of the people he loves—his mother and sister, his children and grandchildren, and most of all, my mother.

The walls are reserved for history. One features black-and-white photographs of the ships he served on during World War II. My favorite shows only the top of the superstructure of the old battleship USS *Mississippi* as she disappeared among the wind-whipped waves that raged around her. The photograph was taken December 10, 1941 as the ship pounded from Iceland toward Norfolk, Virginia, during one of the worst Atlantic storms ever recorded. She was heading for a far worse storm in the Pacific.

The photographs are joined by a colorful, framed document bordered by various sea denizens, real and imagined, certifying that my father, Donald

Clyde Jackson Jr., had been initiated into the "Solemn Mysteries of the Ancient Order of the Deep" and therefore officially graduated from "polly-wog" to "shellback" for crossing the equator in July 1940. It's signed by King Neptune and his scribe, Davy Jones.

Hanging on the wall in one corner is a framed box of bronze-colored medals. The Neutrality Patrol Medal. A medal for the Asiatic-Pacific Campaign. Another for the Philippines Campaign. The Occupation Medal. A Unit Commendation for the officers and crew of the cruiser USS *Santa Fe*. And the Good Conduct Medal, or as he jokes, "the no-discovered-criminal-activities medal." My mother had the display case put together for him as a Christmas present, an indulgence he never would have allowed himself.

No pilgrimage to my father's office would be complete without a pause in front of the gun rack that occupies the largest of the walls. It holds a pot-pourri of weapons, only half of which even work. Of those that do, there's a .22-caliber rifle that was my father's when he was a boy growing up on a farm in Iowa, and a well-used but still capable World War II vintage Japanese rifle with a long, wicked bayonet that my father brought back from the Occupation.

Of my three favorite pieces, the oldest is a muzzle-loading rifle once carried by my great-great-grandfather Jackson, a Civil War veteran with the marvelous first name of Dewilda. The other two are swords. A U.S Navy officer's dress sword with a thin, elegant blade engraved with the images of sea monsters and set in a shiny brass hilt with an ivory handle. It's strictly for show. The other is a Japanese samurai sword, also from the Occupation—the blade a yard long, unadorned, razor-sharp, and created to kill.

On this particular day, my father walked into the room and we got to talking about a vague idea I had for writing a book about his war experiences. He insisted that there wasn't much to tell; like a lot of young men, he was just doing a job that needed to be done. He said he wasn't a hero, though he knew some men who were. But after a bit of cajoling, he opened a closet door and took down a box from a shelf. "This might help," he said.

I began by carefully lifting out various items. Part of what I found I had seen before in some form, such as the typed notes of our family history compiled by my father's mother, Gayle, and sister, Joan. Or I'd heard bits and pieces of some of the stories related to the mementos—of sailing ships and the deaths of children, of terrible Civil War battles, of lost farms and ranches, and of an uncle who had died in France during World War I. But most of what I now saw was new to me.

Letters emerged from the box, the ink having turned brown with time. A young man writing to his parents about the joys of lambing season and his hopes that the railroad would establish a depot near his farm. A rose-colored poster, fragile as a leaf in late autumn, for a farm auction in 1927 offering in fading black letters "a matched team of bay mares" and an "ideal horse for children, wt. 900." Another letter, this one from an eight-year-old boy to his mother that same year telling her about the toy electric motor he had received for Christmas, his anguish hidden in the penciled words because all he had really wanted was his family to be made whole again.

Beneath some of the older papers, I discovered a manila folder containing a collection of stories clipped from newspapers and a magazine in the late spring of 1945. Photographs of a burning aircraft carrier, the USS *Franklin,* jumped from the page. And there, next to the exploding wreck, was my father's ship—the *Santa Fe.*

He had rarely talked about the war, but I'd always been fascinated with my father's naval career. It was practically preordained. My earliest memory is of my father in his dress uniform, going to some official function with my mother at the Norfolk Naval Base when we lived in Virginia. I must have been about five and still recall the thrill of seeing my hero wearing a sword!

Even my earliest memory of my mother, at around the same age, is tied to the Navy. She had called my little sister, Mary, and I into her bedroom to talk and sing—*You are my sunshine, my only sunshine. You make me happy, when skies are gray*—on a small reel-to-reel tape recorder for my father, who was away on "Navy business" in some place called Greenland. I remember the incident mostly because my mother cried and just didn't seem herself—none of us did—until he came home one evening and resumed the ritual of kissing me good night. I had missed the feel of his five o'clock shadow on my cheek and the good, clean, soapy smell of him. I assumed my mother got a kiss as well, because she was happy and singing in the kitchen again that next morning after he got back.

My immersion into the world of the U.S. Navy was augmented in 1962, when I was seven and my father was transferred to Oahu, Hawaii. Of course, we went with him, and I spent the next few years growing up in naval officers' housing on the shores of Pearl Harbor. Every day when I left the house for school or to play, all I had to do was look up to see the gleaming white memorial that stood over the sunken battleship *Arizona* across the channel next to Ford Island.

Most days my best friend, Arthur MacElwee, whose father was a submariner and gone for months at a time, and I bravely fended off the banzai attacks of "the Japs" on the playground built next to those haunted waters. In that neighborhood, we were Navy and Marine kids fighting our fathers' war, recklessly remaining at our guns on the teeter-totter as the Kamikazes came blazing down from out of the sun. We died a million deaths, though of course our line held and our comrades were saved, and we rose at the sound of the dinner bell and thus lived to fight another day.

I liked visiting the *Arizona* memorial whenever visitors arrived from "the mainland." There I would make my way to the far end of the memorial to the wall where the names of the men from the ship who died that Sunday morning were listed in bronze letters on the snowy marble. My eyes would go down the names until I located one in particular, Robert E. Jackson, my father's cousin. It made December 7, 1941, somehow more personal.

As a boy in my father's office, I would pore over the tall blue books that were the war journals for the *Mississippi* and the *Santa Fe,* paying particular attention to the latter, as my father served on her the longest. She was known as the Lucky Lady, which seemed heroic. I was enthralled with the photographs and stories about ships at war: Images of planes racing in over the wave tops, small flames erupting from the machine guns in the wings, larger flames growing from their bellies; ships firing big guns and maneuvering wildly to escape torpedoes and suicidal pilots, ships in flames, ships at the mercy of terrible winds and waves; bodies beneath American flags, ready to be committed to the deep; the skeleton of a ruined Japanese city— Nagasaki.

The *Santa Fe* journal contained several pages about the *Franklin* epic, with excerpts from various newspaper and magazine accounts about what happened on March 19, 1945. Now, looking through the box, I found a copy of a *Collier's* magazine story under the title "Chaplain Courageous," as well as a half dozen clippings from the newspaper accounts about "The Carrier That Refused to Die!"

Fifty miles off the coast of Japan, Task Force 58 was launching an air assault against Shikoku and Kyushu when a Jap bomber dropped out of the low overcast, rocketed in over the bow of the 27,000-ton carrier *Franklin* ("Big Ben") and swept the length of her flight deck. From the Jap's belly two 500-lb. bombs plummeted down . . .

—*Time* Magazine, 5-8-45

No other ship in American history ever survived a like ordeal . . .
—United Press International

In that hell on water, big girders twisted like taffy and melted steel ran like ice cream in the sun. . . . Detonated rockets swept the blazing deck at waist level. . . .

—N.Y. *Herald Tribune*

The cruiser *Santa Fe,* Captain H.C. Fitz, USN, commanding, came up on the starboard side. "Are your magazines flooded?" he flashed. He was thinking of the disaster that overtook the *Santa Fe's* sister ship, *Birmingham,* last fall when she was taking survivors off the stricken *Princeton.* . . .

—*Collier's* Magazine, 6-23-45

I was about to replace the folder when I saw a small, clear plastic envelope lying on the bottom of the box. It contained a circlet of hair about as thick as a finger and the color of clover honey. A luck charm, but what it was doing in the box with a collection of war clippings and family histories was a mystery.

My father returned to the room as I contemplated the possibilities. "What's this doing in here?" I asked, holding up the hair. What follows is the answer.

A Terrible Resolve

July 1853
Edo Bay, Japan
USS Susequehanna

Immaculate in a starched white uniform, Commodore Matthew C. Perry strode from his ship down the gangplank and onto the landing barge as the thirteen big guns on the steam frigate USS *Susquehanna* roared to announce his coming. Near at hand another, even larger steam frigate, the USS *Mississippi,* the most powerful dreadnought in the U.S. fleet, and the sailing sloop USS *Saratoga* stood at ready should the Japanese prove treacherous.

Nearly a week earlier, the Japanese warlord who commanded the local military garrison and his samurai were shocked when the barbarians sailed into the forbidden waters of the Kingdom of Japan with a small but impressive-looking squadron of black-painted warships.

In the thirteenth century, Japanese warriors had repulsed an invasion by a vastly superior Mongol army and navy with the help of two fortuitous storms, or *tai-fun.* The invasions had instilled in the Japanese a sense of nation and of racial pride, as well as a desire to keep themselves isolated from the outside world. When the Europeans found the islands in the 1500s, there had been a period that trading was allowed. But in 1639, the Japanese government, dominated by the warrior class, which feared Western ideas might usurp their authority, closed the country to foreigners "under penalty of death." The only trading allowed was through a small port on the southern end of Kyushu Island called Nagasaki.

The isolation lasted nearly 250 years. Then the black ships appeared on the blue waters of the Pacific. The steam frigates—each one many times larger than the biggest Japanese galley and made of steel, not wood—belched huge clouds of dark smoke as their paddlewheels churned, moving them into the mouth of the bay. The Japanese battlements were well within range of the ships' artillery, but the ships were out of reach of the small cannons on shore.

When the Japanese asked his purpose, Commodore Perry, who commanded the U.S. naval forces in the Pacific, said he was there to hand over "a letter of friendship" from the president of the United States and meant for the emperor's eyes only. The warlord demanded that he sail to Nagasaki like any other foreigner.

A large, forceful man in his fifties, and said to lack any sense of humor, Perry was known as an officer willing to mix diplomacy and military action to achieve his ends. He believed that to protect the United States, the Navy needed to establish bases throughout the Pacific. His arguments had been instrumental in the subsequent establishment of bases on Wake Island and the Midway atoll, halfway across the Pacific to the Orient, as well as at Pearl Harbor on Oahu, one of the finest natural harbors in the world.

A year before sailing to Japan, Perry had warned President Millard Fillmore that the British, who controlled Hong Kong and Singapore, would soon have a monopoly on all trade in the area. He urged that the Navy "take active measures to secure a number of ports of refuge" in Japan, and thus his mission was born.

In preparation, Perry had studied what literature he could locate regarding the Japanese. The press of the day had labeled them "barbaric" and "the least interesting people in the world." But he knew that the Japanese possessed an ancient and complex culture and that they currently lived in a rigidly structured feudal system controlled by warlords and their vassals' samurai class. He knew that those in charge would respect power and little else.

However, he also told the president that he hoped to achieve his goals through diplomacy rather than force. "I believe that if treated with strict justice and gentle kindness," he said, "the Japanese will learn to consider us their friends."

Now, when informed of the Japanese demand that he leave, Perry sent the captain of the *Susquehanna* with his reply. "The commodore will not go to Nagasaki," the captain said. "If this friendly letter of the president to the emperor is not received and duly replied to, he will consider his country insulted and will not hold himself accountable for the consequences."

A compromise was reached and a prince of the royal house was sent to receive the letter. On the day of the meeting, the Japanese went to great lengths to impress the foreigners, but made it clear that for all the pretty pennants, pomp, and ceremony, they were not pleased. As a show of their own military might, they had arrayed an army of more than five thousand infantry, archers, and calvary—including the samurai, with their wicked long swords—around the ceremonial tents.

In answer, Perry selected some two hundred U.S. Marines and another hundred sailors, as well as the ships' bands from both frigates, to accompany him. He ordered the men and their officers to wear their dress uniforms. His entourage was sent ahead on landing barges as the bands played merry tunes as though the whole affair were a lark. When the barges were halfway to shore, the *Susquehanna's* guns boomed like a sudden thunderclap, frightening the horses on shore and certainly getting the attention of the samurai.

The whole meeting lasted less than a half hour. Perry presented the letter from President Fillmore to the emperor asking for three concessions: a coaling station for United States ships; a commercial treaty permitting free trade; and "friendship." If the Japanese did not agree, the letter warned, the commodore before them would feel compelled to call upon the military might of the United States.

When Perry returned in February 1854 for an answer, he was pleased to learn that the emperor had granted his demands. The Japanese had hoped that the gods would intercede, perhaps send their divine winds to blow the barbarians and their black ships into the depths of the ocean. But the seas had remained quiet. So rather than confront the barbarians, the Japanese warlords decided it was better to wait, learn, and remember the humiliation when the time was right.

Instead of the winds of war, Perry's visit brought the winds of change to Japanese society. Western merchandise, language, religion, food, and culture entered the country. And of major significance for the events of the next century, Japan's best and brightest were sent out into the world to learn about Western technology and science, with special attention paid to military advances.

December 8, 1941
Tokyo Bay, Japan
Imperial Japanese Battleship Nagato

Short and barrel-chested, Admiral Isoroku Yamamoto was not an imposing man physically until one drew close and felt his intensity and confidence. Yet, now he fretted while all those around him rejoiced.

True, the great enterprise, his masterpiece, was a success. That morning, the planes from the six huge aircraft carriers of the First Air Fleet had attacked Pearl Harbor in the Hawaiian Islands, where because of the international dateline it was December 7, and delivered a devastating blow to the U.S. Pacific Fleet. What's more, the reports from the attacks against the Philippines, Guam, Malaysia, and the Dutch East Indies were just as encouraging. But not all of the news was good.

Vice Admiral Chuichi Nagumo, the fleet's commander, had not sent a third wave of planes to destroy the American fuel oil depots nor the ship repair facilities on Oahu. The former would have severely hampered the surviving American fleet's ability to wage an aggressive counterattack; the latter would have prevented a quick recovery from the damage inflicted.

Worse, Yamamoto's spies in Hawaii, who had provided such valuable information leading up to the attack, had failed to note that the American aircraft carriers were out to sea and thus escaped the devastation. In fact, it was Nagumo's concern over the whereabouts of the American carriers and their potential threat to his fleet that caused him to withdraw before finishing the job.

Still, the Imperial Japanese Navy had done what it had to do to protect the empire from the arrogant military of the United States and its European allies. In July 1937 the Japanese Army had invaded China from Manchuria, which they had seized for its natural resources they so desperately needed for expansion. But Japanese empire building had bogged down.

After three years of vicious fighting, Chinese General Chiang Kai-shek and his ragtag army had proved to be more difficult to defeat than anticipated, taking advantage of the vast reaches of their homeland to hide and stretch Japanese resources. Along with China, the Japanese admirals and generals coveted the resource-rich European colonies in Southeast Asia and Indonesia for their raw materials, especially oil with which to make gasoline and aviation fuel.

Only the United States presented a real obstacle to their plans. It was hoped that through negotiations the Americans could be persuaded not to interfere with Japan's goals. If not, the war planners knew that for the Southern Operation to be successful, the army and navy would have to accomplish three objectives in a very short amount of time. They would have to take Singapore and its enormous naval base from the British; wrest the Philippines from the Americans to deny them a staging area for a counterattack, as well as a base to interdict the sea routes between Japan and Southeast Asia; and destroy the U.S. Pacific Fleet and its oil reserves at Pearl Harbor.

Isoroku Yamamoto, who had assumed command of Japan's combined fleet in August 1939, was given the task of preparing for war with the United States. He did so reluctantly after arguing against attacking the Americans. The admiral had a deep respect for the potential industrial might of the United States. He knew that if the Americans chose to fight a protracted war, Japan would eventually be overwhelmed by the enemy's superior numbers and resources.

He also held an opinion of Americans as a people not shared by many of his contemporaries. Others within the Imperial High Command saw Americans as "soft" and attached to their creature comforts. But Yamamoto knew better. He had studied English at Harvard in the 1920s and served as a naval attaché in Washington; he knew that the Americans, while isolationist and only just starting to emerge from a devastating depression and drought, could be quite warlike if provoked.

His own people were wrapped up in their mythology of the samurai and the code of Bushido—the way of war—and a belief in divine protection, much of it dating back to the Mongol invasions of the thirteenth century. But the Americans had their own myths through which they saw themselves.

The Americans had Lexington and Concord and the "shot heard 'round the world." They remembered the Alamo. And the waves of men in blue and gray marching recklessly into the cannons on the battlefields of Bull Run and Gettysburg. In World War I, they took pride in the "Last Battalion," whose refusal to surrender—so like Japanese samurai—in a nearly suicidal situation so unnerved the German generals that they had retreated and left the ground to the "insane Americans." Having never lost a war, the Americans didn't believe that they ever could, and the admiral knew that made for a dangerous enemy.

Yamamoto wasn't the only senior officer who argued against attacking the United States, most of the dissenters having also lived and studied abroad and therefore not as swayed by misconceptions about the West. Among them was Vice Admiral Takijiro Onishi, who warned that attacking Pearl Harbor would make the Americans so "insanely mad" they would fight until they were dead or Japan did not exist.

Even Emperor Hirohito—a revered symbol of the nation, but little consulted by the military leaders who ran the country in his name—warned that the "boundless" Pacific would prove as difficult for the navy to control as the vastness of China had proved for the army. But his warning went unheeded.

Driven by a fierce nationalism and convinced of their racial and moral superiority, most of the Japanese high command believed that the Americans wouldn't have the intestinal fortitude for the killing and dying it would take to stop Japan. They had reason to believe they were right. The people of the United States were already publicly opposed to getting involved in what they considered another "European war," let alone a war in the Pacific.

In the end Yamamoto gave up his arguments. He was the descendant of an old samurai family and believed it was Japan's destiny and right to rule Asia. So when he was ordered to formulate a strategy to take the Americans out of the fight, he had done his work with consummate skill. The best hope was for a first-round knockout blow that would force them into a treaty acceding to Japan's expansion in the Pacific.

By mid-1941 events were moving toward an inevitable conclusion. In July 1941 the Japanese sent troops into Indochina. The United States, Great Britain, and the Netherlands responded by imposing an embargo on oil, steel, rubber, and other raw materials to the Japanese, hoping to stall the war effort.

In September the Imperial High Command decided that if a political reversal of the embargo could not be achieved by October, Yamamoto's plan would be set in irretrievable motion. Talks with Washington went nowhere; the Americans were not going to get out of the way. On November 26, 1941, Yamamoto ordered Nagumo to sail with the fleet from the Kurile Islands off northern Japan toward Hawaii.

The Americans had made it almost too easy. They knew that the Japanese consulate in Hawaii was filled with intelligence officers, but because of rights granted under the U.S. Constitution, even to foreigners, spies were free to travel about the islands and gather information on the movement and position of the U.S. fleet.

Just before 6:00 A.M. on December 7 in the eastern Pacific, Nagumo turned the task force into the wind so that the carriers could launch their planes. Wearing headbands emblazoned with the word Hissho, "certain victory," the pilots of the 183 planes of the first wave took off. A second wave of 170 planes took off an hour later. When the first wave arrived a little before 8:00 A.M., they found the U.S. fleet just waking up to a lazy Sunday morning in paradise. It should not have been so easy; for more than a year, right up to twenty minutes before the first plane attacked, there had been warning signs.

But by the time the last Japanese plane left at about 10:00 A.M., eighteen U.S. ships, including eight battleships, had been sunk or severely damaged. About three hundred aircraft had been destroyed or disabled, most of them on the ground. More than 1,100 men were wounded, and 2,400 died— 1,103 of them on the battleship *Arizona,* which erupted and immediately sank after an armor-piercing naval shell dropped from a bomber punched through to the ship's Number Two fourteen-inch gun turret's forward powder magazine.

When word arrived of the incredible victory, Yamamoto was beseiged with congratulations and adulation. Yet, he feared that with the aircraft carriers unaccounted for, the victory ultimately meant defeat. The Americans were staggered but still on their feet. He knew they would react emotionally to what they would consider base treachery. That evening Yamamoto's celebrating subordinates were dumbfounded when he told them, "We have awakened a sleeping giant and have instilled in him a terrible resolve."

LUCKY
LADY

PART I

USS *Santa Fe*

Philadelphia to the Marianas

November 1942–June 1944

CHAPTER ONE

Survivors:
Unfinished Business

December 7, 1941
USS California

S eaman 2nd Class Hardy stood in formation on the port side of the battleship USS *California* waiting for the bugler to blow colors at the raising of the flag. The day was already warm, which just didn't seem natural for December, but this was Hawaii, not frozen Ohio with the bitter winds blowing in off Lake Erie.

A tall, raw-boned steel-mill work's kid from Ohio, his parents had immigrated to the United States from Austria as children with their families in the 1890's. He had spent his whole life on a small farm about thirty miles south of Cleveland until he joined the Navy in 1940. His father and brother worked in the steel mills, but he had grown up walking behind a plow.

The family home lacked electricity and running water, and his mother still cooked on a wood-burning stove, but they did pretty well for themselves when he was a child. Then the Depression came along and his father was lucky to get one day of work per week at the mill.

Hardy quit school after the eleventh-grade, but he didn't want to work in a mill or on a farm, even if he could have found a job that paid. Then a cousin who had recently joined the Navy stopped by one day to show off his uniform. *I want one of those,* Hardy told himself. He also hoped to find a little more adventure than, as he liked to say, "using the ass-end of a horse for a compass." So he pestered his mom into signing the "underage papers" that allowed him to join the Navy on his seventeenth birthday in November 1940.

On a Sunday morning a little more than a year later, he gazed aft at the double line of massive gray battleships tied up side-by-side behind the *California,* a hundred feet off Ford Island, the bit of land that separated the east and west entrances to the harbor. The sight never ceased to amaze him.

Battleship Row they called it, the pride and power of the U.S. Pacific Fleet. He could see the *Oklahoma,* which was right behind the *California,* as well as the *Nevada, Pennsylvania, West Virginia, Maryland, Tennessee* and, at the end of the line, the *Arizona.* Of the four other battleships normally assigned to the U.S. Pacific fleet, the *Colorado* was on the West Coast, but the *Mississippi, Idaho,* and *New Mexico* had been split from the fleet that past spring and sent to the Atlantic to guard convoys.

Except for the somewhat smaller *Oklahoma* and *Nevada,* the battlewagons, as they were known in the fleet, were about 620 feet long, the length of two city blocks, and displaced about thirty-two thousand tons, which wasn't their actual weight but rather the tonnage of water their hulls shoved aside. Built for power, their top, or flank, speed was a modest twenty-one knots, or about twenty-five miles an hour. However, their sixteen- and fourteen-inch big guns could hurl a ton of steel twenty miles and hit a moving ship.

Hardy had no real plans for the day. He didn't like going into Honolulu— nothing much there except expensive restaurants, a few hot and airless movie theaters, smoky bars, and tawdry whorehouses. To be honest, Navy life was more boring than he had anticipated. It was all routine: two weeks at sea running through gunnery practice and other drills, then two weeks back in port, where as a "deckhand" his on-duty hours were spent scrubbing the deck, polishing brass, chipping off old paint, and applying new coats of primer in the never-ending battle against the corrosive effects of seawater.

December 7, 1941, was just another day in "paradise." A few more minutes and the bugle would blow, the band would play "The Star-Spangled Banner," the crew would salute, the Marine color guard would raise the flag, and that would be the end of it. But then Boatswain's Mate 2nd Class Biff Bailey, the fleet boxing champion and pride of the *California,* took a second look at the dark specks that were streaming down toward the harbor from the north and the west and grabbed his bosun's pipe. He blew the signal for "All hands seek shelter!" A moment later, the bugler began sounding General Quarters and the crew scrambled for their battle stations.

Hardy ran, still not comprehending, wondering if this was another drill. But then the world began exploding around him. Guns boomed and barked. Bullets whined, twanged off metal, and thunked into wood and bodies. Bomb concussions slapped the morning air, tossing men and machinery as though they were made of paper. Sailors and officers yelled and cursed and screamed, some cried—after all, most of them were just boys, who up to that morning had only played at war.

Hardy got to his battle station inside Gun Turret #2, which housed two of the big fourteen-inch guns that could heave a two-thousand-pound projectile twenty miles. *Who in the hell would attack us?* he thought as he scrambled down a ladder.

For two hours, he sweated through the attack, feeling helpless with the guns above him of no use against airplanes. Then word came to abandon ship. He climbed back to the main, or weather, deck. The attackers were gone, and the view had changed.

The *Oklahoma* had capsized; only the bottom of her hull showed above the water. Black smoke billowed out of the other ships, especially the *Arizona,* darkening the sky until it was difficult to remember that it was blue up there. Fuel oil burned on top of the water, which was littered with bodies and men struggling toward shore.

The *California* had settled into the mud of the harbor until its weather deck was barely out of the water. But they couldn't abandon ship, because she was surrounded by flames. The ship had also begun to list toward the port side and into deeper waters. Afraid that she would capsize, trapping any men still inside, the crew fought to secure her to the mooring block on the starboard side with whatever ropes and cables they could get their hands on.

While all this was going on, Hardy decided to try to get to the compartment where he slept. His parents had sent him a new Bulova watch, and he wanted to retrieve it from his locker before leaving the ship. Using a lantern for light, he reached the hatch leading down into the compartment and looked in but went no further. The room was filled with water, but what stopped him was the sight of a body, charred beyond recognition, lying on Hardy's bunk. His stomach heaving, he turned and went topside, leaving his watch to the dead.

Fortunately, a breeze came up after about an hour and blew most of the fire on the water toward the stern. When he got the chance, Hardy jumped off near the bow. He came up gagging on the bitter, syrupy fuel oil he had swallowed and swam to Ford Island.

The next day, an officer picked him and several other men for "special duty." They boarded a motor launch and began to slowly cruise around the ruined hulks of Battleship Row, recovering bodies and body parts for burial.

The grim task went on for three days. Some of the other men talked about finding a way to get out of the work, but Hardy shrugged and said, "Go ahead, I'm staying." At least a hundred men were missing and presumed dead from the *California* alone, and he had heard it had been much worse for the crew of the *Arizona*. He would do what he could to see that they received a proper burial; then he hoped he would get a crack at the bastards who had killed them.

Seven days after the attack, Hardy had been assigned to his second ship when a fleet of cruisers and destroyers sailed into Pearl Harbor. The survivors were assembled in a field, where they were told by an officer that the ships needed volunteers to double their peacetime complements to a war footing.

Hardy was standing next to an old salt off the *California* named Hank James, who claimed to be a relative of the famous outlaw Jesse James. "What ship would you pick?" Hardy asked, though James appeared to be in no hurry to volunteer himself.

"Well," James said, giving the matter his deepest consideration, "I once served on the *Astoria,* and she was a hell of a feeder." So on the basis of his teen-aged stomach, Hardy signed up for the *Astoria,* a heavy cruiser commissioned in 1934.

The survivors of Pearl Harbor were scattered throughout the Pacific Fleet, including the new ships that began arriving on what seemed a daily basis. They supplied experience to otherwise green crews—and were a sort of group memory of a peaceful Sunday morning when they were attacked without warning.

As the fleet expanded, the men already in the Navy also received promotions faster than they would have during peacetime. Hardy had been promoted to Seaman 1st Class soon after arriving on the *Astoria*. The next few months, he rarely set foot on land. The cruisers and destroyers combined into task forces with carriers *Enterprise, Lexington,* and *Saratoga*—as well as the *Yorktown* when she returned from the Atlantic with the remaining battleships—on a series of hit-and-run attacks against Japanese-held islands. They would show up at a palm-tree-covered bit of sand and coral at dawn, shell and bomb "the holy hell" out of the "the Japs," as they were now known, for an hour or so, then take off on a high-speed run to arrive at dawn off some other island to shell.

On the *Astoria,* Hardy was assigned to a new battle station, a 1.1-inch antiaircraft gun mount above the bridge. The new position suited him fine. Instead of being enclosed in a turret, the mount was surrounded by a waist-high wall of steel, but otherwise he was out in the open where he could see what was going on.

The gun crews worked as a team. A pointer sat in one seat to raise the four barrels up and down; the trainer sat on the other side and swiveled the guns left and right. Hardy and three other "loaders" stood at the back of the gun; two to place the clips—with four shells to each—in the gun and remove the empties, and two to hand them loaded clips. Behind the mount was a "clip house," where more sailors loaded shells into empty clips.

The gun crew worked with the lookouts and spotters to locate the enemy. When the pointer had the target in his sights, he pulled the trigger and the guns would shoot, each set of twin barrels alternating. The men called the guns, "pom-poms" for the pom-pom-pom sound they made, and the trick was for the loaders to keep the guns supplied so that there would be no break in the rhythm.

Hardy was looking forward to a chance to shoot at those planes with the red dots under their wings. He had a few friends to avenge.

The "surprise" element of the attack on Pearl Harbor might have been a blessing in disguise for the United States. As Admiral Chester A. Nimitz, selected by Roosevelt to assume command of the U.S. Pacific Fleet after the attack, would note in his memoirs, too much of a warning would have been an even greater disaster.

"No one regrets more than I our 3,000 dead," he wrote. "But if Admiral Husband Kimmel ... had had information of the attack 24 hours in advance, he would have sent off all of our forces to meet the Japanese. We had not one aircraft carrier capable of opposing Admiral Nagumo's aircraft carrier formation, and the Japanese would have sunk all our ships on the High Seas. We would have lost 6,000 men and almost all our Pacific Fleet." Instead, within a few weeks, the American aircraft carriers and their escorts of more than twenty cruisers and sixty-five destroyers were carrying out hit-and-run attacks on Japanese installations throughout the Pacific.

Still, every day seemed to bring a new disaster for the Allies. Guam, Wake, Singapore, and Hong Kong fell. The U.S. Army under General Douglas MacArthur, who had squandered nearly eight hours after being told of the attack on Pearl Harbor, was being pushed onto a single peninsula, Bataan, and the island fortress of Corregidor and would be forced to surrender that spring. The Allied navies were nearly wiped out, learning over and over again the hard way that warships could no longer venture out without air cover.

The savage ending of the Battle of the Java Sea helped set the tone for the future of naval warfare in the Pacific. After surviving several encounters in late February 1942, Japanese planes and surface ships finally caught up to the USS *Houston,* a heavy cruiser, in early March. Dead in the water after four torpedo hits, out of ammunition and on fire, the ship was at the mercy of the Japanese. But they had formed a semicircle around her, bathing the smoking ruin and frightened crew with spotlights, then blasted away from point-blank range until the ship went under. Of her 1,068-man crew, only 368 men survived to be captured. The fighting had been no-holds-barred ever after.

The damage done by American carriers and their escorts of cruisers and destroyers was minimal. However, the raids had convinced Yamamoto that to win the war, he had to lure the U.S. fleet into a final "decisive battle." In April 1942 he and his staff came up with another plan to lure the Americans into that battle. This time he wanted to attack the Midway atoll (a group of coral islands surrounding a common lagoon) while sending a diversionary force to invade the Aleutian Islands of Alaska. He told his superiors in the Imperial High Command that the idea was to gain control of a forward airbase between Japan and Hawaii, and conversely, to prevent Midway from being used by the Americans to stage an attack on Japan. The capture of the atoll would also be necessary if they wanted to consider a further suggestion to invade Hawaii and possibly an attack against the West Coast of the United States. His plan was rejected.

Then Lt. Col. James Doolittle and fifteen other B-25 bomber pilots and their crews secretly crossed the Pacific to within seven hundred miles of Japan aboard the USS *Hornet,* a daring sortie with planes that had not been designed to fly from carriers. The Doolittle raid on Tokyo and several other sites caused little damage, except to the Japanese psyche. The population had been told by their leaders that Japan could never be attacked. Now, panicking along with the civilian population, those leaders quickly gave their blessing to Yamamoto's plan to finish off the U.S. fleet.

First, however, the Japanese war planners went forward with another part of their overall plan—to take Port Moresby in New Guinea as a staging area to attack Australia. In early May, a Japanese fleet of three aircraft carriers and their escorts sailed into the Coral Sea. They were met there by an American task force that included the American carriers *Yorktown* and *Lexington,* as well as their protective screen of cruisers and destroyers.

During the Battle of the Coral Sea, the *Astoria,* two more cruisers, and four destroyers were responsible for protecting the big fleet carrier *Yorktown.* Other ships guarded the *Lexington,* a former battlecruiser converted into an aircraft carrier.

Patrolling the sea, waiting for the Japanese to show up, it seemed to Hardy that his gun crew was never off watch. And so much for the *Astoria* being a hell of a feeder—they had been at sea for 102 days without seeing a supply ship, and the men had been cut to half rations as the ship ran low on food. He and the rest of the crew even slept at the guns, curled up on the deck as best they could, thankful that the nights in that part of the world were warm.

The first day of the battle, May 6, actually passed without Hardy knowing it. No one announced that American planes had found and sunk a small, or "light," carrier and a destroyer. Or that the Japanese had tried to retaliate but couldn't find the American task force, which hid in the rainsqualls that swept across the sea.

The next day, each side found the other about mid-morning. So calm that he might have been announcing he was crossing a street, Lt. Cmdr. Joe Taylor, commander of the *Yorktown* torpedo squadron, told his counterpart in the dive-bomber squadron, Lt. Cmdr. William Burch, that he was initiating the attack on a large Japanese carrier. "Okay, Bill, I'm starting in."

About the same time, task force radar operators reported enemy planes sixty miles out, flying high—"Val" dive-bombers, coming fast. On the *Astoria,* Hardy felt his stomach knot with fear. The hit-and-run attacks on the islands had provided little opportunity for Hardy to shoot at Japanese planes, as the *Santa Fe* was usually gone before the enemy arrived. But that changed with the Battle of the Coral Sea. It got worse when radar picked up a second group of planes even closer to the task force. Because the radar beam traveled up at an angle from the ship, it had not at first picked up the "Kate" torpedo bombers flying low over the waves at 250 miles an hour. He wondered how they were going to know whether to look up for dive-bombers or down near the water for the torpedo planes. *And how are we going to stop them either way?*

The Kates arrived first, ignoring the other ships and the American fighters who tried to intercept them as they fanned out to attack the *Yorktown.* The ships' guns began firing. First the five-inch. Then the one-point-ones. Despite his fear, Hardy reacted as he had been trained, and soon he was so busy he forgot to be afraid.

Still, shooting at a speeding airplane from a moving ship was like shooting at an angry bee from a roller coaster. The cruiser turned wildly, heeling around corners like a speedboat, first one way and then another, trying to stay in position to screen the *Yorktown* as the carrier desperately maneuvered to dodge torpedoes. All the gun crews could do was keep pouring steel into the sky in the right direction and hope the attackers ran into it.

The noise was deafening, and smoke from the guns enveloped the ship despite running at flank speed. The tension was so high and the men on the guns so focused that they would continue to blast away at the smoking remains that marked the spot of a downed plane, the shells churning the water white. As planes passed between ships, the gun crews even found themselves shooting at each other, but willing to risk the friendly fire to stop the enemy.

The insanity jumped a couple of notches when the dive-bombers showed up a few minutes later, hurtling down out of the sun to blind the ships' gunners. The crews shot anyway, as fast as the guns could be brought to bear and the loaders could tear out the empties and ram a full clip into place. Planes burst into flames and spiraled into the sea, but the boys on the guns and in the fighters could not stop them all.

Bombs rained down around the frantic *Yorktown*. One near miss lifted the carrier's stern so far out of the water when it exploded that Hardy saw the ship's propellers before it splashed back down. Then a bomb pierced the flight deck and continued on down into the depths of the ship before exploding. Smoke billowed from her flight and hangar decks.

At last, all the enemy planes were knocked down or had turned back for their own carriers. Caught up in the moment, some of the gun crews on the screening ships continued to shoot at the retreating specks, even after they were out of range and the order to cease fire had been given and repeated.

The *Yorktown* was crippled, but she was still moving, her battle flags and the Stars and Stripes whipping in the breeze. The *Lexington* was not as fortunate. Several miles away from the *Astoria*, a huge column of black smoke rose from the stricken carrier.

She looked to Hardy like she was burning from bow to stern. He knew she was finished.

The *Astoria* wasn't around to witness the moment. She and her crew were already escorting the battered *Yorktown* back to Pearl Harbor. It seemed to Hardy that they had taken a hell of a beating, but no one told them whether they had won or lost the battle. *Maybe no one knows,* he thought, *or it's bad news.*

The Battle of the Coral Sea had lasted from May 6 to May 8, and for the first time in history, a confrontation between navies was fought with the crews on the combatant ships never even seeing each other. The nature of war at sea had changed forever with Pearl Harbor; a single plane could sink the mightiest ship.

Both sides suffered similar losses on the Coral Sea. The *Yorktown* was damaged. The *Lexington* was set afire and finally had to be abandoned and then sunk by torpedoes from American destroyers to keep her out of Japanese hands.

The Japanese lost the light carrier *Shoho*; the new large carrier *Shokaku* was badly damaged and forced to return to base for extensive repairs; her sister ship, the *Zuikaku*, was unscathed, but had lost nearly her entire complement of aircraft and also had to retire from the scene.

Despite the damage done to both sides, the battle was an American victory for several reasons. For the first time, the Japanese had been stopped, a psychological boost to the hard-pressed American navy. Strategically, the Japanese were forced to give up their plans to take Port Moresby, and Australia was safe for the moment. But most importantly, the temporary loss of the two big Japanese carriers meant that they were unavailable when Yamamoto sent his fleet to Midway a month later.

On June 4, 1942, at the Battle of Midway, Hardy found himself in yet another naval engagement in which he didn't see an enemy ship—only planes, lots of planes with the red "meatball" of the Empire of the Rising Sun emblazoned on their green fuselages and wings. Again, even though he knew the planes were after the aircraft carriers, he was afraid when he heard that radar had picked them out. Who knew when they might settle for a cruiser?

This time, despite her captain's best efforts to keep her from harm, the *Yorktown* and her crew paid the price. First, dive-bombers hit her three times and stopped her dead in the water—the most frightening, vulnerable position for a ship of war.

Yet, the *Yorktown* did not die easily. Her engineering department managed to get her going again, and it looked like she might live to fight another day. But then a squadron of Japanese torpedo planes arrived. American fighters and ships' guns intercepted most of the Kates, but one kept boring in on the aircraft carrier even after the plane had been turned into a fiery coffin.

Forty-foot-long flames trailed from his plane, but the pilot stayed on course long enough to drop his torpedo. A moment later, the plane and pilot disintegrated, torn to pieces by the guns, but the torpedo ran straight and true into the *Yorktown*. Almost immediately the carrier began to list to the port side as seawater rushed in through the gaping holes in her hull.

Worried that she was about to capsize, the captain ordered the crew to abandon ship. In hindsight, the order would be perceived as premature—a circumstance that would impact the decision making of another carrier captain in the future.

The *Yorktown* remained afloat that night and into the morning, when the decision was made to try to save her. However, the delay allowed a Japanese submarine, on orders from Admiral Yamamoto, to find the stricken ship and sink not only the *Yorktown*, but the destroyer USS *Hamman*, which had tied up alongside, too. More than one hundred men died.

Hardy heard the news back in Pearl Harbor. He had watched as the crew of the *Yorktown* abandoned their vessel, and he felt sorry for them. He knew what it was to lose a ship, and he would again.

However, the Battle of Midway was a staggering defeat for the Japanese, who had four carriers and a cruiser sunk, while the remainder of the fleet was forced to retreat to Japan. They had also lost 3,500 men and 332 aircraft.

The Americans got off light by comparison. They lost 307 men, 147 planes, a destroyer and the *Yorktown*, but the *Enterprise* and *Saratoga* were untouched.

No one knew it yet, but Midway was the turning point in the war of the Pacific. What they did know—from Admiral Raymond Spruance, who became a legend that day as the "winning" admiral to Seaman 1st Class Mike Hardy—was that it was going to be a long and bloody cruise across a wide ocean.

At the insistence of the British and the Russians, the United States had established a "Germany first" policy regarding its war effort. Meanwhile, the Pacific war was divided two main theatres. The North, Central, and South Pacific were the purview of Admiral Nimitz and the Navy. The Southwest Pacific, from Australia to the Philippines, was the domain of the Army under MacArthur, who had bullied Roosevelt into accepting the questionable "necessity" of taking the Philippines to win the war. The general was given a naval fleet, the Seventh, to support his actions.

For the Americans, the strategy was to fight a war of attrition—exchange ships, planes, and lives—with the Japanese until the Germans could be defeated and the industrial might of the United States turned to the Empire of the Rising Sun.

The Japanese had not panicked. Even after the losses at Midway, they still had more naval forces than the combined U.S. Pacific and the Australian fleets.

There were several million seasoned troops in China, Asia and throughout the fortified islands of the western Pacific, the empire's "unsinkable aircraft carriers." As they turned their attention south to isolate Australia, the Japanese war council assured themselves that Midway had been an anomaly.

The dueling strategies collided in August 1942 on the land and sea around a small island in the southeast Solomons called Guadalcanal, where intelligence sources reported that the Japanese were building an airfield.

On August 7, 1942, after a massive naval bombardment, the U.S. Marines under Major-General Alexander Vandegrift landed on Guadalcanal, surprised to meet little opposition, as the defenders had withdrawn into the jungle and hills. The Japanese countered with air attacks from Rabaul in New Britain and Bougainville, and sent a fleet of five heavy cruisers, two light cruisers, and a destroyer to attack the Americans on the landing beaches.

With a false sense of security after the nearly uncontested landing, the U.S. Navy was literally caught sleeping in the early morning hours of August 9 by the Japanese off Savo Island.

In August, the *Astoria* was part of a cruiser division along with the *Vincennes* and *Quincy* that bombarded Guadalcanal for two days in preparation for the Marines landing. After the "gyrenes" got established, the ships withdrew to the waters off Savo to intercept an anticipated counterattack by the Japanese navy.

On the night of August 8, Hardy went to sleep at his gun mount. The seas were calm, the sky clear but moonless. They had been told to expect the Japanese sometime after dawn, but all he cared about after two days of General Quarters was a little shut-eye. He drifted off to sleep, the world at peace beneath the stars of the South Pacific.

A little before 2:00 A.M., he was jolted out of his dreams by the bugler blowing the call to battle stations. The Japanese had arrived early. Searchlights stabbed out of the darkness, illuminating the *Astoria, Vincennes,* and *Quincy.* Red flashes from guns flared in the dark across the water; he felt his ship shudder as if punched.

Hardy could make out the outline of a ship behind one of the blinding searchlights. His gun crew began shooting at the light, which flared and then went out. But the Japanese were shooting back—from both sides of the ship.

In the noise and confusion, he was unaware of the pounding the *Astoria* was taking from the Japanese cruisers. All he knew was that his ship was bathed in flames. The bridge below them and the decks were in flames—even the paint was on fire.

Still, his crew kept shooting until, oddly, the order to cease fire was given. The order was followed by a flash and a roar, and something hard hit his left leg. He looked at where the gun's pointer, a friend of his, had been. All that remained was a pair of legs attached at the hip and still sitting in what remained of the pointer's chair. Another friend lay on the deck, screaming, his legs shredded by shrapnel.

Reaching down, Hardy felt his leg; it was wet with blood. A shell had taken out their gun mount, passing through the pointer and into the magazine behind them. They were lucky that the magazine didn't explode or they would have all died. Instead, what remained of the gun crew crawled down from their useless weapon to try to find a safe place.

The word was passed for the wounded to be taken to the port side, where an old destroyer was alongside to evacuate them. A gangway was placed between the two ships for stretcher bearers and the walking wounded, like Hardy.

The pain from his wound was beginning to hit him as he hobbled over. But when he reached a wardroom that had been set up as an emergency medical clinic, he took one look and kept going. He was only seventeen years old and would never forget the sight of the dismembered arms and legs and other gore on the bloody wardroom deck as the ships' doctors fought to save the lives of other young men.

He found a bunk and lay down. It wasn't until later, when he was sent over to a transport, that anyone looked at his wound. A piece of shrapnel had gone into his thigh just above the knee, creating a hole about an inch wide. Where it came out the other side it had torn a three-inch-wide chunk out of his hamstring. A doctor cleaned the wound, poured sulfa powder into it to fight infection, and told him to see a pharmacist's mate in the morning.

Hardy was long gone when the *Astoria* went down having absorbed sixty-eight hits from 6- and 8-inch guns.

Three American cruisers, the USS *Vincennes, Quincy,* and *Astoria,* as well as the Australian cruiser *Canberra,* were sunk during the Battle of Savo Island. Those who survived the shelling had to deal with more danger in the water.

No one knew where the Japanese had gone. Ships passed in the dark, but the men didn't know if they were friendly or the enemy. Everyone had heard the stories of Japanese crews machine-gunning helpless survivors, and no one wanted to take a chance of hailing the wrong ship.

Another danger was from their own destroyers that criss-crossed through the waters several hours after the battle. Each time one came near enough that the men in the water could see it was American, they hoped they would be plucked from the sea. But the ships could not stop, for fear of becoming easy targets for Japanese submarines known to be in the area. At the same time, the destroyers were dropping depth charges, underwater bombs that would sink to a set level and explode, using water pressure to rupture the hulls of submarines. As the destroyers passed groups of survivors, the men onboard would call out over a bullhorn, warning the swimmers to keep their heads out of the water or risk ear injuries from the explosions.

The third danger was the most frightening—sharks, which soon began to appear, their dark fins slicing through the ebony water. Some men stuck together, kicking and splashing if a shark came near. The main danger seemed to be for the men swimming alone. The groups of men would try to paddle to individuals, only to see the sailor suddenly disappear, as though pulled down from below.

More than twelve hundred men died that night; eight hundred were wounded. U.S. forces were fortunate that the Japanese, who worried that the American carriers were nearby, did not press their advantage and go on to strike the vulnerable U.S. transports lying off the landing beaches.

The first Battle of Savo Island was just the beginning of a series of engagements that as a whole became known as the naval Battle of Guadacanal. The second featured a fight between aircraft carrier fleets in late October in which the carrier *Hornet* was hit repeatedly off the Santa Cruz Islands and sunk.

In November the two navies clashed again. This time the American lost two cruisers. One of them was the *Juneau,* from which seven hundred men died; five of them were from the same family, the Sullivan brothers. However, the Japanese lost a battleship, a cruiser, and seven transports filled with reinforcements for the defenders on Guadalcanal. Thousands of Japanese sailors and soldiers went into the, water where—an indication of how vicious the war on this side of the globe had become—they were machine-gunned from American ships and aircraft to prevent them from swimming to the island. When it was over, the naval Battle of Guadalcanal had been decided in favor of the Allies.

It would take six months, but the Japanese also lost the land battle. Yet, in losing, they subjected the Marines to the horror of suicidally motivated

Japanese troops. During the day, the Japanese would hide and have to be rooted out cave by cave, bush by bush, often with flame-throwers and hand-grenades. But at night the Japanese would rush out of the dark at American positions, waving swords and with fixed bayonets, screaming *"Banzai!"* a traditional greeting and war cry that translated to "May you live ten thousand years!" Most of the Japanese soldiers were mowed down long before reaching the Americans, though some got through and jumped into the foxholes and trenches to kill and die in frenzied hand-to-hand combat.

To the young Marines, whose average age was 19 and wanted nothing so much as to survive, there was one gesture they found more shocking than any other. Sometimes enemy soldiers would burst from the jungle strapped with explosive charges and throw themselves under the treads of tanks or into groups of marines.

This wasn't like the soldier who jumped on a live hand-grenade to protect his comrades. Or died at his machine-gun refusing to surrender. This was suicide and not very effective as a weapon at that.

The Marines didn't know that the suicide bombers were the result of an "official policy" dictated by the Imperial High Command. When the generals realized that they were losing the battle, they had ordered their troops to make themselves into "human bullets" and die for "holy *Yamato*," the ancient name for their country, and for their emperor.

However, the high command at last had mercy on its own troops, and in a daring nighttime operation the Imperial navy succeeded in evacuating the twelve thousand remaining troops from Guadalcanal. But it was the last time the Japanese would make an effort to rescue troops; from there on out, the official policy was to fight until victorious or dead.

When it was all over on the island, the United States had suffered twelve hundred Marine deaths; the same number of sailors had also died on that one night in August in the waters around Savo Island. The Navy lost two carriers (the *Wasp* had also been sunk), eight cruisers, seventeen destroyers, and four transports.

On the other side, the Imperial navy lost one aircraft carrier, two battleships, four cruisers, eleven destroyers, six submarines and sixteen transports. The number of dead was horrific—more than twenty-four thousand Japanese soldiers and sailors.

The Americans could absorb the destruction more than the Japanese. The industrial giant that Yamamoto feared was pouring forth tanks, weapons, planes, and ships—as well as the soldiers, pilots, and sailors to use them.

Not quite two years after the attack on Pearl Harbor, four of the six Japanese fleet carriers that participated were gone and the Japanese shipyards had produced only six more. In that same span of time, American shipyards launched seventeen fleet carriers, ten light carriers, and eighty-six small escort carriers, as well as dozens of new battleships, cruisers, destroyers, and submarines. But as hard-pressed as the Japanese were to match American industry, the most devastating losses from the battles of the Coral Sea, Midway, and Guadalcanal weren't the ships or planes, or even the soldiers. What hurt most were the deaths of hundreds of superbly trained pilots; they were gone and could not be replaced fast enough to keep up with the deaths.

Against the giant and his bitter resolve, the Japanese were faced with surrender or relying on increasingly desperate measures. They opted for the latter, choosing to believe in their own mythology rather than reality—that somehow warriors willing to die for the emperor of a land favored by the gods would find a way to save them all from the barbarians.

Sent back to the States, Hardy received thirty days of "survivor's leave" and went home to Ohio. A lot had changed. For one thing, the family now had electricity, though there was still no running water and his mom still cooked with wood. The steel mills were going great guns, the Depression all but forgotten, and women were working in them.

When his leave was up, Hardy reported to the West Coast for his next assignment. When he got there, he learned he might as well have stayed in Ohio. He and more than four hundred other survivors from the *Astoria*, *Vincennes*, and *Quincy* were being shipped back to the Philadelphia Naval Yard to go aboard a new cruiser, the USS *Santa Fe*.

The train ride across the country was a wild one. They were blooded veterans now, old salts who had met the enemy and lived to tell about it. Still, they didn't know if they'd survive the next encounter, so they made the best of the four days they had on the train. At each stop along the way, they piled out and ran up and down the streets of whatever town they were in, looking for liquor stores and stealing kisses from any young women they met. They had arrived in Philadelphia hung over and resigned to their fates as they lined up to board their "home away from home."

Hardy stood on the pier with his seabag slung over his shoulder looking up at the *Santa Fe*. He'd liked the look of the long and lean cruiser with the white "60" painted on the side. Based on his naval experiences thus far, he figured that she had to be luckier than any ship he'd been on. It didn't matter, he had some unfinished business with the Japanese, and he would have gone on a rowboat.

His leg still bothered him some and he limped up the gangway to the ship's quarterdeck, where he saluted the American flag on the stern and turned to salute the Officer of the Deck, who was checking off the names of the latest arrivals.

"Seaman 1st Class Hardy reporting for duty," he said. "Permission to come aboard, sir?"

CHAPTER TWO

Pearl Harbor 1943: "Man the Guns. Join the Navy."

March 23, 1943
Oahu, Hawaii
USS Santa Fe

*T*weet-tweet-tweeeeeet.
　　At the command of the bos'n's pipe, the crew of the *Santa Fe* straightened from parade rest to rigid attention as their cruiser churned slowly past the shattered hulk of the battleship *Arizona*. They were "manning the rail," dressed in their freshest white uniforms and standing shoulder to shoulder at the lifeline that ran all the way around the weather deck of the ship.

Black neckerchiefs, properly knotted, hung around the necks of the sailors, the ends fluttering in the morning trade winds that caressed the ship. Shoes had been shined until they reflected the Hawaiian sun like mirrors. Even the apprentice seamen, fresh out of boot camp, had by now adopted the myriad ways of wearing their round white sailor's caps—perched on the back of their heads, or tilted off at a jaunty angle, or pugnaciously pushed forward until their eyebrows were covered. But on this day they wore the caps "regulation," squared neatly on top of their heads.

"Manning the rail" was a traditional symbol of respect among navies, sometimes exchanged between ships entering or leaving a foreign port, or passing in review of dignitaries. However, almost on its own, it had become a ritual for U.S. ships entering or leaving Pearl Harbor as they passed the *Arizona* and her entombed crew.

"*Tweet-tweet twoeeet!*" The bos'n piped the command to salute. A thousand-plus right hands snapped up. The American flag flying from the ship's mast was quickly lowered a quarter of the way down the staff—called "dipping the colors"—and then returned to the top. The pipe sounded again, like the call of some shorebird, and their hands returned to their sides.

Wide-eyed, most of them took in the devastation for the first time. *Remember Pearl Harbor!* It wasn't just a battle cry; they were three words that recalled the act that had changed their lives forever. They had been toughened by the Great Depression, had learned to do without and how to pull together. Now, if the posters that had been popping up all over the country—"*. . . we here highly resolve that these dead shall not have died in vain . . . Remember Dec. 7th!*"—were right, it was up to them to save the world. And, guaranteed to raise any red-blooded American boy's ire, they had been told that the Japanese didn't think they had the stomach for a fight.

Fifteen months earlier, most of the young men on the *Santa Fe* were just teenagers emerging from churches, or on their way to the movie theater, or flirting with the girls at the local soda fountain, maybe playing football in the park with their pals. Then newspaper boys began to shout from street corners, "EXTRA! EXTRA! Read all about it! Japs bomb Pearl Harbor!" They were, by and large, a patriotic group, who cheerfully recited the Pledge of Allegiance every morning in their schools' classrooms because they had been taught to love their country. If not insanely angry, the nature of the attack made them fightin' mad. Hawaii was American soil and Americans had been killed in a dastardly "sneak attack."

Many of the boys saw war as an adventure, a chance to prove their mettle and, perhaps, find a new life that up to now, for most, had been dominated by the Depression. As recruiting posters sprang up in the windows of businesses and even homes—*Man the Guns. Join the Navy*—the younger boys champed at the bit. They consumed the latest news of the war in newspapers and from the radio broadcasts of Edward R. Murrow, Walter Winchell, Lowell Thomas, and Gabriel Heater. Black-and-white newsreels played before feature films, and the boys eagerly discussed the marching soldiers, the guns firing, the planes diving, the ships in flames.

Eventually, they got in and were shipped off to boot camp on trains, promising their worried girlfriends and mothers, "We'll have 'em whupped in six months." The Navy was anxious to have them. Vessels of every kind were being launched in record time and record numbers from the shipbuilding yards; the service needed tens of thousands of sailors and officers to man them. The industrial giant Yamamoto had feared was awake, but it was a giant whose ships' companies were comprised mostly of reserve officers and enlisted men, who left their jobs or schools, homes, and families to take on the professional military of the Japanese Empire and the German Thousand-Year Reich.

Some of the "men" manning the *Santa Fe*'s rails that day in Pearl Harbor were not supposed to be there. Apprentice Seaman Al Mancini was the youngest sailor onboard, a week short of his sixteenth birthday. Born in 1927, he had grown up in Greenwich, Connecticut, a wealthy enclave known for its mansions and expansive estates. His family lived on an estate too, but in a caretaker's cottage.

An immigrant from Italy, Mancini's father, Alfredo, was a bricklayer and stonemason by trade. But except for the occasional Works Progress Administration job that called for his talents, there was little work during the Depression. So he took care of lawns for the rich folks, while Al's mother, Angela, worked as a domestic servant.

Despite the obvious contrast between his family's position and the wealthy inhabitants of Greenwich, young Al didn't feel particularly out of place. He attended the public high school—when he went at all, by junior high having already become something of a legend for playing hooky. The rich kids—like George Bush, a boy two years older than him—went to private schools, so he didn't have much interaction with them. But most of the students at the public school came from the working class, the children of the caretakers, mechanics, and maids who looked after the wealthy.

Mancini generally hung out with some of the older boys, also from working-class families, in town, keeping a sharp eye out for the truant officer. His biggest passion was building model aircraft and reading anything he could find about planes. He didn't particularly want to be a pilot, but he did want to work on planes and knew that wouldn't happen in Greenwich.

His father, Alfredo Sr., was a hard man, given to fits of anger that he took out on his "worthless" son. The opportunity for young Al to escape the abuse arrived on December 7, 1941. He was in the library with three other boys that afternoon when a man, obviously shaken, came around the corner and told them that Pearl Harbor had been attacked by the Japanese. Mancini and two of the other boys looked at each other dumbfounded. *Where in the heck is Pearl Harbor?* They had never heard of it. But the fourth boy's brother was on a submarine in the Navy; he knew and told the others.

They decided on the spot that they would all try to get into the service. It was easier for the boys who were seventeen and older. But Mancini was only fourteen. He was going to have to get his parents to lie for him or come up with a forged document.

Before he could put a plan into action, his father died. Mancini figured that his mother would be better off without a teen-aged son to feed. She was only making three dollars a day, sometimes four dollars if she did the laundry. He made a little money caddying at the private golf course, often while he was playing hooky. But it was going to be tough for the two of them if he stayed. He thought that if he could get into the Navy, he could serve his country and maybe, if he survived, learn a trade for when he got out.

Skinny as a street-sign post and only five-foot-eight with a shock of curly black hair, Mancini looked his age, but he had found out that he could obtain birth certificates from the town hall for fifty cents apiece. The names and dates on the certificates were written in pen, which he erased using laundry bleach. It took him several tries at forging the new information, but at last he was satisfied. The birth certificate said he was seventeen, still too young to sign up on his own; but he had figured that with his youthful looks, he was going to need his mother's help to fool the recruiter anyway.

She refused. In fact, she hit the roof, alternately crying and screaming at him. *He was too young to go to war. He was her only child.*

"If you don't let me go, I'm going to run away and join the Merchant Marine," he threatened. He knew that would get her. Greenwich was off the Long Island Sound, where merchant ships had been routinely sunk by German U-boats within sight of the shore, sometimes flaming away on the night horizon. As her son expected, Angela decided that the enemy she did not know was better than the one she did, so she relented and signed the papers.

Rain was pounding on the roof and beating against the windows the day Mancini left home in October 1942, but it was nowhere near as wet outside as on his mother's cheeks. He paused at the back door, watching her cry, wishing he could make it better. But there was nothing to do, he had to go, so he said good-bye. "I'll write," he promised. Then he walked out into the downpour and away he went into the rest of his life.

In June 1941, when the keel of the *Santa Fe* was laid at the New York Ship-building Company Yards in Camden, New Jersey, the United States had been at peace. A year later, when the ship slid down the ways and into the water, the country was fighting a two-ocean war and churning out ships and men as fast as possible.

By the fall of '42, new recruits like Al Mancini were being rushed through boot camp in a matter of a few weeks, even less for some. What they didn't pick up from the chief petty officers who oversaw their training, they could learn from the sailor's "bible," *The Bluejackets' Manual*, published by the U.S. Naval Institute. The book was a mixture of practical knowledge—such as knot tying, first aid, and swimming—and Navy terms and homilies.

Although updated, parts of the books were reminders of the days of sail-ing ships. For instance, young sailors learned that modern ships still had *forecastles*, the small, raised deck over the bow, which had been much more prominent on sailing vessels and was still known better by its old phonetic spelling of *foc'sle*. Lookouts still cried out, "Sail ho," when they saw another ship, even if the other ship was now an aircraft carrier without sails.

Some of the old phrases had new meanings. The book warned that onboard ship, when it was announced either by predetermined schedule or over the public address system that the smoking lamp was "lighted," they were allowed to smoke cigarettes. When it was out, they were to douse them. The funny thing was, there was no such thing as a smoking lamp anymore. "In the old days, before matches were invented," the book noted, "a lamp was lighted at certain times aboard the ship when smoking was permitted. All smokers got their pipes lighted from this lamp. We still have the 'smok-ing lamp' in spirit."

The Navy had its own language, including new words for common items. The gutters that ran around the edge of the main, or *weather,* deck were called *waterways*. *Magazines* weren't for reading; they were compartments where powder or shells were stowed. *Starboard* meant the right side of the ship facing forward; *port* meant the left. The front of the ship was the *bow* and the rear was the *stern,* though if one moved in either direction, he was going either *fore* or *aft*. Propellers were called *screws*.

Boats were small craft that could be hoisted aboard a larger vessel. "Never call a ship a boat," the manual insisted. "It is lubberly," a naval insult for an inexperienced or clumsy sailor. The holes in the ship's sides, which drained the waterways, were *scuppers*. Walls were *bulkheads,* the floor was the *deck,* and the ceiling was an *overhead*.

A good portion of the manual was designed to lay out the guidelines that made life aboard a cramped ship of war more bearable, as well as drill into their heads the message of teamwork and absolute obedience. "The efficiency of any ship depends upon the efficiency of the men aboard her. Good men on poor ships are better than poor men on good ships."

At times, the book assumed the role of the sailors' parents. "Do not get tattooed. It is dangerous, costly, and an awful lot of trouble the rest of your life." Of course, the book didn't note that from admirals to raw recruits, many a seaman had disregarded the advice. The men were cautioned against the use of profanity; urged recruits to be careful when choosing their friends and be on the lookout for those who might indicate a proclivity toward "Moral Turpitude;" and cautioned against "bad women."

The manual also warned of "agents" who tried to get enlisted personnel to give them information about the Navy or activities of the fleet. Mancini was careful to guard his speech for other reasons as well, lest some officer hear his voice crack and start wondering. During boot camp, he earned the nickname "Duck" because he had performed his imitation of the cartoon character Donald Duck singing "Home on the Range" during a talent show.

It was his last performance, especially in front of officers. He wanted to keep a low profile. Every time he was told to report to an officer, his stomach would knot into a ball, as he was sure that his mother had reconsidered and he'd been found out. But Mancini got through camp without his secret being uncovered, even though it would be three years before he shaved for the first time.

The *Santa Fe's* crew was a mix of new hands and old salts. Of the twelve hundred men assigned to the *Santa Fe,* most had never been to sea before. However, more than a fourth of the crew was made up of survivors from the disaster at Savo Island.

The ship was commissioned on November 24, 1942—her first skipper, Capt. Russell Berkey. He was a little on the chubby side, but he walked with a sense of purpose, an ever present cigarette holder clenched in his teeth below a long, pointed nose.

Onboard ship, the captain was the ultimate authority. If the vessel was serving as a flagship for the division, it would have an admiral onboard, who would be in overall command of the group. The admiral would be responsible for dictating where the ships would go and what their responsibilities were. However, the actual operation of the ship, including when and how to use the ship's guns, was the captain's responsibility.

The executive officer served as the ship's administrative officer and was next in the chain of command if the captain was killed, hurt, or ill. However, the Officer of the Deck, one of several junior officers assigned on a rotating schedule, would be on the bridge and under the watchful eye of the captain, responsible for the minute-to-minute operations of the ship.

A light cruiser, the *Santa Fe* was the fifth of the ten-thousand-ton "*Cleveland* class," the class designation given to subsequent editions of the first ship of a particular model, in this case the USS *Cleveland*. The *Cleveland* class could carry 120 days worth of provisions and enough fuel oil to steam ten thousand miles. After the lesson of Pearl Harbor, they were built with the new naval warfare in mind, which depended on screening ships to surround and protect the offensive force of aircraft carriers. The cruisers were fast—capable of speeds in excess of thirty-two knots (about thirty-eight miles an hour)—and loaded with antiaircraft firepower far exceeding any prewar ship.

Like her sister ships, the *Santa Fe* was 608 feet from bow to stern and only 63 feet at her widest point amidships. The middle third of the ship was dominated by the fore and aft superstructure—a sort of steel apartment building with two towers that rose high above the weather deck.

On the first deck of the fore superstructure were compartments for Radio One, also known as Radio Central, the main radio receiving room on the ship, which also held the equipment for encryption and decryption of coded messages. The next level up housed the admiral's plot room and the flag bridge, as well as the admiral's sea cabin in the rear, which was used only if there was a "flag officer," an admiral, onboard.

The third level was the enclosed main bridge, or pilothouse, the primary area for the command and navigation of the ship. It was from there that most captains directed the ship, viewing the sea through a series of portholes, with a member of the quartermaster's division usually at the helm. It also housed the chart room, where the navigators plotted the ship's course, and the captain's sea cabin.

Above the main bridge was an "open" bridge, an open-air platform from which the captain could also command and maneuver the ship in the open air. On top of it all was "Spot One" for the antiaircraft gun director and the director for the main battery six-inch guns.

Rising above the superstructure was the main mast, which held large and small radar antennas—one for air detection and the other for navigation—

and a horizontal yardarm from which signal flags were attached to guide-wires called *halyards*. The flags were used to communicate between ships during daylight hours without having to use the radio, mostly for maneuvering instructions such as changes in speed and direction.

The first deck on the shorter aft superstructure contained maintenance and repair shops for radar. The next was given over to Radio Two, which served as an emergency backup for Radio One and was the ship's main transmitter room for long distance radio communications. Above that was an alternate, or emergency, open bridge from which the ship could be maneuvered if the main pilothouse was destroyed in an attack.

The *Santa Fe* had been outfitted with the latest radar, of which there were three types. The first was for navigational radar, used mostly to keep track of ships and obstructions within a ten-mile range. The second was a longer-range surface radar, used mostly to detect ships, but because it scanned close to the surface of the water, it could sometimes pick up the approach of low-flying aircraft. The third was the antiaircraft radar for detection of planes. The readings from the radar antennae were displayed on separate screens in the radar room, the contacts represented by lighted dots, or "pips," on the screens. Transponders on friendly planes and ships differentiated them on the screens from foes.

The information from the radar was then relayed to those other parts of the ship that needed to know—such as the bridge and the Combat Information Center, a compartment in the interior of the ship that gathered the incoming data and disseminated it from there. Those other areas also had their own "repeater" screens, but they displayed only one type of radar or the other—surface or air—changing back and forth by means of a selector switch located at each viewing station.

Between the "foremast" and "aftermast" superstructures were the ship's two smokestacks. At the stern of the ship was a catapult for launching the Kingfisher pontoon planes the ship carried for observation and rescues. There was also a crane for plucking the plane from the sea after it landed.

Otherwise, looking at the outside of the ship, the most notable structures were the big guns that jutted from boxlike steel turrets: a dozen six-inch, .47-caliber "rifles," capable of shooting ten miles, for bombardment and ship-to-ship duels, and another dozen five-inch .38-caliber guns for the same purpose, as well as long-range antiaircraft protection. For medium and close-range work there were rapid-fire antiaircraft guns—the new 40-millimeter twins and quads that replaced the one-point-ones and 20-millimeter heavy machine guns.

As with all U.S. cruisers, the *Santa Fe* was named after an American city.
Those of her sailors who gave it any thought believed that the name boded
well—particularly the Catholics who knew it translated in English to *Holy
Faith*—but there were mixed feelings among the superstitious older hands
when they heard about her launching. The problem was that when the ship
was christened by Caroline Chavez of Santa Fe, the niece of U.S. Senator
Dennis Chavez of New Mexico, she didn't use the traditional bottle of champagne. Instead, the raven-haired beauty struck the bow with a bottle of water
taken from the Santa Fe River and blessed by the archbishop of Santa Fe.

The ship's company, officers, and enlisted men were divided into departments and then divisions within those departments: damage control, navigation, communications, engineering, supply, medical, gunnery. Each
department and division had its own officers, who fell into two main cat-
egories: commissioned officers and "warrant" officers, or the so-called mustang officers, who had risen through the ranks from seamen or firemen and
were generally the experts in the various technologies used on the ship. The
petty officers—noncommissioned like Army sergeants—were responsible
for the hands-on direction of the enlisted men.

On a ship of war, all of the other departments were dedicated to the support of the largest and most important division: gunnery. Of the twelve hundred men in the ship's company, seven hundred of them would be in
gunnery, and even then, other members of the crew would be needed to
man all the guns during General Quarters.

With so many of the crew in the gunnery, that division's members would
fulfill a lot of other functions onboard when not actually manning or maintaining the guns. They would stand security watches; handle the lines and
hoses for fueling, as well as loading ammunition and stores; assist with mooring and anchoring; and they bore the brunt of keeping the *Santa Fe* shipshape.

Those members of the crew who had never served on a Navy ship before
were assigned first to the X Division when they came onboard. The X Division essentially showed them the ropes of shipboard life, including where
they ate—enlisted men in the mess halls and the officers in a wardroom,
fed by galleys that would have to produce thirty-six hundred meals a day;
and where they slept—in bunks that during the day folded up against the
bulkheads. They were given tours of the ship from the fire rooms to the
bridge, the foc'sle to the fantail. They practiced the routes they would take
to reach their battle stations *on the double,* even in the dark of night.

The new seamen and firemen were surprised at some of the amenities. The ship was essentially a small town. There was a laundry and a post office. The ship showed movies when not in a combat zone, with screenings on the deck or in the messhall for enlisted men, or in the wardrooms for the officers. There was a well stocked library and a small chapel. A favorite was the ship's store, where for nominal prices they could buy personal necessities such as razors and deodorant, or incidentals like cigarettes, candy, Coca-Cola, root beers, and even an ice-cream cone from the "gedunk" store, the Navy version of a soda fountain. The money from the ship's store, they were told, went to provide the free services of a tailor, a cobbler, and a barbershop.

The new men soon discovered that the veterans enjoyed having fun at their expense, but no one was sure what to make of the news that the survivors from the *Astoria, Vincennes,* and *Quincy* had started a pool, betting on the date when the *Santa Fe* would be sunk—winner take all . . . if he survived.

The *Santa Fe* reported for duty February 28, 1943, six months ahead of schedule and already a tight, well-run ship. On March 1 the ship left the East Coast for the last time. Then it was through the Panama Canal and, after a brief stop in San Pedro, California, headed west for Hawaiian waters, entering Pearl Harbor for the first time on March 23, 1943, with her crew manning the rails.

It was all a grand adventure for Mancini. When the ship passed through the Panama Canal, he had spotted a young soldier standing guard duty at one of the locks and recognized him as a boy from Greenwich; they had caddied together at the golf course. Mancini waved and called out; the soldier stared, then broke into a grin. He waved and called back, but neither could hear the other. *Small world,* Mancini thought happily as the ship passed into the vastness of the Pacific Ocean.

He loved the Navy. A lonely only child, he now had a thousand big brothers looking out for him. He told some of his new friends the truth about his age after he came onboard, but knew that they would never tell; they were shipmates and that was a bond stronger than blood. The Navy, he was learning, was just like that—let a seaman be treated unfairly at a local establishment or catch some guy from one of the other services jumping him, and his entire division would be down there on the double to tear the place or person apart. Attack one, might as well attack them all.

When he thought about it, that was sort of what had happened after the Japanese attacked Pearl Harbor. The whole country had seemed to pull together. Differences between rich and poor, Democrats and Republicans, even between different races and ethnic groups seemed to have been set aside to unite against the common enemy. Sailors and Marines might call each other "swabbie" and "gyrene," respectively, and many a bar had been destroyed as they brawled over real and imagined slights, but mention "the Japs" or "the Krauts" and they stood shoulder to shoulder.

When he went aboard the *Santa Fe,* Mancini was assigned to the L Division as a surface lookout on the forward part of the foremast superstructure right above the bridge. His job was to scan the surface of the ocean in front of the ship for enemy vessels, hazards such as floating mines or the wake of approaching torpedoes, or periscopes that indicated the presence of a submarine.

Then one day he had attended airplane recognition class in the mess hall and had quickly rattled off the names of the planes from the pictures of their silhouettes. His boyhood fascination with airplanes paid off, as after that display he had been assigned to air lookout on the topmost platform of the foremast. Now his job was to scan the sky with binoculars, looking for enemy planes. He liked the change—anything to do with planes was all right by him—though he still hoped to find a way to become part of the crews that took care of the Kingfishers.

Pearl Harbor was probably the first thing that took the smile off Mancini's face since he had joined. As they passed the *Arizona,* he noticed that fuel oil was still leaking, staining the water with a sickly rainbow. He had seen the newsreels, but they were nothing compared to real battleships, smoke-stained and shattered, lying in shallow water, their superstructures tipped drunkenly to the side.

"Welcome to Paradise, boys," a grizzled old chief petty officer growled as the crew returned to parade rest. "Rich folks spend a lot of money to come here. But you're lucky, the Navy brought you for free."

The chief wasn't smiling, and nobody else felt like laughing.

CHAPTER THREE

The Battle of Sitkan Pip:
A Terrible Responsibility

July 22, 1943
Attu, Alaska
USS Santa Fe

H old your fire!" Captain Russell Berkey's command came across loud and clear in Lt. Warren Harding's headset while all around the *Santa Fe,* the guns of a half dozen other warships thundered. Flames jumped from the muzzles of the big barrels of American battleships and cruisers, illuminating the bottoms of the low-lying clouds and making the ships stand out in sudden relief before the dark closed in again between volleys. Steel projectiles weighing as much as a car and loaded with explosives were hurled through the night—fused, armor-piercing shells following red tracers on a rainbow trajectory toward a spot miles in the distance.

Only the *Santa Fe* did not shoot. Gunnery Officer Harding's men on the aft six-inch main battery were ready and, he knew, had to be wondering. Finally, after waiting and plowing around the fog-bound northern Pacific for four months with nothing to show for it, they were face-to-face with the enemy—a whole Japanese fleet of cruisers and destroyers from what they had been told—and yet the captain ordered them to "Hold your fire!"

After arriving at Pearl Harbor in March, the ship remained in Hawaiian waters drilling for three weeks. Then Berkey had received orders to proceed north to the Aleutians and help kick the soldiers of the Empire of the Rising Sun off their perch in North America.

In June 1942, Japanese troops had invaded the islands of Attu and Kiska—craggy, barren, windswept rocks at the bottom of the Aleutian chain. Admiral Yamamoto had hoped that this diversionary force would trick the Americans into splitting their fleet before the Battle of Midway. The ruse didn't work, but Yamamoto's troops landed virtually unopposed and had been left to sit ever since.

In April 1943, the time had come to oust them. Steaming north from Hawaii in the company of three destroyers, the *Santa Fe* relieved the heavy cruiser *Salt Lake City,* which had been severely damaged in a battle with the Japanese northern fleet. The *Santa Fe* joined Cruiser Division 1, or CruDiv1, which also included the *Richmond* and the *Detroit.*

Since the *Santa Fe* arrived, other than the occasional submarine contact and a few bombardments of treeless islands the crew often couldn't see because of the omnipresent fog, there had been little action. That didn't mean there was no danger or stress. The gray mists that lay over the ocean off the Aleutian chain could be as thick and wet as balls of soaked cotton and difficult to navigate through.

When he wasn't directing his guns from atop the superstructure, Harding served four-hour watches on the bridge as one of the officers of the deck. That meant that at times he was responsible for guiding the ten-thousand-ton warship through fog at high speeds while trying to coordinate its movements with other equally half-blind ships. He was only twenty-three years old, and the weight of having the well-being of twelve hundred other young men resting on his shoulders was enormous. A small mistake on his part, and they could all end up in the frigid waters. Sometimes hours after some of his watches were over, he would still be so tense it was difficult to drink a cup of coffee without spilling it on himself.

Dealing with the stress wasn't something his instructors with the Navy Reserve Officers Training Corps, NROTC, at the University of California–Berkeley had talked about before the war. Who would have thought they had to? Back then, all he really wanted to be was a businessman, like his father.

Warren Harding had been born in Brooklyn in February 1920, but his father, a young banking executive, moved his family to Oakland, California, in 1923 to pursue other banking opportunities. Harry Harding had done well for himself out West, and in 1928 formed his own investment firm. The timing, however, was unfortunate, as the stock market crashed a year later, ruining the firm and putting him out of work.

Still, the Depression wasn't the hardship for the Hardings that it was for many others. Harry had to scramble to find odd jobs to keep cash coming in, but the family had other resources. During the prosperous years, they had bought a summer home in Walnut Creek, a small town about twenty miles east of Oakland in the coastal range. When the Depression hit, Harding's parents decided to move there and rent out their home in Oakland.

The fall after his high school graduation in June 1937, Warren went on to the University of California–Berkeley as an economics major. The university was a land-grant college, which for all male students meant that they had to take Reserve Officers Training, either with the Army or Navy. ROTC required a two- or four-year commitment, respectively, as a reserve officer after graduation.

By the late 1930s, Congress had finally gotten around to modernizing the fleet, authorizing the shipyards to start building, including a line of immense new aircraft carriers; faster, more powerful battleships; and speedy light cruisers. But most of them weren't out of the shipyards yet, and everything pointed to the fact that the Navy was soon going to need the new ships, as well as the men to command and man them.

Harding had no real desire to serve in the military. But at the same time, he was unusual among his peers in that he had kept up with what was happening in the rest of the world. He knew that if the country went to war, the government would soon call up the reserve officers from the college programs. Deciding he would rather do his fighting from the deck of a ship than from a foxhole, he signed up for the Navy program.

Early on during Harding's senior year, a captain who taught one of the NROTC classes kept encouraging the students to consider active duty after graduation. The further into the year they got, however, the more urgent he became. Where he once began his spiel with, "If you volunteer for a year's active duty. . . ," by the time Harding was ready to graduate in May 1941, the captain began his talks with, "*When* you volunteer for a year's active duty . . ."

Rather than wait to be called to active duty, Harding and about half of his class volunteered. The same day they received their college diplomas, they were commissioned as ensigns in the United States Navy.

In July of 1941 Harding was assigned to the cruiser USS *Brooklyn* as a gunnery officer for the six-inch guns in Turret #3 on the foredeck of the ship. He also stood watch as the Junior Officer of the Deck, essentially learning the position on the job, which included occasionally taking the wheel from the helmsman.

The *Brooklyn* had been assigned to the Neutrality Patrol, guarding the waters around the Azores from German U-boats with the aircraft carrier USS *Ranger* and a cadre of destroyers. Several times the task force made contact with German submarines only to have them slip away before they could be attacked.

In the fall, the *Brooklyn* transferred to the Caribbean to chase U-boats that were hunting in the waters near the Panama Canal, waiting for cargo ships to be funneled toward them.

In early December 1941 the *Brooklyn* was in a Bermuda drydock for repairs after burning out a turbine. That first Sunday of the month, Harding and a couple of friends from the ship attended church services in town and then went to the beach to swim and relax. Later that afternoon, they were strolling leisurely on their way back to their temporary quarters when they passed the house of the pastor whose sermon they had heard that morning. They waved when they saw him out in his yard.

"Have you heard the news?" he called to them. "The Japs bombed Pearl Harbor!"

So it's begun, Harding thought as he and the others hurried back to the base. He wasn't surprised that America would now be in a real war instead of the cat-and-mouse games they'd been playing with the Germans. Nor was he surprised that the Japanese had struck first—they had a hell of a Navy and were itching for a fight with their only real competition in the Pacific. However, he was shocked that they had been able to pull off the attack so effectively over such a great distance.

Still, there was nothing to do but roll with the punches and hit back. Harding had confidence in his Navy, confidence in the officers he served under and with, and confidence in the men who served under him. If the Japanese wanted a fight, they had found one.

The *Brooklyn's* war, however, remained in the Atlantic. As soon as she could leave drydock, the ship returned to New York, where she was employed in patrolling the coast and escorting convoys to Great Britain.

It was a homecoming of sorts for Harding, who had been three when he left New York with his family. He still had aunts, uncles, and cousins living in Brooklyn, and they took him into their homes and treated him as a son. The whole country seemed to be undergoing a transformation—there was fear, yes, but there was also resolve and a coming together in the face of adversity.

Everybody seemed to want to contribute to the war effort. Harding's girlfriend, Josephine Kitts, whom he had met on the Berkeley campus, called from California to tell him she had quit school to work at the Mare Island Naval Shipyard in Vallejo, northeast of San Francisco. Recruiters for the shipyards had appeared on campus one day, asking for help. They said that with all the able-bodied young men going into the service, the Navy needed women to fill their places and she had volunteered. She had been given a quick course in drafting and put to work.

Harding wondered how the public would react if they knew how close the war in the Atlantic was to their shores—that in fact, the war was already there. Those on the eastern seaboard occasionally saw plumes of smoke on the horizon, or flames if it was night, from torpedoed ships. But the public had not seen how the waters along the coast were strewn with debris and bodies.

The true extent of the U-boat depredations and acts of sabotage in places like U.S. shipyards didn't make it past the wartime censors, or only surfaced in the press long after the fact. The government worried about the impact such things might have on the public's morale.

Americans looked at other Americans and wondered; it was frightening to think that the enemy was living and working in the United States, blending in with everyone else. But it was also disturbing to many like Harding to realize that part of the aftermath of Pearl Harbor was a blow to American civil liberties, especially as they applied to people of Japanese descent living in the United States.

In Walnut Creek, he had grown up with *Nisei*, second-generation Japanese Americans, including one of his best friends, George Kanagaki. He had known them to be industrious, hard-working neighbors with the same dreams as any other Americans. Now, he was hearing from Jo, as well as reading in the newspapers, that the Japanese Americans were being rounded up and sent to internment camps.

Harding didn't like it, but he also understood it. Up until the Battle of Midway, there was a real threat that Hawaii and even the West Coast might be invaded—not something that was a concern with Germany at that time. The U.S. government was also very aware from Japanese radio broadcasts that the enemy was still receiving reports of U.S. Navy ship movements in and out of ports on the West Coast and Hawaii from Japanese residents more loyal to the emperor than to the president.

There also had been reports of Japanese immigrants celebrating after the attack on Pearl Harbor and of older Japanese residents, in particular, swearing allegiance to the emperor. They weren't in the majority, but these actions were enough to inflame passions. Even Americans, who loathed the idea of singling out a people based on race, recognized that the war effort was vulnerable to acts of spies and saboteurs.

An enemy one never saw was hard to defend against. And the one time then-Lt. (j.g.) Harding did see a U-boat on the surface, his ship had to stay with its convoy. In August 1942 the *Brooklyn* and several destroyers were escorting the *Aquitania,* a British luxury liner converted into a transport, from England to New York to pick up troops. They had been moving fairly fast, twenty-five knots, as they zigzagged across the Atlantic. The reason for the evasive maneuvers was clear as they made their approach to the New York harbor; even a mere five miles from the shore, the water was littered with the flotsam and jetsam of ships that had been sunk by the Germans.

Even though the crew could see the safety of the United States coastline, danger remained all around them. The destroyers, which were equipped with sonar to detect objects beneath the water, reported submarine contacts to either side, ahead, and behind. But for the time being, the Germans left the small convoy alone, wary of the warships.

Other ships trying to reach New York were not as fortunate, as the men on the *Brooklyn* discovered when they spotted a surfaced U-boat in the distance, casually shelling a Norwegian cargo ship that had been making its way up the Jersey coast. Using binoculars, Harding, who was standing watch as the Officer of the Deck, could see the crew of the German raider some three miles away as they pumped round after round into the defenseless cargo ship. A puff of smoke would appear from the submarine's gun, followed a few seconds later by the muffled report of the gun across the water.

Every man on the *Brooklyn* burned to go after the submarine. But they couldn't detour to save a lone merchant ship. Their job was to get the transport safely to New York so that it could be filled with troops and escorted back to England. Assisting the defenseless ship would have endangered too many lives. German submarines hunted in packs, and they could have been setting a trap for the *Brooklyn* using the Norwegian vessel as bait.

It grated on Harding. Leaving behind a ship in distress was not what had been taught him in the NROTC. He was learning the terrible responsibilities of command.

In September, Harding received orders to report to the Philadelphia Navy Yard for assignment to a new cruiser, the *Santa Fe*. He was now a full lieutenant and would be the gunnery officer for the aft main battery of six-inch guns; he would also be expected to again stand watches as the Officer of the Deck.

However, he had a little liberty first and there was something important he wanted to attend to before he went away to sea. Toward the end of his senior year at the university, he and Jo Kitts had talked about getting married, but decided to postpone until after the war they both knew was coming. It was the sensible thing to do. But now that the war was upon them, they realized that there might not be any more time to be young and in love.

Kitts quit her job and moved to Philadelphia. They were wed in New York City on October 3, 1942, in a small Episcopal church with just a few family members in attendance. They then found an apartment in a house in Philadelphia—just a room with a hot plate for cooking, but it was home for five months.

In February they knew that their time together, at least for the foreseeable future, was nearly over. The ship had been on its shakedown cruise, and it was only a matter of days before Warren would have to leave for the war.

There was no mystery about where he was going, though the word had not been passed officially. He knew because of how the ship was being painted.

The Navy had a number of different paint schemes, called "measures," for its ships, depending on the circumstances and the ship's location. For instance, the traditional peacetime gray the public usually associated with naval vessels was "Measure 13." But during wartime, the ships were painted differently in an effort to make them more difficult to see at a distance. In the Atlantic Fleet, the hulls were painted a dark gray with a light gray superstructure to blend in with the dark seas and hazy skies.

The Pacific Fleet, perhaps because the biggest danger was from the air, were generally painted a dark blue-gray, the new color of the *Santa Fe*. That meant Harding was going to fight the Japanese.

Leaving Jo had been hard, but Harding was kept busy enough just trying to do his job. The *Santa Fe* had a good crew, and he was confident they would get even better fast. He thought it was lucky that more than a third of her crew, including several men in his division, were survivors from the *Vincennes*, *Astoria*, and *Quincy*. They had been through the worst of it and would be a steadying force for the younger men. He did notice one little quirk about them. Until the *Santa Fe* reached the Aleutians, where it was too cold to do so, many of the survivors preferred to sleep up on the weather deck rather than in their berths down below. Easier to get off the ship that way, one of his Savo Island veterans explained.

The *Santa Fe* finally got to fire her guns at the enemy when she was assigned to bombard *Attu*. Even then, there wasn't a whole lot of excitement—some inaccurate return fire from the defenders, and a "bogey" on the radar that turned out to be an American B-25 bomber on patrol. A "bogey" was an unidentified "pip" on the radar; a "bandit" was a plane confirmed to be the enemy. The unsuspecting pilot was fortunate to have been identified before the nervous gun crews let loose.

The bombardment apparently impressed the Japanese, however, including "Tokyo Rose"—the mysterious, sexy, and somewhat dangerous woman who broadcast in lilting English exaggerated reports of Allied defeats and Japanese victories.

Radio Tokyo often was the only source of commercial radio the ships could pick up for entertainment. By this time in 1943, the sailors didn't realize that there wasn't really a single "Tokyo Rose." She was a myth created by the imaginations of Allied soldiers and sailors in the Pacific, who lumped nearly two dozen female voices coming out of Japanese radio programming into a single persona.

Whoever "Tokyo Rose" was, she played great music on the air, the latest big band sounds, and her assertions about Allied losses were usually so ludicrous that it was like listening to a comedy show. The day after the Attu bombardment, the crew listened in with great amusement as she announced that the island had been shelled "by a 'battleship' of the 'Santa Fe' class.' " The crew of the light cruiser got a kick out of that—the mighty "battleship" *Santa Fe* was there to set matters right.

Otherwise, life in the Aleutians was pretty boring. The *Santa Fe's* crew was fortunate to have arrived in the northern climes after the worst of the winter storms were over. Their biggest weather problem was the fog, which could keep the area socked in for days without a break. The heaving, gray waters around the dozens of large and small islands that make up the Aleutian chain were difficult enough to navigate through, much less when the horizon ended only a few feet from the ship. Maneuvering in concert with other ships without being able to see them was a risky proposition. Radar was still imperfect—in fog, rain, sleet, and snow a ship might not show up clearly.

The stressful job of guiding the ship at such times often fell on the young Officers of the Deck, like Harding, who had control of the ship's course and speed for their four-hour watches. It was their nerve-wracking job to maintain the ship's position relative to other ships in the formation. A small mistake maneuvering or a malfunction on a radar screen might lead to a collision that in the icy waters could cost the lives of hundreds of sailors and nearly did that May on the *Santa Fe.*

The cruiser division had been plowing through moderate seas off Attu one night in a fog so dense that men at the lookout stations could hardly see the water right below them, much less any distance into the gloom. A little after 10:00 P.M., Captain Berkey ordered that collision mats—thick, rubber pads that hung from the weather deck down to the waterline—be rigged. An hour later, the lookouts who were trying to peer through the gloom nearly jumped out of their foul-weather gear as collision warning horns blared, and the ship suddenly turned hard to port.

Somewhere in the dark, but frighteningly near, some other ship's horns were blasting as well, coming closer. Then an immense dark gray shape suddenly materialized; a hundred feet away, a battleship was bearing down on the starboard side of the *Santa Fe.* If it hit them, the bigger ship would tear the cruiser in two.

The helmsmen on both ships desperately tried to turn away from each other, but a disaster looked unavoidable. Above the frantic blowing horns, someone yelled over a bullhorn, "STAND BY FOR COLLISION TO STARBOARD!"

The vessels were turning, but too slow it seemed. The men on the deck braced for the impact as they looked at the cold, dark waters below them and wondered how long they would last if their ship sank.

At the last possible moment, the bow of the battleship swung past the stern of the *Santa Fe,* the ships clearing one another with only about ten feet to spare. As the leviathan disappeared back into the night, the cruiser's crew relaxed their white-knuckle grips, shook their heads, and whistled. *Man, that was damn lucky.*

By the summer, the Japanese had proved much less frightening than the weather and their own Navy, at least to the men on the *Santa Fe.* The U.S. Army, however, didn't have it as easy with the Japanese. On May 11 the *Santa Fe* and the other cruisers in its division were stationed about sixty miles off Attu, while the Army's 4th and 7th Infantry Divisions landed to recapture the island. The cruiser division was to thwart any attempts by the Japanese Imperial Navy to interfere. No such attempts were made and the division was ordered to return to base on May 24.

However, the GIs were slogging through shin-deep mud and under constant mortar and machine-gun fire with their only cover being holes filled with icy water. The fighting was often at close quarters—dirty work with rifle butts and bayonets—as the Japanese gave ground only grudgingly. But at last on May 28, the American soldiers were poised at the head of a valley leading down to the port of Chichagof Island and the last of the enemy garrison.

Shortly after midnight, the Japanese, shouting *"Banzai!"* charged madly up the valley and into the face of withering artillery and machine-gun fire. Most of the Japanese were slaughtered long before they reached the American lines. Those who were not killed outright took their own lives rather than surrender.

First Guadalcanal and now Attu, the suicidal charges of the enemy were beginning to look like more than some random decision by an insane Japanese commander. The impression such tactics left on the American soldiers was that the enemy was some kind of "mad dog" fanatic who didn't value human life—not his own, nor anyone else's. Unable to fathom the reasoning, the Americans and their allies derisively referred to the Japanese suicide soldiers as "Banzai Joes."

Suicidal attacks weren't of much concern to the U.S. Navy; their counterparts in the Imperial navy didn't seem to have the same tendencies as the army. Both sides had witnessed instances in which a wounded naval pilot, or one who knew he had no hope of returning to his base because of damage to his plane, attempted to crash into a ship as a last measure. Both sides had also sent squadrons of planes at the enemy knowing full well that few, if any, would return. But those pilots were not trying to kill themselves when they left to attack the enemy; their deaths occurred in the flow of the battle.

When the young sailors and officers of the U.S. Navy, who missed their families, wives, and girlfriends, heard about what the Army experienced at Chichagof, they couldn't imagine why the Japanese soldier seemed to want to die and for no good reason. The battle was over—any civilized man, they agreed, would have surrendered.

In all, the *Santa Fe* spent four months patrolling the Aleutian waters without seeing an enemy ship or plane. Then in July, the cruiser division's patrol duties shifted to the waters around the island of Kiska, where the second Japanese garrison was still entrenched.

On July 3 radar contact was made with a Japanese submarine on the surface ahead in the fog. The cruiser fired a few volleys from the main battery and the contact promptly disappeared from the radar, but the crew had no idea if the sub was hit. There was no debris or oil slick on top of the water.

It looked like the ship's first tour of duty might end without really ever facing the enemy. But then the night arrived that would go down in the storied annals of U.S. Naval history as the "Battle of Sitkan Pip."

On July 22 the cruisers were joined by the battleships *Mississippi* and the *Wisconsin* in shelling Kiska to soften up the defenses prior to the planned invasion in mid-August. The ships then moved to intercept a strong force of Japanese cruisers and destroyers reported to be on their way to give battle that night.

The crew *Santa Fe* was both excited and scared, as were the crews of the other ships. Messages flew back and forth between the battleships and cruisers—which called each other by code names such as Lava, Joe, Cable, and for the *Santa Fe*, Lyric, so that the enemy listening in wouldn't know what ships they were fighting.

Daylight faded and darkness crept over the gray sea and overcast sky. All was quiet until just after midnight when one of the other ships reported a "possible surface contact" on its radar screen. Within minutes they were all were reporting "pips" on their screens as well. It had to be the Japanese task force! With a tremendous roar, every gun that could be brought to bear on the targets began shooting.

Only the *Santa Fe* remained quiet. "Hold your fire!" Captain Berkey ordered. On the aft superstructure, Harding got the order and repeated it to his men in the turrets but with a smile.

Radar wasn't perfect, at least not for identifying ships. It had been known to pick up such harmless "enemies" as flocks of Arctic puffins, a peculiar and colorful little bird about the size of a rabbit, when a big flock rested on the waves. Excited gunnery officers had been known to blast the "pip" only to learn later that instead of flotsam and jetsam from an enemy ship, the target area was littered with feathers.

In this instance, the *Santa Fe*'s radar crew had seen the "pip," too. But equipped with newer, improved radar, they had correctly identified the "enemy ships" as "side lobes," or false reflections from the nearby island of Sitkan.

The barrage finally stopped after the other ships noticed that no one was shooting back nor apparently being hit. Embarassed, the radar operators on the other vessels had also finally noticed that the "enemy ships" had not moved on the screen during the shelling.

Of course, holding their fire gave the *Santa Fe* crew bragging rights over the "nervous Nellies," who had been shooting at ghosts. One wag even penned a sardonic poem that appeared in the fleet newsletter, titled *"The Battle of Sitkan Pip."*

Hush my children! Button your lip,
And I'll tell you the Battle of Sitkan Pip.
It all began in the early morn,
When Lava took his bugle and blew the horn,
Then Joe gave vent to his pent-up ire,
Pulled on his pants and opened fire.
He was quickly followed by Lava and Cable,
Who poured it out for all they were able.
At last, old Crystal with nothing to do,
Added her voice with a salvo or two.
Only Lyric, calm and serene,
Sat down on her duff with not a pip on her screen.
And so until morning with infinite care,
Lava, dear Lava, found pips everywhere.
At last came the sunrise a blessing so sweet,
So hush my dear children—please go to sleep.

Only later did the crew learn the reason that the expected counterattack never materialized. On August 15, American troops landed on Kiska, but the Japanese garrison was gone. Two Japanese light cruisers and ten destroyers had slipped in under the cover of the fog and removed the fifty-one hundred defenders. The empire's invasion of North America had been over for two weeks before U.S. forces were aware of the Japanese departure.

In September, Rear Admiral Laurance Tombs DuBose shifted his flag from the USS *Birmingham*, another of the *Cleveland*-class light cruisers, to the *Santa Fe*, which was fresh from an overhaul at Pearl Harbor after returning from the Aleutians. The two vessels and their sister ship, the USS *Mobile*, made up Cruiser Division 13. CruDiv13 was assigned to Task Force 15, which included the aircraft carriers USS *Princeton, Belleau Wood,* and a brand-new USS *Lexington.*

On September 17, after several days at sea, the task force suddenly turned and made a high speed run for Tarawa, a small atoll in the Gilbert Islands near the equator. About 3:30 on the morning of the eighteenth, the carrier planes took off and headed for the target. The Japanese were caught sleeping and most of their planes were destroyed on the ground. By mid-afternoon, the last of the American planes had been recovered, and the task force sped away as quickly as it had arrived.

During the attack, the cruisers had remained with the carriers providing air defense in case of a counterattack. The crews never even got to see the atoll, nor a single enemy plane. By the time Japanese planes arrived from other bases, the task force was long gone. The younger crewmembers, who were itching for a fight, were disappointed, but the veterans from the *Vincennes, Astoria,* and *Quincy* told them to be patient—the Japanese would not always be late.

In the meantime, the older hands eagerly looked forward to a more cheerful event, a different rite of passage. Leaving Tarawa, the task force headed south toward the equator to throw off any Japanese pursuit. For a sailor, the equator was not just an imaginary line that divided the northern and southern hemispheres, but also a dividing line in his career as a man of the sea.

Since the days of sailing ships, sailors had given special import to the first crossing of the equator. Until that day, a seaman—whether he was the captain of the ship or the most novice deckhand—was nothing but a low and pitiful "pollywog," a mere landlubber. Afterwards, he was a "shellback," a real sailor.

Getting through the day was the problem for the pollywog. "By the law of the sea," on the day of the crossing, the shellbacks took over control of the ship's activities with the primary mission of initiating the pollywogs into the "Solemn Mysteries of the Ancient Order of the Deep." Essentially, it was a day of hazing a college fraternity would have envied.

With the firing of the ship's guns, the blasting of her horns, and the cheers of the shellbacks, Captain Berkey announced over the ship's loudspeakers, "Stand by for a bump when the equator is reached." It was the signal the shellbacks had been waiting for as they produced clubs, bats, and paddles and began hunting pollywogs.

Some of the shellbacks got out razors and scissors and began shaving the heads, totally or partially, of the pollywogs. Then the Royal Party, made up of shellbacks in whatever outlandish costume they could put together, appeared. King Neptune, with his trident, crown, and long, flowing hair, was accompanied by his queen, as well as the "ersatz Princess," the Royal Baby (dressed in a large diaper and kerchief on his head), the Royal Jesters, the Royal Judge, and the king's scribe, Davy Jones. They set up their court on the main deck aft.

After first being hosed down with saltwater while lying on the deck, a "symbol of their complete prostration," the "guilty novices" crawled to the court through a paddle line. As blows to their rear ends hurried them along, they were required to chant, "I'm a lowly, slimy pollywog." After bowing to King Neptune and kneeling at the queen's feet, the initiates were made to drink a foul concoction from the Royal Baby's bottle and kiss his ample and hairy belly. The victims then were placed under the custody of the Royal Executioner. Charges were read against each man, and after a "fair" trial the judge sentenced each to "the works."

After a long day, the pollywogs had one last challenge to meet. They had to crawl through a long, canvas chute filled with garbage, oil, and bilge water until finally—bruised from stem to stern, half blinded by fuel oil and smelling like something dead—they emerged on the other end as changed men. Now, they too were shellbacks and heartily welcomed into the fraternity, dreaming of the day when it would be their turn to cross the equator with a ship full of pollywogs.

The festivities allowed the crew to blow off some steam. For a little while, they were just teenagers and young men again, but it was more than just youthful hijinks on the high seas. The former pollywogs were now truly a part of the crew—a family of brothers, each reliant on the next man to do his job as part of a team so that they could all go back to their homes someday.

For now, they shared a common home, the *Santa Fe*, the ship of Holy Faith. But a ship without her crew was nothing except cold steel, empty corridors, and silent compartments. With men onboard, she was almost a living entity, and the crew even thought of her that way in the special relationship sailors have always had with their ships.

Sometimes a mother. Sometimes a girlfriend. Sometimes a bitch. They referred to the ship as "she"—a woman, at once temperamental and nurturing—and were proud of her looks and abilities, as they might once have been proud of their high school prom dates. Her heart beat with the pounding of their feet on her decks and ladders; their laughter in the mess halls was her laughter; her passageways spoke with the sound of their voices.

Their loneliness and fears, their triumphs and tragedies would become part of her soul.

CHAPTER FOUR

Bougainville to Tarawa: For a Bit of Coral

November 8, 1943
Bougainville, Solomon Islands

A quarter-moon dimly lit the sea as dark columns of rain squalls swept across the inky surface of the water. Bolts of lightning stabbed down, adding to the tension the crew of the *Santa Fe* felt as they waited for the Japanese.

The ship was steaming northwest of the island of Bougainville in the Solomons accompanied by two other light cruisers and a half-dozen destroyers. That the Japanese would come, there was no doubt. Behind the ships, U.S. Marines had waded ashore at Empress Augusta Bay, where the main Japanese forces on the island could not get at them easily. The enemy had to attack from their fortress at Rabaul in the north, or concede the landings nearly uncontested.

They'd already tried once with a task force of cruisers and destroyers and had been driven off. But what would they send this time? Planes or ships or both? No one knew.

The waiting was the worst of it. To calm his men, Captain Berkey spoke periodically to the crew over the public address system as a father figure comforting his sons. "Just do what you've been trained to do; the man next to you is counting on it." He tried to lighten the mood by announcing a ten-dollar prize would go to the lookout who spotted the first Japanese plane.

Around the ship, men coped with the stress in different ways. Some men talked or laughed away their jitters, telling jokes they'd all heard a dozen times before. "I heard that up at Attu there was a woman behind every tree … only problem was, there were no trees."

Or, there was the one about the new "boot" in the fire room who looked at the speed gauge and noticed the setting marked "flank speed." "Oh my Gawd!," he exclaimed. "This ship goes sideways!"

Or, they laughed over the story of the young seaman who was taken by his more experienced shipmates to what he thought was a USO show in Honolulu and found himself instead in the seedy lobby of a run-down hotel. When a woman in a red negligee appeared at the top of the stairs above the lobby and bawled out, "Who's next?", he'd asked if she was one of the "entertainers."

A few of the "old salts" amused themselves and frightened "first-timers" with horror stories about sinkings in "The Slot," the narrow band of water that ran between the parallel lines of islands that made up the Solomons. Men who escaped their ships, the veterans said, had to deal with sharks and large saltwater crocodiles that cruised the warm waters. Then, lowering their voices and looking around as if the enemy was listening, they added that even if survivors managed to get past the sharks and the crocs, the islands were infested with fanatical Japanese troops who made a sport of hacking ship-wrecked sailors to pieces with their samurai swords.

Of course—some other older hand was bound to chime in—sailors only had to worry about the crocs and the swords if they weren't trapped belowdecks when their ship went down. A few who'd been on ships that had been sunk recounted having to abandon men when watertight hatches were damaged and couldn't be opened. "We could hear them pounding."

Others passed the time writing letters, which would be passed to a destroyer the next time one came alongside with mail bags. To conserve paper for the war effort, most letters were sent on "V-mail," tissue-thin sheets, folded over so there was no need for an envelope; they could be sent to or from servicemen for free.

As the night wore on, the tension grew until men were wishing aloud that the Japanese would just show up and get it over with. Except those with the dark senses of humor, many of the veterans kept their own nerves in check and tried to calm the uninitiated men who were about to experience their baptism of fire.

Down in the fire rooms, the experienced men on the Black Gang told the nervous younger sailors to ignore what would be going on "topside." A part of the Engineering Department, the Black Gang was responsible for the fuel oil burners that heated water in enormous boilers to create steam. The steam was then transferred by pipes to the control room, where it was used to turn the turbines that spun the shafts that rotated the propellers. The bridge communicated how much power was needed by "ringing up" the control room with a system of bells. They had better have the steam pressure up and ready to make the ship jump at a moment's notice, or they'd be the ones in hot water with the captain.

No one seemed quite sure where the nickname "Black Gang" came from. The joke was that it was because they "never saw the light of day." But most likely it was a holdover from the days of Commodore Perry, when the steam that turned the paddlewheels of the frigates was generated by coal-fired furnaces. The Black Gang was still known for faces smeared with the ubiquitous fuel oil.

Now, some of those younger grimed faces nodded when the old chief petty officers told them, "You've got a job to do. What goes on up there is none of your concern."

Deep in the interior of the ship, in a windowless, gray room, "fire control" personnel tried to concentrate in the "plotting room." Fire control had nothing to do with fires, but rather the targeting and shooting of the ship's guns. Their weapon was a World War II innovation that would one day revolutionize the world: a computer. Although computers were in their infancy, the ship's machine would take the information from the radar operators and "plot" the path and speed of the enemy ship or plane so that the ship's guns could be brought to bear.

Up on the deck, Mike Hardy quietly talked to the other men in the gun director's tub about what it had been like at the battles of the Coral Sea and Midway. Since coming aboard the *Santa Fe*, his battle station was in the tub, spotting for a "quad" four-barreled 40-millimeter, amidships on the port side, and one deck above the gun. "We didn't know whether to look up for dive-bombers or down for torpedo planes, but we got through it all right," he said.

Of course the other men knew that the last time Hardy had been in a battle in the Solomons, it had not turned out all right. That night his ship, the *Astoria*, was sunk.

It had been two months since the raid on Tarawa and the subsequent festivities crossing the equator. Five days after returning to Pearl Harbor that September, they'd only had five days in port before they were underway again as part of a carrier task force sent to hit Wake Island.

In the early days of the war, Wake had become a symbol of American courage, an Alamo surrounded by water. The Japanese attacked on December 8, 1941, expecting to rout the small garrison, but were surprised by the fierce resistance of the Marines.

However, F4F Wildcats were no match for the Mitsubishi-built Japanese Zeros; they lacked the "Zeke's" maneuverability and firepower.

The Marine pilots had no chance, but they kept climbing back into their planes and rising to meet the enemy. The very last of them was shot down on December 23. After that, there was nothing to interfere with the relentless pounding the remaining American defenders took from the air and the sea until they were finally overrun.

Two years had passed, but the American task force intended that payback be hell. During the attack, most of the Japanese aircraft were destroyed on the ground. A few Zeros managed to take off, but to their surprise they met a superior American fighter plane, the new Grumman F6F Hellcat. The Zero could still turn quicker, but with its 2,000-horsepower engine, the Hellcat could outclimb and outdive its opponent, and its six .50-caliber guns provided a lot more firepower than the Zeke's four 20-millimeter guns. This was the first time the Hellcats and Zeros mixed it up; the Americans didn't lose a plane, while the Japanese were blasted from the sky.

After the carrier planes cleared the airspace above Wake, the battleships and cruisers arrived about noon and began to shell buildings, gun emplacements, fuel storage tanks, ammunition dumps, and airfields. The cruiser division, with the *Santa Fe* in the lead, came at the atoll from the north, bombarding as they steamed parallel to the beach. They then made a pass from the west, turned, and made another from the east.

The Japanese tried to fight back against the ships with their shore guns. Their fire was irregular but fairly accurate. Twice during the bombardment, the cruisers had to take evasive action after near misses indicated that the gunners on shore were getting the range.

Then a shell from a large gun roared between the *Santa Fe's* two smokestacks only about twenty feet above the deck. The ship was lucky. The crew ducked and then watched with their jaws dropping as the projectile exploded harmlessly in the water a hundred feet beyond the ship. They then returned fire until the gun emplacements on shore were silenced.

With Wake burning, the task force sailed back to Pearl Harbor. CruDiv13 was then assigned to the newly created Fifth Fleet under Admiral Raymond Spruance, who'd taken over command of the fleet at Midway and won the day.

On October 20, 1944, Captain Berkey called a ship's inspection. The announcement produced the requisite grumbling from the crew who didn't want to stand in rows in their dress whites in the hot Hawaiian sun for God-knew-how-long, waiting for the captain to look them over and dismiss them.

It was going to be their last day in port, as they'd been told they'd be shipping out again in the morning.

The crew, however, loved Berkey. They liked the way he talked to them over the public address system before they sailed into action and let them know what to expect. Then, when the situation allowed, he updated his "boys" about what was happening.

When he took command of the *Santa Fe*, Berkey had been pleased to note how many of his men were already veterans of the Pacific war. A third of them had ships sunk beneath their feet, which meant they'd seen about the worst of it and knew what to expect. He'd called the inspection to present one of them with award earned during the Battle of Savo Island.

Water Tender 2nd Class Jim Hunter had tried to get out of the inspection by volunteering to stand another member of the Black Gang's shift so that he could stay in the fire room. As a water tender, he was responsible for monitoring the level of water in the boilers by watching a glass gauge with one hand poised on a valve. The trick was to keep just the right amount of water in the boilers—too much and the excess steam pressure could tear up the turbines, too little and the boilers would overheat and explode like bombs.

Another sailor, however, was sent to fetch him. Cursing and grumbling, Hunter arrived on the weather deck, where the ship's company was standing at attention in formation. Berkey was pinning a Purple Heart, given to men wounded in action against the enemy, on another survivor from the Savo Island debacle as Hunter found his spot in line.

Hunter didn't wait long before the captain approached and presented him with the Purple Heart for the burns he had suffered on the *Vincennes* while a hatch to prevent seawater from reaching the sinking ship's boilers, while the ship was near the surface and the men in the water. The captain began to turn away and then acted as though he had just remembered something else.

"Oh, yes," he said loud enough for the crew to hear, "I have another one here for you—the Silver Star." The medal was given for conspicuous gallantry "in keeping with the highest traditions of the United States Naval Service." It had been awarded to Hunter for his heroics climbing back down in the burning ship to close the hatch, which had probably saved many lives, as well as assisting injured and drowning shipmates as the *Vincennes* was being abandoned.

The crew was absolutely quiet and therefore it was easy to hear Hunter when he groused, "All right, but it's the last one I'm gonna take." The other men in line smiled and tried not to laugh, but even the captain chuckled;

it had never ceased to amaze him how matter-of-fact these young men were about the job they were doing. They didn't see themselves as heroes, and he loved them for it.

After the ceremony, Berkey spoke to Hunter privately. "You've done your part," the captain told him. "Say the word, and I'll send you home."

The young sailor thought about it for a moment. He'd been away at war for nearly two years and many aspects of shipboard life were getting pretty old. A lot of it was just plain boring; work a shift, then go up top for a breath of fresh air and stare at miles and miles of featureless ocean. There was always the fear that a torpedo would burst through the side of the ship; then he and the other members of the Black Gang, at least those not killed by the blast, would drown in the dark like rats.

Plenty of times, he had wished the ship would go back to the States for a breather. But he wasn't one of those guys who confessed in moments of homesickness that he missed his mother. He had joined the Navy right after Pearl Harbor to do a job and that job wasn't finished. Besides, some of the younger guys were still learning the ropes, and who was going to keep the ship moving if all the veterans jumped ship?

"I didn't come out here to go home now," he told the captain. "I think I'll stay a bit longer."

October 1944
Bougainville

When the *Santa Fe* crew left Pearl Harbor again the next day, they were told that the ship was bound for the Fiji–New Hebrides area to participate in fleet training exercises to prepare for the invasion of the Gilbert Islands. But they were heading into more trouble than anticipated because of decisions that had been made at the highest levels eleven months earlier.

In January 1943, when the *Santa Fe* was still being outfitted, President Roosevelt and British Prime Minister Winston Churchill met at Casablanca to hammer out a cohesive strategic policy. Probably the most significant political decision was their agreement on a policy of "total surrender" from their enemies. Germany, Italy, and Japan were to be left without the means of waging a war of aggression again.

There were also several specific military strategies that came out of the conference. One was that the Allied invasion of Europe would begin with Italy. Another was the necessity of keeping General Chiang Kai-shek's Chinese army in the war by keeping the supply routes through Burma and India.

The third strategy dealt with how to prosecute the war in the Pacific. The first step had been to take back the Aleutians. With that accomplished, the rest of the Pacific was divided into two main theaters of operations. The Southwest Pacific, from Australia to the Philippines, was the domain of the Army under General MacArthur. The Central and North Pacific were the responsibility of the Fifth Fleet—from the Gilbert Islands through the Marshalls, then the Marianas, and up in a line to the Bonin Islands of Chichi Jima, Haha Jima, and Iwo Jima, and finally Okinawa and the home islands of Japan.

Admiral Ernest King, the commander-in-chief of the Navy, reorganized the Pacific Fleet and its Allied components into three main fleets. The Seventh Fleet was placed under MacArthur's overall command to support his troops in New Guinea, the first step to returning to the Philippines as he had pledged.

In conjunction with MacArthur's plans, Admiral William "Bull" Halsey was placed in command of the Third Fleet and charged with taking the remaining Solomon Islands following the fall of Guadalcanal. His eventual goal was to capture the Japanese fortress of Rabaul in New Britain.

The Fifth Fleet, under the command of Spruance, represented the rest of the Navy's presence in the Pacific. The Navy, with its Marine ground forces, planned to island-"hop"—isolating some without bothering to capture them, while attacking others selected for their strategic value as airbases for the next push.

Beginning in the southern Pacific, the American forces would fight their way north on two parallel tracks: MacArthur up the west; the Fifth Fleet up through the Central Pacific, converging at the Philippines. Once the Philippines were regained, Japanese shipping and movement south could be stopped, and the Philippine airbases would be a threat to both Japanese-held Formosa and Japan itself.

For the Fifth Fleet that meant a lot of water to cover. To keep the Japanese guessing where the next attack would occur and keep their defenses stretched thin, the Navy created "fast attack carrier" task forces. These were made possible by the addition of the massive *Essex*-class fleet carriers, each displacing twenty-seven thousand tons and capable of speeds up to thirty-five knots, making them the fastest major warships on the seas. The new behemoths, twenty-four of which had been ordered from the shipyards, carried a hundred planes in three squadrons: thirty-six fighters, thirty-six dive-bombers, and eighteen torpedo planes.

Each task force consisted of two, or sometimes three, of the large, or fleet, carriers; one or two light carriers; two battleships; six cruisers; and eighteen destroyers. There were also supply task groups comprised of fuel, ammunition and stores ships, cruisers and destroyers for defense, as well as small "escort" carriers, which carried replacement planes for the fleet carriers, along with their own air defenses known as the Combat Air Patrol, or CAP.

The September and October attacks on Tarawa in the Gilbert Islands and on Wake Island were warm-ups to work out the coordination between the carriers and surface ships. The first big test for the Fifth Fleet would be when it returned to the Gilberts.

In the meantime MacArthur's troops were slogging their way through New Guinea as Halsey moved his fleet north through the Solomons. Halsey intended to take Bougainville, already the site of one of Japan's most devastating losses of the war, before the ships and Marines arrived.

In April the Japanese were in the midst of counterattacking the Allied forces in the Solomons, when Admiral Yamamoto decided he needed to look over the situation himself. But U.S. Navy codebreakers intercepted the message announcing when his plane would arrive.

Flying at the extreme range of their fuel supply, Marine pilots in P-38 Lightning fighters flew from Guadalcanal to intercept the admiral. They ambushed his plane just as it was landing, and when they left, Japan's best military strategist was dead.

Prime Minister Hideki Tojo, whose military government had seized power, and the Imperial High Command still believed they could win the war. They withdrew their forces to a defensive line extending from the Kurile Islands north of Japan to the Marianas in Micronesia to New Guinea and Burma. They planned to bide their time until the moment was right for the "decisive victory" that their late admiral knew was necessary for Japan to keep its empire.

In the meantime, their strategy would be to kill as many American servicemen as possible and see if the enemy had the stomach for the bloodshed. As part of that strategy, in September the Japanese high command established the "New Operational Policy." From that point on, their garrisons were considered "immovable." There would be no more Guadalcanal-style evacuations, unless it was to fall back to a more defensible place for a last stand. There would be no surrender; Japanese troops would fight until victorious or dead.

So far the Japanese soldiers and sailors in the Solomons had given a fierce account of themselves as the Third Fleet moved north. Then on November 1 the Marines under Major General Vandegrift, of Guadalcanal fame, skirted the heavily defended southern end of Bougainville and landed on the weakly defended west side at Empress Augusta Bay. The Japanese responded by sending a force of four cruisers and six destroyers to attack the invaders' ships, but they were driven off with the loss of a cruiser and destroyer.

However, Halsey's cruisers were also battered during the fight and needed a breather. A call went out for help.

November 6, 1944
Bougainville

As the Fifth Fleet headed for the waters between Fiji and the New Hebrides, they crossed the equator on November 1 with the usual initiation festivities. This time, however, there were only a few pollywogs on the *Santa Fe* (having just joined the ship in Pearl Harbor) to bear the brunt of the hazing.

The fun was over too soon—at least for the shellbacks—as CruDiv13's mission unexpectedly grew more serious. The division had hardly arrived in the training area when the cruiser division commander, Admiral DuBose, received new orders. The cruisers and a squadron of four destroyers were to separate from the fleet and head northwest for Espirutu Santo, an island in the New Hebrides, to refuel and then relieve CruDiv12 at Bougainville.

The two divisions rendezvoused on November 7, and CruDiv13 took over escort duties of guarding the transports bringing reinforcements to Empress Augusta Bay. After they delivered their charges on the eighth without incident, the cruisers and destroyers proceeded twenty-five miles northwest.

Berkey addressed the crew. They would be stationing themselves to block any attempt by the Japanese to break through and attack the landing beaches, he said. Such an attack might come by sea or air, or both. They would all have to be vigilant and do their duty when called upon.

All was quiet until late in the afternoon, when lookouts spotted a Japanese "snooper," a scout plane skirting the formation. He was well out of range of the five-inch guns and soon disappeared, back in the direction of the Japanese base at Rabaul. "Giving our location to every Jap south of Tokyo," the veterans muttered. They knew that the attack would come at night, and they would be without any air cover from American fighter planes because Halsey's carriers had withdrawn from the area.

As the sun set in the west, Berkey gave the command for the crew to report to General Quarters, Condition 1, meaning every gun was manned, every man was at his battle station, and the ship was buttoned up tight. Throughout the vessel, hatches and watertight doors were slammed shut and dogged with steel bars to prevent their being opened; they would remain so until the captain said otherwise.

The Japanese waited until a little after 10 P.M. Then the men in the plotting room saw them—twenty-five, maybe thirty pips on the radar, coming fast. The twin-engined "Betty" bombers flew low so that they would be hard to see against the dark waters. Any higher and they would have been silhouetted, even against the weak starlight.

Guided by radar, the Santa Fe's five-inch guns opened up first. But not all of the planes appeared on the screens; they flew too low, just above the waves, and were soon too close for the five-inch guns. Stopping them fell to the crews on the 40-millimeter twin and quad mounts, and the 20-millimeter machine guns, most of which were manned by the ship's Marine contingent. The forties and twenties weren't guided automatically by radar, just by the lookouts who searched the darkness for the telltale blue flames of the planes' engine exhaust—their only clue to the planes' whereabouts.

Mike Hardy was one of those straining his eyes to see. The 40-millimeter guns were guided by a "director" who sat next to Hardy, both men plus a lookout surrounded by a waist-high wall of steel. Looking through a scope, the director placed his hands around what looked somewhat like the grips on a motorcycle's handlebars. From there he could make the barrels on the gun below him move back and forth and up and down electronically as he followed a plane through the scope. When he had a plane in range, he pulled the trigger on the handlebar and the guns below would start shooting.

Voices came over Hardy's headgear. *Bandit two points off the bow! Bandit coming starboard side! Two of 'em port side!* The forties started up—a deeper POM-POM-POM than the one-point-ones—then the twenties began to chatter. He saw exhaust flames and pointed them out to the director, who swiveled the gun and shot.

As usual, Hardy had experienced a case of nerves when Berkey announced that the Japanese were on the way. He had looked around for the director and the lookout, a Marine sergeant, but couldn't see well enough in the dark to tell if they were scared, too. But when they began to shoot, Hardy's fears trailed out into the night along with the red tracers. He was okay as long as he was fighting back.

The Japanese Bettys attacked at 250 miles an hour, their guns blazing as they maneuvered to drop their torpedoes and bombs. The American cruisers, led by the *Santa Fe,* twisted and swerved wildly at thirty knots, trying to turn their bows into the paths of approaching planes to present less of a target.

In the fire rooms the Black Gang stayed busy answering calls for more power, less power, power to one propeller or another. *All ahead full. Full back port.*

At times, the planes flew so low that they could have struck the smokestacks. Dark shapes roared past and the men tensed, wondering if a torpedo was on the way. Bombs exploded in the water around the ship, sending up huge geysers of water.

However, the American guns were taking a toll. Time and again, a line of tracers would end with a burst of flame and a plane would streak like a meteor across the sky until crashing into the ocean, where its fuel would continue to burn on the surface.

One plane was hit repeatedly but kept coming for the *Santa Fe,* even when flames consumed it and shells from a dozen guns tore into it. With a roar like a speeding train, the plane passed over the bow of the ship almost eye-level with the men on the bridge and crashed into the water on the other side.

The crewmembers who saw the plane waited for the explosion of its torpedo, which they thought must have been launched before the plane went down. The moment passed and the men out in the open breathed easier. But down inside the ship near the forward five-inch gun ammunition room, there was a loud CLANG! of metal striking metal. With their hearts in their throats the men waited for the explosion, but the torpedo was a dud.

The attacks continued for nearly two hours, and the night might have gone worse for the Americans, but the ships were able to dip in and out of rainsqualls that hid them from the planes. After the Japanese left, Berkey cautioned the men that the battle might not be over. Physically exhausted and emotionally spent, the men tried to rest at their battle stations. The quiet didn't last long; two hours later, the Japanese were back again with a dozen planes.

Seaman 1st Class Al Mancini's only warning that his short life was in danger again was when he saw the tiny flames from the wing guns of a Betty that was coming right at him. Even then, he didn't duck fast enough.

A lot had happened to him since he left his mother crying at the kitchen table back in Greenwich. Not all of it related to the war. On his sixteenth birthday, a week after arriving at Pearl Harbor in March 1943, a couple of buddies who knew his secret took him into Honolulu for what they said would be a "three-minute movie."

Little did he know, at least until they arrived, that "three-minute movies" were government-run whorehouses—three dollars for three minutes with one of the hostesses, hence the name. It was the first time he ever saw a woman with a tattoo.

If Mancini was nervous then, it was nothing compared to waiting for the Japanese to show up that night off Bougainville. It didn't help that he was paired with a fellow from Milwaukee named Pete, one of the survivors from the *Vincennes*. Some of the Savo Island veterans Mancini had met seemed exceptionally calm, but others were like Pete, excitable and nervous, even when there was nothing to worry about. Pete considered himself a man of the world and took great delight in being a bad influence on his younger shipmates. He smoked cigarettes one after the other and got Mancini into the habit by repeatedly offering him one.

Following the first wave of attacks that night, Pete acted like a pot ready to boil over, chain-smoking and pacing. Then the second wave arrived, dropping flares over the ships and attacking from the dark outside the circle of light. That's when Mancini spotted the Betty coming at him, its guns spitting fire and bullets. There was so much noise and confusion as the ship turned hard that Mancini was hardly aware of the bullets that tore into the ship around him and Pete. Then the plane was gone.

Pete looked at him in the failing light of the flares. "What are you sweatin' for?" the older sailor said, grinning.

"I'm not sweatin'," Mancini replied. He put his hand up to his face and felt something wet and sticky. He looked at his hand; it was red with blood. He saw then that the edge of the waist-high metal wall around his station was jagged where it had been struck by bullets.

Some of the metal splinters had struck him in the face and scalp, but a couple of inches higher up and he would have been cut in two by the bullets. There wasn't any pain, nor was he losing a lot of blood, so he stayed at his battle station for the remainder of the fight. The older hands could say what they wanted about the *Santa Fe* being christened with holy water, but as far as he was concerned she was a lucky ship.

The *Birmingham* wasn't as fortunate. She was struck by two torpedoes, but the damage was contained by her watertight compartments. She was back under full steam when the second wave came in. Then to the crew's horror, the *Mobile,* which was following behind, launched a star shell that illuminated the area right over the *Birmingham.* A Japanese pilot responded like a moth to a flame, hitting one of the ship's gun turrets with a bomb.

The damage was slight, however, and her casualties were confined to one of her Marines, who had been manning a 20-millimeter and was blown overboard by the blast. Unfortunately, with enemy planes still in the area, the ship could not stop to look for a single man in the dark sea without risking the rest of the crew.

At last, the Japanese—the few who survived the ships' guns at any rate—returned to Rabaul. After reveille that morning, Captain Berkey assembled the crew and presented the ten-dollar prize to the lookout who had spotted the first plane. The skipper then held up a piece of the torpedo rack that had dropped onto the ship from the blazing plane that had passed overhead.

All told, twenty enemy planes had been shot down by the American cruisers and destroyers during the two attacks. In such hectic circumstances, with more than one ship often firing at the same target, it was difficult to tell which ship should get credit for a "kill," and in all likelihood, many of the Japanese losses were the result of combined fire from more than one ship. However, later that day, the *Santa Fe's* painter was authorized to paint three red-and-white Japanese flags below the silhouette image of a Betty on the side of the pilothouse, the "official" tally for the ship.

The crew patted each other on the back and recounted the most exciting moments. They were now all blooded warriors. They had done their jobs, as Berkey pointed out when he passed a message along from the commander of the transport ships back at Empress Augusta Bay: "Thanks for keeping the bastards off our necks."

November 20, 1943
Tarawa

Someone had made a mistake. From his position high atop the *Santa Fe's* superstructure, Lt. Warren Harding watched in horror as the young Marines struggled toward the beach only to be mown down in the water by machine guns and mortars. With the morning's landings on the Tarawa and Makin atolls in the Gilbert Islands, the long, bloody road through the Central Pacific was under way. And from what Harding could see through the range finder he used to spot targets as a gunnery officer, it had not begun well.

Up to this point, ground battles in the Pacific had been through the mountainous jungles of Guadalcanal, New Guinea, and Bougainville. Tarawa and Makin were two of sixteen atolls in the Gilberts, low-lying isles of coral and sand, scarcely above sea level. Hardly worth fighting for, except that the Japanese airstrips on them had to be neutralized and turned around for the fleet's own use before moving on to the more important target of the Marshall Islands to the northwest.

Coconut palms, a few hardy grasses, and indifferent shrubs were the only vegetation on the atolls. But what natural defenses they lacked in vegetation and terrain, the Japanese made up for with reinforced concrete pillboxes and blockhouses, connected by a network of tunnels, and built to defend Prime Minister Tojo's "unsinkable aircraft carriers."

That morning, the battleship *Maryland,* risen from the ruins of Pearl Harbor, and the *Santa Fe* were assigned to cover the Second Marine Division's landing on Betio, the largest island in the Tarawa atoll. Only a half mile across at its widest point and two miles long, yard for yard it was destined to host some of the bloodiest fighting of the war.

Two hours of steady shelling with high explosives had stripped the fronds from the coconut trees and shattered their trunks, until they were nothing more than big sticks jutting from the sand. Watching from a ship, Harding wondered how any human being could have survived. But the battle for the island had then turned into a series of mishaps and mistakes by the Americans.

First, the bombardment wasn't as effective as it appeared. The *Maryland* had guns capable of hitting targets twenty miles away, but she was only two miles out and the barrels of the sixteen-inch guns were nearly horizontal when they were fired. The result was that the projectiles came in flat, and unless they actually hit a raised obstruction such as a blockhouse, they often skipped off the island without exploding.

Second, the surface ships and carrier air forces had failed to coordinate their schedules, and the American planes showed up a half hour late. Then the Marine landing craft were supposed to arrive immediately after the bombardment, while the Japanese still had their heads down. But the boats were also late getting started, and the enemy had emerged from their fortifications, waiting for the Marines to land.

To compound it all, the planners misjudged the tides. The landing craft were supposed to drop the men close to the shore, in shallow water. But the boats got hung up on the outer reef, a hundred yards from the shore, where they were easy targets for Japanese artillery. The Marines had to jump out and wade slowly to the beach.

Half a mile away from the landings, Harding felt a wave of pity wash over him as he witnessed so many young men being massacred by presighted and overlapping machine-gun and mortar fire. His range finders made it appear that the battle was only a hundred feet or so from his position, and he could see individuals and groups of men clearly as bullets stitched small geysers through the water until intercepting their bodies. Hundreds of dark forms that he knew had once been teenagers and young men in their early twenties now floated in the bloody water.

A few made it to shore, but they were pinned down behind a small sea-wall. Harding was now in Spot One and in overall command of the main battery. He wanted to call them up now and blast away at the Japanese. Yet, there was nothing he could do until he received orders, and none were forthcoming. He hadn't felt so helpless since watching the German U-boat shell the Norwegian merchant ship in August 1942, and that was not nearly so horrific.

A couple weeks earlier, during the night battle off Bougainville, Harding had had a ringside seat on top of the superstructure and nothing much else to do but watch. The crew got a good laugh the next night when Tokyo Rose came on the radio. They were at first surprised when she admitted that the Japanese had lost "fifteen planes." However, she cooed, the brave fliers of the empire had not died in vain. They had taken "three battleships, two aircraft carriers, seven cruisers, thirteen destroyers, and an unknown number of transports" down with them.

Thanks to Captain Berkey's reports, the men all knew that only the *Birmingham* had actually been hit. The ship would be out of action for a while, but her own captain had joked after the broadcast in a message to the rest of the division, "apparently one American cruiser looks like an entire fleet to the Japs."

Harding was envious of the *Birmingham's* crew getting to go back stateside for a while. He missed his wife, Jo. They wrote often, but he wasn't allowed to say much about where he was or what the ship had been doing. If he slipped up and revealed too much, the military censors who read all the V-mail would have physically cut it out of the letter. So their messages to each other dealt with the little things.

Harding had to limit himself to talking about the weather—unbearably hot and humid—or the funny or mundane aspects of life at sea. Mostly, he just told Jo how much he missed her and tried to reassure her that his spirits and those of his shipmates were high. There would be no telling her, therefore, how his spirits had sunk to an all-time low after the fight at Bougainville when he saw the carnage at Betio. Or how he felt guilty for being glad that he was not one of those young men struggling to the beach.

The crew heard later that the first wave of Marines had suffered 75 percent casualties and that subsequent waves suffered from 40 to 50 percent. Harding would have guessed the numbers to be higher. Every man onboard burned to do something to help, but not until the next day, after the Marines had been reinforced and were able to establish a real foothold, was the ship called in to take out individual Japanese emplacements.

Berkey brought the *Santa Fe* as close as he could to the shore to blast away at the Japanese, risking return fire from well-entrenched shore batteries, including eight-inch coastal defense guns brought from the fall of Singapore. Even one of the cruiser's Kingfisher pilots got into the act. Lt. (j.g.) Theodore Buzanoski was flying low over the island relaying target locations to the ship when he spotted an ammunition dump. He took a run at the dump and released a bomb he carried, scoring a direct hit that sent the ammunition skyrocketing in massive detonations.

The battle for Betio lasted for three days and would set the brutal tone for the campaign through the rest of the Central Pacific and beyond. Having watched their comrades being slaughtered, the Marines who survived were in no mood to show mercy, nor were the Japanese inclined to ask for it. It was a war of extermination, a war fought with flamethrowers, hand grenades, and canister shot; a war in which bulldozers were used to bury the Japanese in their redoubts, after which gasoline was poured down air vents, followed by explosives.

On the night of the third and final day of resistance, the remaining Japanese defenders mounted a suicide charge. Some managed to reach the American lines, where the fighting degenerated into bloody hand-to-hand combat.

The victory was costly for the Americans, but the Japanese paid a much more terrible price for defeat. When the Stars and Stripes was finally raised on a shattered palm tree, proclaiming the battle over, more than a thousand Marines were dead and another two thousand wounded. Of the five thousand defenders, one officer and sixteen soldiers were captured; all the rest were killed or took their own lives.

By then, the *Santa Fe* had already departed, having expended the ammunition for her six- and five-inch guns. Back on the open ocean Harding had been struck by its beauty and peacefulness. The way the sun slipped from the blue and green waters in the morning and the way it set at night in a glory of colors, after which the stars, with no competition from civilization, sparkled like diamonds on black velvet. Dolphins played in the bow's wake, racing along with the warship, unafraid of her terrible power. Yet Harding knew that he might never again be able to look at the ocean without seeing Marines dying for a bit of coral that no one had ever heard of before.

CHAPTER FIVE

My Father: A Lucky Man

December 15, 1943
Pearl Harbor, Hawaii

Captain Berkey ambled down the lines of sailors and officers who stood at attention on the pier next to the *Santa Fe*. Occasionally, he stopped to point out some flaw, such as a nonregulation haircut or a handkerchief improperly knotted, but mostly he smiled or said a few quiet words to his "boys."

Behind him, Captain Jerauld Wright strolled stiffly, as though his long legs ached to move faster. Tall and angular, thin almost to the point of gaunt, he fixed each man he passed with his hawklike eyes but spoke to no one. They were not his men, yet.

Six days earlier, after two months of operations, the *Santa Fe* sailed back into Pearl Harbor. Now, standing at attention in their dress whites, the crew was about to lose the only captain many of them had known as Wright prepared to relieve Berkey of his command.

The men had greeted the news of Berkey's transfer—he had been promoted to rear admiral—with sadness and apprehension. The skipper was popular with the crew, a father figure for many who were away from home for the first time, including parental warnings like, "Don't try to drink all the whiskey in Honolulu the first day . . . your stomach has forgotten what it's like." However, he also ran a tight, disciplined ship and asked that each man perform his job up to expectations. Most importantly, he had taken them into battle and brought them back out safely.

No one knew much about this new captain—what kind of a ship he ran or how he would react when the bullets and bombs started flying again. Any lingering ideas that the war would be over soon or that the Japanese would give up had disappeared in the bloody surf at Tarawa. And the crew knew that the danger wasn't all on land.

A little after 5:00 A.M., November 22, the day after they had sailed from the atoll, the escort carrier USS *Liscome Bay* was attacked by a submarine off Butaritari Island near Makin. A torpedo struck near the stern of the ship—a so-called jeep carrier used mainly to provide air protection for convoys and transports, as well as replacement planes for those lost from the big carriers. A few moments after the first explosion, the aircraft bomb magazine detonated, sinking the ship within minutes. Two hundred and seventy-two men were saved by other U.S. ships, but six hundred and forty-six men died in the shark-infested waters.

The dead included Mess Cook 3rd Class Doris "Dorie" Miller. A "colored" sailor onboard the battleship USS *West Virginia* at Pearl Harbor on December 7, 1941, Miller had manned a machine gun to defend his blazing ship and was credited with shooting down a Zero. His heroism earned him the Navy Cross, the service's highest honor and a first for a member of his race. In this war, like any other, the good were dying young.

After participating in raids against the Marshall Islands, the next step toward Tokyo, the *Santa Fe* and the rest of CruDiv13 were ordered back to Pearl Harbor. The news was welcome to the cruisers' crews, as they had been at sea almost constantly since October 13. Still, it was with mixed emotions that they sailed into the harbor on December 9, saluting the spot where the *Arizona* rested; two years after the bombing, no part of the ship could be seen above water, as the superstructure had been removed.

The men were excited to get solid land beneath their feet for more than a couple of hours, go out for dinner, drink a few beers, and maybe catch sight of a girl in a dress that wasn't made of burlap sacking like what was worn by the native women on the atolls. But they were starting to wonder when they might get to go stateside. They knew of ships that had seen far less action but were allowed to head home for one reason or another. The order sending the *Santa Fe* back to the States seemed to have been lost in the shuffle.

Nevertheless, the crew was relieved to learn that they would be in port for two weeks, maybe more, as the ship would be undergoing renovations. Some of that included new equipment of a secretive nature. The only real evidence of it they saw was a new antenna, which only a few of them knew had to do with "radar." Even in December 1943, unless their job was directly connected to the "secret weapon," not many regular crewmembers knew much about the technology, other than that it had to do with detecting enemy planes and ships.

When the installation was completed on the *Santa Fe* there were three different kinds of radar systems onboard the ship. Two of these were improved long-range radars. The navigational radar searched the azimuth, or surface of the ocean, for such things as ships, islands, shorelines, and harbor entrances. The other long-range radar was used to detect airborne targets, including those beyond the horizon over the curvature of the earth.

The third, and newest, addition was short-range, high-definition fire-control radar that was used for acquiring accurate target information for the firing of the surface target and antiaircraft guns. The new radar was hooked up to the 40-millimeters, which were now entirely aimed and fired by the gun director, who, looking through a viewfinder, placed the radar pip of an enemy plane within a donut and pulled the trigger. It wasn't automatic, but it beat doing it all by sight with pointers and trainers trying to aim the guns.

The acquisition of the new technology required having someone aboard who knew how to operate and maintain it. Reporting for that duty on the same day as the change-of-command ceremonies transferring the responsibility of the ship to Captain Wright was a twenty-four-year-old warrant officer named Don Jackson.

The *Santa Fe* was a new vessel for him, but Jackson had served for a short time under Wright and respected him. It had been more than two years since he'd last seen the new skipper, and he was a mere petty officer third class then, so he was surprised now when Wright stopped in front of him and looked closely at his face. "I know you," the captain said.

"Yes, sir," Jackson replied. "And I know you, too. From the *Mississippi,* sir."

For the briefest of moments, Wright allowed a quick grin to tug at the corners of his mouth. "Yes," he replied, "the *Mississippi.*"

The captain strode on, leaving Jackson to recall those days on the battleship *Mississippi,* before there was a war, when they were all still free to pursue their dreams.

Donald Clyde Jackson Jr., was born September 16, 1919 in the small South Dakota farmhouse with only a neighbor woman to assist his mother at his birth. The first eight years of his life had been happy ones, even if the family kept moving from one failed South Dakota farm to the next. But by February 17, 1927, his father, who was known by his middle name, Clyde, finally admitted that he wasn't ever going to make in that state as a farmer and held a public auction to get rid of nearly everything his family owned.

They loaded what little was left in a old Ford truck and moved to Hot Springs, South Dakota when Clyde found a job in a lumber mill. Moving from school to school was hard on young Donald, but it never crossed his mind that his family was poor. There wasn't ever any "cash money" for extras, but living on farms and even in Hot Springs there was always enough to eat. He didn't wear shoes when the weather was warm, to save them for the winter, and his meager wardrobe was mostly hand-me-downs. But his clothes were clean and well-mended.

Don had his family and that was what was important to an active little boy. Clyde Jackson was a quiet, gentle man who loved to wrestle with his son on the floor. The boy also adored his mother, Gayle, and doted on his baby sister, Joan. But not everyone was as happy. Years later, Clyde and Gayle would each blame the other for what happened and after a few months in Hot Springs, she took the children and went to live with her parents in Winner, South Dakota.

The boy missed his father and so was overjoyed when Clyde showed up a few weeks later, driving a beatup Model T Ford. As far as Don was concerned, now that his family was back together, all was right with the world. But it wasn't right between his folks.

The morning after he arrived, Clyde walked back out of the house, got in his car, and started to drive away. When Don saw his father leaving, he took off running after the car. His father saw him in the rearview mirror and stopped to let the boy catch up. Don climbed in the car and without anything more than the clothes he was wearing, left with his father, not knowing it would be three years before he saw his mother and sister again, and then only briefly.

Clyde Jackson headed east, back home to Malvern, Iowa where he and his son moved in with his mother, Mina, and stepfather Barney McFall. The older couple did their best to let Don know he was loved, but the little boy was lonely for his mother and sister and often cried himself to sleep.

He held onto the hope that his parents would reconcile. Shortly after Christmas 1927, he wrote to his mother, ostensibly to tell her about the gifts he'd received—especially his favorite present, an electric motor he had to assemble himself—then got to what was really on his mind. "We will not be coming to S. Dakota anymore, so if you want to see us, come here." The plea was as plain as he could make it, but it did no good; his family was broken and there was no putting it back together again.

Don Jackson grew up like any farmboy. He woke at 5:30 in the morning and was soon out in the cold, dark barn milking the cows, moving on to feed the hogs and sheep, before shoveling the manure out of the stalls and pens. Only then did he come in for breakfast and to get ready for school. Mina would pack him a lunch and send him off wearing the same clothes he did his chores in, a daily uniform of denim overalls and chambray shirts.

It was a hard life, and sometimes dangerous. His grandfather, William, was killed by lightning while mending his fences just moments after telling his hired hand that it was "the easiest death a man could suffer."

As he had in South Dakota, Don attended a one-room schoolhouse until high school. He was bright and loved books, but nobody pushed him on his school work. Like his father and father's father on down the line, he was expected to be a farmer.

Childhood passed into adolescence, and although he continued to miss his mother and sister, he was not otherwise dissatisfied with his life. As a farm kid, there were always chores to do when school was over. But Sundays after church were for playing baseball in a pasture and for ice-cream socials during strawberry season. There were the county and state fairs, which provided a chance for the teen-agers from different parts of the region or state to meet and sometimes start courting.

Patriotic holidays were big events, big as Christmas. The residents of Mills County were still grieving their losses in the Great War, but it was with pride. Everybody flew the flag on Armistice Day and the Fourth of July, when men, women, and children gathered to cheer the veterans as they paraded though Malvern—most in their Doughboy uniforms and a few old codgers left over from the Civil War. The cemeteries would blossom with fresh cut flowers, and flags were placed on the graves of those who hadn't made it back like Don's uncle, Russell, his mother's younger brother.

In 1932, Franklin Delano Roosevelt was elected president and inherited an economy gone awry, which was soon known as the Great Depression. Adding to the stress, at least as far as farmers were concerned, the bad economy coincided with a multi-year drought. Although not hit as badly as the so-called Dust Bowl areas further south and west, the dry years hurt Iowa farmers, too. A day would begin sunny and clear but by afternoon the sky would be tinted brown with topsoil and the sun would appear as a weak orange ball.

Crops failed and farmers with them as banks—those that hadn't gone under themselves—weren't loaning money for something as iffy as a good crop. Across the country nearly three in four farmers lost their land and Mills County was no different. But town or country, everyone scrambled to find work, even kids were expected to pitch in to help their families.

Beginning at age twelve, Don stared working for his uncle, Ivan, on his farm during the summers. His father's younger brother and his wife, Viola, cared for him like a son, treating him with the same love and affection that he'd missed with his own family. It was through watching Ivan and Viola and the McFalls that he learned what a strong, committed marriage should be and, as he got older, knew that he wanted the same thing for himself someday.

Ivan was more Don's male role model than his own father, who was gone for extended periods trying to find work as a sheep-shearer and farmhand. Ivan was what they called a straight-shooter, but he wasn't much of a church-goer. The way he saw it, a man should be judged by what he did outside a church more than what he said inside of one.

Don Jackson attended high school in Malvern. The big, three-story red-brick building was the first school he'd ever attended with more than one classroom. That's were he realized that a lot of the town kids didn't have it any better than he did, and some had it worse.

One of his new friends, Willard Milliken came from a family so poor that his folks couldn't afford to take care of him, so he'd been taken in by a farm family. Tall and thin, Willard was a dreamer, always playing with model air-planes and talking about how some day he'd be a pilot.

Another friend from town, Devere Knight, was the son of an often unem-ployed house painter. The family basically lived hand-to-mouth and Devere, short, stocky, a constellation of freckles smeared across his open, honest face, had probably never owned a new article of clothing in his life.

Jackson admired that neither Milliken nor Knight ever complained about their lot in life. They had great senses of humor and were brimming with confidence that they had bright futures, all they had to do was work hard and then reach out to grab them.

Jackson had graduated from high school in the spring of 1937, envious of his classmates who were going on to college. Most of them were from families who lived in town; farm kids like him were supposed to grow up to be farmers. However, a toy electric motor he had received ten years earlier for Christmas had sparked a continuing interest in electronics, and Jackson wanted to be an electrical engineer. But there had never been a college graduate in his family, and there was no money to produce one now.

Still, he hadn't given up on the idea, and he had hoped to save enough someday to enroll. Realizing he wasn't going to get there on the dollar a day he was making as a farm hand, Jackson had decided to leave Iowa. He had always wanted to see the ocean, and a friend, Dwight Horton, whose family had moved from Malvern to Woodinville, outside of Seattle, wrote and told him he could get a job working with him on truck farms. Horton claimed that they would be making the extraordinary sum of "thirty cents an hour!" for ten-hour days.

So Jackson climbed on the 1935 Harley-Davidson Model 74 motorcycle he had bought for $150 that summer and first headed north into South Dakota before turning west. Five-foot-nine and 150 pounds with his leather riding boots on, he was lean and strong, a handsome eighteen-year-old with dark, wavy hair and piercing brown eyes beneath the cloth helmet and goggles he wore. He carried everything he owned with him—his work clothes, a suede leather coat, and thirty dollars in his pockets.

There weren't many other travelers on the northern highway; the Depression's great migration to California mostly followed the southern routes. But it was a good road composed of small stones in asphalt called a "macadam highway," built by the Work Progress Administration, or WPA, one of Roosevelt's "New Deal" programs to employ the population in public works to give them both an income and self-esteem. Most of the roads that fed into it were still dirt, and the few people he saw along the way were usually on horseback.

Reaching Woodinville, Jackson got a job as promised picking vegetables on a truck farm, bent over for hours at a time as the sweat soaked his clothes and poured from his forehead. But he was used to manual labor and thirty cents an hour was a decent wage. In fact, when he received his first paycheck, Jackson felt flush enough to go in with Horton and, for a grand total of twenty-five dollars, purchased a 1925 Model T so they could pal around together "in style."

At the first opportunity, Jackson insisted they head down to Puget Sound. He marveled when they arrived, and he sniffed the salt air for the first time. The Puget Sound was the biggest expanse of water he had ever seen, but what really caught his imagination were the huge ships. He wondered what it would be like to sail across the ocean on one and visit exotic ports.

He was so enamored with the ships and the thought of going to sea that he talked Horton and another friend, Bill Dill, into driving down to the local U.S. Coast Guard station to enlist. There were positions available, but first they had to pass a physical. Jackson got through his with no problems. But Horton had a heart murmur. And Dill couldn't pass the vision test—or as Jackson and Horton teased him, "you're blind in one eye and can't see out of the other." Although Jackson could have gone in on his own, he decided not to leave without his buddies so it was back to the truck farm.

The harvest season lasted until mid-November, after which Jackson decided to go back to South Dakota. He showed up at his mother's just before Thanksgiving and soon had two jobs: one at a local filling station, working for a family of three brothers, and a second driving a gravel truck at night for a WPA road construction project. He worked for the brothers from 6:00 A.M. to 6:00 P.M., then had an hour off before reporting to the WPA at 7:00 for an eight-hour shift.

Unfortunately, the jobs didn't last. He was fired from the WPA because he had no dependents; married men with families, several of whom showed up after him, had priority. He also knew that his job at the filling station was temporary, since he had just been filling in for one of the brothers who was off on his honeymoon. He needed to think about his future, and that's where a filling station customer, Petty Officer 1st Class Shumway of the United States Navy, came into the picture.

A sixteen-year veteran of the Navy, Shumway ran the recruiting office next to the station. Recognizing that the young man who began dropping by to ask questions was the serious sort, Shumway didn't regale him with "sea stories," but emphasized the educational opportunities the Navy offered. He noted that a business course Jackson had taken in high school, in which he had learned to type, would be very useful for getting a better position onboard a ship than the average seaman, and despite what people said, a war was coming. And it was better to serve in the Navy, where you always knew where your bed was and could count on warm meals, than "slogging through the mud with a rifle."

Jackson agreed it was a good point. Still the threat of war wasn't what concerned him. He wasn't getting anywhere in Deadwood City, and at the rate he was going, he was never going to be able to afford college. He thought that if he joined the Navy and saved his money, he could serve a four-year stint, do his patriotic duty if war came, and put aside enough to pursue a college degree when he got out. In the meantime, he would satisfy his curiosity about the ocean and, as the posters in the recruiting office promised, "See the World."

By February 1938 Jackson was ready to sign on the dotted line, but Deadwood City was just a subrecruiting station. The closest place to enlist was Omaha, Nebraska. So he hunkered down against a bitter wind and rolled back the throttle of the Harley. Small towns ticked by—Sturgis, Rapid City and Wall, Kodoka, Murdo, and Chamberlain. He saw few people on the streets, as if they too were waiting for spring and the end of the Depression to wake up from the long winter. But in the meantime, America slept, her sons safe at home. The troubles blowing against the rest of the world seemed far away.

Jackson rolled into Omaha to find out that there were 150 applicants for only fifteen spots in the recruiting class. A peacetime Navy could afford to be selective and took only the best applicants, based on physical and written tests. Jackson thought he did pretty well on the tests, but still was relieved when told that he would be one of the new recruits.

Reporting back to the Navy recruiting station in Omaha, he and the other recruits were sworn in and herded onto a train to be shipped off to the U.S. Naval Training Station at Great Lakes, Illinois, outside of Chicago. The new arrivals were quarantined for two weeks to prevent the spread of infectious diseases and given vaccinations against smallpox and typhoid. They were the first vaccinations Jackson had ever received, and his arms swelled up like balloons. The worst part about the medical care, however, was the visit to the dentist. He had never been before and learned that he had something called "cavities," three of them. Without anything to deaden the pain, the dentist immediately began drilling into his teeth, a tortuous process that got worse as the drill bit grew hotter. When the torment was over, he figured that if he could survive a trip to the dentist, he could survive anything.

Still, he thought that being in the Navy was a pretty good deal. He was impressed with the clothing and other gear the Navy had given him. "About $107 worth," he wrote to his mother and sister. "All of it new and very good stuff." And more than he had ever owned in his entire life.

Out of boot camp after twelve weeks, Jackson was pleased when told to report to the battleship USS *Mississippi*. Everyone knew that the battleships were the favored ships of the fleet—not only were they roomier and less turbulent in rough seas than smaller vessels, but they also had better food and more amenities, such as nightly movies and ice cream.

At that time in June 1938, the *Mississippi* was in drydock at the Bremerton Navy Yard near Seattle. Seeing the ship out of the water, Jackson was surprised by how much of the *Mississippi* wouldn't show when she was afloat—like an iceberg, two-thirds of the ship would be beneath the surface.

As with all new seamen, he was first assigned to the X Division to learn how to get about on the ship. The X Division indoctrination included hearing about the history of the ship and its predecessors. He learned that the first *Mississippi* had been a steam frigate designed by Commodore Matthew Perry and was the backbone of the squadron that in 1853–54 forced Japan to open her doors to commerce and contact with the West.

After about a month onboard, Jackson learned that Shumway had been right about his typing skills being an asset. When one of the ship's communications officers found out about his ability, Jackson was given the opportunity to go to the onboard radio operators school as a radio "striker," meaning he was in training for an operator's position. One task of the radio operators was to transmit and receive wireless radio messages using International Morse Code. Receiving the coded messages wasn't too difficult, as they were transmitted by shore stations at the relatively slow speed of eighteen to twenty words a minute. However, regular voice broadcasts required typing speeds of thirty-five words a minute.

One nice aspect of his new position as a radio striker was that he was excused from a lot of the common "deckhand" chores like cleaning, painting, and scraping. Two more radio strikers, Wilbur Ellis and Tommy Savin, joined him. They were a couple of nervous types who chain-smoked cigarettes, but they were good guys and he liked working with them.

Jackson's first skipper was then-Captain Raymond Spruance. The future admiral was quiet and soft-spoken, but had a commanding presence that inspired confidence in his men. Even though it was peacetime, he demanded that his ship and his crew be ready for war. When the overhaul was finished, the *Mississippi* left Puget Sound for Long Beach, where the Pacific Fleet battleships were berthed.

Jackson adjusted easily to the routine of two weeks drilling at sea, followed by two weeks back in port. As a farm boy he was used to getting up early and working long hours that were never over at some prescribed time, but only when the job was finished.

Life onboard a warship was strictly regimented by the calls of a bugle from the moment reveille blew in the morning to rouse the crew from their hammocks. Each series of notes meant something different. There was a call to General Quarters. A call to eat. A call for fire drills. A call to church. At the end of the day, the bugle sounded again to turn out the lights and then, finally, taps was played. *Day is done, gone the sun . . .*

The hardest thing for new crewmembers was adjusting to a near total lack of privacy. The ship's company numbered about eleven hundred men, and that was its peacetime complement; in time of war that number would be closer to eighteen hundred. As a seaman, Jackson slept in a hammock in a compartment on the third deck (two ladders down from the weather deck), side by side and head to toe with fourteen other men in hammocks that were strung up at night and taken down in the morning. He'd had no problems with seasickness and found that sleeping in a hammock actually helped alleviate the feeling of the ocean's motion, as it hung nearly stationary while the ship rolled from side to side. Each sailor got a locker in the compartment to store his gear, but there was nothing to sit on.

They ate in mess compartments, which doubled as sleeping compartments, sitting on long benches at ten-man tables while the mess cooks—junior members of the ship's crew who rotated in and out of the position—brought out large tureens of food, which were handed to senior men first and then passed on to the others.

The "head" was just a long trough through which seawater passed; the only seat was two parallel boards with a space between them suspended over the trough. There were common bathing and laundry compartments. The ship made its own fresh water from seawater with a desalinization plant. But the boilers, which could not use saltwater, had first priority for fresh water and often there wasn't enough for the crew. Daily reminders to conserve fresh water permeated the bulletin boards around the ship.

Jackson had learned in boot camp that the privilege of taking a freshwater shower onboard a ship was to be coupled with efficiency: turn the water on, get wet, turn it off, soap up, turn it back on to rinse, get out. It wasn't as if anyone really wanted to tarry in the shower onboard ships, as hot water was limited. Each crewman was issued a four-gallon bucket that he could fill with fresh water and then heat by placing it beneath a steam valve—that's all the warm water he got to shave, bathe, and do laundry.

In 1940 the Pacific Fleet was moved to Pearl Harbor. Promoted to rear admiral and assigned to a cruiser division, Spruance left the ship and moved on toward his place in history. Jackson—now a petty officer third class, which meant more responsibility, a little more pay, and a cot instead of a hammock— remained on the *Mississippi*. After two years at sea, he became a shell-back when the battleship crossed the equator on July 24, 1940, during fleet exercises.

For Jackson, getting along in the Navy was a simple matter of following the rules and doing his job as well as he could, even if it meant simply keeping his duty station dusted. The Navy was a real stickler for cleanliness onboard its ships. Part of that was to keep the crew busy, so they were always cleaning, scraping off old paint and applying new coats, oiling and lubricating, waxing and "swabbing" decks. They were also expected to keep themselves and their clothing clean, if for no other reason than that it made life more bearable in cramped quarters. But there was also a deeper lesson— a man who paid attention to details in everyday life might someday pay attention to a detail that could save his ship and shipmates.

Of course, some officers were more finicky than others. In late 1940 the ship's executive officer, then-Cmdr. Jerauld Wright, took over command of the *Mississippi* when Captain Theodore Wilkinson was hospitalized.

An academy man, Wright was known to be a real tiger about keeping the *Mississippi* shipshape. The skipper, who held himself almost painfully erect in the presence of the ship's company, wasn't one of the more outgoing captains. But the men knew he was straightforward and fair in his dealings with them. The ship ran smoothly with him in command, which was about all they could ask.

Jackson found that the Navy was full of memorable characters like Wright. Probably the most colorful as a group were the old-timers who had served "on China Station." They had mostly been on river gunboats, like the USS *Panay*, which the Japanese shot up "accidentally" in 1937 and then apologized for causing an international "incident."

A tough, weather-beaten bunch, most of these men proudly displayed on their hairy arms and chests proof that they had ignored the warnings in the *Bluejackets' Manual* about tattoos. Many were walking cliches of sailors: They drank like fish, smoked like chimneys, swore blue streaks, associated with "bad women," and fought for the fun of it when on liberty. But they also knew what they were doing aboard a ship, and while Jackson thought little of their vices, he respected their seamanship and listened raptly when they talked about the places they had been. He found their descriptions so fascinating that after his promotion to petty officer third class, he put in for a transfer to China Station. He was disappointed when the Navy said it needed him right where he was, on the *Mississippi*.

Sometimes the crew's conversation during meals or while shooting the breeze on deck would turn to the threat of war. The newspapers and politicians seemed to think that the real concern was the Germans; most dismissed the Japanese as racially and militarily inferior. General MacArthur even boasted that he could hold the Philippines "indefinitely" against the Japanese if they were foolish enough to attack.

Many of the sailors and officers aboard the *Mississippi* were of the same mind. The Germans would be tough, they said, but if the Japanese tried something, the U.S. Navy would take care of "the little yellow bastards" in short order. About the only ones who dissented were the China Station men. When it came time to a fight, they said, the Navy would find itself with its hands full trying to cope with "the Japs."

When the fleet arrived at Pearl Harbor to be based permanently, it was hard for Jackson to imagine that the Japanese could pose much of a threat to such an awesome display of power: the battleships moored side by side; the four big Pacific Fleet carriers—*Enterprise, Saratoga, Lexington,* and *Yorktown*—and their complements of fighters, dive-bombers, and torpedo planes; the dozens of cruisers, destroyers, and submarines.

The harbor itself was beautiful—the waters a clear azure and teeming with fish—ringed in by the green, mist-enshrouded Koolau mountain range to the north. Rows of palm trees waved from Ford Island, which separated the east and west mouths of the harbor and housed the men and planes of the naval air wings when they weren't aboard the carriers. The island's senior officers quarters of generous homes and lawns manicured by Filipino servants provided a pleasant backdrop for the men manning the ships on adjacent Battleship Row.

If the *Mississippi* wasn't at sea, every third day from 4:00 P.M. to midnight and every third Saturday or Sunday from noon to midnight, Jackson had liberty ashore. He would take the train to Honolulu to catch a movie or maybe have dinner with some of his shipmates.

Jackson took in all the usual sightseeing tours and saw what there was to see of Honolulu, but was soon bored with it all. He wasn't much of a drinker, and he had preferred to bank the seventy-two dollars a month he was making after another promotion to petty officer second class. He was making plans for the future but had decided against trying to get into the Naval Academy at Annapolis, a thought when he first joined, after his tour of duty was up in March 1942. Instead, he was going to leave the service and go to college; if he were frugal, he figured he would have more than enough money saved by then.

So for most of his recreation, he chose those activities that didn't cost anything. The ship showed a movie every night in the open air on the fantail of the ship if the weather was nice or in the mess hall (for the enlisted men) and wardrooms (for the officers) if it rained. The ship also sponsored "smokers," boxing and wrestling matches with crews from other ships, and there were swimming pools on base.

Otherwise, when Jackson got liberty he spent his time exploring the less-traveled areas of Oahu. Very little of the island was developed or inhabited, and there were miles and miles of white sand beaches where he could walk or swim and not see many other people.

Jackson's favorite place to go was the Navy rest-and-recreation camp for enlisted men at Nanakuli Beach. There wasn't much to it. The men ate in groups beneath large tents, and each man was assigned to a small "pup" tent with a single cot. But it was right off the water, where he could spend all day bodysurfing, being tossed about by the waves, absorbing the calming effects of the sea and the sun. Then, worn out, he would happily retire to his tent to read a book and then fall asleep beneath the mosquito netting.

Onboard the ship, one of the high points breaking up the daily grind was getting letters from home. In one letter, Jackson's father wrote that Willard Millikin, the friend who had been adopted by a farm family and was always playing with model airplanes, had gone away to war. Apparently, Millikin had first tried to join the U.S. Army Air Corps but was turned down, so he had traveled to Canada, where he enlisted with the Royal Canadian Air

Force. Now he was flying Spitfire fighter planes against the Germans in what was being called the Battle of Britain.

In late 1940, Jackson received another letter from his father, telling him that a cousin, Robert E. Jackson, was also at Pearl Harbor and stationed aboard the battleship *Arizona*. He had never met Robert, although his cousin had lived in a nearby part of Iowa, but when he got the chance, Jackson went over to the *Arizona* for a visit. Several years younger, Robert was a yeoman, who was essentially working as a secretary for the captain or one of the other officers. The two cousins visited for a couple of hours on the weather deck, talking about their families and the places they both knew, before Don had to go.

Other than a few more such visits, there really wasn't much of a chance for the the two to get to know each other. Their ships were rarely in port at the same time, and events were unfolding that would change both of their lives forever.

In early May 1941, an order came through to transfer two *Mississippi* radio operators to the *Arizona*. Wilbur Ellis and Tommy Savin were told to pack their seabags and go. Jackson was permitted to stay, due to a stroke of luck. Six months earlier, a warrant officer had asked him if he wanted to learn how to repair radio transmitters and receivers. Always interested in anything new to do with electronics, he had agreed. So when the order came through to transfer two radio operators, the communications division officer sent the other two, because Jackson had the more comprehensive training.

Ellis and Savin groused about having to go to the *Arizona*. Every ship becomes a community, and having to transfer was like moving from one town to another because of a sudden, unwanted job relocation. It meant leaving friends and workmates—in a word, home—for strangers and unfamiliar surroundings.

Jackson was relieved to stay. It would have been nice to get to know his cousin better, but his friends were on the *Mississippi*.

In late May 1941, not long after Ellis and Savin left, the *Mississippi* was participating in sea exercises with two other battleships, the *New Mexico* and the *Idaho,* when a destroyer appeared from over the horizon. Quickly coming alongside each of the battleships, the destroyer sent over a packet of secret "guard mail," and then steamed away again.

Within a half hour the battleships separated, each with an escort of several destroyers, and steamed out of sight of one another. Only as the ship approached the Panama Canal was the crew told that they were on their way to Guantanamo Bay, Cuba. The old-timers gave each other knowing looks: Guantanamo was the training base for the Atlantic Fleet.

The *Mississippi* passed through the canal and headed east for Cuba, where she was rejoined by the other two battleships and their escorts. Reaching the base, the ships were placed in drydock and repainted so that the hulls were dark gray, almost black, while the superstructure received a coat of hazy gray. The crews knew then that they would be escorting convoys to help the British, but it wouldn't be to guard against submarines, a job for which battleships were poorly equipped. The scuttlebutt was that they had been sent in the hopes that they might run across the German battleships *Bismarck* and *Scharnhorst,* which had been wreaking havoc with the convoys.

Of course, the outcome of such a meeting was anything but certain, yet that uncertainty may have been the basis for a plan. The German raiders were more modern—faster with bigger guns and more armor plating. The Americans would not have backed down from a fight, and if it happened that one were sunk, President Roosevelt might have the international incident he needed to enrage the American public and drag a reluctant country into the fray.

Throughout the summer, the *Mississippi* escorted convoys from Argentia, Newfoundland, to Hvalfjordur, Iceland. However, other than the occasional submarine contact, there were no incidents between the battleship and the German navy.

In September 1941 the *Mississippi* docked in Newport, Rhode Island, to give the crew a break from their duties. One day, as Jackson was working in the radio transmitter room, the division officer called and asked him to report to his office.

"We need to send a radio operator who knows how to repair radio equipment to attend telephone school, and I'd like you to volunteer," the officer said.

The request didn't make sense. Telephone school was for interior communication electricians, not radiomen, who took care of the ship's external communications. But the officer said he didn't know any more about it, except that it was a big secret and that when the school was through with him, Jackson would be returning to the ship.

Intrigued by the secretive nature of the request, Jackson did volunteer and an hour later left the *Mississippi* carrying his seabag and a train ticket to New York City. Once in the city, he was sent to the receiving ship *Seat-*

tle, where he discovered that he wasn't the only radio operator being sent to the school. There were a couple dozen men from a number of warships, all wondering what was up with the "telephone school." More mystery was added when they were issued identification cards that included photographs and fingerprints, nothing they had ever experienced before. But still no one would tell them where they were going or why.

They cooled their heels for a week, until late one afternoon they were told to get their gear together and board a train heading north. The conductor told them that they were going to Buffalo, in upstate New York, but when they woke up in the morning, they discovered that they were in the small town of Clinton, Ontario.

The bewildered radio operators departed the train and were met on the platform by Royal Canadian Air Force personnel, who escorted them to a bus. The bus took them out into the countryside, arriving at last at a military compound an a flat open area, surrounded by a tall, chain-link fence topped with barbed wire. A sign outside the gate identified the site as Royal Air Force Flying School No. 31.

The Americans were taken to a barracks, where they were told to leave their gear before heading to the base's auditorium. An officer with a British accent stepped to the podium. They'd been brought to RAF Flying School No. 31, he said, for a top-secret project—learning how to operate and maintain a new technology, Radio Detection and Ranging, or "radar."

"You are not to repeat the word 'radar' or write it down," he said. "And that goes for after you leave here and until you're given permission by your superiors to do so." During their stay, they would be allowed to go into town once a week, but they were to tell the locals nothing about why they were there.

In the fall of 1941 nothing in their experience had prepared the men for the idea of sending a radio beam, which they were all familiar with, out to detect air and surface targets. Not only that, they were told, the technology could be used to direct a ship's guns to destroy those targets. The new "magic eye" saw through clouds and at night, and gazed over distances no human lookout could match.

When the month of training was up, the radio operators were sent back to their ships with the understanding that the new technology would be installed on them soon. Arriving in Newfoundland aboard a seaplane tender, Jackson learned that the *Mississippi* had already sailed with a convoy for Iceland. He would have to catch up to her aboard the USS *Sturtevant,* an ancient "four-piper" (as in four smokestacks) destroyer left over from World War I.

The *Sturtevant* left without knowing that convoying in the Atlantic had taken a new twist. A little more than a week earlier, a destroyer, USS *Kearney,* had been torpedoed by a German U-boat, killing eleven men and injuring twice that many. The *Sturtevant,* however, was soon dealing with another powerful enemy, a storm.

It wasn't a particularly violent storm, at least not for the Atlantic, and Jackson knew he would have hardly noticed the weather aboard the *Mississippi.* With her great size and deep hull, the battleship would have plowed through even the rough seas with hardly a shudder.

However, there was a saying in the Navy that destroyers rolled and pitched even when in drydock, "out of habit." The *Sturtevant* didn't so much slice through the water as she cork-screwed, tilting wildly to starboard, then wildly to port and back again as she pushed ahead through the waves. In the meantime, the bow would shoot out of the water when she reached the top of a wave and then slam back down with a bone-jarring crash.

Jackson had never been seasick before, but now he made up for it. He wasn't even able to crawl off somewhere to be alone with his misery, having to work in the radio room during the crossing. Just to keep from sliding across the compartment whenever the ship rolled required fastening his chair to the radio equipment desk with lanyards. For two days, he sat at the radio receiver desk with a bucket between his feet and his stomach trying to turn inside out.

After his ordeal, Jackson was relieved to reach the harbor at Hvalfjordur and see the *Mississippi* lying peacefully at anchor. He had a whole new respect for the men who manned the "tin cans," as the destroyers were called, but he had no desire to become one of them.

The feeling intensified when he saw the *Kearney* tied up alongside a repair ship and was told she'd been torpedoed. But that wasn't the worst of it. In the early morning hours of October 31, another destroyer, the USS *Reuben James,* which had been in the convoy ahead of the *Sturtevant,* was sunk by a U-boat. A torpedo had ripped into the destroyer's side and detonated in an ammunition magazine, which exploded and tore the ship apart. It was a miracle that forty-four crewmembers were saved from the icy waters; one hundred others perished.

The *Reuben James* was the first American naval vessel sunk in a war that had yet to be declared. The two attacks angered Jackson and his shipmates.

The American public might have wanted to stay out of the fight, but as far as the sailors and officers onboard the *Mississippi* were concerned, they prayed for the chance to shoot at anything German. They were surprised when war officially arrived, not in the Atlantic, but a half a world away and without warning.

"Yesterday, December 7, 1941—a date which will live in infamy—the United States of America was suddenly and deliberately attacked by naval and air forces of the Empire of Japan."

Petty Officer 1st Class Jackson sat with the other radio operators on the *Mississippi,* somberly listening to Roosevelt's address to the nation. Off to one side, several of the older radio operators typed as fast as they could, transcribing the president's speech as it was transmitted in International Morse Code. The usual crew was complemented by the presence of a yeoman who knew shorthand and could take down the president's voice broadcast. The atmosphere was clear of any interference, and Roosevelt came through loud and clear, voicing a defiance and anger they all felt.

It was hard to believe how fast their lives had just changed. The afternoon before, a quiet Sunday in that part of the world, Jackson had gone ashore to take a walk and think about his future. Hiking was about all the ships' crews were allowed to do in Iceland, which despite its name was generally green and pastoral. The local population barely tolerated the presence of foreign ships, and the crews had been told to stay away from them.

Jackson had other things on his mind than the ruddy-faced natives. Ninety days. Ninety days and he was through with his four-year obligation to the Navy. He had kept his nose clean and done his job, been promoted, and saved his money. He was making eighty-four dollars a month now and had enough put away that he would be able to afford college when he got out. The rest of his life was laid out like stepping stones across a river: He would get his degree, find a job in electrical engineering, meet a nice young woman, get married, have kids, a home, a future. Then over a period of about two hours, it had all changed. He returned from his walk and heard the news about Pearl Harbor. The stepping stones had just been swept beneath the rising tide of war.

His chief concern when he was told about the attack was for the men he had known. He had learned that the *Arizona* had been hit by a bomb that pierced through to one of the forward ammunition magazines. According to the reports, the damage had been devastating and the ship sunk with the loss of many lives.

No one had provided a whole lot of details after that, but Jackson considered the time and day of the attack. Most of the crew would have been resting or carrying on with their morning duties, and he knew in his heart then that Ellis, Savin, and his cousin Robert would not have survived.

Information about the Japanese operation was incomplete and all of the men were baffled. How were the Japanese, so far from their home bases, able to surprise the fleet? Obviously, part of the answer was through deceit and treachery, as Roosevelt was noting in his speech.

> The United States was at peace with that Nation and, at the solicitation of Japan, was still in conversation with its Government and its Emperor looking toward the maintenance of peace in the Pacific. Indeed, one hour after Japanese air squadrons had commenced bombing in Oahu, the Japanese Ambassador to the United States and his colleague delivered to the Secretary of State a formal reply to a recent American message. While this reply stated that it seemed useless to continue the existing diplomatic negotiations, it contained no threat or hint of war or armed attack.
>
> It will be recorded that the distance of Hawaii from Japan makes it obvious that the attack was deliberately planned many days or even weeks ago. During the intervening time, the Japanese government had deliberately sought to deceive the United States by false statements and expressions of hope for continued peace.

The *Mississippi* had been ordered to wait until the morning of December 8 before heading west. No one knew for sure, even in Washington, D.C., the true extent of the damage, and the British were also going to have to find a way to replace the Americans on the convoys.

Even after they left the harbor and sailed into the cold, gray waters of the Atlantic, there were more questions than answers, the big one being: *What now?* It sounded as though all the battleships of the Pacific Fleet were on the bottom of Pearl Harbor. But what would the Japanese do? Invade Hawaii? The West Coast? If so, what was there to stop them?

> Always will we remember the character of the onslaught against us. No matter how long it may take us to overcome this premeditated

invasion, the American people in their righteous might will win through to absolute victory.

I believe I interpret the will of the Congress and of the people when I assert that we will not only defend ourselves to the uttermost but will make very certain that this form of treachery shall never endanger us again.

No one could say how long it was going to take to defeat the Japanese, or even if they could. Jackson now held no illusions that he was only ninety days from finishing his Navy career, nor did he want out. His dream would have to be put on hold; his country was in mortal danger, and his people had always responded to that call.

Of Scot and Scot-Irish descent, Jackson's ancestors had left their home isles from the early 1700s to the mid-1800s for a variety of reasons—famine, religious freedom, politics—to see what lay on the other side of the ocean. But mostly they had left to find some piece of land to call their own.

Few generations escaped war. They had served in the Revolutionary War and the War of 1812. Then in 1862, Jackson's great-grandfather DeWilda Cargill Jackson, joined the Union cause with his two brothers, riding with the 4th Volunteer Iowa cavalry during the Civil War. They could have said it wasn't their fight; they were simple farmers on the western edge of what was then the frontier—not southern cotton merchants nor northern textile mill owners, not politicians trying to get elected nor professional soldiers trying to be promoted. They had never owned a slave. They fought in part because slavery was wrong; but more than that, because their country asked for their help. There was a price to be paid for those gently rolling Iowa hills thick with stalks of corn, for the scent of newly turned soil warming in the sun—a price to be paid for the land and for the opportunity.

Miraculously, all three brothers survived and returned to their farms. But many others—cousins, uncles, friends, as well as many on his mother's side—did not. They filled graves from Vicksburg to Gettysburg.

Jackson's family paid the price again in July 1918 during the previous world war when one his mother's brother, Russell Burks, was killed by a sniper's bullet.

The *Malvern Leader* noted in Burk's obituary: "He was a splendid specimen of young American manhood—clean, capable, courteous and painstaking—and we can well understand the hold he had secured in the affections of his Major."

"He has made the Supreme Sacrifice upon his country's altar, and he did it willingly, gladly, bravely. Our sorrow over his loss is great and the ache in the hearts of parents and friends will always remain; but the pride we have in his bravery and fearlessness, as he placed his young life and all that he had in the service of his country, our country, that he loved so well and served so faithfully, surpasses all else and will last as long as time."

Jackson had never met Russell, having been born a year after his death, but he understood why his uncle believed he had to go. There was that debt.

> Hostilities exist. There is no blinking at the fact that our people, our territory, and our interests are in grave danger. With confidence in our armed forces—with the unbounded determination of our people— we will gain the inevitable triumph, so help us God.

Roosevelt's "inevitable triumph" seemed a long way off as the *Mississippi* steamed for the East Coast with an escort of destroyers and ran into one of the worst Atlantic storms in recorded history. They were sailing into an uncertain future in which even the winds seemed to have turned against them.

The *Mississippi* and her escorts rode out the storm and limped into the naval shipyard at Norfolk, Virginia, for resupplies and new equipment designed to meet the threat of the new era in naval warfare. One-point-one "pompom" antiaircraft guns were added to her weaponry, and unknown to the crew and even most officers, the new secret weapon, radar, was also installed. Only Jackson and a young lieutenant knew what it was, as well as how to maintain the equipment and train operators to use it, which they hurriedly began to do.

As soon as the new guns and the radar were in place, the *Mississippi* left for the Panama Canal, passing through the locks and entering the Pacific on January 6. The ship moved north taking its time, training the gunners on the new antiaircraft guns, and entered San Francisco Bay, its new home port, on January 22.

When the *Mississippi* arrived, Californians seemed to have settled into the routine of supporting each other and the war movement, dutifully accepting sacrifices and inconveniences, all while going about their lives as normally as possible. The West Coast was under blackout conditions, and even the windows of private homes had to be covered so that no light leaked out at night to guide enemy ships or planes. But inside those homes, families still listened to *Fibber McGee and Molly* or *Jack Benny* on the radio, as well as the war broadcasts; they gathered with friends and drew closer.

The Navy took precautions with its remaining battleships. Whenever they were in port, the *Mississippi* and the others were docked between piers, rather than being anchored out in the bay, so that they could not be easily torpedoed. Vulnerable to air attacks, they were kept out of the shooting war at first. Even as the aircraft carriers, cruisers, and destroyers began their hit-and-run tactics, the battleships were mostly escorting supply convoys to Hawaii and back again with the empties.

They didn't enter Pearl Harbor, nor did they stay long in Hawaiian waters. They may have itched for a fight but weren't present at the Coral Sea battle. And at Midway, the *Mississippi* and the other old warhorses were stationed west of Hawaii as the last line of defense if the Japanese won. The line would not have held for long; without air support from carriers, the battleships and their crews would have been annihilated without ever even seeing an enemy ship. However, the Japanese lost at Midway and the threat of an early invasion sank with the Imperial carriers.

In August 1942, the *Mississippi* entered Pearl Harbor for the first time since leaving in May 1941. Jackson was shocked to see that the once-clear waters and shores of the harbor were now fouled with black fuel oil. Worse still was the sight of Battleship Row—the *Oklahoma* capsized with its belly exposed to the sky, the *Arizona* beneath the surface with only her scarred superstructure showing above the water.

The crew manned the rail trying to remember Pearl Harbor as they had known it in peace. Jackson had learned from his father that his cousin Robert had been reported missing and presumed dead. The names of Wilbur Ellis and Tommy Savin had also appeared on the casualty lists. He was angered not just by their deaths, but by the manner of them. The men who had died were not at war nor aware of any danger when, without warning, men from a foreign land had dropped bombs on them.

Jackson felt sorry for all the young men whose dreams had ended that day, but he also felt a resolve growing inside. The Japanese, joined by the Germans and Italians, had started this war, but the United States would finish it. Old ships like the *California* and *West Virginia*, which the enemy had boasted were gone but were now being raised from the harbor mud. They would avenge their murdered sailors with the help of their sisters, such as the *Mississippi*, and the new ships at the yards were already splashing at a record pace.

When the *Mississippi* returned to sea, Jackson did not go with her. He had been promoted to warrant officer, but there were no positions on the ship for another, so he was sent back to the Treasure Island electronics school in San Francisco Bay.

Leaving his ship, the only one he'd ever known, was wrenching. The *Mississippi* had been his home for four years and he felt attached to her; his friends were onboard, he knew her passageways and the feel of her decks beneath his feet. Now there was only the unknown. However, there was one bright spot about being sent to Treasure Island. Her name was Charlotte Grace Gates.

She'd been born on Christmas Day 1925 in her maternal grandparents' home in Malvern, Iowa, the second daughter for Betty and Paul Gates. Her red-haired sister, Peggy, was a year older, but the girls were nearly inseparable and people often took them for twins. The little brother, Bobby, was born two years after Charlotte.

Paul Gates had a good job in Nebraska, where the family actually lived, as an assistant manager for a young oil company called Standard. But at the urging of his brother, who was in management with Rath Meat Packing Co., in Southern California persuaded him in 1937 to move to "God's Country . . . the Golden State."

Twelve-year-old Charlotte would always remember the trek across country for the gypsy caravans they saw along the road and the herds of sheep that crossed the highways, holding up traffic for hours. At the border between Nevada and California, they came upon an orange juice vendor— five cents for all a person could drink. He must have lost money that day just on the two girls. But California indeed looked like the golden state, where fruit practically threw itself onto one's laps.

During the three years the family lived in Southern California, Charlotte and Peggy learned to jitterbug and spent many an evening dancing to Big Band music at the Pasadena Civic Auditorium and the Palladium—all for a quarter a night. They swung to Glenn Miller, Tommy and Jimmy Dorsey, and listened to singers Martha Tilton, Betty Hutton, and a skinny kid all the girls loved, Frank Sinatra.

Triple-decker ice cream cones were five cents and chocolate sundaes were fifteen at Alhambra's famous "Leo's Ice Cream Parlor," which was walking distance from their home. For even cheaper entertainment, their mother would take them to the corner of Hollywood and Vine to watch out for the movie stars.

Another cheap pastime was going to Long Beach on Sundays and riding Navy launches out to the big battleships and carriers in the harbor, which allowed visitors to come onboard. The pretty blond and red-head were more than welcomed by the sailors stuck onboard without liberty.

The two girls attended a private Catholic girls school where they both excelled at art. Peggy as a violinist and Charlotte in the fine arts. Charlotte even won a national art contest in 1939 for her painting of the Disney character Jiminy Cricket standing on top of a globe above the words, "World Peace." She received the magnificent sum of three dollars and fifty cents as her award.

However, finding a good job wasn't as easy as it had sounded for Paul Gates. In the early summer of 1940, he found better work in northern California and moved the family to Redwood City.

When school started, Charlotte and Peggy felt like they'd moved into a different culture. The kids in Redwood City didn't even know how to jitterbug; they still enjoyed Big Band music, but it was all ballroom dancing. Still, the girls got their fill by dancing to records during the lunch breaks on a outdoor stage.

On the morning of December 7, 1941, the three Gates children were just returning from Sunday School and were standing in the front yard of their home when their dad came running out, waving his arms and shouting, "The Japs bombed Pearl Harbor!" But what she would remember most from that time was the next day at school, listening to Roosevelt give his "day of infamy" speech. They were all standing by their desks at attention trying to hear the radio over the public address system when she glanced at the Japanese-American girl next to her. The girl made no sound, but large tears were rolling down her cheeks. The next day, the girl was gone, and Charlotte never saw her again, but she would never forget how sorry she felt for her classmate.

Missing her sister who was a year ahead of her, Charlotte graduated early from high school in January 1942. The girls tried not to let the war spoil all their fun. They still danced whenever they got the chance—only now they had to wear shoes with cardboard soles because all the leather was going to make boots and shoes for "the boys" in the military. Nylons were next to impossible to get, so they used a cream someone had developed to "tan" their legs and then drews lines down the back to imitate seams.

The Gates family was patriotic to the core. Paul Gates, who'd been stymied in his attempt to get a officer's commission in the Army, worked as the Civil Defense warden for the neighborhood making sure, among other things, that everyone observed the blackout conditions at night, so "the Japs" wouldn't know where to find them. Charlotte was so patriotic that one day when her sister walked in on her taking a bath as the Star-Spangled Banner came over the radio, Peggy found her standing at attention, soap bubbles and all, with her hand over her heart. She was quite thrilled the day the handsome young sailor stopped by the house, looking for her grandmother.

It was in March 1942. Jackson had been on his way to Palo Alto, about seventy miles straight south of San Francisco, to see a girl he had known in high school. But he stopped in Redwood City, about halfway, at his mother's request to look up an old friend of hers from Malvern.

Walking up to the house, he knocked on the door, which was opened by a pretty blond teenager. She was wearing a white blouse and brown slacks and sported a pageboy haircut that framed her merry blue eyes.

After he had explained the reason for his visit, she let him in and introduced herself as Charlotte. She had been doing her history home-work, she said, pointing to papers and books spread out over the living room floor.

The whole family was at home: her grandmother, Martha; her parents, Betty and Paul; her cute, redheaded sister, Peggy; and her little brother, Bob. When they had all fussed over him for a few minutes, Jackson explained that he couldn't stay long. Disappointed, Betty suggested that if he had time on the way back to his ship, he should stop in again for dinner.

Jackson went to Palo Alto to see the other girl. But the more he thought about dinner at the Gates's home, the better it sounded, so he cut the date short and soon was back at the Gates's door. Betty was an excellent cook and insisted on second and third helpings for the sailor in their midst. He enjoyed being around a family, so he was pleased when Betty invited him to come back soon "and feel free to bring a friend." On his next day off, he went back to the Gates's home and brought Earl Watts, his best friend from the *Mississippi*.

Tall and dark-haired, Watts was another Iowa boy, who had been on the ship about six months in 1939 when he had walked up to Jackson and extended a big hand. "Don't I know you?" he had grinned.

Jackson had seen the sailor around and thought his face looked familiar. Now he recognized Watts as another farm kid from a community near Malvern. In fact, Watts was a well-known high school athlete in the region— a "big league" softball player who was paid by a local trucking firm to play ball for its team.

The two young shipmates were soon the best of friends. Both were "straight shooters," who carried their farming work ethic to their shipboard responsibilities. They believed in working quietly and efficiently without trying to call a lot of attention to themselves, unlike some others who were always bucking for promotion. Their superiors, however, had recognized their abilities, and both men had worked their way through the ranks quickly.

Watts had it rough growing up. His father had abandoned the family one night when Earl was a little boy. He went out to buy cough syrup for one of Earl's siblings and simply never came back. Forced to raise the kids alone, his mother struggled to keep their heads above water. But she had done her best, and Earl had turned out to be a fine young man.

Soon both young men were welcome fixtures in the Gates household, where they could take off the uniforms for a bit and wear "civvies," while enjoying a family life and home-cooked meals. The young men were becoming such a part of the family that sometimes they stayed for a night or two when the *Mississippi* was in port.

The Gates girls were certainly lively company. They never seemed to stop laughing, especially when together, and they liked to team up to pull pranks on the flustered sailors, like dousing them with perfume so their shipmates would wonder where they had been, and with whom, when they got back to the ship.

Of course, the sailors assured themselves, they thought of the girls only as friends. After all, Jackson was twenty-two, Watts was twenty-three, and Charlotte and Peggy were sixteen and seventeen, respectively, and too young for romance.

The girls even went out on dates with high school boys from time to time when the sailors were visiting. Once, near the end of the school year in the spring of 1942, Jackson was staying at the house for a couple of days, when Charlotte dropped a hint that she was in a real bind. It seemed that her English teacher had promised her an "A" for his class if she would type up his master's thesis for him. The problem was, she said, batting those baby blues at Jackson, she was supposed to go to her high school prom that night— only now she was going to have to stay home in order to finish typing the papers if she wanted that "A."

"Go on, have a good time. I'll type them for you," Jackson offered gallantly.

She had looked in on him before leaving on her date that night. He was in the guest bedroom typing when she knocked on the door and entered. She was wearing her prom dress, and he thought that she looked drop-dead gorgeous, but he couldn't tell her that. They were *just friends.* She thanked him for helping her out, and they wished each other good night. She left with her date, he returned to typing the papers, but for some reason he found it hard to concentrate.

When he left the *Mississippi* several months later and transferred to Treasure Island, the young couple began to officially "date." A war was raging, however, and like romances all over the country, theirs was postponed when in January 1943 he was transferred back to the Naval Research Laboratory in Washington, D.C., for advanced courses in electronics, including the latest innovations in radar. There he had remained for nine months, but he and Charlotte wrote to each other and, as with so many couples during the war, began to fall in love by mail—though neither admitted it to the other yet.

In November 1943, Jackson returned to the Bay area with orders to report to the light cruiser USS *Santa Fe* for duty. He was happy about the assignment; he had wanted to serve on a cruiser. He liked their looks, especially some of the older versions that had the long, pointed "cutter" bow, like the USS *Indianapolis,* which he had often seen tied up at Long Beach.

While he waited for transportation to his new ship, he accepted an offer from Betty and Paul Gates to stay in their house. Charlotte wasn't living there anymore. She had graduated from high school early in January 1943 and enrolled in a cadet nursing program at Saint Luke's Hospital in San Francisco. The nursing program kept her busy, and her curfew allowed her out only until 10:00 P.M. But they saw as much of each other as they could for the next five weeks.

He wooed her with gardenias he could buy from street vendors for a nickel and with steak. The student nurses were required to turn over their sugar and meat rationing cards to the hospital administrators, who then used them for the interns and residents. So he took her, and sometimes one of her best friends, Carole Jespersen, to Fisherman's Wharf, the only place in town to get a steak. The double date cost him plenty out of his college fund, but with a pretty blond on each arm he was the envy of battalions of sailors and soldiers walking the streets of San Francisco.

However, it all came to an end when Jackson received orders to embark on a cargo ship for transportation to the port—the Navy wasn't saying which—where the *Santa Fe* would next call.

Jackson was ready to go. Everything in his life—college, a career, a family— would remain on hold until the war was over. It was time to finish it, one way or the other.

The worst part was leaving Charlotte. They had both known he would soon have to go back to sea again, fight in the war, and that maybe he wouldn't return. So they hadn't talked much about the future; they cared about each other and were going to have to leave it at that for the time being.

Knowing he would not be there for her eighteenth birthday later in December, Jackson took Charlotte and her parents to the bar on the top of the famous Mark Hopkins Hotel for the breathtaking view of the city, the bay, and the Golden Gate and San Francisco Bridges. Eighteen was the legal drinking age in California, but no one questioned him when he bought Charlotte her first cocktail—a Tom Collins, because she wanted the maraschino cherry.

Later they went to dinner in downtown San Francisco, where again he was the envy of the other young men and she the envy of the young women. Charlotte was a beautiful young woman with a figure that would have made one of the famous pinup girls jealous; he was a handsome young naval officer, splendid and dashing in his uniform.

Charlotte's parents agreed that they made a lovely couple. They could all only hope it would work out someday. Before he left, Jackson took Betty aside. He had cut an advertisement from a magazine, which he pressed into her hands along with money. The ad was for cedar "hope chests," which were traditionally given to young women to collect the sorts of things they would eventually need to start a household, as noted by the ad: "The Love Gift that says: 'Darling—you are mine forever.' This Christmas give her the gift that starts the home."

The advertisement pictured a drawing of a dreamy eyed young woman in front of an open chest filled with linens and towels. Down in the corner was a soldier with a rifle in hand, looking up at her, beneath the words, "She's who I'm fighting for."

A hope chest wasn't an engagement ring. But in a way it was a more solid commitment to the future than a diamond would have been. And Jackson figured that if he didn't come back, she could still use it when she found someone else.

Charlotte had something of her own she wanted to give him. On the last night before he was scheduled to leave, they went out to dinner. When he walked her back to the nurses' dormitory, she handed him a small silver-and-turquoise ring her parents had brought her from Mexico in 1937. "For luck," she said with tears in her eyes and kissed him goodnight . . . and good-bye.

On December 15, 1943, when Jackson reported to the *Santa Fe* in time for the change-of-command ceremony, he wore the ring on a chain around his neck that also held his identification dog tags. He knew he was lucky just to be alive.

If the Navy hadn't rejected his request for China Station in 1940, he would have been trapped there and either killed or captured when the war broke out. Then if the warrant officer on the *Mississippi* hadn't asked if he wanted to learn how to fix radio transmitters, it could have been him transferred to the *Arizona,* and then he would have been aboard the ship on December 7, 1941. And the *Mississippi* could have just as easily been kept at Pearl Harbor while some other battleship was sent to the Atlantic.

Instead, he was aboard a fast, modern, well-armed ship of war that was fully capable of defending herself, as well as her charges—the aircraft carriers. And he thought that she had a good skipper, even though he learned that some of the men weren't sure what to make of Wright. They thought he was standoffish, even rude, to the point where he didn't always return their, "Good morning, sir!"

Jackson was aware that Wright wasn't terribly sociable, but also knew that part of that stemmed from being partly deaf after all those years exposed to the blasts of the battleship guns. Unless he was looking at whomever was speaking, he didn't always catch what was said and avoided long conversations.

However, Wright won over a few more men as they were leaving for the war zone. The crew was a little forlorn, as the ship had taken a quick trip back to California, arriving New Year's Day 1944, to pick up a convoy headed for the invasion of the Marshall Islands, and they had all been given five days of liberty. They would have liked more.

"Sit back, boys, and relax," Wright told them as the shoreline of their country disappeared on the eastern horizon. "You've got a ringside seat at the greatest show on Earth. We're going to hit 'em with everything we've got. We'll throw oranges, pineapples, flower pots—whatever it takes."

Jackson smiled. *Oranges, pineapples, and flower pots?* He rubbed the ring beneath his shirt—so far his luck was holding up pretty well.

PART II

USS *Franklin*

Newport News to Saipan

December 1943–August 1944

CHAPTER SIX

Big Ben, the Flattop:
With Revenge in Mind

January 31, 1944
Norfolk Navy Yard, Portsmouth, Virginia

W hen he thought no one was watching, Jimmy Shoemaker Jr.
slipped out of the door of the captain's cabin. His father, Captain James Shoemaker Sr., and mother, Frances Shoemaker, were
entertaining the "important visitors" following the commissioning of his
father's ship, the USS *Franklin.* Jimmy and his brother had been dressed up
in their Sunday School clothes and told to be on their best behavior, but
he was bored. Besides what did they expect from a ten-year-old boy with
the opportunity to inspect an aircraft carrier?

Jimmy was proud of his father and knew how excited he had been to
finally get "his ship," the USS *Franklin,* CV-13, the newest carrier in the fleet.
But the boy was also a little sad to learn that his daddy would be going away
now to the war, though he tried to understand and be brave. Frankly, the
family's attitude from his mother on down was "Godspeed and go kill some
Japs." Some of that stemmed from the fact that as a family, they had already
seen more of the war than most American civilians ever would.

It began for them that horrible morning in December 1941, when Jimmy
and his older brother, Tommy, were in their bedroom in the house on Ford
Island reading the Sunday comics. Suddenly, outside there arose a terrible
commotion of explosions and guns and sirens and bugles, as well as the
sounds of a swarm of planes passing overhead. The brothers ran into the
backyard just as a silver plane with a large red dot on the wing darted above
the palm trees surrounding their home.

"Jeez, that's a Japanese plane!" exclaimed Tommy, who at eleven years old,
three years older than Jimmy, was much more in the know about such things.

They had run back into the house to find their father, who was the commander of the naval air station on Ford Island. He was dressed and sitting on the bed, tying his shoes.

"I want you boys to go to the admiral's bomb shelter," he said. The boys knew what he meant. The house at the end of the block in the officers' housing area had been built over an old gun emplacement that had been turned into a shelter.

The boys ran outside and took off across the yards, skittering from house to house and avoiding a large open area. The sound of explosions and guns firing was a continuous roar behind them, and black smoke filled the air as they reached the admiral's house without incident.

Their mother was not as lucky. Frances Shoemaker decided to take the most direct route to the bomb shelter across the open area, running with the boys' six-month-old sister, Katya, in her arms.

When she was halfway across the open space, a two-seater Japanese plane swept in at treetop level. The pilot apparently recognized that she was not a military target, but the tail gunner either could not see her well, or had no such compunctions about whom he shot. He swung his guns toward her fleeing figure and let off a stream of bullets. Chunks of sod and dirt flew up around her, but somehow she and her child were spared. Then the plane was gone. She ran into the bomb shelter, wild-eyed, clutching her little girl, but really more angry than frightened when she told the boys about her harrowing experience. Frances Shoemaker was a Navy wife through and through.

Several hours later, Jimmy's father showed up at the shelter and told them that he believed it was safe to leave. He was carrying a Thompson submachine gun and wearing a steel helmet. All morning, he had been fighting fires and he looked exhausted, his face blackened by soot. He was limping where a bullet had struck his foot. When he removed the helmet, they saw that his hair had been burned off the top of his head—from flaming pitch off a burning building, he said, after which he had found the helmet.

"Thank God, the air wings weren't here or it would have been worse," he told Frances as the boys listened.

Leaving the bomb shelter, the family had walked back to their home to find that it had been turned into an emergency medical facility. The kids and their mother also learned that they had apparently had another narrow escape that morning. When the *Arizona* erupted at 8:10 A.M., a large steel chunk of the ship had flown into the air and crashed back down through the roof of their house.

Now the rooms were filled to overflowing with wounded men. Dozens had been laid out on the lawn on top of blankets and sheets. Jimmy could see that many of them had been horribly burned; they had tried to swim through the burning fuel oil to the shore. Tearing himself from the tragic scene, he and his brother walked around to the other side of the house, where they could see what remained of Battleship Row some two hundred yards distant. Closest to them was the *Arizona,* with her superstructure tilted to the side as a huge plume of black smoke boiled into the sky.

The boys' mother soon rounded the boys up to take them to the bachelor officers' quarters, a sort of dormitory used by the air wings when the carriers were in port. Frances and her children spent a fearful night huddled in a hallway. Anytime they started to drift off to sleep, they were startled awake by antiaircraft batteries engaged in frenzied shooting. The gunners were all a little trigger-happy with the rumors that the Japanese might send in troops to follow up the air attack. The one-point-ones tore up the quiet of the night, their rhythmic pounding accented by occasional machine-gun fire.

In the spring of 1942, Captain Shoemaker and his family moved to Virginia when he was appointed commander of the naval air station at Norfolk. He wanted a carrier but had to wait until the fall of 1943.

A little more than two years later, Jimmy wandered off into his father's ship. He wanted to be a naval officer like his father and, of course, officers inspected ships.

There were a lot of sailors and civilians onboard that day for the ceremonies, so no one noticed one small towheaded boy peering into every compartment and nook. Having never met a ladder he wouldn't climb up or down, Jimmy kept going deeper until there weren't so many people around. That's when he realized that he was lost.

Fortunately, there wasn't enough time to panic. "Now hear this," the ship intercom squawked. "Any member of the ship's crew who observes a ten-year-old boy on the ship is to immediately apprehend him and promptly deliver him to the captain's cabin."

A moment later, Jimmy was nabbed by two sailors, who asked if he was the captain's son. When he confessed, they led him by the hand up several levels to the cabin and presented him to his father's Marine orderly. The orderly in turn escorted him into the presence of the captain, who scowled.

"Where the hell have you been?" he demanded.

"I wandered off and got lost," the boy replied honestly. "I don't know where I was, but the *Franklin* sure is big!"

The captain's face softened; he knew what it was to be a boy and to fall in love with ships. He was 15 years old when he entered the U.S. Naval Academy.

It was no accident that the keel for Hull No. 396 had been laid a year earlier on December 7, 1942. She was being built—at a cost of $63 million—with revenge in mind. Ten months later, on October 14, 1943, in record time for a ship that size, the hull was floated from the ways and christened the USS *Franklin* with a bottle of champagne struck across her bow by Lt. Cmdr. Mildred H. McAfee, the director of the Navy Women's Reserve, or WAVES.

The *Franklin* was the fifth *Essex*-class carrier, and she was also the fifth United States naval vessel to be given the name. The original *Franklin* was actually a fishing schooner, on loan to the Continental Army from her owners and renamed for the patriot Benjamin Franklin in 1775. Her captain was under orders from Gen. George Washington to seek out and destroy British shipping, as well as to help supply the ragtag American army.

The early *Franklin*'s most famous adventure occurred when the ship, commanded by Captain James Mugford of Marblehead, Massachusetts, caught up to the British transport HMS *Hope,* and forced his majesty's ship—laden with seventy-five tons of gunpowder and a thousand muskets—into American-held Boston Harbor. Mugford accomplished the feat right under the noses of much larger, better-armed British men-o'-war that were supposed to be blockading the harbor.

The next *Franklin* was a brig built for the new Navy in Philadelphia in 1775. She weighed in at 155 tons and was armed with eight cannons. Unfortunately, her greatest claim to fame was being captured in 1802 by the infamous Barbary pirates, who terrorized Mediterranean shipping from their bases in several Islamic states of North Africa. The United States and Great Britain put the pirates out of business soon afterward during the so-called Tripolitan Wars, which were immortalized in the U.S. Marine Corps Hymn. *From the Halls of Montezuma to the shores of Tripoli. . .* Neither the third nor fourth *Franklin* saw much in the way of military action.

When aircraft carriers came into being in the 1920s, the U.S. Navy decided that it would name them after famous ships or important battles fought by Americans. So although the original *Franklin* was named in honor of the patriot, subsequent ships were named for their predecessors, and thus the carrier was not the USS *Benjamin Franklin*. Only later would her crew affectionately nickname their home upon the seas "Big Ben."

The aircraft carrier *Franklin* easily dwarfed her namesakes. She was 872 feet long—nearly three city blocks—and her flight deck floated nearly 70 feet above the waterline.

A carrier's most notable feature was of course the flight deck, for which they were called "flattops." Some countries, such as Great Britain, built their flight decks of steel. However, the flight decks of American carriers were comprised of oak planking. The reasons were threefold: Wood insulated the ship from the sun better than steel; it conserved steel; and it reduced skidding by planes that made rough landings.

Rising from amidships on the starboard side of the flight deck was the other most identifiable part of a carrier, the "island" superstructure, which housed the bridge and other navigational and command areas similar to the superstructure on other types of warships.

In cross section, the interior of the ship from the island on down looked like a multistoried apartment complex connected by a maze of passageways, hatches, and ladders. At the bow of the ship, beneath the flight deck was an open "front porch," the aircraft carrier version of the foc'sle. It housed the powerful winches that raised and lowered the chain attached to the ship's massive anchors. Beneath the foc'sle were compartments for storage of the anchor chains, paint, crew berthing, a barber shop, and tens of thousands of gallons of potable water provided by the ship's evaporators, which distilled seawater.

Immediately below the flight deck and running the length of the island structure was the gallery deck. It contained the pilot "ready rooms"—where pilots would be briefed before takeoff and after landing—as well as the Combat Information Center, the radio receiving and transmitting rooms, and some of the officers' quarters.

Beginning about a quarter of the way back from the bow beneath the flight deck was the main deck of a carrier, otherwise known as the hangar deck. This armor-plated deck was actually more important to the structural integrity of the ship than the flight deck; the flight deck could be all but destroyed, rendering the ship useless for offensive purposes, but it would still be seaworthy as long as the hangar deck was intact.

Thirty feet from deck to the ceiling, or "overhead," the hangar itself was a big warehouselike area that stretched almost the remaining length of the carrier. It was sectioned into five parts by steel bulkheads, each with a door large enough to roll a plane through. The hangar deck could be opened to the air during daylight hours by raising steel curtains. The curtains were lowered at night to allow the crew to work on aircraft while still keeping light from giving away the ship's position.

While at sea, of the hundred or so planes in the ship's complement, three-fourths would be parked aft on the flight deck. The rest would be kept in the hangar, which also served as the repair facility. Three elevators ferried the planes between the hangar and flight decks: the forward, or No. 1, elevator was at the end of the hangar closest to the bow; the midships, No. 2, elevator was actually on the port side of the flight deck (and sometimes called the deck-edge elevator); and the aft, No. 3, elevator was toward the stern end.

At the stern and separated from the hangar deck by a bulkhead was the back porch, or fantail. The fantail of a carrier was traditionally a popular gathering spot for off-duty sailors; it was also used to store various materiel, including rows of oxygen tanks for the planes' aviators, as well as welders' torches.

The "second deck," just beneath the hangar deck, was largely given over to the crew's sleeping quarters. The bunks were tiered three and four high, sometimes with just enough room on the top bunk for a thin man to slide in. Privacy was nonexistent, as the narrow aisles between the long rows of bunks were also the main passageways that ran fore and aft.

The crew would eat on the "third deck" in cafeteria-style mess halls or in several smaller compartments off the main halls. There the mess cooks would serve ten thousand meals a day, including fresh bread from the ship's bakery. Officers, including pilots, would eat in wardrooms on the second deck, where they were served by "colored" mess stewards at tables set with linen napkins and fine silverware.

Down in the depths of the ship were the fuel and ammunition holds. Also below the waterline were the fire and control rooms that powered the ship. The *Franklin* was not just one of the largest warships in the world, she was also one of the fastest with a top speed of thirty-three knots, nearly forty miles an hour.

As awe-inspiring as any ship in the world at that time, the *Franklin* was already obsolete by the time she was launched. The day before she touched the water, Secretary of the Navy Frank Knox had announced that the Navy would build three new "super" aircraft carriers. They would weigh in at forty-five thousand tons, as big as the new *Iowa*-class battleships and yet another reminder that carriers had replaced the dreadnoughts as the most important capital ships.

But it would be years before the new carriers arrived, and in the meantime, the *Essex*-class carriers were the most powerful ships afloat. Still, they were nothing but steel tubs without men.

The backbone of the *Franklin's* crew—about six hundred petty officers—arrived in Newport News in October to begin acquainting themselves with the ship. Many of them had seen their first service during World War I or in the peacetime Navy between the wars, and were veterans of two years of fighting in the current war. They all had different stories about how they came to be in the Navy, but few had originally joined looking for a fight.

Chief Petty Officer Raymond Blair's motivation was his allergies. Born on a farm in Nebraska in 1910, he had been the oldest of twelve children, charged with looking out for the little ones. His brothers and sisters loved him dearly; he was a gentle boy with an easy sense of humor, and enjoyed going off by himself to draw and write. In high school he entered a contest to design a mascot for Planters Peanuts and won the five-dollar first prize for the top-hatted peanut character that would eventually become "Mr. Peanut."

After high school, Blair left Nebraska and his family for health reasons. Since age twelve, he had worked on neighbors' farms to help his parents with the bills. But he suffered terribly from allergies to goldenrod, ragweed, and dust—all of which were abundant in in the Cornhusker State.

Hoping some other place would be easier on his sinuses, he wandered around before reaching California and signing up for the Navy in 1937. He didn't come home when he got leave, but he wrote often to tell his family about his adventures. Sea duty, he said, was good for his allergies, and he had no problems "until I hit shore."

Six feet tall and broad-shouldered, with brown hair and eyes, Blair married a young woman, Beverly, he had met in California. He continued to work on his art when he had a few minutes alone and was even doing fill-in drawing for Walt Disney's animation studios. His job on the *Franklin* was going to be working for the ship's newspaper, a vocation he enjoyed. In fact, whenever he was in a new port, he liked to visit city newspapers and thought about pursuing journalism when he returned to civilian life.

By the fall of 1943, when he was assigned to the *Franklin,* Raymond and Beverly had a four-year-old son, Bruce. Blair had hardly seen his son after the war began; he had been on a cruiser and constantly at sea. So he was pleased when sent to precommissioning preparations for the new carrier in October, knowing he would have at least a few precious months with his family.

Most of the rest of the *Franklin's* crew showed up in November, the majority fresh from boot camp. If a cruiser such as the *Santa Fe* was a small town, the *Franklin* was a bustling metropolis. When underway, there would be more than three thousand men onboard; two-thirds of them the ship's officers and crew, the other third the pilots and their radiomen and gunners who made up the air group.

They came from all walks of life and every corner of American soil, including Puerto Rico, as well as Guam and the Philippines. Most of them had been kids when Pearl Harbor was bombed and were now barely out of high school and had no concept of what they were going to face.

Seaman 2nd Class Ernest "Scotty" Scott peered around the dock, looking for the ship that was supposed to be there. At least that's what the driver of the truck that deposited him and a half dozen other "boots" at 1:00 A.M. in the rain had said. Only seventeen years old, he was wet and miserable from riding in the back of the open truck, but all he could see in the dark and drizzle were big gray buildings.

"Where's the ship?" he asked a guard who was standing nearby.

The man gave him an amused smile. "You're lookin' at her, dummy," he said and nodded over his shoulder.

Scott looked up, his jaw dropping at the same time. What he thought was an immense gray wall was actually the hull of the largest ship he had ever seen, which was saying something, as he had worked in the shipbuilding yard in Bath, Maine, until a month earlier. He realized then that he was standing about halfway down the length of the vessel. If this had been his birthday, April Fool's Day, he might have figured someone was playing a trick on him: *How could anything that big move through water?* But it was November and this was no joke.

Scott had been born and raised in Woodland, Maine, on the Saint Croix River near the Canadian border. Woodland was little more than a village, whose population of three thousand or so relied on the surrounding natural resources for their livelihoods—woodsmen, rivermen, lumberjacks, and mill workers. His grandfathers had worked in the lumber mills and his father worked in the town paper mill.

Woodland was the sort of place where there was never any great rush to get anywhere special, or to start today what could be put off until the next . . . week. Nobody was starving, but nobody had a lot of money either.

The woods of northeastern Maine were a grand place for a boy, and Scott was constantly outdoors, always up to some exploration or adventure with his best friend, Eddie Carlisle. There were baseball games in Father Hanscom's field, swimming "bollicky"—in the nude—whenever possible, or fishing at the "Sortin' Gap," a favorite spot on the Saint Croix. For excitement, the boys could steal apples from Charlie Blaney's orchard—the fact that he would knock the tar out of them if he could catch them made it worth the effort—or hunt deer, rabbit, and girls.

Of the girls, Scott was sweetest on Vivian Cox. They had known each other since they were children; in fact, when they were eight years old, he told everyone he knew that they were going to get married someday. She was a great friend, as close as he was to Carlisle, which was saying a lot. By high school he would have liked to have been even closer, but he didn't quite know how to get the words out to make her "his girl."

Besides, he was having too much fun chasing girls who weren't quite so hard to catch. Or trying to talk local characters Earl Cox and Billy Burton out of a few bottles of their "tiger sweat," home-brewed beer that they had been known to flavor with everything from raisins to moose meat.

On the evening of December 7, 1941, Scott walked into the kitchen of the Leland home looking for his friend Kenny Leland. The family was sitting at the table, listening to the radio. Kenny glanced up when he came in and told him the news. "We're in a war with Japan."

Kenny's parents, Ev and Es Leland looked worried. "They'll be taking the boys," Ev noted.

However, the boys thought the news was exciting. Not until Gabriel Heater of the Mutual Broadcasting System, one of the popular radio commentators of the time and known for his emotional deliveries, came on and mournfully began his broadcast, "Ah, there's bad news tonight . . . ," did they grow more somber. In the past, Heater had almost invariably opened his show, "Ah, there's good news tonight . . ."

Jee-zus, Scott thought, it sounded like there was nothing to stop the Japanese from invading California! By the time Heater finished, Scott was plenty scared.

Pretty soon, however, Woodland was cleaned out of young men of military age who either enlisted or waited to get their draft number called. Anytime one of the boys came home on leave from training camp was an excuse for a party. However, as the war news continued to grow grimmer, there was the feeling that these might be the last good times many of the boys would ever have in their hometown. Splendid in their new uniforms, they knew where they were headed and what was in store for them. But they tried their best not to let on how scared they might be, especially around their folks.

In late 1942 Scott got a job with the Bath Ironworks on the coast of Maine. If there was anything good about the war, it was that it had stuck a nail in the coffin of the Depression and put a lot of people to work. He was given a job helping build destroyers, but the more he worked on the ships, the more he wanted to see what it might be like to go to sea.

When he turned seventeen, in April 1942, Scott started pestering his parents to sign the underage consent form to let him join the Navy. But his mother wouldn't listen to reason, and kept saying that she wasn't going to let her only son go off to war.

Figuring it was only a matter of time before he wore her down, Scott sold Eddie Carlisle, who was a year younger, on the idea, too. Still hampered by a childhood bout with rheumatic fever, Carlisle had a reputation for always being "in the right place at the wrong time." If the boys crossed a frozen waterway in the winter, it didn't matter who went first or last, Eddie was guaranteed to be the one who fell through the ice. But he was the younger brother Scott had never had—being saddled with three sisters instead—and they were inseparable. Carlisle told him that if he would wait until he graduated from high school, "I'll sign up with you."

In October, Scott's parents finally relented and signed the consent form. He and Carlisle, whose father had died young and whose stepfather had no use for him, enlisted and were sent off to boot camp together. Scott's only regret as they boarded the train for Newport News, Rhode Island, was that he had no "understanding" with Vivian Cox.

The first days of boot camp, Scott and Carlisle found themselves sitting "bollicky" in a corridor on a long wooden bench with a lot of other naked young men waiting for their turn to pass through a green door at the end of the hallway. Every few minutes, someone behind the green door would yell, "NEXT!" and a recruit would stand and go in.

Eventually it was Scott's turn, and he entered the room, closing the door behind him at the command of a lieutenant sitting behind a desk. The officer was a sickly looking man with a small, pencil-thin moustache, who fired a series of questions at Scott as he remained at attention in his birthday suit.

"Do you like women?" the officer began.

"Yes, sir."

"Do you like little girls?"

"Yes, sir," Scott replied, then considered what the officer was driving at. "I mean, no, sir. How do you mean that, sir?"

The officer ignored his confusion and went to his next question. "Have you ever had sexual intercourse with a woman?"

"Yes, sir—Well, sir," he stammered, "not a woman, but a girl, sir."

"More than one?"

"Yes, sir."

"Ever had intercourse with an animal?"

"No, sir. Not that I know of."

The officer asked him if he ever masturbated. How often? How many times in a row? Did he enjoy it? Did he feel guilty?

Scott did his best to keep up. "Yes, sir. I don't remember, sir.—What?"

Finally, the officer was finished. "That's all," he said. "NEXT!"

A little later, Carlisle caught up with him back in line. Eddie looked a little dazed by the questioning and not much better when he saw they were going to have blood drawn. His nerves really frayed when the biggest guy in the room fainted as the corpsman plunged a needle into his arm.

Before it was their turn, a doctor approached and told them to put their hands out, palms down. Carlisle's were shaking like leaves in the wind. "You nervous, kid?" the doctor asked him.

"N-n-n-n-o-o-o, sir," Carlisle stuttered.

"You always chew your nails like that?"

"Sometimes sir."

"Okay," the doctor said, "you go stand over there with that group."

Watching his best friend cross the room, Scott suddenly got the feeling he would never see Carlisle again and for the first time felt like bawling. But he saw that Carlisle looked like he felt and needed encouragement. He was going to yell to his pal that everything would be all right, but then Carlisle's group was hustled out of the room.

There wasn't much time to worry about what was happening with his friend. Those who remained were allowed to dress, sorted into companies, and hurried out onto a field, where they were lined up and introduced to their company commanders—the chief petty officers who would be in charge of their training.

Scott's company commander, a nice-looking young chief petty officer, greeted them in what he later learned was the traditional Navy manner, by screaming at the top of his lungs.

"I'VE BEEN IN THIS MAN'S NAVY FOR EIGHT YEARS!" the chief bellowed. "EIGHT YEARS . . . TRAINED THIRTY-TWO COMPANIES AND HAD A GODDAMN GOOD RECORD UP TO NOW!

He whirled on the quivering recruits. "YOU'D THINK A RECORD LIKE THAT OUGHTA BE REWARDED SOMEHOW, BUT 'OH NO,' THEY SEND ME THE GODDAMNDEST BUNCH OF HALF-ASSED PANSIES EVER SPAWNED AND TELL ME TO MAKE SAILORS OUT OF THEM!"

The man was practically frothing at the mouth, a little vein in his forehead bulging as he continued. "LOOK AT ME, YOU ASSHOLES! I'M GONNA HAUNT THE LIVIN' HELL OUTTA YOU FOR THE NEXT TWELVE WEEKS. . . . I DON'T LOOK LIKE A BAD GUY NOW, DO I?" He paused as if to allow any of them to challenge the assertion, then went on when there were no takers. "WELL, I'M A PRICK ALL THE WAY THROUGH, AND YOU'RE GONNA HATE MY GODDAMN GUTS. BUT YOU'RE GONNA DO IT BY THE NUMBERS!"

Later in boot camp, when Scott had figured out that the chief wasn't a half-bad fellow, he thought the "greeting" was probably meant to do just what it had—get their attention. Listen close and they might learn what they needed to learn to survive the months and years ahead.

Just learning to survive the first few nights sleeping in a hammock was enough of a chore. And morning would come all too early with the voice of the chief, "Awww-right you guys, drop your cocks and grab your socks! Reville! Outta them sacks!"

Scott didn't see Carlisle again until the middle of the second week. Then one night a little before lights out, he heard a familiar voice. "Where the hell are ya, Scotty?"

Overjoyed, Scott rushed up and grabbed his friend around the neck. "Goddamnit, Ed, where the hell have you been? Have I ever missed you, ya homely mug."

Carlisle explained that he and the others had been taken to a building called "Ward C" for observation. "Jeezus, them guys is all nuts over there," he said. "One of them kept bangin' his head against the wall every morning, and then telling the doctor he had violent headaches.

"One of those guys was always standin' with his ear to the wall. Then this mornin', he asked me to come and listen. I did, and I told him I didn't hear a damn thing. He says, 'Yeah, it's been like that since I got here.'"

A doctor had finally asked Carlisle if he wanted to be discharged from the Navy or stay in. "I told him I'd be glad to stay in if they'd just let me the hell outta that place."

Carlisle was assigned to another company, but they got to see each other after the day's classes and chores were through. Occasionally their companies drilled together, too, and Scott was present one day when Eddie caught an earful from his company commander. That chief was a tough SOB whose men swore probably hated his own mother. "If he has one," they added.

After ten weeks of training, and just when it seemed they couldn't stand another day without getting off the base, the boots were granted a few hours of liberty in Newport News. The young men saw themselves as horny, hard-fisted, hell-bent-for-leather veterans now, ready to take the town by storm—only to learn that the merchants of Newport News had seen thousands like them and had figured out how to get their hands on the sailors' pay with the least amount of damage to their property and daughters.

After boot camp, Scott and Carlisle caught the train back to Maine and a bus home to Woodland. Scott didn't tell his family he was coming home and was delighted with their surprised and happy greeting. While home, he went out several times with Vivian, planning to ask her to be his girl; but again, he couldn't quite figure out how to say it. Then the week was over and he had to leave.

When they got back to Newport News, the two young men received their assignments—Scott was being sent to electrician's school and Carlisle was to join the crew of a new aircraft carrier, the USS *Franklin*. They were disappointed. It was probably too much to hope that they would be sent to the same ship, but now that it wasn't going to happen they realized they had counted on it. Scott felt that Carlisle, with his penchant for getting himself into trouble, needed looking after and worried that no one else would do it for him. Therefore, they were both delighted when a couple of the other men assigned to the *Franklin* went AWOL—Absent Without Leave—and Scott was reassigned to the ship.

Even then, Carlisle ended up going to the ship first when Scott came down with the flu and was sent to the hospital. A week later, Scott and several other stragglers were put on the back of a truck for the ride down to the Norfolk Navy Yard.

As he looked up at the *Franklin*, Scott wondered, *How the heck am I ever going to find my way around in there?* But as he considered the challenge, he realized that Eddie Carlisle was going to need more looking after than originally anticipated. With that in mind, he shouldered his seabag and followed the others to find a way onboard

The next day, he found Carlisle and learned that his friend had been assigned to the gunnery division and would help operate a 40-millimeter antiaircraft gun. That sounded dangerous and he wasn't happy about it, but he wasn't any more pleased with his first assignment to the yeoman's pool. He didn't want to be a secretary, or as he described it to Eddie, "a ball-bearing WAVE."

Scott only lasted a couple of weeks, which he spent arguing with the first class petty officers, who seemed to enjoy finding something new for him to clean just so they could mess it up again. His "disposition" got him sent to the Combat Information Center, which as the "brains" of the ship seemed more interesting—until he was handed a bucket of soapy water and a rag and told to "scrub them bulkheads, boy."

A few more choice words from the unhappy sailor, and he found himself quickly reassigned to Fire Room Number Two. He'd managed to smart-mouth his way onto the Black Gang just as the ship was preparing to make its trial runs in Chesapeake Bay, so the boilers were going full tilt the first time he climbed through the hatch and for the first time looked down on the noisy cavern that was to be his new "home."

Jee-zus, he thought, beads of sweat already popping out on his face, *it's hotter than the hinges of hell down here*. But the heat wasn't what had him doubting his own intelligence for being so mouthy. Instead of typing up reports in some nice compartment up in the superstructure, he had been told that the *top* of the boilers were nineteen feet below the water line. It looked like twice as much as that down to where the fireroom crew stood watching him. *What chance do we have if a torpedo hits us?* he wondered.

Scott got his answer from a tall, blond man leaning up against one of the rails below. The Black Gang had seen the same look on the faces of nearly every new member who came through the hatch for the first time and realized where they were in relation to where the ocean was. Now, the blond man, Fireman 1st Class "Swede" Hanson, pretended like he was playing the violin while his compatriots laughed.

"You sing 'em, dear," he shouted up to Scott, "and I'll play 'em."

While Seaman Scott was trying to figure out a way to get his friend, Eddie Carlisle, off the antiaircraft guns, Steward's Mate 2nd Class Matthew Little was wishing the Navy had seen fit to put him on one. He wanted to fight—not serve breakfast, lunch, and dinner to officers, and then when the shooting started have to climb down into a hole and pass ammunition. But on that ship, a "colored" man didn't get to fire the guns.

When Little showed up at Norfolk after boot camp, he was as impressed by the size of the ship as a small town boy from Anderson, South Carolina, could be. Born in June 1925, a descendant of slaves brought to America from Africa, his grandfathers and father were all sharecroppers, working other men's lands for some of the produce and perhaps a little cash money. He had never been more than a few miles from the weathered one-room cabin he shared with his parents, two brothers, and two sisters.

They were as poor as the overworked soil they farmed. But the Littles were a close-knit family, who worked hard in the fields—including after school—and laughed just as hard. They didn't have much for entertainment except a radio and each other, but that was enough. On Sundays no one had to work, except his mother and sisters in the kitchen, and there would be a big family dinner, after which they would all sit around and listen to radio programs. And that's where they were when the announcer said that Pearl Harbor had been bombed.

The reaction in the Little household that evening was much the same as it was throughout the United States. Shock. Confusion. *Where is Pearl Harbor?* And then a growing anger—*their* country had been attacked. They had all prayed for world peace at church, but these Japanese folks crept in like killers in the night and bombed *their* boys.

For whites, it might have been difficult to comprehend why "colored" families like the Littles were so patriotic. The Negroes had been stolen from their homes in Africa—beaten, murdered, raped—transported over a wide and frightening ocean to be sold into slavery. Yes, the Civil War had liberated them from their chains, but only to be shackled by poverty and inferior opportunities. They were treated as second-class citizens, or worse—the Ku Klux Klan was alive and well in Anderson. A few Negro activists even argued that the grandsons of former slaves owed nothing to the country of their oppressors.

But that wasn't how the Littles looked at it, nor most of the other families they knew. Their young men enlisted after the attack as quickly as the white boys. Granted, military service was a job and a way out of poverty, but for many, patriotism was the primary motivation. They may have been wronged, but it was still their country—a place where even a black man could dream of a better life, at least for his children.

There was no hesitation for Matthew Little. On his eighteenth birthday, in 1943, he walked into town and registered for the draft. A tall, thin-as-a-beanpole young man, he was excited about going away to war. He had never been more than a few miles from Anderson and wanted to see some of the world.

Matthew Little also dreamed of better things than working another man's farm. But he had no idea how he would accomplish his dreams. Neither of his folks had much education, but they insisted that their children attend school, first in the nearby one-room grammar school and then at Green Street High School in town.

Both schools were all "colored;" the white kids attended their own. He liked school, but classes for the boys and girls in colored high schools ended at the eleventh grade. Only the white kids went on through the twelfth grade and graduated with a diploma.

Little knew that he had to escape Anderson and find someplace where he could go back to high school for that final year and graduate. After that he would find a way to scrape together enough money to attend Benedict College in South Carolina, an all-colored school famous for turning out "teachers and preachers." But then the war came along.

When he joined up, Little wasn't worried about the possibility of danger; in fact, he couldn't imagine anything *bad* could happen to him. He even told the draft board that he was hoping that he could get into the U.S. Marine Corps, whose exploits at Guadalcanal were already the stuff of legend. He said he wanted to fight.

The government's response was to put him in the Navy. Initially disappointed, he decided that the Navy still seemed a lot more exciting than helping his dad hoe.

On the day he left for boot camp, Little's father took him aside. "Do your duty as best you can, son," the older man said. "And son, be a man."

Matthew nodded but wasn't entirely sure what his father meant by the remark. He was already a man, wasn't he? Eighteen years old and ready for whatever adventure came his way. He hoped that after boot camp he would be assigned to a warship and get to shoot the big guns at airplanes, like he had seen a few times in the newsreels. Black-and-white images of tiny dark objects darting across the screen, gun crews in battle helmets pointing and shooting, planes trailing smoke as they fell into the ocean.

Boot camp wasn't so bad. The Navy fed him well, and practically everything he'd seen since leaving Anderson was new and exciting. However, his naval career began on a sad note when one night he got a call from home. His mother had passed away. She had always been there for him—comforting him as a child, telling him to believe in himself, seek an education, dream his dreams. Now she was gone without him even getting to say good-bye.

Still, Little knew that his mother would have wanted him to go on. Despite his grief, he did well in boot camp. He had been sent to gunnery classes and was one of the better shots. When he was assigned to the *Franklin,* he thought he would get put on a gun crew. But he was disappointed; there were no black gun crews on the ship.

Instead, when he arrived for the ship's precommissioning school, he was assigned to be a steward's mate, one of the men who cleaned officers' compartments, did their laundry, served their food. His battle station would be in one of the ammunition holds deep inside the ship and one of the most dangerous places to be during combat—no one survived an explosion when surrounded by ammunition. His job would be passing five-inch shells hand-to-hand with other black men to the conveyor that would take them up to the guns.

Little resented the discrimination. But he kept his mouth shut; his eyes, ears, and mind open; and did as he was told.

On a wintry December day when Captain Shoemaker introduced himself to the *Franklin's* crew, he had concluded his speech to the crew with, "Six months from now you will have seen what your first Jap looks like. . . . Good hunting!"

Shivering in the cold, Matthew Little, the son of a sharecropper and the descendant of slaves, figured that in six months' time, maybe a little longer, he would get a chance to prove himself as good as any man. Like most of the black sailors onboard, he had heard about Dorie Miller, the mess cook who had distinguished himself at Pearl Harbor and won the Navy Cross. *If he could do it,* Little thought, *then so can I.* He didn't know that a month earlier, Miller had been killed when his ship, the USS *Liscome Bay,* was torpedoed near Tarawa. The idea that heroes sometimes died young had not yet crossed his mind.

January 31, 1944
Norfolk Navy Yard, Portsmouth, Virginia

The day the USS *Franklin* was commissioned and little Jimmy Shoemaker got lost deep in her bowels was also bitterly cold and gray with the half-light of winter. Nevertheless, a large crowd of visitors and dignitaries had assembled on the flight deck to hear the day's speeches.

Assistant Secretary of the Navy Artemus L. Gates, a World War I navy pilot, was to be the featured main speaker. But it was a message sent by Captain Mildred McAfee of the WAVES, who couldn't attend the commissioning of the ship that she had christened, that the crew would recall on an even darker day in the future. "Its men will make the name forever glorious by your skill, your valor, your maintenance for your ship of the proud traditions of the Navy on sea and in the air."

Meanwhile, the ship's crew shivered in their dress blue uniforms and peacoats, wishing the speeches would end soon as they stood at attention on the island, as well as on the flight and hangar decks. The only crewmembers with seats were the musicians in the ship's band, who had done their best, despite blue lips and numb fingers, to entertain the guests. Watching and listening with pride was their "manager," Lt. (j.g.) E. Robert Wassman, who knew better than most that this was not just any old Navy band.

When the *Franklin* left for the war, she would be taking along "The Best Band in the Land." The label was no idle boast, either. While other large ships like carriers and battleships often had bands for entertainment, they were mostly comprised of regular Navy men and crewmembers. But the *Franklin's* band was largely made up of former professional musicians from some of the well-known big bands of the era who had been drafted or enlisted at the outbreak of the war. The band had been assembled a year earlier and a lottery held to decide which commanding officer of a naval air station would win their services. Shoemaker had drawn the lucky number during his tenure as commanding officer at Norfolk.

The band's leader was Musician 1st Class Saxie Dowell, who in civilian life had been acclaimed for his arrangements of "Playmates" and "Three Little Fishes." Another of the *Franklin* band's claims to fame was Musician 2nd Class Deane Kincaide, a native of Houston, Texas, who played saxophone and clarinet for the Navy. But before the war he'd been better known for his arrangements with the bands of Tommy Dorsey and Benny Goodman. His hits included "Bugle Call Rag," "Dixie Land Band," and "Boogie Woogie." His arrangement of "Hawaiian War Chant" had been one of the most popular songs on the radio when Uncle Sam came calling.

The crew of the *Franklin* had heard different stories about the band's reaction to the news that the captain had been granted command of an aircraft carrier and planned on taking them with him. Up to that point, their military service had been pretty cushy—playing music at the officers' club, while living off base with their wives and girlfriends.

One version was that Dowell and others had been dismayed. However, Kincaide had a different account of at least the bandleader's reaction. According to Kincaide, when Shoemaker got his orders to assume command of the *Franklin,* he had immediately called Saxie to tell him. "Dowell, I've got a ship!"

"Why, Cap'n," Dowell, a native of North Carolina, was said to have drawled, "I sho' wish we could go with you."

Whether it was mere politeness or a genuine interest in going to sea, Dowell's wish was granted. The question was which division to put the band in. Onboard a ship, every man was expected to pull his weight. The musicians, who did nothing on shore but play music, were going to have to have regular duties, including manning their battle stations, which in their case meant assisting the medical staff.

Shoemaker decided to put them in the navigation division, because that's where the ship's buglers were assigned. The navigator, Cmdr. Benjamin "Benny" Moore, didn't want anything to do with them, so he passed them on to Wassman. But as a card-carrying union musician himself, the twenty-three-year-old Wassman was delighted to accept the responsibility. In a way, he was following a family tradition.

Born in August 1920 in New York City, he was the only son of a hardware and theatrical equipment business owner. Both sides of his family had immigrated from Europe in the middle of the previous century: the Wassmans from Germany and the Shermans from Holland. His great-grandfather, Gustaf Sherman, although just a boy, had served in the Union army as a bugler. He had even earned himself a trip to the White House when he stopped a runaway horse carrying President Lincoln's young son, Todd, when the president was touring a battlefield.

Wassman had played guitar in bands since high school and as a student at Columbia University, including for some of the big-name bandleaders of the time, like Sid Caesar, who played clarinet and was not yet known as a comedian. But there was a more serious side to Wassman as well.

In 1939, as an engineering major, he started a civilian pilot training program at Columbia. Although there was no ROTC program at Columbia, the government was sponsoring such programs so that if war came there would be a reserve of trained pilots available. He knew that the United States could not stay out of the war indefinitely, nor did he think it should. It angered him that the Germans were sinking U.S. merchant ships without repercussions, and he believed the United States should give up any pretense at neutrality and save Great Britain. He didn't pay much attention to the Japanese warmongering, though the news from China was disturbing. *Germany first,* he thought.

In late October 1941, he tried to turn his thoughts into action. He attended a recruiting party thrown by the Royal Canadian Air Force at the Waldorf-Astoria Hotel to find American pilots willing to help fight the Battle of Britain. Impressed by the fancy uniforms and gold flight wings—as well as relishing the opportunity to get in the fight—he signed up on the spot. However, before he was called to report for his physical, the Japanese bombed Pearl Harbor.

Wassman and his Delta Phi fraternity brothers gathered that evening in their fraternity house to listen to the radio accounts of the disaster. They were incensed and patriotic fever ran high. They all swore that on Monday they would enlist.

The next morning, Wassman called the commandant of the Third Naval District. "I'm a pilot and engineering student at Columbia," he said. "Can you use me?" A few days later, the centerfold photograph in the *New York News* showed the "young patriot from Columbia" being sworn in by the commandant.

Within days he was off to three months of preflight training in Georgia, where he quickly demonstrated that he was already an able pilot. From there he was sent to operational training—learning how to fly dive-bombers and fighters—in Jacksonville, Florida, under commanding officer Benjamin Moore.

Health issues nearly cost Wassman his commission and delayed his training program. While Wassman waited to be reassigned, Moore suggested that he attend air navigation school for officers who would be needed on aircraft carriers—not to fly, but to assist the pilots with getting to and from their targets. Navigating over an open ocean with no landmarks was no easy task. Nor did aircraft carriers linger in the area after launches; they followed a predesigned course that avoided being easy pickings for enemy submarines and aircraft, but they also arrived at an exact spot in the ocean at a prearranged time to retrieve their aircraft.

A few months later, Moore, who had just been assigned as the navigator of the new carrier *Franklin,* brought his protégé onboard as the navigation division officer, a nice promotion. However, Wassman's first job was to proceed to Newport, Virginia, and pick up some of the crew who would be part of the division and then escort them to Newport News for precommissioning classes.

When he arrived in Newport, Wassman met up with a dozen or so quartermasters, who assisted the navigator with charts and sometimes manned the helm. He also located the twenty-two musicians from the band. The quartermasters were happy enough, but a number of the musicians griped at him for most of the train trip. Sea duty? They were jazz musicians, not sailors, for God's sake—used to smoky bars and late nights, not salt air and reveille at 5:00 A.M.

On January 31 the band sat huddled against the cold like everyone else listening to the speeches, and wishing they were in one of those smoky bars. The *Franklin* was at last ready to take the final steps that would lead her to the Pacific to face the Japanese. She had been painted in a camouflage pattern using white, gray, and black paint to break up the solid outline of her sides; shapes that from a great distance might resemble the silhouette of supply ships, and therefore not as alluring targets, were part of the design.

The captain spoke to the crew—the sons of mill workers and business tycoons, musicians and farmers, the descendants of slaves and native peoples and European immigrants—of their mutual obligation as American fighting men.

We have followed the final stages of construction of this great ship, and know from personal observation that in a material sense she is as nearly perfect as possible. Today our *Franklin* becomes a unit of our Navy, and we are charged with the large responsibility of training ourselves to have complete knowledge of all the potentialities of our ship, to the end that she will soon be ready to take her place in the line of battle.

This is no easy task. The ship's company and the air group together compose the most complex combat team in the world. Knowing this, we in the *Franklin* highly resolve that the trust reposed in us shall prove to have been well justified, and that our ship will join the Fleet ready in all respects to strike hard, again and again, until the enemies of this great nation shall have been beaten to their knees.

CHAPTER SEVEN

Aviators and Airedales: Air Group 13

March 14, 1944
Chesapeake Bay, Virginia

L t. (j.g.) E. John Weil circled five hundred feet above the huge new aircraft carrier in his Curtis SB2C Helldiver, cruising first along the starboard side going in the same direction as the ship, before turning to pass down the port side. He was in a group of three dive-bombers flying in echelon, or a staggered formation, so that each plane was just behind and off the wing of the plane in front. As they swept past the ship's island, Weil pushed a lever that hydraulically lowered his wheels and flaps for landing, then reached for another lever and manually lowered the tail hook.

All of five-foot-seven and 115 pounds, Weil was already an experienced combat pilot, with an Air Medal earned at Bougainville that fall when he dove through antiaircraft fire to put a bomb through the deck of a light cruiser. Still, there was something nerve-wracking about landing on a new ship for the first time, and he wanted to make a good impression.

He was twenty-five years old—the same age as Minnesota farm boy Charles A. Lindbergh had been in 1927 when Weil, then seven, and his parents had watched the famous aviator fly over the city of Paris to complete his historic flight across the Atlantic. Weil's father owned an import-export business in Manhattan, and the family had moved to Paris so that his father could work with his uncles, who handled the business on that side of the Atlantic. Back then the world had been at peace, and the sound of an airplane flying over a European city was no more alarming than a dove's flight.

The Weil family didn't like Paris and returned to New York City after a year. Not long afterward, the stock market had crashed and the country was in the throes of the Great Depression. His family didn't struggle like some of the people he saw on the streets selling apples or pencils or anything to make a buck, or in the newspaper photographs of the hungry men, women, and children standing in bread lines.

The Weils lived in a nice apartment and John attended a private school, though on scholarship. There had been the one alarming day when he had come home and found his father weeping like a child because of the financial reverses he had suffered. But mostly the Depression was a matter of tightening their belts—such as his father buying an apple and a Hershey bar for his lunch every day from a street peddler rather than going to a restaurant for a businessman's lunch.

After high school John was accepted to the University of Pennsylvania, where he attended the prestigious Wharton School of Business. But he didn't like college much and was beginning to see the writing on the wall. The war was raging in Europe by 1940, and it was obvious the United States was being sucked into it like a leaf down a storm drain.

He didn't want to go down that drain in the Army, so in July 1941 he left school and signed up to become a naval aviator. He had the requisite two years of college and had reached the age of twenty-one that the Navy required at the time.

After receiving his "wings of gold" identifying him as a Navy pilot in June 1942, Weil was sent to the Naval Air Station in San Diego where he was assigned to Advanced Carrier Training Group (ACTG) as a dive-bomber. He was soon introduced to the Douglas Dauntless SBD. The two-seater—one seat for the pilot and one for the rear-facing tailgunner/radioman—was an easy, forgiving plane to fly and accurate in a dive. But a dive-bombing attack still depended on precision and coordination among the planes.

Dive-bombers flew in divisions of six, with two sections of three planes each. They would cruise at an altitude of about fourteen thousand feet to a maximum of seventeen thousand feet until spotting the targets. Then each would begin to point his nose down to lose altitude. As the plane picked up speed, the pilot opened the cockpit in case he and the gunner needed to bail out quickly.

About twelve thousand feet, the first plane in line would open his dive flaps and "peel off" to attack the target, followed by the others at intervals of a few seconds. The dive flaps, in conjunction with the normal flaps in the wings, actually helped slow the plane so that it could be controlled; even then it would exceed 260 miles an hour, with the noise of the wind and engine roaring in the canopy.

Diving as steeply as possible to make it more difficult to defend against required that the pilot, hanging by his seat belt, point the nose of the plane straight down. However, because of the lift created by the wind passing over the wings, the actual path of the plane would be closer to a 70-degree angle.

In order to dive down and have the path intersect the target, the pilots placed the target in the viewfinder of a "telescope" and adjusted their flight accordingly. As Weil soon learned, it was one thing to lock on to a stationary target, quite another to hit one that was moving, such as a ship taking evasive maneuvers. Striking a turning, twisting warship required constant adjustments to keep the target in the viewfinder. Too radical an adjustment and the plane would "skid," like a car in too tight a turn, so that even with the target in the sight, the bomb would fly off in the direction of the skid's momentum.

The margin for error was slight and not just from the standpoint of striking the target. The pilot had to release his bomb at approximately three thousand to twenty-five hundred feet and then, in a matter of seconds, pull out of the dive to level off by one thousand feet. The closer the pilot got to the target before releasing the bomb, the greater his accuracy, but it also put him and his gunner at risk of being consumed by the blast of their own weapon, or not being able to recover from the dive in time.

Pulling out placed a lot of force on the plane and its crew—three to four "g"s, or three to four times the normal effect of the earth's gravity. Riding this edge of disaster or triumph was an adrenaline rush most of the men had never felt before, or would feel again if they survived beyond the war. But at least the pilots could see where they were going; the tail gunner faced backward, looking up at the sky, and had no idea how close to the ground or water the plane might be in its screaming descent.

Having learned to dive, Weil and the other aviators had a new challenge, learning to land on a moving platform that teetered with the pitch and swell of the oceans—an aircraft carrier. But the Navy wasn't going to risk a real ship on rookies. So first they practiced landing on a "field carrier," a flight-deck-sized area that had been marked off on the ground. Only when they could land and take off in the prescribed space were they allowed to try a ship—in the case of Weil's initial attempt, the Navy's first escort carrier, the USS *Long Island*.

To assist with both landing and taking off, the carrier would turn into the wind and adjust its speed so that there was a fairly constant thirty-two knots of air moving down the flight deck. So if the wind was moving at fifteen knots, the ship would cruise at seventeen to have enough passing over the wings and providing lift as the planes took off over the bow. Or conversely, helping slow the planes coming in from the stern to land.

As they prepared to land, the planes circled the carrier like bees waiting in line to return to the hive, dropping steadily lower as each plane in front touched down and was moved out of the way for the next. On the final circle, after passing first on the starboard side moving in the same direction as the ship, then on the port side in the opposite direction, the landing plane made one last 180-degree turn to line up with the flight deck.

About halfway through the turn, the pilot started watching the landing signal officer, who stood on the signal deck platform, a small ramp on the port side and near the stern that extended beyond the flight deck. A net hung below the platform just in case the signal deck officer and his crew had to jump for their lives to get out of the way of an errant plane.

The LSO carried two large, bright-orange paddles (or at night, lights) he used to give directions and correct approaches. If the pilot was unable to adjust in time, the LSO would give him the "wave off" signal by rapidly crossing his paddles, at which point the flyer would have to increase his power, pull up, and try the approach again.

However, if all was in order, when the plane was just about over the deck and still about twenty feet in the air, the LSO would signal for the pilot to cut his engine. The pilot would then put his tail down and try to snare one of a half dozen "arresting cables" strung out across the deck with the hook on the plane's tail. The arresting cables were on a hydraulic retrieval system that allowed them to give with a plane's momentum. If the pilot missed the cable with the hook, he would crash into a barrier of more cables raised to keep him from piling into any planes parked on the bow of the ship.

As soon as the plane jerked to a stop, a member of the deck crew would rush out and release the cable from the tail hook. The plane would then be rolled in front of the barrier so that the next plane could land. The teamwork had to be exacting, as the goal was to land planes about twenty seconds apart. Any pilot who couldn't regularly snag a cable wasn't going to last long on a carrier, and some pretty decent pilots never got the hang of landing on a moving ship. Some would die trying. However, with his gunner, Aviation Radioman/Machinist's Mate 3rd Class Lou Kufelt, along for the ride, Weil quickly made six landings and takeoffs from the *Long Island* without a hitch and became "carrier qualified."

Learning to dive-bomb and to take off and land on carriers was dangerous work, even without enemy fire. Recognizing the high level of stress, the Navy made allowances for the highly trained young men to let off steam. In October, Weil was assigned to join Bombing Squadron 11 (VB-11). His squadron was blessed with a particularly understanding skipper, Lt. Cmdr.

Weldon Hamilton, a mustang officer who had been at the Coral Sea battle and understood the pressure they were under.

Typical of how Hamilton looked after his pilots was his handling of a young officer appointed to get the pilots physically fit. One day the officer entered Hamilton's office and complained that the men had told him to "shove it" when he tried to encourage them to participate in group exercise. The squadron commander calmly told the junior officer to return to his quarters and get into his formal dress uniform if he wanted to lodge a complaint.

The skipper hoped the diversion would allow the officer to cool down. But when the man, properly attired, returned and complained again, Hamilton laid it on the line. "Listen to me, fella," he stormed. "All I want my pilots to do is fly, drink, and chase dames.

"With all that going on, they don't have time for your nonsense. Now get the hell out of my office." It was the sort of reaction for which the men loved Hamilton . . . and there was no more talk of calisthenics.

VB-11 was assigned to replace the air group then serving aboard the carrier *Hornet,* the ship that had carried Doolittle and his raiders to strike at Japan and that was now in the middle of the fight for Guadalcanal.

Every man took the news differently. Some couldn't wait to get into the fight; no one was going to win any medals in San Diego. Others greeted it as a grim fact of life that they were going to have to kill or be killed. Each man also had to confront his own doubts about how he would face the rigors and fears of combat. But they had been trained to do a job, and they were all ready to go.

Any excitement, however, turned to disappointment in November when they learned that the *Hornet* had been sunk off the Santa Cruz Islands. Not until Easter of 1943 did they finally get into combat—as land-based planes flying out of Henderson Field on Guadalcanal. By now the battle for the island was over except for mopping up duties, so their targets were other islands in the Solomons, including one run to Bougainville where Weil sent a five-hundred-pound bomb through the deck of a light cruiser, which erupted in flames and black smoke. The attack earned Weil an Air Medal for bravery.

In all, Bombing Squadron 11 carried out more than sixty missions during its four-month tour, including patrolling for submarines, losing a handful of pilots and gunners. The antiaircraft fire from the Japanese seemed haphazard and generally ineffective, and the day of the Zero's dominance in the skies, if not over, were greatly diminished.

The air group returned to the States in August 1943. Six pilots—Weil, William Bonnar, "Dutch" Bomberger, Joe Eisenhuth, Kilmer Bortz, and Dick Harding—were all transferred to a new dive-bomber squadron in the newly created Air Group 13. They were pleased to learn that the air group had been assigned to one of the big new *Essex*-class carriers, the *Franklin,* which meant they would be in the thick of things as the United States pressed on to Japan.

Now-Lieutenant Weil, who had lost fifteen pounds in the South Pacific to dysentery and hepatitis A, got a new ARM 3rd class tail gunner named Lou Horton, an eighteen-year-old redhead from Lynn, Massachusetts. Weil didn't know much more about him than that.

The crewmen in both the dive-bombers and torpedo planes were enlisted men who had been recruited from their boot camp classes. It was an odd fact that the pilots and their crews, who depended so intimately on the other's abilities during combat, essentially had very little contact once they stepped away from the plane.

Lt. Cmdr. R. L. Kibbe, a Naval Academy man, led the dive-bomber squadron VB-13. He was well liked by the other pilots but had no combat experience; in fact, of the thirty-six pilots in the squadron, only nine had seen any action, including the six from VB-11.

They trained stateside at Naval Air Station Wildwood in New Jersey for the rest of the year on their own, until January, when the three squadrons—dive-bombers, fighters, and torpedo planes—that would comprise Air Group 13 were all brought to Oceana Naval Air Station near Norfolk, where the *Franklin* was docked. The group was under the overall command of Cmdr. Charles C. Howerton, nicknamed "Sunshine" due to his cheery disposition—a handsome, dapper officer who carried a swagger stick.

While the ship underwent its final sea trials and awaited commissioning, the squadrons practiced working together. They were all flying the latest planes. There was the Grumman "Avenger" torpedo plane (TBF), faster and more powerful than the old Devastators that had provided so much easy fodder for Japanese Zeros early in the war. The fighters were the new F6F Hellcats, or just "Sixes" to their pilots and ground crews.

The Navy presented the VB-13 pilots with a new "improved" dive-bomber, the "Helldiver" SB2C. The "Beast," as it was quickly nicknamed, wasn't as stable or easy to fly as the Dauntless. But it was billed as being bigger and faster with more range and firepower—including 20-millimeter "cannons" in the wings, and larger bomb capacity. The bombs were also carried inside a bomb bay rather than strapped to the underbelly, cutting down on drag. The target sighting system was now electronic and built into the windshield as a pattern rather than the old telescopic sights that had injured many pilots upon crashing. Another big advantage for a carrier plane, the Beast's wings folded up, meaning more could be stored on the flight or hangar deck.

The first SB2Cs didn't live up to the hype. They had Wright engines, which proved to be not as stable as the old Dauntless Pratt-Whitneys, and a number of planes crashed on take-off because of insufficient power. The Beast didn't fit the advertising until the Navy switched over to SB2C-3s, which had more horsepower and four-bladed propellers instead of three-bladed. That solved the power problem but they were still more difficult to fly than their predecessor.

Finally on March 14, 1944, the air group got the word that the *Franklin* was ready for her shakedown cruise, and they were to fly aboard for the first time. The first man to land on her was already one of the most colorful characters in the fleet for both his combat heroics and his onshore carousing.

Born in Danville, Illinois, Joseph Franklin Taylor had graduated from the Naval Academy at Annapolis, Maryland, in 1927. Two years later he earned his wings at the naval air station at Pensacola, Florida. Before the war, he had flown from the *Langley* and *Lexington,* then in May 1941, he was given command of Torpedo Squadron 3 aboard the *Yorktown.* The ship had been in the Atlantic, protecting convoys, when the news about Pearl Harbor hit the radio waves.

Taylor and his squadron had been among the first to strike back at the Japanese, participating in the raids against Japanese ships in the Gilbert and Marshall Islands in February 1942. Those raids were followed by another against shipping in New Guinea, when Taylor took his squadron thirty miles beyond the target area to attack and destroy a seaplane aircraft carrier.

Taylor, a lieutenant commander at the time, and his men distinguished themselves again on May 4, shortly before the Battle of the Coral Sea, by striking at Japanese shipping in Tulagi Harbor. Despite the frustration of "dud" torpedoes, which could not withstand a drop of more than fifty feet or a flight speed of more than 120 miles an hour—two and a half times slower than the pursuing Zeros, eight Japanese ships, mostly cargo and munitions vessels, were sunk.

On May 7, Taylor and his squadron had been in on the combined attack that sank the light carrier *Shoho* at the outset of the Battle of the Coral Sea.

The next morning, the squadron was the first to attack the *Shokaku,* a brand-new twenty-six-thousand-ton carrier when at 10:57 Taylor radioed his counterpart with the dive-bomber squadron, Lt. Cmdr. William O. Burch Jr., with the laconic statement, "Okay, Bill, I'm starting in."

Taylor was awarded the Navy Cross for his role at the Battle of the Coral Sea; he was then presented with a Gold Star in lieu of a second Navy Cross for the earlier attacks against the Japanese in New Guinea. His subsequent actions at Midway earned him a Bronze Star for gallantry, and a Purple Heart when he was wounded slightly by shrapnel after staying on the burning *York-town* to organize the fire-fighting crews that tried to save the ship.

Taylor was held by his men in equal parts of affection and awe. "He's part Indian," one of the pilots told Quentin Reynolds, a war correspondent for *Collier's* magazine. "That's what makes him so tough." Another noted that he had been a test pilot. "Hell, he can fly anything with wings!"

"Yeah," another had chimed in. "Joe was on the *Yorktown* when she got it, but nothing much happened to him. The guy is indestructible."

Dark-haired and rakishly handsome, a cigarette dangling from his lips almost constantly, Taylor's appetite for booze, dames, and late nights while ashore was legendary. He was also a wonderful pilot and floated the new Avenger onto the flight deck of the *Franklin* like a seabird alighting on a piece of flotsam.

It was the last time he would land on the ship. He parked the Avenger and climbed down to assume his spot on the bridge as the ship's air officer, which is where he was when Weil took his place in the landing circle above the waters of Chesapeake Bay.

Weil completed his turn back to the ship and lined up with the flight deck, on which a large "13" had been painted. There were a lot of 13s associated with the ship. The ship was CV-13. It was Air Group 13—with the fighters, VF-13; the torpedo planes, VT-13; and the dive-bombers, VB-13. Weil's squadron had been formed on October 13, 1944.

The superstitious may have felt that the ship was numerically doomed before it left Norfolk. But Captain Shoemaker had told the crew when he introduced himself in December that 13 was his lucky number. Weil, who caught the first cable and also made a perfect landing, figured they would all find out soon enough.

May 15, 1944
Balboa, Panama

Aviation Radioman 2nd Class Samuel Plonsky climbed down from his radio operator's seat in the Avenger torpedo bomber and knelt down on the glass floor of the belly turret. He knew it was safe, but it always made him nervous to see all that water rushing past at a couple hundred miles an hour and a hundred feet below.

During most of a flight, Plonsky's position was up inside the abdomen of the plane, facing forward on a bench toward his radio equipment. But when his plane was attacking or being attacked, his job was to crawl down into the turret and kneel. One reason was so that during a torpedo or bombing attack he could bend forward and look up at the belly of the plane to make sure whichever weapon they were carrying dropped properly from the bomb bay. The second reason enabled him to turn around to use the turret's rear-facing .30-caliber machine gun to either fend off other aircraft or strafe targets below and behind the plane.

Plonsky had left his seat this time when his pilot, Ensign Robert Freligh, told him to get ready to make a torpedo run at the dam that held the water supply for a nearby city. Above him, in the ball turret on top of the plane, he could hear Aviation Machinist's Mate 2nd Class Peter Sanchez checking his twin .50-caliber machine gun, his eyes peeled for any enemy aircraft above them.

Plonsky felt his heart pounding, the excitement of the moment building as the plane dropped lower and raced across the wave tops. As far as he was concerned, life as a Navy combat air crewman was a pretty grand adventure—especially for a nice Jewish boy from a pleasant middle-class neighborhood of Boston. With a lot of hard work and long hours, his father made a good living as a shoe wholesaler, even during the Depression. Sam certainly hadn't suffered, except from a bad case of acne and maybe from a little boredom. Life up to that point had been pleasant but dull.

Pearl Harbor had certainly changed that. He wanted to sign up right away, but he was only seventeen and his mother wouldn't hear of him joining early. She said it was because he needed to graduate from high school first. But after he graduated in the spring of '42, she just wouldn't discuss it—he suspected because his older brother, Fivee, had died of appendicitis a few years earlier, and Sam was now her only child.

So he had to wait until his eighteenth birthday—Halloween, October 31, 1942—to join the Navy. But he was in for another disappointment. He had always wanted to fly and hoped he would be sent to pilot training, but they weren't taking guys straight out of high school yet. However, when he got through boot camp, and they asked him what he wanted to do, he replied, "Navy Air Corps," without hesitation. So they sent him to aviation radio and gunnery school to fly aboard a torpedo plane as a combat air crewman.

Plonsky came out of the school gung-ho and ready to go kill "those dirty Japs" for what they had done at Pearl Harbor. As far as he was concerned, the Japanese were no better than the Nazis, and everybody knew what Hitler and his murderers had been doing to Jews in Europe. He certainly had heard enough down at the temple, and that was even before the worst of the news about the concentration camps and ovens started leaking out of Europe, which he heard about after he joined.

When Air Group 13 flew aboard in March, he was there with Freligh and Sanchez to set the world right again. But the ship wasn't quite ready.

With her planes onboard, the *Franklin* left Newport for her shakedown cruise escorted by two destroyers. Heading into the Caribbean, the carrier operated off Trinidad in the British West Indies for a month.

The *Franklin* returned to Virginia for final equipment modifications and installment, and for farewells. The men were excited, most of them not more than a year or two out of high school and embarking on the biggest adventure of their lives.

They would never again be as innocent. But most of the crew were still hardly more than boys when they gathered on the evening of April 24, 1944, in their compartments around radios to listen to a salute addressed to them by bandleader Fred Waring and his Pennsylvanians. The crew had been invited to send in their requests, and there was also a special arrangement of a new song written by Waring's friend, Musician 1st Class Saxie Dowell, a jazzy, if a little hokey, number called "Big Ben the Flattop."

We're the *Franklin,* the *Franklin,*
Statesman of the Sea;
We legislate with fighting planes;
And we're making history.
No wind nor wave nor deadly foe
Can stand against our might;
Our scrappin' crew will bring her through

With that good old Navy fight.

Chorus: Big Ben the Flattop! Mistress of the sea and sky;
With every ounce of strength we'll help her fighting aces fly;
As from our decks those motors roar and rocket off to sea,
We'll give a mighty, heartfelt cheer for—
Her Wings of Victory!

As the ship slipped away from its berth, the dock was lined with the wives and girlfriends and families of many of the men. Some of the wives, especially those with children, were settled and would remain in the area. Some would leave to live with their families while their husbands remained at sea. Others planned to move to the West Coast to be within visiting distance if the ship returned during the war.

Plonsky watched the distance to the dock grow, wishing his girlfriend, Mimi Gordon, had been there to send him off with a kiss. But her father wouldn't let her; she was too young to be traveling from Boston to Norfolk— or across town for that matter. She was only fifteen.

They had been sweet on each other for three years, since she was twelve and he was fifteen. On the day of one of Mimi's older cousin's Bar Mitzvah, a slim and dapper Samuel Plonsky strolled into the party.

All the girls began vying for his attention, even if he had his share of pimples. He was the oldest boy there and splendid in a zoot suit, Mimi was captivated, but as a mere twelve-year-old, he didn't give her a second look.

The next summer, Plonsky got a job making deliveries for Mimi's uncle, who was in the wholesale fruit business. One day when she was visiting his office, Sam saw her and asked if she wanted to ride along while he went about his errands. The rest, as she told her friends, was history.

Before he left for aviation school, he and Mimi had exchanged friendship rings. But her father thought that at age fifteen she was too young to be "going steady," even if he was several hundred miles away.

Sam Plonsky got around the parental censorship by writing his love letters to her in Morse Code—a lot of dotted and dashed *I love yous*—which he had to learn as an aviation radioman. When his letters arrived, she would sit down with her Girl Scout handbook and decode them dot by dot and dash by dash. She thought he was just *so* romantic—especially when he wrote to tell her how he had painted "Mimi" in the shape of a heart on his plane with black paint, "right above the door" where he entered so that he could touch it before every takeoff. It was for luck, he said, though he didn't figure he'd need it—but being a little superstitious, he figured it couldn't hurt.

The two other members of the plane's crew looked at the ten-inch heart painted on the dark blue fuselage and shook their heads. Sanchez was like a big brother to Plonsky. The wise-cracking Chicago native, who was one year older chronologically and ten in experience, was always teasing him about "his babe, Mimi . . . ohhh, Mimi." But then he would pat Sam on the back and add, "Don't worry . . . we'll get you back to her."

After leaving Norfolk, the *Franklin* sailed down and into the Caribbean, then headed west for the Panama Canal. While still a hundred miles away, Shoemaker ordered the air group to pull a simulated surprise attack on the U.S. Army bases guarding the militarily sensitive area.

A Detroit product, Freligh was a hell of a pilot as he demonstrated attacking the defenseless dam. To throw off the imaginary "gunners," he would drop down so low that it seemed the belly turret would soon be dragging in the water; then he would pop up to fifty or a hundred feet, then swoop low again, all the while darting from side to side like a bat catching insects. When the dam holding back the reservoir's water was right in front of the plane, a couple hundred yards out, Freligh stopped his jitterbugging and held the plane steady to drop the torpedo. "Torpedo away!" he called out over the headphones.

Plonsky looked up at the bomb bay, watching for the single, fourteen-foot long, three-foot-wide tube to drop into the water and streak for the dam. Of course nothing happened, though that night in the ready rooms they claimed a direct hit. Next up, he said, a Jap ship.

On June 5 the *Franklin* slipped into Pearl Harbor with her crew assembled on the flight deck to pay homage to the *Arizona*. At the command of the bos'n's pipe, they had saluted as the *Franklin*'s flag was briefly dipped.

Wide-eyed Aviation Coxswain 3rd Class Frank Turner stared hard at where they had been told the famous battleship now rested. But he couldn't see anything, just oil-slicked water over a shadow that he guessed must have been the ship. In fact, he had to look close to see any evidence of the attack. He was a little disappointed. Growing up with the newsreels of the ships belching black smoke, he had expected to see more damage still in evidence. However, he was moved by the ceremony of manning the lines and flag dipping for the *Arizona*'s dead.

Turner had been born and raised in the Bronx, the son of a New York City firefighter. The Turners were Irish Catholics and lived right off the Grand Concourse, the main thoroughfare through the Bronx, surrounded by stores and six- to eight-story apartment buildings and private homes.

During the Depression and the years leading up to the war, they had occupied the main floor of a house (another family lived upstairs) across the concourse from Saint Phillips Church. Frank's parents had been married in that church, and as a youth he had served as an altar boy.

The Bronx was a true melting pot, with strong Irish, Italian, and Jewish blocks. There were also quite a few Negroes on the north end of the borough, but Turner and his friends never had any problems with them. They were just some more fellas to challenge to a game of stickball in the streets, or baseball on a vacant lot they cleaned up to make a ball field. Nobody had much money, and they all sweated the same on hot summer days when the city broiled. He only saw trouble between different people when Hitler came to power and some of the men in the German neighborhood started wearing strange brown uniforms and then armbands with swastikas. There seemed to be a lot of fights wherever those guys turned up.

Turner spent much of his boyhood down at the firehouse, especially after his father, Frank Sr., got transferred from Harlem to the station a few blocks from their home. His mother used to send him to the station with his father's lunch and supper, which was fine by him.

Like most boys, Turner thought his father was a hero, but only *his* dad had the medals to prove it. One was the Silver Star for bravery he had earned during World War I when he was in the Army and voluntarily rushed out into no-man's-land to repair a telephone line between the frontlines and his artillery unit. When his son asked about his war years, Frank Sr. replied that they were not something he wished to recall. War was not something to look forward to, he said, but sometimes it was a duty, "and when your country calls, you go."

After he got home from the war, Frank Sr. earned more medals as a New York City fireman; these were for saving people—rushing into burning buildings, risking his own life to save theirs. He seemed to his son to be prouder of the firefighter awards than the Silver Star. He was patriotic and belonged to the department's American Legion post, but when he marched in the parades down Fifth Avenue, he wore his fire department uniform, not his Army clothes.

During the Depression, he stayed on the job even when the paychecks were irregular. And in the mid-1930s, he was made battalion chief, responsible for five station houses. Even in the supervisory role of battalion chief, Frank Sr. never stopped acting like a hero. One night in 1938, his son heard over the radio that there was a big fire at a housing development built by the Works Progress Administration in the eastside of the Bronx. He figured his father was probably there, overseeing the fire companies, but the next morning there was a photograph in the newspaper of his father. Wearing his white battalion chief's helmet, he was emerging from the blazing building with a child in his arms.

Even as a teenager attending Cardinal Hays Catholic High School, Frank Jr. still enjoyed going down to the station house to hang out with "the guys." So he happily complied that Sunday late afternoon on December 7, 1941, when his mother asked him to take some paperwork to his father. He arrived at the station to find the men gathered around the radio, shaking their heads.

After the "day of infamy," Frank couldn't wait to sign up. "I'm going to enlist," he announced to his parents toward the end of his senior year in high school. His mother, Katherine, wouldn't hear of it—he was her only boy and she wasn't going to see him march off to war.

When she wasn't around, his father took him aside. "I know you're going to go," he said. "But I want you to finish high school. And there's one more thing, I don't want you going into the infantry. You're joining the Army Air Corps or the Navy."

Frank Jr. graduated from high school in May 1943, but wouldn't turn seventeen until September. As the day of his birthday approached, his mother was still resisting. But his father now took his side. Frank Jr. could hear him sometimes at night, talking to his mother in the kitchen. *He's going to go. Better he pick which branch.* There were plenty of tears, but at last she relented. He was sworn in the day after his birthday.

Near the end of boot camp, Turner and his classmates were given the aptitude test, and he noted that he enjoyed airplanes. The Navy sent him straight from boot camp to an escort carrier, the USS *Charger,* which was being used to carrier-qualify new pilots. He was assigned to the flight deck crew, nicknamed "Airedales," to be trained as a plane handler. He was part of the crew that moved the planes for launching and then retrieved them upon landing; then they spotted them again in the proper order, and in the requested numbers, on the flight deck in preparation for the next strike.

The plane handlers were just one component of a flight deck crew whose movements at times looked like a large, complicated ballet. And a colorful one. Turner's gang wore blue hats and blue shirts. The guys in red shirts loaded the "ammo" on the planes—the bombs and rockets and bullets. The planes were fueled by men in purple shirts. Men in yellow were called plane directors and guided the planes as they taxied to the launching point.

The colors served the essential purpose of identifying who was responsible for what jobs on the flight deck in a world of whirling propellers, intense noise, and dangerous weapons. Within weeks, Turner had seen men walk into propellers in a moment of confusion or loss of focus. He was on the deck during landings one day when an arresting cable snapped. The suddenly loose ends whipped back like angry snakes and cut the head off a sailor across the deck from him as clean as a knife would have.

The *Charger* only had a few planes on the deck at a time. The danger ratcheted way up when Turner was transferred to the *Franklin* air group in the fall of 1943 and the squadrons started practicing landings and takeoffs. Then there might be few dozen planes of all kinds moving about the flight deck, with more waiting below in the hangar to be brought up by the elevators. Accidents increased, and so did the bloody deaths.

Preparing for a mission, the flight deck was set up as strategically as a game of chess. The heaviest planes, the torpedo bombers, were spotted at the stern of the flight deck, because they needed the extra space on the runway to lift off. Next were the dive-bombers and at the front were the fighters. How many of each depended on what the mission called for—if they were going after shipping, or attacking facilities on land, one might call for more torpedo planes, one for dive-bombers or for more fighters.

The deck crew referred to a plotting board in the island structure to put the pieces in place and took pride in their efficiency. Then someone would die and remind them it wasn't a game after all.

When the *Franklin* reached Hawaiian waters, the air group was sent to the naval air station at Puunene on the island of Maui. There they encountered other air groups that were still waiting to be assigned to a carrier and worried that someone might claim seniority and bump them off the *Franklin*. Everyone wanted into the fight.

The air group's fears were for naught, and they joined the ship when she sailed from Pearl Harbor on June 15. The confidence of the men on the carrier was echoed in a man-on-the-street interview that ran in the ship's newspaper, the *Franklin Forum*.

The "Roving Reporter" had asked: *When do you think the war will be over?*

Commander F. K. Smith, the senior medical officer, replied, "It won't be over before the next two years. I figure it will take this long, as much as I hate to say it. I think the Japs will have to be corralled before they will give up."

Lt. Cmdr P. Speer, an aide to the executive officer, voiced an opinion shared by the veterans who had seen enough of the world: "The war will be over two weeks before I get home for good."

Lt. Cmdr. W. H. Kreamer, a communications officer, said, "I believe that although the fighting may stop in the Pacific theater by late Spring of 1946 so far as the United States is concerned, the Japs will remain unsubjugated in their home islands indefinitely because of the great difference between the Occidental and Oriental character."

Chief Boatswain's Mate J. F. Sheppard was a little less intellectual: "Don't know when the war will be over," he said, "but when it is, I want to be in Tokyo using Tojo for a Yo-Yo with an abundant audience of Geisha girls."

The *Franklin* arrived at the Eniwetok lagoon on June 20 to join up with the Fifth Fleet. The lagoon, however, was nearly empty. They didn't know it, but at that moment, the fleet was far to the north in the second day of a battle that someday would have enormous consequences for the war in general and the *Franklin* in particular. Officially, the event was recorded as the First Battle of the Philippine Sea. But the first day at least became better known as The Great Marianas Turkey Shoot.

Of course, the crew of the *Franklin* knew nothing of the battle, as that evening they listened with amusement to Tokyo Rose announcing that the USS *Franklin* had been sunk with a massive loss of life in some battle to the north.

The *Franklin Forum* wasted no time making light of it in the next edition under the headline: TOJO THE FIBBER IS CAUGHT RED-HANDED

The crew of the USS *Franklin* was reminded of none other than Mark Twain himself when it heard over the radio . . . a Japanese broadcast blandly announcing the sinking of this great aircraft carrier.

Twain, it will be remembered, upon hearing an erroneous report of his death, said, "The reports of my death are greatly exaggerated."

So, we feel we are not without ample precedent in emphatically stating that the reports of our sinking are greatly exaggerated.

One young bluejacket who had been several decks below all after-noon jumped to his feet when he heard Tojo's broadcast and said, "Hell, I'm going up topside to see for myself."

It would not be the last time, not by a long shot, that Tokyo Rose would announce the demise of the *Franklin*. A couple of times, she was nearly right.

CHAPTER EIGHT

Iwo Jima to Saipan: Fireworks and Flies

July 4, 1944
Iwo Jima, Bonin Islands

Price! Price! Was that you or that other son of a bitch?" Cmdr. Charles Howerton, the skipper of Air Group 13, squirmed in the cockpit of his F6F Hellcat, trying to see behind him, where a plume of flame and smoke rose from the surface of the ocean.

"Sunshine" Howerton had taken off from the *Franklin* that morning accompanied by his wingman, Ensign Calvin Price, to observe the air group as they bombed and strafed the Japanese forces on a small island about six hundred miles south of Japan called Iwo Jima. The *Franklin* was celebrating the Fourth of July with deadly fireworks as part of Task Force 58, the striking arm of the immense Fifth Fleet. Now he worried that his attempt to aid two downed flyers had cost his young wingman his life.

In June, when the carrier dropped anchor in the Eniwetok lagoon, there were only a few supply vessels and the hospital ship, USS *Hope,* present. Those first few days seemed like an idyllic vacation for the crew, who had no clue that a few months earlier, thousands of young men—twenty thousand of them Japanese—had died fighting for possession of the atoll.

The crew was allowed to dive and swim from the ship after the captain ascertained that there weren't supposed to be any sharks in the lagoon (though Marines armed with carbines were posted just in case). One-fourth of the men at a time also received liberty passes to one of the atoll's islands; there they explored the white sand beaches and made their first attempts at breaking open coconuts for the milk and sweet white meat.

Soon, however, they were put to work carting supplies and ammunition onboard. After several days, the crew wondered when the rest of the fleet would show up so that they could set sail and do something a little more exciting.

The only word they had of the fleet was Tokyo Rose's report that the task force, including the *Franklin,* had been destroyed in the Philippine Sea. But since they knew part of that wasn't true and the officers didn't seem too concerned, they didn't worry either. However, some did find it a little disturbing that Tokyo Rose even knew they were in the vicinity, which meant there were still Japanese spies watching ships come and go from Pearl Harbor.

On the fourth morning, the crew hopped out of bed at the bugle call for reveille and discovered that overnight the lagoon had filled with hundreds of ships of all sizes. There were other *Essex*-class carriers such as the *Wasp, Hornet,* and *Intrepid,* plus older warhorses like the *Enterprise,* as well as light carriers and escort carriers. Everywhere they looked were battleships, cruisers, and destroyers, as well as hundreds of supply, fuel, and ammunition ships. PT (patrol torpedo) boats and launches skittered about like water bugs on a pond.

The task force stayed put until the end of June, when it again steamed from the lagoon to run at flank speed toward the Bonin Islands of Haha Jima, Chichi Jima, and Iwo Jima. The men on the *Franklin* were proud to learn that their vessel had been selected to serve as the flagship for Task Group 58.2, one of four that made up the task force, under Rear Admiral Ralph E. Davison, a Naval Academy graduate and veteran of the early Pacific campaigns.

Task Group 58.2 also included the *Wasp,* as well as the light carriers USS *Monterey* and USS *Cabot.* The concentric circles of screening ships included the cruisers USS *Boston,* USS *Baltimore,* USS *San Diego,* and USS *San Juan,* and a new USS *Vincennes* protected them. Patrolling the outer rim were a dozen destroyers, one of which was named USS *The Sullivans,* after the five brothers who had died aboard the *Juneau* in November 1942 at the final naval clash of the battle for Guadalcanal.

Wasp. Hornet. Lexington. Yorktown. Vincennes. The Sullivans. The Navy paid homage to its fallen ships and men by naming new vessels after them. The practice had the added advantage of confusing and disheartening the Japanese. The United States kept pouring ships into the fray in seemingly endless numbers, including resurrecting the ghosts of those they thought had been destroyed at Pearl Harbor.

In the two years since Midway, shipyards in Japan had turned out only six aircraft carriers. During the same period, U.S. builders had more than doubled that number in huge fleet carriers, plus ten light carriers and eighty-six escort carriers. The United States enjoyed the same disparity turning out tanks, guns, and planes.

The American advantage was growing daily. Still, the Japanese refused to sue for peace or give up. Instead, illogically, they fought more fanatically than before, sending thousands of their troops and hundreds of their pilots to die in battles they had no hope of winning—or even affecting the outcome of the war.

The United States, on the other hand, was methodical in its dissection of the empire. The attack on the Bonins—part of Japan's "inner" defense ring—had several purposes. The islands were within striking distance for the Japanese of Saipan and the next step in the campaign, the Philippines. The Americans wanted to eliminate or reduce the Bonins' effectiveness as air bases.

A second purpose was to send a message to the Japanese government and military that the war had progressed to the point where the Allies could strike anywhere at anytime and that surrender was the only viable option. If they failed to heed the warning, the Bonins were also within striking distance of Tokyo. Eventually, they were going to have to capture one of the "Jimas" to use as an advance base for fighters to escort the long-range B-29 bombers that would be based in the Marianas once Saipan, Tinian, Rota, and Guam were in American hands.

The new men on the *Franklin* got their first small taste of combat the day before the July 4 strike when the task force moved to within three hundred miles of the Bonins. A long-range Japanese bomber attacked the task group, dropping two bombs that narrowly missed a destroyer, then fled. With the element of surprise gone, the new *Essex*-class *Hornet* launched fighter planes to attack Iwo Jima, where they knocked down a dozen Zeros, or Zekes, as they tried to take off, and destroyed many more on the ground.

The next morning, General Quarters sounded at 4:30. The ship's crew scrambled for their battle stations, as the aircrews hurried to ready the planes while the pilots and their combat crews were briefed in ready rooms. An hour later, the entire task force turned as one into the wind and the carriers began launching planes.

Howerton was flying with a ringside view of the attack with Calvin Price, a young pilot from Missouri, on his wing when he spotted two figures in the water. They were wearing yellow Mae West life jackets of the sort used only by U.S. Navy fliers. The fliers waved as he swooped in low and slow to look them over. Satisfied they were Navy pilots, he relayed their position so that a destroyer could pick them up.

Circling, he decided to drop his own life raft for them. But freeing the raft from where it was stored was no easy feat. Compressed into a tight square, it was sandwiched between his parachute, on which he sat, and the seat cushion. In the cramped quarters of a Hellcat, he discovered that pulling out the raft while flying the plane was better suited to a contortionist. He finally managed to get the raft out from under him and prepared to drop it close to the downed aviators when he noticed the Zero flying above and to the side, apparently unaware of his presence.

The commander tried to toss the raft out of the open cockpit at the same time as he began to increase speed, climbing into a steep turn and to bring his sights to bear on the enemy fighter. But the raft wouldn't cooperate and got stuck half in and half out of the cockpit. Still, he managed to swing around behind the Zero. He knew he couldn't miss as he squeezed the trigger and waited for the bullets and tracers to spit from his wing guns—except nothing happened; his guns were jammed.

Suddenly hunter turned to hunted as the Zero wheeled and came for him. Desperate, Howerton shoved the raft out of the cockpit and then tried to climb away from the enemy, but his Hellcat wouldn't respond. Looking back, he was dismayed to see that the life raft was now wrapped around the tail of his plane and knew that the Japanese pilot would soon have him dead to rights. Then out of the corner of his eye he noticed Price break off and start back for the Japanese fighter.

A few moments later, even as he shook the raft off his tail, Howerton saw that a plane was going down in flames, but he couldn't tell which one. *If that's Price, it's my fault,* he thought. They were supposed to be maintaining radio silence, but he flipped the switch and yelled into the mike, "Price! Price! Was that you or that other son of a bitch?" He was relieved to hear Price's slow Missouri twang assure him that it had been "the other one, sir."

The escapade made for a good yarn that evening in the pilots' wardroom. "I didn't know what that Jap was going to do," Howerton later regaled his audience, "but I hoped he wouldn't take offense at my trying to get him." He cursed his guns for spoiling what would have been an easy shot "for an old Texas duck hunter."

All in all it was an exciting and rewarding first day in combat, the recounting of which was filled with humor and bravado.

Cmdr. Wilson M. "Cap" Coleman, the commanding officer of the fighter squadron, had ventured off in pursuit of an escaping plane and flew to within sight of Japan, a first for an Allied pilot since the Doolittle raid in 1942. He was chased back by three Zekes, whose pilots then found the tables turned when the combat air patrol roared in to Coleman's rescue, "splashing" all three.

The stunt was the sort of thing that could have landed Coleman in hot water, but Captain Shoemaker decided his fighter commander's exploits would be good for the crew's morale and had the squadron leader describe his experience over the public address system. "I was so close, I just had to see it," Coleman explained.

Not all the stories, of course, were funny or ended happily. While enemy fighter opposition was light and easily turned aside by the Hellcats, the anti-aircraft fire was intense for the bombers and torpedo planes. Some of the veteran pilots viewed the vigor of the ack-ack with alarm, based on earlier experiences in which Japanese antiaircraft fire was disorganized and largely ineffective. These Japanese gunners seemed to have developed a new system in which their fire was much more concentrated and accurate than in the past.

With regret, Lt. John Weil learned that Lt. Milton "Milt" Bonar, who had been with him on Guadalcanal, and Bonar's gunner, ARM 3rd Class Al Loenthal, had been reported missing and were presumed dead. Others in their flight had seen them knocked from the sky into the ocean by antiaircraft fire.

The Japanese guns' proficiency had surprised Weil. Over the Iwo Jima harbor, his wing leader spied a ship and they had peeled off into their dives. The sky suddenly appeared to bloom with a field of black poppies as the shells from the Japanese guns exploded all around the plane. Passing through the gauntlet of smoke and steel shards seemed a matter of pure luck. He thought that the bomb he dropped was on target, but he didn't stick around to find out with all the ack-ack flying about. He sped away, jinking for all he was worth to throw off the gunners.

Sad though the deaths of Bonar and Loenthal were, Weil didn't allow himself to dwell on the loss. Death had been a part of being a naval aviator since his days as a cadet. He figured there had been more fatalities from training accidents and operational failures, such as landings, than from enemy action. They were in a war, and anytime a pilot and his crew went up there was a good chance they wouldn't be coming back.

Six pilots, including Weil and Bonar, had transferred from Air Group 11. Now there were five. How many would be left when it was over, only God knew—and He wasn't saying. But neither was Weil asking; he was there to do a job, and he just had to get through one day at a time until it was finished.

The ship's company was also reminded that working onboard the carrier didn't guarantee they were safe. That afternoon a plane came in off center, missed the arresting cables, and struck the barrier. Normally, the incident would have ended there. However, the pilot failed to cut his engine and the plane spun off the barrier toward the island as men scrambled to get out of the way.

A sailor who shouldn't have even been on the flight deck, but was there "sight-seeing," ducked inside a door on the aft end of the island as the plane moved toward him. He may have felt safe inside the steel compartment, but the spinning propeller of the plane cut through the quarter-inch steel plating like scissors through paper, killing him.

The bodies of Bonar and Loenthal were not recovered for the memorial service held on the ship that evening. Only the remains of the hapless sailor—sewn into a canvas bag and weighted down with a five-inch shell—slid off a board from beneath an American flag to drop into the ocean below. There, the chaplain intoned, his soul would rest until Judgment Day ". . . when the sea shall give up her dead."

July 7, 1944
Guam, Marianas Islands

Floating in a life raft at night in the Philippine Sea, *Franklin* fighter pilot Lt. Willard Gove thought he might be as good as dead. His Hellcat rested on the bottom of the ocean a mile north of Guam, which was in the opposite direction of where the current was taking him. He figured he was on his way to China, a couple thousand miles to the northwest—not that it mattered, he would never survive the trip.

After the fireworks at Iwo Jima, the task force had quickly withdrawn and headed south at flank speed for Guam, which, following the June invasion of Saipan, was the next target in the Marianas. Before the war, the island had been a U.S. territory, its citizens allowed to travel and work freely in the United States (though not given the right to vote for the president). Three years later, the Fifth Fleet, the U.S. Marine Corps, and the U.S. Army were poised to take it back. The American reinvasion was planned for July 12, and the air groups were told to spend the week leading up to the attack obliterating the Japanese defenses.

The planes from Task Group 58.2, which included the *Franklin*, got a good start that day, sinking two destroyers, three destroyer escorts, and two medium tankers, as well as other smaller tankers and freighters. Eighty-nine Japanese planes were demolished, fifty-seven of them on the ground.

It was no "milk run," though. Twenty-two American planes had been shot down, one of them Gove's. He had been leading a flight of Hellcats over Guam, shooting up airfields, fuel and ammunition depots, and troop concentrations as they appeared. They had just passed the island heading north to return to the ship at about 4:00 in the afternoon when there was a slight jolt. Oil began spraying over the front of the cockpit so that he couldn't see in that direction, but looking out the side he saw there was a hole in his wing and that his plane was on fire. He knew from the oil and the sudden loss of power that he had also taken a hit in the engine—he was going to have to ditch.

Gove cranked open the cockpit so that he could see as he brought the plane down in the water without power—a "dead stick" landing. He was thrown forward against his harness, but as soon as the motion of the plane stopped, he scrambled to get out. The Hellcat was a powerful son of a gun, but it got that power from a big engine that would take the plane down like a rock.

In fact, the squadron had suffered its first casualty two days before the strike against Iwo Jima when its executive officer, Lt. Cmdr. Kelly Blair, spun into the water short of the ship when returning from combat air patrol duty. The landing wasn't too hard, and those watching from the air and the ship expected to see him pop the canopy and get out. But to their horror, the plane sank with no sign of Blair. Later, the other fighter pilots speculated that he may have had his shoulder harness too loose when he landed and struck his head, knocking him out cold.

Or Blair may have had trouble extricating himself from the cockpit, as Gove was experiencing. Gove worked quickly to disconnect himself from the oxygen supply and the radio; then he released the seat belt and the shoulder harness. He popped the canopy the rest of the way off, stood up with his parachute still attached, and pulled up the life raft that formed part of his seat. He climbed out of the cockpit and pulled the inflation device on the raft as he jumped into the water. By the time he turned around, the plane was already gone—maybe thirty seconds had elapsed between landing in the water and the plane sinking.

His troubles were far from over, however, as he now had a hard time getting into the little raft. Weighed down by his flight clothes, including a heavy pair of shoes, he couldn't quite pull himself up before the raft moved away and dumped him back in the water. Twice he went under and had to struggle back up, choking on seawater, certain he was drowning. Then he started to go under again. *Not a third time, Gove, go under a third time and you're dead.* He had heard that old wive's tale somewhere and now, along with finally ridding himself of the shoes, it gave him the energy for one last attempt to get in the raft. This time he succeeded.

Exhausted, Gove took a moment to catch his breath before looking up. He saw that he was a half mile to a mile offshore from Agana, the capital of the island. Overhead, another Hellcat—he was pretty sure it was Ensign Roger L'Estrange's—circled and then left in the direction he knew was the *Franklin.*

At first he was afraid the Japanese would try to pick him up, and he checked his .38-caliber pistol, determined to fight it out if they did. But no enemy boats appeared as the current took him farther from the island, toward the northwest.

Night falls fast in the tropics and that night it seemed to fall faster than normal. Pretty soon all he could see was the black outline of the island, the dark, shimmering surface of the ocean, and a few billion stars above his head. He was wet and cold, but grateful that at least he was in the warm waters of Micronesia; if he had crashed in the Atlantic, he would have never survived the cold. Now the question was whether he would survive the night.

He didn't know it, but a couple hundred miles to the north and east, other men were also locked in a life-and-death struggle. Only this was on a massive scale, as the fight for Saipan was reaching its horrific climax.

Before the June 15 invasion, the Imperial High Command declared the island "indispensable" to the defense of Japan, a mere twelve hundred miles away. Japanese soldiers and airmen were to achieve victory or die trying. So beginning in the early morning hours following the American landing, the Japanese had launched a series of banzai attacks against U.S. Marine and Army positions on an almost nightly basis. But it wasn't just the mass suicide night attacks that were so chilling.

During the day, American troops learned to watch every bush and shadow in the jungle. Strapping explosives to their bodies, Japanese soldiers were hiding and waiting for the opportunity to break from cover and hurl themselves beneath a tank or into a group of American soldiers. Even wounded

Japanese soldiers were booby-trapped to explode when approached by U.S. medical corpsmen.

Even as Lt. Will Gove floated in the dark, wondering what the dawn would bring, the last major battle for Saipan was fought. A little before 5:00 A.M., Japanese bugles sounded and more than four thousand soldiers of the Empire of the Rising Sun poured out of the hills from their caves and bunkers and jungle hiding places. Ill-equipped and poorly supplied, they carried empty rifles, bamboo spears, knives, rocks, and sometimes nothing at all, as they ran toward the American front lines, screaming, "Banzai!" Their sheer numbers and the ferocity of the attack broke through in several places. American soldiers found themselves fighting for their lives in isolated pockets as the Japanese swept around them and poured onto the coastal plain.

For a time it looked like the Japanese might push the Americans into the sea. But like a wave washing up against a seawall, they rushed up to the American artillery positions, and there the charge was broken. The big guns fired round after round of high explosive and canister shot into the masses of Japanese soldiers, who were sometimes only a few yards in front of the muzzles. Their bodies piled up until the gunners had to move their weapons in order to shoot around the carnage.

By dawn's early light, the battle was over. More than four hundred American soldiers had been killed, but the Japanese dead numbered 4,311. In the tangle of bodies, some of the wounded still lived, hideously maimed, crawling or simply staring up at the tropical sun, sucking in ragged breaths, waiting for death. Meanwhile, the survivors wandered the killing fields, hollow-eyed as though still living the nightmare, or sometimes dispatching the wounded and searching for souvenirs.

As the same sun rose in the east, Gove was taken by the beauty of the morning. The light tinted the clouds pink and red, as gray rainsqualls glided like cloistered monks across the blue-green waters. He felt as though he floated into an enormous cathedral. Never much of a churchgoer, he prayed, *Hey God, get me out of here and I'll go to church every Sunday.*

Only, where was *here?* He had expected to see Guam, but the only thing in sight was ocean in all directions. During the night, he had heard a twin-engine plane pass overhead, and he considered whether to fire his service revolver, which was loaded with tracer bullets. But he worried that the plane might be Japanese, so he made no attempt to send up a signal.

Now he wondered if anybody was even looking for him. And if they were, how would they find him, an insignificant speck in an immense and unforgiving sea?

It looked like the squadron would lose its third pilot in less than a week. First Blair, then his friend Lt. Johnny Johnson had been shot down at Iwo, now Gove.

A descendant of pilgrims who had landed in one of the ships closely following the *Mayflower*, Gove had been born in Walpole, Massachusetts on September 16, 1919. His father worked for Gove's grandfather in his hardware store and was also the owner, and undertaker, for a funeral business.

After high school, Gove went on to the Worcester Polytechnic Institute, where he graduated with a degree in electrical engineering. But what he really wanted to do was fly, having joined the civilian pilot training program sponsored by the government. Then in his senior year on campus in 1939, he saw a movie, *Wings of Gold,* which had been produced by the U.S. Navy, and he was hooked—he wanted to be a fighter pilot on an aircraft carrier.

On December 7, 1941, he was an instructor at the Navy's combat pilot training center in Kingsville, Texas. The base commander was Cmdr. Charles "Sunshine" Howerton.

Gove and five other instructors were all living the good life with a house on the beach, which they called "The Snake Pit," carousing and drinking way too much. They were at the house, sleeping off another Saturday night, when they got the sobering news that Pearl Harbor had been attacked.

Of course, they all immediately volunteered for combat duty. They had friends at Pearl. But the Navy told them that they were needed right where they were—getting other pilots ready to fight the war.

The U.S. Navy aviation program was behind the eight ball. The Japanese pilots already had a half dozen years or more of combat experience from beating up on the Chinese. The enemy also had better planes, including the Zero, which could run circles around any fighter the United States had.

However, training centers like Kingsville began turning out top-notch pilots by the hundreds. The new recruits were among the best America had to offer, boys who had been in college and were often star athletes, picked for their physical abilities. Some even played professional sports, like baseball great Ted Williams, who did his combat training at Kingsville. These were the men who would stem, and then turn, the tide of the air war in the Pacific. They were able to do so in part due to a strategy built upon a concept that was as American as apple pie and Americans' penchant for organized sports—and that was teamwork.

The best Navy fighter, the F4F Wildcat, was no match for the Zero one-on-one. However, Lt. Cmdr. John Thach, who had commanded the fighter squadron from the *Lexington* during the Battle of the Coral Sea and the *Yorktown*'s fighters at Midway, developed a system of interlocking mutual support, called the "Thach Weave," that negated the Zero's superiority.

Thach changed the normal Navy fighter formation from two three-plane "sections" to two two-plane sections. When confronted by the enemy, these sections would deploy abreast of each other at a distance equal to the turning radius of Wildcats. When a section was attacked, it would turn toward another section, bringing the enemy, who was following, right into the guns of the second section.

As long as they stuck together in the weave, the American pilots could beat the Zeros, which did have some design disadvantages from the rugged Wildcats. To increase speed and maneuverability, the Zero's builders left out armor. The plane also lacked the self-sealing fuel tanks that the American planes had. It didn't take many hits to light up a Zeke like a Roman candle on the Fourth of July.

The Zero was still a fine plane, but air superiority had swung irrevocably to the American side even before the F6F Hellcats arrived. Thanks to the Thach Weave, by 1943 the Wildcats were racking up a 14-to-1 "kill ratio" over the Zeros.

Of course, part of that had to do with the declining abilities of Japanese aviators. Most of the best Imperial pilots were dead. With rare exception, they flew combat missions until they were shot down, and the battles of the Coral Sea, Midway, the Solomons, and dozens of lesser known others had claimed them. Those who replaced the veterans got younger—recruited as early as age fourteen—and had less training than their predecessors, as the Japanese military tried to push them through abbreviated programs.

On the other side, by the fall of 1943, American pilots, especially those selected for carrier duty, were the best-trained in the world. The age and education requirements for U.S. Navy pilot training had dropped from the pre-war twenty-one years old and two years in college to eighteen years old and a high school education. But the cadets spent almost two years in training before they saw combat, easily logging more than twice and even three times as many hours as the new Japanese recruits.

The Japanese had few experienced pilots left to lead the raw recruits. But the new American squadrons, like VF-13, tended to be a mix of newcomers and experienced combat veterans. Unlike the Japanese, American pilots were rotated back to the States after completing each tour to refresh, retrain, and await reassignment. Once an American pilot finished two tours of combat duty, he would be transferred back for a stateside tour of duty, usually training new pilots. There was not the same hopelessness of simply fighting until one died that the Japanese pilot had to come to terms with.

As the war wore on, Gove kept asking for combat duty. In the meantime, he kept practicing, including perfecting his bombing technique until he could plant a warhead on a target the size of a bed. Then finally, in the fall of 1943 he was granted his request and sent to Atlantic City, where VF-13 was being formed, for assignment to the new carrier, USS *Franklin*.

The pilots, who called themselves "The Smashers," were a bunch of juiced-up, smart-assed aviators who acted like they owned the world and all the women and booze in it. If there was a greater bunch of guys in the world, Gove didn't know where he would find them.

The skipper, Cmdr. "Cap" Coleman was a Naval Academy man and a true Southern gentleman. He was something of a fundamentalist Christian, but he knew that his "boys" were not going to take much preaching about their wild ways. However, his skill as a pilot and his dedication to their training, as well as his courtly manner, made him a well-liked skipper.

They were certainly a collection of characters. Lt. (j.g.) Bill Bowen was a former All-American fullback for the Ole Miss, University of Mississippi, football team. He would get a couple of drinks in him and then go find someone, anyone, to fight. Ensign A. J. "Betty" Pope was a little guy and the wiseacre of the squadron, who seemed to take particular delight in needling Ensign Calvin Price, a big, taciturn guy from Missouri.

There was boyish Ensign Roger L'Estrange, whose French Canadian family had somehow ended up in New Hampshire before the war. They were certainly doing their share of contributing to their new country—his brother was a captain in the U.S. Marines.

Lt. A. C. "Stud" Hudson considered himself to be the group's "ladies' man," hence the nickname. He had been a pilot for an airline company before the war and claimed to have had sex with the stewardesses in the cockpit during flights. The fact that he had a wife and infant daughter in Ohio didn't seem to slow him down either.

One of Gove's best friends was Lt. Johnny Johnson. Calm, cool, Johnson looked like he could be a leading man for Hollywood. He could also fly anything with wings and was widely regarded as one of the best fighter pilots in the fleet, until he was shot down.

Every fighter pilot who wasn't blinded by youth or convinced of his own immortality knew that sooner or later even the best of them would die. Sooner or later the enemy would drop in behind them and squeeze off the shot that would send them down in flames. Or a mechanical failure would drop them into the water. There were no services for aviators—none of the "burial at sea" ceremonies the sailors got; there was no body.

Drifting in the raft, Gove knew that he faced a long, excruciating death with no water or protection from the tropical sun—if the Japanese didn't find him first. He didn't know that even as he was making promises to God his friends were looking for him.

In particular, Cmdr. Coleman wasn't going to let one of his boys go without trying. Gove had been right—L'Estrange saw him ditch and get into the raft and had gone back to the *Franklin* to report the news. That night, Coleman had done two things—he prayed for Gove, and he sat down with one of the officers on Admiral Davison's staff who was an expert on tides and wind.

Just before dawn, Coleman, Howerton, and their two wingmen were launched by catapult from the *Franklin*. They flew over to the cruiser USS *Boston*, which launched its two Kingfisher seaplanes, and the six were off to look for Gove based on the estimates Cap and the admiral's man had worked out that night.

Still, it was an awfully large ocean. Looking for one man in a tiny raft was akin to looking for a particular seashell on a beach. They had to fly nearly two hundred miles to reach the area they thought Gove might have drifted to, approximately twenty miles northwest of Guam. When they reached the area, the fighters flew abreast about two hundred feet apart, sweeping back and forth as the seaplanes flew behind.

They had about reached the end of the fuel range without seeing anything when Howerton reluctantly noted that it was time to head back.

"One more minute," Coleman asked. The air group commander agreed; after all, he had known Gove since before the war. The extra minute was all it took. One of the wingmen spotted Gove.

The first Gove knew of his imminent rescue was the roar of the four F6Fs flying overhead. A minute later, Kingfisher pilot Lt. (j.g.) Fred Rigdon plopped down near him and taxied up until a pontoon was right next to the raft. However, Gove was too exhausted by his ordeal to climb out of the raft unassisted, so Rigdon got down and helped him.

Gove slept most of the way back to the *Boston*. There Rigdon landed in a smooth slick created by the ship turning and taxied up onto a mat that had been lowered over the side. When he had hooked onto the mat, the ship's crane was swung out and a hook lowered to be fastened onto the King-fisher, which was then hauled aboard.

Onboard, Gove posed for a photograph in his bare feet with his rescuer and the ship's commanding officer. Then a doctor took a quick look at him and said there was nothing wrong that a little sleep and food wouldn't cure. A little later, Gove was transferred to a destroyer via a "breeches buoy," which he thought looked like a large diaper hanging from a rope, by which he was pulled over to the smaller ship. The destroyer's crew was then delighted to deliver him to the *Franklin* by the same manner, in exchange for the tradi-tional treat of ice cream from the carrier's gedunk.

Once back aboard his own ship, Gove was told to go get some sleep. He was about to walk into the island structure when he saw a familiar figure in a Hellcat just getting ready to taxi into position to take off. He walked over and wiggled the aileron on the Hellcat's wing. Feeling the control stick move in his hands, "Cap" Coleman looked out of the cockpit, smiled, and gave Gove a thumbs-up.

By July 9, the *Franklin's* pilots were complaining about the lack of worth-while targets on Guam. The Japanese had tunneled into the hillsides or were lying in wait in the jungle. The top brass knew that the Japanese had large shore batteries in the hills overlooking the landing beaches, but they were well hidden. The Navy needed something to lure the Japanese gunners into revealing themselves, but it would have to be a prize worth giving away their positions.

The scuttlebutt onboard the *Franklin* was that there was going to be a lot-tery to see which carrier would sail close enough to Guam to draw the fire of the defenders' big guns. They knew that the rumor was true, and that the *Franklin* had lost the lottery, when they saw Admiral Davison and his staff "transfer the flag" to the *Hornet*.

As soon as the admiral was gone, the *Franklin* and the destroyer *The Sul-livans* headed toward Guam. The island grew near that evening and tensions rose. Every man aboard the aircraft carrier knew that the ship was a float-ing gas tank with enough munitions onboard to vaporize them and the ves-sel if she took a hit in her ammunition magazines from the big guns.

The *Franklin* must have made a tempting target—a huge, dark silhou-ette against the lighter night sky. But the Japanese apparently knew why the ship was there and held their fire. However, the gambit worked in another sense. As the American ships drew close, someone began signaling with a light from the jungle. Using semaphore, the signaler was able to convince the destroyer to send in a boat to pick him up from beach.

His name was Robert Twiggs, a petty officer who had been stationed on Guam when the war broke out. He had refused to surrender and instead took to the hills where, with the courageous help of some of the native Guamanians, he had been hiding since December 10, 1941. He had made his stay useful by learning the position of Japanese guns and troop movements. Beginning the next day, the task force pilots had plenty of new targets to attack. Twiggs's information was so valuable that the invasion was postponed while the planes wreaked havoc on the defenses.

During the next ten days, the combat operations on the ship settled into a routine. Before dawn the task groups, sailing about twelve miles apart, would move to a launch point a few hundred miles from the target to begin launching planes. Then, when the day's work was finished and the planes recovered, the ships would reverse course and sail away from the islands and their defenders to a rendezvous point several hundred miles away to be refueled and replenished if necessary. About midnight, the ships would change course again to be at the launch point by dawn.

The first planes to take off were the fighters assigned to that day's combat air patrol, which circled above the ships, ready to intercept Japanese attackers. These Hellcats were launched by means of catapults at the bow of the ship. The flight deck Airedales would then turn their attention to the rest of the planes as the pilots hurried from the ready rooms to join their crews at planes that had been assigned to them for that strike.

After a "deck full" was sent off, the Airedales brought the planes for the next strike up from the hangar and positioned them on the flight deck. When the first strike was on its way back, the next would be sent off, and then the crew would stand by to recover the first planes.

When a plane landed, it would be hurriedly moved ahead of the barrier onto the bow area of the flight deck. After all the planes from a strike were recovered, they had to be moved either by hand or with small, motorized carts called "mules" or "tugs." If they were to make another strike that day, the planes were moved to the aft end, where they would have to be gassed, armed, and ready to go before the preceding strike force returned. Planes that were not needed, or were damaged by enemy fire or crash landings, would be sent to the hangar via the elevators—the fighters down elevators

No. 1 and No. 2, the dive-bombers down elevator No. 2 (the deck-edge elevator), and the torpedo planes down elevator No. 3. A plane too badly damaged to be fixed was simply "deep-sixed" by shoving it over the side.

It had been one thing to accomplish all this during training, another to do it in the heat of battle. Onboard the ship, there didn't seem to be much danger from the Japanese except for the occasional submarine alert. The destroyers dealt with the submarines, and the combat air patrol, simply known as CAP, took care of enemy aircraft. However, the hectic activity on the flight and hangar decks, where the rush to get the planes ready or retrieved amid the din of dozens of powerful engines warming up, magnified the danger many times over.

When he first came onboard the *Franklin* with the air group in February, Coxswain Frank Turner had been assigned to help teach new Airedales how to safely go about their jobs. But no matter what he and the other experienced men tried to impart, more men were killed on the flight deck of the *Franklin* than in the air during the month of July. A sailor walked into a spinning propeller and was decapitated. Another was sitting on one of the mules, waiting to tow planes to the stern, when a landing plane overshot the barrier and struck him.

Turner was on the flight deck one day when an Airedale was killed by bullets from one of their own planes. Before landing, the pilots were supposed to run through a checklist that included disarming the guns, but with the adrenaline still pumping from his sortie, this pilot had forgotten. He also still had his thumb on the trigger when the Airedales began folding his wings before moving the plane.

The plane may have lurched, but suddenly the air was torn by the staccato sound of the guns going off. Bursts from machine guns and even the occasional five-inch rocket jostling free and whistling up the flight deck were fairly common incidents. Usually everybody just hit the deck until it was safe to stand up, shaking their heads over another close call. But this time one of the Airedales was standing right in front of one of the guns, and the big bullets cut him nearly in two at the waist. He lived just long enough to tell his comrades, "Now, I'll never get to go home."

Fortunately, not every mistake ended badly. Just before sunrise on July 18, Lt. Cmdr. James Moy, a ship's physician, was hurrying to get to his battle station on the flight deck when he ran into one of the guardrails erected at night around the edge of the flight deck. He flipped over the rail and out into space over the water.

The seventy-foot fall to the ocean could have killed or stunned him. Moy had been a diver in college, however, and managed to gather himself quickly enough to enter the water cleanly. He came up sputtering in a black ocean with his ship sailing swiftly past. His life jacket was at his battle station, but he did have a small emergency whistle, which he began blowing. An alert crewmember heard the whistle over the pounding of the engines. "Man overboard, port side," he yelled into the ship's intercom.

A strong swimmer, Moy rid himself of his shoes and pants. He then buttoned his collar around his neck and, holding out the front of his shirt, forced air into it, creating a makeshift life vest, as they'd been taught in boot camp. Still, he was in the middle of a very large, dark ocean, and all sailors were aware of the sharks that followed the ships, looking for garbage—and anything else worth eating . The carrier could not stop for a single man, due to the danger from submarines, nor turn fast enough, but Moy was lucky— a trailing destroyer found him.

The next morning as the "tin can" pulled alongside the *Franklin* to return the doctor, Captain Shoemaker decided to have a little fun and teach a lesson to the crew as well. He had all hands muster to witness Moy's delivery via the breeches buoy. Then as the doctor, looking rather sheepish, was pulled across, the captain announced over the public address system, "Stand by to retrieve some dumb-ass seaman who fell over the side."

The crew clapped and whistled as the doctor, who was well-liked, arrived back onboard "wet and cheery," according to the next *Franklin Forum*. "Authoritative sources report that Dr. 'Wrong-way' Moy no longer is permitted on the flight deck without a good stout line fastened about his waist."

Although the official version was that Moy was trying to find a new route to his battle station, he later confided to Turner that he had perhaps had a little too much Schnapps with some of the pilots who were celebrating prior to his dunking. Fortunately, the guard rail had been up, he said, or he might have landed more awkwardly and been too stunned or hurt to blow his whistle.

Every day there seemed to be some new way to get killed onboard an aircraft carrier. One of the more unnerving was the afternoon a torpedo bomber returned with a thousand-pound bomb, capable of sinking a ship, hung up on its bomb rack.

On landing, the still-armed bomb was knocked loose and went skidding along the flight deck as Airedales scattered. The bomb finally came to a rest and lay on the deck, no one knowing if it was about to blow or not. "Three swabbies finally threw it overboard," one of the flight deck crew wrote that night in his diary. "This sure is a lucky ship."

If the danger wasn't bad enough, life at sea simply wasn't comfortable. Even on a ship as large as an aircraft carrier, space was at a minimum.

The discomfort increased in the tropics, where the heat and humidity combined to turn the inside of the ship—even with the ventilation fans going—into a sweltering oven.

Dealing with the heat was one thing during the day while working and moving, but sleeping on one of the tiered bunks deep inside the ship was nearly impossible on some nights. So the men tried to find ways to sleep outside. No one was supposed to sleep on the flight deck, but the officers tended to look the other way when the men dragged their mattresses out on deck and used their life jackets for pillows. As long as they packed up and were gone before reveille sounded in the morning, no one hassled them.

Still, despite the hardships, there was also a beauty to their surroundings that belied the horrible things that were occurring on that wide expanse of water. Dolphins played in the waves created by the bow as though escorting the ship. Flying fish took to the air, flashing in the sun. Young men who had never expected to see the ocean a few years earlier witnessed the sun rise red and promising from the water in the east and set flaming orange and gold that same day in the west.

Whenever he could get away from his duties, Steward's Mate 1st Class Matthew Little enjoyed going up on the flight deck to watch the sunsets or, better yet, to enjoy the cooler night air and look at the stars in the western Pacific. He missed his family back in the little sharecropper's cabin in South Carolina that seemed at times part of another world. He longed to talk to his father and feel the arms of his mother, though he knew he would never see her again.

Sometimes it was hard to believe he was fighting a war with so much that was lovely surrounding him. At least it was hard until General Quarters sounded and he raced for the ammunition hold, where he passed the five-inch shells and tried to keep his mind off how he would escape if something went wrong.

All in all, he enjoyed life aboard the ship. There were movies on the hangar deck, ice-cream cones from the gedunk, and basketball games with his shipmates. In the beginning, he had resented that the Navy thought him fit only to serve meals or pass ammunition. But if there were bigots onboard the *Franklin,* and he knew that there probably were, he was never bothered by anyone. Neither the white enlisted men nor the officers onboard the *Franklin* had ever mistreated him because he was "colored."

He and the 150 other men of his race onboard had their own church and chaplain, but otherwise the *Franklin* was not segregated as some ships still were. There were no separate toilet facilities marked "colored" or "white." He didn't know it, but the fact was that around the fleet it was the white sailors and officers who were taking down the symbols of segregation, as familiarity bred not contempt, but respect, and the color bar blurred among brothers in arms.

After her commissioning, the original crew were all presented with a certificate identifying them as "plank owners," a Navy tradition to establish a bond between men and their ships dating back to the time of sailing vessels when the decks of ships were built entirely of wood planking. No one who came aboard later could ever be a plank owner; only the first crew could "own" a piece of the *Franklin.* White or black, they took pride in her—pride in the accomplishments of her pilots and also in their own ability to work as a team.

When it came right down to it, "plank owner" Little knew that a white officer could die onboard the *Franklin* just as easily as a black mess steward. They shared the hardships and the dangers and the laughter of young men. They had come out here together, and if they were going to get back to their cities and towns and farms, and back to their dreams of the future, they were going to have to rely on each other and on their ship, "Big Ben." He still wished he could man one of the guns, but now it was for more than the excitement or glory. When the Japanese came gunning, he wanted to shoot back to protect the place he and the others called home.

Fostering that sense of community was the job of the ship's newspaper, the *Franklin Forum,* of which Raymond Blair was the associate editor.

Published once a week, the *Forum* covered a wide variety of topics. There were biographies of various ship's officers and crewmembers—one of Shoemaker was followed by another of Chief Boatswain's Mate Anthony Wayne, a fleet boxing and wrestling champion, who in 1940 had gone with Admiral Richard E. Byrd on the Antarctic expedition to the South Pole.

The paper covered shipboard entertainment from amateur shows to the weekly offerings of Saxie Dowell and the ship's band. It also offered sports scores and stories from the ship's teams, as well as highlights from the professional teams in the States, especially baseball scores, which the radio operators picked up from the International Morse Code. The May 14, 1944, edition had included a story about how at the National Association of Basketball Coaches were considering rule changes to prevent taller players from "turning the game into a sport of the giants."

The *Forum* encouraged the men to submit their own writings for publication and provided an outlet for the ship's poets.

There were regular admonitions from one of the ship's ministers, such as the March 31 column from Chaplain E. J. Harkin titled "Who Is The Tough Man?"

> Any derelict can throw away his money. Any dope can get drunk, or contract a venereal disease. The tough man, however, is a man who has formed good character and maintains his self-respect by clean living. He's a man who has disciplined his life to conform to definite moral laws."

This being the Navy, the preaching was balanced with cartoons and corny jokes, which ran under the logo AIR FU. Of course, most of them dealt with the things dearest to a sailor's heart: girls, liberty, and food, with the occasional bit of political humor.

Hayes: "I'm forgetting girls."
Humphreys: "So am I. I'm for getting some as soon as possible."

Big Ben Mess Cook: "So you complained of finding sand in your soup?"
Seaman 2nd Class: "Yes."
Mess Cook: "Did you enlist to serve your country, or complain about the soup?"
Seaman: "To serve my country, not to eat it."

Selectee: "They can't make me fight."
Draft Board Chairman: "Maybe not, but they can take you where the fighting is and let you use your own judgment."

A good deal of the humor in the newspaper was supplied by the mishaps and adventures of the ship's company, such as Moy's sudden departure from the flight deck.

The V-mail censors even supplied some, once giving the newspaper part of a letter written by a young sailor from the backwoods of Tennessee. "Dear Pa: I'm in a tight spot—cooped up here in this ship with guns and ammunition, submarines and bombers and Yankees all around me. Tell Ma not to worry."

Those who worked on the newspaper occasionally tossed in their own sense of wry humor, such as the notice: "JOIN THE NAVY AND SEE THE WORLD— Paid Advertisement."

Of course, the *Forum* had its serious side. The stories in it from the States were often a reminder to the men that even in the short time they had been gone, their country was undergoing massive social changes that would affect them greatly upon their return. Women were in the workforce. The population was moving away from the rural areas and into the cities as America industrialized. Those who stayed in the country, and for one reason or another weren't in the military, were buying up surrounding farms. Others were taking over businesses.

The war had certainly ended the Depression. Everybody seemed to have a good job, everybody was getting ahead, while the sailors were stuck on an aircraft carrier in the middle of an ocean. Many of the men wondered if there would be anything left for them when they got home, including girls.

Still, most would not have left their ship. They believed in what they were doing—that, like the politicians said, they were making the world safe for democracy, ridding the world of dictators and war. They were fighting, and they were also using some of their small wages to buy war bonds to help the effort. The newspaper encouraged their patriotism, even printing a clip-and-send Fourth of July letter for the folks back home. The writer recalled the Independence Day celebrations of his childhood with its fireworks in light of that day's attack on Iwo Jima.

> Those fire-crackers and sky-rockets I enjoyed so much in my younger days have become a tool of destruction against the enemy who endangers our reasons for celebrating this date. . . . The thought foremost in my mind is, "Will we appreciate and take advantage of all the bloodshed and sorrow caused to achieve this freedom?"

A battle won is not of much value if the victory is not complete. Will we complete our coming victory by using this lesson as a precaution in the future?

Let us hope that we will not make the sad mistake of our forefathers. We cannot let the terms of peace be such as to breed or permit another war.

Your loving son . . .

In the same edition, the Roving Reporter asked: What are your plans for after the war?

Some dreamed big. Lt. (j.g.) G. M. Orner, an exchange fighter pilot from Southern Rhodesia in Africa, said, "I'm going home to Southern Rhodesia, and if conditions are favorable, I plan to return to gold mining, in which I was engaged before entering the Navy."

Others seemed to have found a new home. Seaman 1st Class Joseph Yurcho, a ship's barber, said he was signing back up with the Navy. "There'll be too many guys looking for jobs when the war is over, and I believe the Navy will be a good career."

Boatswain's Mate 2nd Class H. C. Billings wanted to return to his farm five miles out of Bloomington, Indiana. "To my wife, and a three-months old son I've never seen."

Lt. (j.g.) E. Robert Wassman planned on going back to Columbia to finish his engineering degree. Matthew Little was sending money back to South Carolina to help support his family. But he was also putting some aside so that when he got back he could finish his high school education and go on to Benedict College. Preacher or teacher, either one sounded pretty good to him.

Some had simpler plans. Water Tender 2nd Class "Scotty" Scott knew he would take the first train or bus he could get back to Maine, hitchhike if he had to, and marry Vivian. Anything after that would be gravy. His pal Eddie Carlisle couldn't be bothered with such long-range plans; he was just going to take it one day at a time and see what life had to offer.

Lt. John Weil figured that he would be due a long vacation on a beach somewhere. But as a dive-bomber pilot, just making it back was enough to worry about.

Coxswain Frank Turner's father wanted him to join the fire department. But Frank was interested in airplanes, flying them and fixing them; he would just have to find a way to break the news to his dad.

A job in journalism would have suited Chief Petty Officer Raymond Blair, or maybe working for Walt Disney studios. But what really mattered was getting home to his wife and watching his son grow up to be a man. Now that was worth dreaming about.

Petty Officer 2nd Class Edwin Garrison hoped he would get to go to college to study chemistry after the war. However, school was about the last thing on his mind as he stared off at the dense green jungles and rocky cliffs of Saipan about a mile distant.

It was August 2 and the *Franklin* was anchored offshore to take on supplies before heading to its next target. He batted absently at a fly, then another and another. He wrinkled his nose; the wind was blowing from the island to the ship, bringing with it a sickly sweet smell, as of something rotting in the tropical sun. He wished he had a cigarette to cover up the cloying stench of the island. He had been a two-packs-a-day man when the ship left Norfolk, but he had quit when the ship left Pearl Harbor, bound for the combat zone.

Born in 1920, Garrison had spent the first seven years of his life in the tiny little town of Fountain Inn, a stop along the road that existed mainly as a way station for the railroad. But his life was about to be altered by a traumatic experience.

His father ran the teletyping office at the railroad station, until one night when a man named Carl shot and killed him during a robbery. Carl pawned the watch he took off his victim, which is what led to his arrest and conviction. He would have received the death penalty, but Garrison's mother asked the judge to spare him and so his father's killer got life in prison instead.

After his father's death, Garrison, his brother, two sisters, and mother went to live with his maternal grandparents in nearby Simpsonville. Even as a child, he worked picking cotton and in his grandfather's general store to help support his family.

While living at his grandparents' home, he met their neighbor, Sam Slone, who had a reputation for being dishonest and was widely regarded as "the meanest man ever." However, he seemed to like Edwin and often talked to him while the boy was out doing his chores. Slone's wife had died, and as a result, he had tried to commit suicide on several different occasions. He confided to Edwin that if he ever wanted to kill himself, the best way would be to drown. "After you fill your lungs with water, you have no more pain," he said. "And the feeling you have as you go to sleep with all of the beautiful lights you see is wonderful."

There was no money for college after high school, so Garrison had gone to work for a chemical company. However, on his twenty-first birthday, in 1941, he received a notice to register for the peacetime draft. He soon learned he was going to be sent to the Army for eighteen months of military training. It was clear to him that the United States would soon be at war, so he broke every speed limit driving to Greenville, South Carolina, to enlist in the Navy. There was only one difficulty: He was six-foot-two, but only weighed 137 pounds, one pound less than the minimum. The recruiters stuffed three bananas and a quart of milk down him and signed him up.

After basic training, Garrison asked to be sent to aircraft metalsmith school and then to be assigned to a fighter squadron, caring for their planes. In September 1942 he was assigned to the new escort carrier USS *Santee*. In October the ship was with the Allied invasion force landing in North Africa and six months later at the invasion of Sicily.

When the *Franklin* crew was being assembled in the fall of 1943, a call went out for aircraft metalsmiths, and Garrison found himself assigned to the new ship. When the ship sailed for the Pacific, he was only too happy to leave Norfolk. He had never liked the town before the war, when all the better hotels and restaurants had signs in the windows, "NO DOGS OR SAILORS ALLOWED." Of course after Pearl Harbor, everybody became patriotic, and the business folks couldn't do enough for the men in uniform. But he thought the changing attitude of the citizenry of Norfolk was two-faced and thought *good riddance* as he sailed out of Chesapeake Bay and into the Atlantic.

The Navy had trained him to be a metalsmith, which included doing any possible sort of metal work on the ship. His real job was to patch together airplanes that had been hit by enemy fire, but one day during the campaign to prepare Guam for invasion, Garrison had used his new skills to create a "secret weapon."

The idea came to him one day when he was talking to an ordnance man and a pilot, who was complaining that the antipersonnel bombs he was dropping on Japanese troops weren't having much of an effect. The bombs were striking the soft sand and burrowing in before blowing up, the pilot said.

Instead of the blast and shrapnel spreading out over a wide area for maximum effect, the sand was directing the blast upward at a steep angle. A Japanese soldier could be standing within a few feet of a bomb explosion and not be hit. The ordnance man explained that he had tried setting timers on the bombs so that there was no delay on impact, but even at that the sand was too soft.

"What if I made an extension?" Garrison said. He explained his idea to weld an eight-foot-long section of metal tubing on the nose of the bomb so that the warhead would explode while still several feet off the ground.

"Make one and let me try it," the pilot replied.

Garrison set to work and the next morning had the new bomb ready to go. The pilot returned from his sortie elated with the results. "It took out an area half the size of a football field," he gushed. He and his squadron mates wanted more.

All that night, Garrison and other metalsmiths worked on the new bombs and had a supply ready to go for the morning's raids. Again the bombs exceeded expectations, perhaps performing too well. They were making more the next night when they received word that the Japanese commanders on Guam had issued a warning over the radio.

They demanded that the U.S. flyers stop dropping the new "secret weapon" or they would use poisonous gas when the invasion began. The U.S. brass took the threat seriously. One of the most horrific weapons of World War I, the use of gas in warfare had since been banned by the Geneva Convention. But the Japanese had never signed on to the agreement and felt bound by it only when it met with their aims. They had already used gas against Chinese troops, and no one doubted they were capable of it again. An order came down from Captain Shoemaker to stop working on the new bombs and dump any of the unused weapons over the side.

The men on Big Ben were beginning to feel confident, almost cocky, that their ship and CAP could handle any attack. After all, the first month of combat had passed without the ship being struck by so much as a single enemy bullet.

As he smelled the air coming to him from Saipan, Garrison knew that not everyone was so lucky. Although the battle for Saipan had been declared officially over on July 9, the Marines and Army were still mopping up isolated pockets of resistance. The white coral beaches and green jungles had sopped up a lot of blood. Nearly 3,000 Americans had been killed and another 10,000 wounded. The Japanese had fared much worse with 24,000 dead and 3,600 missing, but only 1,780 prisoners taken.

Among the Japanese dead were General Yoshituyu Saito, who commanded the island defense before drawing his own blood with his sword and then ordering his adjutant to shoot him on the night of the final battle. In a nearby bunker, Admiral Chuichi Nagumo, who nearly three years earlier had sent the Imperial First Fleet planes to attack Pearl Harbor, also took his life. That score had been settled.

U.S. soldiers had also looked on in horror as Japanese civilians, including whole families, threw themselves from a cliff onto the jagged rocks below rather than be captured. Of course, the American way was to make light of traumatic events that otherwise would have invoked only nightmares, including a story filed by one of the war correspondents and reprinted in the *Franklin Forum* in late July:

SAIPAN—On the eve of the assault upon this island, a medical officer called members of a Marine artillery unit together and warned them:

In the surf they must beware of sharks, barracuda, sea snakes, anemones, razor-sharp coral, polluted waters, poison fish and, of all things, giant clams capable of snapping on a man like a bear trap.

Ashore, the men must take precautions against leprosy, typhus, filiarisis, yaws, typhoid and paratyphoid fevers, dengue fever, dysentery, an assortment of skin and eye infections, saw grass or saber grass, a wide variety of insects, snakes and giant lizards.

They were instructed to eat nothing growing on the island, nor to drink its waters, or to approach its inhabitants.

At the conclusion of his lecture, the doctor asked if there were any questions. A private raised his hand.

"Yes?" queried the doctor.

"Sir," said the private, "why don't we let the Japs have the island?"

The reality of Saipan, however, was anything but humorous. Attempts to bury the incredible number of Japanese dead using bulldozers to dig huge trenches couldn't keep the smell of death from permeating the air or wafting out to the task group that anchored offshore a month after the last major battle.

Worse than the smell, Garrison thought, were the flies—huge, black carrion flies with monstrous green eyes. They were following the ammunition and supply barges out to the ship from the island until the foul air was swarming with them.

Divine Winds

August 1274
Beijing, China

The Emperor Kubla Khan grew angrier as he studied a map of his world, focusing on a string of islands to the east of China. The grandson of the great conqueror Genghis Khan, he ruled the vast Mongol Empire from the shores of the Korean peninsula to the western steppes of Russia. No other empire of the time was as large, as rich, or as powerful. Few dared oppose him—except for the obstinate people of those insignificant islands racked by volcanoes and earthquakes. That he did not rule Yamato, the ancient name for Japan, made him insanely mad.

Eight years earlier, he had sent his ambassadors there to demand tribute. It was obvious that the Japanese were no match for his vast resources of men, ships, and other weapons of war. But the shogun, the military ruler of Japan who commanded in the name of the emperor, paid tribute by returning the ambassadors' heads in baskets.

The Khan then assembled some 450 ships and a Mongol and Korean army of 40,000 men in a bay on the southern end of the Korean peninsula. When the preparations were complete, he ordered them to sail across the Korea Straits to teach a lesson in humility to the insolent Japanese.

When the main force of the Mongol army sailed into Hakata Bay, it met with no opposition. Vastly outnumbered and unprepared, the Japanese shogun, whose title loosely translated to "barbarian-defeating general," knew that to fight on that ground would have been suicidal without purpose. So the Mongol troops were allowed an uncontested landing. With no enemy to thwart them, the invaders set about murdering and brutalizing the locals, raping the women, and laying waste to the land.

Yet, as the great army prepared to march inland, a *tai-fun* swept in from the China Sea. In the face of the storm, the Mongol army at Hakata Bay hurriedly boarded their ships and made for open water. The ships' captains knew that if caught in the bay, the ships' anchors would not hold and the fleet would founder. There would be no room for maneuvering to avoid the rocks, the shore, or each other. Only in the wide expanse of the Sea of Japan could they hope to ride out the storm. But they were in the path of a wild wind greater than any they had faced before.

Waves higher than the tallest masts tossed the ships. The wind shrieked in the rigging and blew so viciously that ocean spray could cause a man's face to bleed. Half the ships were overturned, smashed to tinder by waves, or simply swallowed whole, slipping into the dark deep. Thousands of men struggled in the frothing waters with no hope of rescue.

When at last the storm passed, what remained of the scattered and devastated Mongol fleet turned for home, the invasion literally drowned. The Japanese rejoiced. Surely the gods had demonstrated that they were a favored people, their emperor a deity.

Enraged by the turn of events, Kubla Khan sent more ambassadors, this time demanding that the Japanese pay tribute and swear their loyalty to him. He promised them friendship, peace, and prosperity if they acceded to his wishes, or the total destruction of their homeland and death or enslavement if they did not comply. The Japanese demonstrated their loyalty by sending more heads in baskets back to China.

Hot anger turned to cold, calculating fury. The Khan took his time assembling another fleet to follow up on his threat. Then in June 1281 he launched an armada of 4,000 ships, carrying more than 140,000 superbly armed warriors across the straits. Their sails stretched from horizon to horizon, and at the end of their voyage the ships crammed into Hakata Bay until it was filled.

The Japanese, however, had not been idle in the intervening years. They had raised a great stone wall along the seashore to hold back the superb Mongol cavalry. From behind these walls, they intended to fight to the death as the emperor, through the shogun, commanded. As the Mongols came at them, the vastly outnumbered defenders reacted with superhuman ferocity. Samurai blades rang on steel and sank into leather, muscle, and bone. Men screamed in agony and in victory as blood painted the shore red and tinted the waters pink.

For two months the Japanese held against the barbarian invaders. The battles that raged would inspire some of the most enduring tales of the samurai; their names and deeds would be woven into the culture of Japan, known to every child and adult. Still, in the third month it became obvious that the invaders were about to overwhelm the Japanese with their superior numbers and resources. Bleeding and exhausted, the samurai prepared for death. They sent clippings of their hair home to loved ones, and to show that they intended to fight until victorious or dead, tied a white scarf, the *hachimaki,* around their heads. The ritual scarves had been inscribed with mystical verses to give them courage and invoke the gods' assistance. If nothing else, the samurai were determined to kill as many of the enemy as possible before they fell.

The fatalistic preparations proved unnecessary. On the morning of August 15 a wind arose, bringing with it roiling clouds that darkened the skies like spilled ink on parchment. Again the Mongol fleet tried to make for the open sea. But crowded together as they were, escape was slow, and before the fleet could make much headway the wind and a tidal surge forced them back into the bay. In the fury of the *tai-fun,* many of the ships were swamped or dashed into each other and onto the shore.

Tens of thousands of the invaders died that day. Thousands drowned. Others struggled to the beach, where they were slaughtered by the defenders. Only a tattered remnant of the mighty armada returned to China to tell the tales of fanatical warriors and demonic winds that snatched away sure victory.

Again the Japanese rejoiced and praised their gods for deliverance. The people believed then that Japan could never be successfully invaded, not so long as Yamato was protected by resolute warriors, willing to die for the emperor, and by the divine winds, which in their language they called *kamikaze.*

October 13, 1944
Luzon, Philippines

On a late afternoon nearly seven hundred years after the thwarted Mongol invasions, a rumpled little Imperial Japanese Navy admiral surprised his staff by striding across the Mabalacat airfield and climbing into the cockpit of a twin-engine Betty torpedo plane. The weather matched the admiral's mood. All day, rainsqualls had swept across the region and mists swirled like ghosts of Japan's departed samurai beneath a leaden sky.

Rear Admiral Masafumi Arima removed all insignia of his rank and announced that he would lead the next strike against the American fleet. His subordinates tried to dissuade him, but it was obvious that he had made some special preparations: The Japanese word for knife, *naifu,* had been hastily painted in white on the olive green fuselage of the plane. But still his officers did not comprehend what it was he intended.

Hard-working, meticulous, but somewhat rumpled from sleeping in his uniform over the past few harried days of constant attacks by the Americans, Arima was a man caught between two eras and two cultures. He had been raised in England, attended their public schools, and as a young man, begun his military training with the British Royal Navy. But he was also steeped in Bushido, "the way of war," the codified behavior for samurai that first flourished in the twelfth century. At Bushido's core was an unquestioning willingness to die for a deified, and omnipotent, emperor.

Arima intended to live up to that that duty by dying.

After the Japanese military seized power from the civilian government in 1936, they promoted Bushido and the legends of the samurai as a sort of cultural inheritance to their people. They pointed out to opponents who predicted disaster with their imperialistic rhetoric that Japan had never lost a war, nor been successfully invaded. And at first the leadership had indeed seemed prescient.

After the Mongol invasions in the thirteenth century were turned back, Japan had remained isolated from China for nearly a hundred years. But in 1931 it was Japan that sent its troops into Manchuria in northern China, a land rich in the natural resources that Japan lacked, beginning the long war to turn China into a vassal state.

When the war with the Americans and their allies erupted, the Imperial Japanese Army and Navy gained an almost mystical reputation at home given the easy early victories over the arrogant West. The Japanese soldier, sailor, and airman was said to be imbued with the ancient virtues of the old samurai.

However, there was a darker side to Bushido as it was interpreted by the Japanese leadership and passed down to the lowliest soldier. One that bred an arrogance born of a perceived racial and moral superiority. One that precipitated horrific atrocities by Japanese troops throughout the war, and earlier in the 1930s—epitomized by the Rape of Nanking in which more than two hundred thousand Chinese, mostly civilians, were killed in an orgy of rape and murder, as well as the use of bubonic plague-infested wheat dropped on Chinese cities.

This darker side of Bushido also sealed the fates of tens of thousands of young men who died inhumanely or unnecessarily—Allied prisoners of war, as well as Japanese soldiers, sailors, and airmen . Written into the Japanese military code of behavior was the insistence on death before surrender as the only honorable substitute for victory. As such, prisoners of war were considered beneath contempt. But this belief also caused the militarily pointless, suicidal slaughter of Japanese troops on islands the length and breadth of the Pacific from Attu to Guadalcanal to Saipan.

The concept of suicide missions was not new, nor particularly Japanese. Almost every culture had a variation on the story of heroes knowingly sacrificing themselves for king, country, or sometimes simply their honor—the Spartans at Thermopylae; the Charge of the Light Brigade at Balaclava; Davy Crockett, Jim Bowie and Col. William Travis and 186 others at the Alamo. And almost every culture also had its tale of the wounded warrior, knowing he was doomed, fighting to his last breath to take as many of his enemies with him as possible.

Japanese history was replete with heroic last stands. The Japanese belief system—encouraged by the military government—held that an honorable death in battle would be rewarded with an eternal place among Japan's war heroes at the Yasukuni Shrine near the Imperial Palace. There were even instances in which suicide missions had been successful as military tactics. During the Russo-Japanese War of 1903, Japanese units staged suicide attacks in Manchuria that had unnerved their numerically and technologically superior enemy and resulted in victory. During World War I, a Japanese suicide force assailed the "impenetrable" fortress of Qingdao and to the surprise of themselves, the leaders who sent them, and their enemy, they had captured the fortress.

In the Second World War, however, the banzai ground attacks had little real military significance other than the slaughter of young Japanese men. Some were spur of the moment, or the last gesture during a campaign's final days. However, on Saipan, as previously on Guadalcanal, it became official policy when the Japanese military leaders ordered their troops to turn themselves into "human bullets."

The battle for Saipan also introduced a new suicide tactic—this one in the air—the *taitori,* or ramming attack. Again, the concept of crashing into the enemy as a desperate last measure was not entirely new. Both sides, in fact, had pilots who, with their planes in flames, perhaps already mortally wounded, attempted one last act of defiance by seeking to crash into a ship or a concentration of enemy forces.

The *taitori* attacks, however, were being undertaken by Japanese pilots who were not wounded, whose planes were still airworthy, against American planes. The Japanese pilots, frustrated by the U.S. fighter planes that thwarted traditional attacks, were ramming American bombers in midair. And some wanted to take it a step further.

Among the Japanese navy pilots in particular, there was a strong cadre who argued that the only way to stop the Americans was to crash-dive their ships. Chief among the proponents of the *Toko*, or "special attack" concept was Vice Admiral Takijiro Onishi. Before Pearl Harbor, Onishi had warned his countrymen that attacking the Americans would make them so "insanely mad" they would fight to the bitter end. Now that the end of the war was looking bitter indeed for Japan, with the Americans calling for "unconditional surrender," he believed that only the most drastic measures would stop the enemy from successfully invading his homeland.

The sorry state of affairs of the Japanese air corps, he thought, made such measures necessary. The problem wasn't airplane production. The factories—such as Mitsubishi Motors—were still turning out several thousand planes a month. The problem was the lack of experienced pilots to fly them.

After the Battle of the Philippine Sea in June, and what the Americans were derisively calling the Great Marianas Turkey Shoot, there were few pilots left in Japan's navy who were capable of landing or taking off from an aircraft carrier. The young men coming in were certainly eager and brave, but there was no time to prepare them properly.

Onishi knew that the new pilots couldn't be expected to fly well enough to hit a wildly maneuvering warship with a bomb or torpedo, much less fend off the combat air patrols that hovered above the American fleet. He believed that the only effective way for these young pilots to strike a blow for the emperor was for them to give their lives.

The solution, Onishi told his superiors, was for pilots in their fuel- and bomb-laden aircraft to forget the strategy and technical complexities of traditional attacks and bore straight into the American ships like an arrow to the heart. The best targets, he argued, would be the big aircraft carriers, for without them the landings on Japanese-held islands would be much more difficult for the Americans, maybe impossible.

The special attack had several advantages over the traditional attack, he said. The pilot would not have to concern himself with the precision timing of a dive-bombing attack or torpedo run. Nor would he have to worry about when to pull out of the dive or turn away. The pilot would have a singular purpose—no breaking from his task to engage enemy fighters in aerial combat or trying to evade the combat air patrol and the ships' guns any more than necessary to achieve his goal. Psychologically, the pilot would not be hampered by thoughts of survival if he knew from the outset that the success of his mission depended on him dying. And the Americans, who placed such an inordinately high value on a single life, would be terrorized.

Onishi's idea was popular with the pilots and some of his colleagues, such as Rear Admiral Arima. However, his arguments didn't sway his superiors; suicide tactics had already been tried on the ground without success. The human bullets had failed to stop the Americans on Saipan. When the island fell, Prime Minister Tojo, who had been under increasing criticism for the policy, was forced into retirement (though he continued to hold sway with the Army). The new regime, while staunchly in favor of continuing the war, promised that never again would it consider using human bullets. To insist that troops fight to the last man and engage in banzai attacks was asking enough; they were not prepared to create units committed solely to suicide. Not yet.

After the fall of Saipan, the Japanese war strategy was to withdraw into the "inner empire" defensive perimeter of the Philippines, the coastal regions of China, Korea, the Bonin Islands, and Okinawa. Their carriers were no longer effective as offensive weapons, but they still had a powerful surface Navy and a huge Army, including one million men in China, two million in Japan, and hundreds of thousands on the fortresslike islands that dotted the sea routes to the home islands. If the cost of victory for the Americans was high enough in terms of lives and resources, the war planners felt their enemy could still be bloodied into accepting a peace agreement that would leave the emperor on his throne, the army and navy intact, and the inner empire and the home islands unsullied by foreign invaders.

Even the most optimistic no longer believed that they could win the war, but surely they could dictate something other than unconditional surrender. Toward that end, the military leaders adopted a strategy by which their forces would win the "decisive victory" envisioned by their great fallen admiral, Yamamoto. They called it the Sho plan. Although, they did not know where the Americans planned to attack next—the Philippines, Formosa, Okinawa, or even the home islands—the plan was designed to work under any contingency.

The Sho plan involved attacking the American landing forces from three different directions with the still-powerful surface fleet, which included the largest battleships ever built. It was a complex plan that would depend on impeccable timing and resolute leadership, but the biggest hurdle would be negating American air power so that the surface ships could move close enough to attack the American landing forces. To accomplish this, they would sacrifice their remaining aircraft carriers as a "bait fleet" to pull the American aircraft carriers away from the landing site long enough for the surface fleet to slip in and attack, destroying whatever support fleet was left to protect the landing. Then the American troops on shore would be caught between the Japanese defenders and the powerful guns of the Imperial fleet. The invading force would be slaughtered.

Seeing an opportunity, Onishi promoted the use of a special attack unit into the Sho plan. He argued that a couple dozen dedicated pilots could ram the American aircraft carriers and put them out of commission, possibly even sink them, even before the bait force had to be used.

The idea was tempting to the Imperial war council of generals and admirals. If it worked, the Americans would be decimated on the sea and blasted to bits on the land, their juggernaut would stall, and they would have to consider making peace. Or, if not inducing a peace agreement, then such a massive defeat would make the Americans have to pull back to regroup, buying more time to train pilots and produce planes.

Still, the war council balked. By mid-October, Onishi's request had not won formal approval, though some previously opposed to the idea were at least listening. He kept up hope that his plan would be executed, especially when told he had a new assignment upon which the fate of the empire hinged.

On the afternoon of October 13, Onishi flew to Manila to take command of the First Air Fleet, which would be responsible for the naval air defense of the Philippines, from Vice Admiral Kimpei Teraoka, who was thought by the Imperial High Command to have lost his taste for fighting. But even as Onishi was landing, he did not know that his strategy had already been implemented by his friend and supporter Admiral Arima.

As commander of the 26th Air Flotilla, Arima knew better than most the deficiencies of the new pilots in the fall of 1944. Just trying to get them and their planes to the front was a challenge. More than a third of the new pilots who took off from Japan for the Philippines or Formosa never arrived. They were either lost at sea (having learned little about navigation in their abbreviated training classes), or were picked off by the American fighter pilots before they could arrive at the bases.

Arima had seen enough. For the past four days, American carrier planes had bombed and strafed the Japanese airfields in the Philippines and Formosa with little effective opposition. The Japanese air corps was being blasted on the ground and in the air with few successes. The little admiral had gone repeatedly to Teraoka for permission to take the remaining planes and make a special attack, only to be politely rebuffed. But when Teraoka left for Manila to meet Onishi, Arima seized the opportunity while his superior was absent.

Into the overcast and troubled skies, he led a group of about ninety planes. He knew that after the American planes attacked the Philippines or Formosa they would head back for the fleet, so the trick would be to follow them without being intercepted by the American combat air patrol. Once in the air over their ships, the returning American flyers would circle their aircraft carriers as they waited to land. With weather conditions limiting visibility and with so many planes in the air and the hectic pace of landing operations, Arima hoped that he and his pilots might circle unnoticed, as though they were American planes returning to the carriers themselves, until they found the right moment to attack.

Instead of approaching the fleet in one large group, which would have been easy for the American radar operators to spot, Arima had the squadrons split into small groups of four or five planes. Still, most of the Japanese planes that afternoon were intercepted by the combat air patrol and shot down or forced to retreat without even seeing the American fleet.

However, Arima's torpedo bomber and the three others that accompanied him spotted an American task group 240 miles from Manila. In the center of the group was a large aircraft carrier with the numeral 13 painted on its flight deck and on the sides of its island structure. The task force was turned into the wind and running in a straight line to retrieve its aircraft, a most vulnerable time.

Circling until he saw his opening between the screen of cruisers and destroyers, Arima suddenly peeled off and began a traditional torpedo run at the port side of the carrier, followed at roughly one-minute intervals by his companions. He dropped down to wavetop level. The lookouts on the ships spotted him and the guns began to fire; all around him, the air was filled with splotches of black smoke.

The gods could not have arranged more perfect circumstances. He and his men were inside the protective circle, forcing the ships to fire at each other in order to bring their guns to bear on the attackers. Still, the anti-aircraft fire only intensified with the lighter, rapid-fire guns joining the bigger guns; brilliant tracers arced toward Arima like shooting stars, as the carrier loomed ahead of him. He jinked to the left and the right, up and down, following the ship as its captain tried desperately to take her out of harm's way.

Approximately five hundred yards out, Arima dropped his torpedo, which ran straight for the aft end of the huge ship. The captain on the carrier turned hard to port—actually toward Arima—to swing the stern of the ship away from the onrushing torpedo. Arima turned to follow the maneuvering ship rather than pull up and away as was expected. He rose suddenly so that he could plunge into the wooden flight deck, the ship's most vulnerable spot. Despite the swarm of flying steel that flew out to greet him, he must have still been alive in the moments before he reached the ship, because his wing guns were firing.

Miles away, beyond the circle of ships, Japanese spotter planes witnessed the admiral's charge with surprise, and then with admiration for his courage and audacity. They left to return to the Philippines with the story, which spread like wildfire from airfield to airfield and to the headquarters of the First Fleet. That's where Onishi heard the news with grim satisfaction. No one knew yet what to call Arima's sacrifice, but the kamikaze had returned in Japan's hour of need.

PART III

The USS *Franklin* and *Santa Fe*

The Philippines

October–December 1944

CHAPTER NINE

The Winds of War

October 13, 1944
Philippine Sea
USS Franklin

Aviation Coxswain 2nd Class Frank Turner emerged from the island onto the flight deck after checking the board that showed where planes were to be placed for the next morning strikes. Pausing outside the hatch, he took note of the low clouds and dark line of rainsqualls drifting across the Philippine Sea. All day long, he'd worried that the weather would provide a place to hide for "bogeys," but none had come close to the *Franklin*. Still, it would be dark soon, the Japs' favorite time to attack.

The *Franklin* was turned into the wind to retrieve the last of her daytime guardians. In an hour or so, the night-fighters would be launched from the catapults at the bow of the ship. He could see the black dots of the CAP against the gray sky swarming around the carriers of the air group like excited hornets. He was glad that they were friendly hornets.

Aircraft carriers were at their most vulnerable during takeoffs and landings. The ship had to stop its defensive zigzagging and run in a straight line, making it an easier target for aircraft and submarines. So the less time spent making corrections, the safer the ship and its crew were.

In early August, Task Group 58.1—which included the large carriers *Franklin* and *Enterprise*, as well as the light carriers *San Jacinto* and *Belleau Wood*—left the flies and stench of Saipan and steamed at flank speed for the Bonins.

Arriving in those waters one month to the day after the Fourth-of-July raid on Iwo Jima, the ships encountered nasty weather for flying. But the same drenching rains, high winds, and rough seas probably lulled the Japanese into a sense of complacency, and they were again taken by surprise when

the task group launched raids against Chichi Jima, the most heavily fortified of the Bonins.

The *Franklin's* planes surprised a convoy of cargo ships, escorted by a light
cruiser and a destroyer, trying to slip out of the Futami Ko harbor. The
cruiser and several cargo ships were soon burning and settling into the water.

The other carriers' air groups caught up to another convoy of cargo ships
and tankers, escorted by a half dozen destroyers, near the small island of
Ototo Jima. However, the weather played hell with their attacks and a single bomb struck only one ship.

After recovering their planes, the other carriers decided that the weather
made it too hazardous to try any more launches that day and halted flight
operations. But Shoemaker wasn't about to let the convoy escape and
ordered another strike. The targets didn't have the glamour of aircraft carriers or battleships, but he knew that this war wasn't being won by sinking
warships; it was being won by cutting off supply lines and strangling the
enemy's ability to wage war. The last strike left at 4:00 that afternoon, launching during a break in the rain.

Locating the convoy, Hellcat fighters went after the destroyers, two
of which blew up and sank within minutes. A third was left dead in the
water and on fire. The dive-bombers accounted for two cargo ships, and
the torpedo planes sank four more, before the air group had to return to
the ship.

With darkness and the weather closing in, flight operations on the *Franklin*
were finished for the day. But one of the task group's screening cruiser divisions, CruDiv13 led by its flagship the USS *Santa Fe,* was sent racing through
the storm to finish off what remained of the convoy. The reports came back
later that night that of the eighteen to twenty Japanese ships that set out from
Chichi Jima, only one old destroyer may have survived.

The next day, the *Franklin* was again the only carrier to launch air strikes
and just one at that. Before a second strike could be sent, the weather dete-
riorated until the storm waves were breaking over the flight deck, and the
ship's aerology department warned that a full-fledged typhoon might be on
the way. So the task group turned and headed south for Eniwetok to the
relief of the destroyers, which had struggled to keep their screening positions while the waves slapped them around.

The raid had been an enormous success. But it also "proved our most
expensive in that we definitely lost three pilots and one aircrewman," according to the August 7 "Plan of the Day," a daily memorandum posted through-

out the ship that included the day's activities schedule and noting the outcome of incidents from previous days.

The memo reported that the Hellcat squadron had lost flight leader Lt. A. C. Hudson and one of the youngest fighter pilots onboard, Ensign Roger L'Estrange. It also noted that L'Estrange had provided air cover for the invasion of Guam by the Marines, one of whom was his brother, a captain.

The Chichi Jima raid proved costly to the dive-bombers as well. Lt. Cmdr. Carl Holmstrom, the well-liked executive officer of the squadron, and his gunner, Walter Brooks, had been hit by antiaircraft fire and were seen crashing into the waters of the harbor.

"While these shipmates are all reported as 'missing,' little hope is held for them," the memo noted. "We of the *Franklin* deeply regret their loss."

A torpedo plane had also been shot down during the last raid. "However, there is hope that some or all members of the crew escaped: Lt. (j.g.) H. F. McCue, the pilot, Aviation Ordnance Mate 3rd Class W. D. Hever, the radioman; and ARM 3rd Class R. T. Robinette, the gunner . . . we are hopefully awaiting word of their rescue."

Putting death in the proper perspective aboard a warship, the plan didn't deviate from its usual postings, such as the routine for the morning—reveille at 4:00 A.M., air bedding at 6:00 and breakfast at 7:00—standard duties from 8:00 to noon. After noon and for the remainder of the voyage to Eniwetok, it noted, work hours would be spent on "field day," meaning all hands would "turn to" to help clean and polish the *Franklin* "in order that our ship may be highly presentable on arrival. We will certainly have visitors from other ships and may receive a flag [an admiral]."

The ship pulled into the Eniwetok lagoon on August 9, joining hundreds of other ships, including five more fleet carriers and as many light carriers, as well as divisions of battleships, cruisers, destroyers and support vessels called "ships of the train." The Plan of the Day notice included the announcement that the movie *Hitler's Madmen*, starring Alan Curtis, Patricia Morisson, Ralph Morgan, and John Carradine, would be playing at 7:00 P.M.

Sunbathing would be permitted, according to the Plan of the Day, for off-duty personnel on the flight deck—the aft end reserved for enlisted men and the forward end for officers. "Sunbathing is not permitted in the walkways nor on gun stations at any time."

The *Franklin* remained at Eniwetok for two weeks undergoing an overhaul, while the men were allowed trips to Runit Island. Like most other islands in an atoll, Runit was a strip of coral sand, the tops of its coconut trees blasted away by the shelling that preceded the invasion. There wasn't much to do but swim, walk on the white coral beaches, make attempts at splitting coconuts, and play softball or volleyball. Still, it was the first solid land the crew had stepped on in two months and a welcome respite from life on a ship.

September 1944

When the *Franklin* departed, it was as part of a "new" fleet. Admiral Raymond Spruance had been recalled to Hawaii for a breather and to map out strategy to follow the upcoming invasion of the Philippines. Admiral William "Bull" Halsey took over to coordinate the fleet's support activities for MacArthur's long-promised return. Actually, very little changed except that the Fifth Fleet was now called the Third Fleet, and Task Force 58 became Task Force 38, with the *Franklin* the flagship for Task Group 38.1.

Starting where it left off, the task force flew 91 sorties against Iwo Jima on the first and second of September. The air attacks were followed up by the cruisers and destroyers, which moved in close to pound the island from the sea. Then it was off to the Caroline Islands, the home of several major Japanese bases, which stood in the way of the Philippine campaign. The Navy also wanted the Ulithi atoll's lagoon, an immense 112-square-mile natural anchorage in the Carolines that could hold a thousand ships and was a thousand miles closer to the Philippines than Eniwetok.

There followed a succession of raids launched at the islands of Yap and Palau. Then on September 10, the task force attacked the island of Peleliu in the Carolines in preparation for the Marine invasion, which was scheduled to begin five days later.

On the day of the invasion, the aerial bombardment was coordinated with a massive shelling by the cruisers and battleships offshore, lasting even after the Marines began to hit the beach. According to the U.S. war planners, Peleliu was supposed to be a pushover, and indeed that appeared to be the case as the Marines landed with little opposition. But then the Japanese began to emerge from their caves and bunkers dug into the high ground that overlooked the landing beaches and began to rain artillery and mortar fire down on the leathernecks, as well as taking out landing barges filled with reinforcements. The battle became so intense and the American losses so grievous that the scheduled invasion of nearby Anguar Island had to be postponed.

Task Force 38.1 air groups tried to help the Marines by flying strikes whenever the "gyrenes" called for help. Over the course of the week preceding and during the invasion, the *Franklin's* planes dropped 256 tons of bombs on Peleliu. But at last, the task group ran out of munitions and aviation gas and had to turn over its support duties to a fresh task group.

This time the *Franklin* kept heading south beyond Eniwetok, bound for Manus in the Admiralty chain for resupply and some real R&R away from the front line. The men felt good about their first extended duty on the front. Except for a few accidents that a fellow could avoid if he paid attention, the *Franklin* was a lucky ship—more than two months in combat and they had never had to fire the guns at an attacking plane yet. There had been the occasional submarine alert, but no torpedoes streaking beneath the waves. Even the more fearful among them talked about the raids against the Japanese as "milk runs."

Traveling to Manus meant that the ship crossed the equator, with the resulting initiations into King Neptune's realm. The initiations were no easy task on the *Franklin* considering that for every shellback there were forty pollywogs, who occasionally turned the tables on their tormentors.

Upon liberty at Manus each enlisted man was allotted two cans of warm beer. Nondrinkers found themselves to be extremely popular with their drinking comrades, at least until they had given away their share. Most found that after a long stint without any alcoholic beverages, two beers in the tropical heat did the trick. The officers, however, headed for their own club, where their allotment was eight beers, served on ice.

At least there was time to sit under a coconut palm and write a letter home. Some of the ship's crew had found ingenious ways to let their folks at home know where they'd been although they were prohibited from writing about the ships' activities or travels in letters home.

Before he left the small farming community of Zumbrota, Minnesota, one of the ship's "weathermen," Aerologist Mate 2nd Class Jim Erredge, had worked out a code with his parents so that they could chart the movements of the *Franklin* on a large National Geographic Magazine map of the Pacific they hung on a wall of the family room. Disguised within age-old complaints and homesick ramblings of sailors, the code was quite simple: He'd write about the numbers of sheep or cattle back home and reference them to certain pastures that related to points on a compass. The numbers were really the latitude and longitude, and the compass directions further pinpointed the ship's travels.

Dear Ma,

Here is another note from out of the blue so to speak. . . . Boy could I ever go for a good meal of vegetables from the garden: Our chow certainly has not been anything to brag about lately. They are even getting so they cut down on the quantity as well as quality. That's when I think things are getting bad. My mouth really waters when I think of corn on the cob, fresh carrots, strawberries, and stuff like that.

How are the lambs doing now that they are on grass? Bet the flock of a hundred and forty keeps the grass pretty well chewed down. Why don't you try keeping most of them over in the east lot and leave about twenty-five in the home pasture?

Not all of the crew was allowed on shore at one time. Liberty was granted according to which "watch"—starboard or port—a sailor was on. The best part was getting out of work. Those enlisted men who remained onboard were put to work loading supplies and ammunition in the sweltering heat.

A number of command changes occurred on Manus for the *Franklin*. Commander Day, the executive officer, was promoted and given command of a new escort carrier. The navigator, Cmdr. Benny Moore, was promoted to executive officer, and Cmdr. Henry Hale transferred from the light carrier *San Jacinto* to take over as navigator. "Sunshine" Howerton left the ship to become the air officer on another carrier, and dive-bomber squadron leader Kibbe was put in his place as air group commander.

All too soon, the task group left for the Carolines. Ulithi and other key islands in the region had fallen, although the Japanese held on at bloody Peleliu. However, the task group didn't pull into the Ulithi atoll, but spent a week in the storm-tossed seas waiting to rendezvous with the rest of the Third Fleet.

October 1944

Task Force 38 showed up and was now comprised of three task groups, which translated into six *Essex*-class carriers, another half dozen light carriers, eight battleships, twenty cruisers, and a hundred destroyers. They proceeded to steam north, each task group spread out in circles covering over a dozen square miles of ocean and separated from the other task groups by a dozen more miles.

The armada followed behind a typhoon that was raging out of the South China Sea toward Okinawa and Formosa, the rains and clouds hiding the black and slate warships as they approached the gateway to Japan. The backside of a typhoon was the least dangerous place to be, but the winds were still blowing up to sixty knots, or seventy-two miles an hour, and the waves rose so high that the destroyers would disappear from view into the troughs between them.

The task force's high-speed run brought the ships about equidistant between Okinawa, Formosa, and Luzon, the northernmost main island in the Philippines chain. They were sticking their heads in the lion's mouth. Up to this point in the war, the aircraft carriers had been dealing with naval aircraft from carriers or those flying from tiny strips on small islands. Now the major air bases of the empire were in a position to reinforce and support each other. But the storm had once again shielded the Americans' approach.

To further ensure secrecy, American fighters ranged far ahead of the task force, ambushing six Japanese sentinel planes without the enemy having seen a single ship. However, there was a moment of concern when a destroyer picked up two Japanese fishermen in a small boat. They were transferred to the *Franklin,* which had a brig, for questioning; the ship's officers were worried they might have had a radio on their boat and warned their countrymen. Two days later, the carrier pulled up alongside a tanker to refuel and transfer the prisoners. The first was sent across in a breeches buoy without incident; but the second prisoner managed to loosen his bonds and jumped out midway between the two ships. The officer in charge of the hangar deck drew his handgun and fired; he missed, but the prisoner quickly disappeared in the churning water between the two ships and didn't surface again.

On the morning of October 9, more than two hundred Hellcat fighters, most of them armed with six-inch rockets, climbed from a dozen flight decks to attack Okinawa, a banana-shaped island located almost exactly the same distance—about 350 miles—from Japan, Formosa, and the coast of China. They caught most of the Japanese planes on the ground and shot down the few that managed to take off. With the defender's airplanes and airfields decimated, the Americans went about bombing fuel depots and ammunition dumps until a black pall of smoke hung over the length of the island when the last American plane left.

The Japanese regrouped after dusk and sent search planes and squadrons of torpedo planes to find the American fleet. Once again they were at a disadvantage. While they searched for a blacked-out fleet on a dark ocean, American night fighters stalked the Japanese planes. The night fighters were Hellcats with radar mounted on the wings, a technology the Japanese did not possess. Guided to the Japanese squadrons by the more powerful radar on the ships, the Hellcats then used their own radar to hunt down the Japanese like bats hunting bugs in the dark. The Japanese never found the fleet, and many never made it back to their airfields.

The next day at sunrise, a thousand American fighters, dive-bombers, and torpedo planes again lashed out at Okinawa and Nansei Shoto, a small island on the southern end of the Japanese archipelago. The Imperial High Command was infuriated. It was one thing to lose Saipan, a distant colony, and for the Bonins to be under frequent attack—though that was practically in their backyard—but Okinawa, which the Japanese had invaded in the mid-eighteenth century, and Nansei Shoto were considered home grounds.

That night the Japanese were back out in force. This time they found the fleet, but again met the night fighters and withering fire from the ships' guns and none made it through to complete an attack. The only casualty suffered by the men on the *Franklin* was the sleep they lost from having to jump out of their bunks to report to their battle stations several times during the night.

On October 11, Task Group 38.4, with the *Franklin* as its flagship, broke off from the rest of the task force to attack a seaplane base on Luzon. The Bonins. Okinawa. Nansei Shoto. And now the Philippines. Halsey wanted to mix it up and keep the Japanese guessing where the next strike would hit, preventing them from concentrating their forces.

The next day, the *Franklin* was in real danger—but from American planes, not Japanese—because it was the carrier's "day in the hole." The idea was to designate one carrier to be used by all damaged aircraft, no matter what ship they launched from, so that crash landings would not put more than one of the ships out of commission at a time.

If a plane was too badly damaged, the pilot might be ordered to land in the water close to one of the destroyer "lifeguards." But water landings were dangerous if for no other reason than the pilot or crew might not make it out of the aircraft before it sank. However, if it looked like the plane could be repaired, or if an aviator was hurt and unlikely to survive a water landing, the pilot could be directed to the carrier whose turn it was for a day in the hole.

A day in the hole was universally disliked, as it was dangerous for the flight deck crew, as well as the ship. It turned out to be a hectic day for the *Franklin,* as the strikes were against well-guarded Formosa, where the Japanese put up a fierce fight with their Zeros and antiaircraft guns. Soon pilots from the *Franklin* and other carriers were calling in, using the ship's code name for the day "Buick" (changed every twenty-four hours to confuse the Japanese). Their calls were broadcast over the ship's loud-speakers so that the flight deck crew would know what to expect. "Buick! Buick! My right aileron is missing." "Buick! My fuselage is all shot up and my gunner's hit!" However, there were no crashes that took the *Franklin* out of action.

In the afternoon, the Japanese tried to reinforce their decimated squadrons on Formosa by sending a hundred planes from the Philippines. However, they were spotted by the task force's radar and twenty American fighters were scrambled to intercept them. The Hellcats caught the enemy seventy miles out and pursued them, knocking them out of the air one after the other. Only a few survived to land on Formosa, and those only because the Americans were low on fuel and had to turn back.

Once again squadrons of Japanese torpedo bombers sped out to attack the fleet that night, and once again no U.S. ships were hit, but that didn't stop Tokyo Rose from declaring a major victory later that night. Imperial pilots, she said, had sunk fifteen U.S. carriers, including the *Franklin,* as well as seven battleships.

"Twenty thousand U.S. sailors were sent swimming," she purred. "Why don't you nice American boys give up, and you can all be home for Christmas?"

The crew got a kick out of that. Heck, the wind had been more danger-ous than the Japanese on that day.

The next day, October 13, the *Franklin's* planes concentrated again on For-mosa. By the time the last strike was over in the late afternoon, thousands of fires were raging all over the island. No one knew it, but the strikes had been a signal for MacArthur's Eighth Army and the Seventh Fleet to set out from Manus, bound for the Philippines.

It was also a sign Rear Admiral Arima had been waiting for to climb in a torpedo bomber and fly out to find the American fleet.

In the late afternoon of October 13, Turner watched as the last of the com-bat air patrol fighters was coming in. As soon as they were all down, he and the rest of the plane spotters' real labors would begin—organizing the deck for the next day's mission.

Captain Shoemaker had relaxed General Quarters to Condition 3, which meant some of the guns—particularly the forties—were manned, as were the fire control stations. But most of the rest of the crew was relieved to go get some chow and rest, while those still working buttoned up the ship for the night, pulling down the hangar deck curtains to prevent light from escaping.

Of course, Turner and the other Airedales still had plenty of work left before they could relax, thanks to the lousy weather. The seas had been rough for nearly the entire trip since they had left Manus and joined up with Halsey and the rest of the Third Fleet. Now, the ship rode up and down on the big swells like an enormous, slow-motion roller-coaster, unusual for a ship the size of the *Franklin*. Normally, the ship plowed through even moderately rough seas steady as you please.

Combined with the wind and rain, the movement made a difficult and dangerous job that much harder and more hazardous. The flight deck crew was exhausted. They had been launching and landing planes all day. Sending a flight out when they heard that a previous flight was returning, loading the next with fuel, bullets, rockets, and bombs, and then sending them out again. Such a day was tough enough without a long night of extra work because of the rough weather.

In good conditions, Lt. Fred Harris, who oversaw the flight deck crew, would have studied the requirements for the next day's strikes and told the men what planes he needed and where. Then after the last of the afternoon's flights was retrieved, the Airedales would begin moving them to the aft end, or down into the hangar. If there were no major accidents, they could be done by eight, in time to get a little warm chow before hitting the sack.

However, in foul weather the Airedales also had to tie the planes down to hooks inset in the wooden deck to keep them from being knocked into each other or the ocean by waves or wind. They might not finish until 1:00 A.M. or later. Then if they were hungry, they had to beg a cook for some bread and cold cuts—a round amalgam of pressed mystery meat the ship's company commonly referred to as "horse cock," which came with a green slime coating owing to poor refrigeration.

As young and energetic as they were, one day of bad weather flight operations wasn't too hard on them. But after four days of pushing planes around in the rain and not getting finished until the early morning hours, all the men wanted to do was take a shower and go to bed. Sometimes fatigue ruled out the shower, and they fell straight into their bunks without bothering to remove their clothes. Before the sun came up, they would be roused to begin the merry-go-round of flight operations all over again.

As he stepped out onto the rain-soaked deck, Turner was worried. He knew that exhausted men made more mistakes, especially when the ship was rocking and the deck was wet. He was tired of seeing what happened when men lost focus. He had seen them walk, crouched down, with their faces averted to avoid prop wash beneath the wings of taxiing planes and forget to keep a hand on a landing strut. They wouldn't know then when the pilot applied the brakes and would walk straight into the spinning propeller.

Even the wind could be dangerous on the flight deck. Sudden gusts had been known to carry unwary men overboard. If they were lucky, someone saw them go and a destroyer could be sent to retrieve them. Still, it meant surviving a seventy-foot fall into heavy seas. They were all required to wear life jackets while on the flight deck, but not every man overboard was found.

The most frightening enemy was fire—surrounded as they were by planes filled with high-octane aviation fuel and loaded with munitions of all sorts. A potentially devastating conflagration was possible at any time without warning.

Turner hoped that another long night—as October 13 was shaping up to be—wouldn't end with a tired Airedale getting hurt. He wasn't worried about the Japanese. All day long, task force planes had hammered Formosa, and the Japanese had tried to get at the fleet but none had made it past the combat air patrol. In fact, the *Franklin* had yet to be attacked by an enemy plane.

At the moment, everything appeared to be calm and under control. A little bit aft from where he stood, Turner saw a pal of his from his days on the *Charger,* AMM 1st Class Harold Stancil, kneeling at the rear of an F6F Hellcat in the middle of the flight deck. Stancil had just released the plane's tail hook from the arresting cable so that the pilot could taxi forward beyond the lowered crash barrier.

The lookouts were squinting up at the clouds at the small black dots that circled but no one seemed anxious about the possibility of an attack. A Marine on a 20-millimeter machine gun across the flight deck from where he stood stared attentively out over the ocean.

Suddenly, a voice he recognized as belonging to the air officer, Cmdr. Joe Taylor, yelled down to him. "Hey, Turner! Get yer butt out of there. . . . They're coming in!"

At the same time, the guns began firing, and not just those on the *Franklin.* The entire task group seemed to be shooting. Turner spun in the direction

Taylor pointed. At first, he didn't see anything except hundreds of puffs of black smoke against the gray sky. Then he saw them, flying low over the water . . . twin-engine Betty torpedo planes. The first was already within two carrier lengths of the ship and a moment later, a long, dark cylinder dropped from the plane.

Time seemed to slow down. He saw the white streak of the torpedo's wake beneath the water running straight for the *Franklin*. He saw Stancil running across the deck away from the onrushing plane. Behind him and off to the side, the Landing Signal Officer, Lt. Dan Winters, was also running.

The Marine on the machine-gun was standing his ground, his body shaking as he blasted away. *He's got to be knockin' the bejeezus out of that plane,* Turner thought.

But the plane kept coming. Tiny flames flickered from guns in the wings and its belly gun. Then the plane was on fire, but the pilot kept the carrier in his sights.

Turner suddenly realized that the pilot intended to crash into the ship. And what's more, he seemed to have picked out Frank's spot, as his final destination. But others would feel that way, too.

"Where is everybody, Ed?" asked Water Tender 2nd Class Ernest Scott. They had just finished dinner and were back in Eddie Carlisle's compartment, shooting the breeze, when Scott had noticed that nobody else was around. Privacy of any sort was unusual, especially that time of the evening—something had to be up.

Scott's attitude after being assigned to the Black Gang in December 1943 had not improved right away—in part because he had fallen in with a couple of slackers who suggested that the petty officers could be ignored with impunity. As a result, he was handed every menial job the "POs" could think of; worst of all was when they sent him off for a tour of duty working in the mess halls during the shakedown cruise.

Mess hall duty was a never-ending misery of scrubbing, cleaning, and carrying the various pots and pans, plates and trays, and cups and silverware from nearly ten thousand breakfasts, lunches, and dinners. They scooped the garbage into fifty-gallon drums and carted them to the huge garbage disposal, nicknamed "Gravel Gertie," on the second deck to be ground up and spit out the side of the ship. Then there were the countless hours preparing hip-deep mounds of celery and carrots and potatoes for the crew's consumption.

Mess hall duty meant getting up before everyone else and often going to bed after the rest had turned in. One day he spent five hours breaking eggs for the cooks until, he groused, he was suffering from "shell shock." He was not amused to see that every fifth egg or so seemed just a few days short of hatching. When he complained about adding them to the mix, the cook told him to "Just shuddup and stir." The fresh eggs wouldn't last long—and Scott, like every other sailor onboard, would come to hate powdered eggs—but at least the reconstituted eggs hadn't "feathered out."

The only good thing about mess hall duty was meeting Fireman 1st Class Chuck Berringer, a muscular, clean-cut boy from Zanesville, Ohio, who would become one of Scott's closest shipboard friends. While on duty, he and Berringer spent a good deal of their creative thoughts on how they were going to get rid of the master at arms who ran the mess hall, a "skinny bastard" named Macabee. The man was a petty tyrant, who enjoyed making a miserable job worse—such as the evening they all came down with the "back door trots" from eating spoiled chicken ala king, but he still made them stay up all night cleaning silverware. The man was so mean, Berringer joked, "Even his own mother won't write to him."

Berringer was in charge of running Gravel Gertie. Every so often, he would throw stainless steel silverware into the three-foot wide maw of the garbage disposal. Gravel Gertie made a horrible racket as she ground them up, which would cause Macabee to run over and demand to know what caused the problem. Berringer kidded Scott that one of those days he might get Macabee to lean over to look in the disposal and . . . Months later the pair wondered if someone else got a similar idea after Macabee mysteriously disappeared one night.

After returning to Norfolk from the shakedown cruise in April, the crew got four days leave. It wasn't really enough time to go home to Maine, but Scott told Carlisle he was thinking of going anyway.

Carlisle tried to talk him out of it. "Jeez, Scotty, you'll get your ass in a sling if you go AWOL."

"Yeah, I know," Scott replied, "but you heard the 'old man' say we'll be fighting off Jap planes a month from now, and we might never get home again."

Scott promised Carlisle he wouldn't go AWOL, but after he had spent his time in Woodland, he couldn't quite get himself to leave. After a week, his father asked how much time he had left and Scott told him the truth: He was already three days late.

"Well, boy, it's your hide," his father said. "You know them better than I do, but the longer you're over, the rougher it'll be. Better think about it."

Scott knew he had to go back, too. Not so much because the Navy would come looking for him, but Carlisle was still back with the ship, and Eddie was going to need looking after.

Still, before he left he wanted to talk to Vivian Cox about the future. He might not be coming back from the Pacific, but if he did, he wanted to know if she would wait for him. His father noticed him mooning around and guessed at the problem. "It's none of my business, but why don't you tell Vivian what the score is?"

Scott thought about it. Vivian had been over to the house more often than usual since he got home; maybe she was hoping he would ask. So he took her out again on a date and this time managed to blurt out the words. Her response was that she liked him a lot, too—but she didn't want to get "tied down" just then. "But we could date and write to each other," she suggested.

Suddenly, going back to the *Franklin* got easier as he figured there was nothing keeping him in Woodland anymore. He promised Vivian that he would write to her, but he wondered how much "dating" she thought they were going to do when he was in the Pacific getting shot at by Japs.

When Scott got back to the ship, he was sent to the brig—a small jail with several tiny cells on the fourth deck—for ten days while he waited to be brought to a Captain's Mast, a sort of mini-trial for minor offenses. He was offered the services of an officer to serve as his lawyer, but he figured that he was guilty and might as well throw himself on the mercy of the captain. Shoemaker gave him ten more days in the brig on rations of bread and water, except every third day when he would be given full rations.

Hot, stifling, and crowded, the brig was a miserable place to spend the better part of a month. But it gave Scott the chance to consider how he had been acting and where it had gotten him so far. Back when Pearl Harbor was bombed, he couldn't wait to enlist. But now that he was in the Navy, he was messing up. He decided that maybe the slackers were wrong; maybe he needed to buckle down and do what he was asked.

Besides, Eddie needed him. Scott was lying on his bunk one night, looking forward to his release from the brig the next day, when there was a loud crash from down the hall where the ladder leading to the third deck was located. He listened to the Marine who guarded the brig speak angrily to whoever was causing the commotion. Then he heard a familiar voice— though obviously one under the influence of alcohol—shout back.

"Goddamnit, my buddy's in there," Carlisle yelled, "and I'm gonna see him if I have to lick the whole goddam Marine Corps!"

The Marine guard told Carlisle to shut up. "Or I'll clobber you."

Scott figured he better intervene before Carlisle got hurt. He yelled to the guard to let his friend visit. "I'll get him to quiet down."

The Marine considered the options and agreed. "Okay, one minute, that's all," he said.

A moment later, Carlisle entered the brig crawling on his hands and knees. He had apparently made the most of the crew's last night of liberty in Norfolk before they shipped out. Scott reached through the bars of his cell and grabbed Carlisle under the arms and lifted him to his feet. "Ed, I'm getting out of here in the morning if you don't screw it up for me," he said.

Carlisle's face crumpled and tears began to flow down his cheeks. "Okay, Scotty, okay," he slurred. "Just remember I love ya."

Scott smiled and patted his friend on the shoulder. "Okay, Eddie," he said, turning him around and pointing him toward the door. "Now hit the sack, will you, and I'll see ya in the morning."

Carlisle staggered out of the brig and immediately fell over several trash cans in the passageway, which woke up the mess cooks who slept in a nearby compartment. They cursed the drunken sailor, who returned the invective. "Blow it out your seabags!" he yelled as he fumbled his way to the ladder and noisily climbed back to the third deck.

Scott lay back down on his bunk and thought about his loyal friend. *That Eddie*, he shook his head, *he's one helluva guy.*

After the ship stopped briefly in California, Scott noticed that one of the other men from the fire room, Sawaski, was sporting a new tattoo depicting a black cat—back arched, hair standing on end—perched on a large numeral 13. "What's that supposed to mean?" he asked.

Scott got a response typical for Sawaski, who ever since he had known him had contended that he wasn't "going anywhere on this pig iron bastard, much less the Pacific," though he had obviously made it that far. Now, he replied, "This pig iron sunnavabitch is too chicken-shit to be sunk. Got more luck in her guts than a nine-lived cat. And this here is CV-13 ain't it? Half of the crew's got the same tattoo."

The petty officers and other ranking enlisted men on in the fire room noticed Scott's new attitude. Every so often, Water Tender 1st Class John Frajman started telling Scott to knock off whatever menial cleaning job he was doing so that he could learn how the boilers worked.

A "regular Navy" man, "Shanghai" Frajman had served on China Station before the war. He would talk for hours about battling hordes of Chinese insurgents while on a "fury boat," one of the gunboats that patrolled the big rivers in China to protect American interests. He was a big, rugged guy and no threat to replace any of the leading men in Hollywood when it came to looks.

Initially, Scott had disliked him intensely. Now that he was getting to know Frajman, he still didn't like him all that much, but he respected him. The man knew everything there was to know about—as Frajman put it— "keeping this old tub moving."

Scott had to admit, "Shanghai" could be pretty funny. He had a nickname for everyone. Because Scott was also the name of a popular brand of toilet paper, Frajman decided that from there on out, he would be called "Shit-house." Max Nettnay was Maxine. Paul Betz was "Pauline." Two more sailors from Maine—Paul Dalton and Keith Roberts—became "Birdlegs" and "Chessy Cat." The former because he was skinny as a noodle, the latter because he was always leaning against something, loafing and smiling like the Cheshire cat.

The more Scott learned from the older hands like Frajman, the more he liked being a member of the Black Gang. He actually made water tender 3rd class, a real job with responsibilities, and felt reasonably safe in the warm environs of the fire room.

The big fear for the men working in the bottom of the ship once they entered the war were torpedoes. During General Quarters, they were locked down in their compartment with not much hope of getting out if they took a "fish" below the waterline. But for all that, Scott felt it was more dangerous up top.

Not all the danger was from the Japanese. Scott was on the flight deck one day between shifts, watching the planes land, when a Hellcat came in so hard that it bounced over the crash barrier. The fighter landed almost on top of an Airedale sitting on one of the small tractors they used to pull the planes around, and its still spinning propeller neatly lopped off his head.

Scott was struck by both the horror of the man's death and how quickly the flight crew recovered and went on about their business. The body was quickly removed, the blood washed over the side of the ship, and they were back in business. "Respot the flight deck, prepare for flight operations," said a voice over the loudspeaker. Apparently, the flight deck crew moved a little too slow responding, so the voice added, "Get the lead out of your asses!"

Another afternoon one of the other members of the Black Gang entered the fire room looking a little pale. He said he had been on the flight deck, watching some of the Airedales who were chatting near a parked Hellcat. A plane captain, a man responsible for making sure that a particular plane was in working order, was toying with the gun switches when he let off a quick burst. Three .50-caliber bullets tore into the stomach and upper thigh of a young Airedale who had been standing in front of the wing. There was nothing anybody could do to save him. "It must'a taken an hour for him to die," the shaken sailor said.

So far there had been no attacks by Japanese planes on the *Franklin*, but Scott worried about Carlisle being with a gun mount just off the flight deck. That was too dangerous for Scott's liking.

He and Carlisle knew they were lucky to be on the same ship. They were meeting lots of "swell fellas" like Berringer and Water Tender 2nd Class Lem Hall, a soft-spoken, redheaded boy from Virginia. But Eddie Carlisle remained his best friend, and they spent as much time together as their schedules would allow.

In the late afternoon of October 13, they had returned from chow and were talking in Eddie's compartment when Scott noticed that nobody else was around and asked his friend about it. Before his friend could answer, they both bolted upright at the sound of the five-inch guns going off. Then the forties.

"What the hell's goin' on?" Scott asked.

"Jeez, I don't know," Carlisle replied. "Ain't supposed to be any practicing around here. I better get the hell up on the gun!"

The two young men exited the compartment and took off running toward the stern of the ship to get up on the fantail. They climbed the ladder to the hangar deck and had just stepped through the hatch when they saw the Betty barreling in on the port side.

Carlisle ran for a ladder and began to scramble up to reach his gun on the flight deck. But Scott stayed to watch from the fantail. He could see tracers from a half dozen guns intersecting the plane but nothing seemed to faze it. A torpedo dropped from the plane's belly. He expected to see the bomber pull up, but it instead it kept coming—*right at me*, he thought.

Then the plane passed out of sight overhead, followed by a terrible racket from the flight deck that sounded as though some hopped-up Maine lumberjack was trying to chop his way through the wood. Scott spun to look off the other side of the hangar deck and saw what was left of the plane hurtle off the starboard edge of the ship. A mass of flames, it rocketed up and then turned over and roared down into the sea. *That guy was nuts,* he thought. He had no idea he was staring at the final act of desperation of a Japanese admiral and the beginning of a new way to wage war.

There was no time for anyone to think about the ramifications of what they had seen. Four more torpedo planes were barreling across the water, staggered at one-minute intervals. One was turned away by the fire from cruisers and destroyers trying to protect the aircraft carriers *Franklin, Enterprise, Belleau Wood,* and *Cabot.*

As another Betty homed in on the *Franklin,* fighter pilot A. J. Pope saw what was happening and pulled out of his landing pattern despite being almost out of fuel. Pope flew through the murderous fire of his own ships and shot the torpedo bomber out of the air before it could release its torpedo, and then got the hell out of there before his own guys knocked him down.

Another plane passed in front of the *Franklin* heading for one of the other aircraft carriers, but was blown from the sky by the ships' guns. The last pilot, however, dropped his torpedo on a perfect course to intercept the *Franklin.* Perhaps believing he'd done his damage there, he hedgehopped over the bow of the carrier and made for the *Enterprise,* which was steaming about a thousand yards away. The plane was between the two carriers so the gun crews of each ship had no choice but to fire in each other's direction, their shells raking the other with "friendly fire." The bomber made it about half way to the *Enterprise* before it was torn to pieces part way between the two ships.

Meanwhile, its torpedo ran straight and true, and if the Franklin had continued to move forward the fish would have hit the ship. But Shoemaker kept his cool. He ordered *Right, full rudder* and personally rang up, *Back full* on the starboard engines. Slowly, the mighty ship slowed, then stopped, and then reversed its course, picking up speed as the bow pulled away from the path of the torpedo, which passed within fifteen yards.

Smoke billowed from the flight deck of the *Franklin.* However, the damage looked much worse than it was.

The suicide plane had come in at too slight an angle to punch through the deck. As it hit, it bounced several times, its whirling propeller chewing up hunks of wood before the plane continued off the port side of the ship and crashed into the sea where its fuel continued to burn on the surface.

Other than a dozen hash marks from the propeller, quickly fixed by the ship's carpenters, the flight deck was hardly damaged. A plane had to be jettisoned over the side. But otherwise, they'd been lucky.

Naturally, the suicide attack was the talk of the ship that night. Some of the flight deck crew swore they could see inside the cockpit and knew the pilot was dead when he hit the ship. But his belly gunner, they claimed, kept shooting even after the plane skittered off the starboard side. Feeling the swagger of battle-tested veterans now, each man had his story of what he was doing when the attack came.

When Scott found Carlisle, he was still as white as a ghost. Carlisle recounted for him how he had gone up the first ladder and reached a platform about halfway to the flight deck and was about to climb the next ladder when he tripped and fell. Typical Eddie. This time, however, his clumsiness proved fortuitous.

"I could hear the bullets hitting the ship all around me. I closed my eyes, thinking, '*Oh, my God. This is it,*'" he told Scott. Then the plane and the bullets were past him; he opened his eyes and checked for damage. Finding none on his person, he picked himself up and went to look for where the bullets had struck. "I'd have been dead if I'd been on that other ladder."

Scott congratulated his friend on his clumsiness. Good ol' Eddie—always in the right place at the wrong time. He didn't know what he would do if something happened to his best pal, and he didn't want to think about it.

Everyone's favorite story was that of Lieutenant Winters, who said he saw the plane coming and knew that if he stayed on the signal officer's platform, he was going to get hit. So he took off running across the flight deck, the Betty hot on his tail. He heard the bullets plunking into the planking behind him and, at the last moment, dove face down.

The plane bounced off the deck, its left wing sheared off, the tip just brushing Winters as it went flying past. With near surgical precision, it had torn the seat out of his pants so that when he stood up and ran to the starboard side to see what happened to the plane, his rear end was exposed. Still, he had looked at the smoke and flames rising from the water, then turned to the bridge and gave a thumbs-up.

"Scratch another Betty!" he yelled as though he, or his derriere, had been responsible for its demise. The men told the story and retold it. Some took up a collection to pay for a tattoo on Winter's butt; they thought that a Japanese flag, like those painted on the side of a ship when it shot a plane down, would be appropriate. The lieutenant politely turned down their offer.

The next time the crew saw some of the guys from the *Enterprise,* they joshed them about having shot up the *Franklin's* hangar deck curtains when the fourth plane passed between the ships. The *Enterprise* crew countered that the *Franklin's* gunners had demolished a couple of their whaleboats. It was all good for a laugh, this time.

In all the excitement, there was one sobering note. Harold Stancil had been hit by the plane or a piece of flying debris and killed. He was buried at sea that evening, the first member of the *Franklin's* crew to die in combat.

Those who attended the services on the fantail, like his pal Frank Turner, watched the canvas bag holding Stancil's body slip from beneath the flag and wondered how many more such burials there might be before it was over. Turner had cut out a piece of the Betty's wing that showed the red meatball of the Rising Sun. How many more times would they lift their voices to sing the *U.S. Navy Hymn?*

> Eternal Father, strong to save,
> Whose arm doth bind the restless wave
> Who bidd'st the mighty ocean deep,
> Its own appointed limits keep;
> O hear us when we cry to thee
> For those in peril on the sea.

CHAPTER TEN

The Lucky Lady

October 16, 1944
Philippine Sea
USS Santa Fe

The "Jill" torpedo bomber fishtailed like a car on snow as the Japanese pilot swerved back and forth to throw off the aim of the gunners on the cruiser he had singled out. White tracers intersected the plane's path, and dozens of antiaircraft shells exploded in black puffs around it until there seemed to be no clear space through which the pilot could fly. Yet he kept coming while the gunners on the *Santa Fe* blasted away with everything they had—fives, forties, twenties. The booms, poms, and hammering blended into a continuous, discordant roar. Gunpowder smoke enveloped the ship as she ran, twisted, and turned at flank speed, her decks quivering from the pounding of her engines and guns.

I'm hitting him, Hardy thought. *Damnit, I know I'm hitting him.* A half dozen times at least, he had seen flashes on the plane after he had pulled the trigger on his four-barreled "quad" 40-millimeter. The forties were a big improvement over the one-point-ones he had manned on the doomed *Astoria* back in '42. But this plane was apparently impervious to the best efforts of a ship designed to stop aircraft with its guns and the latest radar.

At that moment, Hardy didn't need radar, or a lookout, to tell him where to locate the target. The enemy was right in front and ripping toward him at more than 280 miles an hour, firing its own guns and carrying a fourteen-foot-long torpedo.

The Jill was the second attacker the gun crews had had to fend off in the past five minutes. The first—a fast, twin-engined Japanese torpedo plane of a type they had never seen before—broke through the combat air patrol. After first making a run at the *Santa Fe*, the plane swerved to put a fish into the already wounded cruiser USS *Houston*, a thousand yards off the port beam.

Then this single-engine, Mitsubishi-built Jill slipped in and, skimming just above the waves, headed straight for the middle of the *Santa Fe's* starboard side. The plane was difficult to see—a dark circle for the nose and the thin lines for wings—against a gray sky and slate-colored ocean. Still, the radar-guided five-inch guns put so many shells around the plane that at times it looked like the Jill had been swallowed by a black cloud, only to emerge a moment later.

When the plane was three thousand yards out, Hardy and the other 40-millimeter gun directors on the starboard side were told to commence firing. The plane raced another thousand yards and the twenties opened up. The ocean in front, beneath, and behind the plane was turned into a frothing cauldron by the flying steel, some of which had to be passing through the plane. And still it kept coming.

Several hundred yards out, the pilot released his torpedo. Men onboard the ship watched in horrified fascination as the white arrow of the weapon's wake streaked beneath the surface toward them.

Hardy was so busy he didn't see the torpedo drop, though he heard about it over his headset. He had no time to worry about it; he had to try to stop the plane, which instead of veering away or rising to pass over the top of the ship stayed on course. The guns were having some effect; a moment after the torpedo fell, flames appeared beneath the fuselage of the plane. But neither the bullets nor the flames deterred the pilot.

As Hardy fired, the ship swung hard to port, steering away from the onrushing plane and torpedo. The plane fell astern, but Hardy followed it in the viewfinder and kept shooting until the brake that prevented the gun from turning too far and firing into the aft superstructure stopped him. He lost sight of the plane.

Suddenly, the Jill roared past him, heading in the same direction as the ship. The bomber passed Hardy's position at eye level, a mass of flames starting from just behind the cockpit. It passed so close that he thought a wingtip might touch the ship. He could see the face of the pilot—the man was looking forward, his eyes fixed on the bow as if he were trying to outrace the ship to some finish line ahead.

Before Hardy could recover to shoot again, the plane sped around the forward superstructure and out of his sight. A moment later, he ducked at the sound of a large explosion from the stern. A few heartbeats ticked away, and then there was another explosion near the bow and oily black smoke began pouring back over the ship. He heard men screaming from that direction.

Up to this point, he and the rest of the crew had thought of the *Santa Fe* as a lucky ship. It was the blessed water from the river in New Mexico, according to the superstitious older hands who had changed their original opinion. But Hardy figured that her luck had just run out.

Even among the other crews of the fleet, the *Santa Fe* had a reputation for getting in and out of hot spots without a scratch. In fact, CruDiv13 as a whole—the *Santa Fe, Birmingham,* and *Mobile*—all seemed to be sailing, as the sailors like to say when wishing each other well, with "fair winds and a following sea." Except for the attack when the *Birmingham* got hit near Bougainville—causing only minor damage and one fatality—they had all escaped harm.

Yet, of the three, the *Santa Fe* had been in on every engagement in the Central Pacific campaign and had her share of brushes with potential disaster. There was only one tragedy to mar her perfect record. When her crew suffered its first losses, the sea was responsible, not the Japanese. The ship spent most of May in the Marshalls, anchoring in the Kwajalein lagoon between excursions, at which time she had passed the 100,000-mile mark, enough to have circled the Earth more than four times.

The ship was anchored at Kwajalein one afternoon when three hundred crewmembers were allowed to go ashore for a few hours liberty. An LCI (Landing Craft Infantry) was assigned to carry the men to the shore; however, for reasons never made clear, the boat's pilot stopped a hundred yards out and told the sailors to get out and swim.

The men clambered over the side and began to make their way through the chest-deep water, but a strong tide was flowing away from the shore and carried some men off into deeper water. The muggy tropical air soon filled with desperate calls for help. When heads were later counted on the beach, three men had drowned.

The sailors were buried in the island's military cemetery, a sobering experience for the other young men, who had to that point escaped war's worst aspects. But the superstitious among them pointed out that the drownings weren't combat deaths, they didn't count against the *Santa Fe*'s luck.

Following the Great Marianas Turkey Shoot in June, the cruiser division had been assigned to Task Group 58.1, with its brand new carrier *Franklin*.

They had joined in the fireworks at Iwo Jima on the Fourth of July, closing on the island to shell Japanese air installations.

There the ship's luck had extended to its aviators. They had wrapped up the bombardment when the Kingfisher flown by Lt. Bill Henderschot came tearing around from the other side of Mount Suribachi. On his tail were three Zeros, each of them jockeying to get into position behind the plane to shoot it down.

Henderschot dove and dodged to escape the Zekes, which poured bullets after the little seaplane. But by all logic, and the expectations of the *Santa Fe's* crew, who could see the events unfolding, the pilot and his radioman, Art "Granny" Hickman, should have died. The Kingfisher was slower, less maneuverable, and had much less firepower than a Zero, one of the finest planes of the war.

Hickman knew it too and threw back the canopy and stood up in the plane with his .30-caliber machine gun. When a Zeke lined up for the kill, he emptied the gun into the Japanese plane. He had intended it to be a last great act of defiance, but to his surprise, as well as everyone else's, the fighter burst into flames and crashed into the ocean. The remaining Zeros were finished off by the ships' guns and the combat air patrol.

Henderschot landed the Kingfisher as the crew of the *Santa Fe* cheered. But its pontoons had been shot so full of holes, the plane sank almost immediately. The two soggy—but happy to be alive—aviators were fished out of the sea by a destroyer.

August 4, 1944
Chichi Jima

The *Santa Fe* and her sister ships in the division certainly brought a different sort of luck to the enemy. With the weather growing worse, the carrier planes were grounded, so the division and a squadron of destroyers were sent to hunt for the Japanese convoy trying to escape the Bonins. That led to a long stern chase through rough seas at thirty knots, the ships and men taking a pounding as they crashed through the waves.

With daylight nearly gone at about 7:30 P.M., radar picked up what appeared to be a light cruiser or large Japanese destroyer up ahead nine miles. The ship seemed to be hanging back, waiting for the pursuers.

The *Santa Fe* was leading the pack when the cruisers opened up on the Japanese vessel, which turned in S-shapes at twenty-eight knots trying to avoid the barrages. Several times, the Japanese captain wheeled to rush back toward his pursuers, who had to then drop back to stay out of his torpedo range. When he got close enough, he let loose a salvo from his guns; the fire was light but fairly accurate, splashing into the water around the cruisers.

As the firing and maneuvering continued, Captain Jerauld Wright addressed the crew over the public address system, informing them of what was going on. Occasionally in the past, Admiral DuBose had also addressed the crew, so the crew wasn't surprised this time when he also talked to them about the chase. "He's a good skipper," the admiral said, complimenting the Japanese captain. "He's hanging back to protect the other ships."

The Japanese were game for a fight. But their ship didn't have the fire-power of its pursuers, who could stand off and shell them from a safe distance. More than an hour after the shooting started, the Japanese destroyer was all but done in. She was limping along at ten knots, absorbing hit after hit as the cruisers used their superior radar to pinpoint the ship's location in the dark.

At last, DuBose ordered the destroyers ahead to finish off the vessel. They rushed in but soon reported that the enemy ship had slipped beneath the waves before they could close for the kill. All there was left to do was fish a few survivors out of the dark, wind-whipped seas for interrogation. They identified the ship as the *Matsu* and said that most of the crew of more than a hundred men had gone down with the ship, including seventy young midshipmen from the Japanese Naval Academy on their first cruise.

The *Santa Fe's* crew never saw the destroyer they sank, or the sailors treading water. So they didn't have to linger over the images of the men, most of them about the same age, or even younger, who were left to their fates in an uncaring sea. The hard fact of naval warfare, especially in the Pacific, was that the winner sailed on, the losers rarely were rescued.

With the Japanese destroyer out of the way, the hunters set off after the rest of the convoy, which was soon caught. By the time it was over, the *Santa Fe* was credited with sinking the *Matsu*, as well as a large landing barge filled with troops, who were also left to struggle in the water, two cargo ships, and two supply barges. The division and accompanying destroyers pursued the convoy to within 350 miles of mainland Japan, the closest a surface ship had been since the war began. The crew was relieved when they finally turned back and put more distance between themselves and the Land of the Rising Sun.

The next morning, the *Santa Fe* and her sisters were back with the task group off Chichi Jima. With the air groups still prisoners of the weather, the cruiser division moved in to blockade the harbor and blast away at the ships that remained trapped inside. As she passed across the mouth of the harbor, shells from a large gun on a mountainside straddled the *Santa Fe*. Captain Wright immediately gave orders to take evasive maneuvers before the Japanese gunners, who had the range, put a shot between the first two. Then the ship's main battery opened up on the shore installation. When the smoke and dust cleared, the Japanese gun had been silenced.

Once again the ship's good luck had held. They had dodged planes, mines, torpedoes, and shore batteries all without losing a man.

September 9, 1944
Bislig Bay, Philippines

Back at Eniwetok, following the raids in the Bonins, the Fifth Fleet and Task Force 58 were renamed the Third Fleet and Task Force 38, respectively, and placed under the command of "Bull" Halsey. CruDiv 13—the *Santa Fe, Birmingham,* and *Mobile*—was assigned to Task Group 38.3. Their primary duty was to protect and support the aircraft carriers *Langley, Essex, Princeton,* and *Lexington,* all new since the war and two named for ships that had been sunk during it.

The men were sorry to see Admiral Raymond Spruance relieved. Halsey had a good reputation for being a "fighting admiral" coming out of the campaign in the Solomons. However, he was also seen as more impetuous and careless, where Spruance kept his cool and carefully analyzed problems before committing men to danger.

Under Halsey the Third Fleet went after the Carolines, the main objective being to secure the use of the Ulithi atoll, with its enormous lagoon, as the fleet's staging area for the invasion of the Philippines. Everyone knew that the battle for the Philippines would be a bad one. The archipelago was defended by nearly a hundred thousand Japanese soldiers, thousands of aircraft, and was within reach of the Japanese fleet and the airfields on Formosa, Okinawa, and Japan itself. There were many in the American military establishment—including Nimitz—who questioned the military necessity of taking the Philippines instead of proceeding right to the Bonins and Japan. But MacArthur had threatened Roosevelt with dire public backlash if he "abandoned" the Philippines. So the decision to go ahead with the invasion was made, with the Third Fleet assigned to support the general's plans.

On the morning of September 9, carrier planes attacking the Philippine island of Mindanao spotted a convoy of forty Japanese supply ships sneaking along the coast, hoping to avoid detection. By the time the American planes ran low on fuel and had to return to the carriers, eighteen of the Japanese ships were sunk or burning. The *Santa Fe* and *Birmingham,* in the company of four destroyers, were sent to finish the rest.

When the warships arrived shortly before noon, the remaining twenty-two ships were attempting to hide in two small bays. This was the first time anyone from the surface fleet had actually seen the Philippines since the spring of 1942, but they weren't there to sightsee.

At first the American cruisers and destroyers passed back and forth across the mouths of the two bays, pumping shells into the enemy ships. Then they entered the bays and closed the range—sometimes to within a couple hundred yards—so that even the 40- and 20-millimeter gun crews could shoot. The Japanese ships were only lightly armed and attempts to shoot back were met with overwhelming firepower.

The annihilation of the convoy was merciless and complete. But any remorse about the plight of the Japanese sailors was tempered by the knowledge that the supplies carried by those ships would have been used to help kill American soldiers and sailors.

There wasn't a lot of sympathy anyway for an enemy who, if the stories coming from spies and escapees from the Philippine prison camps were true, sent defenseless men on death marches and had committed the wholesale murders of prisoners, military and civilian alike. The bitterness ran so deep that the Marines on one of the 20-millimeter crews threw "Joe cups," coffee mugs, at Japanese sailors struggling in the spilled fuel oil of their sinking vessels.

The Americans pounded away at the trapped ships for nearly two hours until each was either a pillar of smoke and fire or a tomb on the bottom of the bay. By the time it was over, the *Santa Fe* had fired 1,789 rounds of six- and five-inch shells, as well as thousands more from the forties and twenties. Her guns had raked fifteen different ships; four of them sank immediately and three were left burning fiercely. The *Birmingham* and the destroyers accounted for the remaining ships.

A few survivors were plucked from the water for questioning. They said they had been trying to get from Japan to their destination in the southern

Philippines for more than three months, running from port to port and hiding during the day to avoid detection. They seemed relieved that the journey, and the war, was over for them.

The war, however, wasn't over for the *Santa Fe* crew, who got little rest
over the next month. They had refueled at sea on the tenth, and then headed
back to Mindanao for more shelling. On the twelfth, four more battleships—
the *Alabama, Massachusetts, Washington,* and *Indiana*—joined the task force.
The brass was concerned that while the Japanese carriers were ineffective,
the Japanese surface fleet was still formidable, led by the "unsinkable" super
battleships the *Yamato* and *Musashi.* No one knew when they would appear,
but sooner or later they would come out and fight.

October 2–15, 1944
Philippine Sea

From the harassment of the Japanese in the Philippines to the bombardment
duties during the invasion of Peleliu and back to the Philippines again, the
Santa Fe was constantly on the move. But finally, on October 2 she steamed
into the Ulithi lagoon for a breather and supplies. The crew looked forward
to liberty, just to feel solid ground again, even if it was on a miserable little
bit of coral. But their hopes were dashed when fleet aerologists reported that
a typhoon was on the way and expected to hit Ulithi. The fleet was told to
move out. If they tried to ride out the storm in the lagoon, their anchors
might not hold and they would risk foundering or crashing into one another
without much room to maneuver.

The *Santa Fe* quickly finished loading its "bullets, bolts, and beans" and
was gone again in a few hours. The fleet tried to outrun the storm and generally succeeded, though there were frightening hours spent fighting through
monstrous waves that submerged the weather decks and rolled the ships
to precarious angles.

On October 10 the fleet had recovered from the storm and moved into
position to attack the airfields and other installations on Formosa, Okinawa,
and the Philippines. The Japanese fought back. Just after sunset on the
twelfth, radar operators reported dozens of enemy planes approaching the
fleet. Their tactic this time was to light up the ocean with flares and then
attack the task groups from a variety of directions.

The *Santa Fe* saw little action, as the Japanese concentrated on other task
groups. Most of the night, her lookouts watched the distant flash of guns,

the night sky occasionally punctuated by a distant burst of orange flame and a meteor streaking down into the dark ocean as planes were shot down one after another. Still, it didn't stop Tokyo Rose from boasting about "twenty thousand U.S. sailors sent swimming."

On the thirteenth, the Japanese finally attained a limited success. First the carriers *Franklin* and *Belleau Wood* were hit, which caused a stir among senior officers all the way up to Halsey's staff when they heard about the manner of the attacks. Apparently, the pilots had not tried to escape after launching their torpedoes, but intentionally crashed their planes into the flight decks of the carriers, as though that was what they had intended from the outset. However, Halsey and the others decided that the "suicide attacks" must have been the work of a couple of zealots, an aberration.

Later that evening the Japanese attacked in a more traditional manner. One of them put a torpedo into the USS *Canberra,* which was taken under tow by another cruiser. The *Santa Fe's* division and a half dozen destroyers were assigned to escort the two stricken cruisers to the Ulithi atoll. Under tow the group could make only four knots. Fortunately, the admirals were thoughtful enough to include the light carrier USS *Cabot* to provide air cover.

The next day, the Japanese broke from their nighttime pattern by attacking in the morning with dozens of planes. The ashen sky was soon swarming with fighters and bombers locked in deadly struggles. The cruisers and destroyers ran in circles around their charges, blowing black smoke from the smokestacks—created by cutting off oxygen to the burners—to make it difficult for an enemy pilot to get a good look at the targets.

The *Cabot's* fighter planes kept the Japanese at bay until nightfall, when a torpedo plane broke through and made a run at the *Canberra.* The plane had nearly reached the point where it would release its torpedo at the helpless ship when the *Santa Fe's* guns caught up to it and sent the plane crashing into the sea in flames. The attacks continued until near midnight. A dozen Japanese planes had been shot down, though with so many ships shooting, only the *Santa Fe* was officially credited with a kill.

The cruisers and destroyers had fended off the enemy, the *Canberra* was still afloat and the job of towing her was handed off to a fleet tugboat while the warships continued their protective circling. However, they were soon joined by the cruiser *Houston,* which had been struck by a torpedo and two bombs during the night while screening for another task group. The new addition was listing to starboard, with only about three feet showing above the hungry Pacific, and wallowed like a pig in mud behind the USS *Boston,* a heavy cruiser that had her under tow.

If the *Santa Fe* was a lucky ship, others were the opposite. The saying went that some ships "couldn't get out of port without getting hit." Even some names seemed unlucky; two good examples were the *Canberra* and the *Houston,* both of which had been named for ships sunk earlier in the war.

At four knots, the convoy was an easy target. A long, telltale slick of fuel oil stretched back toward Formosa, a greasy dark finger pointing straight at them even in rough seas. The Japanese redoubled their efforts, but they were rebuffed again by the defenders, which had been joined by more destroyers and another light carrier, the USS *Cowpens.*

The plight of the stricken cruisers and their shepherds gave the American admirals an idea. The night after the *Houston* was hit, Tokyo Rose had come on the air to boast, of course, of another great victory for the Imperial Japanese Navy. This time she announced the "annihilation" of the Third Fleet. Twenty carriers and most of their supporting cast had been sunk, she said. The sea was awash in smoldering wrecks and doomed sailors.

Onboard the "sunk" ships and smoldering wrecks, the young men laughed and shook their heads. *What would she come up with next? Good thing she played great music.* But the American brass thought that maybe the Japanese would believe their own propaganda and, with the right enticement, make a mistake. They decided to use the *Canberra* and *Houston,* as well as their escorts, as a bait force to lure the Japanese into committing their air corps and surface ships to finishing off the supposedly devastated Third Fleet. Once they took the bait, the fleet would rise from the ashes and pounce.

In the meantime, the bait force would be sitting ducks. The cripples wouldn't even be able to take evasive action, but it wasn't just the cripples that would be in danger. Although the *Santa Fe* and her fellow guardians steamed around the slow-moving convoy at twenty knots, their overall forward progress was no faster than the *Canberra* and *Houston.* If the Japanese fleet or its submarines found one, they would find them all.

The crew of the *Santa Fe* took their designation as one piece of the bait being offered to the Japanese with good humor. A ship's painter drew a large hook and worm on the second smokestack until an admiral sent a message by semaphore demanding that it be removed.

The plan almost worked. On October 15, Japanese battleships and cruisers steamed out of their ports, while their jubilant airmen got ready to assist in the slaughter of the remnants of the Third Fleet. However, a Japanese scout plane missed the bait fleet and found the real fleet instead and warned headquarters in time. The Imperial Navy turned tail and ran from the ships that Tokyo Rose claimed had been sunk.

However, that had not stopped the Japanese air corps from continuing to try to reach the stricken ships and their escorts. They attacked in waves, their tactic since Pearl Harbor. Their officers knew that most would be shot down by the American combat air patrol, but one or two or three might make it through to strike a telling blow. It was almost suicidal to attack the American fleet, but not quite.

On the morning of October 16, the captain of the *Houston* asked to transfer two hundred nonessential personnel to the *Santa Fe,* just in case something went wrong. When they came aboard, a half dozen members of the *Houston*'s Marine contingent begged to be allowed to man one of the *Santa Fe*'s 20-millimeter gun mounts, in case the "dirty Japs" came back for their ship. Captain Wright understood the sentiment and allowed them to take over a gun position on the bow.

All morning long, the *Cowpens'* and *Cabot*'s fighter pilots kept the Japanese attackers away. But the *Santa Fe*'s crew was getting jittery. They hadn't had much sleep over the past few days. It seemed that every time they closed their eyes, the General Quarters alarm would sound. Even when Captain Wright relaxed the posture to Condition 3, meaning most of the crew was free to go about their normal duties or relax for a few minutes, the gun and fire control crews remained on duty, red-rimmed eyes scanning the skies, trying to differentiate between friend and foe.

That afternoon, a "Frances," a new type of twin-engine Japanese torpedo bomber, evaded the combat air patrol and plunged through the antiaircraft fire heading first for the *Santa Fe.* The plane was faster than the task group's gunners were used to—the Japanese apparently were not so beaten as to have stopped developing new weapons—and it threw their aim off. But the pilot was driven off, or perhaps noticed an easier target, and changed his trajectory toward the *Houston.*

The crew on the *Santa Fe* watched with horrified fascination as the torpedo dropped from the plane and raced for the *Houston.* The plane sped beyond the ship and was gone with the ink spots from the five-inch shells polka-dotting the sky well astern of the fleeing bomber. A few moments later the torpedo struck near the stern of the *Houston,* from which a sixty-foot-high ball of flame erupted. But there was no time to respond to the stricken ship, as a Jill torpedo plane suddenly appeared over the wave tops, heading straight for the starboard side of the *Santa Fe.*

The sky swarmed with racing black specks of torpedo planes and dive-bombers as Cpl. Fred P. "Andy" Anderson swung his 20-millimeter machine gun, trying to catch up to the streaking aircraft. He stood behind the gun, which was on the port fantail of the *Santa Fe,* strapped into a leather harness. As he fired, his body shook with the recoil of the gun—the 20-millimeter could go through a sixty-round magazine in thirty seconds.

As soon he emptied a magazine, his loader, Pfc. Paul Yeager, who was standing on his right, yanked it out and slapped in another. Standing next to Anderson on his left was the trunnion operator, Pfc Fritz Huebner, who raised and lowered the gun. When Anderson needed to shoot high, Huebner would raise the gun so that Anderson could crouch under it to get maximum elevation on his gun's barrel; or, conversely, Huebner would lower the gun so that Anderson could stand upright and depress the barrel to shoot low.

Suddenly, the ship swung hard to port, kicking up a surging wall of wake. Anderson looked over his shoulder and saw the reason—a Jill torpedo bomber coming in low on the starboard side. He spun his gun around so that he was shooting across the fantail at the plane, which dropped its torpedo. Every gun on the ship seemed to be ripping into the plane—literally shredding pieces into the air—as it flew. But the plane wasn't stopping.

The middle of a war seemed an odd place for a young man born in Friendship, Tennessee, a small farming community, in October 1917. Fred Anderson was the fourth child and third son of Frank Anderson, a carpenter, and Ora Hill Anderson. Times were tough even before the Depression for the entire Anderson clan. Frank's father sold horse-drawn buggies and was slowly being squeezed out of business by automobiles. Nor was carpentry paying the bills. So in 1922, Frank moved his wife and children to the big city of Memphis, where he started a new life as an ironworker.

After graduation from South Side High School in 1937, Anderson hired on at the newly opened Firestone Tire and Rubber Co. plant. There he worked on the assembly line for thirty-two cents an hour, a tidy sum that paid for the 1937 Lafayette he drove. The girls found him charming—with an engaging, chipped-tooth smile—including fourteen-year-old Leta Fay Thompson, the cousin of one of Anderson's friends. She met him in the early spring of 1942 when she came to Memphis to visit her relatives, though of course she was too young for anything except the exchange of pleasantries and developing a schoolgirl crush.

Older girls and cars had to be put on hold when Anderson enlisted in the United States Marine Corps in June 1942. He knew he was going to be drafted and didn't want to surrender to the whims of the Army. Having seen the 1936 film *Pride of the Marines,* starring Charles Bickford, he had decided he wanted to do his fighting with "the best."

Anderson arrived for boot camp at the Marine Corps base at Parris Island, South Carolina, aboard a bus with other recruits. At the base front gate, they passed another bus heading in the opposite direction filled with Marines who had just finished their training. Most of them were on their way to the vicious battles in the Pacific, but when they saw the new recruits, they were the ones yelling, "You'll be *sorrrrreeeee!*"

Boot camp was every bit of hell he thought it would be. But when Anderson volunteered for sea school—a plum post for Marines assigned to naval vessels—his request was granted. The Marines had been a part of the Navy since their creation in 1775, serving as both a landing force and as guards and gunners aboard ships. By the 1940s, those who assaulted the beaches were part of the fleet marine force, otherwise known as "grunts." Those who served on the ships were the seagoing marines, who served as orderlies for captains, guarded prisoners, and manned antiaircraft guns. They had been nicknamed "seagoing bellhops," by sailors, who were kidding them about their assignment of standing guard outside the captain's cabin when the ship was in port.

After the twelve-week boot camp was finished, "Andy," as he was known to his Marine buddies, was sent to the school in Portsmouth, Virginia, where he was introduced to life aboard a man-of-war, learning the customs and terminology of the U.S. Navy. Then it was on to Philadelphia for Anderson and Paul Yeager, a friend he had met in boot camp, to join the crew of a new cruiser, the USS *Santa Fe.* They were told that as part of the ship's first crew, they were plank owners, ostensibly one of the owners of the teakwood planks covering the weather deck.

So far from family and friends, Anderson, like many of his shipmates, fastened on to anything from home. Therefore, he had been pleasantly surprised one day after the ship returned to Pearl Harbor after the Aleutians campaign. He and some of the other Marines were leaning over the rail inspecting some of the new Marine recruits lined up on the dock when he recognized one as a young man he had seen around the Firestone Plant in Memphis. He and Pfc. Walter "Whit" Whitby were soon fast friends—sometimes in the middle of the Pacific it was fun just to recall a particular street or an old hangout with someone who knew what he was talking about.

By the same token, he kept a photograph of Leta Thompson taped to the inside of the locker door. She had started writing to him after he shipped out, not as a girlfriend but because it was a common, "patriotic thing to do." When convoys of servicemen on the way to the front passed through the towns and cities of America, girls would stand on the curb and both parties would throw their addresses to each other. Many a romance was born in such a manner, but Leta was just a teenaged pen pal, someone who could give him the familiar news from home.

He had to admit that duty onboard a ship was pretty nice by comparison to what many other Marines were enduring. But there was certainly no foxhole to jump into on October 16, 1944, when the Jill raged in toward the *Santa Fe,* letting loose a torpedo that streaked toward the ship.

Through the sight of his smoking gun, Anderson saw the shredded torpedo plane roar past, its engine still revving but clearly on its last legs as the pilot tried to turn to keep up with the ship. An enormous explosion in the ship's wake sent an immense geyser of smoke and water into the air. But the Marine kept tracking the plane and shooting until the bomber disappeared forward beyond the superstructure. Then there was another explosion and a ball of flame rose from the bow.

Oh no, he thought, *we're hit!* He wondered how bad the damage was and if they would have to abandon ship. He had expected to feel more of a jarring blow—but then, the *Santa Fe* had never been hit before, so he didn't know.

Observers on other ships saw the torpedo drop and the plane trying to crash into the cruiser. There was an explosion and then another. The bow of the *Santa Fe* disappeared in a wall of flames and a huge plume of black smoke. They all knew then that her luck had run out. Then the cruiser materialized from the smoke, steaming hard, still twisting and turning like a saddle bronc at a rodeo and apparently unscathed.

It seemed like a miracle, but what they had just witnessed was a magnificent piece of seamanship by Captain Wright. He had turned the stern *into* the approaching torpedo so that the wall of wake caused by the churning propellers detonated the warhead.

At the same time, by ringing up *all ahead full* on the starboard propellers and *full back* on the port, Wright swung the bow of the ship away from the onrushing plane fast enough that the damaged Jill couldn't keep up. The plane just barely missed and crashed into the sea slightly ahead of the bow and where the ship would have been without such a radical maneuver.

Still, the *Santa Fe* did not escape entirely. The bomber struck the water just a few feet from the foc'sle. Its momentum splashed flaming gasoline over the 20-millimeter gun manned by the Marines from the *Houston,* as well as over several members of the ship's crew and Marines who had stayed to watch the crew. A half dozen men were turned into human torches.

Crewmembers rushed forward to their aid; one of those was seventeen-year-old Aviation Machinist's Mate 2nd Class Al Mancini. While others bitched and moaned about the Navy, Mancini loved every minute of it. He wasn't half as afraid of the Japanese as he was of his mother, even two years after he snuck into the service, pulling the pin on his naval career. He regularly sent her money—in part because he was a good son, and partly to show her how well he was doing.

In return, Angela Mancini sent her son food. He didn't have the heart to tell her that perishables like Italian pepperoni sausages were spoiled by the time they arrived in the tropics. "The guys and I loved it," he wrote when she would ask if he enjoyed the food.

Other than living in fear of being discovered, life couldn't have been better as far as he was concerned. Sure there were some unpleasant moments, like the hideous flies that had swarmed all over the ship when they had anchored off Saipan in August, but the guys on the ship were his family now.

Mancini had even managed to finagle his way onto the crew that took care of the seaplanes and thought he had died and gone to heaven. The transfer occurred just before the July 4 attack on Iwo Jima. He had watched the whole battle between the Zeros and the Kingfisher, sure that he was about to see one of his beloved planes—and its crew—blasted from the sky. When Art Hickman instead hit one of the Zeros, Mancini had jumped around with his pals as if the little seaplane had knocked down an entire squadron.

In the interim, he had learned a lot about planes and how they operated, so he couldn't believe that the Jill was still flying when it went soared past where he was standing. Fire had stripped the plane down to where he could see the ribs of its airframe, but the pilot somehow managed to keep it under control.

Mancini felt the explosion that lifted the ship in the stern, even as he watched the plane disappear up beyond the bow. Another explosion ripped the air, which was suddenly filled with black, acrid smoke that hurt his eyes and throat. Because his battle station was now with the repair crew on the weather deck near the bridge, he was one of the first to arrive on the foc'sle. He recognized the first injured man he came to, a shipmate named Al Lamprin, who had been badly burned and was lying on the deck in agony, his clothes still smoking.

"Duck, help me," Lamprin said, reaching up and calling Mancini by his nickname.

Mancini reached down and grabbed his friend by his forearms, only to have the young man's blackened skin come off in his hands. For the first time, Al wished he were back home in Greenwich.

•

The flames were doused on the foc'sle and the injured men taken to sick bay, but there was little time for the *Santa Fe's* crew to reflect on the miracle of their delivery. For the remainder of the day, the Japanese kept coming, trying to finish the job they had started on the *Canberra* and the *Houston,* which stayed afloat even after the second torpedo. However, between the ships' guns and the combat air patrol, no more planes made it through the screen.

At sunset the raids stopped. The gray skies were for the moment free of danger when the *Santa Fe's* crew participated in her first burial at sea; one of the *Houston's* Marines had died from his burns.

Only afterward did the crew have time to rehash the day's events. Every man seemed to have a story about the "crazy Jap" pilot who tried to crash his plane into the ship. They hoped that there weren't many more like him around. On the other hand, the men's estimation of Captain Wright increased considerably. He had kept most of them out of harm's way, and that gave them the confidence he would do it again when the time came.

The old salts noted again that there had still not been a combat fatality among the crew—the Marine who died (and another who would follow by the next morning) had been from the *Houston.* The *Santa Fe* was still the luckiest ship in the Navy, they said. She was, as she became known to the fleet, the Lucky Lady.

CHAPTER ELEVEN

A Taste of War

October 15, 1944
USS Franklin

Hopping down from the wing of the Hellcat, Aviation Coxswain Frank Turner gave a thumbs-up to the pilot he had been talking to as the plane's engine warmed up. The noise on the flight deck was deafening as several dozen other pilots revved the engines of their planes amid a cloud of blue exhaust smoke.

Running to the port side of the ship near the deck-edge, or No. 2, elevator, Turner jumped down four feet onto the catwalk and turned around to watch the planes depart.

After taking a pounding the day before, the Japanese had regrouped and changed their tactics, attacking the fleet in the morning. Thanks to radar, however, the combat air patrol was ready for them and the initial waves of attackers were dispersed or shot down.

All morning long, the gray sky was slashed with vapor trails of dueling planes, punctuated by exclamation-point trails of darker smoke where planes had plummeted into the ocean. But the bogeys never got close to the ships, and Turner was confident the CAP would keep the Japs at bay during daylight hours, though after the torpedo plane attack on the thirteenth, it was no longer a sure thing in anyone's mind.

In the meantime, the task group was hitting Manila again 150 miles to the west. By 10:30 A.M., the *Franklin* had already launched one deck load of planes, and the second was ready to go. Turner wanted them out of there with no problems. This was the dangerous time for the ship. She was running in a straight line, and almost half of her complement of planes was on the flight deck, fully armed and filled with high-octane aviation fuel.

"Attention on deck! Cut your engines! They're coming in!" Once again, the voice of Cmdr. Joe Taylor on the loudspeakers jolted Turner into searching the skies. About the same time, someone nearby shouted, "Look up!" He did and saw three dive-bombers plunging down toward the ship. He didn't need to hear the roar of Big Ben's guns—seemingly all firing at once until the whole ship was shaking like a building in an earthquake—or the sudden heeling over as the ship began evasive maneuvers to know the planes weren't American.

Turner signaled to the pilot to cut his engine and pointed up. The pilot did as told and jumped out of his plane and ran across the deck for the island structure. Two other plane spotters who had been standing with Turner took off running—one heading aft on the catwalk, the other for a hatch opening leading from the walkway into the hangar. Frank followed on his heels.

The first plane panicked in the face of the antiaircraft fire and dropped his bomb from too high up. It landed in the water, well short of the carrier, as the pilot fled only to be shot down by the combat air patrol. The other two planes bore down through the antiaircraft fire. The second plane's bomb just missed off the starboard side, shaking the ship.

As he reached the hatch opening, Turner felt, rather than saw, the third bomb go past where they had been standing. With a massive roar, a searing blast tossed him into space.

When the bugle call for General Quarters sounded and the guns erupted, AMM 2nd Class Edwin Garrison and another aviation metalsmith, Henry Long, crouched behind a large machine, part of the arresting cable gear, near the portside edge of the hangar deck. When a bomb exploded in the water some distance from the ship, Long took a pack of cigarettes, Chesterfields, from his shirt pocket and offered one.

Garrison shook his head. "Nah, I quit," he yelled above the din of the guns. It didn't surprise him that they were under attack again—the Philippines were going to be hell to take back. On Manus, he had talked with one of the *Franklin's* medical corpsmen, who had just returned to the ship after picking up supplies on the island. The corpsman said he had been shown a ten-thousand-bed field hospital, row after row of neatly made-up cots. But the spooky thing was, the corpsman confided, there was no one in the beds, the medical staff was just getting ready for the invasion.

Knowing the invasion was coming, the Japanese seemed to be increasingly desperate, at least to a sailor like Garrison. Two days ago, he had been on the hangar deck on the other side of the ship when the torpedo planes attacked. He was watching the fourth plane that had hopped over the bow and was heading for the *Belleau Wood* when a friend of his, C. J. Sangster, hurried by.

"Hey, where you going?" Garrison shouted.

Sangster pulled up short and looked back. "Battle stations," he yelled.

At that moment, an errant stream of 20-millimeter bullets from the light carrier *San Jacinta,* which was shooting at the plane, ripped into the *Franklin's* steel plating a few yards beyond Sangster. His eyes got bigger when he realized that if he hadn't stopped to answer Garrison, he would have been torn in half. He grinned. "Thanks for saving my life!" he shouted and ran on.

Now, two days later, Garrison was wondering if he was going to need someone to save his life when a second bomb exploded in the water on the starboard side. The blast made the entire ship shudder. "I'll take that cigarette," he said. He lit the Chesterfield and stuck it in his mouth.

That's when the third bomb struck the edge of the No. 2 elevator. It continued down and exploded just as it hit the waterline next to the ship. Although two hundred feet from the explosion, the concussion blew the cigarette out of Garrison's mouth. But he didn't have time to go looking for it.

Flying pieces of metal split open the gas tanks of several of the planes on the hangar deck. Fuel poured out and immediately caught fire.

Garrison and Long rushed out from their hiding place and, grabbing a fire hose, began trying to wash the flaming liquid overboard. Their task was made more difficult and dangerous, however, due to the motion of the ship. The *Franklin* was still zigzagging through evasive maneuvers. When it tilted away from the men with the hose, it was relatively easy to wash the flaming liquid off the side of the ship; but when the ship leaned in their direction, they found themselves running for their lives from the flames.

Every time it looked like they were making ground, the ship would turn the other way and they had to run. On one of those occasions, Garrison took refuge behind a bulkhead and spotted a telephone. He picked it up and called up to the bridge. "Do you think you could put the ship into a turn long enough for us to wash the fire overboard?" he asked.

"Sure can," was the reply. A moment later, Garrison had to brace himself as the ship turned so hard that he wondered if the *Franklin* would capsize. However, after he and the other firefighters regained their balance, it took less than a minute to spray the remaining fuel and flames over the side.

The third bomb killed eight men—two of them torpedo plane pilots who had been sightseeing on the catwalk of the deck-edge elevator. The explosion wounded twenty-seven others, including Frank Turner. The force of the blast threw him through the hatch and into some cables and wiring hanging down above the hangar deck. He dangled there, unable to move, with wounds to his face and right arm and a chunk of shrapnel in his shoulder. When rescuers were finally able to extricate him, he was taken down to sick bay to get patched up.

Bruised and battered, Turner considered himself fortunate among the men who had been standing in the vicinity of the deck-side elevator. Along with the two pilots, the plane spotter who took off running aft had been killed. The other spotter with Turner, who had entered the hatch before him, caught a load of shrapnel in his guts; he was heavily sedated when Turner saw him in the sick bay.

Another Airedale friend Turner had known since his days on the *Charger,* Leo Balwick, walked into the sick bay with a piece of metal sticking out of his helmet. The other end of the piece was embedded in his skull, from which he was bleeding like a stuck pig. Balwick wasn't in much pain and had wanted to remove his helmet out on the flight deck, but horrified shipmates urged him to keep it on until a doctor could take a look. He ended up needing surgery to remove the scrap of metal and the helmet.

The damage to the ship, however, was slight and flight operations were quickly resumed. As were the Japanese attempts to finish the ship.

About an hour after the attack, Garrison found himself sitting at his workbench in the metal shop smoking a cigarette. He didn't remember lighting it or even how the pack got into his shirt pocket. Reminding himself that he had stopped smoking, he walked over to the porthole and threw the pack overboard. His latest effort to quit, however, was short-lived.

At about 2:00 P.M., Captain Shoemaker came on the public address system to tell the crew that more enemy planes were on the way. A lot more. Radar had picked up fifty bogeys approaching from the northwest, and another thirty from the southwest. He told the crew to be alert and ready, but not to worry, the combat air patrol would handle the situation.

"We couldn't handle five this morning," Garrison muttered, "and here comes eighty?" He bummed a pack of cigarettes off of another sailor.

Five minutes and several cigarettes later, Shoemaker reported that the enemy planes were now fifty miles away—a distance they could cover in ten minutes if left alone. But as the captain pointed out, they were about to be intercepted by the CAP.

After another five minutes and a few more cigarettes, the report was that the enemy was forty miles away but under attack. Ten more minutes passed. Garrison expected to hear the General Quarters alarm and the firing of the guns at any moment. But then Shoemaker spoke again: The combat air patrol had taken care of the problem and the pilots were on their way home. "Prepare to land aircraft."

Garrison looked at the pack of cigarettes in his hand. Twenty minutes and half of them were gone. *I'll quit after the war,* he decided, and put the rest of the pack in his pocket.

The radio in Gove's helmet crackled suddenly with a warning. "Tallyho! Bandits at Angels Eleven!"

Gove looked in the direction of Angels Eleven. "Angels" meant at altitude, or above their position. Eleven would have been the placement of the hour hand if he had been looking at a clock. He saw sixteen, maybe eighteen, Zekes diving out of the sun.

As the senior fighter pilot in the air that afternoon, Gove was the flight leader, responsible for himself and eleven other Hellcats and their pilots. They were in a tight spot—outnumbered and the Japs had the advantage of the higher elevation and the sun at their backs.

The deaths were mounting in the squadron. Gove personally had lost three roommates. Two of them—A. C. "Stud" Hudson and Roger L'Estrange—went down in rapid succession in August at Chichi Jima. The weather then had been horrible for flying, but it was the antiaircraft fire that got them.

Like most of the other fighter pilots, Gove made two strikes on August 4, sinking a cargo ship on one of them. But he wasn't flying with Hudson and didn't learn of his death until that evening in the ready room when the pilots gathered for their debriefing. The Air Combat Information (ACI) officer told them all he knew. Hudson had been leading a strafing attack on one of the destroyers when his plane was hit by fire from the ship's guns. Plane and destroyer exploded at the same time, so Hudson got credit for the ship; he would probably be up for the Distinguished Flying Cross, a lot of good it would do him now.

Hudson's squadron mates slouched silently in their chairs. There wasn't much to say. It wasn't like they could pack their bags and go home now. The officer went on to talk about the day's other events and what the morning might bring.

Later, Gove packed up Hudson's personal effects to be sent home to his wife and baby girl. There wasn't much to send, the pilots traveled light and didn't even have their winter flying gear. There were a few photographs of a pretty woman and an infant and that was about it. There wasn't much time for reflection, however, as that night Gove had a new roommate, L'Estrange, and the next morning they were back in their planes waiting to take off.

The weather was still lousy on August 5, and the *Franklin's* air group was the only one to launch. Gove and his cohorts spent two and a half hours diving through antiaircraft fire to shoot up fuel and ammunition dumps around the harbor. When they returned to the ship, it was pitching up and down in the high seas. As the ship would head down into a trough, waves would break over the flight deck, which was normally sixty feet above the water.

Taking off had been difficult enough, though not as tough for the fighters as for the heavier dive-bombers and torpedo planes. The F6F had a lot of power, and depending on how far back on the deck one was spotted before takeoff, a Hellcat could lift off before it ran out of real estate. However, if there wasn't enough runway, especially in the case of the heavier planes, departing aircraft actually dropped off the end of the carrier to gain enough speed to pull up and away.

In rough seas, the flight signal officer, Lt. Dan Winters, had to time the rise and fall of the deck to make sure the planes had enough clearance for the dangerous takeoffs. But he got them off that morning with no problems.

Of course, landing was always worse, especially under those conditions. None of the pilots in Gove's group, including him, had ever tried anything like it. And every one of them hesitated when approaching the rocking deck and had to be waved off by Winters. When the last of them missed, the flight signal officer shouted at them over the radio: "Listen up, you sons of bitches! Watch me, not the deck, *I'll* tell you when to cut 'em. . . . got it?"

They circled back around and the next time kept their eyes on Winters. The lieutenant got them lined up and then, at precisely the right moment to match the motion of the ship, signaled for them to cut their engines. He dropped every one of them onto the deck light as a feather, or at least the carrier landing equivalent.

Gove was relieved to be back. However, he soon learned that his new roommate hadn't made it. The ACI officer told the pilots that L'Estrange's plane had been hit by antiaircraft fire and burst into flames before crashing into the waters of the harbor. Again the ready room was quiet; a few men shook their heads.

L'Estrange was one of the youngest members of the squadron. He had been one of the new breed of pilot who had entered flight training right out of high school and had only received his commission in June 1943. When the Marines stormed the beaches of its former territory on July 21, 1944, L'Estrange had helped clear the way for his brother, a Marine captain in the first wave.

For the second night in a row, Gove packed the few personal items his roommate had left in their room. He was struck by the irony of L'Estrange fretting over his older brother, who had survived the invasion, when it was Roger who wouldn't be going home to their mother and sister.

Gove barely met his third roommate, Lt. Wade Winecoff, in September before he was gone. Winecoff was a replacement pilot, but he never made it back from his first mission in the Carolines. He'd had no time to unpack any personal effects.

The deaths were sad and costly. Naval aviators were among the country's best and brightest—selected for their physical and mental abilities. On a personal level, the men in his squadron were more like brothers than even friends. They had grown up together. Got drunk together. Chased women together. Flew together. Fought together. Watched out for one another, and packed up each other's personal belongings to send home to their survivors when darkness fell over the Pacific and the pilots did not return. But once they were gone, Gove didn't give them a lot of thought.

A combat pilot couldn't afford to spend a lot of time mourning dead friends or worrying about what could happen the next time he went up. He needed to stay focused on his job or it might be his name on the ACI's clipboard. The Navy didn't even perform the traditional burial at sea services for downed aviators, just a brief note in the Plan of the Day and a mention at Sunday services. Most of the time there was nothing left to commit to the deep from beneath a flag. They were simply listed as "missing in action," or "missing and presumed dead." All Gove could do about it was try to get the damned war over with that much sooner. And that meant killing other men, shooting down their planes, blowing up their buildings, sinking their ships.

So he and the others fought their way through the Central Pacific without looking back. Chichi Jima. Yap. Palau. Peleliu. The resistance they met in the air was determined but ineffective.

As a former flight instructor, Gove, who received the Air Medal for sinking the ship at Chichi Jima, knew that the young pilots coming in—eager to show their meddle "before it's all over," and spoiling for a fight—were the best trained combat pilots in the world, though he knew the Marines would haggle with him about that. And these young men were being teamed with guys like himself, who after more than fifty missions still looked forward to the adrenaline-pumped excitement of combat and were now the pilots with the experience that the Japanese used to have.

At least as many pilots were dying of "operational" problems as the efforts of the Japanese. After his experience off Guam, Gove particularly identified with those who had to ditch in the water. A destroyer or submarine would pick up about half of them. But the others didn't make it out of the cockpits before their planes sank. The simple fact of a combat aviator's life was that he could die in a wide variety of ways.

Some seemed to have more lives, however, than the proverbial cat. One day in August, Johnny Johnson showed up onboard again. He had been shot down off Iwo Jima in July and picked up by a submarine, he said. Of course, he wouldn't have been Johnny without returning with wild tales of having been dropped off at Saipan, where he went hunting with Marines in the caves for holdout Japanese soldiers. It had taken him more than a month to get back to his ship.

One of the more unusual attempts on Gove's life occurred October 13 as he and Lt. (j.g.) Bill Bowen were flying in tandem over Formosa. They had spent the previous day shooting up targets on the ground and were disappointed not to find more planes in the air.

They were flying in loose formation over the ocean about thirty feet apart and "looking for trouble." Gove was shocked nearly out of his cockpit when he glanced over at Bowen in time to see a large, dark cylindrical object drop between them from above, missing their wingtips by no more than ten feet.

"Where in the hell did that come from?" Bowen yelled.

Glancing up, they saw a Zero peel away and flee toward Formosa. Somehow the Japanese pilot crept up on them until he was flying a mere two hun-

dred feet above their heads. Then for some strange reason, he had tried to hit them with a bomb.

Gove and Bowen threw their planes' overdrives from first into second and roared in pursuit of the Zero. But before they could get close enough, the Zero disappeared into a cloud shrouding one of the island's mountain peaks.

They circled above the mountain, waiting for their prey to emerge from the cloud cover. But they didn't see him again and thought he had either given them the slip or, more likely, planted himself into the mountainside.

Gove was back on the ship on October 13 when the Japanese torpedo bomber pilot tried to put himself through the flight deck. But he was already in the ready room when General Quarters sounded, so he didn't get to see the heroics of his wingman, Ensign A. J. Pope.

Later in the ready room, the tale of the Zero that tried to bomb Gove and Bowen was a hit with the other pilots. But they were upstaged by Pope and by the strange tale of the Japanese pilot who had tried to crash the flight deck. It sounded like this pilot intended to commit suicide from the beginning. They figured that he had to have been some lone nut who had gone over the edge, battle fatigue maybe.

As far as the attack went the ship was okay, and Gove thought it was a good thing that the crew had finally been given a little taste of what war was about. Up to this point, the aviators went off and fought the battles and then came back to a ship that might as well have been on a pleasure cruise. He knew it took a crew working together for the air group to do its job, but he had lost a lot of friends and the crew needed to know just how serious the situation was, how quickly their own lives could end.

Death was an everyday companion for aviators, and there didn't even seem to be time to talk to God about watching over them. After his night at sea in the raft, Gove had promised he would attend Sunday services, but he was usually so busy flying and fighting that he was never quite sure what day of the week it was.

The day after the torpedo plane attack on the *Franklin*, October 14, Gove was flying alone, high above Manila when two "Tony" dive-bombers jumped him. The big planes were slower, but they were well armed and there were two of them. He maneuvered so that they could not both come at him at once, and then looped so that he could come in from behind one. His target tried to dive away as its rear gunner fired a volley of shots at him. But Gove had the plane in his sights and pulled the trigger. The burst from the fifty calibers caused pieces of the plane to fly off, and the rear gunner stopped shooting. Desperately, the pilot tried to turn, but another burst from the Hell-cat and there was a puff of smoke, then flames. One more and the plane disintegrated in midair.

A stream of tracers flew past Gove, an unnecessary reminder that there was a second dive-bomber to deal with. He dove and turned, faster than the Tony could manage. Again he maneuvered to come up behind the enemy plane. The slugs from his guns tore into the fuselage and ate up the wings with their red "meatball." The Tony started to smoke and veered off into a long spin that took it down into the sea, where it exploded.

Gove gave one last look at the two columns of smoke rising from the water and left to meet Bowen at their preset rendezvous point above Manila Bay. He was flying low near the water when he was attacked again. This time by two older-model "Oscar" dive-bombers.

Normally, the Hellcat would have trumped even a pair of Oscars, but this time Gove was in trouble—he didn't have any more ammunition. Still, he figured, the Japanese pilots didn't know that, and with no better ideas coming to him at that moment, he wheeled and charged straight at them. One of the Oscar pilots panicked and tried to turn away but lost control of his plane and spun into the bay. Gove looked around quickly for the second enemy plane but saw he had nothing to worry about. Bowen had arrived and shot down the other Oscar.

Gove was credited that day with three planes—two he had shot down and one, his squadron mates laughed, he had "scared to death." But even that didn't earn him a rest, not that he wanted one.

The next afternoon, the fifteenth, he was leading the flight, looking for enemy aircraft reported to be heading for the fleet, when the Zeros came at them from out of the sun. He immediately gave his wingmen the hand signal to deploy into the Thach Weave formation. The section of planes behind followed their lead.

The battle was a clear example of how far Japanese pilot training had fallen. The enemy pilots had started with the advantage of elevation and the sun but had not used it well. They didn't lack courage, but instead of working together, they flew around individually, trying to engage in dogfights only to be lured into the trap of the weave.

When it was over, ten Zeros had been shot down and the rest had fled. As the flight leader, Gove didn't fire his guns once during the melee. Instead, he had directed the weave—a complicated task with that many planes covering for each other—sort of like a football quarterback calling the plays at the line of scrimmage in a two-minute drill. However, he couldn't control everything that went on in the heat of battle and, though it wasn't Gove's fault, a lack of discipline had cost the squadron another pilot.

Young, athletic, and tough, Ensign F. A. Beckman broke from the weave to pursue a fleeing Zero. The rule was that once a pilot left the weave, he was on his own. But "Becky," who wanted to "shoot one of those sons of bitches," had been talking about it for days, and it cost him his life.

Later, when the ACI officer told them that Beckman's plane had been seen crashing into Manila Bay, Gove looked around the ready room at his quiet comrades, each lost in their own thoughts. He hoped the younger pilots got the message: Don't leave the weave.

Sometimes the most valuable lessons were also the most cruel.

In the course of the one-day battle on October 15, the task group shot down eighty-four planes. Of the enemy casualties, the *Franklin's* fighters accounted for twenty-nine, and its gunners had been given credit for shooting down the plane that killed their shipmates with its bomb.

That night Tokyo Rose broadcast that once again the USS *Franklin* had been sent to the bottom of the sea "with great loss of life." The men shook their heads, and a few laughed, but most of the ship's company listened to her somberly. The old girl was closer to being right than any of them cared to think about. That last bomb had come within a few feet of hitting a flight deck full of tightly packed planes, each filled with a couple hundred gallons of aviation fuel and jammed to the gills with bombs, rockets, torpedoes, and machine gun bullets.

They were an older, more sober group of men as they prepared to turn in that night. The taste of war was still bitter in their mouths.

Before taps was played, Shoemaker reminded the ship's company that some of the day's casualties had been men who instead of taking cover had wanted to watch the action.

"You are to take no foolish unnecessary chances." The captain paused; he wasn't trying to be cruel, but it was his job to get his men and his ship through the war. "It's sometimes easier to defeat the enemy than our own stupidity."

CHAPTER TWELVE

Upon His Country's Altar

October 24, 1944
USS Santa Fe

The eruption of an immense mushroom cloud of white smoke on the horizon halted Jackson in his tracks as he was hurrying back to his battle station in Radio Two. *That much smoke . . . has to be a big ship,* he thought. *Maybe a carrier.* And it appeared that lightning had struck the same place twice.

Earlier, he had seen a column of darker smoke rising from that spot, which he estimated to be twenty miles away. Then the column shrank until it was just a thin smudge against the clouds, as the ship's crew apparently got the fire under control. But whatever disaster had befallen the ship the first time, it looked like it had gotten a lot worse now. The thought passed with a wave of sadness. That much smoke and fire also meant that lives had been lost.

Shortly after he saw the first smoke that morning, he had also noted that the *Santa Fe's* sister ship, the *Birmingham,* wasn't with the division anymore. Now he reasoned that she might have been sent to help the stricken ship— fight fires, provide an escort, maybe take off survivors as the *Santa Fe* had done a week earlier for the *Houston.*

If that were true, they might not see the *Birmingham* for a while. CruDiv13 had been stuck with the bait force for five days, almost always at General Quarters, as they crawled toward Ulithi. They had traveled 170 miles from Formosa and were looking at a journey of more than a thousand. The worst day for Jackson had been the sixteenth, when the torpedo plane attacked and he and the others under his command had been cooped up in the radio room, where he could only hear what was happening outside.

First there was the General Quarters alarm and then the five-inch guns began booming. At that point the men in the radio room weren't worried; it probably meant that the gunners were aiming at a plane in the distance, but not necessarily one that was after the *Santa Fe.* The men still continued their conversations—the latest news from home, a letter from a girl, the first bar they planned to hit when they got back to the States.

When the forties started in with their rhythmic pom-pom-pom and the ship picked up speed and began cutting S-turns, they paid more attention—the *Santa Fe* may have been singled out by a plane. The small talk continued, only now it was stilted, tending to drift off. Then the guns ceased firing and they relaxed. The conversation picked up as they smiled and poured another cup of Joe.

The peace didn't last long. A few minutes after the initial shooting stopped, it started again. The fives opened up. Then the forties kicked in and were almost immediately joined by the twenties, barking like guard dogs with a burglar on the premises. The ship shuddered as every ounce of horsepower was coaxed out of the turbines and the captain threw her into evasive turns.

The enemy was too close. Jackson looked around. The men's faces betrayed their common fear. They were turned toward the starboard bulkhead, the direction the guns were firing. Death, if it came, would burst in from there. They braced for impact as the ship tilted hard to port and the roaring of the guns reached a crescendo outside.

When the guns suddenly stopped firing and the ship's engine slowed to the familiar hum of cruising speed, the effect was much like waking from a nightmare. The men dared to exhale. Smiled. Shook their heads, pursed their lips and whistled. *Man, must have been a close one.*

How close they learned shortly afterward when the captain spoke over the public address system. The ship had indeed had a narrow escape and, sadly, the *Santa Fe* had suffered her first combat fatality—a member of the *Houston's* Marine contingent.

In a few days, someone back in the States—some family, some woman, some child—hoping for a letter from a son or a husband or a father would instead receive a telegram. Sometimes they were delivered by military chaplains. Sometimes by taxi. Or by Western Union messengers riding bicycles.

However they arrived, telegrams were never good news. "The Secretary of the Navy regrets to inform you that . . ."

What impressed Don Jackson about his shipmates was that the vast majority of the men manning U.S. ships were not professional soldiers. They weren't even "regular Navy," who like him had joined up before the war for economic reasons.

They were in the reserves, ordinary citizens—some of them whose families had been Americans for generations, some whose parents, or even themselves, had hardly stepped off the boat from some foreign land. They were businessmen and engineers, like he still dreamed of becoming. Or scientists and teachers, farmers and laborers.

Many were boys just out of high school who until December 7, 1941, only talked about killing when it was the Yankees "killing" the Red Sox. They had no idea what they wanted to be when they grew up, but they wanted the chance to find out.

The young men in Radio Two weren't world conquerors; they were regular guys like Jackson's boss, Lt. Norm Utecht, the ship's communications officer, a Harvard graduate and well into his career as a businessman when called up. They were guys like Charlie Matta, a steel mill worker's kid from McKeesport, Pennsylvania, who was striking to be a radio operator on Jackson's crew—always talking about his girl back home, reminiscing about the days when excitement to him was meeting her halfway across the bridge that spanned the river between their two smoky mill towns.

They were guys with names like Kennedy and Krawszun. L'Hommedieu, Li Santi, and Locke. Montgomery and Montoya. They were Protestants and Catholics and Jews.

Not everything was perfect back home. There were contentious issues of race and gender. Of fair wages for the working man. And fair treatment for the Indians. But by and large the men on the ships, and in the trenches, and in the air knew it was better than what their counterparts had in Germany, Italy, Japan, and for that matter their ally, the Soviet Union. And if the war had shown the world—especially the despots and world conquerors—one thing, it was: Hit one American, might as well have hit them all.

They would put aside their differences, the rancor of their politics, and the issues that divided them until the common threat had been dealt with. They had been thought soft. But on dozens of beaches, forests, and hills from Normandy to Peleliu, above the skies of Italy and Iwo Jima, and across the world's oceans from the North Sea to the Philippine Sea, they had proved themselves tougher than their enemies had imagined. Jackson was proud to serve with these men as the *Santa Fe* rejoined the task force off the Philippines after escorting the *Canberra* and *Houston* halfway to Ulithi on the eve of the largest naval battle in the history of the world.

October 21, 1944

The general made good on his promise when more than 170,000 troops of the U.S. Sixth Army landed on the island of Leyte in the middle of the Philippine archipelago. Offshore, MacArthur had at his disposal the Seventh Fleet, comprised of old battleships, many of them resurrected from the destruction of Pearl Harbor, and escort carriers, whose air wings were designed to support troop landings with strafing assignments and antipersonnel bombs. The Third Fleet, as represented by Task Force 38, was assigned the responsibility of supporting the Sixth Army by destroying the enemy's airplanes and airfields, as well as thwarting any counterattacks against the landing beaches by the Imperial Japanese Navy.

The monsoon season was in full swing. Rain fell in sheets and then suddenly gave way to a sweltering sun that would make steam rise from the ocean and from the soaked men manning the ships' guns. Typhoons sometimes raged out of the South China Sea, which stirred up the waters for a thousand miles with their angry winds. Rainsqualls swept across the sea like gray monks hurrying to vespers.

The invasion of Leyte was the signal the Japanese were waiting to set into motion the Sho plan. Simple in concept, the plan was complex in logistics and carried with it the potential for enormous victory and enormous failure for both sides.

The Japanese First Fleet—consisting of two battleships, six cruisers, and a host of screening destroyers—was to rush through the Surigao Straits between Leyte and Mindanao and fall upon the transports and invading troops on the beaches.

At the same time, the Japanese Second Fleet—comprised of the two super battleships, *Yamato* and *Musashi,* plus three older battleships, ten cruisers, and eleven destroyers—were to drive through the San Bernardino Straits between Samar and Luzon. They would then steam south to cut the invasion force's supply line to Ulithi. Thus, the American troops on shore would be first isolated, and then pounded into oblivion from the sea, the air, and the land.

In order for the plan to work, the Japanese fleets had to exercise complete coordination and create a diversion. The Imperial admirals believed their surface fleet was a match for American battleships and cruisers. However, the biggest obstacle to the success of the plan was negating American air power so that the surface fleet could get close enough to the American landing forces to use its big guns.

To that end, they were willing to sacrifice their remaining four operational aircraft carriers as a bait fleet to pull the American aircraft carriers away from the Gulf of Leyte. The bait fleet included two old battleships, eight cruisers, and six destroyers, which were to escort the four carriers south from Japan to a point a hundred miles north of the Philippines.

When the moment was most auspicious, the few pilots experienced enough to fly from an aircraft carrier would launch to find the enemy and, perhaps, strike a telling blow. However, the main purpose of the planes and the fleet was to lure the American carriers north. The Japanese expected to lose the carriers and perhaps the rest of the ships. But it would be worth it—the carriers were nearly useless anyway—if it meant the First and Second Fleets could isolate and attack the landing beaches. They were fortunate that they faced the impetuous Admiral Halsey, who could be expected to rise to the bait, rather than the cooler Spruance.

Almost lost in the excitement of last-minute preparations for the upcoming battle was the advent of a new weapon. Two days before the American invasion of Leyte, on the night of October 19, Vice Admiral Takejiro Onishi flew from Manila to the Mabalacat airfield. A week earlier, the airfield had been under the command of Admiral Arima, who had the word *Naifu* painted on his plane and then heroically smashed his aircraft into an American aircraft carrier. Onishi now hoped that his colleague's sacrifice would encourage the pilots at Mabalacat to volunteer for a very special sort of mission.

Word of Arima's deed—which grew in the telling to where his final plunge had sunk the carrier—had spread quickly throughout the Japanese air corps, particularly the navy. His example had led to other pilots taking his path to martyrdom. Japanese spotter planes reported that on October 16, a torpedo bomber had destroyed or severely damaged a light cruiser (the *Santa Fe*) that had been guarding a convoy of wounded warships.

Admiral Onishi praised the enthusiasm of the *Toko,* "special," attacks. But that night when he spoke to the officers of the base's air corps, he talked about the need to harness that spirit into a unified plan. The special attacks pilot should not attempt to make a conventional attack, releasing his torpedo or bomb, but plunge with the weapon into the ship. Only then would their sacrifices not be in vain; only then would the enemy's navy be swept from the western Pacific.

Onishi argued that the detractors of his plan, and there were many, were quibbling over a minor difference. It was suicide anyway, he said, to send the current crop of half-trained pilots to attack the American fleet by conventional means. They were dying by the hundreds. At least his way they might strike an important blow. One man in one plane, he said, could—with the help of the gods—sink a carrier. Or, at the very least, knock one out of flight operations for a week while the deck was repaired.

In the end, nobody had a better option for dealing with the carriers if the ruse of the bait fleet failed. If Onishi's pilots were even partly successful, a week's time was all the First and Second Fleets would need to wipe out the enemy landing forces and convince the Americans to abandon their demand for unconditional surrender. A few even dared hope that just as Midway had turned to tide of the war toward the Allies, this upcoming battle would reverse the flow back to the holy cause of the emperor. They might still rule Asia.

Aware of his countrymen's prediliction for grand gestures, Onishi wrapped the reality of the mission in mysticism and mythology. On October 21, the day selected for the first sorties, he made another trip to Mabalacat field, where he read aloud from a scroll he had beautifully inscribed in caligraphy, an art form for which he was famous in Japan.

Kyo sakite, asu chiru
Hana no wagami ka na
Ikade sono ka wo kiyoku todomen

Blossoming today, tomorrow scattered;
Life is like a delicate flower;
Could one expect the fragrance to last forever?

Onishi signed the scroll as a member of the special attack corps, as if he considered himself one of them, his fate irretrievably tied to theirs. He told the pilots, who puffed up with pride at the thought, that while they would not live to see the results of their courage, he would personally tell the emperor of their deeds. And at the moment of their deaths, he said, their souls would fly to the Yasukuni Shrine to be worshipped by future generations of Japanese. Theirs was a holy cause, he said. "You are already gods. You are no longer to concern yourselves with the affairs of men."

After all that, however, the special attack corps got off to a desultory beginning. The pilots waited most of the twenty-first for scout planes to locate the American fleet. Finally, the information arrived in the afternoon. The pilots ran for their planes and took off to the cheers of the other pilots, who would have to wait their turn, and the ground crews, who would have to keep patching together airplanes and airfields to keep the program going. *Banzai! May you live ten thousand years! Banzai!*

Those who remained behind waited for word of their heroic deeds and glorious deaths. However, the results were disappointing. The pilots could not find the fleet and had to return, red-faced. Their superiors assured them they would soon get another chance to die for the emperor.

There was one pilot that day who accomplished his mission. He was not part of the corps, but certainly one with them in spirit. That morning as the Seventh Fleet stood off the landing beaches at Leyte and American troops poured ashore, a Japanese plane appeared out of the fog. The pilot flew just above the waves, and there was no warning of his approach from the radar operators.

Startled American gun crews jumped for their weapons, but it was too late. At the last moment, the pilot flew up and straight into the foremast of the Australian cruiser HMAS *Australia*. A ball of fire engulfed the bridge, killing the ship's captain and nineteen seaman, as well as wounding an Australian commodore and fifty-three other men.

The plane had come out of nowhere, but what surprised everyone most was that the pilot made no attempt to drop a bomb and then get away. The attack had been suicidal from beginning to end, though not even the Japanese could find a record of which of their pilots made the spontaneous demonstration of fealty. He was not officially connected to Onishi's special attack corps, which had not yet taken off.

Onishi's pilots would indeed get their opportunities over the next few days to prove the efficacy of his plan. As they left the airfields, never to return, the admiral thought that such poetic self-sacrifice had to have a special name—something less grim than "certain death unit" and more emotionally appealing than "special attack corps." One of Onishi's staff noted that the symbols for "special attack" written in Chinese caligraphy also looked like the symbols for "divine" and "wind."

The coincidence was perfect. Every child in Japan knew the story of how the country had been saved from the Mongol barbarians by the gods, who had sent a terrible wind to destroy their enemy. Japan, holy Yamato, would prevail so long as there were resolute warriors willing to die for the emperor and the protection of those divine winds, now in human form—the *kamikaze*.

October 23, 1944

A long time would pass before the American Navy would become familiar with the name kamikaze. At the opening of the battle for the Philippines, they weren't aware that there were certain-death units, organized to commit suicide by careening into their ships. The separate incidents earlier in October just confirmed the American belief that the Japanese were crazy, that they had no regard for human life.

On the night of October 23, the combined Seventh and Third Fleets received word from U.S. submarines in the South China Sea that large elements of the Japanese navy were on the move toward the Philippines. One task group, which included the fleet carriers *Franklin* and *Enterprise,* wheeled and steamed westward to meet the threat.

The remaining task groups remained behind to the northeast of Leyte, opposite Luzon, to support the troops. A little before midnight, the crews were called to battle stations when bogeys appeared on the radar. But the planes were "snoopers," who circled twenty to twenty-five miles away, reporting on ship movements while avoiding American night fighters.

The enemy waited until dawn to attack. The task force carriers had already launched the morning's first strikes when all hell broke loose. At 6:10 the Combat Information Center reported that forty Japanese planes were on the way from the south. A few minutes later, the CIC passed the word that another thirty were approaching from the northwest.

The combat air patrol intercepted the first waves and broke up the attack. But the Japanese kept throwing more planes of every sort into the fray. The CAP couldn't get them all. Zekes, Jills, Judys, Emilys, Oscars, and the speedy new Frances torpedo bombers pierced the eight-mile circle of destroyer pickets and bore in on the carriers at the center.

Radar screens were so cluttered with "pips" that it was impossible for the CIC to identify them well enough for automatic sighting. The gunners were told they would have to rely on visual recognition; the lookouts with binoculars would have to try to identify planes moving at nearly three hundred miles an hour.

At about 9:30, the crew of the *Santa Fe* noticed a column of black smoke on the horizon. A ship, a large one by the size of the plume, must have been hit. But their attention was soon diverted by a Japanese bomber that had appeared overhead, diving on the destroyer USS *Healey,* which lay several hundred yards away off the cruiser's port beam. The plane appeared to have the *Healey* dead to rights. Its engine screaming above the cacaphony of guns, the plane was just about to release its bomb when the *Santa Fe's* forties knocked it off course. The bomb barely missed the *Healey,* and the plane flew off, trailing smoke, and finally crashed in the distance.

All morning long, planes fell out of the sky in flames. So many ships were shooting at them it was almost impossible to tell which struck the killing blow. However, the *Santa Fe* was given partial credit for hitting another plane, which then tried to limp away from the battle but was set upon and torn apart by Hellcats. About 11:00 A.M. there was a brief lull, but the Japanese returned at noon with renewed vigor.

Time and again, the *Santa Fe* came under attack. An hour after the battle resumed, an Emily dive-bomber dove at the ship only to be driven off into the waiting guns of the CAP. A little later, every gun on the ship was firing as she was attacked simultaneously by a torpedo plane and three dive-bombers.

Bombs exploded all around the ship. The men belowdecks watched with fear as the bulkheads wavered from the concussions like they were made of rubber sheets. But the ship, their lucky ship, remained unharmed and, with the help of her sister ships and the combat air patrol, knocked the attackers into the ocean.

The *Santa Fe* was a difficult target, as Captain Wright drove the ship like he was commanding a speedboat, heeling her over in such hard turns that crewmembers on the weather deck thought they could have touched the water if they had reached over the side. At the same time, the gunners poured it on until the forties got so hot the gun crews could not touch the empty brass shells to toss them overboard and had to let them pile up on the deck.

Throughout the action, the ship's chaplain, Lt. Cmdr. Seth Russell, like a play-by-play man working a game between the Brooklyn Dodgers and Saint Louis Cardinals, kept a running account on the public address system for the men who couldn't see the action. The well-liked chaplain, the crew agreed later, called a mean battle.

During the heat of the fighting, Jackson was called to the bridge to remedy a glitch with the radar. While he was there, a Japanese plane made a run at the ship. The admiral, DuBose, who was also on the bridge, crouched behind a metal wall and pointed at the intruder, shouting, "Git him! Git him! Git him!" While comical, everyone knew better than to laugh at an admiral while he was standing, or crouching, nearby.

Jackson was returning to Radio Two when he noticed the second blossoming of smoke on the horizon. He thought of the lives lost—the families back home who would be receiving the telegrams. He wondered which ship was beneath the cloud.

The USS Princeton *and* Birmingham

A little after 9:30 that morning, a dive-bomber broke through the fighter screen and planted a five-hundred-pound bomb through the flight deck of the light carrier *Princeton*. The bomb continued down into the hangar deck before it exploded, rupturing the gas tanks of the planes waiting there, spilling aviation fuel across the deck. The fuel ignited and spread to ammunition lockers and stacked bombs, setting them off.

Belching black smoke and racked by explosions, the ship dropped out of formation. As Jackson had surmised, the *Birmingham* was ordered to go alongside the stricken carrier to help fight fires and remove survivors if necessary.

The first attempt of the *Birmingham* to aid the *Princeton* was delayed by first a submarine alert and then by another air raid as the Japanese tried to finish the job. The cruiser had to pull quickly away, circle, and return after the attacker was shot down. The *Birmingham* idled to within fifty feet, stopped, and began to douse the flames with fire hoses.

Several hundred members of the cruiser's crew were on the main deck, many helping with the fire hoses, but many others were just watching. It had been a year since their ship had been hit off Bougainville. Memories fade, and like most young men, they were heedless of the danger.

After a while, the fires on the *Princeton* seemed to be under control. But then the world of the sailors on the deck of the *Birmingham* blew apart with a roar and a wave of blinding white heat. A fire burning in the *Princeton's* interior had reached an ammunition magazine on a lower deck.

The cataclysmic explosion blew the stern off the carrier and shoved the *Birmingham* violently sideways as if the ship was no more than a child's toy in a bathtub. A storm of fire and flying metal swept over the cruiser. In the time it takes for a thought to form, men disintegrated as if they had never existed; others were blown into the water to drown, or thrown against steel bulkheads, where they lay crumpled like ragdolls.

The neat and scrubbed deck of the *Birmingham* was transformed into a slaughterhouse of bodies, many burned and torn beyond recognition. Streams of blood poured into the waterways and drained from the scuppers, running in red rivulets down the hull.

A tall column of white-gray smoke rose like a tombstone over the two ships, visible for fifty miles. Unconcerned with the battle raging above them, sharks responded quickly to the blood in the water. Marines with rifles were posted to keep the predators away from the men, not always successfully, as destroyers hurriedly lowered whaleboats to pluck survivors from the sea.

Hours later, when the survivors had mustered for roll call and the wounded had been accounted for, it was determined that the cruiser had suffered the more grievous losses: 239 men from the *Birmingham* had died and another 400 were wounded; half of the ship's company had been wiped out in a heartbeat. Damage to the ship, however, had not affected her seaworthiness, and she soon got underway for Ulithi with what remained of her crew. She was going to be out of the war for a while, but as much to replace her missing men as to repair the wounds to her steel.

The *Princeton's* crew fared better; 108 had died and several dozen had been wounded. But the blast ended any hope of saving the carrier, and her captain ordered his remaining men to abandon ship. In the tradition of navies around the world, he was the last to leave.

The end came quickly then. A U.S. destroyer moved in and sank the ship with a brace of torpedoes as survivors of the *Princeton,* aboard other ships now, wept while watching her go down.

The Battle of Leyte Gulf

October 24, 1944
USS Franklin

ARM 3rd Class Sam Plonsky touched the heart he had painted on the Avenger's dark blue fuselage as Pete Sanchez walked up from behind and patted him on the shoulder.

"Don't worry," Sanchez said, "we'll get you home to her." The turret gunner stepped past him into the side door of the plane and wiggled up through the top turret opening into his position.

Satisfied that the "Mimi" ritual had been followed to the letter, the nineteen-year-old Plonsky climbed in after his fellow crewmember and took his seat on the radio operator's bench facing forward. He and Mimi had been growing closer through their correspondence. In fact, all he could think about was going home and marrying his "babe"—at least when he wasn't fretting about getting killed.

After flying past the Zeros and through the flak at Iwo Jima, Guam, Haha Jima, and the Carolines, he wasn't as gung-ho as he had been back in '42 when he couldn't wait to enlist. At first the war had been a big adventure, and he didn't give much thought to the killing or dying going on all around him. The possibility of his own death didn't really start to hit until he noticed how many of the *Franklin's* planes weren't coming back from missions. He gave it more thought whenever his plane got really bounced around by the ack-ack and would land on the ship with holes in the wings and fuselage.

Plonsky still felt that he had a job to do, but it wasn't fun anymore. In fact, he was sure that the more often he flew, the greater the odds were that the next time or the time after that, would be the last. Now every time the Avenger took off from the carrier, he would wonder if he was going to come back and would pray: *God, don't let anything happen to me. . . . You can't let anything happen to me. . . . God, please . . . let me get home to Mimi.*

Anything that could increase his chances of getting home in one piece was worthwhile. Without fail, he touched the "Mimi" heart above the door of the plane every time he got in, and he waited for Sanchez to tell him not to worry. He also kept the Navy prayer book, a small volume of loose sheets held together with a string, in the front pocket of his flight jacket for luck.

However, Plonsky did not like the way things had been going lately. There had been a few close calls and not all of them in the air.

On October 13 he had been standing on the hangar deck when the torpedo planes attacked. He didn't see the plane that tried to crash the flight deck, but he had stood transfixed, watching as one of the torpedoes launched at the ship rushed toward him like a big silver fish. The torpedo struck the ship directly below his position and would have probably killed him except that this "fish" bounced off the hull without exploding.

That day—a Friday the thirteenth, he had noted—had been a rough one all around. In his logbook, he had written that the morning raid on Manila had been particularly bad. "Most rugged one yet . . . lots of ack-ack . . . four Jap planes jumped us," he wrote. "I think I got one . . . but I'm not sure."

Then just that afternoon, as VT-13 combat crews gathered in their ready room to be briefed on the mission, he had taken a seat next to another radio operator/gunner he hadn't seen before. There was nothing unusual about that—as guys went down, they were replaced by new men, often right out of flight school. But when he introduced himself this time, the new man paled.

"You don't want to talk to me," he said. "I'm your replacement."

Plonsky had no idea what that meant, nor did the other young man; it was just what he had been told. But there was no time to look into it as the briefing officer entered and told them they were being sent after what sounded like the entire Japanese fleet.

The night before, U.S. submarines in the South China Sea had spotted major elements, including battleships, of the Japanese fleet on the move. The subs had done their part, sticking torpedoes into three cruisers, two of which sank, and the third was burning and on the run when last seen.

In the morning, Task Force 38.4—the *Franklin, Enterprise, Belleau Wood,* and *San Jacinto*—launched planes to search the numerous water passages that separated the Philippine islands of Samar, Leyte, Cebu, and Negros. Several hours went by with no luck, but then a searcher discovered two enemy destroyers and a cruiser, apparently scouts for the main fleet. The Hellcats arrived first and roared in to hit the ships with rockets,

bombs, and machine-gun fire. Within minutes, the cruiser had capsized and sunk. And by the time the fighters left, the two destroyers were on fire and listing.

The second strike, which included Plonsky's section, waited until after noon for their turn as the search planes scoured the area for the main force. When at last the searchers found the Japanese Second Fleet, they identified four battleships, including the *Yamato* and *Musashi,* the largest warships in the world, as well as a bunch of cruisers and destroyers.

The enemy was in the Sibuyan Sea just 150 miles west of the San Bernardino Straits. At the command "pilots and crews to your planes," Plonsky and the others took off running for the flight deck. He and Sanchez had gone through their ritual and climbed in the plane.

Above him, Sanchez situated himself in the ball turret and closed the armor-plated hatch between them. Plonsky could hear him checking out his twin .50-caliber machine guns. Compared to Sanchez's weapons, his own little .30-caliber was a peashooter, but he was glad he got to shoot back when the Japs started trying to kill him.

Up ahead, his pilot, Ensign Robert Freligh revved the engines and taxied the plane to where he was directed. Then with a lurch, the plane began to move down the flight deck, picking up speed. There was still that initial nauseating drop when they ran out of room at the end of the flight deck, before the plane gained enough speed to climb up away from the grasping waves.

As they joined the squadron above the fleet, Plonsky went through his litany. *God, don't let anything happen to me. . . . You can't let anything happen to me. . . . God, please . . . let me get home to Mimi.*

Like sharks smelling blood in the water, the air wing of Task Group 38.4 swarmed to the Sibuyan Sea. Helldivers, Hellcats, and the Avenger torpedo planes all came blazing in at the Japanese battleship fleet.

As Freligh followed the flight leader into the approach, Plonsky climbed down from his radio operator's bench and knelt on the floor of the turret so that he could watch the bomb bay. He still didn't like standing on the Plexiglass, but it was his job so he did it.

From that vantage, he could also see out the side windows of the belly turret and noticed a friend, ARM 3rd Class Eugene "Red" Black, waving to him from the belly turret of the plane next to his. He smiled and waved back. At that moment, an antiaircraft shell pierced the bottom of his friend's plane. Plonsky saw it explode in the cockpit where the pilot had been sitting and watched with horror as Black's plane flipped over and plunged toward the sea.

Plonsky had to shake himself out of the shock. He still had that job to do and needed to put Black's terrified face out of his mind. Their flight leader picked out a heavy cruiser and began his run. Freligh followed, losing altitude until they were only a few feet above the sea.

Black puffs of flak exploded on either side of the plane, which rocked from the buffeting by the closest explosions. As they swooped in on the ship, Freligh swerved back and forth to throw off the Japanese gunners. Then the plane stopped weaving to launch the torpedo.

With the torpedo gone, Plonsky turned and grabbed the handles of his machine gun and peered out the gun port. As the plane rose and swept over the ship, he saw men running on the deck below. He aimed at them and pulled the trigger. The tracers reached the ship even as a geyser of water erupted on the other side of the cruiser. The torpedo had found its mark. Sanchez let out a happy yelp.

We made it, Plonsky thought as he stood and climbed back into his radio operator's chair. In the next moment, the plane was struck by two antiaircraft shells. One hit the engine, filling the Avenger with smoke and spraying oil over the canopy, making it difficult for Freligh to see. The second shell came up through the bottom of the belly turret, shredding Plonsky's right hand, which he held up in disbelief as blood spouted over his face and chest.

In shock, Plonsky looked out the side window and saw a Hellcat pull up next to them. The fighter pilot gave a thumbs-down; he could see the damage better than they and was telling them they had to get out.

"You guys want me to climb to 500 feet so that you can jump?" Freligh asked. It was a brave offer. He would have to stay with the burning plane until the other two were clear, and it might blow at any moment. But normally it would be safer than a water landing.

"We can't," yelled Sanchez, who had opened the turret hatch and looked down. "Sam's hurt bad. He'll never make it." He knew that even if Plonsky bailed and made it to the water, he would never survive on his own. "We better ditch."

"Okay," Freligh agreed. "I'm going to put her down in the water."

Plonsky opened the side door and prepared to get out as soon as the plane stopped. As Freligh eased the aircraft toward the water, the young radioman

Chief Warrant Officer Donald C. Jackson Jr.
and Charlotte Gates were married April 22, 1945
at the Stanford University chapel.

Vivian Cox with Ernest Scott and Eddie Carlisle
back home in Woodland, Maine in July 1946.
The buddies took on the dangers of manning
a ship sailing into harm's way.

Lt. Warren Harding and his wife, Jo, in Los Angeles when the USS *Santa Fe* docked
for a few days in January 1944 before leaving again for fifteen months.
The *Santa Fe* set U. S. Naval records for frontline service, while gaining a
reputation as a phenomenally lucky ship.

Chief Warrant Officer Donald C. Jackson Jr., in cap, peers over the left shoulder of radio operator Charles Matta with other members of his crew in the crowded confines of Radio Two aboard the USS Santa Fe.

Lt. (jg) E. John Weil, second row far left, with the other members of Dive-bomber Group 11 that transferred after a tour on Guadalcanal to Dive-bomber Group 13, pictured here aboard the USS Franklin.

Warrant Officer Donald C. Jackson Jr., second row far left, with other communications officers from the USS Santa Fe pose with beers on the island of Mog Mog in the Ulithi Atoll in May 1945. The lagoon, encompassed by the islands that formed the sarcastically called "Paradise with Beer," could hold a thousand ships.

The USS *Franklin* is turned into the wind and preparing to retrieve
a flight as two F6F Hellcat fighters, with belly tanks, standby.
(PHOTO COURTESY OF WILLARD GOVE)

Built to participate with fast attack aircraft carrier task groups, the 10,000-ton light cruiser USS *Santa Fe*
was commissioned on November 24, 1942. She engaged the enemy from the Aleutians to the Solomon Islands
to the shores of Japan, steaming nearly 300,000 miles before being decommissioned in 1946.
(U.S. NAVAL ARCHIVES PHOTOGRAPH COURTESY OF BILL ANDERSON)

On October 16, 1944, the USS *Santa Fe* was attacked by a "Jill" torpedo plane that made it past combat air patrol and screening ships. Tracers intersected the flight path of the attacking plane as five-inch anti-aircraft shells exploded, but the plane kept coming and tried to crash into the ship in one last suicidal gesture by the pilot.

Burial service at sea, October 13, 1944.
The *Franklin* lost 916 men during the Pacific campaign while the *Santa Fe* lost none despite beginning her frontline fighting in early 1943.

Kamikaze attack on the *Franklin* October 30, 1944. Fifty-six men were killed. Earlier, mid-October suicide plane attacks on the USS *Santa Fe* and *Franklin* signaled the beginning of the kamikaze era that would continue and pick up momentum as the war went on.

(U.S. NAVAL ARCHIVES PHOTOGRAPH COURTESY OF RAY BAILEY)

(U.S. NAVAL ARCHIVES PHOTOGRAPH COURTESY OF RAY BAILEY)

Looking down through a large hole in the flight deck, after a hit by a kamikaze, October 30, 1944. Petty Officer 2nd Class Edwin Garrison, the tall man in the center of the flight deck beneath the girder, is showing Admiral Bull Halsey (the shorter man to his right) the kamikaze damage, hoping the *Franklin* will be sent home for repairs.

(U.S. NAVAL ARCHIVES PHOTOGRAPH COURTESY OF RAY BAILEY)

Starboard side view, with 13 degree list. Big Ben is almost to the point of capsizing and lies dead in the water 52 miles off Kyushu, Japan as the crew attempts to smother the fires.

Explosion on the flight deck, tossing debris high into the air as men fight fire, aft of island, March 19, 1945. Two 500-pound bombs pierced through the flight deck to the hangar deck where they exploded, setting off ammunition and fuel stores.

USS *Franklin* engulfed in smoke from the first bomb explosion, March 19, 1945. Aircraft carriers were considered symbols of supreme power by the Japanese high command.

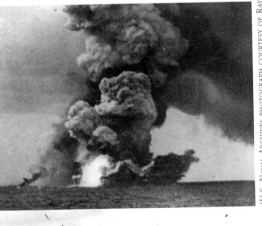

(U.S. NAVAL ARCHIVES PHOTOGRAPH COURTESY OF RAY BAILEY)

(U.S. NAVAL ARCHIVES PHOTOGRAPH COURTESY OF RAY BAILEY)

Starboard side, bow to stern view of USS *Franklin*,
taken from the USS *Santa Fe*, March 19, 1945.

Close view of wounded on the
flight deck while some are being
helped over the antenna to the
USS *Santa Fe*. The men who
weren't forced by fire and
explosions into the water, or
didn't transfer to the *Santa Fe*,
stayed onboard the *Franklin* until
all the fires were put out.

(U.S. NAVAL ARCHIVES PHOTOGRAPH COURTESY OF RAY BAILEY)

Father Joseph T. O'Callahan giving last rites to crewman Robert Blanchard aboard the USS *Franklin*, March 19, 1945. One of the most famous photos of the war, most people who remember it don't know that Blanchard survived.

(U.S. NAVAL ARCHIVES PHOTOGRAPH COURTESY OF RAY BAILEY)

USS *Franklin* survivors sprawled on the aft deck of the USS *Santa Fe*, March 19, 1945. The crew of the *Franklin* became the most decorated in U.S. Naval history, including two Congressional Medal of Honor winners, O'Callahan and Lt. (jg) Donald Gary; as well as twenty Navy Crosses and twenty-three Silver Stars. The captain of the *Santa Fe* was awarded the Navy Cross, and three of her crew won the Silver Star and another four the Bronze Medal; the ship's crew was awarded a unit commendation for their actions in saving the *Franklin* and her crew.

thought he heard beautiful music surrounding him. He found himself thinking of his brother, "Fivee," who had died from appendicitis a few years earlier. "Please Fivee . . . don't let me die . . . let me get home to Mimi."

He was still begging Fivee for help when the plane hit the water. The sea rushed in through the belly turret, which had been shattered by the flak. Plonsky thought he was going to drown, but a moment later he was in the clear as the nose of the plane went down and the tail went up. Seizing the chance, he jumped out of the door and into the sea.

After the plane stopped, Freligh released the canopy above his head and threw out the one-man life raft that was part of his seat. Sanchez also popped open his escape hatch in the turret and scrambled to get out. They knew they only had about thirty seconds before the plane sank. Sanchez got free. But Freligh's parachute was caught on something in the cockpit as the plane began to go down. He would have drowned, but Sanchez got to him quickly, cutting the pilot free with his survival knife.

They had escaped but had a new fear. Plonsky's hand was torn open. His forefinger hung down with frayed tendons exposed. The rest of his fingers were cut open as well, and he could see the layers of muscle and the bone. However, the biggest worry at that moment was the blood draining into the water. They had all heard stories about the ferocity of the sharks that inhabited the warm waters around the Philippines.

The three young men decided they would all hold onto the life raft while Plonsky kept his bleeding hand inside its tube to catch the blood. They also had to find a way to slow the bleeding or he would weaken and drown. But the first aid kit was with the larger life raft that had gone down with the plane, and they had nothing to make a tourniquet. Then Plonsky remembered the Navy prayer book in his flight jacket or, more specifically, the string used to hold the pages together. His comrades fished it out of his pocket and tied the string tightly above his wrist to stem the flow of blood.

One problem solved seemed to give way to another. They were about a half mile from the main Philippine island of Luzon, a stronghold of the Japanese. They did not relish the idea of being captured, or executed on the spot, by the Japanese. Still, better to reach the jungle and hope to run into some friendly natives than remain in shark-infested waters with a bleeding man. So they tried to paddle toward the distant green canopy, but try as they might, they got no closer.

Exhausted, they gave up and floated for hours, expecting at any time to see gray fins swimming toward them or hear the engine of a Japanese plane arriving to strafe them in the water. They certainly weren't expecting the canoes that appeared in the distance. As the canoes drew closer, the aviators pulled out their .38-caliber service revolvers, wondering if the water-logged weapons would still shoot. They told each other to save a last bullet for themselves rather than be taken by the Japanese.

When the canoes were near enough, they could see that the occupants—small, brown-skinned, dark-haired men in tattered shirts and shorts—were not Japanese. But they didn't know if these natives were friendly or hostile.

Apparently, the canoeists were assessing the aviators' intentions as well as they circled the life raft and the three aviators at a distance. Finally, one of the men in the lead canoe yelled, "Americano? Americano? . . . We Filipino."

"Yes. Yes," the aviators yelled back. "We're Americans." That seemed to satisfy the men in the canoes, who moved in quickly to help them from the water.

The rescuers quickly transferred the Americans to a small fishing boat that appeared and had them lie down in the bottom. They were then covered with woven grass mats, which, the Filipinos made clear, was to hide them from any nosey Japanese patrols.

Upon landing on Luzon, the aviators were quickly led to a nearly deserted village predominantly comprised of thatched huts. Their hosts, several of whom spoke a halting English, explained that they were guerilla fighters. This had been their village, but now they were forced to hide deep in the jungle with their families to avoid the Japanese. They only came down to the beach to fish, help rescue American fighters, and occasionally snipe at Japanese patrols.

That evening they were joined by other guerillas. They brought with them three more American flyers from a different carrier, who had been downed in the same attack on the Japanese fleet and been picked up by a fisherman. The other Americans had managed to salvage their large raft, which had medical supplies, including a seven-day dose of antibiotic sulfa pills they gladly gave to Plonsky. But he still needed to have his hand taken care of properly or it would soon turn gangrenous and have to be amputated.

"You're going to have to shoot me before you amputate my hand," Plonsky said. He did not want to go back to Mimi without all his parts.

Plonsky was in luck. One of the few occupants left in the village was a doctor, who lived in the only wooden house, which is where the guerillas took him and his comrade. The doctor looked at his hand and shook his head. There wasn't much he could do. He had few medical supplies—no sutures and no painkillers. The best he could do was clean the wound, try his best to put the hand back together, bind it and then hope it healed without developing gangrene.

The doctor brought out the last item in his medical inventory, a bottle of alcohol, which he proceeded to pour over Plonsky's hand while the other men held him down. They didn't have to restrain him long, because as soon as the alcohol washed over the wound and the pain hit, he passed out like somebody had clobbered him with a baseball bat. He woke with his hand throbbing inside a tightly bound bandage.

For dinner that night they were each handed a half coconut shell full of rice. Sanchez looked at his and made a face. "Look in yours," he said.

Plonsky looked and made a similar face. Ants were crawling all over the rice. But before he could toss it out, Freligh gave him an order. "Eat it," the pilot said. So Plonsky did as he was told, swallowing the starchy rice and its small inhabitants without chewing.

Later the men were taken to a hut to sleep while the Filipinos stood guard. Worn out, Plonsky nodded right off to sleep on the bamboo floor despite the pain in his hand. He woke several hours later, yelling and feeling as though someone were sticking him with hot needles.

A light was fetched, and the next thing he knew he was grabbed by the other men, rushed outside, and placed in the nearby river. The others had seen what woke him—he was covered with red ants that had been drawn to the blood on his clothes and body. The men washed the ants, and the blood, from his body, the water soothing the pain of the bites.

When he had recovered somewhat from his ordeal, seated in the river, Plonsky looked around. The moon was up over the jungle, illuminating the banks. He had to shake his head and blink to make sure he wasn't seeing things, because no more than fifty feet away, several crocodiles lay on the bank next to the water. He quickly decided he had bathed long enough.

Back in the hut, he thought of his replacement back onboard the *Franklin*. *The Navy had certainly arranged that right.* And he wondered how Mimi would take the news when the telegram arrived at his parents house saying that he was missing in action. *This'll probably kill my mom,* he thought, *especially after losing Fivee.*

Surrounded by the sounds of an alien jungle, alone and very homesick, he was just a skinny Jewish kid with acne, the son of a shoe wholesaler from Massachusetts. What in the hell was he doing in a thatched hut guarded by

Filipino guerillas, eating and being eaten by ants, and then eyed by what
he assumed were hungry crocodiles? He was a week away from his twentieth birthday—and hoping he lived long enough to see it.

October 24-25, 1944
Philippine Sea

Even as Plonsky fell back asleep on the night of October 24, events were
unfolding that could, and would, determine the lives of tens of thousands
of young men like him.

The Japanese Second Fleet had paid a high price for knocking down a
few planes like Plonsky's. Its admiral, Takeo Kurita, had been told he would
have land-based air support to protect his ships. But the planes were sparse
and showed up late. Nor did the new secret weapon, the special attack corps,
find and attack the U.S. carriers, at least not the ones sending the planes
after Kurita's fleet.

So the Japanese learned the hard lesson they had taught everyone else
in the early years of the war: Ships without air cover were doomed when
the enemy's planes showed up. In the course of the attack, the reputedly
unsinkable battleship *Musashi* was hit by ten bombs and an incredible nineteen torpedoes before turning over and plunging beneath the surface.

The battleship's sister, the *Yamato,* also took a hit from a dive-bomber and
spent the rest of the afternoon trying to escape the bombs and torpedoes
of others. Two heavy cruisers were struck repeatedly with bombs and torpedoes and left dead in the water. And a light cruiser was hit by a single
torpedo, exploded spectacularly, and sank within seconds. The battered fleet
reversed course and sought to escape to the west.

The Sho plan was already in disarray, but then Admiral Halsey nearly
managed to save the day for the Japanese. While the attacks on the Second
Fleet were still ongoing, scout planes reported to Halsey on his flagship, the
USS *New Jersey,* that a powerful enemy carrier force (the Japanese Third
Fleet) had been spotted two hundred miles off the northern tip of Luzon.
This was the bait fleet, and Halsey rose to it like a trout to an artificial fly.

Having missed the battles of the Coral Sea and Midway, the admiral was
now determined to make up for it. He believed that it was a carrier-based
plane that had bombed the *Princeton* that morning, and that those carriers
represented a bigger threat than Kurita's "defeated" fleet.

The plane had actually come from the Philippines. The fact was, the Japanese carriers had launched all seventy-six of their aircraft and none of them did any damage to the American fleet. The few who even survived were so poorly trained that they had to land on airstrips in the Philippines because, lacking even rudimentary navigational skills, they would have struggled to find their carriers, much less land on them. But the novice pilots had accomplished their real purpose, and that was to goad Halsey into precipitous action.

It was almost 5:00 P.M. when American scout planes spotted the Japanese bait force, 190 miles to the northeast. They reported a force of four aircraft carriers escorted by four battleships, six to ten cruisers, and a dozen destroyers.

Halsey licked his chops. The ships had to be the last remnant of the once mighty Japanese carrier fleet. Here was the opportunity to exorcise once and for all the demons that had attacked Pearl Harbor. But there was one problem, the Third Fleet's orders were to guard the northern approach to the landing beaches on Leyte.

The Seventh Fleet was already divided in two. The battleships and some of the screening destroyers, as well as a pack of PT boats, were in the south in case the enemy tried to force his way through the Surigao Straits. The second half of the Seventh—the escort carriers and troop transports, as well as their screen of destroyers and destroyer escorts (a smaller, more lightly armed version of their bigger cousins)—was in Leyte Gulf, closest to the troops. However, this force was intended to support the men on shore and was not equipped to deal with an attack from naval forces.

Halsey believed that any threat from the Japanese through the San Bernardino Straits, north of Leyte Gulf, had been dealt with. During the morning of the twenty-fourth, the carrier *Franklin's* task group had discovered the Japanese surface force that included the *Yamato* and *Musashi* in the Sibuyan Sea. The task group's planes attacked the Japanese fleet and claimed that what they didn't sink or leave burning had turned around and was steaming for home.

The Japanese surface fleet in the Sibuyan Sea probably had taken all the punishment it could handle for a while, Halsey reasoned. The Seventh's battlewagons were watching the south, and he thought the escort carriers could handle any smaller threat. Still, he could have split his fleet. Despite having allowed one of his larger task groups to leave for Ulithi to resupply, he had plenty of vessels—including six modern battleships, as well as eight fleet carriers and as many light carriers, plus their planes—to accomplish both purposes, guarding the San Bernardino Straits *and* going after the Japanese carrier fleet.

In fact, Halsey indicated in a message that day to Admiral Kincaid of the Seventh Fleet that he was planning on forming a new task force of surface ships, Task Force 34. The task force would be built around the battleships for the express duty of guarding the straits. But then he ordered the Third Fleet, including the battleships, to steam north to search out and destroy the Japanese carriers.

Halsey, who hoped to get close enough, with the *New Jersey* and the other battleships, to the Japanese carriers to sink them with surface fire, would later explain to Admiral Nimitz that he felt it was "childish" to wait around the straits for an enemy he did not think would show again. So he abandoned his post and took the entire Third Fleet with him to the north, leaving the San Bernardino Straits unguarded and the invasion beaches on Leyte only lightly defended by the escort carriers and a few destroyers of the Seventh Fleet.

The *Franklin* and the rest of Task Group 38.4 was told to break off the pursuit of the Japanese in the Sibuyan Sea and join up with the rest of the task force, which was heading north to find the Japanese carriers. The task groups were slow in forming up, not arriving at the rendevous point until midnight. And even then no one knew exactly where the Japanese carrier fleet was, as the scout planes had lost contact at sunset.

It wasn't until 3:30 in the morning on October 25 that the night fighters located the Japanese fleet, only forty-four miles away. The funny thing was, the enemy ships just seemed to be milling around, almost as though they wanted to be discovered.

The air groups were told to be ready to launch at dawn.

October 24-25, 1944
Surigao Straits

In the meantime, the Seventh Fleet's "muscle" was far to the south of the landing beaches, meeting another threat. U.S. submarines had reported that the Japanese First Fleet—two older battleships, six cruisers, and a half dozen destroyers—were moving toward the Surigao Straits between Leyte and Mindanao. If they succeeded in getting through the straits, they would arrive off the landing beaches in a matter of another hour or so. But at about 10:00 that night, the Japanese ran into some old friends.

As the Japanese vessels, divided into two "striking forces," one trailing the other by a dozen miles, steamed through the narrow straits in a single column, they were beset by American PT boats and destroyers. The small ships soon sank one of the battleships and damaged or sank all but one cruiser and a destroyer from the first striking force.

When the remaining battleship plus the cruiser and destroyer emerged from the straits, the Seventh Fleet's six battleships were waiting. Five of these had been raised from the mud of Pearl Harbor; the sixth was the *Mississippi*. Old and slow, the ships had been mostly relegated to the job of shore bombardment through the course of the war. On this night, however, they finally tasted revenge.

The American ships had pulled off the classic naval maneuver of "crossing the T," in which their battle line formed the horizontal top of the letter, the Japanese the vertical line. It allowed the Americans to pour decimating broadsides into the Japanese ships as they came forward in a line. Volley after volley of one-ton projectiles were hurled at the Japanese ships. When the smoke cleared, the Imperial battleship and cruiser were sinking, though somehow the destroyer escaped to the west.

When the second Japanese striking force entered the straits, its commander saw the burning and sinking hulks of his predecessors and lost his nerve. However, he couldn't escape harassment by American PT boats. One Japanese cruiser was lost to a torpedo and another severely damaged when it ran into an already burning cruiser during all of the confusion.

At daybreak, there was little left of the Japanese First Fleet except for a couple of smoldering wrecks, which were finished off, as well as oil slicks, debris, and the bodies of thousands of Japanese sailors, living and dead. The day was not won though, and in fact was close to being lost.

Rear Admiral Jesse Oldendorf, in command of the U.S. ships at the Surigao Straits, had just recalled his vessels from chasing the remnants of the Japanese fleet when, a little after 7:30 A.M on October 25, he received an urgent message from Admiral Kincaid in the north.

The escort carriers were being attacked by a strong force of Japanese surface ships off the east coast of Samar Island. If the enemy broke through, the American troops on Leyte's shores would be slaughtered. But Oldendorf was a long way from Samar, his ships were nearly out of ammunition, and he was wondering what in the hell had happened to Halsey.

Colored puffs of smoke like fireworks on the Fourth of July burst gaily around the dive-bombers as they began to peel off into their attacks. Pink. Blue. Black. Gray. Lt. E. John Weil thought they looked spectacular, but was fully aware of their murderous intent.

The American pilots had heard that the Japanese were receiving anti-aircraft equipment and training from the Germans, who had been perfecting their techniques for years. Instead of trying to track planes like a hunter leads a running deer, the Germans divided the air space above them into grids, then the guns assigned to a grid tried to fill it with pieces of steel and let the bombers fly into it.

Whatever the enemy was doing, the pilots all noticed that they were getting more accurate. On October 12, Lt. Rupe Weber, who'd replaced Lt. Cmdr. Carl Holstrom as the squadron's executive officer, failed to return with his gunner, James Hatt, after leading the strike against Formosa. The day before the current mission, the squadron lost another plane and its crew when the air wing caught the Japanese in the Sibuyan Sea. Lt. (j.g.) Marshall "Barney" Barnett and his gunner, Leonard Pickens, didn't make it back.

Still, there was nothing for the surviving air crews to do but climb in their planes and take off again at dawn when Task Force 38 turned into the wind and began launching deck load after deck load of Hellcats, Helldivers, and Avengers.

Today was the first time Weil had seen the different colored antiaircraft smoke, but he recognized its significance: Different colors represented different altitudes, giving the gunners on the ships below a better gauge on how to hit the planes.

Up ahead was the first group, led by VB-13 skipper Lt. Chuck Skinner with Lt.(j.g.) Tom Norek, the youngest member of the Franklin's dive-bomber squadron, and his gunner, Harry Steele, on his wing. Weil followed as the leader of the second section.

The squadron began its high speed, nose down approach when suddenly Norek's plane disappeared in a ball of flame and smoke. The rest of the division didn't falter though and on cue peeled off for the ships.

Weil focused on his flying and kept an eye on the prize—a hit on a carrier. There was an unwritten rule in the Navy that planting one on a carrier was good for a Navy Cross, the highest honor in that branch of the service and only one step below the Medal of Honor. But as large a target as a carrier was standing still, it was hell to hit when on the move.

The ship was moving at flank speed while its captain jerked it through a series of hard turns. Just like a car flying around a tight corner on a gravel road, the stern of the ship "skidded" around before the vessel was off on a new course.

A dive-bomber pilot trying to adjust to the ship's gyrations had to be careful that his plane didn't also "skid." Releasing the bomb during a skid would assure the pilot of missing the target. However, correcting the skid and trying to continue with the bombing run would also increase the danger. The closer to the ship he got, the better chance he had of hitting it, but the better target he also made for the ship's guns. The bomb blast from the plane that preceded him might reach up and swat him from the sky. Or he might not be able to pull out of the dive before he ran out of room and crashed into the sea.

Now Weil's plane went into a skid as he tried to keep the carrier in his bombsight. By the time he got it corrected, he was below twenty-five hundred feet and knew he was pushing the envelope if he continued the attack. But he wanted a hit on the carrier in the worst way, as the ultimate goal of every dive-bomber from the moment they began training. And he wanted to give one back to the Japs for his lost friends. He focused on the ship and released his bomb.

Behind him, his tail-gunner, Lou Horton, whooped. "Direct hit, sir!" he yelled into the mike. But there was no time for self-congratulations. By the time he pulled out he was down to two hundred feet where he stayed, jinking and swerving as he passed right alongside one of the Japanese battleships. The massive ship's masts towered high above and he could see the flashes of the guns, some of which were even shooting down to try to shoot the dive-bomber.

Hitting the carrier was akin to kicking an ant hill, the ship's gunners poured flak at his retreating plane. Because there were few fighters to deal with, Horton was shooting a camera instead of his machine guns. He snapped off a frame just as a shell exploded near the tail of the plane. Ten feet closer and they would have joined Norek.

Later in the ready room, the dive-bomber pilots all agreed that the morning's antiaircraft fire was the worst they'd ever seen. They'd lost three planes and their crews including Lt. Jack Finrow, a good friend who'd already served a combat tour aboard the "Big E," the famous *Enterprise,* and his tail-gunner, Henry "Hank" Borja.

The rest considered themselves lucky. The squadron logbook would note that no one could understand "why it was not fifteen or twenty times that number." Weil knew he would be recommended for the Navy Cross, but he would have preferred to have kept his lost squadron mates.

October 25, 1944

By afternoon, Task Force 38 had sunk the large aircraft carrier *Zuikaku,* the last of the six carriers that had attacked Pearl Harbor, as well as two more light carriers. Another light carrier was left afloat but not moving, and several cruisers were on fire or sinking.

The two old battleships and several more cruisers and destroyers were seen fleeing to the north, trying to escape. As the pilots wondered what the next step would be, there was a surprise announcement. The fleet was turning around and heading south as fast as possible.

During the night, the Japanese Second Fleet under Admiral Kurita had regrouped and turned back for the San Bernardino Straits. On the way, he received a message from Admiral Soemu Toyoda, the commander in chief of the Japanese fleet: "All forces will dash to the attack, trusting in divine assistance." He knew that he was expected to succeed or die trying.

Kurita commanded a still powerful force of four battleships, including the *Yamato,* which had recovered from its wounding, as well as six heavy cruisers, two light cruisers, and a dozen destroyers. With or without divine assistance, he should have sicceeded.

The Japanese fleet's arrival off Samar that morning was not a surprise. But Halsey and his staff ignored reports from night fighters that at least some elements of the "defeated" fleet had reversed course and were in the straits. The American admiral assumed that the threat wouldn't be significant and instead pressed his own attacks against the Japanese carriers.

When Kincaid sent his message to Oldendorf that morning, he also pleaded with Halsey for help. But "Bull" ignored the requests for nearly three hours, while his planes chewed up the nearly toothless fleet of aircraft carriers.

Halsey did nothing to rectify his blunder until a message arrived from Admiral Chester Nimitz, the commander in chief of the Pacific Fleet: WHERE IS, REPEAT, WHERE IS TASK FORCE 34? THE WORLD WONDERS.

Only then did Halsey break off and head south, leaving four cruisers and a division of destroyers to chase after the crippled remains of the bait fleet.

CHAPTER FOURTEEN

Desperate Times, Desperate Measures

October 24
Philippine Sea
USS Santa Fe

Commence firing!" At the word from Captain Jerauld Wright, the twelve six-inch guns on the *Santa Fe* thunderclapped as one.

Fifty feet from the closest turret, Gunnery Officer Warren Harding felt the ship tremble beneath his feet. The force of the volley wasn't as violent as it would have been on one of the battleships, where the sixteen-inch guns fired simultaneously would move a thirty-thousand-ton ship sideways in the water. But four turrets with three barrels each could hurl a lot of steel and explosives across the water toward the "light" aircraft carrier floating on the horizon. The destructive capability was magnified by the addition of the guns from the other three cruisers in the division, including two "heavies" with eight-inch guns.

At his battle station high atop the *Santa Fe's* superstructure, Harding watched through his range finders as the first salvo fell short of the carrier. Despite radar and computers, fire control—which had to do with firing the ship's guns, not flame suppression—sometimes needed the human touch for minor adjustments. "Up one hundred," he said into the microphone that connected him to the plotting room.

The guns boomed again, belching smoke and flames from their muzzles. On the weather deck below, the crews manning the open 40-millimeter gun tubs cringed from the concussion; they liked to complain that muzzle flashes burned the hair off their heads even though they wore battle helmets.

Harding saw the armor-piercing projectiles find their marks. They punctured the flight deck, the island, and the hull of the Japanese ship before exploding and sending debris high in the air and out over the water. He informed "plot" that there would not be the need for any more corrections. The guns could fire at will.

Now each turret fired as quickly as its crew could ram a shell and a bag of gunpowder up the three barrels and close the breeches. Each barrel's discharge was staggered from its mates by a half second—first the left, then the right, then the center—so that the projectiles would not interfere with each other's flight.

Harding had a great gunnery crew. A turret could get three salvos in the air before the first one hit the target.

Stopped dead in the water by earlier attacks from U.S. carrier planes, the Japanese carrier made an easy target—a big steel box, sitting still on the water, silhouetted against the dying light of the day. He watched as Japanese sailors swarmed over the flight deck, running first this way and then that, trying to avoid shells they couldn't see coming. They slid down hand lines that had been lowered from the deck into the sea, or just jumped. He saw them floundering in the water, trying to swim away from their doomed ship.

Their struggles brought to mind the image of the Japanese sailors he had seen in the water off Saipan back in August. The *Santa Fe* had been steaming slowly through the area when the ship came upon a hundred or so survivors from a Japanese destroyer that had been sunk the night before. The men were treading water in sodden life jackets or clinging to floating objects. He could see individual faces through the range finders and was struck by their looks of resignation and hopelessness. They knew there was no Japanese navy coming to their rescue, nor were they likely to be picked up by American ships.

This was a cruel war, especially for the losers. Some of the gunners on the 20-millimeters tried to shoot at the enemy sailors, but they were too close to the ship and the barrels couldn't be depressed enough. Harding was glad they couldn't, it just seemed unnecessary.

Now, looking at the aircraft carrier as the guns roared and the ship absorbed hit after hit, catching on fire as men flung themselves into the sea, Harding felt like a bully. He had to remind himself that twenty-four hours earlier, it had been an American aircraft carrier, the *Princeton,* that was on fire and American sailors dying.

The crew of the *Santa Fe* had not heard of the *Princeton* disaster until later that evening. ComCru13, which was now comprised of the light cruisers *Santa Fe* and *Mobile* and the heavy cruisers *Wichita* and *New Orleans,* was chasing north with the rest of the Third Fleet to find a Japanese carrier task force.

Captain Wright came on the loudspeakers to let them know what caused the smoke they had seen on the horizon earlier in the day. The *Princeton* had been hit. "There was an explosion in an ammunition hold," he said. "They had to sink her." There was no mention of the *Birmingham*, except a message that the cruiser's surgeon, who was consulting aboard the *Santa Fe*, was needed immediately back on his ship. A destroyer was sent to pick him up.

Earlier this morning, Harding had watched as hundreds of American planes formed up in the sky above the task force before heading north, where the Japanese carriers had been spotted. It was an impressive sight and, he noted, one the Japanese did not respond to with air attacks of their own. But that didn't mean the U.S. aviators had it easy.

Planes returned badly shot up. Missing their landing gear. Trailing smoke. Engines sputtering. Some landed in the water, occasionally cartwheeling in. Even those pilots who managed a belly landing didn't always get out of their planes on time, and the destroyers rushing to the downed planes weren't always quick enough to help.

The Japanese bait fleet fled north toward Japan with the Third Fleet in hot pursuit. Then all of a sudden in the early afternoon, word came down from the top that the task force was packing up and heading down south.

Harding had wondered why the main body of the fleet left in such a hurry, thinking it couldn't have been good news.

Three hundred miles to the south, Halsey's worst nightmare had come true. At 6:45 that morning, a fighter pilot from one of the Seventh Fleet escort carriers on routine patrol north of the Gulf of Leyte was shocked to see four Japanese battleships and eight cruisers speeding south, only a few hours from the American landing beaches. He reported his discovery and, without waiting for help, single-handedly attacked the Japanese ships. His action was significant as, believing the single plane might have been the precursor to a concentrated attack, the enemy ships went into a defensive, antiaircraft posture—akin to circling the wagons—delaying their southern course.

At the time, Rear Admiral Clifton Sprague was in command of the northernmost of three Seventh Fleet escort carrier task groups in the Gulf of Leyte. When he saw the masts of the Japanese battleships and cruisers appear on the horizon shortly after the warning from the fighter pilot, he figured his men and his ships were doomed.

Sprague also wondered why. He and the other commanders of the Seventh Fleet task groups had been operating under the assumption that Halsey's Third Fleet was guarding the north. In particular, that the battleships of Task Group 34 were in the San Bernardino Straits.

Sprague's ships were no match for the force they faced. If the faster Japanese battleships and cruisers pulled within gun range—about twenty miles for the big ships—they would sink the escort carriers within a few minutes.

All Sprague had to throw at the armada were three destroyers, four destroyer escorts, and a few dozen planes that were not armed with armor-piercing bombs necessary to deal with ships, nor were their pilots trained for such attacks. It was suicide for his forces to stand and fight, but he had no choice. Only a couple of hours from the landing beaches on Leyte, if they couldn't hold off the Japanese warships until help arrived, the slaughter of thousands of American soldiers would commence.

Such a disaster most likely would not have changed the outcome of the war. The United States could produce too many ships, tanks, planes, guns, and men for the Japanese to compete. But losing at Leyte could put the Philippine campaign back months, maybe longer, allowing the Japanese time to build up their defenses. And the massacre of so many U.S. troops might have swayed public opinion to agree to the negotiated settlement the Japanese wanted.

Sprague ordered his small force of destroyers and planes to attack the opposing ships while he tried to maneuver his escort carriers out of the way. The three destroyers—the USS *Hoel, Heermann,* and *Johnston*—launched themselves at the massive battleships, using rainsqualls to their advantage to close to within range of their five-inch guns and torpedoes. They were quickly joined by the destroyer escorts, which had no chance against even the weakest of the Japanese ships.

The American planes—joined by their comrades from the escort carriers to the south—harried the ships with antipersonnel bombs. The bombs were of little use against armor plating, but they were enough to panic the Japanese. When they ran out of bombs, the pilots continued to attack as if armed.

The Japanese command was confused and disorganized. The ferocity, both real and feigned, of the American surface and air attack forced the battleships into evasive maneuvers, further slowing their advance.

Unbelievably, for a brief time the Americans were winning the fight. Three Japanese cruisers were hit and set afire. But as the battle wore on, their losses

began to mount. The scrappy destroyers *Hoel* and *Johnston* and the destroyer escort USS *Samuel B. Roberts* were blown apart by gunfire. Then the escort carrier USS *Gambier Bay* was hit repeatedly and sunk, the only U.S. carrier claimed by gunfire from surface ships in the war.

The Americans fought on bravely, but were about finished. The planes were out of bombs and bullets; the destroyers had used up their torpedoes.

Sprague knew that the Japanese would soon realize they were fighting a paper tiger and then his men would be annihilated. He was amazed that he wasn't already swimming, or worse. Exhausted by the rigors of the two-hour battle, he was wondering how it would end when he heard one of his signalmen yell, "Goddamnit, boys, they're getting away!"

It was truly one of the great lines of the war. But sure enough, the mighty Japanese fleet was inexplicably retreating. Sprague couldn't believe it until his scout planes continued to report that the enemy was running north for the San Bernardino Straits.

What could have been going through Kurita's mind? Perhaps he thought that the unusually fierce resistance meant he had stumbled upon an outlying element of the Third Fleet that was only fighting a temporary holding action until the main force showed up at any minute. Or maybe the two-hour delay caused by Sprague's warriors panicked Kurita, who, already battered by the previous day's air attacks, believed that Halsey would arrive from the north and cut off his retreat through the straits.

Whatever the reason, Kurita knew that the Sho plan was a do-or-die proposition. Retreating wasn't supposed to be an option. But he disengaged and ran, his blunder even bigger than Halsey's. On the brink of one of the most stunning blows of the war, he had snatched defeat from the jaws of victory.

Any help would have been hours away. Only after receiving Nimitz's inquiry—*Where is, repeat, where is Task Force 34? The world wonders*—did Halsey reluctantly turn back from chasing the bait fleet. He was not fast enough to cut off the escape of Kurita's ships, including the *Yamato*, which went home to Japan to brood until some final use might be found for the goliath.

When the *Santa Fe*'s crew learned they had been left behind by the carriers and battleships, they hoped that the Japanese cripples included only other cruisers and destroyers. They had heard there were battleships in this Japanese fleet, and even a crippled battleship, like a wounded bull, was dangerous to a light cruiser.

A little after 4:00 in the afternoon, radar picked up a surface target ten miles ahead. It was a large ship and apparently unable to move.

When it appeared on the horizon, Harding looked at the ship through his range finders. The vessel was a light aircraft carrier—like its American counterparts, built on the hull of a cruiser. He couldn't see any damage to the ship; it wasn't on fire or listing, and appeared to be in no danger of sinking.

The cruisers turned broadside to the carrier. They were not concerned with the sporadic and light gunfire that emanated from the enemy ship and fell well short of the mark. The four turrets of the *Santa Fe*'s main six-inch battery swiveled to bear on the carrier and at DuBose's command commenced firing.

The six-inch guns of the light cruisers and eight-inch guns of the heavies mauled the ship for an hour until at last the carrier slowly listed to port and began to sink. Admiral DuBose ordered the destroyers to move in and finish her with torpedoes "if desirable, but don't waste them."

Five minutes later, the commander of the destroyer division radioed back to the *Santa Fe*: "She is going down and not worth a fish. I am rejoining."

Harding was glad to see the Japanese carrier go under; his six-inch guns alone had sent 281 rounds flying toward the ship, most of them hitting her. He knew the sinking was necessary. There were no planes on the ship's flight deck, but that didn't mean they weren't around and wouldn't be returning. Nor could the ship be left afloat to be salvaged by the Japanese, to kill Americans again some other day.

Still, he felt sorry for the sailors in the water. The crew was probably about the same size as the *Santa Fe*'s. They were human beings, and he took no joy knowing they would probably all die so many miles from their homes and loved ones. But he also recalled looking through those same range finders as young Marines were slaughtered without mercy on the beach at Tarawa, and as the smoke plumed on the horizon the previous morning from the *Princeton*.

It could just as easily have been us, he reminded himself. *We could just as easily have been the ones in the water tonight.* It was just the nature of war that a lot of people were going to die before it would be over and he could go home to Jo, get a job, and raise a family in peace. He and his men hadn't asked for this fight, but they would help finish it if they could.

A few survivors were picked up by a destroyer and brought to the *Santa Fe* for questioning. Before they were taken to the brig, they said their ship was the *Chiyoda*. Later they would be transferred to a ship to be taken to a prisoner of war camp where they would be fed, clothed, and given medical attention. Their shipmates, however, did not fare as well.

Search planes had discovered more enemy vessels, traveling in small groups forty to fifty miles to the north. All of them "going like hell" toward Japan, according to the pilots. As the American cruisers and destroyers turned to give chase, Harding didn't look back as the remaining sailors from the *Chiyoda* were left behind, alone on the surface of a dark and heedless ocean with night closing in.

Later, October 25, 1944

The sun was down when Admiral DuBose's task group closed on the three surface pips picked up on radar. The ships appeared to be waiting for them, a rear guard left to protect the fleeing battleships, which seemed to have lost all of their heart for the fight. The *Santa Fe* and *Mobile* were ordered to take on the nearest of the targets, while the *Wichita* and *New Orleans* shot at the more distant with their bigger guns.

For the next hour, the two light cruisers chased what turned out to be another cruiser. Crashing through the swells at twenty-eight knots, the opponents exchanged volleys in an old-fashioned naval duel. Red tracers from the American ships illuminated the night sky as they arced toward the enemy. A sudden flash at the end of their trajectory, followed by a fire that flared and quickly went out, indicated a hit.

The Japanese ship shot back. Shells splashed ahead of the American cruisers and others whistled overhead.

The Americans fired again and again, running forward in a zigzag pattern so that all the turrets could be brought to bear on the target—sending off a broadside with each turn. More flashes and fires flared in the distance despite the Japanese ship's wild course changes and counterfire.

Wounded, the Japanese cruiser slowed until the *Santa Fe* rushed in alone to within a few thousand yards, almost point-blank for her main batteries, which could hit targets ten miles away. The ship's five-inch guns shot star shells over the Japanese ship, illuminating the enemy ship like an actor on a stage. Then the Lucky Lady poured a series of volleys into the now-blazing wreck.

Four minutes later the Japanese cruiser lay still in the water beneath the eerie glow of the star shells. Destroyers were sent in to finish the ship with torpedoes but again reported that a ship had sunk without their torpedoes to speed the process.

"He has gone down," radioed the skipper of the destroyer USS *Porterfield.* "We were cheated."

"It breaks our hearts," was the reply from DuBose's staff.

Leaving the survivors to fend for themselves as the star shells slowly settled into the water and went out, the *Santa Fe* and *Mobile* turned to resume the hunt. But night fighters reported that the nearest target was forty-two miles to the north and going fast. The cruisers could have gone on, but the destroyers didn't have enough fuel for a thirty-knot stern chase, so the task group had to give up and head south to rejoin the carrier force.

So ended the *Santa Fe's* part in the greatest naval clash in history, the Second Battle of the Philippine Sea, which included the various actions at Surigao Straits, Leyte Gulf, and north of the Philippines. The struggle had featured the only duel between American and Japanese battleships of the war, as well as one of the few times surface ships of any size would fight toe-to-toe.

Over the course of four days, 170 U.S. ships and 1,400 aircraft had destroyed 35 Japanese warships, including one large carrier, three light carriers, three battleships, six heavy cruisers, four light cruisers, and twelve destroyers. An estimated 20,000 Japanese sailors and their officers were killed outright, went down with their ships, or plunged into the water where very few were rescued from the sharks, the sun, and the sea.

The United States lost one light carrier, the *Princeton,* and two escort carriers, two destroyers, and a destroyer escort; a half dozen more ships were damaged, including the *Birmingham.* Hundreds of U.S. sailors died, though most crews from the damaged or sunk ships were saved from the clutches of the ocean.

October 24–25, 1944
The Special Attacks Corps

The Sho plan had turned into a crushing blow for the Japanese. The Imperial Navy essentially ceased to exist as an effective fighting force, except for its aircraft. Never again would its ships be able to contest the U.S. Navy's supremacy on the seas. But there was one major ramification of that statement no one quite understood as yet.

A desperate strategy that actually failed to accomplish its champion's stated goal of knocking the big American carriers out of the fight emerged as one of the few successes for the Japanese. The special attacks corps did more damage to American warships than any of the vaunted battleships or the conventional air attacks, which, except for the mortal wounding of the *Princeton,* had little to show for the loss of hundreds of planes and their aviators.

The contribution of suicidal pilots during the battle began slowly. On the twenty-fourth, a suicide plane struck the fleet tugboat USS *Sonoma,* sinking her. But once again, the plane was not one of Admiral Onishi's volunteers. The Japanese were not even sure, when they heard about the attack, if it was a Navy plane from a different unit or a plane from the Japanese army, some of whose pilots were also enamored with the special attacks concept.

Meanwhile, Onishi's pilots waited day after day for word of the whereabouts of the American carriers. Hour by hour, they had to keep themselves mentally and spiritually prepared to kill themselves, a psychologically exhausting challenge. They finally got their chance mid-morning of October 25.

While Admiral Sprague's group was holding off the main Japanese force to the north, another of the escort carrier task groups farther south was hit by the first of the organized suicide planes. By the time the sailors on the escort carrier USS *Santee* saw the Japanese plane emerge from a low-lying cloud, it was too late to bring their guns to bear. They feared a bombing attack, but the Zero never pulled up or released its bomb. Instead, it tore through the flight deck, creating a 450-square-foot hole. Plane and bomb exploded in the hangar, causing a fire where stored bombs were waiting to be placed on planes. Fortunately, those bombs didn't detonate before the crew put out the fire. However, sixteen *Santee* shipmates were dead, another twenty-seven were wounded, and the ship was put out of action.

A little later, the men on the escort carrier USS *Suwannee* saw the plane that had singled them out. The gunners even managed to hit it when the pilot hesitated before starting his dive. But they couldn't stop him. Dozens of American sailors were killed and wounded when the plane crashed into the flight deck, but the damage was slight and the ship was operating again in two hours.

The escort carriers USS *Kitkun Bay* and *Kalinin Bay* were also hit. The former was slightly damaged, but the latter was put out of action; both crews suffered casualties.

A Zeke delivered the worst blow when it crashed through the flight deck of the escort carrier USS *St. Lo,* which had been named after one of the bloody

Normandy landing beaches. The plane and its bomb exploded on the hangar deck among parked planes, setting off aviation fuel and munitions in a series of spectacular explosions. The flight deck, an elevator, and several entire planes were blown into the sky along with less identifiable debris.

The *St. Lo* sank in less than an hour; 126 of the ship's 898-member crew died. For many of those survivors in the water, the last memory they would have of their ship was one of pride as the Stars and Stripes battle flag was still flying as the waters claimed her. The special attacks corps had claimed their first ship.

In trying to glean anything positive from the fiasco of the Sho plan, the Japanese war council grasped onto the amazing effectiveness of the certain-death units. There would be those who continued to support conventional air attacks as the only honorable course. But the truth was that from the Battle of Leyte Gulf on, the only effective weapon the Japanese had against the U. S. Navy were the divine winds—the *kamikaze*.

CHAPTER FIFTEEN

Kamikaze

October 30, 1944
Philippine Sea, East of Samar
USS Franklin

L t. Willard Gove and the other fighter pilots in the ready room glanced up toward the flight deck at the sudden percussion of the five-inch guns. They weren't used to the sound of antiaircraft fire from this vantage point on the gallery deck. "Let's get the hell out of here," the squadron leader, Commander "Cap" Coleman, said. "You guys follow me; I'm going inside the island."

Gove sighed. He just wanted to get the meeting over with. It was early afternoon and there might still have been time for a mission, or at least a little combat air patrol. He thought "Cap," as courageous a combat pilot as any in the air, was now acting as nervous as a replacement pilot getting ready for his first combat flight.

Coleman had called together the flight leaders to discuss what to do about the pilots who seemed to be having second thoughts about flying combat missions. Most of these men were on their second tours—had even flown in the old F4F Wildcats back when the Zero still ruled the sky—and maybe thought they had taken enough chances. The flight leaders pondered creating a short list of guys to send home a little early. Let some of the new young bucks out of training school get a crack at the Japs. At least that was a nice way to put it.

Gove had no problem with anyone who wanted out, but he didn't really understand not wanting to fly in combat. Personally, at twenty-six years old, he couldn't wait to get back into his Hellcat—the hotter the action, the better.

Coleman had flown more total combat hours (209) and more strikes (51) than anyone in the squadron. As the skipper, he could fly whenever he wanted, which was all the time. Otherwise, only one other man in the squadron—Ensign Dick Huxford—had logged more than Gove's 194 combat hours on this tour. And with forty-four strikes, Gove was tied for second most with two others, Lt. (j.g.) George Orner and Ensign Bob Slingerland; seven others—including Bowen and Pope from his flight group—had forty-three.

Despite having flown nearly sixty total missions, Gove still had that fighter pilot's mentality, a combination of derring-do, aggressiveness, swagger and maybe just a little craziness thrown in. Even getting shot down and stranded in a life raft in the middle of the ocean had slowed him down only long enough to catch up on his sleep. If he sometimes forgot to go to Sunday services, well, he hadn't forgotten his promise to God to attend church more regularly, only delayed its implementation until his life grew a little less hectic.

October had been a busy month, even for Gove. He had flown so often—twenty out of thirty days so far—that days and missions seemed to run together in a hodgepodge of briefings, takeoffs, dogfights, ocean, rockets, beaches, machine-gun fire, jungles, bombing runs, ack-ack, ships, and landings. The logbook he kept religiously was his only reliable source for what happened the previous week. And he had a lot more notations lately about the squadron "losing" pilots.

Actually, since the squadron's executive officer, Lt. Cmdr. Kelly Blair, crashed in June, VF-13 had lost eighteen pilots—almost half the squadron—eight of them in October alone. Often it was the ocean, not the Japanese, that took their lives. About half of the pilots forced to make water landings were picked up by destroyers, seaplanes, or submarines. The other half didn't make it out of their cockpits before their planes plunged to the bottom.

On October 17—three days after Gove shot down the three Japanese planes and two days after he quarterbacked the dismantling of the flock of Zeros—Lt. (j.g.) Joe Kopman had gone down with his plane. But nobody knew why.

Returning from the end of a mission, Kopman radioed in that he was out of fuel and made a nice smooth water landing. The other pilots in his formation expected to see him pop the canopy and climb out. But as the seconds ticked by, there was no sign of Kopman. A destroyer rushed toward the fighter, but before the ship could arrive, the plane stood on its nose, hung for a moment, and then slid beneath the surface. Just like that, Kopman was gone

The next day, Gove was with another pilot who faced a similar fate. The mission on October 18 was pretty much the same as the day before: pound away at the Japanese positions and airfields around Manila while dodging horrific antiaircraft fire and abundant, if not skilled, Japanese pilots.

During the attack, Gove got separated from his companions and headed alone to the rendezvous point about two hundred miles east of the Philippines before heading back to the ship. When he arrived, he saw that there was another Hellcat circling and swung over for a closer look. He smiled when he recognized the pilot, his friend Lt. Johnny Johnson.

As usual, the twenty-six-year-old Johnson looked like he had been in a scrap; his plane was riddled with bullet holes and splattered with oil. He used hand signals to tell Gove that his radio, landing gear, tail hook, and the hydraulic equipment that lifted the heavy Plexiglas canopy were all casualties of the enemy's bullets. To make matters worse, he was almost out of fuel.

Johnson was a little banged up himself; he had caught several fragments in his right arm and right leg. But in typical Johnny Johnson—"if you think I look bad, you should see the other guy"—style, he also signed that he had shot down one of the two Zeros that jumped him.

For all of Johnson's bravado, Gove realized his friend was in a real predicament. He was going to have to crash-land. The question was whether it would be in the water or on the deck of a carrier. If it was the water, Gove knew his friend probably wasn't going to make it; he would never unhook, unstrap, and crank the canopy open manually with his injured arm before the plane sank.

Gove motioned for his friend to follow him back to the *Franklin*. When they got within sight of the ship, he radioed ahead, "I've got an injured chicken that needs to land aboard."

Cmdr. Joe Taylor, the *Franklin's* air officer, talked it over with Captain Shoemaker, who had a tough decision. There were twenty other planes still to land, and if Johnson crashed, they couldn't land and it could even imperil the ship. "Sorry, Will, but no way," Taylor replied. "He's got to land in the water."

"Yeah, but . . . ," Gove explained that Johnson was hurt; he would never get out of the plane.

Taylor repeated the order. It wasn't his choice; the decision was coming down from Shoemaker and the captain could not risk the ship for a single pilot.

"Yeah, but . . . " Every time Gove was told to relay the order to Johnson, he countered with another version of his same argument. If the wounded pilot landed in the water, he would die.

Fortunately, Gove had a sympathetic ear in Taylor. The air officer and Johnson were friends. Taylor talked it over with Shoemaker again. If anybody could bring a plane in at a hundred miles an hour with no wheels and no flaps it was Johnson. The captain nodded, "Okay, bring him in."

The flight deck was cleared and Shoemaker raced the ship into the wind as fast as it would go to help slow the landing plane. Johnson didn't have a tail hook to catch the arresting cables, but he touched down on the plane's belly as lightly as possible, then scraped across the deck and stopped just short of the crash barrier. Afraid that the plane would catch on fire, the flight deck crew rushed to pry him out of the cockpit. As soon as Johnson was out, he used his one good arm to help push the battered aircraft over the side of the ship. The carrier was back in flight operations a few minutes later. And the next day, Johnson, his wounded elbow patched up, and Gove were back in Hellcats when the squadron took off again for Manila.

On October 21, the U.S. 6th Army landed on Leyte. But Gove and the rest of the *Franklin* pilots, except a dozen who were flying combat air patrol above the task group, were grounded while the carrier group withdrew to the east to refuel and take on supplies and ammunition. For Gove it was his first day off after flying the past twelve days straight, one more than any other pilot on the ship.

The break didn't last long. On the night of the twenty-third, American submarines spotted the Japanese fleets heading for the Philippines and the *Franklin* steamed west to intercept, launching at dawn on October 24. Gove wrote cryptically in his logbook about the events of the next two days that covered the Second Battle of the Philippine Sea. For the twenty-fourth he wrote simply: "Combat over Manila Bay." The next day, when the *Franklin* chased north after the Japanese carrier "bait" fleet with Halsey, he jotted: "Fleet Action. Strafed and rocketed light cruiser."

Commander Coleman would prove a little more imaginative, if no less vague, in his description of the attack on the Japanese carrier fleet for the *Franklin Forum*: "I was there all day, and I don't know half of what happened and wouldn't believe half of what I did see, if I hadn't been there."

On the twenty-sixth only a half dozen pilots flew combat air patrol as the carrier task group again withdrew to refuel. But the next morning, three flights of heavily laden fighters—four to a flight—lumbered off the *Franklin's* deck. They were being sent off on a "special mission" to search for Japanese warships still thought to be fleeing east, escaping the failed Japanese attempt to stop the Leyte invasion. The mission was expected to be a long one, so the Hellcats were weighted down with an extra 150-gallon belly tank of fuel, in addition to six rockets and a five-hundred-pound bomb each.

That afternoon, Gove was leading his flight—which included Lt. (j.g.) Bill Bowen and Ensigns A. J. Pope and Bill Nygren—over the collection of smaller islands in the middle of the archipelago when Pope spotted a big, twin-engine Japanese transport below them. They pounced with Pope leading the way, followed by Bowen and Nygren, while Gove hung back. The transport plane's pilot probably didn't see them until his plane was already riddled by fifty-caliber bullets and on fire.

Gove never even shot his guns; he didn't have to—the plane was engulfed in flames and on its way down before he got a chance. He looked up now, however, and saw an even larger, four-engine plane high above them. The group reformed and threw their engines into overdrive to climb up to intercept the big bomber.

They were about a thousand feet from the plane and in attack formation when a worried voice broke in over their Very High Frequency (VHF) radios, surprising the fighter pilots, who usually operated only with hand signals and didn't know anyone else was using "their" frequency.

"Hey, knock it off, you goddamn Hellcats," said the pilot of the bomber they were preparing to shoot down. He was a U.S. Navy pilot flying a new aircraft—the Navy version of a B-24—which is why they hadn't recognized the plane. The fighter pilots gleefully assured the bomber pilot that they *probably* would have seen the star on his wings and fuselage before they opened fire.

As if on cue, a more familiar voice broke in. "Hey, Will, you guys got anything left?" Johnson asked. He was leading a flight over a different sector some sixty miles to the north and had discovered a Japanese cruiser. Johnson said he and his guys had shot up the ship with machine guns and rockets, but they didn't have any bombs left and had since run out of ammunition.

Gove knew that he and his companions had all their bombs and rockets. Their problem was fuel. They had already dropped the extra belly tanks and used a lot of gasoline climbing to reach the bomber. It would be risky— flying north, attacking the cruiser, and then getting back to the *Franklin*. "We'll be right there," he replied.

Low on fuel themselves, Johnson and his team were gone by the time Gove and his guys arrived. Gove looked at his fuel gauge again. He estimated that they had enough, barely, for one pass at the ship.

Like the pilot of the transport plane earlier that afternoon, the captain of the cruiser didn't see the Americans until it was too late to take evasive action, as they dove out of the sun at more than three hundred miles an hour. This time, Gove led the charge dropping from fifteen thousand feet to about six thousand, at which point he released his armor-piercing bomb, then fired his rockets before pulling the trigger to rake the deck with his machine guns as he passed over the cruiser.

After his pass, Gove turned immediately for the *Franklin*, conscious that he was nearly out of gas and more than a hundred miles from the carrier. There wasn't even enough fuel to make another pass to see if he had done any damage. But Pope and Bowen, who had followed him, let him know all about it.

The hundreds of practice bombing runs he had made as an instructor at Kingsville had paid off. "You put it right down his smokestack," Bowen said. It was a figure of speech, but it meant Gove had hit the middle of the ship. His flight mates had seen the flash of the explosion after the bomb pierced the weather deck and dug its way into the bowels of the cruiser before blowing up.

Gove was pleased with the report; it probably meant he had sunk a cruiser. But at that moment, all he really wanted was to reach the carrier before his plane fell out of the sky.

When the fighter pilots spotted the *Franklin*, they didn't bother to get into the landing circle but headed straight for the flight deck. They were running on fumes, but they all made it. Bowen had just enough to bring his plane in and catch the arresting cable before his engine sputtered and quit. Instead of taxiing forward ahead of the crash barrier, his Hellcat had to be pushed.

When Gove logged his hours, he was shocked. The longest he had ever been up before was 4.8 hours, which was on combat air patrol, hovering above the fleet and conserving fuel. This mission had lasted 5.2 hours, a squadron record. VF-13 was lucky four pilots didn't have to be fished out of the drink, which would have meant two of them would have probably drowned.

They heard later that fighters from the *Enterprise* had gone out to finish off the cruiser, and two destroyers reported to be damaged in the same vicinity. When the "Big E" pilots arrived, the cruiser had already gone under, so they sunk the destroyers and went home.

For the next two days, Gove flew combat air patrol over the landing beaches on Leyte. On October 30, the squadron was essentially waiting around to see if the Army needed any help when a task group of fleet fuel tankers about fifty miles north reported they were under attack. A dozen fighters were sent to the rescue. Gove had hoped to go with them, but instead Coleman asked him and a few of the other flight leaders to report to the ready room to discuss what to do about the pilots who kept having "engine trouble" before missions. Nothing was settled when the ship's guns started firing and the skipper decided to move the meeting.

The pilots followed Coleman into the portion of the island structure built below the flight deck and down several ladders to another room. They had hardly settled into their seats when the pounding of the five-inch batteries suddenly picked up their pace and were then augmented by the frantic staccato pops and bangs of the smaller guns.

Coleman dove under a table just as a dull boom rolled through the ship, vibrating right up through his flight shoes. A moment later, the ship's public address system crackled with an urgent call, "All hands on deck!"

On October 30, 1944, the suicide plane attacks were still being viewed as an aberration by the American fleet commanders—a last desperate measure by battle-fatigued Japanese pilots. The sailors and officers on the ships under attack, however, noticed that for an aberration, there were an awful lot of these attacks. Most of them were performed by Zeros, but all sorts of planes were making suicide dives, including the *Suisei* bomber that on October 28 crashed into the cruiser USS *Denver*, causing considerable damage to the superstructure and a dozen casualties.

However, after the sinking of the *St. Lo* on October 25, during the Battle of Leyte Gulf, no other ships had been sunk despite many attempts. These suicidal missions of crazed Japanese pilots were not very effective. Few eyebrows were raised on the twenty-ninth, when a suicide plane struck the *Essex*-class carrier USS *Intrepid*. After all, only ten men were killed and six wounded, and the ship continued with its flight operations within the hour.

All day on the thirtieth, large groups of enemy aircraft hovered at the edge of the *Franklin's* task group—which also included the *Enterprise, Belleau Wood,* and *San Jacinto*—as if sizing up the combat air patrol, but none had come within ten miles. The next afternoon, however, the *Franklin* received the urgent message from the fleet's tankers and the fighters were launched to respond.

After the Hellcats were on their way, the *Franklin* continued cruising along at fifteen knots on light seas with visibility about twelve miles and a high cloud ceiling. Nearly forty-five planes were parked on the flight deck. They were fully gassed and their machine guns armed, but none were carrying any bombs or missiles; another forty-five planes, fueled but not armed, were parked in the hangar. The gasoline supply hoses had been shut off and purged with inert gas.

Meanwhile, radar reported no bogeys in the area, so Captain Shoemaker relaxed General Quarters from Condition I to Condition III to allow some of the men to move about the ship, grab a meal, carry on with their regular duties, or relax before the next engagement. Therefore, while the anti-aircraft guns were manned, not all of the hatches were shut and dogged.

More fighters were being launched from the catapults for combat air patrol when a half dozen Japanese planes—both Zeros and Judy dive-bombers—suddenly appeared high above the task group's radar scans and the CAP. The cruisers and destroyers of the defensive screen closed in tight around the carriers to concentrate their gunfire.

When the Japanese planes approached to within six miles—only about a half minute out—every five-inch gun in the formation began shooting. The Japanese planes circled as the combat air patrol began rising to meet them. Then three of the attackers peeled off and plunged toward the task group as the ships' 40-millimeters, soon joined by the twenties, began to shoot, and the *Franklin* heeled over in a turn to evade the planes.

The combat air patrol couldn't stop the planes in their mad dash as they closed in on the closest carrier in their path, the *Franklin.* But the ship's guns turned the first plane into a mass of flames, and it missed the carrier by twenty feet and splashed into the sea, leaving two more bandits in the sky.

Lt. (j.g.) Robert Wassman was standing at his battle station in the open air of the "secondary con" on the aft part of the island, having just watched the first plane miss the ship. Above the roar of the *Franklin*'s guns, he heard the air officer, Cmdr. Joe Taylor, on his headphones calmly say, "Here he comes." Suddenly, a plane's engine screamed behind him, there was a roar like a passing train, followed by an explosion that shook the ship.

Wassman looked over the side at the flight deck. An enormous hole gaped just to the rear of the island. A black cloud of smoke billowed from the crater; flames leaped forty feet into the air and licked at the planes on the deck. He was supposed to remain at his battle station, but he was damned if he would stand around watching a fire grow on his ship. He climbed over the side of the steel wall that surrounded the con and went down several ladders to the flight deck.

"You men follow me," he yelled to a group of stunned-looking sailors and ran for a fire hose. Spurred to action, the sailors joined him in dragging the hose to the edge of the inferno and began to pour foam on the blaze.

Ripping into the ship just aft of the island at about three hundred miles an hour, the second kamikaze had crashed through the flight and gallery decks and into the hangar, where the plane's five-hundred-pound bomb detonated among the parked planes. Two dozen men died in the initial blast, dozens more were injured.

It almost got worse. The third kamikaze plunged toward the ship, but this pilot released his bomb, which missed the bridge by only a few feet and splashed harmlessly into the ocean. The plane was so low when it pulled out of its dive that some observers on the *Franklin* swore it touched the water. Instead of trying to escape, the pilot now continued his charge through the hail of antiaircraft fire and then rose slightly and crashed into planes parked on the aft end of the *Belleau Wood*. A second carrier was now burning. But the damage to the smaller light carrier was mostly confined to a half dozen planes, and the fire was quickly put out.

The battle on the *Franklin*, however, was just beginning as a thick column of smoke towered high into the gray skies, a beacon for other Japanese planes. The blast ruptured aircraft fuel tanks, causing flames to spread quickly and grow in intensity. Spilled fuel leaked to other decks below the hangar, where it too caught fire; gasoline vapor explosions rocked compartments throughout the interior of the ship.

Twenty minutes after the crash, a massive explosion of gasoline vapors—more powerful than the initial blast—rattled the *Franklin* again. Dozens more men died. But fire-fighting crews fought back with thousands of gallons of seawater and foam.

Down in the hangar deck, the men in the conflagration station—responsible for turning on an overhead sprinkler system—were burned when the blast blew in the windows of their office and then forced to abandon their post by the flames. But not before they turned on the water.

Still, it was thirty minutes before anyone could reenter the hangar to fight the still blazing fires. Even then it was nearly impossible for the men to see what they were doing, and they were forced to wear rescue breathing apparatus—self-contained masks with oxygen bottles that were good for about thirty minutes.

The Japanese were still trying to finish the ship, which had to dodge their attacks while its crew fought the fires. Sailors kept going down, injured by flying pieces of steel or flames or overcome by smoke. But when one went down, another would step up to his place in line on the hoses. Still others carried on with their duties throughout the ship, in spite of their fears that would spike with each explosion.

Steward's Mate 2nd Class Matthew Little had been in his sleeping compartment when General Quarters sounded. He moved quickly as sailors ran down the passageways or scrambled up and down ladders. He wished he were running to the guns up in the open air, but instead he headed for his battle station in an ammunition magazine five decks below.

Shortly after he arrived inside the magazine, Little felt the ship vibrate beneath his feet from the kamikaze crashing through the deck into the hangar. The ship leaned one way and then another, apparently to avoid more planes. Every man in the magazine was conscious of being far below the waterline and in the most vulnerable spot in the ship. A fire would kill them all, as would a torpedo. But no man broke for the hatch to try to escape; instead, they got to work.

Little and his mates passed hundred-pound, five-inch shells to the conveyors running to the men on the guns. When smoke began to pour into the ammunition hold, they donned rescue breathing apparatus masks and kept working, even when the ventilation system shut down and the heat rose until they felt like the fire was right outside the door. Courage meant staying in place and just doing the job.

Meanwhile, as the *Franklin's* sailors and their officers worked to save their ship, a destroyer was ordered to come alongside. After conferring with Captain Shoemaker about the possibility that the *Franklin* might have to be abandoned if the fires grew worse, Admiral Davison transferred his flag, person, and staff to the *Enterprise*. The *Franklin* was at the very least going to be out of action, even if the fires could be controlled, and the admiral needed to carry on the war effort from another ship.

The men on the carrier's flight deck and island watched Davison go and said good riddance; Big Ben was their home, not his. They would save their ship without the help of any admirals.

Deep in the interior of the *Franklin,* a far-off rumble became a roar and smoke began to pour into the fire room through the ventilation system. "Shut the blowers off," yelled the petty officers. "Watch your pressure!"

Although the ship had obviously been hit, it had not yet affected the engineering spaces. One by one they all checked in to damage control, "All secure."

The ship was still moving at twenty-six knots, but gradually the shooting stopped and the Black Gang relaxed a bit. Water Tender 2nd Class Ernest Scott and the other members of the fire room crew were told they couldn't be relieved quite yet, as the third deck above them was flooded from fighting the fires. At last the emergency hatch from the third deck into the fireroom was cracked. A sheet of water flooded down upon the crew, but it passed through the grates in the deck and into the bilge, where it would could be pumped out. The flow quickly tapered off and Petty Officer 1st Class John Frajman poked his craggy face in.

For once, Scott was happy to see Frajman. But the news he got from Jim Dunn, another member of the Black Gang, who had just come down to relieve the watch, was terrible. Dunn told the gang that the ship had been hit by a suicide plane; then turning to Scott, his face betrayed the news before he spoke. The plane, he said, had hit at the base of Eddie Carlisle's gun mount and wiped it out.

"Oh God," Scott groaned. "No, Jim . . ."

Dunn hung his head. "I'm sorry as hell, Scotty, but that's what one of the gunners told me."

Scott felt sick to his stomach. *It can't be,* he thought. *It just can't be. Not Eddie. . .* He burst into tears.

A few minutes later, Frajman came over and patted him on the shoulder. "Go up and eat, Scotty," he said. "You'll have to come back down as soon as you can."

Scott turned from the other man. "I don't want to eat," he said quietly and began to walk away.

But Frajman reached out with a big hand and spun him around. "Look, Scotty, I heard about Ed," he said, his voice still gentle, but firmer. "I'm sorry if it's true, but we gotta keep this barge running. Get your ass up there and eat something."

Scott would have protested further, but the look on Frajman's face told him that the petty officer wasn't going to tolerate any insubordination this time. So Scott climbed up the ladder and out of the fire room onto the third deck. The third deck was awash with eight inches of warm dirty water and only dimly lit with a few emergency battle lanterns placed at long intervals down the passageways. The air smelled of burned fuel and scorched paint.

Scott still didn't plan on eating anything, but he moved toward the mess hall anyway, hoping to find someone who could tell him about Eddie's final moments. He had almost reached the hall when he heard a familiar voice complaining in a Maine accent, "Goddamn bastards walked all over me."

Rushing into the compartment, Scott could just make out the short figure of Eddie Carlisle standing beside a large barrel of canned peaches. Carlisle was talking to several gunners' mates as they shared the barrel's contents, dipping their bare hands in for the syrupy peach halves.

How many times since childhood Scott had seen that face smeared with some sort of sticky juice, he probably couldn't have counted. But this was the best of all. He ran up and grabbed his friend in a bear hug, then slapped him on the back, shook his hand, and hugged him again—all the while exclaiming, "Man, am I glad to see you! Where ya been? I heard you bought the farm."

When Carlisle finally managed to extricate himself from Scott's clutches, he explained how close the rumor came to being true. When the alarm had sounded, he had rushed to his gun mount. His station was in the clipping room—a small compartment where 40-millimeter rounds were loaded into clips. The room was behind and below the main platform of the mount, and

Carlisle's job was to pass the clips through a shoulder-high hatch to a loader standing on the platform.

After the action started, Carlisle said, he was too busy to see much. But it was true that a suicide plane struck near the base of his gun. The concussion blew several men right out of the mount, he said; others were horribly burned by a wave of fire that passed across the guns, cooking the flesh off their hands, arms, and the exposed areas of their faces and necks. The flames had surrounded the gun mount, and the only way for the crew to escape was through the hatch into the ammunition room and out another hatch at the rear.

Of course, Carlisle, with his predilection for being in the right place at the wrong time, decided to peer out of the loading hatch just as the crew was abandoning the gun. "The first guy came through the hatch feet-first and knocked me ass over kettle," he said. "The whole gun crew walked out over me. There oughta' be footprints all over my mug."

Footprints or no, Scott had never been so happy to see a face in all of his life. The two pals walked back toward the galley to see if they could find a cup of coffee. They were just passing an ammunition elevator when Carlisle grabbed Scott's arm and pointed. "Jeez, Scotty, look."

An explosion had knocked the elevator's armored door off its hinges, and it had dropped to the bottom of the shaft on the third deck. A lifeless arm now protruded from beneath the door. The friends hurried away, the coffee forgotten, happy only that the other was alive.

October 31, 1944
Steaming for Ulithi

Fifty-six men died during the attack or in the hours that followed. During the night, their bodies—at least those that had been found and identified—were sewn into canvas bags and weighted with five-inch shells. The next morning they were lined up on the aft end of the flight deck.

"All hands bury the dead." At the officer's command, the crew of the *Franklin* snapped to attention. The American flag atop the superstructure was lowered to half mast, and the crew was ordered to stand at parade rest as the ship's chaplains, Lt. (j.g.) E. J. Harkin, a Catholic priest, and Protestant minister Lt. (j.g.) Clarence Chamberlin, began the services with a reading from the scripture.

Lt. Will Gove stood with the other pilots. After the suicide plane hit, Gove and many of the other pilots responded by running to the hangar and flight decks, where they helped fight the fires. He had been on the hangar deck, digging in with the sailors on either side of him to hold a hose or, later, shoving damaged planes over the edge.

This was the first time he had witnessed the Navy ceremony for burying its dead, and he was impressed. When an aviator didn't return to the ship, he was simply "lost," or "missing," as if he had wandered off someplace and couldn't find his way home. This ceremony was dignified and appropriate. He felt more a part of the ship's company than any day since he had first flown aboard in February.

Every one of the dead men had friends onboard who were now grieving. It suddenly struck Gove how little time he had spent mourning the passing of the pilots in his squadron. They were his brothers, yet he had just been too busy—and maybe that was a good thing—and there had been no such burial services to dredge up those feelings. He recalled the names and faces of his comrades—Blair, Hudson, L'Estrange, Beckman, Magnusson, Kopman, Winecoff, and eleven others.

He felt his anger and disgust rise at the Japanese and their new suicide tactics. Up to now, he had hardly paid attention to the buzz he had heard in passing about the "crazy Japs'" latest trick. When the suicide plane tried to crash the ship on October 13, the fighter pilots had widely regard the attempt as a joke: The dumb bastard couldn't hit a ship, but he had torn the seat out of Lieutenant Winters' pants. It wasn't funny anymore.

Gove knew why the Japanese were resorting to crashing into ships. The new American pilots were coming from the States with six hundred to nearly a thousand hours of flight time already under their belts. He estimated that many of the Japanese pilots he had seen lately couldn't have had more than a couple hundred. They were simply in-capable of fending off the American combat air patrol and attacking ships conventionally.

The Japanese tactic was understandable but also unforgivable. The suicide attacks meant that the Japanese leadership knew they were beat and were just buying more time for themselves by throwing away the lives of their country's young men in a hopeless cause. They wanted only to kill; not win, not defend, just kill. It was an act of cowardice, he thought—not on the part of the pilots, but their leaders.

Gove knew he would have been one of the victims of the attacks if not for Coleman moving the meeting. The suicide plane's bomb and the subsequent fires had all but obliterated the gallery deck ready rooms. When he found his logbook, its edges were burned and the outside covered with soot.

When the chaplains finished with their prayers, the canvas shrouds were brought six at a time to the stern edge of the flight deck and placed onboards beneath American flags. The crew was called back to attention and the command given to salute. The boards were picked up at the head and the bodies slid from beneath the flags and committed to the deep. Six more bodies were placed beneath the flags. *Attention! Salute!* The remains of six young men fell through the air and disappeared in the churning wake of the ship. Six at a time they rested one last moment in the sun and then went into the depths until they were all gone.

A benediction was read, and then as the crew saluted, the seven-man honor guard of Marines fired three volleys. The crack of the rifles was still ringing when the bugler played the first melancholy notes of taps.

Gove made no notations in his logbook for the thirtieth or this day. For the last time he left the Philippine Sea, where nearly sixty young men he didn't know, and eighteen he did, would remain. He knew he would remember the power of the simple ceremony with or without his logbook, and the shapes beneath the American flags, six by six by six.

October 31, 1944
Luzon, Philippines

As the *Franklin* sailed south and east for Ulithi, one of its former torpedo plane radiomen/gunners, Samuel Plonsky, was living the life of a guerilla fighter in the Philippine jungles. In the course of a week, he had been shot down, wounded, clung to a life raft for hours, been rescued by men in canoes, eaten red ants and nearly been eaten by them, managed to escape being devoured by crocodiles, and engaged in several skirmishes with Japanese patrols.

With their hosts and the other downed American aviators, he, his pilot, Robert Freligh, and the top turret gunner, Pete Sanchez, had engaged in several skirmishes with Japanese patrols and consequently been commissioned as lieutenants in the "Luzon Guerillas."

Plonsky figured that he had had about enough adventure for one skinny Jewish kid from Massachusetts. And what he really wanted was to go home to his girlfriend, Mimi. Pete Sanchez assured him that he would get back to her, but Plonsky wondered how long that would take.

The six American aviators rescued by the Filipinos were counting on the guerillas' radio transmitter as their salvation. They had been in contact with MacArthur's troops on Leyte before the aviators were shot down; however, the gasoline generator that powered the transmitter had since run out of fuel.

In the meantime, the Filipinos had treated the Americans like heroes. When his hosts learned that October 31 was Plonsky's twentieth birthday, they threw a party deep in the jungle.

The Americans arrived bedraggled and dirty from the hike over rough terrain—their shoes were rotting off their feet from the muddy trails, their flight clothes were in tatters, and their beards were a week old. The Filipino women disappeared into a hut and emerged a little while later in fresh dresses that they must have put away for special occasions, and were even wearing lipstick! Then the Filipino men changed into dress shirts and clean pants.

By comparison the American aviators looked like bums, but they might as well have been kings. They were given the night's only meat, a "chicken," which they later learned was the spoils of a cockfight between two neighboring villages, and copious quantities of *tuba*, a sort of palm wine. As they ate and drank, their hosts entertained them with native songs played on guitars and ukuleles.

When the Americans were finished eating, the Filipinos asked to hear a song from the United States. After much drunken haggling, the aviators settled on "Show Me the Way to Go Home," making up for talent with boozy effort. *Show me the way to go home . . . I'm tired and I want to go to bed . . . I had a little drink about an hour ago, and it went right to my head . . . Soooooo, show me the way to go home . . .*

The party wore on into the wee hours of the night. One by one the aviators drifted off to sleep while their hosts continued to play their music and dance. Bleary, Plonsky felt his eyelids growing heavy. *Boy, if Mimi could see me now, what would she think?*

She had probably heard by now that he was missing in action, maybe even presumed dead—not falling asleep in a far-off jungle to the sounds of guitars and ukuleles and inebriated voices singing in a foreign language, and all of it blending in with the strange sounds of the jungle. It had certainly been an adventure. But he was ready to go home and marry the girl he dreamed of that night.

November 4, 1944
Ulithi Lagoon

Walking past the *Franklin's* quarterdeck, Petty Officer 1st Class Edwin Garrison noticed that the Officer of the Deck (OOD) was a lieutenant from his division. He stopped to chat, enjoying a few minutes of leisure now that the ship was anchored in the lagoon and most of the cleanup from the suicide plane was finished—at least as much as what the crew could accomplish.

When an aircraft carrier was tied up to a dock or anchored, the quarterdeck was actually a roped-off area on the hangar deck where the ship's company and visitors requested permission of the OOD to leave or come aboard. As the ship was close to a mile from the shore, a boat was required to get back and forth to the principal island of Mog Mog. Leading down from the hangar deck to the water's edge was a removable series of stairways, like a fire escape on a city building.

Garrison and the officer broke off their conversation when a motor launch came around the bow of the ship, flying a dark blue pennant bearing four gold stars. The OOD turned to Garrison and asked, "What is a four-star admiral's gig doing out here?"

"It's got to be Halsey," Garrison replied. With Spruance back in Hawaii, there was only one four-star admiral in these parts: Admiral William "Bull" Halsey.

The Officer of the Deck turned pale as the launch pulled up to the ladder. "He wants to come aboard," he croaked. "Watch the deck for me, I need to go find a photographer."

Garrison was left to wonder why the OOD wasn't trying to find a ranking officer as he prepared to greet the most powerful admiral in the western Pacific. One never knew what one would get with Halsey. He had been known to shed a tear with sailors over the loss of their shipmates; he had also been known to blow up over the tiniest uniform infraction.

Still, Garrison wasn't nervous; meeting Halsey was nothing compared to fighting fires caused by the suicide planes. On October 30, he had been in the metal shop on the port side of the hangar deck when the first explosion crumpled the bulkheads, trapping him in the compartment. He had had to wait for a damage control party to come along with a torch to cut him out.

After the fires were put out, Garrison and the remaining men of his crew were assigned to clean up the section of the hangar deck that included what was left of the suicide pilot and his plane. Some men had already been searching through the rubble, looking for souvenirs.

The pilot was still wearing his cloth helmet and goggles, as well as a white silk scarf around his neck on which was written "U.S. Navy" and some Japanese symbols. Garrison asked the ship's executive officer, Commander Day, who was present for the exhumation, what to do with the body.

"Feed it to the fish," Day said.

"Deep six it," Garrison ordered his crew, who dragged the remains across the deck and flung them into the ocean.

The Japanese pilot had not sunk the carrier, though he had come close. But he did take down a carrier captain. In the Notes section of the Plan of the Day for October 31 was a small announcement: "The Captain has received orders detaching him from command of the *Franklin*. There is no information regarding a new Captain." There were no other details, but the message to the crew was clear: Captain Shoemaker was being blamed for the damage to the carrier. It didn't seem fair to most of them, Shoemaker had steered them out of a number of tight places, and no one could have stopped the suicide plane that day. But it was done, and they wondered what the next captain would be like.

The *Franklin* steamed into the Ulithi atoll on November 2. Two days later, one of the most famous military leaders in the world was boarding Big Ben with only a metalsmith to greet him. Briskly climbing up to the quarterdeck, Halsey stopped to salute the American flag hanging off the stern of the ship before turning to Garrison. Then, in the tradition of United States Navy, he asked for permission to come aboard.

"Permission granted and welcome aboard, sir!" Garrison said, returning his best salute.

"They tell me you have more damage than a repair ship can take care of," the admiral said, "but I need you out here so badly that I decided, since I was passing by, to take a look myself."

Garrison knew the engineering repair crews were due to come onboard soon to assess the damage. Scuttlebutt was that if it was bad enough, they would get sent back to Hawaii. Or, maybe, if they were really lucky, to one of the shipyards on the West Coast.

Hit by a sudden urge to see his mother, Garrison thought that it might be best if he showed the admiral the damage himself. "Yes, sir, come with me," he said. He then led the admiral up the nearest ladder to the flight deck.

A walk around the still gaping hole seemed in order, followed by a tour of the worst sections of the lower decks.

Garrison did the talking. He didn't even have to exaggerate . . . much. The ship was a mess. The flight deck had a thirty-foot-wide hole in it where the suicide plane went through; and a number of smaller holes had been chopped into the planking so that the firefighters could pour water into the gallery deck from above. Stopping at the edge of the big hole, one of the ship's photographers found them and snapped a picture of Garrison, who towered above Halsey, "briefing" the admiral.

Garrison then led Halsey below. The hangar deck, as well as large sections of the second and third decks, was a wasteland of twisted, melted steel. And much of the once-spotless ship was covered with a thick film of oily soot.

Halsey followed the metalsmith with a scowl on his face but not a word until finally he had seen enough. "I'm ready to leave," he snapped. "Show me where I came aboard." Back on the quarterdeck, Halsey paused only long enough to salute the flag before he was gone.

A moment later, Garrison heard the sound of feet running on the deck behind him and looked back. Commander Day and one of the air officers, as well as the Officer of the Deck, were moving "on the double" to the quarterdeck. They arrived just in time to stare disconsolately at the departing launch.

That night Garrison repeated his story about playing tour guide for Halsey to anyone who wanted to listen. With each telling, he only embellished a little, such as his version of his response to Halsey's request to come aboard.

"I told him, 'Permission granted and welcome aboard, but only because you outrank me,'" Garrison said with a straight face. His listeners let him know that they thought he was full of "bull."

The next day, the engineers from the fleet repair shop came aboard to inspect the damage. "We just repair 'em; we don't rebuild 'em," the chief engineer reported to the fleet commander. They were going back to Hawaii . . . and with a little luck, maybe home for Christmas.

CHAPTER SIXTEEN

Typhoon

December 18, 1944
Philippine Sea
USS Santa Fe

J UST WHAT IN THE HECK ARE WE SUPPOSED TO BE LOOKING FOR?" Cpl. Fred "Andy" Anderson yelled, trying to be heard above the shrieking wind by his friend, Pfc. Paul Yeager. The two Marines huddled in a small metal tub called the crow's nest halfway up the rear mast of the *Santa Fe* some sixty feet above the main deck.

About midnight, one of the sergeants had come to Anderson and told him, "Get one of your men and climb up in the crow's nest . . . and keep a sharp eye out." An eye out for what, he and Yeager had no idea. The night was dark as pitch, and about the only thing they could see were the nearest looming black walls of water that surrounded the ship and the whitecaps on top of the waves.

Anderson and Yeager were protected from the worst of the weather by the nearly shoulder-high wall of the crow's nest, which was just big enough for the two of them, and could duck behind the mast to protect their faces from the spray. But the *Santa Fe* didn't just roll, the cruiser also pitched up and down at the same time; the forward movement of the ship more closely resembled a corkscrew going into the cork than a warship slicing through the sea.

As the two Marines clung to their precarious perch, they didn't know—because no one had told them—they were at the mercy of the kamikazes, who their enemy hoped would blow them all away. All they knew was that ever since the Second Battle of the Philippine Sea, if the Japs couldn't get at them, the wind would try.

October 27, 1944

Following the battle, the *Santa Fe* had headed for Ulithi, arriving on October 27. After the events of the past month, the men were looking forward to a few quiet hours on the beaches of Mog Mog. Located on the western side of the atoll, the island was sarcastically referred to by the fleet as the "tropical paradise with beer," where on any given day, ten thousand sailors would be strolling, swimming, playing ball, gambling, brawling, and looking for anyone with another warm beer to sell. Still, for all its drawbacks, it was the only bit of land they were allowed to walk on for a couple thousand miles and a welcome relief from the rolling deck of a ship.

However, when the *Santa Fe's* crew reached Ulithi, it was only to learn that the ships in the lagoon had been placed on Typhoon Condition II, which meant one of the cyclonic storms would hit the atoll within a day or two. The men groaned when liberty was cancelled.

They groaned again when the cruiser division commander, Admiral DuBose, was relieved by Admiral M. S. Deyo. Not that they would miss DuBose—most of the crew, and even officers, had little to do with the admiral or his staff—but they had hoped the new admiral would "break his flag" on another cruiser so they could go home for a bit.

The *Santa Fe* had spent more continuous time on the front line than any other warship in the United States Navy, long before October setting the fleet's "without overhaul" record. Ship and crew were both due a break. But when the explosion of the carrier *Princeton* devastated the *Santa Fe's* sister ship, the *Birmingham,* the pessimists had correctly guessed that they could all kiss the trip back to the States good-bye. Still, they wouldn't have traded places with the *Birmingham's* crew. *Santa Fe* sailors looked at other crewmembers they considered their friends, considered even their brothers— or maybe the best combination of the two, shipmates—and tried to imagine what losing half of them to death or injury would be like.

The *Santa Fe* pulled out on October 29, with Task Group 38.3, which included the fleet carriers *Ticonderoga, Lexington,* and *Essex.* So they were already over the horizon when the burned and battered *Franklin* steamed into the lagoon, put out of action by a single plane.

On November 1, a new captain took command of the *Santa Fe.* After eleven months as the skipper, Captain Jerauld Wright had been awarded the Silver Star for the incident involving the suicide plane, promoted to rear admiral, and relieved of his duties to be "kicked upstairs." During his tenure, the ship had earned six battle stars, representing major sea and air action but not exactly counting every bombardment or plane attack the ship had experienced.

Wright was replaced by Captain Harold C. Fitz. A graduate of the U.S. Naval Academy in 1920, he had also managed his career so that he could earn a law degree from Harvard in 1934. From 1941 to 1943, he had commanded a destroyer division on escort duty in the North Atlantic. Fitz wasn't as "regulation" as Wright, but he had an air of confidence about him on the bridge that the officers and men picked up on immediately. In his first address to the crew, he told them he was pleased to come aboard a ship with such a lucky reputation, but that he knew "luck" was in large part due to their abilities as seamen.

The *Santa Fe* was a lucky ship, but her crew was constantly reminded that their good fortune could disappear with the speed of an onrushing suicide plane or torpedo. On the night of November 3, the task group was steaming off the San Bernardino Straits when the light cruiser USS *Reno*, which had been added to CruDiv13 and was sailing about five hundred yards from the *Santa Fe,* was struck by a submarine torpedo. A few minutes after the attack, another torpedo exploded in the wake of the carrier *Essex.* The *Reno* lost forty-five men and all her power, so the ship and her crew had to be towed fifteen hundred miles back to Ulithi.

However, submarines weren't as much of a concern as the ever increasing number of Japanese suicide planes that attacked the task force. Hit especially hard were the "tin cans," the destroyers that had "picket duty" on the outside of the screening circles. On November 1, the "Banzai Joes" and "Sake Drivers," as the sailors had begun to derisively label the new pilots they both feared and loathed, crashed into the destroyers USS *Claxton* and *Ammen,* killing about a dozen men but causing little damage.

In fact, the *Claxton* was back in action a couple of hours later, picking up survivors after a suicide plane crashed through the deck of the destroyer USS *Abner Read.* Fire had quickly reached the *Abner Read's* magazine, and the ship blew apart and sank within minutes. It was a miracle that only twenty-two members of her crew died.

On November 5, the *Santa Fe's* task group again came under attack by the suicide planes. The carriers' aircraft were striking at Manila when small groups of Japanese planes appeared high above the fleet.

One group of five Japanese planes had not even waited to target the ships. When they saw the American planes heading in for Manila, they dove down into the squadrons, ramming five planes.

Most of the Japanese pilots who continued on to find the ships never reached their targets. They were shot down by the combat air patrol or the ships' guns. But the Americans couldn't stop them all. One suicide plane crashed into the *Lexington's* island, destroying much of the superstructure and killing two dozen men who never saw the enemy coming, only heard the crescendo of five-inch guns, then the forties, then the twenties, then a roar, then nothing.

Despite the blow, the fires being spread by the Japanese plane's aviation fuel were controlled in twenty minutes, and the ship resumed limited flight operations. And while part of her crew was fighting the fire, her gunners knocked down a suicide plane heading for the carrier *Ticonderoga* about eighteen hundred yards ahead. The plane missed the *Ticonderoga* by a mere fifty yards off the port beam.

Only after the battle was over did the *Lexington* limp off for Ulithi. When they arrived, the ship's crew learned that Tokyo Rose was claiming that for the second time in the war a *Lexington* had been sunk. But no one laughed at the exaggeration this time.

Nor were the Japanese limiting their suicide attacks to the air.

The task group sailed into Ulithi again on November 17, happy to be away from the insanity of the suicide planes. The strategy wasn't very effective so far in damage or lives lost, but the intensity of the attacks and their bizarre nature had frayed the crews' nerves. But there was no safe place—not even fifteen hundred miles from the Philippines—not from a fanatic willing to kill himself for a cause.

On the evening of November 20, a brilliant flash of light illuminated the harbor, followed by an enormous blast as shock waves rippled across the water. The huge fleet tanker, USS *Mississinewa,* loaded with 400 thousand gallons of aviation fuel, had erupted in flames and was billowing black clouds of smoke.

Japanese one-man submarines had crept into the lagoon when the anti-submarine nets strung across one of the entrances were pulled aside to allow a destroyer to enter. Loaded with a three-thousand-pound warhead, one of the suicide submarines had rammed the *Mississinewa.* Two more of the submarines were sunk by depth charges from destroyers.

Fifty officers and men from the tanker were killed in the blast or died in the flame-covered water. More would have died except for the heroics of one of the *Santa Fe's* Kingfisher pilots, Lt. Blasé "Zoom Zoom" Zamucen, and his radioman, Hal Evinrude. Assessing the situation as he returned from a mission, Zamucen landed near the stricken ship, then taxied through the inferno as Evinrude threw lifelines to struggling men and pulled them to safety. If there was such a place.

November 25, 1944

It was a banner day for the suicide planes. Sent with their escorts to attack the fleet in five groups of twenty-five planes each, they hit four aircraft carriers. The *Hancock* suffered only minor damage when the gunners blew the plane apart seconds before impact and pieces of burning plane fell on to the flight deck and started fires. Two planes, however, crashed through the flight deck of the *Intrepid,* forcing her to return to Ulithi. Then the light carrier *Cabot* was struck, but with only slight damage and quickly patched.

A few miles away from those attacks, the gunners on the *Santa Fe* were unable to stop a suicide plane that dove on the *Essex.* Fire and black smoke poured from the ship, but the damage was limited because the plane's bomb didn't explode. The cruiser's gun crews did stop the next attempt on the *Essex,* and the carrier was back in business a couple of hours later.

That night, Tokyo Rose boasted of a new "superweapon . . . the kamikaze . . . the divine wind." These warriors of the emperor, she said, had a holy mission to turn the tide of the war against the Americans.

The American brass knew it wasn't as bad as all that, but they finally admitted that they had a real problem. The aircraft carriers were vital to the American strategy for prosecuting the war. If one dangerously dedicated man in a plane could take out an entire aircraft carrier, what might hundreds, even thousands—if Radio Tokyo was to be believed—do to the American fleet? The war could be prolonged months, even years, at the cost of thousands more lives. How many more telegrams expressing regrets for a son or husband or father killed in action could the American public, which financed the entire effort by purchasing war bonds, take before they were willing to settle for something less than "unconditional surrender."

Tokyo Rose claimed that the suicide pilots—these kamikazes—were all volunteers. But the Americans knew better. One captured pilot, whose plane crash-landed near a U.S. ship, said he had not volunteered but had been assigned to one of the "certain death" squadrons right out of flight school—which meant the Japanese military government was committed to this desperate course of action.

Realizing that the Third Fleet needed a break after the attacks of November 25, Halsey recalled the task force to Ulithi while he and his advisers sought an answer to the kamikazes. Arriving in the lagoon on December 2, 1944, the crew of the *Santa Fe* were in a good mood. They were certain that they had just participated in their last combat operation for a while and would get to go home—at least to Hawaii and maybe the States.

So they were duly disappointed when the task force headed out again on December 10 with the *Santa Fe* in her usual position of leading CruDiv13. The optimists onboard assured the others it was for "just one more operation." That would certainly have to be it. The pessimists thought they might never see home again.

When Task Force 38 headed out, Halsey had come up with four "special measures" to deal with the kamikazes. Up to this point the task groups had spread out over such a large area that it was difficult for the combat air patrol to cover the distances between ships fast enough, nor were the ships close enough to cover each other with their antiaircraft guns. So the first special measure was to reorganize the task force into more concentrated groups; instead of four task groups there were now three, each with four or five attack carriers and as many light carriers, two or three battleships, four to five cruisers, and sixteen to twenty destroyers.

The second measure added another layer of responsibility onto the already difficult job of the destroyers. Some of the kamikazes had infiltrated task group airspace by pretending to be American aircraft and assuming a place in the landing circles until the opportunity to attack arose. But now a few of the destroyers—called "Tom Cats"—would be stationed each day between the task groups and the Americans' target. Returning aircraft would be required to turn a full circle above the destroyers for identification purposes, or be considered hostile and attacked.

The third defensive measure was to increase the number of fighter aircraft onboard the big aircraft carriers. Instead of thirty-six fighters, thirty-six dive-bombers, and eighteen torpedo planes, each carrier would now hold seventy-three fighters, and fifteen each of the dive bombers and torpedo planes. The additional fighters were to carry out the final measure, which was to "blanket" enemy airfields during flight operations so that the kamikazes could not get off the ground.

Following his nearly disastrous journey to the north, Halsey had been reminded that the Third Fleet's job was to support MacArthur's landings in the Philippines. "Bull" was not going to let any "Divine Winds" stop him. But he hadn't counted on another sort of wind.

December 17, 1944

In mid-December, Task Force 38 was operating about two hundred miles northeast of Manila with the carriers launching strike after strike despite clouds, fog, and rough seas. The Japanese air forces in the Philippines were being decimated.

On the thirteenth alone, U.S. pilots had shot down 64 planes and destroyed 208 more on the ground; they had also sunk 18 ships and damaged 37 others, mostly tankers and freighters, in an effort to deprive the defenders of fuel and supplies. The success had come at a cost of 54 American planes lost—27 to antiaircraft fire, most of the rest to mechanical or operational problems, and only a few to enemy fighters. But the pace could not be sustained without a break.

On the sixteenth, Halsey ordered the task force to head east to refuel. Despite heavy seas, he hoped the fleet could return as soon as possible. By the morning of the seventeenth, however, the weather was deteriorating rapidly. The Third Fleet, more than 130 vessels from aircraft carriers to ocean-going tugboats, was spread out over two hundred miles of ocean. Refueling was going to be tough.

The ability to supply its armed forces on the land and the sea was one of the major reasons America was winning the Pacific War. By refueling at sea, the American fast-attack carrier task force could carry out dawn-to-dusk missions for several days, then rendezvous some two hundred miles away with the support fleet. In good weather, the entire task force could be refueled and replenished in a day and back at the launch point the next morning.

Refueling was the trickiest part of the supply operation, requiring expert seamanship and teamwork. While moving at speeds of seven to twelve knots—to at least make it somewhat more difficult on enemy submarines—the ship needing fuel maneuvered to within fifty feet of the tanker and matched speeds and direction while fuel hoses were swung between the ships. Too close, especially in rough seas, and a rogue wave or sudden gust of wind might push one ship into the other; too far away and the oil hoses would snap, spraying sticky oil over men, ships, and the sea.

Big ships like the carriers and battleships, and to a lesser degree the cruisers, had large fuel oil reservoirs and didn't have to refill them very often; in fact, they sometimes refueled the smaller ships. But destroyers and destroyer escorts used up a lot of fuel, especially during flight operations, when they scampered like sheepdogs around a flock trying to maintain their screening duties, as well as chasing down submarine contacts and rescuing pilots.

Destroyers also needed to keep their fuel tanks filled to act as ballast in heavy seas. Otherwise, they took in seawater as ballast until they could fuel, delaying that process while the tanks were flushed.

On the morning of the seventeenth, the most pressing concern was the destroyers. The frantic pace of the flight operations had dropped their fuel reserves to dangerously low levels. If they ran out of fuel, they would be at the mercy of the sea and winds, unable to maneuver, and unless they gave up trying to refuel and took on seawater for ballast, they would be subject to intense rolling.

Some destroyers managed to refuel, but by mid-morning, the seas were too heavy and the ships could not maintain the proper relationship with the tankers. Halsey ordered the battleships, including his flagship, the *New Jersey,* to refuel the smaller ships. With the battlewagons' size and maneuverability, the idea was to create a shielded spot out of the wind that would allow the destroyers to take on fuel. But that didn't work either.

A little after 1:00 P.M., with the winds gusting to forty-five knots, or fifty-four miles an hour, and the seas mounting, Halsey suspended refueling operations. He ordered the fleet to a new rendezvous point, 160 miles to the northwest, apparently not realizing he was sending the fleet closer to the storm's path.

Halsey had a large aerology staff, including the fleet aerologist, Cmdr. George Kosco, aboard the *New Jersey.* Armed with the latest weather reports gathered by aircraft from stations scattered from Hawaii to the Marianas, they deduced that the stormy weather was due to a "weak low" and would soon pass. Perhaps because the massive *New Jersey,* with its bulk, hardly shifted in the seas, the admiral wasn't aware of the rough ride the destroyers were already experiencing.

On ships that didn't receive the weather reports, even junior officers had figured out the old-fashioned way—by looking at barometers, as well as the size and direction of ocean swells—that a big storm was headed right for them. Even the ensigns had read enough of the cyclonic storms section in *The American Practical Navigator,* by Nathaniel Bowditch, who had died a hundred years earlier but was still considered the father of U.S. Navy navigation, to know the basic rule of thumb: "If the wind remains steady in direction and increases in force in heavy squalls while the barometer falls rapidly, say, at a greater rate than .03 of an inch per hour, the vessel is probably on or near the track of the storm and in advance of the center," Bowditch wrote. He then went on to recommend, in such instances, "putting as much distance as possible between the ship and the storm center."

The signs pointed to the approach of a typhoon. From the Chinese *tai-fun* for "great wind," typhoons were the western Pacific's version of a hurricane. Arising generally out of the South China Sea, the elliptical storms, covering as much as three hundred square miles of ocean, swirled around a calm center that itself could be ten to twenty miles across. The seas generated by the winds were violent and confused, with gigantic waves charging at each other from different directions; the strongest winds were found just outside the eye of the storm and could blow in excess of 125 knots, or 150 miles an hour, and gust to nearly twice that amount.

The fleet had encountered typhoons before with minimal damage, because they had generally steered clear of them. But Halsey and his staff continued to ignore that this storm was more than a weak low, instead changing the refueling rendezvous point a third time, even closer to where the storm was headed. And every mile in those rough seas was sucking fuel from the destroyers, some of which gave up and pumped in seawater—praying they would have enough fuel to outlast the storm—while others waited, hoping for a quick break in the weather to at least take on a little more fuel.

At 10:00 P.M. on the seventeenth, Halsey again changed the rendezvous point, and again brought the fleet closer to the storm's path. The most powerful, best-equipped navy in the world was blundering into a potential disaster worse than anything the Japanese had been able to do. Halsey based his assessment of the storm's danger on the position of the main body of the fleet. But the *New Jersey* and the big aircraft carriers were the farthest from the storm center. The winds and waves hardly moved the large ships. So the admiral insisted that the entire fleet stay on the same course, rather than each ship trying to find a way out of the storm's path according to its own position.

Closer to the center of the storm, the conditions were much more frightening, especially for the destroyers. The U.S. Bureau of Ships, which was responsible for setting the safety standards for U.S. Navy ships, held that no modern naval vessel could capsize; the destroyers, according to the engineers, could recover from a seventy-degree roll, as measured by a device called an inclinometer. But some of those calculations were on pre–World War II destroyers that had since had several hundred tons of radar equipment and antiaircraft guns added to their tops.

The men on the destroyers in Task Force 38 prayed the engineers were right as their ships rolled to forty-five degrees, then fifty-five degrees, and the weather just kept getting worse. However, rolling wasn't the only problem. The light destroyers tended to labor up large waves rather than plunge through them. The bow would break free of the water at the crest before slamming down with such force that the impact reverberated throughout the vessels.

Even aboard a larger ship like the *Santa Fe,* life was miserable. The winds howled as angry waves beat against the ship. Deep inside the *Santa Fe,* below the raging seas, the Black Gang could hear the tempest—a deep thundering like distant artillery. Walking down a passageway required one foot on a bulkhead and one on the deck to adjust for the tilt. And of course a large portion of the crew was so ill they were useless for any sort of duty.

Up in the swaying crow's nest, Anderson was glad he didn't get seasick. The only time he had felt queasy since the storm began was when he walked into the Marine berthing compartment and found a half dozen men lying on the floor with buckets held up to their faces. When he saw his friend Pfc. Pete Connolly losing what little he may have still had in his stomach, Anderson did an about-face and went outside for fresh air. The view outside, while not nauseating, was certainly more alarming, as he could see six water spouts—the equivalent of tornadoes, only over water—swirling around on the horizon.

Nighttime up in the crow's nest was no less frightening, though at least Anderson couldn't see if there was something horrible bearing down on him, as it did at almost four o'clock on the morning of the eighteenth. The ship had just rolled hard to starboard when there was a roar, and Anderson and Yeager were knocked to the bottom of the crow's nest by a wall of black water. Unseen, a giant wave had rushed in out of the darkness and slammed against the ship.

Fortunately, the ship righted herself and the water had quickly drained from the crow's nest. Gasping from the shock of the cold water, and the moment of terror, the Marines picked themselves up, thankful that the sides of the tub were high enough to prevent them from being washed out. One look at the churning sea when the dawn finally brought some visibility was enough to convince Anderson that any man who went overboard would be lost.

At 5:00 A.M., Halsey canceled the rendezvous and ordered the destroyers to attempt fueling in the lee of the fleet carriers. But by then any maneuvering for the small ships was impossible.

Visibility ranged from zero to a thousand yards and could change in an instant. Surface radar was nearly worthless, and smaller ships disappeared in the troughs between sixty-foot waves. Calls poured in to the fleet commander from ships in desperate straits. Destroyers reported being "in irons"—caught in a trough, swept along in the direction the wind and sea wanted to take them, and unable to fight their way out to stay on course. Light carriers and escort carriers had planes breaking free from their moorings and fires were spreading in the hangar decks.

The winds near the storm center grew to 150 knots and gusted to as many as 200, an incredible 240 miles an hour. At those extremes, the spray had the force of a sandblaster and caused capillary bleeding in the faces of lookouts. Even the fleet carriers reported men being swept from the flight deck by waves or simply blown overboard by gusts.

Still, Halsey took an hour and ten minutes to decide that fueling was impossible. By then, the task force was in even more trouble. Some ships had lost power and were drifting out of control through the fleet, threatening collision; others had power but were still helpless to do anything except try to stay afloat.

Yet, a little after 9:00 A.M., Halsey sent a message to Admiral Nimitz that the fleet had run into a "tropical disturbance," still refusing to recognize that the storm was a full-fledged typhoon. That acknowledgment took another hour, but even then his staff didn't relay the information to any of the other ships' captains. However, Halsey did send a message to MacArthur informing him that the fleet would not be able to dodge the storm and would have to put off hitting targets until the nineteenth.

A warning to the other ships wouldn't have mattered by then anyway. The ships nearest to the storm's path, especially the destroyers, were in a furious fight just to survive. Some were experiencing rolls that exceeded the inclinometers' maximum reading of seventy-five degrees, and the ships were having an increasingly difficult time righting themselves against the pressure of the wind.

A little before noon, Halsey finally gave permission for the other ships to abandon the current bearing and "find the most comfortable course" away from the storm. Even the *New Jersey* was starting to rock a bit in waves kicked up by ninety-three-knot gusts, and had to swerve to avoid ramming a cruiser that had lost power and was adrift.

Onboard the *Santa Fe,* Warrant Officer Don Jackson waited by the doorway leading from the after superstructure until that side of the ship began to rise with the roll. He then quickly opened the watertight door and stepped outside into the storm. It was not a comforting sight. The wind tore wraiths of sea foam from the tops of the waves and flung them into a sky that was as dark and turbulent as the ocean, despite the presence of the morning sun somewhere above the clouds.

Captain Fitz had ordered the ship buttoned down. No one was supposed to break watertight integrity or be on the weather deck without a damn good reason and only after asking permission of the damage control officer. But the "Talk Between Ships" (TBS) radio operator had reported that his equipment on the bridge was malfunctioning, which meant somebody from the radio and radar repair crew had to go fix it. TBS radio—used mostly for maneuvering—was particularly important in this storm, when visibility was poor, the radar signals confused, and some of the task force ships were having difficulty staying on course.

Jackson had decided to handle the situation himself instead of ordering one of his crew to do so. Sometimes the other officers wouldn't listen to an enlisted man, so he preferred avoiding confrontation by going first himself to see what the problem was and then calling for his guys if needed. And ordering another man out in conditions like this to avoid the hassle himself was not the way he operated.

Squinting against the driving rain and spray, Jackson resealed the door and quickly moved forward. He stayed as close to the superstructure as possible and away from the lifelines that had been rigged around the ship. If a sailor lost his balance or a wave swept across the deck, the lifelines were his last chance to save himself.

Jackson preferred not to test his dexterity under those conditions and chose his path carefully. He didn't see anyone else on his journey; even the gun tubs stood empty. At the moment, no one was concerned about the Japanese; the enemy was the storm.

Only this was an enemy they couldn't fight. Jackson and his men, including those who were not on duty, had spent most of the past twenty-four hours in Radio Two. Even if they could have slept through the ship's gyrations, the thought of going below to their berths, where it would be difficult to escape if something went wrong, did not appeal to them. So they hunkered down in the small compartment with their life jackets on to wait out the storm. There they stayed, except when given permission to dodge out of the superstructure to get something to eat. But sandwiches were about the only thing available and were wolfed down while the men braced against a bulkhead.

The men in the radio room had been tense and quiet, lost in their own thoughts. There were no duties Jackson could assign them to keep their minds—or his—off the storm. Keeping their balance and the contents of their stomachs was enough of a task.

He had been engaged in plenty of contemplation himself. He had been thinking a lot about Charlotte Gates, but still wasn't sure about the next step in their relationship. He knew a lot of guys on the ship were talking about getting married to girls they hardly knew. They had been introduced to the girl at a USO dance—maybe just a few days before they shipped out. Or they had started writing to a shipmate's sister or corresponded with one of the girls who sent letters to lonely sailors and soldiers. Now they were "in love" and could hardly wait to get back to the States to tie the knot. His entire generation's courtship was being conducted on the tissue-thin pages of V-mail.

On the other hand, Jackson had spent quite a bit of time with Charlotte and felt he knew her pretty well. Their correspondence had become progressively more romantic, though he was always conscious of the prying eyes of the censors, and he felt that he loved her. She was kind and funny, full of life and beautiful. He always wore her ring on the chain around his neck, and he knew he would never find someone like her again if she decided not to wait for him. But still he hesitated to ask her to marry him.

Part of his indecision was because of the war. He had little control over what might happen to him, and saw no good in making plans when he might not make it back at all. Time and again, he was reminded that the difference between living and dying was a matter of a couple of minutes, or a few feet, or some higher-ranking officer's decision. Or luck.

In October it could just as easily have been the *Santa Fe* ordered to go alongside the burning carrier *Princeton*, rather than her sister ship in the division, the *Birmingham*. If the admiral's flag had been transferred to that unfortunate ship as was scheduled so that the *Santa Fe* could go back to the States for an overhaul, their fates might have well been reversed.

Then one night in November, Jackson had been jarred out of his sleep by the explosion from the *Reno* being torpedoed. Before he could even get his shoes on, the smell of fuel oil from the wounded ship wafted in through the *Santa Fe's* ventilation system. He had donned his life jacket and was rushing down the weather deck to his battle station when they passed the *Reno,* dead in the water and listing. Normally, as the flagship, the *Santa Fe* would have been in the lead of the division and possibly caught the torpedo that killed forty-five men on the *Reno,* but not that night. They'd been lucky. But there was no guarantee that next torpedo would miss the *Santa Fe.* Or the next kamikaze wouldn't burst through the bulkhead of the radio room. But his hesitation with Charlotte had as much to do with his childhood as it did with the uncertainties of war.

Seven years had passed since he climbed on that Harley-Davidson motorcycle in Iowa and rode west into the rest of his life. Three of those years had been lost forever to a war, but he still had his dreams. The war had interrupted his plans to go to college, but he had continued to save his money and expected to enroll when the fighting was over. He also wanted a wife and a family—the type of marriage his uncle and aunt, Ivan and Viola Jackson, had—but the timing was bad now. What if he and Charlotte got married before the war was over and he was killed? She would be a widow. And what if they got married and it didn't last? How could he be sure she was the right one for him when he was thousands of miles away? He didn't want to be responsible for little boys or little girls crying themselves to sleep because their family was broken and couldn't be put back together again. So he had purposely avoided writing anything to her about what sort of future they might have together and concentrated on his job.

At the moment, his job was getting to the bridge so that he could find out what was wrong with the TBS radio. He timed his advance to coincide with the movement of the ship and the waves. As one side began to rise, he crossed the ship in that direction so that he would remain on the high side; then when the ship rolled the other way, he would cross back. Sometimes he looked down across the deck and it looked like he might fall straight into the ocean if he slipped.

At last he reached the forward superstructure and quickly established that the "malfunction" was the radio operator, who needed to turn up the volume. Still he didn't get upset with the sailor, a new man. They had all been "young" and inexperienced once—a long time ago, it seemed.

Returning to Radio Two, he again carefully timed his route. He had seen the inclinometer in the pilothouse register rolls higher than forty degrees—anything over forty-five was past the halfway point. Much farther, he figured, and the ship would just keep going.

As if he needed anything to remind him that he and the other men on the ships of the embattled Third Fleet weren't in control of their destinies, the storm was doing that. This was just not the time, he decided, to be thinking about marriage. Or the future.

In the pilothouse of the *Santa Fe,* Lt. Warren Harding was counting the minutes to the end of his shift at noon. He was the Officer of the Deck on the bridge with Captain Fitz; it had been a long morning, and he needed a break. The lieutenant had confidence in the ship and confidence in the skipper. Fitz had already proved himself a deft ship handler during fueling operations. Still, even a great captain couldn't do much in a storm like this one.

As the wind yammered and screamed around the bridge, waves broke over the bow and submerged the weather deck sixty feet below until only the gun turrets and the superstructure remained above water. Then the ship would lift free again until the next foam-crowned monster tried to smother her.

With the wind blowing from the port side, the *Santa Fe* had a list of five degrees to starboard, even though Fitz had ordered that the long, heavy barrels of the No. 1 main turret be turned to port to counterweight the pressure of the wind. The ship, of course, rolled to both sides, but rolls to the starboard were always greater and the length of time to recover longer because of the wind.

Harding never saw the wave that suddenly shoved the *Santa Fe* over onto her starboard side. In fact, it may have been a combination of waves as the wind blew, making it difficult for the ship to recover from a roll before the next wave was upon them.

All he knew was that suddenly everyone on the bridge was holding on to whatever they could to prevent them from tumbling onto the starboard bulkhead. Farther and farther the ship tilted as the inclinometer reached forty degrees . . . then forty-five, the halfway point . . . then fifty ... at that point the bulkhead was the deck and the deck the bulkhead.

Harding kept waiting for the ship to right herself, but she kept leaning . . . fifty-three degrees . . . She hovered there, fighting to regain her balance as the wind pushed her down like a killer trying to hold his victim's head underwater. Any farther and the smokestacks might dip into a swell on the starboard side, allowing thousands of gallons of seawater to pour down into her boilers.

Slowly, almost imperceptibly at first, the Santa Fe began to lift, as though a creation of steel possessed a will of her own. Back she fought, her turbines throbbing and spinning the shafts that turned the propellers; she drove forward until she was upright and leaning the other way. Harding shook his head—that was close, but it was going to take more than a big wave to put the Lucky Lady down. Other ships and crews were not so fortunate.

When the worst of the typhoon passed about 2:00 P.M. on the eighteenth, it was two hours too late for three destroyers, the USS Hull, Spence, and Monaghan.

At about the same time as the Santa Fe was struggling to right herself from a fifty-three-degree roll, the Hull had gone to seventy degrees. She had begun to right herself when the wind struck her again, pushing her all the way over onto her starboard side as the sea flooded in. The ship had capsized and went down with as many as a hundred men trapped belowdecks and unable to escape.

The 160 men who did get off the ship had to fight the suction that pulled them down as the ship sank, feeling the concussion when her boilers blew beneath them. Most of them wouldn't last the night. Only a dozen of the Hull's 245 men and 18 officers survived.

For some reason, the skipper of the Spence, who had been in command for only a couple of weeks, had not ordered all the watertight doors closed during the worst of the storm. When the ship rolled to forty-seven degrees, the sea poured in through the open hatches and she was unable to right herself. The Spence remained tilted on her side for several minutes, then capsized, broke in half, and went down. Less than two dozen of her crew would be found.

The Monaghan lost all her power due to flooding of her engineering spaces and was then at the mercy of the wind and waves. Rolled, slammed, and bent, her hull structure finally crumbled. About fifty of her men managed to scramble out from belowdecks onto the hull when the ship began to turn over. Some jumped into the sea only to be slammed repeatedly against the metal ship by the waves. Those who survived when the ship finally dove for the bottom soon had to contend with sharks, even in the rough seas. Eventually, six survivors were found, three of whom would perish after their rescue.

The fates of the *Hull* and *Spence* were not known by Halsey until late that night. At 7:00 P.M., the admiral had ordered a thorough search of the area through which the fleet had passed, but the ships were only looking for a few men reported to have been lost overboard from other vessels. Only when the searchers stumbled across some of the survivors from the two destroyers did the magnitude of the tragedy start to register. It would be several more days before the few men left from the *Monaghan* were found and the fate of that ship and her crew also known.

The Third Fleet limped back into Ulithi on Christmas Eve 1944. Nearly seven hundred years earlier, the Mongols had twice been defeated by the *tai-fun* in their attempts to defeat Japan. The winds had not destroyed the American fleet. But poor judgment and reckless decision making by Halsey and his staff when faced with a sailor's oldest enemy, the sea itself, had caused more damage and casualties to the fleet than the First and Second Battles of the Philippine Sea combined.

In addition to the three lost destroyers, three light carriers, six more destroyers, and several destroyer escorts were badly damaged and knocked out of the war—some for weeks and some for months. Also lost were 146 airplanes—more than the entire complement of one of the fleet aircraft carriers.

In fact, not since the Battle of Savo Island in August 1942, when more than twelve hundred American sailors and officers lost their lives, had the American Navy suffered such harm, including that caused by the human "divine winds," the kamikaze. But that would change.

CHAPTER SEVENTEEN

The Farewell

December 3, 1944
San Diego, California

The little boy hid behind his mother's dress when the big man in the dark blue uniform walked into their small home. "Now, Bruce, this is your daddy, come out and say hello," his mother coaxed. But five-year-old Bruce Blair had no memory of this tall stranger and played it safe.

However, the longer he looked at the man—who smiled down at him and then glanced up at his mother as if they had some special understanding—the more intrigued he became. Not so much with the man, but with the shiny gold buttons and interesting patches on his uniform.

The alarm returned when the man's large hands encircled his chest, and Bruce was lifted up until he was face to face with the stranger. Without warning, the man tossed him into the air before catching him again. Panicked, Bruce looked around for his mother. He was afraid, especially when he saw that his mother was crying. But on second glance, he noticed that this seemed to be a different sort of crying; tears rolled down her cheeks, yes, but she was also smiling and laughing. All at once, he felt safe and happy, and he threw his arms around his father's neck and nestled against his chest.

Chief Petty Officer Raymond Blair had understood that his son would see him as a stranger. More than half of the boy's life, he had been away at sea—most of it fighting the Japanese thousands of miles across the ocean. There had been the few months they had all been together that previous fall while waiting for the *Franklin* to be completed and commissioned, but little Bruce could hardly be expected to remember much. Hoping to create some childhood memories of family for the boy, Raymond Blair intended to pack in as much time together as he could before the carrier was repaired and he had to go back to the war.

Fortunately, it looked like the repairs at the Bremerton Navy Yard across Puget Sound from Seattle were going to take a couple of months at least. In the meantime, half the crew at a time was being given twenty-one days leave. As soon as he was able, Blair caught a train south to San Diego to pick up his wife, Beverly, and son and take them back to Washington. He had been billeted in a naval housing area for noncommissioned officers with families, so they would have a small home to themselves.

For a brief moment in time, life was perfect for the Blair family—a father held his little boy in one arm while the other arm circled his wife.

USS Franklin

Captain James Shoemaker was officially relieved of the *Franklin's* command on November 7, 1944, by the forty-seven-year-old Captain Leslie H. Gehres, the first non-academy-educated officer to be given command of one of the big fleet carriers during the war. Four days later, the ship left Ulithi bound for Pearl Harbor.

Most of the crew had respected Shoemaker; although he kept mostly to the bridge and was somewhat removed from the enlisted men, he was always cordial, and they felt he was concerned about their welfare, as well as the ship's. On the other hand, they didn't know quite what to make of Gehres posting his "resume" on the bulletin boards around the ship. "As I know a ship's company is always curious about a new captain, there follows a brief sketch of my naval career to date," the biography began.

Gehres had served in World War I aboard destroyers. He had seen the future and become a naval aviator in 1927 and had served as a fighter pilot, an air officer aboard an aircraft carrier, and had even served under Shoemaker at the naval air station at Pearl Harbor before the war. So far during the war, he had commanded land-based naval air operations, and more recently destroyers, in Alaska. But he had lobbied to get command of an aircraft carrier and was at last given the *Franklin*.

At the bottom of the memorandum to the *Franklin's* crew, Gehres listed his hobby as "being a naval officer." His likes: "The Navy and the people in it." Under "aversions" he listed: "Japs, lazy people, dirty people, noisy people, and smarty-pants boots who imagine they are being 'salty' by showing off ashore, or who snub me by not saluting and thus preventing me from saying 'Good Morning' to them." His immediate ambition: "To get the *Franklin* clean, repaired, and back into action."

Gehres, a big man at six-foot-five and about 250 pounds, closed his message with the notice: "Only within the limits of the quarterdecks do I want officers and men to remain at attention when I am about. In other parts of the ship, only those men within six paces of me need rise and salute—and they may carry on as soon as I have passed them. Men actually working will continue their work unless I stop to speak to them. You have all seen how big I am, so you can realize I really need gangway in the narrow passageways and on ladders, and captains are usually in a hurry."

Gehres quickly let it be known that the way the crew had been functioning would change under his command. The first afternoon at sea, a "captain's inspection" was announced for all hands not on duty. Each division mustered on the flight deck in their dress whites, while the skipper strolled up and down the ranks of men, who tried to look sharp while bracing themselves against the roll of the ship.

The captain gave a short speech praising the crew and Air Group 13, but then got down to business. He announced that clean shirts—with the sleeves buttoned down, not rolled up—and dungarees were the uniform of the day and that sailors' caps would be "squared . . . And you'll show respect to officers by saluting and addressing them as 'Sir.'" The crew glanced at one another. This captain was "regulation"—Shoemaker had been relaxed about squaring the cap and saluting every time an officer came by, at least while they were on the front lines, and such things seemed superfluous.

The captain had rankled some of the crew when he opined to several of his officers, within earshot of some of the enlisted men, that in his opinion a lax attitude among the officers and men had contributed to the kamikaze's success on October 30. Such a lack of discipline, he warned, would not be tolerated under his watch. The comments made their way quickly around the ship as scuttlebutt.

The remark seemed unfair. True, the ship had not been locked down as tight as it could have been, because Shoemaker had relaxed General Quarters to Condition III. But the guns were manned, the combat air patrol was up, and the captain had taken evasive action. They had thrown everything they had against the kamikaze, but nothing was going to stop that kind of fanatical dedication on that day.

The remark also seemed callous to the losses they had suffered. A ship's crew was family; now, Gehres appeared to be saying that the deaths of their brothers in arms had been their fault.

After the carrier reached Pearl Harbor on November 21, the shipyard's engineers decided that the repairs to *Franklin* were going to take months. But their facilities were for ships that could be quickly repaired and returned to the front lines; the *Franklin* would have to go back to the States. Whatever disappointment the crew might have had when no liberty was granted that day for the beaches and nightlife of Waikiki was soon overcome by the news that the *Franklin* would be leaving the next morning for the Bremerton Navy Yard in Puget Sound.

The trip to Bremerton was largely uneventful. The seas grew rougher, but the cooler weather was a relief to all hands who had suffered from heat rash and impetigo in the tropics. They were also cheered by the announcement in the Plan of the Day that the crew had been awarded a unit commendation from Admiral Halsey for their actions to save the carrier after the kamikaze attack. The news came with a pep talk from their new captain.

"Once more, December seventh—Pearl Harbor Day—is coming up. To all of us in the Navy, it is a day never to be forgotten. The 'Yellow Bellies' jumped us without provocation. They asked for it, and thank God, they're getting it. The *Franklin* has had her hand in the delivery. She comes back to the States with an accolade from an admiral we are all proud of—Admiral Halsey of the Third Fleet."

The memorandum also came with a warning. "We are about to encounter one danger which has been strikingly absent for the past five months— VENEREAL DISEASE. All prostitutes and all pick-ups are infected sooner or later, and you have no way of telling whether or not you are being soon or late in your contact with the girl. You may think you know everything about a girl, but you may find out that 'something new' has been added during your absence or between your visits."

Night had fallen by the time the *Franklin* docked in Bremerton on November 28. The first off the ship were the pilots and combat air crewmen of Air Group 13. The "Fighting 13th" had done well. Flying 3,971 sorties, its pilots and crews had destroyed or damaged at least 338 enemy planes; sunk 60 merchant ships and damaged another 66; sunk 15 warships, and damaged 19 more.

They would not be returning to sea with the *Franklin*, however. They were rotating back to the States to regroup, retrain, and await orders for the next assignment. Those pilots who had finished their second tour would be reassigned to a stateside tour, teaching recruits to fly combat missions. The carrier would pick up a new air group after she was repaired.

Buses were waiting on the dock to deliver the men of the air group to the Sand Point Naval Airbase to check in. But some had other ideas.

Dive-bomber pilot Lt. E. John Weil and his buddy Lt. (j.g.) Charlie Emiling tried to give the officers in charge of their transportation the slip. They had almost made it into a taxi that was loitering nearby when one of their shepherds spotted them and personally escorted them to the steps of the bus.

As soon as they got checked in, Weil bolted for freedom with a few of the more adventurous pilots—Emiling, as well as his old mates from VB-11 who had served with him at Guadalcanal, Lieutenants G. K. "Dutch" Bomberger and Joe Eisenhuth. They were soon drinking to excess at a Seattle club.

At four o'clock in the morning, Weil decided to call his parents back in New York City from a phone booth in the club. It was hard to hear over the sound of two drunk women rolling around on the ground and fighting like cats outside the booth, but he recognized his father's voice when he picked up the telephone.

Weil happily slurred that he was in Seattle safe and sound, had got himself a Jap carrier, and would be coming home soon. "That's wonderful, John," his father replied just as Weil's mother picked up another phone line. "But wouldn't it be better if you called back this afternoon?"

Catching the hint, Weil quickly said good-bye and hung up. Besides, it was difficult to focus on talking to his parents when one of the women outside the booth had gained the upper hand and was sitting on her rival's belly knocking the hell out of her. All in all, he thought it was a grand night.

After a couple of days, most of which was spent inebriated, Weil and the others were granted thirty days leave. He caught a commercial flight for the East Coast, stumbling onto the plane miserably hung over, and took a seat next to a pregnant woman. The propellers had hardly started to turn when the woman grabbed a "doggie bag" and got sick. In his state, the only thing that stopped him from joining her was the ignominy of a dive-bomber pilot getting ill on a passenger plane.

VB-13 was broken up. The pilots who had served two combat tours— Weil, Bomberger, and Eisenhuth—along with several other of the more experienced fliers with only one Pacific combat tour were transferred to the airbase at Jacksonville, Florida, to help train new pilots for carrier operations. The rest were sent to other squadrons to prepare for the invasion of Japan.

Weil reported for duty after having spent most of his leave drinking. His nerves were pretty shaky. He figured he was damn lucky to be alive—the squadron had lost seven pilots and their crewmen—every day from here on out was a bonus, and he might as well try and enjoy it.

Fighter pilot Lt. Willard Gove caught a commercial flight home to Massachusetts. It was a time of reflection for him, spent thinking about the squadron mates he had lost. He felt like maybe he should go see their families—at least those of the men he had known best, his brothers in arms, in case their families had any questions he could answer and to express his condolences. But then he wondered if they might not want such a new wound ripped open.

Gove realized that he didn't know much about most of the dead pilots. The life they had led since meeting—first at the airbases getting ready for war and then in the Pacific—was a day-to-day, and sometimes moment-to-moment, existence. They had spent a lot of time together, but not much of it talking about their "other" lives before the war or what they were going to do when it was over. It was as if they had lived in another world in which the past and the future had not mattered—the world of fighter pilots.

When he got home, the feeling of alienation from the "normal" world was exacerbated. It seemed to him that his parents, his friends, and everyone he met, except other veterans, didn't know the first thing about what was really going on in the Pacific or Europe. They kept talking about the "sacrifices" they were making—eating oleo margarine instead of butter, going without meat and new shoes, rationing gasoline, or having difficulty obtaining a bottle of whiskey.

He wanted to tell them about the real sacrifices of guys like Hudson and L'Estrange, but they wouldn't have understood something so far beyond their experience. How could he have explained climbing in the cockpit of a plane day after day to kill or be killed? He couldn't. So instead, he just smiled politely when they talked about "doing without," drank heavily, and then when his leave was up, reported to San Diego where Fighter Squadron 13 was being re-formed.

New pilots were brought in to replace the guys who had finished their second combat tour. The new men were a great bunch of "kids," and probably the best-trained pilots coming out of flight school of any in the world. They reminded him a lot of himself and his old comrades when they were just getting started—hard-drinking, hard-loving, hard-fighting, and anxious to get into action "before it's all over."

Sadly, Gove knew it wouldn't be over until Japan had been invaded, which meant that many of them, as well as the veterans like himself, wouldn't be coming home. While not above a beer and a brawl—he was, after all, still a fighter pilot—Gove left the worst of it to the new guys. He just wasn't the same brash Hellcat jockey who helped his squadron carouse its way through Oceana back in 1943. In fact, he finally found the time to fulfill a promise he had made while floating on a life raft four months earlier and began attending church every Sunday.

December 25, 1944

Mimi Gordon stood on her tiptoes trying to see over the sea of bobbing heads as the crowd departed the train. Many of the passengers were in military uniforms with a wide array of hats and sailor's caps, making it difficult to spot the face she longed to see. Just seventeen years old, she had pretty much grown up with the war.

When she wasn't in school, Mimi filled her days playing tennis and visiting with her friends to talk about fashion, boys, movie stars, and the latest gossip. She loved to dance and had talked her father into buying one of the first phonograph record players in their neighborhood. She and her girlfriends then spent their allowances on 78-speed records so that they could spend hours practicing their dancing—she preferred the jitterbug—in her basement to the big band sounds of Benny Goodman and Tommy Dorsey.

Mimi was also a good student and dreamed of becoming a medical doctor someday. How she would manage that, she didn't know, as her father didn't believe in good little Jewish girls going to college. But that was about the biggest concern in her young life until that Sunday in 1941 when her father let out a yelp and rushed into the room. "We're going to be in a war. The Japanese attacked Pearl Harbor!"

The news had frightened her. She wondered if it meant someone might now try to harm her, especially because she was a Jew. They had been hearing at the temple that Hitler was murdering Jews in Germany and Poland. Even before the attack on Pearl Harbor, at school they made the students practice "air raid drills" by retreating into the basement where they sat cross-legged on the floor with their hands over their heads. She worried that such drills would no longer just be drills.

Of course, Sam Plonsky had never been scared, at least never around her. He had looked very dashing and brave in his uniform with its gold wings when he came home on leave. She thought they were perfect together; they had even blown away the competition at all the dance contests. With guys like her Sam out there taking care of business, her fears diminished and life took on a new sort of normalcy—changed and yet the same.

While Sam was gone, Mimi kept an active social calendar. She and her friends—male and female—formed a club called The Deocs (for "coed" spelled backwards) that got together every Friday to dance at the American Legion Hall. They thought they were, in the vernacular of the day, "the living end."

When she and Sam had exchanged friendship rings before he left on the *Franklin,* Mimi considered herself to be "going steady." But she had also gone along with her father's wishes and dated other boys. One of them was a drummer for the band that played the Friday night dances. He could keep a beat, but even he couldn't measure up to Sam Plonsky.

Sam's letters from the Pacific were so romantic—at least what there was left after the military censors got through with them. Sometimes his mail looked like moths had eaten it. He had to stop writing to her in Morse Code, but he had other ways of letting her know where he was, such as lightly drawing a palm tree on a page to say he was in the South Pacific. He always started his letters the same way, "Hi, Babe," then he would get all mushy. "I love you. . . . I love holding you. . . . We're going to married someday when I get home."

His letters suddenly stopped in early November. But there was no word that something bad had happened to him, and Mimi just thought there was a holdup somewhere in the mail system. However, the mix-up had been at the War Department; his parents never received the telegram saying that he had been shot down and was missing in action.

Neither Sam's parents nor Mimi knew there was anything wrong until a letter arrived at his parents' home in early December from Sam's squadron commander, Lt. Cmdr. L. T. French. "You have no doubt heard that your son, Samuel Plonsky, has been missing in action since October 24, 1944," the letter began. Fortunately, the good news followed. "We just received word that he was picked up by friendly forces. As far as we know, he is safe."

Sam's mother called Mimi and read her the letter. The letter raised more questions than it answered. Missing in action? Did that mean he had been shot down? Who were these friendly forces?

"He's safe," Mimi told Mrs. Plonsky. "He's going to be fine."

"I don't know," his mother fretted. "I don't know."

The older woman could not be convinced, but Mimi was sure that nothing could stop her Sam from coming home. The squadron commander had included Sam's logbook along with some other personal effects, but there were no other explanations. Then a few days before Christmas, the telephone rang at the Plonsky house. Sam's father answered.

"Dad?" said the voice on the other end of the line. It was Sam. He was in California and wanted to come home, but he didn't have any money.

Navy combat airman and guerilla fighter Sam Plonsky and the other members of his plane's crew, Robert Freligh and Pete Sanchez, had spent nearly seven weeks on Luzon. Finally, the Filipino guerillas had been able to capture gasoline to run the generator that powered their radio transmitter. When American forces on Leyte were reached, Plonsky and the others were told to sit tight and they would be picked up as soon as it could be arranged. That turned out to be several weeks—several weeks of skirmishing and dodging Japanese patrols—before they were finally rescued by sea planes just as Japanese patrol boats were closing in.

Plonsky had been taken to a hospital, where the doctors were amazed that his hand had healed so well. There was no infection and it appeared he would suffer no permanent damage beyond the scars.

Arriving back in the States on December 20, Plonsky thought his troubles were over. But there was a problem. While he was gone, the *Franklin* had been hit and his records had been destroyed or lost. The only thing the Navy would give him was a piece of paper saying that he claimed to be missing radioman/gunner Sam Plonsky. But the service wouldn't issue him a new uniform, a train pass, or any money. The Red Cross gave him a shirt and a pair of pants, but he had to ask his father to wire him the money to get home.

"Are you all put together?" his father asked.

Sam understood the vague question. His mother must be nearby, and his father wanted to know if he was going to have to break the news that her remaining son was maimed.

"I was wounded a little," Sam replied, "in my hand."

"You still have ten fingers and two hands?"

"Yes."

"Good." With that, Sam could hear his father call for his mother. "It's Sammy."

Sam waited . . . and waited some more . . . then learned why. "Your mother fainted," his father sighed.

That same morning, Mimi got up and looked at the stockings that her father, though Jewish, hung by the chimney for his children. *The best Christmas present would be for Sam to come home,* she thought. A little later, the Plonskys called to tell her that her wish had been granted.

On Christmas morning, they picked her up and drove with her to Boston's South Station. The day was not as happy for other people. The mood of the country was a somber one. Just when it had seemed that the Germans were on their last legs and the war in Europe nearly over, the enemy had staged a counteroffensive beginning December 16 through Belgium's Ardennes forest. In what was already being called the Battle of the Bulge, American troops had taken a horrible beating with a lot of casualties.

For the past week, bad news had leaped from the headlines of newspapers and the mouths of radio announcers. The whole country was stunned and worried, struck by the realization that the war could drag on, maybe for years.

Yet, what mattered to Mimi Gordon was that her man was coming home. As she strained to get a better view of the platform, she was elbowed aside by Sam's mother, a short but broad-shouldered woman. "Listen," the older woman warned, "I'm his mother, and I'll be getting to him first."

The train arrived and the passengers began to disembark. With so many men in uniform and out, Mimi wondered how she was ever going to spot Sam. Then she saw a skinny figure with a duffle bag slung over his shoulder; she couldn't get a good look at the figure's face, but there was something about the way the bag moved through the crowd that suggested a familiar cocksure saunter. She knew the owner of that walk was the incomparable Sam Plonsky.

When at last he emerged from the crowd, Mimi was surprised by how gaunt he appeared—he would later weigh in at 122 pounds—and his acne seemed to have erupted from whatever diet he had been on. But she thought he was the best-looking sailor in the entire train station. As he hugged his mother, he looked over her shoulder at Mimi and smiled. "Hi, babe," he said, like he had been on a short vacation, and she burst into tears.

That, however, was not quite the end of Sam Plonsky's war story. He had been back for several days and was upstairs sleeping in his parents' home late one morning when a Navy chaplain knocked on the door. Sam's mother thought having a Catholic priest in a Navy uniform show up on her doorstep was a little strange. But she let him in and made him sit down in the living room while she went to fetch coffee and bagels.

When she returned, the chaplain sipped at his drink politely as Sam's mother took a seat next to him. Then his face softened and his eyes welled with tears; he had had to do this far too many times. He cleared his throat and then gently said he'd come to pay his condolences. He had been notified that her dear son, Samuel Plonsky, had been missing in action for nearly two months. The Navy now presumed that he was dead.

The priest waited for the reaction that always came from the mothers—a moment of disbelief, perhaps a mental image of their boy as a child, then the hysterics, or the fainting, or the quiet weeping. But Mrs. Plonsky leaned forward, smiled, and patted him on the knee, "Father, there's good news. My son's upstairs sleeping." She quickly recounted the "miracle" of her son's deliverance.

When she finished, the priest began to cry. After a minute or so, he pulled himself together. Wiping away the tears with a handkerchief, he explained, "I've made a lot of these visits over the past few years. This is the first time one had a happy ending."

The half dozen sailors marched somewhat in order into the lobby of the hotel, toting their seabags and a couple of boxes that clinked suspiciously like bottles of booze.

"Detail, halt!" Chief Petty Officer John Frajman bellowed. "At ease, men. Smoke 'em if you got 'em."

Water Tender 2nd Class Ernest Scott, Eddie Carlisle, Paul "Birdlegs" Dalton, and Lem Hall dropped their bags, taking considerably more care with the boxes, and looked around. The hotel was nothing fancy, but not bad either.

Frajman advanced toward the front desk on somewhat unsteady legs. Behind the desk was a hefty blond woman toward whom the chief now directed his booming voice. "Christine! My ol' Bunkie. Crissake, honey, how the hell are, ya?"

Christine emerged from behind the desk and playfully belted him in the ribs. "Frajman, you old bastard, you ain't changed a bit," she roared right back. "Whatcha drinkin'?"

Scott looked on at the greeting with delight. The big blond woman appeared to be fifty years old if she was a day, but he figured a seasoned sailor like Frajman, who was in his mid-twenties, could have developed a sort of age blindness from being at sea for extended periods of time. Women had certainly been on the minds of the *Franklin's* crew. As soon as they heard they were going to the States, the bragging started. "I'm writing the old lady today, 'Drop them skivvies, honey, I'm coming home,'" one would boast. Another would chime in, "My old lady ain't gonna see nuthin' but the ceiling for the first three days."

The day the *Franklin* entered Puget Sound, the crew was told that they would receive twenty-one days leave, half of the crew at a time.

The men were also warned about saying too much regarding the ship. Battle damage and casualties sustained by the *Franklin* and the manner in which they were received were not supposed to be discussed at all. "You may state that, in her operations, the *Franklin* was under enemy aerial attack several times." Even scuttlebutt they may have heard about future operations was to be secret. "The mere mention or slight remark concerning future operations may mean death to your shipmates, the loss of an American warship, and compromise of an operation. Trust NO ONE in these matters. The enemy REALLY has ears everywhere."

The *Franklin Forum* noted that a special train had been arranged to take the crew from Seattle to Chicago. From there they would have to arrange their own connections to their hometowns. The crew was warned to be on their best behavior; the train had been acquired with "some reluctance" on the part of the railroad, because groups of servicemen in the past had proved "destructive to railroad property."

As quickly as they could get off the ship, the crew swarmed ashore to find telephones to inform those back home when to expect them. Many of the sailors then followed that up heading for the base uniform shop, where they bought the Asiatic Theatre combat ribbon for their dress blue uniforms and three battle stars to pin on it. There had been no official word on the ribbon and battle stars yet, and so technically they weren't supposed to wear them, but what the heck good was going to war if they couldn't show everyone that they had been shot at.

Soon afterward, half the crew—more than twelve hundred young men—left. Twenty-one days later, after the first wave returned from leave, the second group of men was released. A few intimated that they weren't coming back. One of them was "Swede" Hanson, the Black Gang member who had played the imaginary fiddle when Scott entered the fire room for the first time.

The final straw for Hanson had been the morning following the kamikaze attack. Hanson said he had taken his mattress out onto the fantail to sleep that night, noticing in the dark that a lot of other guys had the same idea and were lying under their blankets in rows on the deck. He found a spot among them and lay down. The next morning, he woke up to the sounds of a bosun's pipe and sat upright. The crew was being called to attend the burial at sea ceremonies, and he had been sleeping among the dead, who had been sewn into canvas bags. Ever since that incident, he had sworn, "If this tub ever hits the States again, I'm long gone."

Scott figured Hanson abandoning ship would be no great loss. But he was concerned about Carlisle. Scott was worried that if he stayed up on the gun mount, something bad might happen. He asked Eddie if he would join the Black Gang if it could be arranged. "You might not like it," he warned. "It's below the waterline and all. But everything that's happened so far has been topside."

Carlisle agreed. He was upset, having lost several friends on his gun mount during the kamikaze attack, and wanted to stick with his best friend. Scott talked to his chief, who was only too happy to trade one of the "slackers" in the fire room for Carlisle. The only unfortunate thing for Eddie was that Frajman saddled him with the nickname he used for Scott; they were now "The Shithouse Twins."

Being from the same fire room, Scott, Carlisle, "Birdlegs" Dalton, Keith Robertson—all from Maine—and Lem Hall got to take their leave together. The trip across the country was a continuous poker game and drinking binge. The last time they had taken a train, they were fresh out of bootcamp; now, they were "old salts," blooded and ready to prove they were men. And at every stop, the wild scramble for liquor stores or back-alley booze peddlers would begin. No matter how bad the whiskey, Birdlegs Dalton would take a swig and announce it was the "finest kind."

The party seemed to reach a climax the night Lem Hall came wobbling down the aisle of the train car to ask Scott if he'd seen Carlisle. Eddie had consumed a little too much "finest kind," and Hall was concerned that he might have wandered right off the moving train. They looked for him everywhere with no luck. Then Scott looked in the women's restroom where, sure enough, Carlisle was on his knees with his head in the toilet.

When Scott returned to their seats, he found Birdlegs sitting next to an angry looking young woman who seemed none too thrilled with his amorous advances. Birdlegs had polished off more than his share of several bottles and apparently believed that made him a regular Romeo. His half-lidded eyes and slurred speech, however, got him nowhere with the young woman, and he eventually gave up and passed out.

Scott found Lem Hall curled up on a seat and fast asleep with his head on the lap of what had to have been a 70-year-old woman who sat next to him. Hall had a smile on his face, and the odd thing was, so did she as she stroked his hair like he was a small child.

Hall got off the train in Chicago. When the other four sailors reached Maine, they split up. Scott and Carlisle caught another train to Bangor from which they planned to take the bus to Woodland.

Scott had been home for several days when his father asked why he was avoiding his old girlfriend, Vivian. The question confused him. He wasn't avoiding her, he just figured that nothing was going to happen between the two of them. She was in high school and had boyfriends, and he'd about given up on her. But when his dad told him she'd been by several times when he was away, hope rekindled the old flame, and he called to ask her out.

They saw a lot of each other over the next few weeks. One night toward the end of his leave, they were returning from the movies when Scott pulled his father's car over to the side of the road. He'd proposed to her once when they were eight years old, and now he wanted her answer.

Knowing the question was coming, Vivian had been giving it some thought. She'd worked in a Rhode Island zipper factory that summer and had seen a bit of the world outside of Maine before returning for her final year of high school. She was considering going to college. Still, she loved him, pretty much had since childhood.

And Scott seemed to have grown up a lot since joining the Navy. He was more mature and seemed to know what he wanted, which was to settle down when the war was over and start a family. He had brought her home a pretty, black and blue dress for Christmas; he even got the size right, and there was something to be said for a man who had an eye for clothes.

She just wasn't sure she wanted to get married, at least not right away. So she hedged a little and said she'd marry him after she graduated from high school. That would give them both a chance to think it over.

The answer was as good as Scott thought he was going to get, so the next day, he and his mother drove to the bigger town of Bath and picked out an engagement ring. He was a happy sailor when he and Carlisle caught the train back to Chicago. There they met up with a tired but happy Lem Hall and did their best to finish off any of the "finest kind" they could get their hands on for remainder of the trip.

All in all, Bremerton wasn't bad duty. They had to work every day, cleaning up the ship behind the repair crews; as well as load and store supplies. But life was certainly more comfortable than it had been when they were out at sea.

Upon arrival at the navy yard, they'd been moved into barracks onshore and ate together in a large mess hall. Starved for milk, fresh fruit, and vegetables during their months in the Pacific, they now made up for it with gusto. The crew also got liberty every other night and the occasional weekend pass.

Their time in the States was drawing to a close when Scott and the others agreed to accompany Frajman, who'd appointed himself "captain" of the expedition, to Seattle for a night of hard drinking in the little hotel run by his former "bunkie," Christine.

Despite her close former association with the chief, the blond desk clerk said she couldn't get them a room until checkout time at midnight. The announcement did not dampen Frajman's enthusiasm for his mission.

"Break out the stores and pass the rations," he commanded. "We'll drink just enough to keep up our strength." His crew happily carried out his order, although they opted for more than just a little strengthening.

At fifteen minutes to midnight, Frajman assembled his compatriots outside the room they'd been assigned and told them to "stand by to ram." He then knocked on the door and when the departing guest answered they all barged in and tossed his bags out into the hall. Closing the door on the man who cursed them from the landing, the chief announced that the "boarding party had secured the ship."

Frajman was having a grand time. "Now hear this, Lem, you and Maxine dog the escape hatch and guard same . . . repel all boarders," he ordered. "Bird, fresh rations all around. Shithouse, draw the captain's bath—the captain will now soak his barnacles."

The orders brought out the first dissent among the crew. In the beginning, the younger men had taken his commands good-naturedly. But the more intoxicated they got, the more they were losing interest in following his orders. "Shithouse" had better things to do than draw the captain's bath; so it was that Frajman climbed out of his clothes and lumbered into the bathroom where he lowered himself into the empty tub. Nonplussed, he gave new orders to Carlisle. "Chief engineer, blow all ballast and open the main line."

Carlisle turned on the hot water faucet—which gurgled, hissed, belched, and finally coughed up a blast of steam that hit Frajman in the small of his broad back. "JEEZUS H. CARRIST, SECURE THE FIRES!" the chief bellowed. "AND GET ME OUT OF THIS GODDAMN TUB!"

The steam scalded Frajman pretty well, and the other sailors knew it had to hurt like hell. On the other hand, no one seemed overly concerned as it took several of them in their inebriated state to haul his bulk out of the tub and steer him toward a bed where he lay down on his stomach. "Oh, you bastards," he lamented as they broke up in giggles. "It's mutiny, that's what it is. Mutiny. I'll nail your asses to the yardarm for this. Gimme that goddam jug."

Dalton took a swig from the bottle and handed it to the ailing chief. "Finest kind," Birdlegs said with a laugh. Frajman took a long swig, handed the bottle back and passed out. The mutineers continued their assault on the ship's "stores" until well into the morning before they joined their fallen leader.

January 31, 1945
Bremerton, Washington

Snow fell outside the small home on the base near the Bremerton Naval Yard as the taxi cab pulled up outside and honked. The chill morning was still dark, though quite a few of the houses had lights on as other men prepared to leave their families.

Inside his home, Chief Petty Officer Raymond Blair stood with his wife at the doorway of their son's room, listening to the sounds of the sleeping child.

Raymond Blair had taken his little family back up to Bremerton on the train. He hoped that his son would have good memories of that Christmas season—memories that they could share together someday. Like how Raymond had held him up high so that he could see the train cars being coupled and uncoupled from the platform when they reached Portland, Oregon. Or the morning the two of them had trudged into the woods to cut down a Christmas tree for their tiny living room.

Certainly they would all remember Christmas Eve when Beverly opened the front door, and there mewing in the newly fallen snow was a tiny white kitten that had appeared as though by magic. She'd brought the kitten in, and Bruce had discovered it curled up beneath the tree on Christmas morning, the best present he had ever received.

Sadly, it was a fleeting gift. A few days later, the kitten got out of the house and disappeared. The family had searched for the tiny feline, Bruce going as far as his five-year-old legs would carry him, but to no avail. The Christmas kitten had walked off into the place where memories are kept. Now, Raymond Blair had to leave as well.

Repairs on the *Franklin* were completed on January 28, 1945. Gehres and the crew took her out into the sound to test her engines and other equipment. Then they had returned to the dock where the men were instructed to collect their gear, say their goodbyes, and report back on the morning of January 31 ready to sail.

Early that morning, Chief Petty Officer Raymond Blair rose and dressed in his uniform. His seabag waited by the door as he stood in his son's doorway and Beverly leaned up against his shoulder. He crossed the room to his son's bedside and looked down on the boy.

The cab honked outside. Blair leaned over and inhaled the sweet perfume of a sleeping child. He had to go and finish his job so that children like his son could rest peacefully in their beds without fear of tyrants or suicidal fanatics in airplanes. Kissing the boy's cheek, he stood tall in his uniform with the shiny brass buttons and left the room. There was time for one last tender kiss from his wife, and then he walked out the door to that place where the Christmas kitten went and was gone.

LAND OF THE RISING SUN

The Pilot

The Japanese pilot hid in the clouds two thousand feet above the Pacific Ocean, peering down through occasional breaks in the cover. Somewhere in all the thousands of square miles of lead-colored ocean below was the American fleet with its hated aircraft carriers.

He flew a *Yokosuka* dive-bomber, known to the Americans as a "Judy," a two-seater and one of the fastest dive-bombers of the war with a powerful Mitsubishi-built engine. Like the American dive-bombers, it carried a radioman-gunner, who sat behind the pilot facing the rear in front of machine guns. The olive green aircraft with the red dot of the rising sun on its fuselage and wings was also armed with machine guns in the wings and two armor-piercing, five-hundred-pound bombs.

Who this pilot was, who he loved and who may have loved him, what he had accomplished in his life and in this ugly war, all would be lost to history. But he was probably one of the few experienced pilots left in the Japanese air corps, because he was not a kamikaze. Most of them by March 1945 were hardly more than poorly trained teenagers and not expected to survive their first flight, whether they found the enemy or not.

This pilot would not try to kill himself. However, he probably held no illusions that he would survive the war, even if he made it through this day. Every soldier and sailor owed his life to country and Emperor. But he would attack, drop his bombs, and then try to make his escape—only to rearm and attack again until the arrogant enemy finally stopped him.

Up to the moment when his soul was enshrined at the Yasukuni memorial, his goal was to take as many American lives as he could. And, if the Shinto gods of war smiled on him, sink an aircraft carrier.

The cult of the kamikaze, shrouded by a veil of mysticism and patriotic rhetoric, grew quickly following the Second Battle of the Philippine Sea. Beginning in early November, Lt. General Kyoji Tomonaga, who commanded one of the army groups in the Philippines, began giving the same speech to departing kamikazes from his units:

> When men decide to die like you they can move the heart of the Emperor. And I can assure you that the death of every one of you will move the Emperor. It will do more . . . it will even change the history of the world.
>
> I know what you feel now as you put the sorrows and joys of life behind you because the Emperor's fortunes are failing. Do not worry about what happens when you die and what you leave behind you— for you will become gods. Soon I hope to have the privilege of joining you in glorious death.

The Emperor labeled the kamikazes "national heroes." The suicide pilots were told that they were defenders of the "divine nation" and that they would be dying for a "holy cause" and the "glory of his majesty."

Kamikaze organization and preparation became more ritualized. In addition to wearing white *hachimaki* around their heads, they were sent off with elaborate ceremonies capped by drinks of sake said to have been sent by the Emperor. The different units took on colorful names. Cherry Blossoms. Heaven Sent. Devotion. Auspicious Clouds. And the Soldiers of the Gods.

The Japanese military bought into the kamikaze concept with such fervor that they sought new ways to have their soldiers and sailors kill themselves. One was the *Oka* "flying bomb," a rocket-propelled missile dropped from the belly of a Betty bomber and guided by a human pilot. Although one did tear a destroyer in half, the rest did so little damage that American sailors and pilots derisively referred to them by the Japanese word *Bakha* bomb, or "foolish" bomb.

One new method by sea was the "human torpedoes," the *Kaiten,* or one-man suicide submarines. Most sank, however, before reaching their destinations, and the sinking of the U.S. fleet tanker, the *Mississinewa,* was the sole success.

In the battle for the Philippines, the Japanese attacked using small "suicide boats" made of plywood and powered by automobile engines. The boats were intended to carry depth charges into the American fleet at night and drop them as close to ships as possible, while their crews fired on the surprised enemy with machine guns and hand grenades. These, however, were intercepted and blown from the water before they could do much damage.

Beginning in the summer of 1944, a new terror had appeared in the skies over Japan: the B-29 Superfortress. The huge new bombers flew so high that the only way to reach them was to take everything—radios, parachutes, guns—out of the Zeros, which left the pilots only one option: *taiatori*, the ramming attack. They had some successes, but not enough to prevent the "*B-san*," as the Japanese respectfully referred to the bomber, from beginning the wholesale destruction of the Japanese war industry.

It was the original concept of the kamikaze pilot plunging with his plane into ships that was having the greatest impact on the American military. Of course, the proponents of the kamikaze tactics—most notably Admiral Onishi—inflated the numbers to make their case with the Imperial High Command and the emperor. They claimed that from the first special attacks in the fall of 1944 to January 1945, five carriers, one battleship, five cruisers, three destroyers, and twenty-three transports had been sent to the bottom. And, they said, hundreds of other American ships had been damaged.

After his own kamikaze failed to knock out any of the large aircraft carriers during the Second Battle of the Philippine Sea, Admiral Onishi doubted whether even his drastic strategy could alter the course of the war. But he still believed it was the only chance to win some sort of negotiated surrender that would leave the inner empire intact and prevent the home islands from invasion. So he preached that the kamikaze would not just sink the enemy's ships, it would break their morale and will to fight.

The propaganda worked; by the beginning of 1945, the high command had decided that most of the nation's air corps—other than a few planes held back for scouting, escorting kamikazes, or conventional attacks by the remaining experienced pilots—would all be converted into special attack units.

The kamikaze was certainly the most effective weapon left to the Japanese navy, which could no longer face the Americans on the seas. On January 4, Onishi got one of the results he was hoping for when a bomber made it past the combat air patrol and dove on the escort carrier USS *Ommaney Bay* in the Sulu Sea. The pilot came in so fast that the ship's crew had no time to react before the bomber clipped the island and crashed through the flight deck into the hangar deck. The plane and the first of its bombs exploded on impact, while the second bomb continued down into the forward engine room where it exploded. The ship was soon blazing out of control.

The fire spread to ammunition and bombs, causing them to detonate, in turn chasing away the destroyers that pulled up alongside to pour water on the flames. At last the ship's captain had no choice but to order his crew to abandon ship, which most did before the fires reached the torpedo stowage area and set off an enormous explosion. Otherwise, the casualties would have been higher; as it was, 158 men were killed or wounded. Shortly after midnight, the destroyer USS *Burns* put the carrier out of her misery with a torpedo.

The sinking was exactly what Onishi had claimed could happen: one plane in exchange for one ship. However, further Japanese claims of success were greatly inflated compared to what the U.S. Navy actually lost.

Still, in that period of time more American ships had been sunk and damaged by the kamikazes than in all other previous naval engagements of the war, including Pearl Harbor. While the seven hundred deaths from the typhoon in December was the single greatest loss of life in the Navy since 1942, the casualties from the suicide bombers had, in the first three months of 1945, surpassed that number.

However, the drain on human life and resources was harder on the Japanese than the Americans. The truth was that on any given mission, only a fraction of the kamikazes even found the fleet; a smaller number made it past the combat air patrol; and an even tinier percentage survived the ships' antiaircraft fire to attack. Another truth was that ramming a moving ship amid the gunfire and at such incredible velocities was more difficult than imagined, and most struck nothing but ocean.

Meanwhile, the makeup of the special attack units was changing. In the beginning, Onishi's naval aviators had clamored for the "honor." After the army embraced the idea, its pilots too volunteered with enthusiasm. But those early volunteers were gone. In the three-month period of operations in defense of the Philippines, the Japanese army sent 719 special attack pilots to their deaths; the navy, another 480. Those numbers did not include those lost in conventional air attacks, which almost always ended with the same result for the pilots.

By March 1945, the "voluntary" nature of the kamikaze program was mostly illusion. Draftees and college students, who had so far escaped the war with deferments, were placed in the "certain death" units according to the program's needs. Some of these so-called volunteers were in their middle teens. Still, most accepted their fates with resignation as faithful sons and as loyal subjects ready to die for the emperor.

The culture of suicide was building. On February 19, 1945, the U.S. Marines landed on Iwo Jima. Before the battle was over nearly a month later, nearly twenty thousand Japanese soldiers were dead and only a couple dozen, too injured or ill to fight, were captured. But five thousand U.S. Marines had also died and twice that many had been wounded.

Despite such a massive loss of life in a hopeless cause, there was no public outcry in Japan about the sacrifice of so many young men. Part of the silence was due to fear of the military government, as well as strict press censorship that left out the worst details, or described the losses in glowing patriotic terms. But also, the maxim that *a true samurai must live always prepared to die,* had been drilled into the minds of schoolchildren and adults since the 1930s. Therefore such acts were not considered suicide as much as patriotic self-sacrifice for emperor, for country, for family.

The truth of the matter was, the Japanese people were being set up to commit national suicide. In mid-January, Onishi admitted as much when he established the *Kamikaze Tobetsu Kogekita Niitakatai,* or the Divine Wind Special Attack Bombing Squadron Niitaka Unit. The unit had been named for the mountain in Formosa that had been used by Admiral Yamamoto as the code word to launch the attack against Pearl Harbor.

"This special attack unit will produce," Onishi declared to the young fliers. "Moreover, even if by any chance you are defeated, you will have kept Japan from becoming a ruined country." He promised that their deaths would inspire the entire nation to resist the invasion of the homeland. Millions of men, women, and children would sacrifice themselves, as the pilots would be sacrificing themselves, he said, to annihilate the enemy.

If they got the chance. On March 9, the B-29s appeared above Tokyo and dropped incendiary bombs on a city built largely of wood. Eighty-four thousand people, many of them women and children, died that night as firestorms swept through a quarter of a million homes.

Still, the Japanese military leaders were not willing to surrender. After all, they still had a massive army in China, as well as all those troops that had been left to shift for themselves on islands that the Americans had leapfrogged. The production plants were still producing two thousand planes a month that could be used to stop the *B-sans* and the U.S. Navy. And they still believed that the divine winds, the kamikaze, could save them if they could just get to the American aircraft carriers. The civilian population would just have to endure until the enemy had suffered enough.

Not everyone in Japan supported continuing the war. But the peace council's voice was always drowned out by the men who could not face the ignomity of defeat. Nor was everyone enamoured of the kamikazes—seeing them for what they were, the last desperate measure of a losing cause. These dissenters, many of them the traditional pilots, called the kamikazes "the crazy men" and were just as determined to show that they could still attack with conventional means and be as effective.

The two strategies got the chance to prove their comparative worth in mid-March. On the seventeenth, the American fleet was spotted only a hundred miles south of Kyushu and steaming for holy Japan. Before dawn the next day, twenty-seven kamikazes and twenty-five conventional bombers took off from their bases to attack. The escort planes reported that three American carriers had been hit. But none of the attackers—conventional or kamikaze—came back. Nor did the Americans leave.

The next day, the nineteenth, the American fleet of more than a dozen aircraft carriers was again located just before dawn. The Americans began launching strikes against targets around the Inland Sea, which until then the Japanese had considered inviolate. The Japanese responded again by sending dozens of conventional bombers, as well as kamikazes. They didn't have far to go, as the arrogant Americans were now only sixty miles off the coast of Kyushu.

The cloud cover hid the Japanese pilot from his enemies. However, the clouds also prevented him from seeing below, so occasionally he dropped down for a look around.

Under the ceiling, visibility was excellent. He could see his country from that height, perhaps he even tried to pick out the region where his family may have lived. But he couldn't linger for long, the combat air patrol or the lookouts on the ships might see him before he was ready.

His heart must have skipped when a little before 7:00 A.M., he dropped beneath the clouds and saw an American carrier group spread out like a banquet a few miles ahead of him. He would have noted the destroyers on the outer perimeter and the cruisers inside of them, and there in the middle was the prize, a group of four aircraft carriers.

The pilot's luck was excellent. The carriers were at their most vulnerable— turned into the wind to launch their aircraft.

He swung around so that he was approaching one of the largest carriers— the one with the numeral 13 on its flight deck—and broke from the cloud cover just a thousand yards from his target. He did not hesitate nor worry any longer about the combat air patrol. By the time they caught up to him, he knew it would be too late. Only the ships' antiaircraft guns could stop him now. He pushed the yoke forward and began to dive. He may have even yelled, *"Banzai!"* May you live ten thousand years!

PART IV

The USS *Franklin* and *Santa Fe*

Japan

March 19, 1945

CHAPTER EIGHTEEN

The Calm Before the Storm

March 19, 1945
Sixty miles off Kyushu, Japan
USS Franklin

In the moments before the lights went out, Steward's Mate 1st Class Matthew Little was surveying the wardroom, where a couple dozen officers were enjoying their breakfasts as he stood against a bulkhead in his starched white coat and neatly pressed dress blue pants. He was tired and could have used a cup of coffee himself to ward off the yawns. The crew had been up most of the night—actually, most of the last couple of nights— as the task force steamed into Japanese waters.

The bugle call to General Quarters had sounded every few hours as Japanese scout planes tested the edges of the task group's perimeter. Little and most of the other "colored" sailors hustled down to an ammunition hold to await the order to start passing ammunition.

No attacks materialized. Each time a threat disappeared from the radar screens, the men were allowed to return to their bunks, only to have the scene repeated a couple of hours later. It seemed to Little that his eyes would hardly close before the alarm sounded again and the public address system would start blaring, "All hands! Man your battle stations! All hands! Man your battle stations!" And he would be off and running for the ladders that led down into the bowels of the ship.

As a result, Little's wake-up call that morning seemed to come earlier than usual. He and the other mess stewards and cooks always had to get up an hour before reveille to get dressed, eat their breakfasts, and then prepare the wardrooms for dining before the officers arrived. The places around the tables had to be set with neatly folded linen napkins, china, and silverware, all of it laid out just so. Quite different than the cafeteria-style eating arrangements of the enlisted men with their tin plates and cups and the long tables. But, he had noticed, the officers generally ate the same food as everyone else.

Despite their lack of sleep, the officers were in good spirits—laughing over their coffee and grousing good-naturedly about "powdered eggs, again?" The *Franklin* was back in the fight, and the attacks on the Japanese mainland the day before had gone well with expectations that today's operations would equal or surpass previous successes. So far the precursor to the invasion of Japan had been easy.

Still, there was an undercurrent of nervousness, exacerbated by the fatigue, which gave an edge to the banter in the wardrooms and the mess halls. They were just sixty miles from the Japanese home island of Kyushu— a distance, the veterans pointed out to the new men, that a kamikaze traveling several hundred miles an hour could cover in a few minutes—"Just like the one that got us in October."

Little was worried, but he kept his fears in check. He didn't want to be down in an ammunition hold when a bomb or a kamikaze burrowed into the ship. Still, he wouldn't have been anywhere else than on the *Franklin*. "Big Ben," as the crew called the ship, was his home, his only home now.

When the ship had reached Bremerton, Little took the "special" train to Chicago before switching to a regular line for the trip to South Carolina. On the first leg of the journey, he and the other black sailors rode in the same cars as the white sailors, which had been set aside for military personnel. But there were no military cars on the second leg, and he was not allowed in cars with white civilian passengers. Instead, he had to ride in one reserved for Negroes.

Being on a ship where for the most part he was treated like any other sailor—and rank mattered rather than race—he had almost forgotten the discrimination against "coloreds" back in the States, particularly in the South. Although the ship wasn't entirely desegregated—the 150 other black men attended their own church services, presided over by Lieutenant "Pop" Wright, and they bunked in their own compartments, and Little wasn't allowed to serve on a gun crew, as he would have liked—there wasn't much else that he could see differentiating his life from that of a white sailor. Occasionally some bigot might make a racist comment, but most officers didn't tolerate it and, Little thought, *There's a lot more who do the right thing than do the wrong.*

In the South, old prejudices and customs had not changed much. Colored folks were still expected to step off the sidewalk to let whites pass. A colored man was not supposed to speak to a white woman unless spoken to first. They were to stay in their neighborhoods and their schools; any who tried to better themselves by making their mark in the white man's world were "uppity." Voting was discouraged, sometimes violently, and restaurants and drinking fountains were marked "white only" and "colored only." They were supposed to sit in the back of the bus.

However, the old social system was beginning to crumble, weakened by the experiences of black servicemen like Little. His race had fought for this country since the Revolutionary War—faced the added risk when fighting for the North during the Civil War of being executed if captured—and spilled their blood on the battlefields of France during World War I, even though some of their leaders told them not to fight because of America's racist policies. They had earned the respect of their white counterparts, even if that respect wasn't immediately apparent in social changes following each conflict.

That change would be slow and would take another twenty years to blossom as a civil rights movement. But it germinated during those war years in the hearts and minds of men who fought for their country and would come home wanting a fair shake based on the content of their characters, not the color of their skin.

As he made his way down the sidewalks of Anderson, Little stepped aside for no man, except out of courtesy. He walked tall in his bright white uniform—proud of what it represented, proud of his ship, and proud of himself. With his sailor's cap tipped at a jaunty angle and a seabag over his shoulder, he took his time strolling past old haunts, hoping to run into friends who might admire his new look.

Unfortunately, the town seemed empty of young people, and finally he turned to go to his family's home. He wished his mother were still alive to see him; she would have fussed over him and talked about how good he looked, all filled out on Navy food. But she had died when he was in boot camp. Still, he looked forward to his father's reaction to his arrival.

Little had done his duty and performed a man's work in the heat of battle as part of a team that made a powerful aircraft carrier run like the inner workings of a clock. While he was still looking for that opportunity to really prove himself, he was happy with his life in the Navy and was even thinking about making a career of it. He knew that his mother would have wanted him to continue his education, which had been stopped in the eleventh grade, but he believed that she would have also approved of the Navy.

As he walked to the outskirts of Anderson to catch a ride to his family's one-room shack in the country, Little daydreamed of the surprised looks his father and siblings would have when he walked in the door. He was almost out of town when he at last saw a face he knew, but the man didn't smile back. Instead, he unwittingly broke the sad news. "Sorry you didn't make it home for your dad's funeral," the man commiserated.

The statement hit Little like a sledgehammer. He didn't want to believe it, but it was true; his father had been dead and buried for a week.

The American Red Cross was supposed to notify servicemen of such family tragedies, but there had been a mix-up, and Little felt let down that he had to learn it from somebody off the street. As if moving in a dream, he hitched a ride to the sharecropper's cabin where he had grown up. The place was empty. The sounds of children laughing, his mother cooking, and his father coming in from a hard day's work in the fields drifted like ghosts within the cabin's thin gray walls. But it wasn't his home anymore.

From there he went to look for his brothers and sisters at his relatives' homes and found them living with an aunt. His siblings saw him coming down the street and ran out to greet him with hugs and tears of joy and anguish. The next day, when he went to the cemetery where his parents were buried side by side, more tears stained his brown face. He was so disappointed that it was too late to show them how well he had turned out.

Little spent most of his leave visiting aunts and uncles and friends, all of whom wanted to hear stories of his ship and his voyages among the far-flung islands of the Pacific. He had never traveled more than a few miles from Anderson until he joined the Navy, and neither had most of them. Now they gathered in crowded kitchens to hear of tiny coral islands and coconut palms, and stars that winked like fireflies on moonless nights above a limitless black sea. Of fish that flew through the air and big sharks that prowled in the ship's wake.

Mostly they wanted to hear about the *Franklin*—taller and longer than anything they could imagine, he said. He sort of forgot the admonition about revealing too much—after all, he was among family. His family and friends gave him their rapt attention as he described the call to General Quarters and the mad dash of thousands of men running for their battle stations. Using his hands, he demonstrated how the ship tilted this way and that as it swerved to avoid crazed Japanese pilots intent on crashing into Big Ben. Through his voice, they heard the ominous sound of guns pounding away overhead just as he heard them while passing ammunition deep inside the ship. They shook their heads sadly when he told them about the fifty-six men who had died during the suicide plane attack. And when he talked about how the white officers treated him and the other colored men the same as they treated white sailors, they nodded their heads, surprised. *Imagine that.*

At family gatherings, Little was told time and again told how proud his parents would have been. That they would be smiling down from heaven at what a fine young man their son had become and what a sharp figure he cut in his white uniform. The praise helped him accept that while he would never again see his parents, he could honor the love and support they had given him by being the man they would have wanted him to be. That was his inheritance. They had not owned the land his father farmed or the shack where Little and his brothers and sisters were born. His parents never had anything worth passing on—except a legacy of how to live his life honorably.

When his leave was up, Matthew Little packed his sea bag, anxious to get back to the *Franklin*. His siblings would stay with his aunt, and he would send money back to help out. But the ship was his home now, the crew part of his family. He was ready to face the future, but first he had to help take care of business with the Japanese.

So on the morning of March 19, 1945, he stifled his yawns and smiled when an officer caught his attention. "More coffee, please."

The rearmed and reinvigorated *Franklin* and her crew had stood out from Puget Sound and sailed into the Pacific on January 31, 1945. She had been repainted in a new "measure"—gone was the camouflage, replaced by a dark blue-gray to make it more difficult to spot the ship out of the cold, deep waters of Japan. The command staff had changed as well. In addition to her new skipper, Captain Gehres, the executive officer, Cmdr. Benjamin Moore, was replaced by Cmdr. Joe Taylor, the heroic former air officer. Cmdr. Henry Hale succeeded Taylor as the air officer.

Two days after leaving Puget Sound, the *Franklin* sailed beneath the Golden Gate Bridge and into San Francisco Bay, anchoring off the Alameda Naval Air Station. The purpose of the stop was to pick up the carrier's new air wing: Air Group 5.

On February 7, when the *Franklin* left for Pearl Harbor, the ship was carrying more planes than she had on the first tour, 110 compared to 90. Sixty of the planes were a different sort of fighter than Lieutenant Gove and his comrades in Fighter Squadron 13 had flown—the Hellcats had been replaced by F4U Corsairs. Another difference was that the fighters were flown by Marine instead of Navy pilots. The *Franklin* was also carrying an experimental weapon: a 1,100-pound, ten-foot-long rocket called a "Tiny Tim." The so-called "ship buster" was capable of tearing a vessel in two and was designed to be carried beneath the belly of the Corsair.

There were more than a hundred new crewmembers to replace the men who had been killed, wounded, or since transferred. They were young, patriotic, and, they thought, on a grand adventure. The "old hands," though most of themselves only eighteen months removed from boot camp, looked at each other and rolled their eyes when the "pollywogs" talked about how they had been worried that the war would be over before they got a crack at the Japanese.

In the moments before he lost his boyhood, Water Tender 3rd Class Samuel Rhodes Jr. somehow managed to untie his shoes and climb into his bunk. He was one of the new members of the crew, and all he wanted was a couple hours of uninterrupted sleep.

Born in 1926 in Media, Pennsylvania, Rhodes had often been reminded that he was a ninth-generation Pennsylvanian and that one of his earliest American ancestors had stood with other patriots in the Battle of the Brandywine during the Revolutionary War. "Our family has fought in every war this country has ever been in except one, the Spanish-American War," his father, Sam Sr., told his son. "And that was no big deal . . . Teddy Roosevelt charged up San Juan Hill and it was over."

The senior Rhodes had himself been a top sergeant in the Army, fighting in the trenches of France during World War I, and was the president of the local American Legion chapter. When World War II broke out, there was never a question that his son would serve. In fact, when Sam Jr. graduated high school in June 1944, Sam Rhodes Sr. told his seventeen-year-old son, "You better hurry up and enlist or you'll miss all the action." However, he also advised him, "Don't join the Army. We had to live in trenches, there was never enough to eat, and we had to charge into machine guns. . . . Join the Navy."

So Sam Rhodes Jr. took a bus to Philadelphia and the Navy recruiting station. After boot camp, he had hoped to be assigned to a submarine, but he was sent to "flare back college," where he learned to light off boilers like those he would see aboard a ship as a member of the Black Gang. Sailors gave the school the nickname because if lit improperly, the oil burners would "flare back" and singe the hair off of their arms and faces.

Rhodes was then assigned to the *Franklin,* reporting aboard after the ship left Bremerton and reached San Francisco Bay. A smoker who went through two packs of Lucky Strikes cigarettes a day—after all, everybody, including Humphrey Bogart, smoked—he was concerned that matches might be hard to come by and unreliable on the ocean. So one of the first purchases he made at the ship's store was a silver-colored Zippo lighter. "Lights every time," he boasted to his pals.

Rhodes got an even bigger kick lighting off the boilers, which was done by first using a specialized sort of lighter to start a torch, which was then thrust into the burners that would heat the water to produce the steam. The burners caught with a "WHOOMPF!" and the ship's power plant came alive like the beating of a giant heart.

On the morning of March 19, he had just come off watch when he met a friend, Fireman 1st Class Peter Spalluto, in a passageway. "How about going for some chow?" Spalluto asked.

Rhodes shook his head. Watches were four hours on and four hours off—between that duty schedule and the calls to General Quarters, he hadn't slept in two days. "I'm so tired I can't see straight. I'm going to hit the sack."

After arriving at Pearl Harbor on February 13, the *Franklin* spent the next few weeks in Hawaiian waters. The emphasis remained on air operations, especially as the captain was not happy with the air group's performance with landings and takeoffs, unleashing his famous temper until they got it right.

Finally, on March 3 Gehres pronounced his ship, its crew, and the air group fit for duty and Big Ben was ordered west in the company of the new heavy cruiser USS *Guam.* To any sailor who ventured out onto the flight deck, it seemed that the two ships were alone in a vast ocean. But the truth was that hundreds of Allied ships, most of them American, separated from each other by distances of fifty to a hundred miles, were sailing for Ulithi.

If not for the growing awareness that the ship drew nearer to the war with each swell that passed beneath the hull, the voyage would have been pleasant. The seas were calm, the sunrises and sunsets painted in spectacular arrays of colors—sometimes soft pastels as in a newborn infant's room, other times fluorescent as neon signs.

As the nights grew warmer, men congregated on the flight deck to enjoy the breeze, a smoke, conversation, and the stars above the ocean. The enlisted men were frequently joined by a compact, good-looking, dark-haired man who, like many of them, wore only his boxers as he strolled about the deck enjoying a cigarette. Although there was no insignia to iden-tify his rank or division, the new men could tell by the self-confident man-ner in which he carried himself that he was an officer. They also learned from the way the veterans would straighten up and warmly address him as "Sir" that he was an officer they liked as well as respected.

Some of the first-time sailors thought that he must be one of the pilots, because he regaled them with stories from the early days of the war. He told them about flying in the battles of the Coral Sea and Midway, when young pilots knowingly sacrificed their lives to stop the Japanese. But his stories weren't all just about pilots and flying. He also talked about the bravery of the crews who fought the fires on the doomed aircraft carriers *Lexington* and *Yorktown*.

Almost three years removed from those battles, the newcomers and expe-rienced men hung on every word. *Coral Sea. Midway. Lexington. Yorktown. Enterprise. Hornet.* These were names they knew from the newsreels, leg-endary battles and deeds and ships that were already becoming part of Amer-ican military folklore, like Gettysburg, the Alamo, and John Paul Jones.

After a bit, the officer would bid them good night and leave them to their sailors' talk. "Who was that?" some new man would invariably ask.

"That," the veterans would answer with pride, "was our exec, Commander Joe Taylor . . . toughest pilot in the Navy."

In the moment before he found himself flying through the air on the morn-ing of March 19, all Chief Petty Officer Edwin Garrison wanted was a shower. And personally he was a little upset with Taylor that he was back onboard the *Franklin* at all.

Garrison thought Taylor was a great man and excellent officer, but he had a personal bone to pick with him. On the way from Ulithi to Pearl Harbor following the kamikaze attack in October, he was working on a damaged torpedo plane when Taylor approached and asked if the plane would be ready to fly by the time they reached the States. "If we get to go there," Tay-lor corrected himself as no decision had supposedly been made yet.

"Yes, sir," Garrison replied, "but it won't be able to land on another carrier . . . the tail hook has been shot off."

Taylor said he didn't care; he wasn't planning on landing on a carrier. "If you have it ready to fly two days before we get to the States, I'll fly you to an East Coast naval air station when you get your leave."

Garrison eagerly agreed to the deal. The crew believed that they would be granted "survivor's leave" of twenty to thirty days, and he figured that the one-day plane flight would save him four days of riding a train to Greenville, South Carolina, plus the fare.

The Avenger was ready as requested; however, Garrison's ride to the East Coast never materialized. After Taylor reached Oahu flying the plane, an admiral commandeered it. That was the way things worked in the Navy, so Garrison was not too surprised or disappointed. He figured his hard work would still pay off someday, because now Taylor owed him a favor.

However, when he tried to cash in on that favor, he was sorely disappointed. Shortly after repairs began on the ship in Bremerton, another metalsmith had come aboard and offered Garrison five hundred dollars to swap duty. The other man was attached to a patrol squadron stationed nearby, and he was afraid that the war was going to be over "before I see any action."

"Hell, I'd give you a thousand dollars, if I had it, to get shore duty," replied Garrison, who felt that he had seen quite enough of "the action." He took his new friend to Taylor to ask if they could trade places.

"How much battle experience do you have?" Taylor asked the other man.

"None," he replied.

Taylor glared for a moment at the pair in front of him. "I wouldn't swap him for ten like you," he snapped at the would-be warrior. "Now get off my ship!" The chastened metalsmith scurried for the door. Then Taylor turned on Garrison. "Don't ever bother me with anything like that again."

Therefore, Garrison was feeling a little bitter toward the new executive officer when he took the train home to South Carolina as part of the second wave. He did, however, manage to have a great time. His sister's husband loaned him his car, and an uncle, who was a farmer and had more gas rationing stamps than he needed, gave him the fuel to get around to see what friends were still in the area.

The good times continued after Garrison got back to the ship and was told he had to catch a train down to San Francisco to acquaint himself with the Corsair fighters that would be coming aboard the *Franklin*. When he arrived at the air base, the aviators had finished training and had been granted three weeks leave, as they would probably be gone for the next eighteen months on their tour of duty.

Learning how to patch together the new planes was no great challenge. So essentially Garrison had an extra three weeks to party with a group of friends—men and women—from the town of Santa Rosa. They were all young and seemed to be hell bent on spending the war drinking, dancing, and romancing.

Back onboard the *Franklin* one day, Captain Gehres handed him a photograph of Garrison briefing Admiral Halsey on the damage done by the kamikaze taken when the ship was anchored at Ulithi. "You may want to show this to your grandchildren some day," Gehres said. When Garrison finally received his promotion to Chief Petty Officer on March 1, he concluded that the "old man" might be "hell on wheels," as some of the officers described him, but he ran a good ship.

With his promotion, Garrison's battle station changed from fighting fires on the flight deck to fighting fires on the hangar deck. Otherwise, his job was overseeing a crew that patched airplanes. He had a good group of guys working for him like Aviation Machinist 2nd Class Earl Clouser and AM 3rd Class James Krenske, who were best friends and hardly ever apart. One of Garrison's best friends, AM 2nd Class Fred Holdsworth, also worked for him.

Garrison was surprised that so many of the men had gone home on leave and gotten married. He had advised against it before they left. "If something happens, you don't want to leave a widow," he warned. But they had gone ahead and "got hitched" anyway. He hoped their wives wouldn't regret it.

After battle conditions were relaxed on the morning of March 19, Garrison thought about having something to eat but decided that a shower sounded better than powdered eggs. He was feeling too nervous to eat anyway. The previous morning, he had watched as a big enemy bomber was shot down in the distance, trailing a plume of smoke all the way to the horizon. There was a kind of beauty in the gray spiral of the plane's demise. But he was soon reminded that his own death was as close as the next wave when the ship sailed into an area of floating mines, some coming so close the gunners shot at and exploded those they could see.

Garrison met up with Holdsworth, who thought a shower might revive him too. As they were leaving the hangar deck to go below, they stopped to watch as a kamikaze attacked the *Essex*-class carrier USS *Yorktown*, which was in a task group about four miles off the starboard bow. The plane made it to within about five hundred feet of the carrier's flight deck before the ship's guns turned it into a ball of fire and smoke.

"Boy, that was close," Holdsworth said.

"Yeah," Garrison agreed. "Kind of strange the captain doesn't have us at battle stations."

The two friends shrugged—that was the skipper's business—and continued on down to their compartment on the third deck to grab their razors and towels before heading to the large shower room. Stepping inside the door, they saw that a lot of the other guys had the same idea and a long line had formed for the showers.

"Hell, let's wait until tomorrow," Holdsworth said. Garrison agreed and they stepped back out into the passageway.

The *Franklin* had pulled into the Ulithi anchorage on March 13 after ten days at sea. Even the experienced veterans were awed at the sight of the largest, most powerful armada ever assembled. The ships were gathering for the final push toward Japan, which had already begun with the February 19 invasion of Iwo Jima.

The fanaticism with which the Japanese defended the Bonins, which they considered a part of Japan, was a warning of what would be in store for the Americans whether the next target was Formosa or Okinawa. Or one of the main Japanese islands, such as Kyushu on the southern end of the archipelago.

The American military leaders assumed that for the war to end, Japan would have to be invaded, probably in the fall of 1945, after the Germans were finished. Until then, it was essential that Japanese air power be negated, especially the threat of kamikazes.

On March 14, the American armada, comprised of four, four-carrier task groups, left Ulithi with a mission—code-named Lucky Day—to destroy airbases and ports, as well as seek out and sink the remnants of the Imperial Navy, on and around the Japanese home islands of Kyushu and Honshu.

The vast array of ships was once again under Admiral Raymond Spruance, and the name changed back to the Fifth Fleet. The task force commander was again Marc A. Mitscher, the popular admiral who had once ordered the fleet to "turn on the lights" following the Great Marianas Turkey Shoot so that his pilots could find their way back to the ships. To accomplish his new mission, he intended to sail where no task force had dared go before, almost within sight of the Land of the Rising Sun.

The *Franklin* was placed in Task Group 58.2 and once again made the flagship of Admiral Davison. The admiral had been on the ship until the kamikaze attack in October and had noted in a memo to the crew that he'd enjoyed his time aboard; his only complaint was that the crew had seemed unusually adept at cursing. When some of the veterans of the crew saw the memo, they let go a stream of profanity that would have convinced the admiral they had become even more proficient during his absence. They noted that the last time they had seen Davison, he was being hauled ignominiously via breeches buoy to a destroyer while they stayed behind to save their burning ship.

The rest of the task group was comprised of the *Essex*-class carrier *Hancock;* two light carriers, the *San Jacinto* and *Bataan;* two new battleships, the *Washington* and *North Carolina;* two heavy cruisers, the *Baltimore* and *Pittsburgh;* the light cruiser *Santa Fe;* and two dozen destroyers and destroyer escorts.

The crews were up most of the night of March 16 at General Quarters as the task force steamed north. Spread out over fifty square miles of ocean, the task force had not yet contacted the enemy, though they were aware that submarines lurked in those waters. Several times during the night, nervous lookouts called in torpedo alerts, rousting the crew to its battle stations.

The task force was spotted the next day, March seventeenth, by a long-range Japanese bomber, which fled with its news. With the element of surprise gone, in the early morning of March 18, 1945, Task Force 58 sailed to within a hundred miles of Japan. Ninety-one years earlier, almost to the day, Commodore Matthew Perry had sailed into Tokyo Bay with his black-fleet squadron, the most technologically advanced warships in the world. Now, once again, the American fleet—the most technologically advanced in the world—had returned determined to win unconditional surrender from the enemy. The "Japanese deceit" of Pearl Harbor had ensured that nothing short of that goal would suffice.

Of the Axis powers, the Japanese were almost alone now. The Italians were long out of the war. The Battle of the Bulge had turned out to be the German's last gasp, and the thousand-year Reich was collapsing rapidly after a little over a decade. Soon the entire Allied effort would be turned to the invasion of Japan, but first the Japanese air corps, especially the kamikazes, had to be eliminated.

An hour before dawn on the eighteenth, Captain Gehres turned the ship into the wind and began launching strikes, primarily at the airfields at Kagoshima and Izumi on the island of Kyushu. The Americans went in low to surprise the enemy, who now had a rudimentary radar. If the Americans had looked up, they might have seen the planes with the red dots on the underside of their wings heading in the opposite direction.

In the moments before he would find himself trapped deep inside a ship, Lt. (j.g.) Donald Gary was "twitting" one of his men in the engine room about his three days' growth of whiskers. The captain insisted that the men "look like sailors" and maintain their discipline even as they moved into Japanese waters.

Born in Findlay, Ohio, Gary was an old man compared to most of the crew, most of whom were about half his forty-one years of age. He was already a twenty-four-year veteran when he joined the *Franklin* in Bremerton as a "mustang" engineering officer. He had begun as an enlisted man, working his way up through the ranks until his promotion in November 1943 to a junior grade (j.g.) lieutenant. Along the way, he served aboard several ships, including the battlewagon USS *Idaho,* and the heavy cruiser USS *Indianapolis,* an older ship but still one of the fastest in the fleet, as well as the carrier USS *Enterprise.*

In early December, he had been on temporary assignment in New Jersey when he was told to report to the *Franklin.* Gary's career was winding down. Another five years and he could leave the Navy with a full pension. He was looking forward to retirement; he had missed too much time with his family. He had had to spend that Christmas without them in Bremerton, though it was having a pleasant dinner at the Officers' Club with the ship's navigation division officer, Lt. (j.g.) Robert Wassman.

Gary's duty and battle stations were both in the engine room, but he didn't limit his knowledge of the ship to the areas where he was stationed. He took it upon himself to learn every square inch of the enormous ship. Thin and wiry, he was constantly squeezing through small spaces or poking his nose up ventilation shafts looking for escape routes. They were heading into a forward area, and he had a feeling that the knowledge might come in handy.

When the ship left Ulithi for Japan, the crew's morale seemed a mixture of confidence and nervousness. Gary himself was feeling apprehensive. He had been fighting the Japanese long enough to know that the closer the fleet got to their homeland, the more determined the enemy would be to stop them. His concern was reflected in the letter he wrote home on the night of March 17:

My Dear Wife and Son:

Happy Birthday, sweetheart! If I could only be there to kiss you and try to make you and I both happy. And I believe I could.

Tonight or early tomorrow morning we will send planes off for a strike at the enemy and will ourselves be in battle condition and subject to most anything. If God is willing, we will come out within a few days after doing our best to make those yellow dogs see that they were wrong when they tried to make everyone do as they decreed, and did the sneaky trick they accomplished on Dec. 7, 1941. I'm positive the Lord isn't on the side of such ruthless people.

I have instructed my men on the easiest way out of most any situation and have acquainted myself with all escape routes in case of trouble—which I hope won't come.

If I can't get back to live the kind of a retirement we have dreamed of, I'll leave with the satisfaction of knowing that you will do your utmost to educate our fine son and teach him to be the kind of gentleman we would both be proud of. Tell him again that I have so many things planned for him as he grows older, and I pray that I'll be able to complete those plans and will carry them out as planned. Be a good father to him if I don't get back or else—and better yet—find a husband and father for both of you.

As God is my judge, I love you as much as life and hope it's not asking too much of the Lord to have both of you for a few more years.

Love to you. Love to Kenny.

Gary paused at that point. The words did not seem adequate to dissipate the feeling of doom that troubled him. He thought for a moment, then added:

P.S. There is so much more I'd like to write but can't put it in words. Besides, I think I've let you know how I feel on a day like this. I've felt like this always, sweetheart, but you know me . . . I don't say it often, or don't say things I should say at all.

Love, Don

When he finished, Gary placed the letter in an envelope. He wrote on the outside that it was to be mailed in the event he was killed. He then placed it in the drawer of the desk in his compartment.

The fact that nothing bad happened on the eighteenth did not alleviate his concerns, but part of those jitters he now attributed to being tired. He had been on engine room watch until midnight—then at his battle station most of the rest of the morning. When the battle ready condition was relaxed, he quickly made his way to a junior officer's wardroom where he wolfed down his breakfast. Although he could have used the remaining time to relax in his compartment or take a shower, he knew that this day could not remain as peaceful as the day before and returned to his battle station immediately.

A few minutes after 7:00 A.M., he noticed the unshaven sailor and asked for an explanation. The sailor said that his razor was in an area that had been locked down for several days. Gary accepted the excuse and said the man could use his electric razor, which he kept near at hand in case he was suddenly called to the bridge. The sailor turned to look for a small mirror as Gary plugged the electric razor into a socket.

On the morning of the eighteenth, twenty-seven kamikazes and twenty-five conventional bombers had been launched to find the American fleet. Even as the American planes that had passed below them pounded their airfields, the Japanese pilots spotted the task group that included the carriers *Enterprise*, *Intrepid*, and *Yorktown*.

Most of the Japanese fliers would not get much closer, as the American combat air patrol intercepted and shot them down. The kamikazes were especially vulnerable and were slaughtered by the Corsairs. However, several of the conventional aircraft made it through and scored hits on all three carriers. But the damage and casualties were light and the ships were soon carrying out flight operations.

The *Franklin's* gunners had a quiet day. In fact, none of the ships in Task Group 58.2 was attacked. The Japanese tried but they were all shot down. Big Ben's fighters alone had splashed eighteen planes.

After recovering the last of its planes, Task Force 58 headed away from Japan to meet with the supply task group to refuel and rearm. That night, the pilots' wardroom aboard the *Franklin* was a merry place. Many had just completed their first combat missions and excitedly recounted their attacks on Japanese targets.

Best of all, Air Group 5 had suffered no casualties. Two of the carrier's planes had been forced into the sea, but the aviators were quickly rescued by American submarines. Even the antiaircraft flak over the targets was much less than they had expected. They could hardly wait for the next morning.

In the moments before he found himself crawling on his knees in the dark and praying for deliverance, Lt. Cmdr. Joseph T. O'Callahan S.J. was complaining to Steward's Mate 1st Class Tom Frasure about the "fried bread" he was serving for breakfast. "We don't like fried bread, especially cold," O'Callahan said.

Frasure just grinned. He knew that "Father Joe," as the enlisted men and officers called the ship's new Catholic chaplain, was mostly jibing him. The priest was known for his easygoing nature and always had a kind word for anyone. "That ain't fried bread, sir; that's French toast," Frasure chuckled.

O'Callahan made a face at his breakfast but smiled. He had only been on the Franklin for two weeks and was already a favorite with the men, even the non-Catholics.

For reasons known only to himself, when the ship reached Pearl Harbor, Gehres unceremoniously transferred Chaplains Chamberlin and Harkin. He then asked that two different chaplains be assigned to the ship. The Navy sent Lt. Grimes Gatlin, a Protestant, and O'Callahan, who had already served aboard carriers longer than most of the rest of the crew or its officers.

A member of the Society of Jesuits, O'Callahan had been raised in Boston, in a large Irish-Catholic family. After his father died of a stroke at the young age of forty-nine, the family had moved in with his mother's father, a wealthy businessman.

An excellent athlete and student at Boston College High School, O'Callahan could have gone into business himself. But he felt another calling and joined the Jesuits shortly after graduation.

O'Callahan was almost forty when he volunteered to join the Navy. He certainly didn't have to serve: He was the head of the mathematics department at Holy Cross College in Worcester, Massachusetts. But he knew war was coming and that he would be needed. After the war started, he had another reason. His sister, Alice, who had joined the Maryknoll order of nuns, had been working in the Philippines and was imprisoned by the Japanese.

O'Callahan served aboard the aircraft carrier USS Ranger for two and a half years, as the ship patrolled the Atlantic Ocean and participated in the invasion of North Africa. During that time, he never quite overcame a fear of torpedoes from German U-boats, telling himself "This is it!" every time the ship had to take evasive action to avoid being hit.

His fears were accentuated by the fact that he had suffered from claustrophobia since childhood. Why he chose to sign up for the Navy, as opposed to another, less-enclosed service, was a curiosity. He did not like being in a room in which the doors and windows were closed, yet he had volunteered for sea duty inside what was essentially a big, steel box that regularly had to be buttoned up tight as a drum.

In January 1945, O'Callahan had shore duty at Pearl Harbor, but he was hoping to be assigned to a staff position with the U.S. naval forces in the Philippines, where he thought he might learn about his sister's whereabouts. The family had heard she was in a prison camp, but for three years there had been almost no word whether "La," as she was known to the family, still lived. The battle for the main island of Luzon was raging, and his concerns had grown with press reports that the Japanese were murdering prisoners as they retreated.

However, no staff position was forthcoming. Instead, on March 2 he received orders to proceed "immediately and without delay" to the *Franklin* for duty.

The Pacific War was different than what he had encountered in the Atlantic. Over there it was all about U-boats and torpedoes; in the Pacific, kamikazes were the principal threat. They were on his mind when he decided to celebrate a special Mass on the afternoon of the seventeenth as the ship prepared for combat.

About twelve hundred enlisted men and officers gathered on the foc'sle. The day was cloudy and cold, a brisk wind made the cloths on the altar table flutter beneath the golden chalice that held the wine and the saucer that contained the bread for consecration. He was assisted by this friend, Lt. Cmdr. Bill Fox, one of the ship's physicians and a former altar boy.

The closer the ship had moved to Japan, the more religious some of the men had become. Just that morning the line for confession had stretched almost half the length of the ship. Now as he performed the ceremony, O'Callahan wondered if this was the last Mass that some of these men would ever hear. *It might be the last Mass I ever say, for that matter,* he thought.

O'Callahan didn't know why the previous Catholic chaplain, Harkin, who had been popular with the men, was transferred so suddenly. But Captain Gehres had made it clear when O'Callahan came aboard that as skipper, he wasn't much of "a church-goer" and wouldn't tolerate anything—including religion—that would get between his men and their mission.

However, on the morning of March eighteenth, Gehres was somewhat friendly when O'Callahan saw him on the bridge. The priest noted that he had been pretty good at praying away the torpedoes when he was on the Ranger. "We'll see how I do with the kamikazes," he said.

Gehres nodded, looking up at the sky as though he expected a suicide plane to materialize. "They'll be out after us today," he said.

Whether it was prayers, skill, or luck—or a combination of the three—all the aviators returned alive from the sorties of the eighteenth. But it was with some trepidation that O'Callahan noted that the next day, March 19, marked the Feast of Saint Joseph, the patron saint of a happy death.

O'Callahan was up most of that night again, going out to check on the gun crews, offering words of encouragement, and taking the occasional hasty confession. Deciding that he was hungry, he decided to stop in a ward room to get a cup of coffee and something to eat before reporting to his battle station on the bridge.

He was delighted to see his friend Lt. (j.g.) Lindsey "Red" Morgan already sitting down to breakfast. Before the war, Morgan, a southerner with a slow drawl to match his even temperament, had hopes of becoming a pitcher in the Big Leagues.

Serving them was the steward, Frasure, a seventeen-year-old "colored" boy from Mississippi. Frasure had hoped to be a professional singer before the war broke out.

"That ain't fried bread, sirs," he laughed when the priest complained, "That's French toast."

"It's still cold," O'Callahan replied.

After refueling on the evening of March 18, Task Force 58 had continued to withdraw to the east until midnight when the ships again reversed course and headed back west toward the launching area.

The morning of March 19 found the *Franklin*'s crew exhausted and jittery from a lack of sleep and constant alarms as the ship began its predawn launch preparations. The announcement that they were closing to within sixty miles of the coast of Japan did nothing to calm their nerves.

A little before dawn, Task Group 58.2 turned into the wind and the carriers launched the day's first strike. As soon as the planes were gone, the ships resumed their pattern of zigzagging beneath the cover provided by the combat air patrol.

At 6:49 A.M., the task group turned into the wind again and increased its speed to twenty-four knots to launch first another combat air patrol and then the second strike. The sky was again overcast, with the aerographers reporting a ceiling of about two thousand feet; however, visibility beneath the cloud cover was excellent.

Moments before he was thrust into a scene from hell, Aviation Coxswain 3rd Class Frank Turner Jr. was about to pour himself a cup of coffee. He was in a small room called the "catapult shack" on the third deck, glad to get out of the bitterly cold wind up top that got beneath even his heavy jacket and jumpsuit.

Looking west from the flight deck earlier that morning, he thought he could just see a dark line on the horizon and that curious shadowing and cloud buildup that signified a land mass. Japan. He wondered what the land of his enemy looked like now that spring was coming. Back home in New York City, he figured, the leaves would be starting to bud on the trees in his neighborhood of the Bronx.

When he was home on leave that past December the trees were bare, but the welcome back from family and friends was as warm as summer. When he could finally convince his mother to release him from her embrace, he had worn his uniform down to the fire station house in Harlem where his father had his headquarters as a battalion chief. The firefighters had lined up to shake his hand, slap him on the back, and remark about how "the kid" had grown up. It was both a thrill and a little embarrassing to be lauded like that by guys he had always looked up to as heroes, like his father.

One evening after he had been home for a couple of days, his father nodded toward the door and said, "I feel like a beer. Let's take a walk." They had headed down to the neighborhood pub, O'Reilley's.

Before they all went into the service, Frank would have expected to have seen most of the gang he grew up with at the pub, pouring back a few pints and shooting the breeze. Now there were mostly old men, who welcomed him home but after a time left him alone at a table to talk to his dad.

"So how was it?" his dad asked. He had seen the newsreels, which were starting to show suicide planes crashing into ships.

Turner had not said much about his experiences so far. The burns on his face from the bomb that clipped the deck-edge elevator on October 15 were pretty much healed up, and his eyebrows, which had been singed nearly off, had grown back. He still had small scars on his back where the shrapnel hit him, but he hadn't shown them to anyone, especially not his mother.

Now he told his dad about the day he had been wounded and showed him the scars. He recounted the kamikaze attack that killed fifty-six men and set the ship on fire. And how before that his friend, Harold Stancil, had been killed by another suicide plane.

As his son related the story, Frank Sr. shook his head. He had fought in World War I and knew that war was never as glamorous as portrayed in the movies. But as a firefighter who thought life was so precious that he had often risked his own to save others, he didn't understand throwing one away just to kill.

"You're fighting a different kind of people," he said. "The Germans knew when it was hopeless and would give up. But these people won't quit."

When he got back to Bremerton, Turner learned that he had a new job. He was put in charge of the crew that launched fighter planes for the combat air patrol using the two catapults located on either side of the forward part of the flight deck. The catapults operated through a hydraulic system of pistons and pulleys beneath the flight deck that would "slingshot" planes off the flight deck at more than a hundred knots.

On the morning of March 19, 1945, Turner and his crew made four "cat shots." The last pilot to go was Lt. Col. Charles Weiland, the commanding officer of VMF 452, and as soon as he was off, Turner and crewmate AMM 3rd Class S. J. Ansaldi ran out to retrieve the catapult equipment, which they quickly stored so that it wouldn't interfere with the launching of the main strike force.

No longer needed on the flight deck, Turner suggested to Ansaldi that they go below to the catapult shack "for a cuppa Joe." They went down the ladder, past the foc'sle and to the compartment on the third deck.

Entering the catapult shack, Ansaldi went over to check the equipment in case the captain called for another catapult shot. Turner picked up the "Joe pot" and started to pour himself a cup.

After the combat air patrol was launched, there were still thirty-one planes— Corsairs, Helldivers, and Avengers—on the *Franklin*'s flight deck with their engines running and propellers whirling. The Helldivers and Avengers were armed with four bombs, mostly of the five-hundred-pound variety; the twelve fighters each had a Tiny Tim rocket strapped beneath their bellies. The flight deck crew in the red shirts and hats had filled all the planes with the highly volatile aviation fuel.

Another twenty-two planes waited below on the hangar deck for a third strike. Eleven had been gassed but were not armed: eight of them were in the forward section nearest Elevator One, the other three were amidships close to Elevator Two. Five more Corsairs had been gassed and armed with Tiny Tim rockets: three of them amidships and two aft near Elevator Three. Six more planes waited in the aft section but were neither gassed nor armed with bombs or rockets.

The hangar deck fueling crew was still in the process of topping off the gas tanks of several planes. They weren't really supposed to be fueling while launching aircraft, just in case there was a crash or a bomb came loose and exploded. The hoses were supposed to have been cleared of the aviation fuel with inert gas that wouldn't ignite in case of a fire. But Gehres was all for setting records for the number of sorties that could be flown from the *Franklin,* which meant having the planes on the hangar deck ready to go as soon as those on the flight deck were gone.

Meanwhile, the pilots and their crewmen flying in the third strike fidgeted in their ready rooms, waiting for the announcement. "Pilots to your planes!"

With the combat air patrol up, the *Franklin* began launching the planes of its second strike. One deck below the bridge, task group commander Admiral Davison was in the flag plot with other flag officers, including Admiral Gerald Bogan, who was getting acclimated as Davison's replacement.

The admiral's radar operator declared the screen clear of bogies, and the admiral sent a message suggesting that the task group secure from General Quarters. Whether to take that advice was every captain's decision, and some did not take the chance being so close to Japan.

But Gehres decided to allow his crew to stand down to Condition 3—the guns would be manned, but most of the rest of the crew were free to go about their regular duties or relax. It had been awhile since the men had a hot meal or had a break from the tension because of all the calls to battle stations.

Shipboard routine resumed. In a compartment connected to the captain's office, four men were being interviewed by a war correspondent for *Collier's* magazine who was writing an article about life aboard a carrier. On the fantail, Chaplain Gatlin and executive officer Taylor officiated at the funeral of a seaman who had died the night before of alcohol poisoning from drinking too much "torpedo juice."

Hungry enlisted men hurried to reach the mess halls on the third deck before the line got too long. Their groans upon reaching their destination told those behind them that the day's fare was once again powdered eggs, powdered milk, and the ubiquitous "spiced ham," otherwise known as Spam.

Those who weren't fast enough found themselves standing in rows that wound from the hangar deck through hatches, down double ladders past the Marine sleeping compartment, and below to the mess halls. A couple hundred late arrivals were lined up on the hangar deck—some stood quietly sleepy-eyed, while others joshed and called out to friends like the noisy bunch of teenagers and young men they were a little after 7:00 A.M. on March 19, 1945.

In the moments before he would have otherwise died, Lt. (j.g.) E. Robert Wassman decided he was hungry and stopped at a wardroom on the third deck to eat pancakes. Like many men on the *Franklin* that day, a moment's hesitation, a step one way or the other, a hunger pang, or a desire for sleep determined their fates.

An entirely different twist of fate had befallen Wassman when he went home on leave back in December. When he had first shipped out on the *Franklin,* he didn't want to be "attached" to any woman back home. He was all for meeting "broads"—sleep with some of them, but that was it.

However, back home in New York City, he was sitting one evening next to a friend on a train leaving Grand Central Station when a pretty young woman sat down next to him. He had turned on the charm, and they were soon talking. He had spent the rest of his leave courting Eleanor Humphrey.

When it was time to leave for the war again, he had undergone a transformation of sorts. He wanted to know that there was someone waiting for him to come home to, and that someone was his new girl, Eleanor.

Somehow the relationship made it both more difficult and easier to go back to Bremerton. Instead of jumping back into the wild life, he was just as happy to meet a new friend, Lt. (j.g.) Don Gary, and spend a quiet Christmas dinner together talking about the two women in their lives.

After the kamikaze attack , Captain Shoemaker had given Wassman some heat for leaving his battle station to lead the fire-fighting effort from the flight deck. However, in the finest tradition of the Navy, the captain had then put him in for the Bronze Star for gallantry.

Wassman felt sorry for the members of the ship's band who had had it rough immediately following the attack. Their battle station duties were to help the medical staff as stretcher bearers. Up to that point, neither they nor the rest of the crew had experienced much of the dark side of war. It was almost as though they were on a cruise, playing music, keeping the "passengers" happy. Then all of the sudden they were thrust into the role of retrieving horribly injured and burned crewmembers and bringing them back to the ship's infirmary. Several had decided that they had had enough, and when the ship left Bremerton for the Pacific, they had gone "over the hill." But most of them, including the famous musicians onboard, had sucked it up and returned. Wassman had picked replacements for the deserters from the Navy music school in San Francisco.

Wassman had a new boss, Cmdr. Stephen Jurika, the ship's new navigator. Jurika had served aboard the old carrier USS *Lexington,* including at the Battle of the Coral Sea. The commander was still troubled, he said, because the scuttlebutt was true—there had been sailors alive in her holds when U.S. destroyers were ordered to finish her.

On March 19, 1945, Wassman had just gotten off watch and had come down the ladder from the island accompanied by his yeoman and the yeoman for the executive officer, Joe Taylor. They were on their way to the navigator's office on the third deck when they passed the galley and he smelled breakfast. Suddenly hungry and having a passion for pancakes, he decided to see if any were available. "You fellows go on ahead," he said. "I'm going to grab a bite to eat."

It was a few minutes after seven, and if he had still been at his battle station, Wassman would have heard the warnings. First, that the combat air patrol had intercepted several bandits and shot them down, but weren't sure if they had got them all. Then a message sent from the USS *Hancock* to the *Franklin:* Two of her lookouts reported seeing a Japanese bomber, but the plane had disappeared into the clouds somewhere in front of the *Franklin.*

When he received the message on the bridge, Gehres called his own combat information center and asked if they had a bogey on the radar.

"Negative, sir," was the reply.

Gehres called the admiral's bridge and asked if they had any on their screens. Again the reply was, "Negative."

The captain called his forward lookout station and told the men there to be alert. "Keep your eyes on the edges of the clouds up ahead," he warned. He then gave the officer in control of the antiaircraft guns permission to open fire without further orders on any unidentified aircraft coming at the ship.

A torpedo bomber had just taken off and another was rumbling down the flight deck when suddenly the air was filled with another frantic call from the *Hancock* using the *Franklin's* code name for the day: "DIXIE! DIXIE! There's one coming in on you!"

CHAPTER NINETEEN

The Last Operation

March 19, 1945
Sixty miles off Kyushu, Japan
USS Santa Fe

General Quarters sounded at 5:30 A.M., rousting Chief Warrant Officer Donald C. Jackson from his bunk in the stateroom he shared with another warrant officer. The compartment was near the bow on the second deck below the weather deck, where he could hear a constant hiss as the ten-thousand-ton ship knifed through the waters of the Pacific.

There was just enough room for each man to have a bunk, a clothes locker, and a combination dresser/desk; there was also a wash basin and medicine cabinet. Crowded as they were, the accommodations were certainly better than the hammock Jackson had slept in when he was a mere sailor before the war; the room even had a door for privacy.

The clanging of the GQ alarm—which sounded like someone banging on a sheet of steel with a hammer, rather than the bugle call used by larger ships—was followed by a command over the *Santa Fe's* public address system: "All hands, man your battle stations." Outside the stateroom, there came the sudden added din of the crew running on the steel decks, scrambling up and down ladders, and jumping through hatchways.

Despite the clamor, Jackson wasn't worried. The alarm was a pre-dawn routine onboard the *Santa Fe* whenever the ship was in hostile waters. The lack of gunfire overhead and the absence of evasive maneuvering meant they were not under attack—not yet.

Still, he quickly pulled on a dark gray, long-sleeved shirt, gray trousers, and black shoes. Standing, he slipped the chain that held his identification dogtags and a small silver and turquoise ring beneath his undershirt. He patted on the triangular khaki cap that identified him as an officer, grabbed his lifejacket, and ran out of the room without bothering to button his shirt or tie his shoes.

Although the alarm was routine, time was still of the essence to reach his battle station in Radio Two before the watertight doors were sealed throughout the ship. Once the hatches were closed and dogged, they were supposed to remain that way until conditions were relaxed or permission to exit was granted by the damage control officer. The damage control officer in turn reported such breaches to the skipper, Captain Harold Fitz, and the "old man" liked to run a tight ship. Jackson's position as a warrant officer, assigned to teach and supervise radio and radar technicians, often required him to move about the vessel with his men, even during battle. But he better have a good reason for opening a watertight door, or he would hear about it from his superior, or worse, the captain himself.

To reach his post from the sleeping compartment, Jackson first climbed two narrow ladders and passed through a hatch to the weather deck. He turned to start making his way aft. The sky was overcast and, an hour before dawn, his surroundings were nearly as dark as a shaft in an underground mine. He relied on memory and feel on his way astern past the smokestacks and antiaircraft guns. All around him the shadowy forms of young sailors were manning their battle stations. Few tried to speak above the high-pitched whine of the electric motors in the gun mounts and the roar of the air intake blowers as the Black Gang got the oil burners cranked up.

Up on the bridge, he knew that the captain, the navigator, and other officers were preparing for the moment when the ships of the task group would turn like synchronized swimmers into the wind so that the carriers could launch their planes for the day's first strike against Japan.

The fleet was cruising under blackout conditions to avoid being spotted by enemy aircraft and submarines. He could not see any other ships of Task Group 58.2, but he knew they were out there: the destroyers on the perimeter, the cruisers and battleships inside of them—all protecting the carriers in the middle. In his mind, he could picture the "pips" on the radar screen, each representing a ship, so he had a general sense of where the *Santa Fe* was in relation to the others. The closest was the massive aircraft carrier *Franklin,* which lay off the port side at a distance of about a thousand yards.

Radar had proved to be one of the most important technologies of the conflict as it had been billed before the war when he and other U.S. Navy radio operators were spirited away to Canada to learn how to operate and maintain the equipment. Without it, the Battle of Britain might have been lost and the war in the Pacific much more costly in terms of Allied lives, resources, and time.

In his job, Jackson's greatest concern was the failure rate and availability of vacuum tubes used in the radio and radar transmitters, as well as the breakdown of radio and radar receivers. While in combat areas, radar failures were particularly stressful. He and his men would have to shut off the power to the equipment, locate the defective part and replace it; once the power was turned back on, they had to tune the system and return it to operation. The entire process might take an hour, as new parts or tubes sent from the factories in the States were often defective and had to be discarded.

While repairs were made, the "blind" ship had to rely on other ships in the formation to relay critical target information via Talk Between Ships radio to the *Santa Fe's* combat information center so that the guns could target the enemy in concert with the other ships. Otherwise, spotting any enemy planes was left to the lookouts and the guns had to be controlled manually.

Fortunately, the *Santa Fe's* equipment had failed only a couple of times in the combat zone, and never when the ship was under attack. That reliability was at least in part due to Jackson's efforts, and those of his men, to prevent any potential problems.

Jackson believed that the best way to eliminate problems out at sea was to test and retest the equipment, including the spare parts, while in port. Rather than wait for the ship's overburdened supply officer to get around to looking for what he needed, as soon as the ship anchored he would get the officer to give him requisition orders and then hop in one of the ship's motorized whaleboats and head off to supply ships to pick up what he needed.

Even then he was sometimes stymied by parts shortages caused by the long supply lines from the factories to the western Pacific. So he had learned to cannibalize equipment from other ships that for one reason or another didn't need their equipment anymore. After the *Houston* got hit in October 1944—and obviously would be sent back to the States for repairs—he had taken a couple of his technicians and gone over to the damaged ship. The *Houston* was a newer cruiser and equipped with a more powerful radar transmitter, which Jackson now asked to exchange with the *Santa Fe's* older model. Knowing how difficult it was to find good equipment at the end of a five-thousand-mile supply line, the *Houston's* electronics officer agreed.

Jackson knew more about the equipment than the men above him—including the communications division officer, Lt. Norm Utecht—so he was pretty much left on his own. His quiet efficiency had won him Utecht's commendations, as well as a promotion to chief warrant officer in December. He was also well liked by his men, in part because he was a mustang who had come up through the ranks and knew what it was like to be an enlisted man.

As an officer, he didn't try to be their friend, but neither did he pull rank and act superior. Nor was he like some of the other officers who took credit for everything their men did. Jackson never had any problems with his men and generally thought they were a cut above the standard "swabbie;" they tended to be better educated and motivated to learn what they could in a field of a cutting-edge technology. That didn't mean there weren't some characters on his crew. Two of his young technicians—Charles Matta and Frank Morra—were constantly competing with each other on the hazardous jobs, such as climbing a mast to adjust a radar or radio antenna. Jackson felt he had to be present at such times to ensure that they wore their safety belts and harnesses, or either man would have scampered up without the safety equipment in an effort to beat his buddy to the top.

Hijinks notwithstanding, their efforts were crucial. Under the right conditions, radar could pick up approaching planes a hundred miles away. But radar was not infallible, nor was it a shield. Air search radar had a difficult time spotting aircraft flying close to the surface of the water; navigation radar could at times accomplish the job, but not reliably, because the weather and even the height of the waves could interfere with the low-elevation radar beams. Also, there was no shipboard radar that could detect aircraft that were directly overhead. And even if the radar detected the enemy, the combat air patrol and ships' gunners still had to see a plane moving at several hundred miles an hour and then stop it before it got to the ships.

The new radar transmitter Jackson and his men had "borrowed" from the *Houston* had proved its value, detecting enemy aircraft at greater ranges than ever before. But on March 19, 1945, everyone was a little nervous being so close to Japan, especially with the skies overcast as they had been since the task force steamed north from Ulithi. As the carriers launched their air groups, the radar screens were filled with planes. Most were easy to discern as friendly—they had Friend or Foe transponders on them and were heading on known routes; and enemy planes would be expected to be coming from the direction of Japan. However, it was difficult to spot Japanese planes before they were over the water due to the interference caused by "land clutter" on the screen, and sixty miles didn't allow for much time to react. And if they got past the combat air patrol and above the fleet in that overcast, no radar in the world was going to help.

The crew had been up for most of the past two days at General Quarters and were tired and a little edgy. However, they were in better spirits than what might have otherwise been expected. At long last, the oft-repeated wish of "one more operation" was finally going to come true. On March 9, before they left Ulithi, the commander of CruDiv13, Admiral Deyo, switched his flag to the *Birmingham,* which had returned a month earlier from the States. That meant the Lucky Lady was going back home for an overhaul the crew figured would take at least two months.

As with most warships, the *Santa Fe's* crew was always in a state of flux as old hands left for other posts and new men were brought aboard. The very latest additions were young men, excited about finally getting a chance to serve and wondering when they were going to see their first "Jap." However, most of the longtime members, especially the core group that had been together from the beginning, were tired of the war and of fighting an enemy who did not know when to quit. Jim Hunter, who had won the Silver Star for his heroics during the sinking of the *Vincennes,* finally had enough and asked for a transfer back to the States—teasing the other members of the Black Gang that he would think of them when he was raising his first glass of cold beer in San Francisco.

The rest just kept plugging away. Jackson and several of his men who knew International Morse Code regularly intercepted the news of the day broadcast over commercial airwaves. The language of dots and dashes was used by the Associated Press, United Press, and other wireless news agencies, which the ship could pick up just like the newspapers and radio stations did back home in the States. The news was censored, but by March 1945 it was obvious that the war against the Germans was drawing to an end. Some of the sailors on the *Santa Fe* were already placing bets on when it would all be over in Europe.

Still, "the Japs" fought on, unwilling to concede defeat. The kamikazes came hurtling out of the sun and dancing over the waves, hoping to stay alive only long enough to crash into an American ship. When they did hit, the damage and casualties could be devastating. Almost as bad was their effect on morale. Sailors and soldiers onboard American ships, wanting nothing more than to live and go home, found it hard to comprehend the mindset of an enemy who *wanted* to die.

Many of the *Santa Fe's* enlisted crew belonged to the regular Navy and, like Jackson, had joined before the war to escape the poverty of the Depression and perhaps earn enough to pursue their dreams, which for him had been to go to college. Those who joined after the war started were Navy reservists, meaning they had signed on only for the duration of the war, enlisting out of a sense of patriotism and duty, sometimes coupled with a yearning for adventure. Most now only wanted the war to end so that they could go home, get a job, get married, raise families, own houses and cars or maybe a few hundred acres of farmland so that they could follow in the steps of their fathers and grandfathers.

Jackson was still saving for college, putting away most of the $145 a month he was now making as a chief warrant officer. But he had also made a decision before he left Ulithi for the "last operation"; he had written to Charlotte Gates, the pretty nursing cadet he had left in San Francisco, and asked her to marry him.

Maybe it was the typhoon and the loss of so many men on the destroyers that went down, or the mounting death toll from the kamikazes, but he had reached the conclusion that there simply were no guarantees. Not that a marriage would last. Not that any of them would survive the war. A marriage might not survive personality conflicts, or financial crises, or simply the passage of time. And death could come to anyone at any moment: to a sailor in the path of a diving plane or a typhoon; to a young soldier like his uncle, Russell, in a French apple orchard; or to a farmer like his grandfather, mending a fence when lightning struck five miles away.

Jackson knew that he would be asking a lot of her; the war wasn't over and as soon as the *Santa Fe* was overhauled, they would be heading back for the last big battles, battles he might not survive. But his whole generation had been forced to live for the moment—first by the Great Depression and then by this war. Often the only thing they had had to go on was faith—faith in each other and faith in the future. And like it said in the Bible, there was a time for every purpose under heaven. *A time to be born, and a time to die. . . . A time of war, and a time of peace. . . .* People didn't commit to each other because someone gave them a guarantee that the marriage, or their lives, would last forever. They got married because even in the midst of so much hate, there was also a time to fall in love and make a commitment to the future.

So Jackson wrote to Charlotte, whose ring he wore on the chain around his neck. It wasn't the most romantic of letters, maybe; he was self-conscious about the censors. He noted that he loved her and hoped that she loved him too. His ship would be coming back to the States soon, he said, and while he realized these were difficult times to be thinking of the future—the war not being over and all—maybe she would consider becoming his wife.

Of course, there was the little matter of surviving this operation. The more superstitious members of the crew felt that the *Santa Fe* was pressing her famous good fortune. Luck, they pointed out, could change in a heartbeat, and all anyone had to do to confirm that was look at the *Birmingham*. She had been considered a lucky ship too. Even after being struck by two bombs and a torpedo in the fall of 1943, the cruiser had only lost one man and got to go back to the States for several months for repairs. But then a year later, on October 24, 1944, she had pulled up alongside to assist the burning carrier *Princeton* at the beginning of the Second Battle of the Philippine Sea, and half her crew had been killed when the carrier blew up.

The big carrier steaming off the *Santa Fe's* starboard on the morning of March 19, 1945, the *Franklin,* was another example. The carrier had gone five months without ever being attacked by an enemy plane. Then "Big Ben," as she was known in the fleet, had been hit three times, twice by kamikazes, over a period of less than three weeks. It was anybody's guess what direction the *Franklin's* fate would now turn, but some ships just seemed destined for trouble.

All of their luck would certainly be put to the test now that the fleet was attacking Japan. No American fighting man who had been in the Pacific any length of time doubted that the ferocity of the enemy would escalate the closer they moved to his homeland.

Between the swinging sounds of Benny Goodman and Tommy Dorsey, Tokyo Rose reminded the men on the ships that Japan was a land protected by the gods; gods who had proved in the ancient past that they favored Japan, by sending the divine winds, to destroy any threat. And for the past three months, ever since the typhoon, the kamikazes had tried to prove her right.

January 1945

After recovering from the storm, Task Force 38 had headed northwest from Ulithi on December 30 to neutralize Japanese air power in the Lingayen area of the Philippines. D-Day for the invasion of Luzon, the principal island of the Philippines, with the capital of Manila, had been set for January 9, 1945.

The task force was larger than ever, with fourteen large fleet carriers, the same number of light carriers, eight battleships, fourteen cruisers, seventy-one destroyers, and twenty-five destroyer escorts, along with scores of support ships. It seemed that nothing could stop the armada. The Japanese no longer had a fleet outside of a few nearly useless surface ships like the battleship *Yamato,* which, while still the largest and most powerful warship in the world, could not leave Tokyo Bay without attracting American carrier pilots like hornets to a picnic. But the Japanese had a weapon the Americans had not counted on—the kamikazes.

By now Halsey and the other admirals realized that the advent of the suicide pilots not only wasn't an aberration—a localized set of circumstances surrounding the Battle of Leyte Gulf—but a permanent policy set in place by the Japanese military at the highest levels. Imperial navy and army planes were both participating, and they were taking a terrible toll.

From the first "official" kamikaze attacks on the American carriers *Franklin* and *Belleau Wood* in October up to January, the suicide planes had sunk two small aircraft carriers and damaged more than a dozen others; damaged five battleships and nine cruisers; sunk three destroyers and damaged twenty-eight more, including destroyer escorts; and sunk five troop transports and six supply ships, damaging twenty-two others. More than two thousand sailors were dead and several times that number had been wounded. But the kamikazes were just warming up.

On January 4 a Japanese suicide plane attacked and sank the escort carrier USS *Ommaney Bay* in the Sulu Sea west of the Philippines. On January 5 a Japanese Zero hit the cruiser USS *Louisville,* but only one man was killed and fifty-nine wounded (one of them the captain). About the same time, the Australian cruiser HMAS *Australia* was struck, killing twenty-five men and wounding many more. Both ships remained in the fighting. That same day, a pair of Zeros zoomed in low on the escort carrier USS *Manila Bay;* one was shot down, the other crashed through the flight deck and into the hangar; however, damage was slight.

It was a war of wills as much as bullets and bombs. While Tokyo Rose boasted of the pilots' courage in her nightly broadcasts, they were no more courageous than the gunners who stayed at their posts, blasting away as planes bore in on them. Often their valor was formally recognized only posthumously. Or for that matter, the suicidal pilots were no more steadfast than the men locked inside the ships, who knew when their ship was in serious trouble by the sound of the guns and the feel of the ship's movement, yet continued to do their jobs never knowing if the next instant would be their last. The Japanese aviators were at least convinced that their sacrifice would be rewarded with eternity living it up among Japan's other war heroes; most of the American sailors shared the various faiths of their fathers, but dying in combat assured them of nothing, except that there would be no tomorrow.

Yet the men of the fleet carried on in the best tradition of the U.S. Navy. When a kamikaze struck the bridge of the destroyer USS *Walker* on January 5, its skipper, Capt. George F. Davis, was doused with flaming gasoline. Even as he was carried below in terrible agony, he exhorted his crew to "Save the ship!" The captain died a few hours later from his burns, but his men put out the fires and kept on fighting.

The "Banzai Joes" came back the next morning. They smashed into the bridge of the battleship USS *New Mexico,* killing a dozen officers and enlisted men. Another suicide plane also hit the destroyer USS *Allen M. Sumner,* killing and wounding forty-three men.

The battleship USS *California,* resurrected from Pearl Harbor, suffered a new blow when a kamikaze crashed into her, killing forty-five men and wounding many others. Also, the cruiser USS *Columbia* was hit by a suicide plane that crashed through three of her steel-plated decks before its bomb exploded; the crew suffered ninety-two casualties.

The kamikazes were having the effect the Japanese were hoping for, both militarily and psychologically. The battle for Luzon in the Philippines had not yet started, but in that bloody week leading up to the invasion, the U.S. Navy had suffered its highest losses in a campaign since the naval battles around Guadalcanal. There was talk at the highest levels of abandoning the invasion of Luzon and regrouping until a way could be found to deal with the suicide planes.

Despite the reservations, the Luzon invasion had gone forward as planned. That afternoon, the USS *Mississippi,* having completed its bombardment duties, was lying off its assigned beach when a plane came hurtling over the jungle straight for her. The old battleship had narrowly escaped three kamikaze attacks in the past few days and blasted a half dozen planes from the sky. This time the kamikaze won the fight and nicked the bridge structure with a wing before cartwheeling into the deck. The plane and its bombs exploded as it struck an area with several gun emplacements, killing twenty-six men and wounding sixty-three. On January 10 a kamikaze crashed into the troop transport USS *Du Page*, killing 35 and wounding 153 others though the ship remained afloat and, after dropping off her wounded, finished her mission.

On January 12, only about a quarter of a mile off the Philippine coast, a kamikaze struck the destroyer escort USS *Gilligan*, which caught fire as Japanese soldiers on shore ran down to the beach to watch, shouting, *"Banzai! Banzai!"* But the *Gilligan* was just the beginning of a murderous day that included suicide attacks on the destroyer escort USS *Belknap*, killing and wounding eighty-seven men, and the transport *Kyle V. Johnson*, causing 129 casualties. The next day, two more suicide planes hit the escort carrier USS *Salamaua*, killing and wounding 103 more men.

Yet, for all the carnage, the kamikazes could not blow the Americans away. In fact, they only grew stronger, strong enough to sail where they had not dared even a few months earlier.

On January 13, Admiral Halsey ordered the Third Fleet through the Bashi Channel and into the sea that lay between the Philippines and southern China and Indochina. Guarded also by the Japanese stronghold of Formosa, the South China Sea had been considered by the leadership in Tokyo a "Japanese lake." Tokyo Rose had boasted that American ships would never be allowed to enter the South China Sea.

After the thirteenth, she changed her tune to say that the Americans would never leave with their lives. Halsey had no intention of trying to leave—not until his ships and aircraft spent a week sinking Japanese shipping, as well as blasting shore installations from the air and sea in Mainland China, Hong Kong, and Hainan Island. Then on January 21, Task Force 38 launched more than eleven hundred sorties against the Japanese forces on Formosa.

The Japanese responded by attacking the fleet with both conventional and kamikaze tactics. One bomber dropped two bombs on the light carrier USS *Langley*, but the damage was quickly repaired. The old fleet carrier USS *Saratoga* was not as fortunate. A gasoline-laden kamikaze knifed into the flight deck, blasting its way through to the hangar deck, where planes were being gassed for the next air strike. The flames were still spreading, the ammunition exploding, when another kamikaze got through and crashed into the carrier's island, killing a dozen men and wounding the captain. The fires were eventually quelled, but 345 men had died and the carrier had lost a third of its planes. And still the day wasn't over—the destroyer USS *Maddox* was struck amidships, and another twenty men died.

The Americans had certainly done the greater amount of damage. Hundreds of Japanese planes had been destroyed, and dozens of Japanese supply ships had been sent to the bottom. The boldness with which the fleet sailed from one locale to another was also a message: The "Japanese lake" would never again be safe from American air, surface, or submarine attacks; Japan could be cut off from its troops in Southeast Asia, as well as the coveted natural resources that had precipitated the war in the first place.

On January 21, Halsey decided that the weary Third Fleet had been through enough. Once again, Tokyo Rose was proven wrong when the Americans left the South China Sea with their lives—except for the nearly four hundred young men whose bodies were committed to the deep there from beneath American flags far from their homes.

On January 26, the fleet entered Ulithi, where it reverted back to the Fifth Fleet under Admiral Spruance. The men had mixed feelings about "Bull" Halsey leaving. On one hand, he had pressed the fight with the Japanese, and they were proud of the fact that he had taken them where no Allied surface ship had dared go since December 7, 1941. But they also knew he could be a careless commander. Word had filtered back about the near disaster at Leyte Gulf, and then there were the men lost in the typhoon.

The scuttlebutt in the fleet was that politics had kept the old admiral from being held accountable for the losses in the storm. A court of inquiry had quickly convened after the battered fleet arrived at Ulithi on Christmas Eve. Rumor had it that Halsey himself had commented that he thought he should probably be court-martialed.

After days of testimony by survivors, ship engineers, the admiral's aerographer, and Halsey himself, a briefing was prepared for the court. However, the briefing was obviously weighted toward putting a best light on the admiral's decisions and contained a number of errors—such as making it appear that Halsey and his staff had warned the fleet about the arrival of a typhoon some nineteen hours before the admiral and his people had conceded it was more than a "tropical disturbance."

The court found that "the preponderance of responsibility for the [loss of the three destroyers and their crews] falls on Commander Third Fleet, Admiral William F. Halsey, USN. [But] in analyzing the mistakes, errors and faults included therein, the court classifies them as errors in judgment under stress of war operations and not as offenses."

The Navy had tiptoed around with reason: Halsey was a popular figure with the citizens of the United States. While some in the Navy hierarchy thought he should have been relieved of his command, even forced to retire, the government didn't want to hurt public morale by depriving them of one of their heroes. There were war bond sales to consider.

Whatever the men on the ships felt about Halsey, no one was complaining when Spruance returned to lead the next phase of the fleet's operations. With the Philippine campaign well in hand, the Fifth Fleet was ready for the opening stages of the final battle.

The crew of the *Santa Fe* was much more concerned about when they were going to get a break from the war than what four-star admiral was in charge of the fleet. Every mile that passed set a new fleet "without overhaul" record, but no one seemed to notice, except the men on the record-setting ship.

When the *Santa Fe* arrived at Ulithi on Christmas Eve following the typhoon, the crew had expected their present would be a trip back to the States. Their disappointment was as thick as the humid air when the day after Christmas, their sister ship, the *Mobile*, which had not been at sea as long, "got our yard duty." Even the optimists had a difficult time uttering the encouragement "just one more operation," watching the *Mobile* sail from the lagoon.

Returning from the South China Sea a month later, the crew once again had high hopes that Admiral Deyo would transfer his flag and they would go back. *Surely this time,* they thought. The ship had passed the 220,000 mile mark while off the coast of Indochina, enough to have circumnavigated the globe ten times; the last 100,000 miles of that had been covered in less than a year and almost constantly in combat areas.

They had fended off dozens and shot down a few Japanese planes in the South China Seas, then had a close call with a submarine. One night while cruising through the dark waters with most of the crew asleep in their beds, the ship was struck by a torpedo on the starboard side of the hull up near the bow. The blow from the torpedo, which weighed several tons, was hard enough to knock some men from their bunks onto the decks. Fortunately, the torpedo was a dud and failed to detonate, though it left the old salts muttering that if the Lucky Lady had been a cat, she had just used up another one of her nine lives.

But Deyo remained onboard and the *Santa Fe* again led CruDiv13 when it left Ulithi with Task Force 58 on February 10. Some tried to cope with humor, saying they would apparently be staying in the war zone until the repair and engineering crews ran out of baling wire and bubblegum to hold her together. Or, as the pessimists retorted, until some disaster finally overtook her as it had the *Birmingham*. Some of the men wondered if Deyo was afraid to shift his flag to a ship with such a run of bad luck.

On February 16 the task force sailed to within 150 miles of Tokyo. Over that day and the next, they launched the first carrier attacks against the mainland since Doolittle's raid in 1942. A hundred inexperienced Japanese pilots were sent out against the fleet, but most were shot down by American fighters without ever even seeing an American ship. Three that did make it past the combat air patrol were shot down by the gunners on the ships, including the *Santa Fe*. The main purpose of the American attacks was to destroy aircraft and airfields that could be used to interfere with the invasion of Iwo Jima. Later the crews heard that a total of 240 Japanese planes had been shot down in the air and another 140 destroyed on the ground, while American losses were thirty-two planes.

On the evening of February 18, the *Santa Fe* was detached from the task group and steamed at flank speed all night to arrive off Iwo Jima before dawn the next morning. In the dark, the ship's gun crews prepared for the *Santa Fe*'s twelfth bombardment of an enemy-held island and her third time preparing a beachhead for a Marine landing.

About 6:45 A.M., the *Santa Fe* joined the rest of the invasion force warships in enfilading the beaches. The tempo of her five- and six-inch guns increased as the Marine landing craft approached the beaches. The Marines poured ashore expecting stiff resistance, but were met with an almost eerie lack of opposition. The calm didn't last long; the Japanese general in charge of the defenses was simply waiting for the Americans to mass their men, tanks, and other equipment on the shore before his troops opened up with artillery, mortars, and machine guns that had all been presighted to decimate the landing beaches.

The *Santa Fe* did what she could, shelling Japanese positions continuously until 10:00 A.M., and then stood by for "call fire" requested by the

Marines. Especially devastating was the fire raining down on the Marines from Mount Suribachi, the volcano that dominated the barren island's landscape. It was difficult to stop the Japanese on the heights, as their strategy was to fire and then retreat back into their caves.

Captain Fitz tried to tempt the Japanese out of their holes by maneuvering the *Santa Fe* within two thousand yards of the shore and ordering the ship's guns—including the 40-millimeters, which had never been used for anything except antiaircraft fire before, to rake the sides of the mountain. He hoped to draw the big guns on the mountain into a duel—a dangerous proposition for a ship that was a "sitting duck" with so little room to maneuver. But the Japanese knew what Fitz was trying to do and continued to hide and reserve their fire for the Marines on the beach and the landing craft bringing in the reinforcements.

The ship spent the next three and a half days shelling Japanese positions both day and night, much of it silencing rocket-launching sites and gun emplacements, as well as shooting star shells over the Marine positions all night to stop counterattacks and infiltrators. On February 21 the ship received a message from 4th Marine Division Headquarters: "For your information to pass on to your officers and men. We have learned from personnel who have been ashore that the naval gunfire effect on targets is very satisfactory. Blockhouses, pillboxes, and gun positions have been blown to pieces by the tremendous bombardment. However, there is still plenty of good hunting."

Meanwhile, the kamikazes were out in force after the invasion fleet. The big carrier *Saratoga*, which had only just recovered from being hit in the South China Sea, was attacked late in the afternoon of February 21 by six of the suicide planes. Two were shredded by the antiaircraft fire until they hardly resembled airplanes, and yet they still crashed into the side of the ship, breaking through the steel plating to explode inside her hull. A third crashed into the anchor windlass, a fourth was shot down, and a fifth hit one of the ship's catapults. The sixth was on fire when it too struck the side of the ship. The *Saratoga*'s flight deck was a wreck and air operations were suspended, but the ship otherwise continued to function. Then as darkness fell, five more kamikazes attacked. Only one made it through, but it crashed through the flight deck and its bomb exploded in the hangar, finally knocking the ship out of commission with three hundred casualties and the loss of thirty-six planes.

The escort carrier USS *Lunga Point* was also attacked, first by two torpedo bombers. Their weapons struck the ship but with little effect. A third torpedo plane launched its torpedo, but then crashed into the ship as well, again with negligible damage.

However, another escort carrier, the USS *Bismarck Sea,* paid a higher price. Two kamikazes attacked the ship in the dark, but the crew saw only one, which they shot down. By the time they were aware of the second plane, it was only a thousand feet and a few seconds from impact. It crashed through a deck elevator and fires quickly spread throughout the hangar, setting off bombs and ammunition. Then the entire aft end of the ship blew out in one enormous explosion. Two hundred men died before the captain ordered the crew to abandon the sinking ship.

At mid-morning of the twenty-second, the *Santa Fe,* almost entirely out of ammunition for her big guns, was relieved by the battleship USS *North Carolina.* The cruiser rejoined the carrier task force for the next raids on Tokyo. But after several days of foul weather that kept the planes on the decks, the cruiser's task group was detached and sent to Ulithi to replenish supplies.

March 19, 1945
Sixty miles off Kyushu, Japan

A little after 7:00 A.M., Lt. Warren Harding scanned the overcast sky above him but could see nothing except gray clouds, and that troubled him. A few minutes earlier, the combat air patrol had intercepted several bandits coming from Japan and shot two of them down. But the fighter pilots had radioed in that they thought that at least one bomber had eluded them and was hiding somewhere in the clouds in front of the task group.

Harding was wearing his sweater to ward off the chill. The *Santa Fe* was heading into the wind and the breeze was cold, a big change from the omnipresent heat and humidity the crew had lived with while fighting their way north through the Central Pacific.

The crew was at Condition III, so he was not at his battle station in Spot One, which would have been one level father up on the top of the superstructure. Instead, he was standing his regular 4:00 to 8:00 A.M. watch in a large open-air tub surrounded by a chest-high plate of steel called Sky Forward Lookout, where he was in charge of the five-inch guns.

Harding hoped that radar would locate the bogey, if he was up there. But if the plane was above the radar sweep, he knew it might go undetected.

Then, unless the combat air patrol found the Japanese pilot first, the enemy could close to within two thousand feet before anyone on the ships would see him.

Of course, the big concern was the kamikazes. Even if the suicide planes weren't attacking the *Santa Fe,* shooting at them presented a problem. The Lucky Lady's gunners had to be careful not to follow the planes all the way down, or they would wind up shooting at the ship they were trying to protect. Occasionally it happened, but generally in those last few hundred feet the fight was between the plane and its target. Everyone else had to just stand by and watch—either to cheer when the enemy was destroyed or missed, or groan at the telltale ball of flame and billowing smoke coming from yet another stricken ship.

In order to deal with the tragedies of each day, or the disappointment of not getting to go home, the *Santa Fe's* crew did their best to keep up their sense of humor despite the disappointments of not getting to go home. Even in a war, there were those humorous moments that relieved the day-to-day monotony, as well as those times of fear.

Some of the humor was even a result of the tensions of the war, such as the evening some months before when the task group "came under attack" just after sunset. It was a favorite time for the Japanese to try something, and sure enough the last rays of the sun caught the bogey glimmering just above the horizon. Nervous gunners on the other ships opened up and gave the bogey everything they had: the five-inch, the forties, even the twenties started popping away. Only when the intruder didn't move or get any closer did someone finally realize that they were shooting at the "evening star," otherwise known as the planet Venus, which was twinkling far out of gun range. Just like in the "Battle of Sitkan Pip," the crew of the *Santa Fe* got bragging rights; their radar operators had once again determined there was no danger and the gunners had held their fire.

Another evening, Harding and Lt. Cmdr. George Hawes, the gunnery department officer, were watching a Japanese scout plane that was staying out of range while snooping on the fleet when they came up with an idea. When the snooper showed up again the next day, they had one of the six-inch gun's shells loaded with a timed fuse on the maximum range. The gun was directed to intercept the path of the snooper and on Hawes's order, fired the shell. They knew they had almost no chance of hitting the plane, even with the help of the plotting room. So they were delighted when there was a black puff of smoke at the end of the shell's path and the pilot, apparently not one of the braver members of the Emperor's aviators, took off in a panic, apparently to report that the Americans had a new long-range antiaircraft weapon.

One of Harding's favorite stories that he looked forward to telling his wife, Jo, when he got home occurred a few months earlier on December 9 at Ulithi when it was announced that "Bull" Halsey was coming aboard. Naturally, many of the men were curious to see what the legendary admiral looked like and had crowded to the port side of the ship. There wasn't a problem until word got out that Halsey was accompanied by a pretty young woman—apparently a Navy nurse. The rest of the crew stampeded to catch a glimpse of the first American woman they had seen in a year, causing the ship to list noticeably. Captain Fitz had to order the Officer of the Deck to sound General Quarters to get the crew to disperse.

Some of the stories were only funny in hindsight. Shortly before the Second Battle of the Philippines, a fighter pilot radioed in to the task force that he had sighted a massive enemy fleet steaming toward them. He said he got a good look at the ships and had counted at least fifteen carriers, big and small; six battleships; sixteen cruisers, both heavy and light; and seventy-five destroyers.

Alarm rippled through the fleet. No one knew the Japanese even had that many ships, especially carriers. Where had they come from? And how had they kept them hidden until they could spring what was obviously a well-conceived trap to catch the Americans napping?

Fortunately, the answers were not as troubling as the questions. A faulty compass in the fighter plane had confused the pilot. The ships he had spied were the American task force. The men joked that night that it was a good thing he didn't take it upon himself to launch an attack on the Imperial Japanese Ghost Fleet.

Life on a ship at war was sort of like a baseball game: long periods of inertia, broken up by moments of action so intense that they would be remembered in vivid detail for decades afterwards. Days would pass with nothing for the crew to do except scrub and paint and clean or, if they were in port, carry and store all those tons of supplies and ammunition. Some officers, like Harding, often pitched in to help with the workload in port; it wasn't something they had to do, but the men seemed to appreciate seeing officers step in to help, too.

On March 16, the radio operators had picked up the report that Iwo Jima was secured after a month of bitter fighting. An American flag flew atop

Mount Suribachi, but while the extent of the Marine Corps' casualties had been held back in the news reports, the crewmembers of the *Santa Fe* knew from a personal vantage point offshore when the invasion began that the "gyrenes" had gone through hell.

Harding's own memories of the invasion were poignant. He remembered watching four small gunships go past the *Santa Fe* at a distance of about twenty yards; the gunners on the boats looked excited and proud to be on their mission, which was to rescue a team of Navy frogmen who had gone in early to scout the beaches. A little later, he saw the landing craft returning, only now half the gunners were draped over their gun tubs, dead or wounded.

A couple of days before the bombardment began, a Marine gunnery officer, 1st Lt. J. D. Williams, had come aboard to acquaint himself with the ship's gunnery officers. He was going to go up in one of the *Santa Fe's* Kingfishers to help direct the fleet's fire for his troops below. Williams was a friendly young man from the hills of Tennessee, and Harding liked him.

The day of the invasion, Williams flew as the spotter on two missions with pilots, Lt. R. C. Jenkins and Lt. (j.g.) Blase Zamucen. The Japanese positions were so well camouflaged in the rugged terrain that the planes had to fly only fifteen hundred to two thousand feet above the ground for the spotter to see anything. Moving only a little more than a hundred miles an hour, the plane was an easy target for antiaircraft guns, which kept the pilots hopping to avoid getting hit.

The second morning of the invasion, the Kingfisher was flying over Japanese positions when it took antiaircraft from the ground below. The plane's pilot was Lt. (j.g.) A. Klein, a new pilot. About two hours later, Klein reported that his spotter, Williams, had been wounded.

Klein returned to the ship as quickly as possible, but the young lieutenant had been hit with a full burst of a 40-millimeter and was unconscious by the time the plane was hoisted back aboard. Williams died the next morning just before sunrise.

Klein was despondent. "Why him and not me?" he asked Harding. But of course there was no answer for such a question. All they could do was move on.

Some of the crew noted that Williams had not been a member of the ship's company and therefore the Lucky Lady had still never suffered a combat fatality. But Harding felt he had been one of them—even if for just a couple of days—and was glad that Captain Fitz requested permission to take the ship to a quiet area so that Williams could be buried at sea with full honors.

Harding knew that the crewmembers who dismissed Williams as not being one of their own were not hard-hearted. They clung to the idea that the *Santa Fe* was a lucky ship—that they were safe as long as they were aboard her. Now that they had received official word that they would be going home after this operation, it was almost worse on their nerves—as if they were just waiting for something to go wrong. On the morning of March 19, a little after 7:00 A.M., something did.

Harding saw the plane drop out of the clouds, headed for the *Franklin*. It dove steeply, like a kamikaze. "Commence firing!" he yelled, knowing it was too late for the five-inch. Even the 40-millimeters only got off a couple of rounds before they had to quit or risk hitting the *Franklin*.

The plane was not a kamikaze. Even as the General Quarters alarm sounded, Harding watched as it passed above the carrier's flight deck, disappearing from his sight for a moment as it went behind the island structure, then reappearing off the stern. The Japanese plane fled, and already he could hear the sound of explosions rumbling across the water like a thunderstorm.

CHAPTER TWENTY

The Valley of the Shadow of Death

March 19, 1945
Sixty miles off Kyushu, Japan
USS Franklin

H is Corsair had just cleared the deck of the light aircraft carrier USS *Bataan* when Lt. (j.g.) Locke Trigg Jr. saw the plane slip from the clouds in front of the big carrier *Franklin* a mile ahead of his own ship. He couldn't see any markings but assumed the aircraft was friendly— there was no combat air patrol giving chase nor were the ships' guns firing at it—even when the plane dove for the flattop.

Some guy showboating, Trigg thought and yelled into his mike, "Don't dive on the ships, you nut!" Only when he saw the two bombs drop, one and then the other, did he realize he was mistaken. The "nut" was Japanese.

Trigg turned sharply to pursue what he now realized was a Judy dive-bomber, even as he saw explosions rock the *Franklin* and smoke billowing from its hangar deck. As the ships in the task group shot at the fleeing bomber, he had to fly through a hail of antiaircraft fire, praying that the ships' gunners would be on target and that no one would mistake him for another enemy plane.

The Japanese pilot and Trigg were soon beyond the reach of the ship's guns. For thirty miles, the American played a game of cat and mouse with the enemy pilot, who ducked into clouds and changed course and altitude while working his way toward Japan.

Whenever Trigg could maneuver to get a shot at the plane, he let go a burst from his machine guns, then dodged when the tail gunner shot back. Several times during the chase, he thought he lost his quarry only to have him reappear—sometimes off to the side, sometimes above or below. Finally, he got a clear shot from behind and pulled the trigger and held it for a longer burst. Pieces of the Japanese plane flew off, and the tailgunner stopped shooting as the plane began trailing smoke.

As Trigg closed in for the kill, he was joined by two Marine fighters, momentarily distracting him. At the same time, the Japanese pilot suddenly climbed steeply back into the clouds and disappeared from sight. The American pilots pulled back on their sticks to follow, but just then the Japanese plane dove back out of the clouds past them, spiraling steeply down until it crashed into the water and exploded.

The Japanese pilot and his tail gunner were dead, but they had struck a terrible blow. Trigg wheeled and raced back toward the stricken *Franklin* to help provide air cover. She wasn't hard to find; an immense column of black smoke marked what appeared to be her funeral pyre.

The dive-bomber was so low when it passed down the length of the *Franklin's* flight deck its two five-hundred-pound bombs came in at a twenty-five-degree angle, rather than perpendicularly as they would have if dropped from a greater height. But they had no difficulty piercing the wooden flight deck, which ignited their time-delay fuses.

The first bomb hit just left of the centerline and slightly ahead of the island structure, tearing open a fifteen-square-foot hole as it penetrated to the hangar, where it detonated. The blast punched a six-by-twelve foot hole in the armored hangar deck. Immense pressure from the concussion pushed the No. 1 elevator up and out of its shaft like a huge rocket trying to escape the Earth's gravity. A moment later, it crashed back down in shambles, coming to a rest at a forty-five-degree angle, part of it still jutting above the flight deck. A black cloud of smoke boiled out of the elevator well, and geysers of flame erupted from the starboard side of the hangar deck.

The second bomb struck the aft end of the ship, just behind the No. 3 elevator and amid the planes warming up on the flight deck for takeoff. This bomb also plunged through and exploded among the planes in the hangar below. The force of the blast lifted planes on the flight deck into the air and bounced them around so that their spinning propellers tore into each other and the men near them. Aviation fuel poured out of the ruptured tanks of planes on both decks, racing (or so it seemed to those who watched helplessly) to locate fire.

Less than a minute after the initial detonations, fumes gathering in the hangar deck from the spilled aviation fuel ignited in a searing wave of white heat that whipped from one end of the eight-hundred-foot hangar to the other. The flames shot up the elevator wells and out the sides of the ship, carrying with them pieces of ship, planes, and men.

The fire was accompanied by a massive concussion that burst through the open hatches and down passageways of the ship's interior, tossing men through the spaces as though they were weightless. Bulkheads crumpled like tin foil, and compartments instantaneously compressed floor to ceiling, crushing men as they stood wondering at the sound or lay in their bunks torn from sleep. The chief petty officer's quarters folded in on itself like an accordion file. Never again would Raymond Blair kiss his son, Bruce, or wife, Beverly, good-bye. He had chopped his last Christmas tree, and there would be no more searches for lost Christmas kittens. He would become only a faint memory in a little boy's mind.

Death came instantaneously to hundreds more. Approximately two hundred men waiting to get into the mess halls on the third deck stood in line in the hangar or on the ladders that went down past the Marine compartment. They were all either killed by the concussion or incinerated on the spot by the flames that followed. The blast tore the clothing off their bodies, and those who weren't burned lay naked on the deck as though they had just come from the showers.

On the flight and hangar decks, pilots and their crews were consumed by the fires in their planes, unable to escape. The members of their flight crews who survived the initial blasts scrambled up the wings to rescue them, or in futile attempts to get away from the spreading conflagration, and died as well.

When the vapor exploded on the hangar deck, the ship actually rose from the water then settled back into its torment as acrid, oily-black smoke filled the hangar and enveloped large portions of the flight deck and the island. Confusion reigned. The bugle call to battle stations died halfway through as the ship's external and internal communications were destroyed.

In most areas of the ship, lights blinked and then went out, plunging the windowless interior into darkness lit either by red emergency lights, battery-powered battle lanterns, and flames. The ventilation ducts that normally drew fresh air into the interior of the ship now inhaled the noxious choking smoke, killing men quietly.

Survival in those first moments depended on luck and fate. Rounding a corner or stepping down a ladder meant the difference between life and death for men no more than a few feet from one another. Some men were knocked to the deck by the blast but not hurt, while comrades standing next to them were consumed by fire.

The decision by Edwin Garrison and Fred Holdsworth to put off their showers saved their lives. They had just stepped through the hatchway leading out of the head when the first bomb went off. The concussion blew them like straw in the wind to the far end of the next compartment, slamming them against the bulkhead.

Picking himself up, Garrison ran back to the shower room, but all the men inside were dead and lay in crumpled heaps where they had been thrown. He turned to leave just as Holdsworth staggered up behind him. "There's nothing we can do for them," Garrison said. "We have to try to get to our battle stations."

In an officer's wardroom, Lt. (j.g.) Robert Wassman had happily settled down to a plate of pancakes when he was blasted across the table. Red emergency lights flickered on, revealing a room in shambles. Picking his way past obstacles, he left the wardroom and turned toward his office. But the way was blocked by mangled steel and increasing smoke. He knew then that his yeoman and whoever else were in the office—which would have included him if he had not stopped for breakfast—were dead.

Wassman figured that the best way out was to go forward along the starboard passageway and try to find a way up. As he hurried along, men were tumbling down ladders from the hangar deck, followed by dark clouds of smoke. The clothing of some of the men was on fire, and they screamed in agony and fear. Other sailors were there, however, to put out the fires and spread salve on their burns, so Wassman continued on.

Eventually, he worked his way to a ladder leading up onto the foc'sle and from there up onto a catwalk, where he grabbed a life jacket and a fire hose and jumped onto the flight deck. Rallying several sailors to help him, they headed aft toward the flames.

Some men survived that morning only because they were so worn out that they decided that for once in their young lives they would rather sleep than eat.

Sam Rhodes could have been standing in line on the hangar deck. Instead, he had told his friend Peter Spalluto to go on without him and lay down on his bunk. He had started to drift off to sleep when he was pressed violently against the springs of the bunk above him, then dropped back onto his mattress.

The bugle call to battle stations started and then died as he lay still for a moment gathering his wits. He then sat up, tied his shoes, and ran out of the compartment heading for his fire room. Out in the passageway, he met up with another member of the Black Gang. They ran together toward the ladder that would take them below, but as they passed a ladder leading up, the other man stopped. "I'm not staying down here, I'm going topside," he said.

Watching him scramble up the ladder, Rhodes wondered if he should follow. But just as the other sailor reached the top and stood up, there was another explosion and the man disappeared in the firestorm that swept past the opening.

Running on, Rhodes was joined by another sailor from the fire room who raced along behind him. A few steps further and there was the sound of an explosion behind Rhodes. When he looked back, there was a new hole in the deck and his companion was gone. Terrified, all he could think of was to keep going, but he soon discovered that the way to the fire room was blocked by debris; he would have to go back.

Ernest Scott was another who had decided on sleep rather than breakfast when his pal Eddie Carlisle asked if he wanted to join him for chow. Carlisle left, and Scott lay down on his bunk. He was troubled about a conversation he and Carlisle had had with their friend Chuck Berringer the night before in the mess hall.

"Did you hear Tokyo Rose tonight, Chuck?" Carlisle had asked.

"No. What's she yakkin' about now?"

"She said they knew a task force was off the mainland. Even called the *Franklin* by name. Claimed they had sunk us already."

Berringer didn't answer right away. When he did, the words sent a chill up Scott's spine. "You wanna know something, fellas? I've been thinking, and I might as well say what I've been runnin' through my head. We're gonna get it again . . . and soon. And when we do, I ain't gonna make it this time. Don't ask me how I know, I just know it's coming."

Carlisle tried to dismiss the fatalistic talk. "Aw, hell, we'll live to get heaved out of Sad Sam's more'n once," he said, referring to a favorite sailors' bar in Honolulu. He and Scott exchanged uneasy glances.

"Chuck, that's a helluva thing to say," Scott protested.

Berringer shrugged. "Maybe so, Scotty, but I know it's comin'."

As the three friends stood to leave, Berringer draped his arms around Scott and Carlisle. "Take it easy, guys," he said. "See you in the morning."

During their watch that night, neither Scott nor Carlisle mentioned Berringer's comments. But later back in their compartment, as they were falling asleep, Carlisle murmured, "Jeez, Scotty, I hope he's wrong."

Scott knew exactly what his friend was talking about. "Me too, Ed," he replied. "Me too."

They didn't get much sleep before they were roused to General Quarters. After conditions were relaxed, Carlisle had gone off to breakfast and Scott was back in their compartment still trying to get some sleep and thinking about Berringer's premonition when he was startled awake by a tremendous roar that shook the ship. He had heard the sound before—back on October 30, 1944, when the kamikaze went through the deck—and knew the ship had been hit hard.

Scott leaped from his bunk and had just tied his shoes when he heard a scream from the passageway outside. A sailor staggered in through the hatch and collapsed. Right behind him, "Slim" Rials leaped through the hatch and looked at the fallen man. "Oh God, Scotty, it's Kennedy," he said, referring to one of their fire room comrades. "He's dead!"

Scott looked around; it didn't seem right to leave Kennedy crumpled on the deck of the compartment. He pointed to a litter used for transporting injured men hanging on a bulkhead. "We'll put him in that."

The placed their friend on the litter and carried him into a smaller compartment aft of their compartment. They laid the litter on a desk, wondering what to do next. They could see blood seeping into Kennedy's shirt and dripping from his shoes.

Rials looked at Kennedy. He had been hit in the legs and stomach by shrapnel. "Both of his ankles are broken up," he said. "How the hell did he get so far?"

"I don't know, Slim," Scott said, "but there's nothing we can do for him now. Let's get topside."

Four minutes after the bombs hit, the *Franklin* was still steaming at twenty-four knots. All the boilers were on line and there was no difficulty with steering. Captain Gehres, who had been knocked to the deck by the first blast, ordered the ship to turn hard to starboard so that the wind would carry the flames away from the planes on the flight deck.

Suddenly, the officers on the bridge saw the light carrier *Bataan* appear off the bow through the smoke. Surprised by the *Franklin's* abrupt turn, the *Bataan* was cutting directly across Big Ben's path, and it looked like the speed and momentum of the massive warships would take them into each other. But the helmsmen on both ships spun the wheels as the captains barked out orders to the Black Gangs for radical turns. A disastrous collision was averted by only a few hundred yards—the length of the *Franklin*.

Gehres had to set a new course to direct the wind to push the flames astern and away from the men on the bow who were beginning to fight the fires. The problem with the new course was that the ship was now headed directly toward Japan and its kamikazes. But there were more immediate concerns.

With fires raging out of control, the *Franklin* was a powder keg waiting to blow three thousand men into oblivion. On the flight and hangar decks alone, sixty-six 500-pound bombs, ten 250-pound bombs, and more than a dozen of the 1,000-pound Tiny Tim rockets were strapped on the wings or inside the bellies of the planes and exposed to the flames. That didn't include the hundreds of tons of bombs, rockets, napalm, and ammunition stored in the holds and in ready service lockers about the ship.

As the flames grew beneath the aircraft, a bomb exploded, then another and another. With each explosion, the ship shuddered and vibrated. Heated by the fires, the .50-caliber machine guns in the wings of the planes spewed bullets and tracers across the decks, tearing into men trying to escape or fight the fires. The ammunition for the twenties and forties joined in when the fires reached the ships' antiaircraft gun mounts.

The men on the bridge ducked as two Tiny Tims mounted on Corsairs took off with a terrible shriek and headed for the island. The rockets narrowly missed the structure and continued on, ricocheting madly off the tops of the waves like stones skipped across a pond until they at last plunged in and exploded.

Two more rockets ignited and roared straight down the flight deck and out to sea. A few minutes earlier and they would have caught the *Bataan* broadside as it crossed the bow.

All over the ship, men found themselves staggering through smoke and past twisted metal, stepping over bodies and wondering why they had survived when everyone around them had perished.

Frank Turner had just poured his cup of coffee when a blast of flame and pressure threw him across the catapult room. He rose and rushed to the telephone that connected the room to the bridge. It was dead.

Meanwhile, the heat and smoke were growing intense. There had been no warning of an enemy plane, so he thought one of the Franklin's own aircraft must have dropped a bomb on takeoff.

He and his catapult crewman, Ansaldi, crawled over the twisted metal outside the compartment, trying to find a way to safety. First, they tried to get back through to the hangar deck, but when they reached a hatch, Turner stopped and pointed.

The paint on the bulkhead around the hatch was starting to peel due to the heat on the other side. "We can't go through there," he said grimly, knowing that there had to have been a lot of men in the hangar.

The two men wheeled and went the other direction and after several attempts at finding a way through mangled passageways, climbed out to the foc'sle.

The ship's priest, O'Callahan, and his friend Lt. "Red" Morgan were teasing Steward's Mate 1st Class Frasure about the cold French toast when the lights went out and they were thrown to the deck.

O'Callahan didn't need anyone to tell him that the ship had been hit. He had been anticipating this all those years in the Atlantic aboard the *Ranger*. *This is it,* he thought and said a prayer. He couldn't see as he crawled over the debris on the floor, but his lungs told him that smoke was pouring into the wardroom.

Men were screaming that they were trapped. But over them roared the voice of Morgan. "Calm down!" he ordered. He said he knew a starboard passage to the foc'sle where they ought to be able to escape.

Despite his own claustrophobia, O'Callahan found himself suddenly at peace amid the chaos. He talked to the men who seemed on the verge of panic; they recognized his voice in the dark and were reassured.

Morgan led them to the foc'sle. From there, O'Callahan made his way back to his stateroom, where he picked up a small vial of oil for administering last sacraments and his battle helmet, emblazoned with a white cross. Then he left to find where he might do the most good.

The first place he stopped was a junior officers' berthing compartment which had been converted into a makeshift hospital. It was already filled with burned and injured men. A seventeen-year-old boy recognized him and asked to be held as he confessed. The priest had gathered him in his arms when there was a horrible shrieking noise, a Tiny Tim rocket taking off.

O'Callahan held the boy until he realized he had died. Laying him back down on the bunk, the priest performed last rites. He stood then, hoping he was ready for the task ahead of him.

A trail of flotsam and men bobbed in the wake of the carrier. Many of the men had simply been flicked overboard by the flames and explosions. Others had no choice but to jump as fire threatened to trap them.

Landing in the water, many were sucked beneath the surface by the prop wash of the passing carrier and its massive screws. Tumbling like rags in a washing machine, it was impossible to know which way was up, and some never resurfaced.

The flight deck crew was required to wear life jackets while working, and they fared better than the others in the swells. Many men had been caught unaware without flotation devices and, whether knocked or forced into the ocean, struggled to stay afloat in the cold waters. They collected floating debris and the few life rafts that were thrown overboard, clinging to the sides as they watched their ship sail on belching smoke and shuddering with each new explosion.

Many of the men who made it to the water were injured. Lts. John Vandegrift and C. K. "Cowboy" Faught, both Marine pilots, were standing next to each other in the ready room on the second deck when the bombs hit.

Two dozen other pilots were also gathered there to be briefed for the day's second launch. Originally, they were supposed to attack the airfields, but there had been a change in plans. A spotter plane had reported seeing the superbattleship *Yamato* steaming out of Tokyo Bay. One of the last vestiges of the mighty Imperial Fleet, the battleship might wreak havoc on the task force if it could get close enough to use its big guns. The pilots' mission was to see that the *Yamato* didn't survive the day.

Then, in a fraction of a second, the world turned upside down. The deck beneath their flight boots rose so suddenly from the force of an explosion—a phenomenon known as "deck heave"—that it fractured the feet and ankles of both Vandegrift and Faught. But they were the lucky ones; they were standing next to a bulkhead that partially protected them, while other men were crushed between the rising deck and the overhead. Only one other man survived being in that room.

Unable to stand because of their shattered legs, Vandegrift and Faught crawled over the bodies of their dead comrades and out of the room. They wound up outside on the portside catwalk. The sanctuary was only temporary. The catwalk crossed directly over an opening through which flames from burning aviation fuel and napalm were leaping higher with every second. They were faced with a choice: roast like sausages on a grill, or go over the side—a drop of about eighty-five feet.

Over they went, crying out in pain when their injured legs hit the hard surface of the water. Both men were wearing their flight jackets but neither had on a life jacket. Vandegrift managed to latch onto a small wooden water cask, while Faught caught a seat cushion from one of the planes that had been blown overboard.

Looking up, the scene seemed surreal to Vandegrift as the ship glided by only a few yards away, wreathed in smoke and racked by explosions that rained debris down on him. *God damn!* he thought. *Just like in the friggin' newsreels!*

Soon after the bombs hit, the destroyer USS *Miller* approached the stern of the *Franklin* and began to pour seawater onto the flames with four hoses. But then the ship was summoned to pull alongside the carrier.

About a half hour after the attack, Admirals Davison and Bogan, with several of their staff officers in tow, had climbed the *Franklin's* escape ladder on the starboard side from the flag bridge to the navigation bridge. There, Davison took Gehres aside, though not out of hearing range of officers and crew on the bridge. The admiral said that the time had come for Gehres to consider issuing the order to abandon ship.

Even if the attacking Japanese plane had not radioed home news of his successful strike, the admiral noted, the smoke was sure to attract more enemy fliers, especially the kamikazes. The admiral's chief of staff, a captain with whom Gehres had served in another command, sniffed, "I suggest you abandon her over the starboard side."

The comments angered Gehres. He saw no reason to abandon the ship— not yet. Although her list was increasing, the ship was not in imminent danger of sinking. If his men could get the fires under control, Gehres thought, there might be a chance of saving his ship.

In later years, some of his detractors would speculate that Gehres was loath to abandon the ship because he would have had to abandon any hope of getting another command or being promoted to admiral. Captains who had ships ignominiously sunk beneath their feet—especially $63-million aircraft carriers—found themselves passed over for promotions. The captain of the *Yorktown* was never given command of another carrier, despite his heroic efforts at the battles of the Coral Sea and Midway; his order to abandon ship, in hindsight, was considered premature by the Navy brass.

However, Gehres would contend that he was motivated by another consideration. Although hundreds of men had been making their way to the flight deck, where they were being marshaled to fight the fires, he was certain that many hundreds of others were still alive belowdecks, trapped in the destruction.

Others, he assumed, were still faithfully at their battle stations. But they were unreachable because the ship's internal communications had been almost entirely wiped out and wouldn't know to leave their posts if he gave the order to abandon ship.

In either case, hundreds of men might die if the ship was abandoned. The same destroyers that were busy picking up crewmembers in the water would be ordered to finish the *Franklin* with torpedoes. He and every sailor in the Pacific Fleet knew the stories that had been circulating about the sinking of the *Lexington* following the Battle of the Coral Sea; the navigator, Cmdr. Stephen Jurika, who had been on the ship, had told the officers on the *Franklin* how men had also been trapped belowdecks when it was sunk.

"It's none of your damn business," Gehres growled at the admiral and the chief of staff. "I'm the captain of this ship. . . . You see to it that we have antisubmarine protection and combat air patrol, and we'll get back to work and save this ship."

Whatever the admiral might have thought about such an upbraiding, he shrugged at the captain's remarks. "Well, sorry to leave you like this," he said. "But I've got a war to fight." He told Gehres to order the *Miller* to come alongside to remove him and the other flag officers, as well as whatever enlisted men from his staff who could be found. He said he intended to shift his flag to the *Hancock.*

The destroyer was signaled and Gehres gave the order "all engines, ahead one-third" to slow the carrier down to eight knots. A highline was rigged between the two ships, and the admirals and their staff were toted across the water like gold-braided sacks of mail.

Objectively, the admiral's duty was not to an individual ship but to the remaining ships in the task group and the mission. But leaving did nothing to win him a spot in the hearts of the men on the *Franklin* as they watched him abandon them and their burning ship for the second time in less than a year.

The truth was that deep inside the ship, hundreds of men were trapped. Many of them fell to the deck, overcome by the smoke, and did not rise again; others slowly suffocated in airtight compartments waiting to be rescued. Some considered escape but remained dutifully at their posts. Many of these were in the engineering department, the Black Gang, who stayed in their fire rooms to keep the boilers going and the ship moving.

Quartermaster 2nd Class Holbrook Davis was in charge of several men in the steering engine room aft, a small compartment in the stern and near the very bottom of the ship, where if the bridge lost steering control, the carrier could be maneuvered manually.

That morning Davis was supposed to have been relieved for breakfast, but his relief was late. He was wondering where the other man was when the ship unexpectedly shook as if it had run aground. The bugle began to sound General Quarters but suddenly died, so he knew that they had been attacked and hit. Then the lights went out.

Using battle lanterns to see, he and his men climbed the ladder and secured the watertight hatch above their heads, their only way in or out of the compartment. They then sat in the dark, waiting further developments.

Davis was not the usual sailor. He came from a wealthy New England blue-blood family that had arrived in America in the early 1630s. Three-hundred-plus years later, his uncle was the president of ALCOA, the Aluminum Company of America; his father was vice president.

After high school, Holbrook had gone on to Harvard. He was a sopho-more there when Pearl Harbor was bombed. He had served one year with the American Field Service driving ambulances for the British 8th Army, which at the time was locked in a titanic struggle with the Afrika Korps in North Africa. Then he had returned home and enlisted in the Navy.

After boot camp, he was sent to quartermaster's school, which pleased him. In the Army, the quartermaster was essentially a supply manager. But in the Navy, a quartermaster steered the ship under the direction of the cap-tain or officer of the deck, as well as assisted the navigator and kept the log-book. That meant he might be on the bridge and would therefore get to see the action.

And as a matter of fact, he had been on the bridge, keeping the logbook, when the kamikazes attacked on October 30. He thought that these pilots were dangerously dedicated as first one crashed off the starboard side and then another dove through the flight deck.

However, when the *Franklin* left for its second tour of duty, Davis was assigned to the steering engine room aft, where on the morning of March 19 he and his men sat in the dark, listening to the pounding of the explosions grow louder and more frequent. At first they believed that the *Franklin* was under continuous attack by numerous aircraft and perhaps sub-marines. But as the explosions kept shaking the ship and picked up speed, they realized that it had to be the *Franklin's* own munitions that were going off. And that could mean only one thing—fire, the most feared enemy on a ship.

With no word from above, they discussed whether they should try to leave. *What if the ship was being abandoned? What if they'd been forgotten?* How-ever, there was so much noise from the exploding bombs directly above them—making their ears ring—they decided to stay where they were, at least until the explosions subsided.

While some men like Davis and his companions remained at their battle stations awaiting further orders, others found themselves trapped involuntarily, many of them on the third deck, where most of the crew's sleeping compartments and mess halls were located.

Ernest Scott ended up in his sleeping compartment. He and Rials tried to escape by going aft but met with men coming from that direction who said the way was blocked by fire, as was the way forward. So they had all ended up in the compartment, where Scott was pleased to see his friend Lem Hall, though he was still worried about what had become of Eddie Carlisle.

The ranking crewmember in the compartment was a chief petty officer who shouted out his orders. "You can't go forward," he bellowed, "and you can't go aft. We've got to stay right here and save all the air we can. Dog those hatches!"

The explosions began picking up in frequency. They counted eleven, one right after the other, and thought the ship was being attacked by the entire Japanese air corps. Somehow above the noise they heard someone scratching and clawing at the hatch. Hall looked through the small window. "It's Ed!" he called out to Scott, who started to move toward the hatch.

The chief blocked his way. "No one gets in," he snarled. "No one gets out."

"Goddamnit, Chief," Scott cursed, "You can't leave him out there. He'll strangle in the smoke."

"Can't help that," the chief replied. "Nobody opens that hatch."

Hall pushed the chief aside. "To hell with that noise," he said. "Give me a hand, Scotty."

As Scott moved forward, a tall Marine stepped up and helped them undog the hatch as the chief threatened them all with court-martials. The hatch opened and Carlisle staggered in, falling into Hall's arms coughing and gasping for air.

The men quickly dogged the hatch shut again. "Oh God, Eddie, am I glad to see you," Scott grabbing his friend. "Are you okay?"

Carlisle wiped tears from his eyes. "Yeah, Scotty, I'm okay, but I didn't think I was going to make it for a few minutes there." He and Scott and Hall stood there like lost children with their arms draped around each other. After a bit, Carlisle regained his old sense of humor as he talked about how the first explosion had thrown him headfirst into a fifty-gallon metal coffee urn. When he came to his senses, he tried to run aft but was turned back by smoke, so he cut across the galley to reach their sleeping compartment. Halfway across the galley, there was another tremendous explosion that apparently blew up a food storage area. "Jeez, Scotty, the air was full of pork chops," he said, "I coulda grabbed one anywhere."

About seventy men were crammed into the compartment, sitting on the beds or the floor. The chief petty officer had been right about one thing—there was no outside air source, and they were going to have to remain still and calm until someone got them out of there.

Meanwhile, a similar situation had developed in a small mess compartment off the main mess hall on the opposite side of the third deck. Like moths attracted to a flame, every man who stumbled through that section of the ship was drawn to the weak light of battle lanterns that emanated from a small window in the hatch leading into the room.

Some didn't have far to go. Bandleader Saxie Dowell had been eating breakfast in the mess hall, talking about how he was going to open a nightclub in Chicago after the war when the bombs hit. Others came from either end of the ship, fleeing smoke and fire that they claimed had them all trapped.

Among those who found their way was Dr. James Fuelling, who after securing from General Quarters that morning had gone to the sick bay to consult with the ship's surgeon, Lt. Cmdr. William Fox, about a patient who had come in the night before.

O'Callahan's "altar boy" at the special Mass a couple days earlier, Fox had been the chief surgeon on the medical staff at International Harvester's Milwaukee plant when he enlisted in the Navy in 1942. He was a veteran of the campaigns off Guadalcanal and through the Central Pacific. When the *Franklin* was in Bremerton, Fox went home for Christmas to see his wife, Elsie. He had done his bit and could have asked for a position stateside, but he enjoyed taking care of the men on the ship and had wanted to see them through the war.

The two doctors were discussing the patient when they heard and felt the first explosions. Almost immediately, the fans in the fresh air ducts began to pull smoke into the sick bay. There were thirteen patients in the clinic who could not be moved, so the doctors and corpsmen sealed off the vents.

Fox said he was staying with the patients, but Fuelling knew he might be needed elsewhere. "We'll be here when you come back," Fox smiled as his counterpart turned to go. Fuelling heard the men in the room dog the door behind him.

Running forward on the third deck until he could go no farther in the smoke, Fuelling saw the light in a starboard mess compartment and headed in that direction. He knocked on the hatch door, which was quickly opened to let him in. The door was shut behind him. The smoke in the mess hall was much less dense, and in the dim light of the lanterns he could see that there were already a couple of hundred men gathered inside.

As more men found their way to the compartment, Fuelling realized that they were going to have to conserve air. The compartment's only access to outside air was a vent the size of an orange. He advised the men to sit or squat and remain inactive. "And pray, quietly," he suggested.

One of those was Sam Rhodes, who had stumbled through the dark and smoky passageways until he saw the light. Inside the compartment, he found himself standing next to a sailor whose arms were bleeding. So he took out his knife and cut the sleeves from his dungaree shirt. One of the sleeves he cut in half so that he and the wounded man could tie them around their noses and mouths to filter the smoke. The other sleeve he ripped apart to make tourniquets to staunch the man's wounds.

Men kept stumbling into the mess compartment from different parts of the ship with the same message: There was no way out.

One of the last to find his way to the compartment was Lt. (j.g.) Don Gary. He had just plugged in the electric razor to lend one of his men when he and his crew were knocked off their feet by an explosion.

They struggled to their feet, dazed by the sound and concussion. For just an instant as the lights went out in that part of the ship, Gary felt a sensation of being entirely alone, as though he were falling into a void. All around him it sounded as though the most violent summer thunderstorm imaginable was raging. Almost immediately, smoke filled the compartment. He grabbed a rescue breather and shouted to his men, "Follow me!"

With Gary in the lead, the men had groped their way forward through two compartments when a sailor appeared out of the dark ahead of them. He said that fire had sealed off all routes to that part of the ship. Gary turned and led his men back until they came to the main mess hall. He noted that the components of Tiny Tim rockets were lying about—the mess hall was also used to assemble munitions. He also knew that over by the galley there was an ammunition elevator around which more warheads and bombs of different sizes were stacked, ready to be taken above to the hangar and flight decks. *One of these goes off,* he thought, *and they'll all go off.*

Then he noticed the light coming from the small mess compartment off the main hall and took his men there. Rapping on the hatch, they were allowed into the compartment just as the planes on the hangar deck above began to explode with deafening roars followed by the sound of more ammunition and rockets going off. They had just dogged the doors when someone else rapped on the hatch; three men entered carrying a seriously wounded man, who was handed over to Fuelling.

As Gary looked at the anxious faces of the young men around him, he knew that the fires could spread to the armament in the mess hall at any minute. Or the smoke, which was slowly creeping in despite the sealed hatches, would eventually suffocate them. They had to escape. He went over in his mind the many exploratory trips he had taken through the ship's interior. *There has to be a way,* he thought.

As Gary contemplated escape, men were dying everywhere onboard the ship and in the water. But others were also fighting back on the flight and hangar decks.

The heat and smoke were brutal. Men fighting the fires could only stand so much of it before they passed out. But others stepped forward to take their place, led on the flight deck by men like Red Morgan, Father O'Callahan, and executive officer Cmdr. Joe Taylor, who were organizing men into groups of five or six.

The conflagration was even worse in the hangar. When the bombs hit, the crewmember manning the aviation fuel pumps either fled or was killed. The pumps were still operating, drawing on the twelve thousand gallons of the high octane avgas.

One of the crewmembers fighting the fires on the hangar deck was Matthew Little. He had been literally blown out of his shoes by the concussion that tore the wardroom apart where he was serving breakfast. The ship quivered, then there was another, more powerful explosion. The lights went out and smoke poured into the room. Men around him called out in pain and terror, but choking on the thick smoke, it was all he could do to find his way out.

Little made his way to one of the ladders leading from the mess halls to the forward part of the hangar deck above. In the hellish light of flames, he saw a nightmare. Dead men lay piled at the bottom of the ladder, some of them burned beyond all recognition. One man, charred by the passing maelstrom, still clung to the ladder, looking over his shoulder as though to see death as it reached for him. The ladder was the only way up for Little, who gingerly tried to pull the man to the side only to have the body come apart in his hands.

Emerging on the hangar deck, Little was greeted by more horror. Dead men lay in lines where they had fallen—some were naked or nearly so, stripped by the blast that killed them. Other remains were hardly more than lumps, barely recognizable as human and still smoldering from the fires that had consumed them.

The fires weren't out nor the danger over. The space was filled with thick, dark smoke in which bombs were bursting; bullets from machine guns whined through the air and glanced off metal, the tracer rounds flashing like meteors in the gloom.

The walls of flame seemed to be winning the battle against the small groups of men who fought them. Little considered whether he should jump into the water—he was a poor swimmer and, without a life preserver, thought he would probably drown. But there was more stopping him than that.

Big Ben was his home, the only one he had left with his parents dead and buried in South Carolina. Sure, he had resented that the Navy had not seen fit to let him, a black man, operate the guns so that he could strike directly at the enemy. But even down in his battle station, passing up five-inch ammunition, he had felt part of the ship's community, and now their home— his home—was threatened.

Little forgot about escaping and ran to help man a fire hose, battling the blazes in his stocking feet next to one of the pilots. They stood together against the nearly overwhelming heat, trying to ignore the blasts and bullets—officer and enlisted man, aviator and steward's mate, white and black—and fought for their ship and each other.

Fires and explosions raged all along the eight hundred feet of the hangar deck, but the fantail was pure hell for the men trapped there. Above them, flames engulfed the planes on the stern of the flight deck, so they could not go up. Going forward on the hangar deck was impossible. There was noth-

ing for them to do except fight the fires that threatened the canisters of
napalm and oxygen stored on the fantail, or join those who had already
jumped off the ship.

Edwin Garrison and Fred Holdsworth had headed aft through the dark
and smoke-filled passageways until they reached a compartment that had
an escape hatch that opened onto the fantail. Garrison had hoped they might
find fresh air there. Instead, they found another holocaust, both on the ship
and in the water.

Garrison could see hundreds of men struggling in the wake of the ship.
They floundered in the burning oil and fuel, or struggled to reach debris.
As he watched, some grew weaker and slipped beneath the gray seas.

Life was precarious on the fantail too. Some men cowered behind whatever cover they could find. But others struggled against the fires. The two
friends spotted a 40-millimeter gun crew hurriedly throwing their ammunition overboard as flames licked at their gun tub and ran to help.

They had just about finished that job when a sailor ran up to the group,
pointed to the hangar, and yelled, "Let's put the fire out! Who's gonna
help me?"

"I will," Garrison said. Fighting fires on the hangar deck was his battle
station anyway. Picking up a hose, he and the other man dashed through a
hatch in the bulkhead to the hangar deck, where they were confronted by
towering flames. However, when they tried to turn on the hose, nothing
happened. A third sailor, who had followed them, yelled that he would get
it turned on and ran off.

As he waited, Garrison noticed a Corsair surrounded by fire. The plane
and its Tiny Tim rocket were facing aft, toward the fantail and the men
trapped there. "We need to wet that plane down first," he yelled to his partner, "or a lot of guys are gonna die when that rocket takes off!"

Just then, the sailor who had left to turn on the water touched him on
the back. "NO WATER!" he screamed. Garrison and his partner looked at the
flames around the Corsair and back at each other before dropping the hose
and retreating through the hatch.

The other sailor led the way and didn't stop running when he reached
the end of the ship but jumped right overboard without looking below. But
Garrison got through the hatch and pulled it closed behind him. He had
slammed the first dog home when a bomb on the other side exploded, blowing the hatch cover right through the bulkhead.

Fortunately, Garrison was standing to the side or he would have been struck and killed by the hatch cover. *Then again,* he thought, *if I'd been on the other side, fighting that fire, there wouldn't have been anything left of me to bury.*

There was one good thing about the bomb going off. The explosion turned the Corsair ninety degrees so that when its Tiny Tim ignited a minute later, the huge rocket shot out the starboard side of the hangar over the waves.

Garrison watched the rocket as it roared halfway to the horizon before it hit the water and exploded. But his attention was soon turned to survival when the fantail was rocked by a series of explosions from above. The bombs in the planes on the aft end of the flight deck were going off, blowing holes in the flight deck over their heads. The men ducked for cover as best they could.

After each explosion, someone else would hop up and exclaim, "I can't take another one of those," and run for the side of the ship, jumping overboard. But it wasn't just the bombs. Flaming aviation fuel was spilling over the edge of the flight deck and onto the fantail, bringing with it intense heat and smoke.

Stumbling through the black clouds, Garrison came across seventeen-year-old Stanley Sward from Winter, Wisconsin, who was contemplating jumping into the ocean. "I don't have a life jacket, and I can't swim," Sward said. "But I would rather drown than burn to death. . . . I'll see you in heaven."

The boy started for the edge, but Garrison grabbed him by the arm. "Hold on a minute," he said. "Let me find my friend. He's a good swimmer and between the two of us, we can keep you from drowning until someone picks us up."

Garrison located Holdsworth, who agreed to the plan. They approached the edge, holding hands like schoolchildren at a crossing with Garrison in the middle, Holdsworth on his right and Sward on his left.

Just as Holdsworth stepped over the lifeline to jump, a five-inch magazine exploded and set off a 40-millimeter ammunition locker beside it. Garrison and Sward were protected from the blast by a steel beam. But Holdsworth literally disintegrated in front of them as a storm of fire and flying metal swept past.

All that was left of Holdsworth was the hand that Garrison was still holding. It was all too much for Sward, who jerked loose from Garrison and jumped over the side.

Horrified, Garrison dropped Holdsworth's hand and stepped to the edge, but he couldn't see the water because of all the smoke, and pulled back. *No telling what I might land on,* he thought. Besides, Sward had probably already drowned, so there was no use trying to find him. *If I gotta go over,* he decided, *I'm gonna wait until the last moment.*

By 8:15 A.M., the *Franklin* had assumed a three-degree list to starboard from water poured on the fire by the *Miller,* but she was still moving under her own power. But for how long? Only the two after fire rooms and the after engine room were still on line, and the men in those rooms were reporting that the heat and smoke were becoming unbearable. Already some of them had passed out.

Despite the efforts of men all over the ship, the situation still looked hopeless. Flames shot a hundred feet into the air next to the island, where Gehres and his officers tried to direct the efforts of the men below and keep the ship functioning as best they could.

As the fires multiplied and grew more fierce, the bombs went off in such rapid succession that at times the explosions seemed to roll into one continuous detonation and a massive ball of fire rolled upward to the low-lying clouds. Most of the bombs on the flight deck detonated there, blowing planes overboard, some with pilots still strapped inside, and tearing huge chunks out of the deck. Some bombs, however, fell through newly created holes to the hangar deck below, adding to the carnage and mayhem there.

The explosions aggravated and flung the fires, which raged unabated, turning the ship into a furnace. As one of the war correspondents for the *New York Herald-Tribune* would later write, "In that hell on water, big girders twisted like taffy and melted steel ran like ice cream in the sun."

With each explosion, the ship shuddered and screamed like some wounded metallic animal absorbing mortal blow after mortal blow. Smoke rose thousands of feet into the sky, beckoning more attackers to apply the coup de grace and end her torment.

Ships dozens of miles away reported hearing distinct blasts. All who watched from other ships and saw the smoke and fire and the flashes of each new explosion thought that the carrier was doomed.

The rest of the task force withdrew over the horizon. The *Franklin* was bait now, honey to trap the Japanese pilots who would surely come to claim their prize, a major morale booster for their beleaguered military. Except for a few destroyers and cruisers left to pick up survivors—perhaps to send her to the bottom when she was at last abandoned—Big Ben was left to suffer on her own.

The transfer of Admiral Davison and the rest of the flag officers and personnel took nearly an hour. The courageous officers and crew on the *Miller* held their ship close by, despite the danger from the explosions. Just as the destroyer was pulling away, a Tiny Tim rocket ignited and headed for the destroyer. Fortunately, the missile struck a swell in the ocean and cartwheeled over the ship before splashing down on the other side, or the admiral might have wished he had stayed on the carrier.

With the admiral gone, Gehres shook his fist and cursed at the sky from which the "the goddamn Japs" had come. He knew the Catholic chaplain, O'Callahan, thought of him as "a Godless heathen"; and in truth, he wasn't a big one for attending services and his profanity-laced tirades were legend. But while he didn't make a big show of being religious, neither did he think of himself as irreligious.

Now, as fires and explosions threatened to consume his ship, he was afraid. But then he heard a voice inside his head—a child's voice reciting Psalm 23, a verse he had not thought of since Sunday School. *The Lord is my shepherd I shall not want . . . He leads me beside the still waters . . . Yea, though I walk through the valley of the shadow of death, I will fear no evil . . . Surely goodness and mercy shall follow me . . .* The little voice knew all the words, and as it spoke to him, suddenly he knew that he would be all right.

His ship's crew was another matter. The wounded needed to be transferred and there was no use keeping the air personnel onboard. He signaled the *Miller* and asked that another ship be sent alongside to remove the wounded and those not needed to try to save the ship.

However, Gehres was fully aware of what had happened to the *Birmingham* when the cruiser came to the aid of the blazing *Princeton* that fall. *Two hundred thirty-nine men killed and another 400 wounded; half of the ship's company wiped out in a heartbeat.* If the fires aboard his ship reached the magazines where the bombs and ammunition were stored, the resulting blast would not only doom his ship, but would likely devastate any ship that came close. The only way to reduce the danger was to flood the magazines with seawater. He sent two men for the task; they soon returned, reporting that their mission had been accomplished.

In the meantime, a light cruiser, the *Santa Fe,* lay off the starboard bow, preparing to come alongside. A signalman on the bridge of the cruiser waved his flags to send a message in semaphore: "Are your magazines flooded?" Obviously, the *Princeton* and *Birmingham* were on everyone's minds, and the *Franklin* was so much larger, the potential for disaster so much greater.

Gehres considered his answer. His men said they had turned on the valves to flood the magazines. Still, he had no communication system working that could reach that part of the ship for confirmation. Finally, he had a signalman send his answer: "Am not sure, but believe so."

For a moment, there was no reaction from the cruiser, as though its captain was weighing the ambiguity of the reply. But only for a moment. Then the cruiser began to move toward the carrier.

Satisfied that help was on the way, Gehres gave the order to evacuate all wounded and unnecessary personnel, including the air group. He didn't know it, but the seawater lines to the ammunition magazines had been severed by the blasts. The magazines were dry.

CHAPTER TWENTY-ONE

A Risky Decision

9:00 A.M.
USS Sante Fe

The three sailors perched at the lifeline that ran around the carrier's fantail as if trying to decide between two evils. Fifty feet below was the cold, dark ocean littered with flotsam and slicks of burning fuel. Behind them fires raged.

A hundred yards away, Cpl. Fred "Andy" Anderson, USMC, watched from his battle station at a 20-millimeter machine gun on the stern of the *Santa Fe* as the three men jumped. The sailors hit the water and disappeared beneath the surface. There was an anxious moment—the big ship's propellers were still turning and a man could get caught up in the turbulence and never come up. But the three resurfaced and struck out for the cruiser. where *Santa Fe* crewmembers hauled them aboard.

Not every man trying to escape the *Franklin* was as fortunate. Bodies, both dead and living, floated in a long trail behind the carrier. Anderson was horrified in particular by the fate of one dead sailor, who had somehow got his foot tangled in a rope and hung upside-down from the fantail. The sailor had drowned as the ship rose and fell on the swells, alternately submerging him up to his chest and then lifting him free of the water.

Already it had been a long day, and that following a nearly sleepless night. The Japanese had kept Anderson and everyone else on edge by their feinting on the outskirts of the task force. He had rushed to his battle station at midnight, then tried to go back to sleep when conditions were relaxed again at 1:30. At 3:30 he was standing behind his gun again. That time, the Japanese dropped a couple of flares in the distance—sudden, fierce points of light that floated slowly to the sea. The enemy's planes, not finding a target beneath the lights, melted away before the combat air patrol could catch them.

Anderson didn't give a lot of thought about the men he was fighting. All he knew was that they had to be eliminated before he could go home. Whenever an enemy plane fell smoking from the sky, he cheered along with the other men on the ship, especially if it was a kamikaze. One of the ship's Marines injured by the suicide plane on October 16 had been his friend Walt Whitby.

"Whit" was the trunnion operator for the 20-millimeter machine gun on the starboard bow of the ship. When he first came aboard, Whitby had volunteered for that particular gun, because an old-timer had told him, "Ya'll go on up to the bow. Nothing ever happens on the bow." He said he regretted not turning over his gun to the Marines from the *Houston,* when he saw the suicide plane coming.

"I could see that Jap plain as daylight," he later told Anderson. "I'm sure he was headed for us Marines."

Only the captain's well-timed emergency turn to port stopped the pilot from wiping them all out. Still, Whitby had watched in horror as the plane crashed into the water just below his position. He was knocked onto his back by the force of the explosion as the bow was engulfed in flames. When he stood up again, his face felt like it was still on fire, and the skin hung off his burned left arm like a dish rag. In shock, he had wandered back amidships, where a corpsman found him and made him lie down as he began giving him blood plasma.

Whitby passed out and was unconscious for the next twenty-four hours. When he came to, his burned head had swollen to the size of a basketball. Anderson came to see him in the sick bay and made him feel a whole lot better by announcing, "Whit, you've got a hole in the side of your head that you could put a silver dollar in." But joking aside, he lay a hand on his friend's shoulder and said quietly, "I thought you were gonna die."

While he longed for Tennessee, Anderson was ready to press on to Japan. Anybody who saw what the Marines went through on the beaches of Iwo Jima and what the fleet experienced—particularly the *Saratoga*—offshore from the kamikazes, knew that the Japanese weren't going to give up without a lot more bloodshed on both land and sea. But it was time to get on with it so he could go on with his life.

When the task force sailed into Japanese waters on March 17, Anderson figured they would be seeing a lot more of the suicide planes. But the Japanese had seemed reluctant to attack.

After the 3:30 A.M. episode with the flares, there had been a break from General Quarters until about 5:00. Then the ships' combat information centers reported more bogeys closing in on the task force and again he had raced up the ladder to his gun. That time the Japanese attacked, but they were after another task group twenty miles away. The sight from the *Santa Fe* was spectacular. Thousands of tracer rounds flew like Fourth of July fireworks into the night as the flashes from antiaircraft guns lit up the low-lying clouds. Occasionally there would be a tiny burst of orange up in the sky and a distant trail of fire down to the sea, cheered by the *Santa Fe*'s gunners like fans applauding a home run at a baseball game.

A little later, two flares were dropped near the *Santa Fe*'s task group, but not close enough to reveal the ships as the task group slipped ever nearer to Japan. But the Japs were getting closer.

A little before 6:00 A.M., the *Santa Fe* turned into the wind with the rest of Task Group 58.2 so that the carriers could launch their planes. About the same time, the combat air patrol shot down a bandit just thirty miles from the ships. An hour later, the fighters reported that they were chasing more bogeys headed for the task group. Admiral Davison decided they weren't much of a threat and went ahead with the flight schedule, keeping the ships running in a straight line with the wind coming over their bows.

Five minutes after 7:00, the *Hancock* reported visual contact with a plane that was approaching the *Franklin*. Three minutes later, Big Ben was on fire and exploding.

Anderson saw the attack as he was coming back from breakfast. He had emerged amidships on the weather deck and had just started to make his way back to his battle station on the port side of the fantail when he glanced over at the *Franklin*. Then, for some reason, he had looked up at the layer of clouds ahead of the carrier just as the plane dropped below them. He didn't realize what he was watching until he saw the first bomb drop from the dive-bomber's belly. The Judy disappeared behind the island super-structure, so he didn't see the second bomb drop. The effects of the attack, however, could not be missed.

Loud booms rolled over the water as inky black smoke began to boil out from the carrier's hangar. Anderson ran back to his gun as General Quarters sounded; by the time he had strapped himself into the web harness, the *Franklin* appeared to be burning from her bow to her stern.

The *Franklin* suddenly veered right out of the formation, narrowly missing the light carrier *Bataan*. The *Santa Fe* heeled over to the starboard to stay with the stricken carrier and provide antiaircraft protection.

It wasn't long before the task group's combat information centers started picking up bogeys swarming toward the pillar of smoke that rose two thousand feet into the overcast. So far the combat air patrol, stung by the success against the *Franklin,* had intercepted and shot down the Japanese planes seeking to deliver the coup de grace. But it didn't seem to those who watched from the other ships that another attack was going to be necessary to finish the carrier, which by now was almost totally obscured by the black, billowing cloud.

Reports began to stream in from other ships that men were leaping by the dozens from the carrier to escape the flames or were being blown overboard by explosions. The destroyer USS *Hickox* was ordered to move in to pick up the survivors, but was soon overwhelmed by their numbers and was joined by the destroyers USS *Hunt* and *Tingey.* The destroyer *Miller* also pulled survivors aboard, while pouring water onto the fantail until the heat and danger of explosions became too much and the ship had to back away. Meanwhile, the rest of the task group continued to move apart from the carrier and her escorts.

Captain Fitz of the *Santa Fe* was placed in charge of evacuating the *Franklin's* wounded, even the whole crew if the situation called for it, and fighting the fires on the carrier. He would use his ship's combat information center to direct the dozen fighters provided by the *Hancock* for combat air patrol.

By 8:15 A.M., the cruiser had moved to within a few hundred yards of the stern of the *Franklin* and was waiting for the *Miller,* which had been ordered alongside the carrier to retrieve Admirals Davison and Bogan and their staffs, to move away. The carrier was moving at the snail's pace of eight knots. Following along behind and slightly to starboard, the *Santa Fe* carefully picked her way through the men in the water.

The *Santa Fe*'s crew threw life jackets, life rings, and floater nets to the swimmers; however, the cruiser needed to stay with the carrier and couldn't stop to pick them up, leaving that task to the destroyers. But there were so many men in the water that the destroyers had fallen far behind trying to reach them, and it was clear that some of the struggling men would die before being picked up.

So as Fitz waited for the *Miller* to clear the *Franklin,* he stopped his ship to allow men to swim to her or catch a lifeline tossed by his crew and then be hauled to safety. Some of the *Franklin*'s men were too injured to help themselves and were saved by members of the cruiser's crew, who dived in and brought them to the ship. The worst cases had been so badly burned—sometimes swimming through burning fuel on the surface of the water—that charred skin fell away from their arms and faces like snakes shedding their skins.

As the *Santa Fe* approached the *Franklin,* Anderson pitied the men jumping from the carrier's deck. But they were all in danger. Tiny Tim rockets were leaping out of the smoke. Two of them came skipping over the water toward the *Santa Fe*—close enough that Anderson could hear them slapping the waves and then plunging beneath the surface with a terrible burbling noise. One exploded lifting a tremendous geyser of water, and he figured if a Tiny Tim hit the *Santa Fe,* it would tear the ship in half. The danger magnified when the *Miller* pulled away from the starboard side of the *Franklin.*

The *Santa Fe* roared to life and the ship picked up speed, heading for the *Franklin,* its rockets, and exploding bombs. As the ship drew closer, the public address system crackled with an order from the captain. All hands—except those assigned to fight fires and handle lines on the portside, and those on the starboard side guns—were to go belowdecks. Anderson and the other gunners on the portside, the side most exposed to a blast from the carrier, were ordered to go to the starboard side of the ship and take shelter behind the superstructure.

Captain Harold Fitz stood looking through the portholes of the main bridge at the *Franklin,* weighing the most important decision of his naval career. He had to make a choice to either risk his ship and the life of every man on it, or play it safe and, perhaps, doom the *Franklin* and many of her men.

He knew that others had already decided that the *Franklin* was lost. At 8:36 A.M., Rear Admiral Davison had sent a message to the commander of the task force, Vice Admiral Marc Mitscher, which was relayed to the *Santa Fe:* "Am afraid we will have to abandon her," Davison reported. "Please render all possible assistance. Am on the *Miller.*"

When the *Miller* pulled away from the *Franklin* at 9:00 A.M., Fitz sent the carrier a message using semaphore. There was no other way to communicate with the *Franklin's* captain, as the carrier's external communications were out. But Fitz only wanted to know the answer to one question: "Are your magazines flooded?"

The implication was clear. Every man onboard the *Santa Fe* was aware of what happened to her sister ship, the *Birmingham,* when she had pulled alongside the burning carrier USS *Princeton* back in October '44.

Fitz knew that what could happen now might be worse. The *Princeton* was a CVL, a light carrier built on a cruiser hull. The *Franklin, CV-13,* was twice as large. Big Ben carried a million gallons of fuel oil and 550,000 more gallons of aviation gasoline in her storage tanks. Just back from the States, the carrier's magazines were filled to the brim with armament for the planes, as well as ammunition for the ship's guns.

If the magazines weren't flooded and fires reached them, the *Franklin* and the three thousand-plus men onboard her would disappear in a cataclysmic blast and fireball that could also obliterate any ship that ventured too close. But the answer from the *Franklin's* captain was not what Fitz wanted to hear. *"Not sure, but believe so."* Hardly the reassurance to stake thirteen hundred more lives on.

Fitz thought over his options. A captain's first responsibility was to his ship and his men. He had been told to help rescue the *Franklin's* wounded and assist with fighting the fires. But no one could order him to take his ship alongside the burning aircraft carrier if the risk was too great.

Still, there were the injured men on the *Franklin* to consider. If the fire spread or the ship went down before they could be evacuated, they wouldn't stand a chance. Nor was Fitz inclined to give up on saving the *Franklin,* especially if the crew and her captain were still fighting for the ship.

He knew that the *Franklin's* crew wouldn't be able to do it alone. The worst of the fire was on the hangar deck back toward the stern, where a broken or abandoned pump was pouring aviation gasoline onto the flames, which in turn kept other fires raging. It appeared that the fire-fighting equipment was out of commission on that part of the ship, and the men there had been forced to flee. The *Franklin's* only chance was if another ship got close enough to put out the fuel-fed fire.

With that his decision was made. Fitz waited only long enough for his crew to pull in two more *Franklin* survivors who were hanging on to lines at the stern of the ship; then he gave his orders: he was taking his ship in alongside.

Time was of the essence. The *Franklin* was one big, burning holocaust waiting to happen. Even if the magazines were flooded, there were plenty of bombs, rockets, and other munitions already out of the magazines, as well as her fuel storage, that could send her to the bottom. The Japanese were also sure to home in on the billowing clouds of black smoke and try to finish her. Sinking a big fleet carrier would be an enormous coup for them at this desperate stage of the war, and any ship tied up alongside the slow-moving carrier would also be an easy target with a limited ability to maneuver and only the guns on the starboard side of any use.

Shouting his orders for the helmsman and Black Gang, Fitz pulled his ship up along the starboard side of the *Franklin* and then slowed to match the carrier's eight-knot progress. The two ships were about forty feet apart.

Fitz would have moved in closer, but the *Franklin's* twin starboard radio masts, which otherwise would have been raised upright, had been lowered to their sides, as was normal during flight operations. The three-foot wide beams jutted out into the space between the ships; any closer and they would rip into the cruiser.

We're plenty close enough, Aviation Machinist's Mate 2nd Al Mancini thought as he helped man one of a handful of hoses pouring thick streams of seawater at the *Franklin.* The carrier was listing toward the *Santa Fe,* sending sheets of flaming aviation gasoline cascading down from the flight and hangar decks into the sea between the ships. The fires roared like a thousand blast furnaces so that he couldn't hear the shouts of the man standing next to him. The only good thing about the current situation was that he wasn't cold anymore.

The *Santa Fe* had pulled alongside the *Franklin* and at 9:30 shot "messenger lines" over to the *Franklin* to begin trying to set up the lines for transporting the wounded. The damage control parties had manned the hoses, but the fire fighting got started on the wrong foot. Two of the hoses had been scrubbed so much with saltwater during the war that they had rotted and now burst when filled with pressurized water.

Mancini concentrated on his job so he wouldn't have to think about some of the horrible things he had seen, like the sailor who dangled upside down from the fantail. The explosions didn't bother him as much—they all seemed to roll into the one continuous cacophony of tortured steel and burning fuel. However, he and everyone else ducked when a Tiny Tim rocket suddenly screamed from out of the hangar deck and passed over the *Santa Fe's* crane by only a few feet.

The *Santa Fe* had been fighting the fire for twenty minutes when Fitz realized that the ships weren't close enough. The damage control parties were having a hard time getting enough water on the main fire on the hangar deck, the one fed by the aviation gasoline system.

In one sense, the water was actually having a negative affect. The *Franklin* was listing more with every gallon of water being pumped into her that was finding its way down to the lower decks. But the options were to pour water on the fire or let the ship burn until she blew up or sank. He considered how to get more water on the problem area.

The matter was decided for him a few minutes later. At 9:50 a ready service magazine filled with five-inch gun ammunition blew up on the flight deck. It was the most terrific blast of the morning, tossing entire airplane engines with propellers still attached into the air. Steel and wood rained down on both ships and the water around them as the carrier shuddered as though she had been driven into a wall. Flying pieces of steel severed two of the *Santa Fe's* fire hoses, but miraculously no one was hurt. The Lucky Lady's luck was holding, but for how long?

Ten minutes after the big blast, the *Franklin* reported losing all power and steering. She lurched forward a few hundred more feet like a mortally wounded leviathan, stopped, and then began to wallow and drift.

On the bridge of the *Santa Fe,* Captain Fitz and his helmsman, Quartermaster Jack Goodfellow, fought to keep the cruiser in position. It was imperative that the *Santa Fe* stay parallel to the bigger ship. The crew was beginning to bring wounded over the lines by stretcher and by breeches buoy for those who could stand; there was a danger of the ships parting and breaking the lines, dumping the wounded into the water. But jockey as the captain and his helmsman might, maintaining the ship's position relative to the drifting *Franklin* was impossible.

Reluctantly, Fitz gave the order to back away from the *Franklin,* taking care to swing the bow free of the carrier's radio antenna. Once clear of the other ship, the captain commanded "all ahead full" and the *Santa Fe* responded like a thoroughbred out of the gate. He ordered the cruiser to turn away from the Franklin and swing in a wide circle to the starboard of carrier to come up from behind again. He had an idea—it was even riskier than his earlier decision—but it was the only way he could think of to save Big Ben and her crew.

Ship of Heroes

USS Franklin

Trapped on the fantail, Edwin Garrison knew he was out of time as he watched canisters of napalm burning next to several hundred oxygen bottles. The bottles, stored against the bulkhead between him and the blazing hangar deck, were pressurized at thirty-five hundred pounds per square inch. When they got too hot, they would blow up with tremendous force.

He had seen his friend Fred Holdsworth disintegrate in a blast, and other men killed by smoke and fire. Still, he had decided against going into the water. Until now. The moment had come to leave the ship. He pulled off his clothes so that they wouldn't weigh him down in the water, but left on his helmet and his shoes in case he landed on something he couldn't see.

As he stumbled through the smoke to the edge of the listing ship, Garrison found a young sailor he knew only by his nickname, "Frenchy." The sailor was lying next to the rail with a hole in his chest so large that Garrison could see his heart beating in the gore.

"I'm going over the edge," Garrison told him, then nodded toward the burning napalm. "Those oxygen tanks are going to blow and wipe out everything back here. I don't think you've got a chance either way, but if you want, I'll drop you overboard."

The boy shook his head weakly. "Maybe the fire will go out," he said. "Leave me."

Garrison took his helmet off and placed it under the dying sailor's head and patted him on the shoulder. There was nothing else he could do for him. He ran the remaining few steps to the side, leaping over just as the oxygen bottles blew. The explosion carried him out and upward in an enormous white cloud.

As he fell, he saw a two-man raft in the distance. *God put that one there for me,* he thought as he hit the water. Sputtering, he came to the surface and struck out for the raft. Partway there, he came across another younger sailor. The sailor had a life jacket on, but he had swallowed a lot of seawater and was retching and weak. Garrison grabbed him by the life jacket and half towed, half pushed him to the raft, where they joined eight other men who were hanging on.

In the hours following the attack, hundreds of acts of heroism large and small, recorded and unrecorded, were performed on the *Franklin* and in the sea around her. Men risked their lives for their friends and for strangers, as well as for a ship that seemed doomed to all who saw her agonies.

As the fires raged on the flight deck, Commander Taylor stood amidships while pieces of bombs and rockets whistled over and past him, yelling through the smoke for volunteers to "man the hoses." He calmly led men forward to the edge of the flames, apparently oblivious to the explosions that killed some and sent others sprawling or looking for some place to take cover.

Father Joseph O'Callahan seemed to be everywhere at once. Identifiable by the white cross on his helmet, he ran from place to place administering last rites, comforting and evacuating the wounded, and organizing fire-fighting teams.

But the officers were not the only ones who acted with courage. Common sailors on the flight deck and hangar deck charged the flames with inadequate water pressure in their hoses. Bombs exploded, knocking them to the deck as sharp pieces of metal scythed through the crowds. With each blast, fewer men got back up than had stood before, but they gathered around their leaders and attacked the flames again.

Some acts of heroism were simple gestures of sacrifice for a shipmate. Best friends and fellow yeomen Guido Cavallo of Galloway, West Virginia, and John Brown of Waverly, Illinois, were eating breakfast in the mess hall when the bombs hit. They made it to the fantail, where they were faced with the choice of leaving the ship or burning to death.

Cavallo couldn't swim and had no life preserver. Brown, a poor swimmer, immediately took his life preserver off and threw it to his friend. Cavallo protested the gesture, but Brown wouldn't take it back. "I can swim," he said, "and if I get tired, I can hold on to you."

Cavallo gratefully accepted the life preserver, tied it on and jumped overboard. Bobbing to the surface, he looked up in time to see Brown jump and land in the water near him, but his friend didn't resurface.

Others performed heroically simply by remaining at their posts, just trying to do their jobs as long as possible and despite their fears.

A few minutes after the five-inch gun ready ammunition locker exploded while the cruiser *Santa Fe* was alongside, engine room personnel called the bridge requesting permission to leave their posts. Temperatures had climbed to 130 degrees and smoke was making it impossible to breathe. The men were passing out—if they didn't leave now, they wouldn't leave alive. When the message was relayed to the captain, Gehres gave his permission, but ordered the men to leave the throttles open at eight knots.

A little later, the Black Gang in the fire rooms asked permission to leave as well as conditions had become unbearable. In one fire room, as the temperatures soared and smoke found its way into the compartment, they had tried to remain at their boilers by taking turns lying down in the bilge, where they could suck at fresh air coming in a one-inch vent pipe. But even with that it became impossible to remain. Again the captain gave his permission to evacuate, provided that they left the boilers going. The men did as told, but by ten minutes after ten, the unattended boilers had shut down and the ship lost power.

The men in the engine room and fire room were able to reach the bridge for permission to abandon their posts only because the men in the steering engine room aft had remained at their posts. After the bombs hit the *Franklin*, Quartermaster 2nd Class Holbrook Davis had climbed up a ladder and secured the watertight hatch above them, their only way in or out of the steering room. When the explosions grew worse and the ship began to list, the men—Davis, Bill Hamel, Jim Gudbrandsen, Larry Costa, and Norman Mayer talked about whether they should try to leave. *What if the ship was being abandoned? What if they'd been forgotten?*

Their decision to remain where they were would later become vital.

After the explosions had subsided somewhat, they learned that their sound-powered telephone—the slight electric current needed generated by the sound of a voice—still connected them to the bridge and to the engineering and fire rooms. It was the only interior communications system still operating in the entire ship; however, the bridge and the men in engineering and the fire rooms could talk only to them. So when the men in the fire room wanted permission to abandon their posts, they had to ask Davis, who relayed the message to the bridge.

It did not escape the notice of the men in the steering room that they were the only ones left in the bowels of the ship. For them, there was no escape. They had been told that the deck above them was flooded with water. If they opened the hatch, their compartment would flood and they would likely drown.

There was soon another reason to remain where they were. When the ship lost power, the helmsman also lost the ability to steer the *Franklin* from the bridge. The men might have to turn the rudder for the ship if the engineers got the boilers going again later. In the meantime, O'Callahan, who reported to the bridge during breaks in his other activities, told them to remain as still as possible to conserve their finite amount of air.

"You're in a tough spot," O'Callahan said. "But the captain says he'll get you out and he means just that; he'll get you out. But we can't do it yet.

"So sit tight and pray."

A lot of men were praying in different parts of the ship at that time. Or as Ernest Scott observed, fear had created a lot of "foxhole Christians," only there was no digging a foxhole on a steel ship. Scott had prayed right along with the others, "Dear God, if you'll only get us out of here, I promise . . ." But he was also putting his faith in a young Marine who had left the compartment, promising to come back for them if he could find a way out.

After what felt like an hour or two, the air had grown noticeably stuffier and it had become harder to breathe, even though they had tried to stay calm. Even worse was not knowing what was going on in the rest of the ship, though it sounded bad.

The explosions had grown in number and ferocity until it felt as if the entire Japanese air corps was taking a whack at the ship and that at any moment, the ship might be sunk. Every explosion renewed the panicked cries from some of the men, a few of whom had to be restrained physically.

As pandemonium threatened to break out, the tall Marine who had helped them get Eddie Carlisle into the compartment took charge again.

The Marine's name was Stephen Nowak, the son of Polish immigrants from Worcester, Massachusetts. He had been with the ship from the beginning and had made it a point to know his way around.

When the ship went back to Bremerton, Nowak had borrowed money for the train trip home so that he could marry his girlfriend, Shirley Smith. He promised her when he left that they would have a life together, and he intended on keeping that promise.

He had already had a couple of close calls. When the suicide plane skittered across the deck on October 13, it had gone right over his gunmount, so close he felt he heat from the flames. Then on October 30, he had fired away at the kamikaze and felt sure the pilot was aiming right for him when the plane plunged into the flight deck; a young sailor standing right in front of him was consumed by the burst of flame, every scrap of clothing gone. He had stuck the sailor with one morphine shot after another from the medical kit until the young man stopped screaming and died. In either case, he had been just a few feet from being killed himself.

Nowak knew that they were going to have to find a way out of the compartment or die of suffocation. Or they might drown in the deep with the ship, which was beginning to list enough that it was difficult to stand upright.

During a break in the explosions, they heard a tapping sound from the deck above. It was Morse Code. A signalman in the compartment listened for a moment, then tapped back. He got a response and turned to the chief who had tried to keep them from opening the hatch to rescue Carlisle. "We've got to go forward, Chief," the signalman said. "Everything's going up back aft."

The chief shook his head. "We stay right here till someone comes after us." He had the compartment's only emergency breathing apparatus hung around his neck, but he wasn't going anywhere.

"Goddamnit, Chief," Nowak spoke up. "We can't stay here forever and let the ship sink under us. You've got the only breather on. Why don't you go forward and try to find a way out? We'll stay here till you come back for us."

Again, the chief answered negatively. "We stay here," he said.

"Give me the breather," Nowak asked. "I'll find a way out and come back after you."

"No! Goddamnit!" the chief exploded. "I said no!"

Nowak stepped up to the hatch. "The hell with the breather," he said. "I'll go without it."

The chief ordered him away from the hatch. "Anybody tries to open that hatch, I'll see that he's court-martialed," he warned.

Nowak defiantly opened the hatch with the help of Scott and Lem Hall, who glowered at the chief. As he stepped into the darkness outside, the Marine turned back to the other men in the compartment. "If I can find a way, I'll be back," he said.

How long the Marine was gone, Scott wasn't sure. But the situation was growing more desperate. A rumor circulated that the order to abandon ship had been given, and that when the other men left the ship, destroyers would torpedo the *Franklin* and any man left behind would go down with her.

The ship was listing further, seemingly with every minute. A sailor felt the side of the compartment nearest the water. "It's cold!" he screamed. "We're already under water! We're capsizing!" He continued to scream until another sailor stepped forward and punched him in the jaw; the blow didn't knock him out, but dazed him and stopped his hysterics.

At long last, there was a weak tapping on the hatch. Scott, Hall, and Carlisle ignored the chief's protestations and opened it. It was the Marine, and he looked half dead as they dragged him in. His eyes were swollen nearly shut from the smoke, and he was bleeding in several places. But he had done what he said he would do.

Nowak had made his way through the smoke-filled passages in the dark, relying on memory and feel. Several forays had ended in blocked escape routes, and he had had to retrace his steps. But at last he had found a way out.

Scott marveled at the Marine's courage. He could have played it safe and not returned—it was obvious that the task had almost killed him—but instead, he had kept his promise.

"We can get out of here," Nowak yelled after he stopped retching and caught his breath. "We'll have to go on our hands and knees. Hang on to the belt of the man in front of you. No pushing or shoving or you won't make it."

The men tore up mattresses into strips and dipped them into a bucket of water to wear over their noses and mouths as filters. When all of the water had been soaked up, some of the men used the only moisture they had available and urinated on their strips.

Once they were all ready, the hatch was undogged again and the men followed Nowak into the dark passageway. It was pitch black and there was no escaping the thick smoke.

At one point, Scott thought he couldn't go any farther and stopped, ready to give up. Then somebody hit him hard from behind. It was Lem Hall. "Don't quit now, Scotty," he growled, "or I'll bust your ass for you!"

After what seemed like an eternity, the men passed through a hatch and arrived at a ladder leading to the second deck. They gasped greedily at the cold, fresh air that poured down the opening. The men stopped just long enough to regain their strength and lift several men who had passed out at the hatch, too weak to climb over the coaming. They then climbed up to the second deck and made their way to the foc'sle, where they climbed another ladder and emerged on the flight deck to a whole new sort of hell.

In the starboard mess hall on the other side of the ship, Lt. (j.g.) Don Gary also knew that he had to do something soon to save his life and those of the other men. Every man in that compartment was bathed in sweat as the temperature in the packed room rose to what he estimated to be more than a hundred degrees. Dr. Fuelling had convinced the men to remain inactive to conserve oxygen, but there were several hundred tense and nervous men in the hot compartment and the air was running low.

Each explosion brought another round of panicked cries. Gary couldn't blame the terrified men; it seemed as though the ship was being torn apart. At one point, a bomb exploded near the rear of the compartment, and a moment later there had been a scratching at the hatch. When it was opened, a sailor wearing a rescue breather fell through, bleeding from shrapnel wounds to his left side.

It was that blast that finally convinced Gary he couldn't wait any longer. What if the next bomb went off in the main mess hall among the rockets being assembled? One explosion would set others off and the men would all die. The ship was listing more to the starboard with each passing minute, and he knew that if it continued, the *Franklin* would roll over and sink. As it was, he could hear loose ammunition outside the room falling and rolling as the ship tilted.

It had been about an hour and a half since Gary had entered the compartment. During that time, he had been trying to think of an escape route, grateful for all the hours spent exploring the ship. When several new explosions started to panic the men, he shouted, "I think I know a way out, and if I can make it, I'll be back for you."

Leaving the compartment, Gary adjusted his rescue breather. He flicked on the flashlight he carried but discovered the beam wouldn't penetrate the thick smoke that filled the third deck. Blind, he felt and stumbled his way over rockets and bombs that had fallen from their holders and now littered his path.

He planned to make his way to the air shafts that provided oxygen for burning the fuel in the boiler rooms below. They had to lead to the outside.

However, to reach the entrance to the air shafts, he had to climb down one ladder to the fourth deck. Fires raged down below, and he was nearly driven back up by the heat.

Still blinded by smoke, he groped his way forward until he bumped into the air shaft. He felt for the rungs of another ladder he knew had to be there. He found what he was searching for, but the metal rungs were blistering hot and burned his hands when he grabbed them.

Gary stood for a moment, trying to think if there was another way. There was none. So he sprang up the ladder, trying to move as fast as he could to save his hands. He climbed several flights straight up until he reached a small, horizontal shaft. It was only eighteen inches high and just wide enough for a man to pull himself through, but he could see daylight at the far end.

Invigorated by the fresh air, he crawled through the shaft until he reached the screen at the end, which he knocked out. Looking out, he saw that by grasping a metal rung four feet from the shaft, the men could swing and drop into one of the 40-millimeter gun tubs on the side of the ship. Once there, it would be easy for them to make their way to the forward part of the flight deck.

Like Nowak on the other side of the carrier, Gary could have swung down and saved himself, gone home to his wife and son. Returning to the mess hall below was to court death from smoke, or from an explosion that might set off the ammunition. But he had given his word to his shipmates, so now he took a moment to readjust his breather and went back.

Retracing his steps, Gary broke his flashlight banging on the compartment's hatch. It opened onto a sea of anxious faces, but anxiety turned to hope when he announced that he had found a way out. However, he said, they were going to have to be patient. He consulted with Fuelling and decided he would take ten men on the first trip. If an explosion wrecked the escape route, killing him and the men he led, those remaining in the compartment would have to find another way.

Ten men were selected. "Grab the belt of the man in front," he ordered. "Don't push or pull." He then turned and led them into the smoke, cautioning them to be careful when they approached a rocket or bomb.

When the group reached the ladder where it was necessary to go down to the fourth deck, some of the men balked. They wanted out, not a journey deeper into the bowels of the burning ship. But Gary assured them that it was the only way. He spoke to them calmly, and despite their fears, they followed him down. Soon he had them swinging down into the gun tub and on their way to the flight deck.

Gary watched them go and then turned back. He tried to hurry, worried that the munitions outside of where the trapped men were waiting would go off at any moment. Arriving back at the compartment, he found the entire "congregation" was kneeling in silent prayer. Dr. Fuelling had suggested it to keep them from panicking and to conserve their strength.

This time, Gary took seventy-five men with him. When he turned to go back, it would be for the last time. He was determined to bring the rest of the men with him.

Back in the compartment, Gary had no trouble persuading the nearly two hundred men who remained that they all had to go—and go now. As he prepared to head back out again, he saw Fuelling bending over the wounded man. Gary hadn't thought about how they would evacuate the sailor, but when the doctor looked up at him, he knew there was no reason to now. The young man was dead.

Gary made every one of the men go ahead of him down the shaft to freedom. Finally, with Fuelling going just before him, it was his turn. He emerged from the shaft and swung down into the gun tub. Making his way to the flight deck, he looked up and saw Captain Gehres on the bridge, shouting orders through a bullhorn.

What he was saying was lost in the noise of the disaster, but it was clear that the captain did not intend to abandon his ship. Nor was he the only one determined not to give up the ship. The *Franklin* was dead in the water, drifting toward Japan. Half of her crew was dead or in the water, many others were still trapped in various parts of the ship. But everywhere Gary looked, men were fighting the fires or helping the wounded.

Still, Gary knew that the final choice might be to leave the *Franklin* or die. The ship was listing at what he figured was probably fifteen degrees, and it wouldn't take much more to send her over. Meanwhile, explosions kept hurling pieces of ship, aircraft, and men into the air, while rockets took off shrieking across the deck and over the water. He could see plane engines melting like butter in the flames.

Yet, men on the flight deck were turning to the starboard side and pointing at an even more incredible, and in some ways more frightening, sight. A few hundred yards away, a cruiser was steaming at flank speed straight for the *Franklin*.

The *Santa Fe,* the ship named for the City of Holy Faith, had not abandoned them when she pulled away after the *Franklin* lost power. The Lucky Lady had circled and was coming back, but it looked like her captain intended to ram the burning carrier. So much so that some men on the *Franklin* ran from the starboard side of the ship, sure that a new disaster was about to overtake them.

CHAPTER TWENTY-THREE

Orders, Sir?

USS Santa Fe

Captain Harold Fitz barked a command—"All ahead, twenty-five knots"—and felt his ship immediately surge forward. Good to know that the Black Gang was on their toes. The *Santa Fe* sped across the waves, but he waited until the ship reached the spot he wanted before he spoke again. "Thirty-five degrees northwest and hold tight."

Quartermaster 1st Class Jack Goodfellow checked the bearing he had just been given and thought there had to be a mistake. "Orders, sir?" he asked as if he hadn't heard. Pretending not to hear was the only legitimate means a sailor had of questioning the captain of a ship.

"Thirty-five northwest and hold tight!" Fitz said more firmly.

Goodfellow peered out of the portholes that lined the pilothouse and was quite sure the captain failed to see what he was seeing. The course Fitz requested would carry the *Santa Fe* right into the starboard side of the burning aircraft carrier and at nearly flank speed. "ORDERS, SIR?" Goodfellow dared to ask a second time.

Fitz, who had been looking at the carrier, turned to glower at the quartermaster. Goodfellow was one of the very best on the wheel—a helmsman who felt the movements of the ocean in his feet through the deck of the ship, smoothly rocking to the rhythms and deftly steering the ship with his fingertips. The captain knew that his order might raise eyebrows, but he didn't have time to explain himself. This was going to be a tricky, dangerous maneuver, and he needed the quartermaster doing what he was told, when he was told.

After pulling away from the *Franklin*, Fitz decided that the only way to accomplish his mission was to place his ship right next to the burning carrier—not forty feet away, not twenty, not ten, but up against her, hull to hull. His fire-fighting crews needed to be as near as possible to put the main gasoline blaze out, or it was going to spread, and maybe reach the ammunition magazines. He still had doubts about whether the magazines were flooded; the *Franklin* had suffered enormous internal damage from repeated bomb blasts, which could have easily destroyed the flooding system, and apparently the captain of the carrier had no communications to confirm or deny the status.

The aircraft carrier was probably doomed anyway, but there no chance of saving her if the fires weren't put out. However, that raised another dilemma. The *Franklin* was already listing at more than twelve degrees due to water draining into the starboard compartments of the ship. But the *Santa Fe*'s damage control parties were going to have to pour more water into the carrier to combat the fires. At some point, there would be too much water, and the ship would capsize. Two thousand men still left on the Franklin would be at great risk if the ship "turned turtle"—and that was just the *Franklin*'s crew.

Fitz's plan also put the *Santa Fe* in danger of being damaged by the carrier's two forward radio masts and the 40-millimeter gun sponsons—gun tubs that jutted out from the hull. Because of the list, the mast and sponsons looked to be about level with the cruiser's weather deck and would being moving up and down on the swells. The *Santa Fe* would be lucky if the projecting sponsons of the *Franklin* didn't tear her open like a can opener and leave his ship incapacitated.

So far the weather was favorable. The *Franklin's* bow was pointed essentially north, and there was a light breeze coming from the east, which blew the smoke and flames away from the starboard side, so visibility was good and the seas were calm with only a light swell. But if the swells grew any bigger, the damage caused by the mast and sponsons would be much worse.

A much bigger concern for the Lucky Lady was the *Franklin* rolling over while the cruiser was tied up next to her with heavy lines; the *Santa Fe*— only a third of the massive carrier's size—would be crushed beneath. And if that happened, all the men inside the hulls of the two ships, as well as the men who went into the water and got caught in the suction, would plunge to the bottom with the ships.

The catalog of things that could go wrong seemed endless. Flames still soared the height of the island from the flight deck, and a stream of flaming gasoline continued to pour from the hangar deck as choking black smoke belched from the interior. The closer the ship got, the more danger there was for anyone exposed to burning fuel and shrapnel thrown out by an explosion.

Fitz knew that his crew was aware of what they would be up against. They had already seen entire planes blown over the side of the carrier and the terrifying spectacle of the Tiny Tim "ship buster" rockets bursting out of the smoke. Always there was the specter of the *Princeton* and the *Birmingham*— only now, the hulls of the *Franklin* and *Santa Fe* would be grinding right next to each other. A massive explosion—such as an ammunition magazine or fuel storage tank—on the starboard side of the *Franklin* would thrust into the side of the *Santa Fe*. Both ships would be devastated, maybe sunk.

Then there were the Japanese to consider. The longer the *Santa Fe* remained next to the *Franklin*, the more vulnerable both ships would be to air and submarine attacks. Already the enemy was flocking to the column of smoke like vultures to a wounded animal. Fitz and his crew could see the life-and-death struggles in the distance between the combat air patrol and the *Franklin's* would-be executioners. Other ships in the task group were doing their part as well, judging from the small black dots of antiaircraft fire on the horizon. But all it would take to destroy the *Santa Fe* and *Franklin* was another pilot—skilled or lucky—to slip through as the pilot of the Judy had done two hours earlier. The situation was only getting worse, too, as the *Franklin* was drifting toward Japan, now only about fifty miles away, or about ten minutes as a Zero flew.

Time was working against Fitz. With the potential for a cataclysmic blast, or the Japanese catching them sitting, or the ship capsizing, the captain knew he needed to bring the wounded and any other personnel across faster than his crew was going to be able to manage with lines.

After pulling away when the *Franklin* lost power, Fitz had circled away from the embattled carrier as fast as his ship could move. However, he had had to slow as he approached again because of all the men in the water. Those men were complicating the situation as he stopped the *Santa Fe* several hundred yards behind the drifting *Franklin* to consider his next step. The easiest way to approach the carrier would have been from almost directly behind and just to the *Franklin's* starboard, like a car pulling in alongside an empty curb. But there were far too many men in the water—hundreds—in that area to move through without endangering them.

However, Fitz thought that he had a way to get around them and still come up against the *Franklin*. If he misjudged the approach it might lead to a horrible disaster, but he had to try something.

At 10:40 A.M., Fitz ordered the *Santa Fe* to "back down," reversing away from the *Franklin* in part to discourage the men in the water from heading for the cruiser, and also to maneuver into a different position for his approach. Four minutes later, with the bow pointed almost due north, he gave the order to move ahead at twenty-five knots, or about thirty miles an hour. He needed to move fast so that the ship reacted quicker at the right moment. The quartermaster keeping the logbook noted: "At the time a few men had hold of lines from this ship, but it was necessary to disregard them because of the still very critical situation on the *Franklin*."

Fitz chose a route outside the fan of men spread out behind the carrier. In fact, he had the cruiser steaming parallel to the side of the carrier when he issued the command to turn toward the carrier. "Thirty-five degrees northwest and hold tight!" But his helmsman seemed to be having difficulty hearing him, or was second-guessing him.

"ORDERS, SIR?" Goodfellow had asked for the second time.

"I GAVE YOU AN ORDER, DAMNIT!" Fitz roared. "THIRTY-FIVE DEGREES NORTH-WEST AND HOLD TIGHT!"

Goodfellow bit his lip as he turned the wheel to thirty-five degrees northwest and held tight to that line.

Boatswain's Mate 2nd Class Mike Hardy couldn't believe what he was seeing. One minute the ship was sitting still, pulling in a few survivors from the water, and the next the *Santa Fe* was charging toward the burning aircraft carrier as though the captain intended to ram the big ship.

Although his battle station was normally on a 40-millimeter quad on the starboard side, he was also part of the fifth division. Known as the "Boat Deck Division," their duty station was the deck above the weather deck around the superstructure, where the small boats were stored. It was their responsibility to handle the lines between ships to bring over mail, or set up a breeches buoy to transport personnel, or to transport stretchers with wounded men.

The duty gave Hardy an excellent vantage point to view what was happening, not that he had liked what he had seen so far. It had been with a mixture of frustration, pity, and anger that he had watched sailors on the other ship desperately, and futilely, trying to get away from the flames. Or leaping from the ship into the water and not resurfacing. Or cut down by explosions or rockets or bullets. He would never forget the sailor he had seen dangling upside down from the *Franklin's* fantail; drowned at sea, when he should have been home, going to college, or working on a farm, or starting a family, a career, a life.

Watching the sailor's body dip in and out of the swells, Hardy felt the old anger that had burned in him since Pearl Harbor in early December 1941 when he had spent three days retrieving the bodies of other young men from the oil-fouled waters. As far as he was concerned, the Japanese were an evil people, whose behavior during this war went beyond the pale. With the liberation of the Philippines, they had all learned that the rumors were true about Japanese cruelty, including mass executions of prisoners of war.

The so-called rules of war had not applied in the Pacific. That past summer when the ship had passed through the hundred or so Japanese survivors from a destroyer that had been sunk near Saipan, he and the other gunners on the *Santa Fe* wanted to shoot the men in the water. They were not men they felt mercy toward, nor pity. Most of the guns could not have depressed their barrels low enough to shoot those closest to the ship, but they had been ordered to hold their fire anyway, causing the crews on the guns and on the deck to mutter angrily. "THE SONS OF BITCHES WOULD SHOOT AT US!" a gunner's mate yelled. Others shouted their agreement—the only good Jap was a dead Jap. Hardy supposed it didn't matter; no one was going to rescue the men in the water, but hatred made him want to pull the trigger too.

The kamikaze epitomized his and many others' opinions of the Japanese. Cruel. Inhuman. Life was cheap—their own or anyone else's. Tokyo Rose talked about them like they were heroes. *Better a live fighter than a dead hero*, Hardy thought; in his opinion, the kamikazes were cowards who didn't "fight by the rules." But if that's the way they wanted it, he and his fellow gunners were more than willing to send them off to Shinto Heaven in a blaze of glory.

Hardy was still just as frightened before an engagement as he had been at the Battle of the Coral Sea or the Battle of Midway back in '42. Or Bougainville in '43, or Leyte Gulf in '44. But just like in his first fire fight, once he had the bastards in his sights and pulled the trigger, his fear left him with the bullets. Then nothing else mattered except that the man in the airplane wanted to kill him, and he wanted to kill the man in the airplane. When the planes burst into flames or crashed into the sea, he cheered, they all cheered—it didn't matter who shot it down.

Still, he was tired of it all. Ever since they had heard they were finally going home, there was one thing he looked forward to more than he looked forward to getting away from the Japanese and their insanity. He wanted to sleep. Sleep for hours on end with no calls to General Quarters, no sound of guns, no flaming planes. When one of his buddies asked him what he was going to do when they returned to the States, Hardy replied, "Christ, when I get back I'm gonna climb into the first bunk I can find, go to sleep, and not wake up for at least a day."

There was this one last operation to complete first. But now it looked like saving men was going to be a more dangerous proposition than trying to kill men.

The cruiser bounded across the swells, the bow rising and falling while her decks vibrated from the pounding of her propellers. Closer and closer the *Santa Fe* steamed toward the *Franklin*, as a huge inky black column of smoke from the stricken carrier towered high above the *Santa Fe*, like a warning to stay away. The carrier filled the world in front of the cruiser's crew, roaring like a forest fire, but Fitz was undeterred.

Hardy noted that the starboard edge of the carrier's flight deck would be about even with the top of one of the six-inch gun turrets and the boat deck. He could see men on the flight deck, many of whom were now moving away from the starboard side, some even running in alarm at the *Santa Fe*'s approach.

Since taking command, Fitz had demonstrated that he was a great ship handler. Still, that was during fueling and at Iwo Jima. No one had a clue what he was trying to accomplish now. The men on the *Santa Fe*'s decks cast nervous glances up at the pilothouse and back to the *Franklin,* then up at the pilothouse again. A few began to cry out, *"Turn!"*

They were going to ram the *Franklin* at flank speed! Hardy and the others braced for impact. Then just before the disaster, the ship turned so hard to starboard that men lurched across the deck trying to regain their balance.

Up in the pilothouse, Fitz had ordered an emergency turn. Goodfellow spun the wheel as fast as he could for "right full rudder," the Black Gang was told "full ahead" on both port side screws and full back on the starboard. As the bow swung past the side of the *Franklin,* the stern slid around like it was skidding on gravel. Then, just as the bow carried beyond the carrier, the captain ordered "full back" on all four screws. Instantly, the propellers dug in so hard that the entire ship shuddered, and the fantail of the *Santa Fe* was nearly submerged as the cruiser reversed direction.

A moment later, the weather deck of the *Santa Fe* slipped delicately beneath the tilted flight deck of the *Franklin,* and her hull came alongside the giant as though Fitz were merely parallel parking a car between two other vehicles. It happened so fast that there was a moment of stunned silence from the crews amid the racket of explosions and fires from the carrier. Then the officers and sailors on both ships who had witnessed the feat erupted with wild cheering.

The men around Hardy clapped each other on the back and shouted.

"Did you see what the old man did! Did you see what the old man did!"

"I wouldn't'ta believed it, if I hadn't seen it with my own eyes!"

"Goddamn, that was close!"

"Did you see what the old man did?"

Fitz nudged the *Santa Fe* slightly forward to bring the bow tight into the *Franklin* and told Goodfellow to hold her there. It was ten minutes to 11:00 A.M., nearly four hours after the attack, and the *Franklin* and *Santa Fe* were now essentially a single ship. The captain wasn't going to have to constantly jockey to stay in position with the wallowing carrier, but they would drift toward Japan together and share the same fate.

As Fitz feared, the *Franklin* radio masts began tearing into the *Santa Fe*— the forward mast up near the foc's'le and the second ripping at the lower forward superstructure compartments just above the main deck with the rise and fall of the swells. A bigger problem was one of the 40-millimeter gun sponsons on the Franklin—which had been added in Bremerton to increase the ship's antiaircraft firepower on the starboard side. The sponson rubbed against the *Santa Fe*'s hull just above the waterline, screeching horribly, and forcing the cruiser's stern away so that there was a small gap between the ships.

If Fitz heard the cheers, he didn't waste any time acknowledging them. Orders were given and the fire-fighting and rescue crews jumped into action. Hardy and his division rushed for the side with their lines to hold the ships together and to set up the system for bringing the stretchers across. Fitz's seamanship had momentarily distracted the crew, but they quickly remembered that they were tying up to a burning aircraft carrier and needed to work fast.

A "brow," or two-foot-wide gangplank, was set between the flight deck and the six-inch gun turret where they were about even, and men from the *Franklin* began to cross. Some of them were wounded but others were not. Men were also clambering over the radio masts, and scooting along on the barrels of the *Santa Fe*'s six-inch gun turret that had been turned toward the *Franklin*.

With the line travelers set up, Hardy and his fellows began bringing the most severely wounded over on stretchers and breeches buoys. One of the first stretchers to arrive contained a young sailor, who was told by one of the line crew to get out and walk so that the stretcher could be returned to the *Franklin*.

"You've got to be kidding," Hardy grimaced and pointed. One of the sailor's legs was missing and the other a mash of blood and bone. They got another stretcher and whisked him off to the *Santa Fe*'s sick bay, where the ship's doctor, Lt.Cmdr. Carl Gilman, was already busy at the operating table.

Outside on the boat deck, Hardy noticed the long lines of apparently uninjured men on the forward part of the carrier's flight deck preparing to cross over the brow and radio masts. Before long, he heard that the carrier's air group and other "unnecessary personnel" had been ordered to transfer to the *Santa Fe*. But there also seemed to be some confusion about conditions aboard the *Franklin* and what the crew was being told.

Word was getting around on the *Santa Fe* that some of the men coming over were saying they had been told that the order to abandon ship had been given. A few even claimed that they heard the *Franklin* was about to roll over. Or they had heard that the fires were winning the battle and getting close to the ammunition magazines, and that the magazines weren't flooded. In short, that Big Ben couldn't be saved and they better all—including the *Santa Fe*—get away from the carrier while they still could.

Up in the pilothouse, Lt. Norm Utecht, the ship's communications officer, pondered how to get better communications set up with the *Franklin's* captain. The carrier's radio antenna had been destroyed, and up to now the two ships "talked" by using semaphore or by trying to relay shouted megaphone messages—neither of which was going to suffice if the *Franklin* was to be saved from the fires and the Japanese.

Utecht decided that he better ask the man who best knew the ship's radio and radar equipment. He picked up the sound-powered telephone and called Radio Two. "I need you on the bridge," Utecht said when the phone was answered, "on the double."

Chief Warrant Officer Don Jackson hung up, adjusted his battle helmet, and undogged the watertight door. What he saw exiting the windowless compartment was like going to sleep and then waking up in a nightmare. He was surprised to see the *Franklin*—belching smoke and shaking from detonations—tied up so close; in fact, he was surprised that the carrier was still floating at all.

Earlier, shortly after the Franklin was hit, Jackson had gone outside and was shocked when he saw the carrier. Big Ben was a thousand yards away and looked as though she was being consumed by smoke and fire. Explosions tossed dark specks—he didn't want to think about what they might be—into the gray sky; then the specks would rain down until the water around the ships looked like it was boiling. Even at that distance, an occasional piece struck the *Santa Fe*.

Jackson thought that the *Franklin* was doomed; he didn't see how a ship could suffer so much and survive. The smoke reminded him of the similar plume he had seen when the *Princeton* went off and devastated the *Birmingham*. If the *Santa Fe* was supposed to "render assistance," he knew the same thing could happen, but he still hoped that the *Santa Fe* would do whatever it took to help the men on the *Franklin*. Even if it meant risking all of their lives.

When the captain ordered all personnel to go inside, except those involved in fire fighting, line handling, and the guns on the starboard side, Jackson returned to Radio Two and remained there until he got the call from Utecht almost four hours later. He walked out of the aft superstructure and stopped again at the sight of the aircraft carrier. The *Franklin* was listing so far over that it looked like the ship was being propped up by the *Santa Fe*. A loud protest of metal tearing into metal emanated from where the vessels were rubbing up against each other, but that was not as alarming as the bombs and shells detonating, or the popping and whine of machine gun bullets. Obviously, the fate of the *Birmingham* remained a viable reality.

As he scrambled up to the pilothouse, Jackson wondered if this was the day the Lucky Lady's fortunes would change. He had written to Charlotte asking her to marry him when he got back to the States, but if things took a turn for the worse, he might never know how she would have answered him.

Inside the pilothouse, Jackson reported to Utecht, who explained the situation. There were several reasons why establishing better communications was important. The first order of business was to talk to the captain of the *Franklin* to see if there was a way to get the broken aviation gasoline pump shut off. It had become clear that until the fuel was shut off, the fire would continue to rage and feed the others. They were all in grave danger as long as the *Franklin* continued to burn.

Once the fires were under control, the ships were going to have to try to escape the waters of Japan, and that was going to take a lot of coordination between the *Franklin* and the ships assigned to be her escorts. The heavy cruiser USS *Pittsburgh* had been selected to tow the *Franklin* as soon as it could be arranged, and the destroyers were already circling to provide a screen as well as pick up survivors. But eventually they were going to have to move toward safety as a concerted group, and when night fell, semaphore flags would be useless and signal lights might attract unwanted attention.

Utecht asked Jackson if he could think of an improvement. At that moment, Jackson was looking at the forward part of the *Franklin's* flight deck. Long lines of men stood waiting on the starboard side to cross over to the *Santa Fe*. But there was also a large crowd of men standing and sitting on the raised port side edge of the deck—apparently sent there to counterweight the ship's list to starboard. His attention became fixed on a man standing alone in the middle of the flight deck about halfway between the bow and the island. The man's bright red hair made him stand out, and in that moment, Jackson recognized him.

In January 1943, Jackson and Chief Warrant Officer W. R. Modeen had both been assigned to the Naval Research Laboratory in Washington, D.C., for advanced courses in electronics. Modeen was perhaps ten years older, but they had become friends. Now, there was Modeen on the *Franklin,* and more importantly, he was carrying a TBY, a battery-operated transceiver.

Jackson pointed Modeen out to Utecht and explained the significance. He had made it a point to know where every piece of radio equipment on the ship was located and now knew where he could find another TBY. It was stored in a small compartment above the pilothouse that contained some of the radar equipment. He turned and ran to retrieve the radio without waiting for Utecht's orders.

Climbing up to the open platform above the pilothouse placed Jackson on a high and exposed part of the ship. Although they had declined in frequency, explosions continued to rack the carrier and flung hot shards of metal at the *Santa Fe,* which sounded like hail coming down on the cruiser's superstructure. But he didn't think about the danger, he was just doing his job; it was the guys below—the firefighters and the men helping bring the wounded across, face-to-face with the fires—who were taking the real risks. Not everyone on the *Franklin* was trying to leave—he could see men battling the blazes and carrying ammunition out of burning gun turrets and rolling bombs over the edge.

Everywhere he looked there were heroes. And maybe more importantly, everywhere he looked there were guys just doing what needed to be done. They were all going to have to stay on the job, and count on each other, if they were going to get out of there. The rest of the task group had disappeared over the horizon, leaving two cruisers, five destroyers, the burning aircraft carrier, and a half dozen fighter planes to fend for themselves. The long smoky trails of doomed planes and a horizon polka-dotted with anti-aircraft fire proved the Japanese had not given up trying to claim their prize. It seemed only a matter of time before another would sneak in.

Jackson entered the radar equipment compartment and located the TBY, which he quickly brought back down to Utecht and explained how to find the frequency Modeen was using. Modeen would never know that it was an old friend who connected him to the *Santa Fe,* but he looked up with a smile and a wave when he at last heard a voice on the transceiver's headset. Modeen took off running for the *Franklin's* bridge.

Conditions in the *Santa Fe* pilothouse were even more tense than they had been when he left. A bogey had been picked up by radar some forty miles out and heading their way. The cruiser's combat information center sent the fighter planes to intercept, but the bogey kept changing directions and, for some reason, also disappearing from the radar screens for periods of time.

When the combat air patrol arrived where they should have been able to spot the enemy plane—now only twenty-two miles from the ships—they couldn't locate him in the clouds. Then the bogey faded from the screens.

Two minutes later, it reappeared just seventeen miles away, but was gone again before the fighters could intercept.

The combat air patrol was recalled to circle closer to the ships. No one knew where the enemy plane was, but the pilot would have no trouble locating the *Franklin* from the smoke, which could probably be seen in Japan. The day before, the combat information center had reported intermittent attempts at radar jamming by the Japanese, an effort recalled now as the plane seemingly disappeared.

With his task completed, Jackson returned to his battle station. Worrying about bogeys and escaping was someone else's job, but it felt good to have done something to help. He was back in the relative safety of Radio Two when there was a muffled roar. A five-hundred-pound bomb had exploded, filling the air—including the open area above the pilothouse— with a cloud of hot, whizzing metal.

When the men on the decks lifted their heads again and looked around, they couldn't believe that not a man on the *Santa Fe* had been injured, though some could point to where bits of flying steel had nicked or dented the ship near them. The Lucky Lady was fighting hard to keep her nickname.

There were, however, two casualties of the blast. Hearing reports of the hot metal raining down on the ship, Captain Fitz had decided that the cruiser's Kingfisher planes were a fire hazard. Although they were not gassed, there was some fuel remaining in their tanks and they were armed with a bomb each, as well as machine gun bullets. The catapult on the port side of the cruiser had also been damaged by the flight deck of the carrier, and there was a danger of the plane parked there toppling onto the firefighting crews on the stern. He ordered the planes to be destroyed and jettisoned over the side of the ship.

The captain might as well have asked Aviation Machinist's Mate 2nd Class Al Mancini to kill his best friend. He loved those planes, but was on a damage control party and had to follow orders. Like a farmer approaching his kid's pet turkey at Thanksgiving time, he reluctantly grabbed an axe and approached the "gooney-birds" with a heavy heart.

Mancini tried not to hold it against the captain. He had liked, or at least respected, all three captains who had commanded the *Santa Fe*. The affable Berkey was the perfect skipper to ease a fifteen-year-old boy into manhood—the comforting father figure his own dad had never been.

Not many men had liked Wright, most thought of him as cold. He had earned their respect as a skipper, especially the way his seamanship had saved them from the suicide plane and its torpedo in October at the beginning of the Second Battle of the Philippine Sea. But it was his humanity immediately following that attack that had impressed Mancini.

Mancini's friend Al Lamprin had been badly burned by the flaming gasoline that splashed over the foc'sle. When Mancini tried to help him to his feet, the charred skin of the sailor's forearms had come off in his hands. Later that evening he learned that after Lamprin's injuries were dressed, Wright had ordered that the sailor be brought to his own quarters, giving up his bunk for Lamprin. According to the corpsmen looking after him, the captain had been concerned that if the ship got hit and had to be abandoned, Lamprin would not have made it out of the sick bay. But he would stand a fighting chance from the captain's bunk in the superstructure. Now that was the sort of captain Mancini would have followed to the gates of hell.

Fitz had won him over in another way. The crew had quickly learned to appreciate that the third skipper was probably the best ship handler of the bunch, but he also knew something about handling men. Sailors don't like change, especially an experienced crew aboard a lucky ship, where change might be for the worse. It could take a new captain time to get the men to trust him as they needed to in battle.

Fitz saw his opportunity shortly after the ship arrived in Ulithi following the deadly typhoon. Rivalry between crews on different ships was a tradition in the Navy. Take a few beers, mix in the sun during liberty ashore on Mog Mog, and there was sure to be an exchange of words at the end of the day when the crews were waiting for boats to return them to their ships. Often as not, the words led to brawls.

Most of these were spur of the moment and quickly forgotten. But the crews of certain ships seemed to take a more permanent dislike toward one another, sometimes for reasons they couldn't even remember anymore. The Santa Fe's crew and that of her sister ship, the USS Mobile, had that sort of relationship.

Some of the men on the Santa Fe claimed it had to do with the Mobile's crew being careless in combat. However, accidents happened all the time—indeed, thirteen men on the Mobile were injured when an antiaircraft shell from another ship struck her. In truth, the Mobile and her crew had performed as heroically as any other in CruDiv13.

The antagonism probably had to do with something much more near and dear to the hearts of young men. Jealousy. Since arriving from the Aleutians in 1943, the *Santa Fe* had always been the flagship of the division, with the implication that it was the "better" ship. Meanwhile, there was a perception aboard the *Santa Fe* that the *Mobile* received preferential treatment. The perception increased greatly following the typhoon when the *Santa Fe*'s crew learned that the *Mobile* was being sent home instead of them.

The *Mobile* had not been out as long or been in on as many operations, the men complained. Fitz, who had been in command of the *Santa Fe* for only two months, saw an opportunity to identify with his men. After "Granny" Hickman shot down the Zero over Iwo Jima in July 1944, a small Japanese flag had been painted on the side of the Kingfisher, just like it would have been on a fighter plane. The aircraft had subsequently been badly damaged in the typhoon.

Before the *Mobile* left for the States, the ships exchanged aircraft—the damaged plane going back for repairs. At the last minute, Fitz sent a crew over to the *Mobile* to pointedly paint over the Japanese flag. The message was that the *Mobile*'s air crew wasn't going to get credit for shooting down the Zero. The gesture didn't relieve the sting of watching the *Mobile* leave Ulithi lagoon, but it was just the sort of thing to endear a captain to his crew. It had certainly done the trick for Mancini.

Still, it was hard for him to destroy the planes. In order for the planes to sink so that they would not be in the cruiser's way, Mancini and his comrades hacked into the wings, where the fuel tanks were located, and into the fuselage to eliminate any potential air pockets. Only after they tipped the planes into the water, however, did the men realize they had forgotten to punch holes in the pontoons. Instead of sinking, the planes floated upside down and had to be finished off with bursts from the 20-millimeter machine guns.

With the planes gone, Mancini and the others returned to their firefighting duties. They had five hoses going, trying to put out the gasoline fire, as well as fires surrounding 40-millimeter gun tubs and the two, five-inch gun turrets behind the island. With a loud "CRUMP" of an explosion, one of the turrets had changed the shape of its walls from a square box to almost egglike. They could hear pieces of flying metal humming around inside the turret like a bunch of angry metal bees. He hoped there was nothing left to blow up in the turret, or the next one would shatter like a light bulb and those bees would be set loose.

As they were pouring water on the gasoline blaze, the firefighters yelled at some of the *Franklin* crewmembers they could see to get down to the 40-millimeter gun sponson just a few feet from the fire and throw the ammunition overboard. Flames were already licking at the sponson, and if the shells blew, they could take out the men on the hoses. The *Franklin* men responded quickly and soon had the ammunition overboard. Then small arms ammunition began to go off behind the *Franklin* men. Some of the men on the *Santa Fe* urged them to jump in the water and swim to the cruiser—from their vantage point, the *Franklin* looked like a lost cause. The men on the *Franklin* looked as though they were considering the option, but at last they waved and faded back into their ship.

Then the firefighters finally caught a break. The flow of aviation gas was at last cut off and the water from the hoses was able to extinguish the blaze. They were still in danger—a fact emphasized when an ammunition box exploded shortly afterward, spraying fragments over their heads—but with the main fire out, the two crews could deal with the rest.

When Mancini was finally spelled on his hose, he was exhausted, mentally as well as physically. He hoped to never see scenes again like he had that day. He had been relieved when the ship came alongside the second time and saw that someone had finally cut the line that held the drowned sailor. But there were plenty of other images he would never forget. He would always remember how the flight deck kept tilting farther and farther toward them, and wondering how much longer before it flopped over and squashed the *Santa Fe* like a bug. He had seen the engines of airplanes melting and men blown through the air with their clothes on fire.

In less than two weeks, he would turn eighteen years old. Back home, guys his age were just getting out of high school, whereas he had been in the Navy for more than two years, been in a dozen battles, become a man. He knew that his mother was proud of him, though he was glad she didn't know all of what went on out in the Pacific, or she might have still tried to get him out of the Navy. And maybe, just maybe, his father—that tough bastard who had treated his son like he would never amount to much—would have been proud too.

Despite orders to stay out of harm's way by remaining inside the ship or at least behind the superstructure, many of the sailors and officers on the *Santa*

Fe could not stay put. They wanted to help in any way possible, even if it meant putting their own lives at risk.

As the cruiser scraped alongside the *Franklin,* Marine Cpl. "Andy" Anderson left the safety of the superstructure and went forward to see if he could assist with the rescue effort. It certainly looked like the carrier's crew was abandoning ship and with a growing sense of urgency by some. Most of the men in the lines on the flight deck waited patiently, but others seemed more desperate to get off the ship and rushed across the brow, gun barrels, and radio masts when it was their turn. A few moved too quickly and slipped off the brow or fell from a barrel, crashing hard onto the cruiser's deck, even breaking bones and having to be helped to the sick bay.

Others didn't take the established routes. Sailors were still jumping from the ship into the water and swimming to the fantail or the starboard side of the *Santa Fe,* where the crew helped them aboard. Men on the foc'sle and hangar deck imitated Tarzan and swung across on lines that hung down from the flight deck, and into the waiting arms of the cruiser's crew.

A number of sailors crossed wearing uniforms—officer's uniforms—that were not their own. They said they had been trapped inside the ship, their clothes soaked as they waded through flooded compartments and passageways; then when they had emerged into the chilly wind, a chaplain on the carrier had handed out officers' uniforms so they could stay warm.

There were the occasional humorous incidents, such as when the *Santa Fe's* crew saw an admiral crossing one of the radio masts and scrambled to assist him. Rather, they had *thought* he was an admiral from the jacket and cap he was wearing. They had been saluting and solicited his needs until they looked under the cap and saw that the "admiral" was just another pimply-faced teenager, who had been told to go below to find dry clothes and thought the admiral's would do just fine.

The rumors about the *Franklin's* condition, and what orders had been given for the crew were self-perpetuating. The *Santa Fe's* crew was hearing that the order to abandon ship had been given; they in turn were relaying that news back to isolated pockets of men on the *Franklin* who had no contact with officers on the carrier, and so left on the advice of the cruiser's crew.

The imminent demise of the *Franklin* still seemed a distinct possibility. The carrier was now listing at what some estimated to be 15 degrees, perhaps a little more. The ship couldn't just keep taking on more water; sooner or later the *Franklin* would roll.

Anderson reached a group of *Santa Fe* crewmen who were throwing life-lines out to men treading water off the starboard bow. Some of the swimmers appeared to be just about spent as he stepped up to help haul on the lines. Even onboard and safe, some of the men he helped pull in would not let go of the line and had to have their fingers pried off.

When there were no more men there to help, Anderson continued over to the port side of the ship, working his way back to amidships, where other rescuers were throwing life jackets and lines to men caught in the water between the two ships. Although the distance to the cruiser wasn't great, the water trapped between the two big, wallowing vessels sloshed back and forth, making it difficult to negotiate. Many of the men appeared to be injured or suffering from burns and in danger of drowning, or being carried by waves to where the ships were grinding together.

As Anderson watched, a tall, red-headed sailor from the *Santa Fe* dove into the frothing water with a lifeline and swam quickly to a sailor who was going under. Raymond "Bud" Hilly was an Irish-American kid from Rockaway, New York. His father, a lawyer, had signed the papers to let him join the Navy at age seventeen. A natural entertainer, Hilly had brought many a tear to the eyes of homesick sailors at talent shows onboard the ship with his rendition of "Danny Boy" and its lament for a young man headed off to war.

Oh Danny boy, the pipes, the pipes are calling
From glen to glen, and down the mountain side
The summer's gone, and all the flowers are dying
'tis you, 'tis you must go and I must bide.

Hilly was quickly joined in the cold, frothing water by his friend John Mosso. The pair moved from one flailing sailor to another, tying lifelines under their arms so that the crew on the *Santa Fe* could pull them in. Only when the *Franklin* crewmembers were safe did Hilly and Masso, chilled to the bone and weak, allow themselves to be brought back aboard.

About noon there was a significant change in the men's attitudes. The fire-fighting crews seemed to have gained the upper hand on the fires. While there was still a significant amount of small munitions going off, the big explosions were much less frequent. It was starting to appear that Big Ben might be saved after all. As if to make the point, men motioned to where high up on the aft end of the carrier's superstructure, sometimes obscured by smoke, a large American flag still flew.

Anderson knew that a lot of men had to have died that morning for that flag. He soon learned that he was fortunate not to be among them when he returned to his 20-millimeter gun on the port side of the fantail. The gun was still intact and ready for battle, but the harness that held him in place was hanging by a few threads—sliced to shreds by flying shrapnel.

Lucky for him, he wasn't standing in the harness when that metal passed through it. Lucky to be on a ship that still seemed charmed when it came to the lives of her men.

Lt. Warren Harding and his friend Lt. Bob Zoeller looked up at the overhead when they heard the sound of the explosions. The blasts were muffled and did not seem particularly threatening inside the officers wardroom, where they had gone after Captain Fitz ordered unnecessary personnel to seek shelter inside the ship.

The two young officers had not seen the skipper's feat of seamanship, but they had heard from others who spoke about it in awed tones. It was hard to believe that the *Santa Fe* was now tied up next to the *Franklin*, except for the proximity of the blasts above them and the ominous metal grating sound of something tearing at the hull of the cruiser.

It seemed somehow fitting to Harding that no sooner had the crew of the *Santa Fe* been promised that they would go home at the end of this operation then they had found themselves in their most dangerous situation of the war. They had been told so many times before that the *next* operation would be the last one that Harding had taken this announcement with a grain of salt. He figured the operations would never be over until the Japanese had nothing left to fight with.

It was frustrating that the enemy would not acknowledge that the war was lost and that the killing needed to stop. The Japanese could not hope to accomplish anything now except more death and injury, including to themselves. Their cities were being decimated, civilians as well as their young soldiers and sailors were dying needlessly. Still, it did not shock Harding that they wouldn't give up; they had proved their willingness to die needlessly since the beginning of the war with their insane banzai attacks.

Even with the war lost, they were still a formidable enemy. How many more years, how many more *Franklins*, how many more Iwo Jimas there would be before it was over, Harding didn't want to guess. But if finishing this horrible war meant the *Santa Fe* could not go home just yet, then so be it—he was ready and so, he thought, was the crew. All they could do was fight the battles one at a time, and at the moment the battle was trying to save an aircraft carrier and her crew.

As bad as conditions sounded outside, sitting in the wardroom drinking coffee was worse. Harding and Zoeller decided they had to do something, anything to help, so they went topside. Zoeller pointed to a life raft attached to a bulkhead. "Let's get that loose," he suggested. So the two friends untied the raft and sent it overboard, satisfied to see two survivors climb wearily aboard to await rescue. It wasn't much, but at least they felt they had contributed.

At noon, the captain of the *Franklin* reported that the major fires were under control, even though the destroyer *Hickox* had to move in at the last minute and remove fifteen men who had been fighting a fire on the fantail and been trapped. The *Franklin's* captain indicated that all the wounded and personnel he wanted transferred had been removed. The ship's list had been stabilized at fifteen degrees, and now he and a skeleton crew were ready for the next step—getting out of there.

Before the *Santa Fe* could leave her post of the past hour and a half, her crew had one last chore. The *Pittsburgh* had maneuvered to the front of the *Franklin* and had sent over a "messenger" line that was attached to a seven-inch-thick towing cable. The idea was to use the messenger line to haul the cable up to the carrier's foc'sle, where it could be rigged for towing.

However, the *Franklin's* capstan—an upright, spool-shaped cylinder used to hoist the anchors, or in this case the messenger line and cable—was inoperative. Efforts to lift the dozen tons of cable aboard with just manpower failed. So the messenger line was brought over to be attached to the *Santa Fe's* windlass, another winch used to haul in the big anchors. The job was hazardous for the windlass- and line-handling crews on the *Santa Fe,* who had to constantly dodge the stump of the radio mast that swept back and forth, gouging at the deck and windlass and threatening to crush any man who was not paying attention.

Each minute of delay was adding to the damage suffered by the *Santa Fe,* which had a twelve-foot-long gash in her side, fifteen inches above the water-line where the main plating had been torn loose and the hull's frame bent by the 40-millimeter gun sponson. The ship's carpenter had remedied the injury as best he could by stuffing the hole with mattresses and then shoring the damaged plating and frame with wooden beams. The ship's fighting ability had also been damaged, as the guns along the port side from the forward deck to amidships had been crushed by the carrier's flight deck.

Through it all, Captain Fitz had encouraged Goodfellow to hold the ship tight against the *Franklin* to lessen the movement. As the towing cable was lifted to the *Franklin,* he told his helmsman, "Hit her one more time, and we'll go home." When the towing cable was attached to the carrier and the *Santa Fe* released the messenger line, Fitz made good on his word and to the great relief of his crew gave the order to back his ship away from the *Franklin.*

The fantail of the *Santa Fe* looked like a refugee camp, as it was covered with survivors from the *Franklin,* and there were many more who had been taken below. The final count of those onboard the cruiser was 832 officers and enlisted men, as well as one war correspondent. Of them, 103 had suffered significant injuries requiring medical care, which had quickly overwhelmed the ship's sick bay and forced the medical staff to turn a mess hall into an infirmary and emergency operating room. A few of the casualties had nothing wrong with them physically, but were suffering from "battle fatigue" and were so traumatized that they could not, or would not, give their names.

However, the impression that they were safe was soon broken when the ship's guns began firing shortly after the *Santa Fe* pulled away from the *Franklin.* Harding was walking amidships when the antiaircraft batteries on the starboard side began shooting as men shouted and pointed up toward the sun. All morning long, the Japanese had tried to reach the *Franklin* to finish her off. But the combat air patrol and the screening ships had knocked them down and chased them away. But finally, another Judy dive-bomber had slipped past the defenses and was hurtling down at the barely moving *Franklin, Pittsburgh,* and *Santa Fe.*

The guns on the ships and the plane blazed away at each other. Harding watched with the rest of the men in horror as the dive-bomber pilot dropped his bomb. They all knew that one more direct hit and all their efforts to save the *Franklin* would have been for naught. The *Santa Fe* was also in the dive-bomber's path; a bomb hit to her would have been more devastating than ever with the eight hundred extra men onboard, several hundred of them looking for nonexistent cover on the fantail.

This time, both ships were lucky. Perhaps the pilot couldn't decide between the targets. Or maybe the ships' guns threw off his aim. But the bomb whistled down and struck the water about halfway between the *Santa Fe* and *Franklin,* where it exploded harmlessly.

The pilot pulled out of his dive and tried to escape flying low over the water. He almost made it too. But just as he was about to elude the screen of protective ships, one of the destroyers blasted him into the sea. Onboard the *Franklin* and *Santa Fe,* the haggard crews cheered.

Over the next half hour, two more planes got close enough to pose threats. One was shot down by the combat air patrol just seven miles away from the ships and their cheering crews. Another raced past the stern of the *Santa Fe,* which opened fire but then had to stop shooting because Corsairs were following too close. The U.S. fighters finally tracked the enemy pilot down and sent him tumbling into the sea.

As General Quarters sounded during the attacks, Harding made his way to his battle station, although there would be little call for the ship's big guns. The *Santa Fe* joined the screen of protecting ships, traveling counterclockwise because her port side guns were useless. The *Franklin* under tow by *Pittsburgh* was making less than three knots, and they were only fifty miles from Japan. It was going to be a long night and a long trip home with a war that seemed to be a long way from being over.

CHAPTER TWENTY-FOUR

The Flag's Still Flying!

USS Franklin

Water Tender 3rd Class Sam Rhodes knew he was in a bad spot. The fire on the flight deck had been beaten back to the midpoint of the island, but the bombs continued to explode farther aft, as rockets, bullets, and pieces of shrapnel whistled through the air around him. He was the lead man on one of the fire hoses for the moment, but he was tired and scared, pouring what seemed an insignificant stream of water into a wall of flames and smoke that towered above him like an angry red and black monster.

Thanks to Lieutenant Gary, he had escaped with the nearly three hundred other men trapped in the third deck mess hall for several hours. Some of the men had fallen during the arduous trek and had to be carried by their shipmates, or they collapsed once they hit the flight deck. Most of the injured suffered from smoke inhalation and a few from "battle fatigue." They were transferred to the *Santa Fe,* which was parked alongside the carrier like an admiral's motor launch.

Many of the other men, such as Rhodes, had caught their breath and pitched in to save the ship. There were only two hoses operating on the forward part of the flight deck, so several of the officers, like Cmdr. Joe Taylor and Lt. "Red" Morgan, had organized teams of men to fight the fires in shifts. Two men would man a hose for a few minutes until nearly prostrate from the heat, and then they would be replaced by two more. After a shift, the men would be called over for a shot of "medicine" out of a case of whiskey bottles that had been liberated from the officer's wardrooms, also known as "Officers' Country," and so braced would be ready when it was their turn again.

While manning the hose, Rhodes tried to keep his concentration on the job rather than the crumpled, mangled shapes of dead shipmates that littered the flight deck and were revealed when the smoke would lift. Sometimes the voice of a wounded man would cry out from the smoke for help, and other sailors would rush in, heedless of the danger.

A bomb went off, knocking Rhodes and his partner to the deck. When they picked themselves up, the other man announced that he had had enough. The ship was doomed. "I'm going over the side."

Wearily, Rhodes looked up at the island. The captain was on the bridge shouting orders, apparently not ready to give up his ship. Then the smoke cleared for a moment, and there flying from the aft part of the superstructure was the *Franklin's* "battle flag," the Stars and Stripes. All around the flag, the steel accoutrements of a modern warship—the masts, the radio and radar antennas—were toppled. The flag itself was tattered and burned; Rhodes could see several large holes in the fabric, and yet that piece of cloth waved undaunted. He took courage in the sight and found new strength. He had been a sailor for less than three months, in combat a mere two days, but the *Franklin* was his ship and he wasn't ready to leave her, not while that flag was still flying above her tormented deck.

"Wait," Rhodes said to the other sailor, "the flag's still flying." But just then there was another explosion, and he found himself alone. He fell on the hose to control it and looked behind him. His compatriot was running for the edge of the flight deck. "YOU SON OF A BITCH!" he shouted after the man, who leaped into space, his arms pumping and legs spinning like he was riding a bicycle.

Before Rhodes could despair, another man rushed up and took the deserter's place. That's how it was that day—every time a man faltered or was laid low, another would step into his spot. They were so young, and yet, surrounded by acts of bravery, men who never thought of themselves as heroes, and were indeed afraid, found the courage to do what was required of them.

None were braver than the priest, Lt. Cmdr. Joseph O'Callahan. He moved calmly about the flight deck without so much as ducking when a bomb would explode or a rocket whistled overhead. Other men would fall to the wooden planking and look up to see him standing there and rise to rally around him. If he knelt, it was to administer to a fallen sailor, calling for medical help, or performing last rites if the man was beyond assistance.

When Captain Gehres became concerned that the five-inch gun turret below the bridge was going to blow up due to the fires in the hangar deck below, he spotted O'Callahan and asked him to get men to hose down the ammunition. The priest had run off into the smoke and returned shortly leading a dozen men. The hoses were needed for fighting the fire on the deck, so the priest had decided on the next best option. In spite of his claustrophobia, which made the turret an even more fearsome place to him, the chaplain entered with the men and they passed the hot ammunition out of the turret and over the side of the ship.

The act was no small matter. If the ammunition had detonated, the bridge would have been destroyed and then, lacking a captain, the ship would have surely been abandoned. "That's got to be the bravest man I've ever seen," Gehres remarked to the other men on the bridge as he watched the chaplain.

O'Callahan was tireless. He heard there was a five-hundred-pound bomb lying on the hangar deck, unexploded but unstable, as it had been exposed to the flames for hours. There was no telling when one more bomb blast would be the final blow for the *Franklin*, or what sailor might be passing by when it went off. He went to find someone to help him get rid of it and located Sam Rhodes, who was taking a breather from his fire-fighting duties.

Rhodes accompanied the priest down the ladder into the hangar. They located the bomb and began to roll it carefully toward the edge of the hangar deck. The metal casing of the weapon was hot, so hot that Rhodes felt like he was placing his hands on a heated skillet and told the priest he didn't know if he could continue.

"We don't have much farther to go," O'Callahan encouraged him, though his own hands were seared as well. At last they reached the edge and dumped the bomb into the ocean. The priest smiled and patted him on the shoulder and for the moment, Rhodes forgot the pain in his hands.

Lt. (j.g.) Robert Wassman was on the bridge looking down at the *Santa Fe* when he heard a voice from below. One of his men from the navigation division, Quartermaster 2nd Class Clifton Martin, was waving from the deck of the cruiser.

"Lieutenant Wassman! Lieutenant Wassman! Here I am," Martin shouted. "Shall I come back aboard, sir?" He had been blown overboard by an explosion and picked up by the *Santa Fe,* but he wanted back aboard the burning ship.

"Hell, no!" Wassman yelled back. "Stay where you are." They had all the men they needed for the few hoses that were in operation. There was nothing for Martin to do, and from the sounds of it, they all might still have to abandon ship.

Martin looked disappointed but stepped back into the crowd of men on the cruiser. Wassman had other concerns. He had been fighting fires all morning but recently reported to the bridge, where he heard the navigator, Cmdr. Jurika, asking if anybody knew the maximum list the ship could tolerate before it rolled over. Someone said that the shipbuilder's manual claimed nineteen degrees.

Captain Gehres turned to Jurika and asked if he thought he ought to let the men on the forward part of the flight deck, those not involved in fighting the fires or rescue efforts, abandon ship. "Not yet," Jurika replied. They would have to keep an eye, however, on the inclinometer. Within an hour after the attack, the list had been eight degrees and climbed at a rate of more than one degree an hour since.

With all the talk of capsizing and abandoning ship, Wassman's thoughts turned to his men trapped in the steering engine room aft, where they had been told to sit tight because of the flooding on the decks above them. He recalled Jurika's tale about the sinking of the *Lexington* and how men had been trapped belowdecks when their own destroyers finished her off. The men now trapped had remained in their position without panicking, relaying messages to the engineering spaces, which eventually had to be abandoned, and being told that they would not be forgotten.

Wassman wasn't going to allow them to be forgotten now. He announced that he was going to find a way to get to those men and get them out. When the superior officers looked at him blankly, he grew agitated and demanded that rescue breathing apparatus be located so that he could negotiate the smoke-filled depths of the ship.

Two breathers were located and Wassman left with Quartermaster 2nd Class Gilbert Abbott. A native of Sayre, Pennsylvania, Abbott had been one of the men led to safety by Lieutenant (j.g.) Gary. He knew what it was like to be trapped in the dark, running out of air to breathe, while it sounded for all the world like the ship was being torn apart. After his escape, he had been one of those on the telephone to the men in the steering engine room aft who had assured the men that the ship wasn't being abandoned. "And if we do, we'll come get you first," Abbott told them, and now he too intended to keep his word.

Wassman and Abbott made their way out of the island. Going aft on the burning flight deck was impossible, so they found a hatch leading down to the second deck, which ran beneath the hangar deck. From there, they began to work towards the stern, picking and choosing their way through the shattered and flooded passageways and compartments.

Without the rescue breathers, the two men wouldn't have lasted five minutes on their dark and smoke-filled journey. Often their way was blocked and they had to retrace their steps—locate more of the breathers—and then try to find another way. At times, they reached flooded compartments and had to open the doors and let the water flood into where they stood so that they could go forward. All the while, the bulkheads shivered and shook from the explosions overhead in the hangar.

It took several hours, but they at last reached the spaces above the steering room aft. However, they knew that taking the men back the way they'd come wouldn't be possible; they didn't have enough breathers. So they needed to find a shorter route to fresh air and safety.

Continuing aft, the two found a way to the fantail, which by now had been abandoned. The destruction was incredible, steel had twisted and melted. Bodies lay everywhere—some burned beyond all recognition or torn to pieces, others as though they had simply gone to sleep.

Just as they were about to head back for the trapped men, Wassman and Abbott heard a cry of pain and traced it to a gun sponson where they found a badly injured sailor. As they picked him up using a blanket as a stretcher, the sailor smiled and weakly began to sing, "*Happy Days Are Here Again.*"

They hauled the wounded sailor up to the flight deck. The fires had abated, but just walking was treacherous on the tilting deck. The heat from the fires had melted the tar used to coat the wooden planking, which made the footing as slippery as ice. Once, Wassman began sliding toward one of the gaping holes ripped into the deck by the explosions. The wounded man pointed and said, "Help the lieutenant," just in time for Abbott to grab him.

They finally reached the island where other men were recruited to help with the wounded man. Grabbing more rescue breathers, Wassman turned to go, but Abbott was done. He'd had an operation on his arms only a couple of days before, and the stitches had split; he was bleeding profusely. But another of the lieutenant's men, Quartermaster 1st Class Virgil Ryan, volunteered to go back with him for the men left behind.

Captain Gehres would later describe the maneuvering of the *Santa Fe's* Captain Fitz as "the most daring piece of seamanship I've ever witnessed." But the carrier skipper's mind blackened with anger when he saw what appeared to be able-bodied men from his ship fleeing to the relative safety of the cruiser.

Gehres's orders to the department heads who could be located by messengers was to "stand by to transfer all wounded and evacuate all personnel not required to fight from the ship." But he had not given a general order to abandon ship. He was particularly incensed to see a great many men in officers' uniforms crossing to the cruiser, while common sailors fought so valiantly for the ship.

However, most of those who left were not abandoning the ship out of cowardice. The destruction of the ship's internal communications system was responsible for a lot of the confusion. The captain's orders were relayed by messengers who often couldn't find the department heads, or anyone else in charge for that matter, and then spread by word of mouth. Many of the men who jumped into the water to reach the cruiser, or swung across on ropes, were cut off from any senior officers. They were on a ship that seemed on the verge of rolling over or blowing apart at the seams and based their decisions on what they saw, as well as the rumors.

Early on they had witnessed the exodus of Admirals Davison and Bogan, along with the rest of the flag officers and their enlisted personnel. Frightened sailors, noncommissioned officers, and officers reported having "heard" that the order to abandon ship had been given. The rumors gained credence when they saw the *Santa Fe* take such drastic, and dangerous, measures to come alongside. Then they watched as other men, including quite a few in officers' clothing, scrambled over the radio antennas and brow. Suddenly, the destroyers they could see in the distance looked ominous; the tin cans were only waiting for the order, some theorized, to sink Big Ben.

Part of the confusion regarding the "officers" abandoning ship could be blamed on O'Callahan. The men clawing their way out from the interior of the ship were often soaked to the bone by their own sweat or by the water poured onto the fires that flooded passageways, sometimes chest deep. Those from the engineering spaces had been subjected to temperatures as high as 130 degrees and emerged to outside air temperatures in the low 50s on a cloudy, breezy day. They stood shivering uncontrollably, and hypothermia—the sometimes fatal loss of core body temperature—became a risk.

O'Callahan tried to help the men with a shot of brandy or whiskey—actually a bad idea for hypothermia but certainly cheering—and told the men to change into dry clothing he had sent others to gather. The third deck, where the enlisted men were quartered, was unreachable and much of it was water-logged anyway; the only quantities of dry clothing had come from officers' staterooms on the gallery and second decks on the forward part of the ship. Many of the "officers" seen on the *Santa Fe* by Gehres and others were actually enlisted men.

Some of the *Santa Fe*'s crew, who had also heard the rumors, encouraged the exodus from the *Franklin*. They too had seen the "officers," and were anxious to get away from the carrier before it exploded or the Japanese returned.

Aviation Coxswain Frank Turner was told by a chief petty officer that the ship's air officer, Cmdr. Henry Hale, had ordered all nonessential personnel, which included the flight deck crew, to leave the ship with the air group. Turner had been taking a breather on the foc'sle from helping fight the fires when the chief said he better get moving because the *Santa Fe* was getting ready to cast off.

Turner hesitated. He was no coward. Like the other Airedales, he had performed one of the most dangerous jobs aboard the ship with courage. He had also been wounded during the kamikaze attack in October. His first inclination was to stay with the *Franklin,* but the chief reminded him that the captain had given the order.

The men on the cruiser saw him at the rail and called up to him. The *Santa Fe* was beginning to back away from the *Franklin*. At the last moment, he grabbed one of the lines hanging down from the flight deck and swung across into the waiting arms of the rescuers.

Beginning a few minutes after the initial attack until about the time the *Santa Fe* pulled away, an estimated sixty of the sixty-six 500-pound bombs, and probably eight of the ten 250-pound bombs loaded on the flight deck's planes exploded. A definite count was not possible, because some planes were blown overboard by detonations next to them without their bombs going off.

Most of the bombs exploded beneath the planes, tearing holes in the flight deck. Some fell through the holes created by previous explosions and burst on the hangar deck below. All twelve Tiny Tims on the flight deck ignited. Most left the ship, terrifying the men on the vessels that had drawn in to assist, especially the *Santa Fe,* which had several rockets pass within a few feet. A few blew up beneath the Corsairs. Four of five Tiny Tims attached to planes in the hangar exploded there.

Other ships in the *Franklin's* task group and other task groups, more than twenty miles away and over the horizon, reported hearing distinct explosions until they evolved into one continuous roar. Anyone who heard the sound and understood what was happening was convinced that there would be nothing left of the *Franklin* to save.

In addition to the bombs and rockets, ready storage lockers filled with ammunition for the planes' .50-caliber machine guns, as well as the ship's 20-millimeter, 40-millimeter, and five-inch guns, exploded as flames enveloped them. They continued to shoot and explode for several hours after the big munitions stopped.

Water Tender 2nd Class Ernest Scott escaped from the third deck thanks to the heroics of Marine corporal Stephen Nowak, only to find that the flight deck wasn't any safer. In some ways, it was more dangerous with all the bombs going off and bullets and rockets flying. But everywhere he looked he saw a ship of heroes.

Scott didn't stand around gawking for long. An officer grabbed him and Eddie Carlisle and told them to climb down a ladder on the starboard side of the ship into a 40-millimeter gun sponson. The fires from the broken aviation gas pump were closing in on the tub, and they were to throw the ammunition overboard before it exploded.

The trio was doing as told when a small arms locker behind them began to explode. Individual rounds flew around their heads as though they were under fire by an army. Seeing this, some of the sailors manning the hoses on the *Santa Fe*—separated from them by fifteen feet of sloshing sea—urged them to jump into the water. "We'll throw you a line," they said.

Scott considered the offer. Across the way, he could see that a great many of the *Franklin's* crew were already there. The cruiser represented safety, behind him were hundreds of dead and wounded men, fire and explosions.

On the other hand, the water looked dangerous too. The *Santa Fe's* propellers were still turning to keep the ship hard against the *Franklin.* He was afraid that if he jumped in, he might get caught up in the churn created by the massive propellers. He waved to the crew and shook his head, he was going to stay with his own ship.

However, it didn't look like he was going to be able to stay where he was either. The ship was now listing so far over that the sponson was touching the water; soon he was going to be in the ocean, like it or not, and perhaps with a thirty-thousand-ton aircraft carrier on top of him. When the order to abandon the sponson was passed down, he and Carlisle gladly obeyed.

Wet and chilled from the waves that splashed over the edge of the sponson, Scott was one of those who benefited when O'Callahan handed out dry officers' uniforms. He continued to be impressed with the priest's tireless efforts—actually with both chaplains, as the Protestant chaplain, Lt. Grimes Gatlin was also fighting fires and tending to the wounded.

He had never seen two braver men and couldn't have agreed more with the chief petty officer, who, when a sailor questioned which denomination a dying sailor wanted present, growled, "What the hell difference does it make which chaplain you find? It's the same God, ain't it?"

Many of the most courageous acts of courage had few witnesses or went unrecorded in the official reports. In another part of the ship, Steward's Mate 1st Class Matthew Little prayed for the same God to help him deal with the latest task set before him. He had continued to fight the fires barefoot, even as the metal deck beneath him grew so hot that the water boiled.

Yet that was easier than what he had been asked to do once the fires were under control and the explosions subsided. He was told to search for wounded men and bring them to the wardrooms that had been converted to medical clinics.

So he had scoured the hangar deck, picking up men—some of them missing limbs, or torn open, or so severely burned that their race could not be identified—and brought them to the doctors and corpsmen. When he could find no more on the hangar deck, he went down below into the dark, wet, smoky third deck to look for others, identifying the living by feeling for them among the dead.

When he had left his family home in South Carolina, his father urged him to "be a man." If there was any doubt before that Matthew Little had quickly grown up to be the sort of man his father would have been proud of, it would have been dispelled by the sight of him staggering through the smoke with a wounded sailor in his arms.

The *Santa Fe* had taken on more than 800 men from the *Franklin*. The five ships of Destroyer Division 104—the *Hunt, Marshall, Hickox, Tingey,* and *Miller*—picked up another 850; the *Hunt,* 442 of them and the *Marshall* another 212. To rescue men from the sea, the destroyers had often slowed, or even stopped, leaving themselves vulnerable to attacks from planes or submarines. In between their lifeguard duties, they had circled the heavy ships like guard dogs protecting a flock, while the combat air patrol flew overhead, keeping one eye out for bandits and another trained on the ocean looking for survivors. The men in the water were spread out over several miles, making their rescue a prolonged ordeal. While the swells were not huge, they had grown during the course of the day and with tides and currents had scattered the men.

Many died before the destroyers could reach them, some before they even hit the water. The sailors on the destroyers also found dozens floating in their life jackets with broken necks because they had jumped from the decks with their battle helmets strapped to their chins. Many others drowned— sometimes quickly, having been knocked unconscious first, or in panicky attempts to stay afloat, or, more slowly, succumbing to exhaustion and hypothermia.

Not all the brave deeds that day were accomplished by the men on the ships. In the water, men struggled not just to save their own lives, but those of their shipmates, fighting to hold a semiconscious friend's head above water or forcing them to move to stay warm. Sometimes men were picked up still trying to save shipmates who had long since perished.

For some, there was nothing they could do once they were rescued but remember the sacrifice a friend or a stranger made for them. When Yeoman 2nd Class Guido Cavallo was picked up by a destroyer after nearly seven hours in the water, he was still looking for his friend Yeoman 2nd Class John Brown, who had given him his life jacket before they jumped.

Those in the water combated many fears. Of drowning. Of sharks. Of the unknown depths of the ocean. But the worst was that the Japanese would find them first. They had all heard the stories of Japanese planes and ships machine-gunning helpless sailors, or, worse, of capturing Americans only to torture and behead them.

Edwin Garrison had ended up holding onto the sides of his raft with nine other men. The others were convinced that they were going to be strafed by a Japanese plane. But they were all members of the Black Gang and didn't know one type of aircraft from another, so they weren't sure which of the black dots swarming around in the air were dangerous.

Garrison had taught himself to recognize all Allied planes by name. He figured that those he didn't know would be the enemy. When his comrades started panicking every time they saw a plane, he told them they only had to worry if he yelled "Dive!" Then they were to go down as deep as they could and count to ten before coming back up.

Knowing that an enemy pilot would start shooting on a strafing run while still more than a hundred yards from his target, Garrison figured that he would wait until he saw the guns firing before he gave the command to dive. To calm the others, he started to point out the different planes in view. "That one's ours. So's that one. The one coming our way is ours too." Then he spotted one he didn't recognize. "That one's not ours," he said.

A moment later, the unidentified "bogey" flapped its wings, and he realized it was a seabird. He looked around to tell the others, but none were in sight. One by one they came back to the surface, gasping; two stayed down so long, he worried that they had drowned.

"Wait until I tell you to dive," he said. "Otherwise, you'll come up too soon and be shot." As it turned out, he never had to give the command. They did see one Japanese plane make a run at the *Franklin,* but it was shot down to their cheers by an American fighter plane.

Garrison wondered how things were on the *Franklin,* which was in the distance but had apparently stopped moving. He saw two destroyers off her port side and figured that they were just waiting to finish her off. He was so intent on watching the carrier that he didn't notice the motor launch from the destroyer *Hunt* until it was nearly on top of them.

"Is there anybody else you've seen?" the coxswain asked after they climbed into his boat. Garrison told him about a dead pilot who was floating nearby, but the coxswain said, "I'll pick him up later. You guys are so cold you're going to shake my boat apart. I'm going to take you to my ship."

Only then did Garrison notice how cold he was; he couldn't stop shivering and figured his face was probably as blue as his companions' faces. It took him a moment to recognize another man he new as "Sears," who had been picked up a few minutes before his group.

When they reached the *Hunt,* they climbed up a cargo net that had been lowered down the side of the ship. Just as Sears began to climb, a wave pushed the launch against the side of the destroyer, crushing his foot as he screamed. Otherwise, they had all escaped their ordeal without a scratch.

Climbing onboard, Garrison was met by a corpsman who handed him a cup of tomato soup. "Drink this, it'll warm you up," he said. Garrison did as told and drank it down greedily. He was so cold that he didn't notice how hot the liquid was until the next day when the skin peeled from the roof of his mouth.

A sailor named J. B. Alt took the nude Garrison to his locker and gave the naked man his last pair of undershorts. Alt then escorted him to a sleeping compartment. Garrison was walking toward a bunk when he felt a tap on top of his head. Looking up, he saw Stanley Sward, the Wisconsin sailor who had been with him when Fred Holdsworth died. "You'll never know how glad I am to see you," he said.

Garrison smiled. "So is this heaven?" he asked remembering Sward's fear of drowning.

"Better," Sward replied. They both laughed until they fell into exhausted sleep.

It took nearly six frightening hours in the dark before Lt. (j.g.) Robert Wassman and Quartermaster 1st Class Virgil Ryan were ready to bring the men out from the steering engine room aft. They'd worked their way back from the hangar deck, looking for alternate routes, and done the best they could, but it still wasn't going to be easy. The smoke was thick and moving through the passageways and compartments involved a lot of climbing and crawling through the maze of twisted steel. In places, the water was still chest deep.

Small flashlights and battle lanterns were their only illumination and the beams often could not pierce the dense smoke. Then again, sometimes it was better not to see too clearly as they pushed aside the bodies of their shipmates. They wondered how many more—both living and dead—might be somewhere in depths of the ship; the dead no longer caring, the living wondering if anyone would find them before it was too late. To get through the fear and sorrow, Wassman and Ryan focused on saving those they could.

Every man on the *Franklin* owed a debt of gratitude to the men in the steering engine room aft. Early on they'd kept the bridge in touch with the Black Gang in the fire rooms and engineering spaces. But they'd performed another even more valuable service later when the *Pittsburgh* began to tow the *Franklin*. The cruiser had struggled to tow the carrier because of the list so that they could head south away from Japan and toward Ulithi. Even pulling at the carrier from a right angle wasn't doing the job so long as the *Franklin's* rudder was stuck in the center position. Abbott, who'd insisted on being the one who stayed in contact with the men and relaying the occasional message to them from Wassman, had been advising them to lie quietly and not exert themselves. But now he had to reverse himself at the request of the captain. "Boys, I need you to manually turn the rudder," he said, explaining the situation.

Turning the rudder by hand required the effort of all the men hauling on a chain. Even working quickly the task took a half hour of heavy exertion to accomplish. Then they learned that they had turned the rudder the wrong way and had to go all the way back the other direction. But at last the *Pittsburgh* was able to pull the carrier in a wide circle and began to head south.

Wassman was worried that the men were running out of air. Dr. Fuelling had said that given the size of the compartment, the men would probably last twenty-four hours if they were calm and absolutely still. The young lieutenant figured that under the circumstances it was a lot to have asked the men to remain calm, and then turning the rudder had certainly used their oxygen more quickly.

The danger of capsizing had been alleviated when Lt. (j.g.) Stanley Graham found a way to transfer thousands of gallons of fuel oil from the starboard side to the port side. Graham, who had also been instrumental in leading the firefighting crews on the hangar deck, had then set a crew to manually opening vents on the port side of the ship to counterbalance with seawater.

By late in the afternoon, the major fires also were pretty much out. A few smoldered here and there, and every once in a while, one would flare back up, requiring the damage control parties to rush back out with the hoses. But the explosions had finally stopped.

The principal danger now was the Japanese. The enemy knew that there was a wounded aircraft carrier only fifty miles from their coast, and they weren't going to give up. The issue was more than one side's efforts to save an aircraft carrier and the other side's determination to sink one. What happened to the *Franklin* could affect the entire war.

If the Japanese military could just sink one of the big American attack carriers, it would be a tremendous morale booster for their people. It would be proof that a single plane could stop a carrier; if they could stop the carriers, they could stop the invasion of Japan. So inspired, the people of Japan could be encouraged to fight on and put up with whatever the Americans wanted to dish out. The Japanese military leaders could also hope, having never quite given up on the idea that Americans were "soft," that the deaths of several thousand sailors in one blow would demoralize the American public. A deal might still be struck.

The American military wanted to give the enemy no such glimmer of hope. As Japanese cities, including Tokyo, suffered, they knew that the peace faction was gaining a larger voice, but the power was still in the hands of the war council. The Japanese people—and most importantly, the emperor—needed to be convinced that nothing short of the complete destruction of Japan was the price of continuing the war. Sinking an American aircraft carrier might cause them to believe otherwise. The Japanese would be back for the *Franklin*—that was a given.

Wassman wanted the men out of the steering room before nightfall. The Japanese knew that their best chance of slipping past the combat air patrol and the gunners on the ships would be in the dark.

As he had worked his way towards the men in the bottom of the ship, Wassman thanked the former captain of the *Franklin*, James Shoemaker, who had insisted that his junior officers know their way around the ship. As a result he knew every passage, every ladder, every possible way down, without that knowledge he might have never reached the men in time.

When Wassman and Ryan at last reached the hatch that led down into steering engine room aft, they rapped on the metal, trying to send a message to the men below in Morse Code. They had drained most of the water from the room into other compartments, but there was still quite a bit, and they needed to be careful when the hatch was opened. They were also going to have to move as efficiently as possible to get through the foul air of passageways.

Down below, Holbrook Davis, Bill Hamel, Jim Gudbrandsen, Larry Costa, and Norman Mayer heard the metal banging with joy. There had been some pretty dark moments in that black hole. When the second dive-bomber dropped his bomb a hundred feet in from the *Franklin*, the ship had literally been lifted partway out of the water and when it settled was listing even more. They had heard the bomb and felt its effects. If this was a new series of attacks by the Japanese, they knew the ship could not sustain much more damage.

Their spirits were lifted when they heard that Wassman was coming for them. But when hour after hour passed with no sign of the lieutenant and the room grew noticeably stuffier, they began to wonder if he would reach them in time.

They recognized that the rhythmic rapping on the hatch was Morse Code, but none of them knew it. They rapped back but in a way that told Wassman that they didn't understand. The lieutenant sent Ryan back to the island to tell the men to open the hatch, but only a little at first to allow the water to drain down into their compartment slowly. They were also to remove their life jackets, as many of the spaces they would have to traverse were barely enough to fit through.

The sun was setting, about 7:00 P.M., when Wassman triumphantly reported to the bridge with the five men from the steering engine room aft. Three of the men were nearly unconscious from smoke inhalation and the stress of the day, but they all managed to salute the captain.

Gehres saluted them back and sent his Marine orderly to fetch a bottle of "medicinal" Scotch to toast their contribution to saving Big Ben.

Thanks to the men in the steering engine room aft, the *Franklin* was heading in the right direction. Progress was slow, however, a mere three knots, and by nightfall the ship was only ten miles or so from where they had started with the *Pittsburgh*. Not far enough. Intermittently, fires would break out, a beacon for any Japanese planes or submarines hunting in the area.

Gehres knew that if his ship was to survive, they would have to get her moving under her own power. Lieutenant Gary was asked to rise above and beyond the call of duty. Then again, he had been doing so all day.

After leading the men from the mess hall below, he had immediately set to work fixing the damaged water pumps to bring more fire hoses on line. Then he had heard that more men were trapped in a forward machinery room, and he had gone for them. When he got there, eight men were dead in one compartment from asphyxiation, but he located eight others, whom he led to safety.

At 9:30 P.M., the bridge received a report from Gary and two other ship's engineers who had been sent to assess the damage in the fire rooms. Gary's biggest concern when he got down to the fire rooms was that the water and oil that had seeped down from above would have reached the burners mounted four feet above the deck. He was relieved to see that it hadn't and thought that despite ruptured pipes that leaked steam and some oil mixed in with the water, one of the boilers in particular could be fired up right away, and the others brought back on line in fairly short order. However, if the boiler was going to be lit, he was going to need a team from the Black Gang to operate it.

About 10:30, Gary had returned to the flight deck, where he approached a group of men gathered on the flight deck and asked if any of them were members of the Black Gang. A dozen men stepped forward. He told them to fetch some battle lanterns and report back to him. When the men returned and asked where they were going, he said, "We're going below to see if we can get one of the boilers going."

Among the men who stepped forward was Sam Rhodes. He had had about all the excitement he wanted for one day. Trapped belowdecks. Fighting fires while ducking explosions. But he had done his duty. Now, however, he blanched at the thought of heading back down into the dark bowels of the *Franklin*. Less than twelve hours earlier, he had feared he might never get out and didn't want to go back now. The ship seemed dead to him; for the first time in months, the boilers had been silenced, and he missed the reassuring vibration of her power plant. But it was Lieutenant Gary who was asking, the man who said he would lead them to safety and had done it. He was the sort of officer, Rhodes decided, that he would follow into the depths of hell. Which, he thought wryly, was a pretty good description of where they were going to go.

The trip down to the fire room took nearly an hour as they climbed and crawled their way through the tangled mess, waded through drowned passages, and tried to ignore bodies. At last they reached their destination and cleared away the debris from around the boiler.

Gary checked the equipment and said he thought the oil burner was operable. The men with him certainly hoped so; otherwise, if there was a leak or something was broken, they might be about to start a whole new fire that could doom the ship. There was only one other problem: No one could find the device used to light the wick to ignite the oil burners.

They were going to have to send someone back into the tangled mess of a ship to find a flame. But then Rhodes remembered his trusty Zippo lighter. He brought it out of his pocket and flicked open the top, and like always, it lit the first time. Rhodes got the honor of lighting the wick and shoving it into the oil burner. For a moment, nothing happened, then with a gigantic "WHOOSH" the burner ignited.

"We got fire!" the men shouted and began dancing a crazy jig around the dark fire room. They stopped their celebration to listen to the familiar sound of the burner heating up the water that would drive the turbines that would turn the shafts that would spin the propellers so that they could get the hell away from Japan. As Rhodes closed his Zippo and stuck it back in his pocket, he thought it sounded like the heart of the *Franklin* was beating again.

The importance of getting the boiler working was demonstrated about an hour later, when members of the crew who were outside began to point toward the north. Twenty miles back in the direction they had come from, thousands of tracers were streaking into the sky while orange puffs of anti-aircraft shells exploded, making the night seem almost festive. Almost—heading in the opposite direction, the flaming trails of dying airplanes plunged toward the sea.

They would learn the next day that the Japanese had sent forty-five planes to find the *Franklin*—a ship that Tokyo Rose crowed had been sent that day to the bottom of the sea with a great loss of life. The planes arrived about where the *Franklin* would have been if the *Pittsburgh* had not taken the ship under tow. But instead of a burned-out aircraft carrier dead in the water, the enemy had run into a carrier task group that had waited in ambush.

Forty-one of the Japanese planes were shot down. The Americans did not get away unscathed; two more big carriers, the *Essex* and *Wasp*, were hit and joined the *Franklin* and her screening ships on the twentieth. The former suffered only slight damage and light casualties, though enough that she needed to retire to Ulithi for quick repairs; the *Wasp*, however, was hit by a bomb that pierced the flight and hangar decks, exploding in a mess hall, killing more than one hundred men. But the Japanese were denied their prize, the *Franklin*.

Still, it was a close call. A couple of hours earlier, a fire had broken out again on the fantail. The crew had rushed to quell the flames, and the destroyer *Miller* had pulled up to the stern to help with its hoses. If the fire had erupted when the Japanese were seeking the *Franklin*, the fires would have summoned them like moths to a lightbulb.

As it was, the Japanese had come too close to finding them again. So it was with great relief that about 1:00 A.M. on March 20, 1945, enough steam had been generated and the gigantic propellers of the *Franklin* began to turn again. Still, there was a long way to go—they were only seventy miles from Japan and more than two thousand to Ulithi. They were not out of danger yet.

AFTERMATH

CHAPTER 25

The 704 Club

March 20, 1945
USS Franklin

L ooking down from a 40-millimeter gun tub mounted above the main bridge, Gunner's Mate 2nd Class Ben Ricks watched the officer who was sitting on the flight deck with the small battery-operated transceiver. That radio was the gun crew's only connection with the other ships that surrounded the *Franklin* or, more importantly, with the other ships' combat information centers. The officer would be the first to know which direction any bandits would be coming from.

They could use all the advance warning they could get. The four-barreled "quad" was the only working gun on the ship, but the gun wasn't fully operational, because all of the electronic controls and radar tracking had been knocked out, and the ship was still in range of the Japanese air corps.

When he left his home in Ashland, Oregon, Ricks had been worried that all the action would be over before he could get into the fighting. He had enlisted in the Navy as soon as he graduated from high school in June 1944, hoping to be a torpedo man on a submarine. Instead, the Navy sent him to gunnery school and assigned him to the *Franklin* while the ship was in Bremerton for repairs after the kamikaze hit. The ship had lasted two days in the combat zone, and that was plenty enough fighting for Ricks.

When the bombs hit, he was in the mess hall with his best friend and fellow gunner's mate Luke Oliver, from Hopewell Junction, New York. They had tried to get to their battle stations on the guns, but ended up in the mess hall where they started. Eventually, they were led to safety by Lieutenant Gary.

Ricks had fought the fires and was one of the men who had gone with Father O'Callahan into the five-inch gun turret to dispose of the ammunition. Then he and Oliver had been assigned to the 40-millimeter above the bridge along with Gunner's Mate 1st Class Mike Gowden, Staff Sgt. Bob Dixon of the Marine Corps, Gunner's Mate 3rd Class Robert Oxley, Yeoman 3rd Class Wilfred Williams, SSML 3rd Class Charles Finkenster, who worked in the laundry, and Wells Wilson and William Albrecht, both of rated seaman second class.

They had spent a tense night huddled around their gun and praying that the damage control parties would extinguish the fires that occasionally flared up before the Japs saw them. They were young men, most of them on their first tour, and their conversations to pass the time involved a lot of bravado and heroic recounting of the day's events. But there were also long silences as they stared out at the now-threatening darkness, wondering if they were going to make it home again. To calm their nerves, they had smoked a lot, slipping into an ammunition storage space beneath the gun mount so that the glow of their cigarettes wouldn't attract any unwanted attention. When they ran out of cigarettes, Ricks went to find more and hit the jackpot on the second deck, where he found forty-four packs in an open locker. They were all gone by morning.

When the sun came up in the morning, it was encouraging to see that the *Santa Fe* and *Pittsburgh* had been joined by two more cruisers, the USS *Guam* and *Alaska,* as well as two more destroyers. But the most comforting change from the low point of the day before was to once again feel the familiar vibration of the ship's power plant and propellers and see the traces of smoke coming out of her stacks.

The engineering crews had continued working through the night to bring more boilers on line, and by noon the ship was making nearly fifteen knots with the aid of the *Pittsburgh.* A little later, the officer with the transceiver informed the *Pittsburgh* that the *Franklin* had built up enough speed to cast off and proceed on her own.

The transceiver had been invaluable after someone on the *Santa Fe* had noticed one of the *Franklin's* communications warrant officers, W. R. Modeen, standing on the flight deck with the equipment and a line of communication was established. It was the *Franklin's* only access to radar information and made it easier to maneuver in concert—such as defensive zigzagging—with the screen of ships surrounding her. The equipment was especially important at night, when semaphore was useless and they didn't dare risk using signal lights. Because the transceiver worked only in a "line of sight" situation, the officer assigned to relay the messages sat or stood in the most open spot on the ship, the flight deck.

By the afternoon of the twentieth, Ricks and his comrades had been on the gun for nearly twenty-four hours without much of a break. But as he shifted his gaze from the officer with the transceiver to other men on the flight deck, he wouldn't have traded places. What particularly caught his attention were the black mess stewards picking their way through the wreckage on the flight deck, stopping occasionally to scoop objects up and place them in the trash cans they carted. It had taken Ricks a minute to figure out what they were doing, but then he realized they had been given the onerous task of cleaning up human remains. He shivered at the thought and was glad he was no closer.

Ricks's attention snapped back to the officer with the transceiver when the man stood up and ran for the bridge. There were bogeys in the area, a lot of them, he yelled. The combat air patrol had intercepted the planes, but the gunners needed to keep a sharp eye out. Before long, the gun crew could see tiny black dots racing through the gray sky. Wispy trails of smoke spiraled down into the sea, indicating the American fighters were on the job. But the bogeys appeared to be pressing closer, as demonstrated when they could see the small white geysers made by Japanese planes crashing into the water.

The combat air patrol couldn't keep them all out. The officer with the transceiver shouted that a bandit had slipped past the fighters and was coming in somewhere on the starboard side.

The men anxiously scanned that direction, looking up and down from the low-lying clouds to the slate-colored waves. Gowden was the gun captain, he would do the shooting. Oxley was the pointer who would raise the barrels up and down; Ricks was the trainer, responsible for swinging the barrels back and forth. Oliver, Albrecht, and Wilson were the loaders, while the rest of the crew served to hand up ammunition or put the shells in the clips.

Suddenly, Wilson pointed up. "There he is!"

The men swung the barrels toward the target and Gowden yelled, "Commence firing."

The Zero dove fast, carrying a five-hundred-pound bomb. The screening ships took him under fire but soon had to stop for fear of hitting the *Franklin*—it was between the men on the single quad and the pilot in a contest of who would blink first. The closer the pilot got, the surer he was of hitting his target, but the greater the risk of catching a 40-millimeter shell.

The *Franklin* gunners fired as fast as they could. Cordite smoke surrounded the mount, and the deck shook from the gun's pounding. Nothing else existed except the gun and the incoming plane, and the gun crew could have sworn that the pilot was aiming for them, not the ship.

The enemy flyer was experienced and talented. He dipped and wove at nearly three hundred miles an hour. Small flames flickered from the guns in its wings, tearing into the carrier. Closer and closer he flew until it seemed he couldn't miss. Those who saw the Zero coming braced themselves—the thought racing through dozens of minds that the *Franklin* could not take another direct hit. Still, the gun crew did not give up and kept pouring round after round at the plane until the pilot blinked. But only by a matter of feet.

If he had been a kamikaze, they might not have stopped him. But he wasn't, and just before he could have crashed into the ship the gunners forced him to pull up prematurely and release his bomb.

Time seemed to stand still for Ricks, the world suddenly grown quiet as he watched the bomb—black and shiny—sail twenty feet above the flight deck behind the island and a hundred feet beyond into the sea. The explosion lifted the carrier up, but the ship settled back into the water and kept steaming forward.

Meanwhile, the Zero had crossed over the flight deck, and the pilot was trying to make his getaway by flying low just above the waves. The screening ships again tried to shoot him down, but somehow he eluded both the antiaircraft fire and the combat air patrol that chased him. He headed back to Japan to fight again another day.

The gun crew were still mopping the sweat from their brows and congratulating themselves when a head popped over the edge of the gun tub. The face belonged to the captain's orderly, Pvt. Wallace "Wally" Klimkiewicz, who had climbed the ladder on the outside of the pilothouse.

"The captain says, 'Good work, boys,'" he shouted.

The captain's compliment made them smile. But it was a comment they heard later that made them laugh. Apparently, one of the other men on the flight deck who had ducked for cover lifted his head after the explosion and complained, "What's he want, blood?"

The Japanese had missed one excellent opportunity to finish the *Franklin*, but they didn't give up. A little after 4:00 P.M., a dozen more bandits were intercepted forty-eight miles away, and all of them shot down. A half hour later, another dozen were splashed fifty-eight miles to the northwest; then more again at six o'clock, except these closed to within eighteen miles before the Corsairs finished the last of them.

As night closed in, the men on the *Franklin* began to hope that they had seen the last of the Japanese air corps. The ship was now steaming at a respectable twenty knots, surrounded by her watchdogs, and 170 miles away from Japan.

By dawn on the twenty-first, they were three hundred miles from the Land of the Rising Sun. A few last long-range bombers tried to find them, but they were easily vanquished by the combat air patrol. Once again, Tokyo Rose got it wrong—the *Franklin* had survived.

Escaping the Japanese, however, was not enough for Gehres. He was determined to bring the carrier back to the States to be repaired and sent back to the war.

The morning after the disaster, before Ricks and his shipmates turned away the coup de grace, Captain Gehres had ordered the crew to muster on the flight deck for a head count. Those needed in the engineering rooms, the crew on the guns, a few of the more lightly injured who had not been evacuated but were still incapacitated, were excused.

The men who assembled on the flight deck numbered 286 officers and enlisted men—out of slightly more than 3,000 who had been on the ship when she was hit. The number who mustered on the deck would be significant later.

At the assembly, Gehres read messages to the crew sent over by the skippers of some of their screening ships, including Captain Fitz of the *Santa Fe,* who radioed: "Congratulations on heroic work and outstanding efficiency of yourself and men in getting your ship underway and saving her. It is an example we will never forget."

The *Franklin's* captain had closed with a little pep talk of his own. He informed his men that others—including Admiral Davison—had suggested in their darkest hour that they should abandon ship.

> Yesterday we were given up for lost. Today we are hailed as heroes. I am a proud man, proud to say that I served with you.
>
> But I am also a very stiff-necked officer. The watchword will be work and more work from now on. If there is a man who thinks he cannot stand up to such a schedule, let him say so now and I will transfer him to another ship. When we get home, I will see that each of you gets a well-deserved rest.
>
> Our first and most important task is to find, identify, and bury the dead. Then we will clean up the ship. I will not have a dirty ship. Secure from quarters and hop to it.

The men had a monumental task before them. The two five-hundred-pound bombs dropped by the Judy had set off more than forty tons of munitions and thousands of gallons of aviation fuel. The effects of both were everywhere.

The flight deck had been demolished aft of the third elevator where all the planes had been parked—dozens of holes, some larger than a plane, had been punched through the wood planks. The middle section of the deck was extensively damaged as well, forward to the first elevator, which hung partly out of the shaft at an awkward angle. Two-thirds of the deck from the island on back had been in flames, and the steel frame beneath the wood was warped and buckled.

On the flight and hangar decks, aircraft were melted into solid lumps of metal. The hangar was a junkyard of grotesquely twisted steel, ruptured piping, and dangling cables. The lower decks were little more than a mass of torn and twisted passages and crushed compartments, all awash in filthy water.

Except for those engaged in keeping the ship moving, the crew set to work throwing debris over the side and pumping water out of passages and compartments below. The captain worked them to exhaustion, believing it would keep their minds off the horrors they had witnessed and fears they had felt on March 19.

The hardest job went to those assigned to locate the bodies of their shipmates, many of which were inaccessible behind ruined steel and flooded areas. The hangar and passageways reeked of burned flesh, which, as the days began to pass and the ship moved into warmer southern climes, was mingled with the smell of rotting corpses.

As Ricks had noted, many of the ship's black crewmembers were assigned the job of picking up pieces of bodies—often nothing more than a lump of charred meat and bone that had once been a young man.

Steward's Mate 1st Class Matthew Little was among those given the task. As he worked, Little felt as though he were walking in a bad dream. All around his ship, his home, men had died in every way imaginable. Some had been crushed between decks or bulkheads and had to be cut and pried from their steel tombs. Others had been ripped apart by bullets and explosion. Many had died of smoke inhalation or asphyxiation in airtight compartments from which they could not escape.

The worst were those who had burned and whose bodies crumbled when touched, like statues made of ash. Some of them could only be swept up with a broom. The pilots who had died in their cockpits were particularly haunting. Their blackened faces stretched in agony, and their fingers still clawed at their harnesses.

The U.S. Navy had told Little that he was not good enough to shoot the guns at the enemy. While he had met with few instances of outright racism from his white shipmates, he knew there were those who thought that "colored" men would freeze in combat. Now, he was good enough to find their bodies—white men and black men and men whose ethnicity couldn't be determined—and bring them to the fantail for burial. He didn't care what race they were or what beliefs they might have held; he was just looking out for his shipmates so that they could be put to rest in the sea.

However, the "colored" men weren't the only ones assigned to the job of locating the dead. As a group, the members of "The Best Band in the Land" were also involved, because it was their battle station's duty to help the medical staff as stretcher bearers. Like Little, they had at first served to bring the wounded to the emergency medical facilities, but when there were no more wounded, their job evolved into transporting the dead.

Other men found themselves saddled with the disagreeable task because they were standing in the wrong place at the wrong time when an officer happened by who had been assigned to take some men and search an area of the ship. The progress of the "death details" was aggravatingly slow. Much of the delay was caused by the amount of water belowdecks that had to be pumped out before passageways could be entered and compartments checked. It wasn't until the third day that a party led by Dr. Fuelling was able to reach the sick bay where he had last seen Dr. George Fox, who had stayed behind with thirteen patients when the bombs began to explode. Water Tender 2nd Class Ernest Scott and several other sailors were assigned to accompany Fuelling.

"Scotty" had already been down into the bowels of the ship beginning that first night after the attack. Sleepless but with no real assignment for the moment, he had grabbed a battle lantern and made his way down to the third deck, where he found Eddie Carlisle looking for something to eat. Not finding it, the two friends continued on to the hatch leading down into their fire room, where they heard voices. They went in and found a half dozen men trying to get one of the boilers lit. The men were in unusually good spirits, having liberated several bottles of liquor from "Officers' Country."

The next morning, the twentieth, Scott had mustered with 285 others on the flight deck to listen to Gehres talk about how he had ignored Admiral Davison's suggestion to abandon the ship. Scott's head hurt due to a hangover, but it was all he could do not to laugh out loud when one of his ship-mates muttered under his breath, "How come we didn't know we were so goddamn brave?"

Three days later when he accompanied Fuelling down to the infirmary, Scott didn't think of it as being brave. They had to pound the dogs off the hatch, which had warped from the heat and concussions and couldn't be opened normally. Just inside the door, looking like they had fallen asleep on the deck, lay the bodies of Dr. Fox and his corpsman. The sight saddened the searchers although they had feared the worst; the physician had been popular with the crew.

The compartment was dry and otherwise . . . empty. The searchers were confounded. They knew there had been thirteen patients in the infirmary when the bombs hit, yet there was no sign of them. The mystery was solved when the search team opened the door to a small shower room in the back of the infirmary. The upright bodies of the patients were packed into the room like sardines. Several of them tumbled out when the door swung open. There wasn't a mark on any of them, nor any clue why they had all crowded into the shower room, except maybe to escape the heat that sealed them in their tomb.

The next step was to remove the bodies, but Scott could not bring him-self to touch a dead man. He sat immobilized until Dr. Fuelling approached and said gently, "Come on, son, it has to be done, and I can't do it alone." The kindliness, as well as the sadness in the doctor's voice, shamed Scott into overcoming his squeamishness.

By keeping his mind blank, Scott was able to help carry the bodies from the infirmary to a ladder leading up onto the hangar deck. Then they started to pull and push the dead up the ladder into the hangar. He was doing okay until they tried to get the body of a huge man up the ladder.

Scott had his arms fully extended over his head trying to push the corpse up the ladder when his upturned face was suddenly covered with some sort of fluid. He didn't know what it was—really did not want to know—or where it came from, except he was sure that there had not been any water in the infirmary and that all the victims had been dry. The shock was too much; he dropped back down the ladder and vomited.

Another physician at the top of the ladder, Dr. Moy, who had once stepped off the flight deck at night into the ocean, yelled down, "Send him topside." When he was finished retching, Scott climbed weakly up the ladder, where the doctor handed him a bottle of whiskey. "Drink and sit," he commanded.

Scott did as ordered and after a bit began to feel better. He stood up, walked over to the hatch, and climbed back down to finish what he had started. But he didn't think of it as being brave.

The bodies of the men from the infirmary were carried to the fantail. Like monks converging on a church, men walked slowly from all over the ship carrying stretchers or bags or barrels filled with the remains of their shipmates.

Waiting on the fantail were the two chaplains, Gatlin and O'Callahan. In the first day following the bombing, they had tried to perform the traditional burial at sea—sewing the victim into a canvas bag weighted with a shell. But there were too many—with more arriving every few minutes—there was not enough canvas, and the living had to move more quickly as the dead began to decompose, creating a health hazard.

The chaplains removed the victims' dog tags—if they still existed, as many had been melted into small lumps of tin—for identification and to determine what faith, if any, the victim had espoused. If the dead man was Protestant, Gatlin said a few words. O'Callahan did the same for the Catholics and, because he also knew the Hebrew service for the dead, the Jews. Then the bodies—sometimes just parts of bodies—were dropped without a bag or weight overboard to float off in the carrier's wake.

By the evening of March 21, the chaplains had sent 251 bodies over the side. With so much carnage and exhausted by the work, little wonder that many of the crew listened with disdain as on March 22 Gehres read a congratulatory message from Admiral Davison. "I am on a stranger's door, but I claim you again with pride," said the message. "Battered though you may be, you are still my child. Great work. Davison."

The men shrugged and turned back to their tasks. Justifiably or not from a military standpoint, their "father" hadn't been so anxious to claim them when they were fighting for their lives and their vessel. In fact, if the order to abandon ship had been given when he suggested, hundreds of them might not have survived the torpedoes of their own destroyers.

The Japanese had not been able to sink the *Franklin,* but as would soon become clear, they had divided her crew emotionally, as well as physically.

When he left the carrier and swung aboard the *Santa Fe,* Aviation Coxswain Frank Turner had looked back at his ship before going below on the cruiser. The carrier was still belching smoke and exploding; he thought that the *Franklin* was doomed.

Exhausted, he had gone to sleep that night assuming the ship was already gone. But the next morning, when the survivors from the *Franklin* gathered for breakfast, a *Santa Fe* officer announced that not only had their ship remained afloat, she was steaming again under her own power. The mess hall erupted with cheers.

The *Santa Fe* escorted the *Franklin* part way to Ulithi then was relieved to proceed ahead, arriving before the bigger ship. The *Franklin* men were sent ashore to wait, and the main topic of conversation was about getting back onboard the carrier for what would obviously be a trip home.

However, Captain Gehres had other plans for them. When the *Franklin* steamed into the Ulithi lagoon on March 24, he assembled the crew again and read another message, this one from the Fifth Fleet commander himself, Admiral Spruance. "The courage, fortitude and ability of you and your crew in saving and bringing back *Franklin* for future use against the enemy cannot be too highly praised." He told the crew that he had replied, "We're down by the tail, but our heads are up."

Outwardly, Gehres accepted the accolades. He said nothing of it to those sending them, but inwardly he seethed when he thought about the men he considered to have deserted the ship. In fact, two days before arriving at Ulithi, he had told his executive officer, Cmdr. Joe Taylor, to draft and post a memorandum that would apply to the men who left the ship, listing "offenses punishable by death" in a time of war.

The list included disobeying the lawful order of a superior officer. "Or, in time of battle, displays cowardice, or keeps out of danger to which he should expose himself; or, in time of battle, deserts his duty or station; or fails to encourage, in his own person, his inferior officers and men to fight courageously." The memorandum further warned that any man found in possession of property not his own, "particularly property or clothing of any officer," would be subject to court-martial.

As the *Franklin* steamed toward Ulithi, Gehres had no intention of allowing any of the officers or men who left the ship to return. But some of his other officers convinced him that they needed about one hundred men who had been on the *Santa Fe* or one of the destroyers to get the ship back to Pearl Harbor and from there to the States. When the ship arrived in the lagoon, those men were told to report to the *Franklin*, which most did happily until they learned that they were under suspicion and that some of them might be charged as "deserters."

Every officer who came aboard was handed a form to fill out that stated: "The Commanding Officer requires an immediate explanation in writing as to when, where, and why, you able-bodied and uninjured left this vessel while she was in action and seriously damaged when no order had been issued to abandon ship." The forms were signed by Gehres.

One who received the form was Lt. (j.g.) Donald Kallstrom, an Air Department officer. He wrote on the form that he had been trapped by smoke and flames near the island structure and had to jump from the starboard side of ship about 8:45 A.M. or die. "Personally, I felt like a traitor at leaving the ship," he wrote. "But even though I had no life jacket on, it was the only thing I could do under the circumstances."

Kallstrom said he was picked up by the destroyer *Hunt* about 9:30 A.M. "I would like to take this occasion to add that the morale of our officers in the water was superb, and the deportment and *esprit-de-corps* of our 400 men on the USS *Hunt* was gratifying to all of the USS *Franklin's* officers aboard. The wounded especially carried on magnificently."

Gehres wasn't interested in the esprit-de-corps of his men on the *Hunt,* or the opinions of officers he planned to bring up on charges. Kallstrom and the others were told that they would be charged with desertion and abandonment of station.

Not all of the enlisted men brought back onboard were treated the same either. Cmdr. Joe Taylor brought some of his men back with nothing said. The commanding officer of the ship's Marine detachment told Gehres flat-out that his men were coming back aboard and that he wouldn't support any attempts to charge them with desertion. The Marines were onboard to fight the Japs, not fires, he said.

When the *Franklin* left Ulithi bound for Hawaii on March 26, Gehres reported that there were 704 officers and men onboard. The remaining men who left the carrier on March 19, he said, would have to be transported back to Pearl Harbor aboard other ships.

On the way to Pearl Harbor, 704 men were given cards signed by Gehres that proclaimed them to be members of the "Big Ben 704 Club." The requisite for being a member of the club was that the bearer could have never left the ship after the attack. That card would divide the crew as no shipboard debate between the men from the north or south, the east or west, between white man or black man, college-educated or illiterate laborer had done.

Aviation Coxswain Frank Turner told the "club members" what they could do with their cards, and it wasn't pleasant. He was back onboard the carrier, because when the ship reached Ulithi, Lt. Fred Harris, who oversaw the flight deck crew, asked that the Airedales be allowed to return. Of all the divisions on the ship, the flight deck crew had suffered the most fatalities; most of them had been on the deck, preparing to launch when the fires swept through them.

Turner had gladly returned to the *Franklin* and burst into tears when he came back aboard and saw the damage. A lot of his friends had been on the flight deck that morning; most of them were gone now. He thought that the remaining crew would be reunited, and he was shocked to learn how the captain felt.

When Gehres issued the club cards, Turner didn't get one, nor did the other men who came aboard in Ulithi. But it was the whole idea of the club that made him angry.

Half of the men who left the ship had landed in the water and were simply fortunate if they didn't drown. And he figured that the vast majority of those who went across to the *Santa Fe,* like himself, had simply followed what they at least believed had been orders. Now, he and others like him were outcasts on their own ship.

Eternal Father, strong to save . . . On April 2, a memorial service was held on the flight deck of the Franklin to honor the dead and comfort the men who lived. As the men sang the Navy Hymn, Chaplain Gatlin looked out on the assembly and was shocked to see so many blank faces and empty eyes.

. . . whose arm hath bound the restless wave . . . All the way to Hawaii, Gehres worked the men hard to keep them from dwelling on the men who had died. But it was difficult to ignore the nearly constant procession of men carrying bodies toward the fantail, bodies that were increasingly located by smell.

Who bids the mighty ocean deep its own appointed limits keep . . . It was hard for the chaplain to believe that only a month earlier, the *Franklin* had sailed from Pearl Harbor a ship full of boys on a grand adventure and was now returning crewed by weary, battle-scarred old men.

. . . oh hear us when we cry to thee . . . When it was his turn to speak, Gatlin decided to talk about Jesus rising from the dead. "And because He lives, we can live. We can win a victory over ourselves and over the powers of evil." As he looked into the tired faces of the crew, he hoped that someday they would be able to regain their youth, forget the horrors of war, and go on with their lives. . . . *for those in peril on the sea.*

The next morning, April 3, the *Franklin* returned to Hawaii. The men had done their best to locate dress white uniforms and get themselves ready to "stand at quarters" on the flight deck as the ship sailed into the harbor. The band—which had lost most of its instruments and several of its members—even managed to put together a "jugs, whistles, pots and pans band" of sort, and on a cue from O'Callahan as the ship approached the pier played the tune for "The Old Gray Mare, She Ain't What She Used to Be." Only now the crew had been given a different set of words to sing for "The Old Big Ben, She Ain't What She Used to Be."

A welcoming party of some fifty young women of the Navy Women's Reserves, or WAVES, stood on the pier in their light blue uniforms waving. They too began singing as the ship approached. The eyes of the men onboard filled with tears as they caught the words to "America the Beautiful" drifting over the water toward them. *"Oh beautiful for spacious skies, for amber waves of grain . . ."*

The ship drew closer and one by one the women's voices faltered as it became apparent that the *Franklin* and her crew had suffered some horrible catastrophe. The words were replaced by small cries of anguish as the women pointed to the battered island, the torn, smoke-darkened hull, and the decimated ranks of men.

However, the women's sympathy was quickly replaced by alarm. At the entrance to the harbor, the ship had picked up a harbor pilot familiar with the waters and the handling of big ships in tight quarters. It was his job to take over from the captain and tell the engine rooms what speed and directions the helmsman would need to steer the ship to its pier. But Gehres dismissed the pilot, saying he had brought in plenty of ships and that he would dock the *Franklin* himself.

However, Gehres misjudged the distance and came in too fast. The captain tried to reverse the engines, but it was too late; the *Franklin* was going to ram the pier. The WAVES and a mooring party that stood by to help tie the ship to the pier ran for their lives. The carrier slammed in, knocking the giant pilings askew and sending concrete flying. The mooring party on the ship, which had prepared to throw lines to their counterparts on the dock, tumbled to the deck. They couldn't throw their lines, but there was no one left on the pier anyway.

Although too late to avoid the collision, reversing the propellers pulled the ship back out into the channel. Embarrassed, Gehres was furious at the mooring party and blamed them for not getting the ship tied up in spite of the mishap. He insisted on trying again and this time docked the ship without incident.

Looking at the ship, spectators on the pier—from admirals to seamen—thought it was a miracle the carrier had survived. But there was one more miracle as far as O'Callahan was concerned. He was looking at the pier when he spotted the district chaplain, Father Sheehy, an old friend. "Hi, Joe!" Sheehy yelled up when he saw O'Callahan. "I came down to tell you that yesterday we received definite word that your sister is alive in Manila!"

The chaplain rejoiced, but the captain was still fuming. Gehres had not mellowed in his feelings toward the officers and men who had left the ship. When those men arrived at Pearl Harbor aboard other ships and asked to be allowed to return, he refused. He even declined to let them onboard to collect their personal belongings. Not until a group of the men went to former chaplain Lt. E. J. Harkin and asked him to intercede on their behalf did the captain relent a little. Gehres said they could come aboard for twenty minutes to gather what they could find of their things, but then they were to "get the hell off my ship."

A few of the sailors left saying "good-bye and good riddance." Even if they'd had a choice of ships now, they would have picked a lucky one like the *Santa Fe,* with Fitz for a skipper. Not a snake-bit carrier like the *Franklin,* with a captain who they felt was trying to transfer the focus of any inquiry into the ship's destruction on them and away from himself.

Edwin Garrison had no desire to go back aboard the *Franklin,* or any other ship for that matter. The night of his rescue, he had been sleeping when he was awakened by a commotion. A doctor was amputating the foot of his friend Sears, which had been crushed between the rescue boat and ship as he was climbing aboard. A ship's photographer who had been recruited to help the doctor kept saying, "I can't do this," to which the physician replied, "Keep holding it."

Sears told him the next day that he didn't mind losing his foot. "People in Chicago love sailors," he said of his hometown. "I put this leg up on a bar, and I'll never have to pay for another drink."

Garrison had arrived in Hawaii aboard one of the ships used to transport the remaining *Franklin* crewmembers who Gehres no longer felt belonged aboard the carrier. At night the ship, and later the barracks in Hawaii, could be hellish with the nightmares of men like Garrison who suffered what the doctors called "combat fatigue."

Loud noises startled Garrison into sweats. "I don't get much sleep," he told a Navy doctor at Pearl Harbor. Even if he dozed off, one of the other *Franklin* survivors was sure to wake him. "We still fight the war all night in our sleep, and it seems like somebody is always screaming."

The doctor told him that there was nothing he could do to help him with battle fatigue. But he could make sure he didn't go to sea again. Garrison considered asking the doctor for permission to return to sea duty only once, when that July the heavy cruiser USS *Indianapolis* pulled into the harbor. She was a beautiful ship, and he wondered if her ship's company might need a metalsmith. But the cruiser was in port on some sort of secret business—judging by the top security around the ship—and was gone before he could inquire.

Most of the men who had left the *Franklin,* however, complained bitterly about not being allowed to rejoin their ship. The carrier and her crew would return to the States for a heroes' welcome, but they had been unfairly branded as cowards and were going to remain behind in barracks. Rumors swirled. Some said they heard that Gehres was recommending they be sent back into the combat zone aboard noncombat ships. They were all going to be charged with desertion, some said. Or at least the captain was going to court-martial the officers, regardless of the circumstances under which they left the ship.

Meanwhile, the officers and men who remained on the *Franklin* reacted to the captain's treatment of their former shipmates in different ways. A number of them were so disgusted that they threw their 704 Club cards off the ship. They had been proud of their efforts to save Big Ben, but this injustice had left them with a foul taste in their mouths.

Lt. Robert Wassman thought that the captain's blanket treatment of the men was a sad, and unnecessary, ending to what was an otherwise epic tale of heroism. He thought of his quartermaster, Clifton Martin, who had been blown overboard and had asked to come back while the ship was still burning. Martin had not been allowed to return.

However, others agreed with Gehres. Whatever the other men's reasons, those who left the ship were deserters and cowards. Some men agreed with the captain to a point.

Water Tender 3rd Class Sam Rhodes had a simple litmus test. Those who left the ship should not be allowed back on, he thought, unless on the day of the attack they were "wet or wounded."

The *Franklin* left Pearl Harbor on April 8. The last body was discovered on April 27 and buried at sea off the coast of New England.

The next morning, the *Franklin* sailed into New York Harbor with her scarred American battle flag flying, having traveled more than twelve thousand miles from Japan. The ship was greeted by fireboats shooting streams of water into the sky, while other ships, military and civilian, tooted their horns and blew their whistles. Planes buzzed above on honorary fly-bys.

The crew once again stood at quarters, many with tears rolling down their cheeks at the sight of the Statue of Liberty. As tugs pushed and pulled her into the Brooklyn Navy Yard, the men who worked there nodded toward the ship, and the yard grew quiet for the first time since the war started. Tough men, hard as the steel they worked, they too wept at the sight.

No other ship in U.S. Navy history had suffered so much damage and survived. Of her officers and crew on March 19, 1945, 724 had died and another 265 had been wounded. Those who lived and brought her back had a right to be proud, but for some that pride was dampened by a memorandum put out by Captain Gehres the morning the ship entered the harbor.

The memorandum contained the usual warnings to "guard your tongues and pens." They were not to discuss "with anyone" the damage, or casualties, or even the other ships involved in the action. The command for secrecy was normal; it was some parts of the rest of the memorandum that the men questioned.

"Never forget that we did not bring out the *Franklin* by ourselves and other ships and crews deserve as much credit as we do," the captain wrote. "Had it not been for the really heroic work of the *Santa Fe,* the *Pittsburg,* and all those destroyers who helped us, towed us, and guarded us we would never have gotten away. And if it had not been for the other task groups whose guns and planes fought off large groups of enemy aircraft reportedly after us, we would never have gotten away."

The men could not have agreed more with those sentiments. However, Gehres then seemed to indicate that they had done something wrong. "Never forget that we did not go out there to save a damaged ship," the captain wrote. "We went to damage the enemy and when we became a casualty, we upset plans and operations by that much.

"Wars are not won by saving damaged ships but by those which are still out there fighting day and night. So when you are allowed to talk about all this, be modest and humble. That we are alive where so many of our shipmates are not, it is largely a matter of luck, so do not be puffed up about it. That we are in the States with a chance to see our families is a great privilege and it behooves every one of us to realize and remember that the rest of the fleet is out there pitching, winning a hard tough battle without any help from us."

The men shook their heads. They had not asked to be bombed or lose more than seven hundred shipmates. So they didn't know quite how to take the captain's final words, which seemed a back-handed compliment at best. "You have all worked very hard on the way home, and in my opinion the job you've done in clearing away the wreckage and getting the ship ready to enter the yard is really more to your credit than putting out the fires in the first place. That kind of hard dirty work really counts, even though it doesn't bring commendatory messages or medals."

Despite the captain's admonition and while the details of the *Franklin's* ordeal were kept from the public, the crew were treated like heroes. Several parties were thrown for the crew at hotels, including one at the ritzy Waldorf-Astoria hosted by Lady Astor herself. Most were also able to enjoy the revelry when on May 7, 1945, the Germans surrendered.

However, not all of the men who had served on the *Franklin* were as free to celebrate. The men who were left in Hawaii were placed in barracks, away from other sailors, while the Navy tried to decide what to do with them in light of Gehres's charges.

In New York, the ship had hardly docked when the Brooklyn Navy Yard's Office of the Permanent Defense Counsel of the General Court Martial was filled with junior officers from the *Franklin*. They had been charged with desertion and abandonment of station.

The commanding officer of the defense counsel, Lt. Cmdr. Samuel Wolf, listened carefully to their stories and concluded that a grave injustice was being committed by the captain of the *Franklin*. For one thing, the numbers didn't add up that all the men were being treated equally.

According to a message from Gehres to Admirals Nimitz and King on March 21, the ship had aboard it "by latest count, 103 officers and 589 enlisted men . . . including two officers and men unfit for duty." Those numbers together equaled 692.

When the *Franklin* left Ulithi, Gehres reported 704 officers and men onboard. If nothing else that was twelve more men than he had claimed on March 21. However, the captain's numbers were confused beyond a mere dozen.

If there were 704 men onboard when the ship left Ulithi and 704 in the club he had formed, then Gehres was indicating that every man onboard the ship that pulled into New York Harbor had never left the ship. But the lawyer knew better than that from interviews with the officers and other men he sent his investigators to speak with.

What Wolf learned was that beginning the day after the bombing, certain officers on the *Franklin* had requested that some men in their divisions be brought over from the screening ships. No log was kept, but estimates later ranged from dozens to hundreds of men (accounting, some suggested, for the sudden jump in numbers from the 286-plus who mustered on the morning of the twentieth).

Then when the carrier reached Ulithi, approximately one hundred men were brought back onboard. Some of them were being held accountable for leaving the ship; but some weren't—although like Frank Turner, they may not have received 704 cards. If for the sake of argument, every one of the 704 "club members" had never left the ship, then apparently Gehres wasn't counting the men who had been brought back aboard while underway and at Ulithi. They didn't exist. It was either that, or the 704 did include men who had left the ship. If so, then everyone else whose actions were similar but had not been allowed back onboard—or worse, were being charged with desertion—were being treated differently.

At the same time, the Navy was quietly conducting its own investigation. Investigators talked to Lt. (j.g.) Robert Wassman and asked him if he had seen men abandoning the ship "in direct disobedience of orders."

"Hell, no," Wassman replied. He thought it was a shame that the captain was casting a blanket accusation over all those men; especially when the captain's actions during the fight to save the crew, as well as those who fought with him, was truly the stuff of an epic tale of heroism. As far as he knew, the men who were forced into the water—like his quartermaster, Clifton Martin—were saving their lives. If those who exited onto the *Santa Fe* weren't supposed to, he told the investigators, he saw no senior officer trying to stop them. "And there were plenty there."

Wassman was a member of the 704 Club. But, he said, only about four hundred of them had never left the ship. He knew because it had been one of his responsibilities to count heads while the ship was enroute to Ulithi.

What then to make of Gehres's report of 692 men on March 21? Wassman said that the captain had asked his officers for lists of the men they wanted to rejoin the ship. Perhaps the captain included those names in his report.

Wassman told the investigators that he thought the remaining survivors weren't brought back onboard because their weren't enough facilities on the ruined ship to care for them—until he heard about the captain's anger.

Wolf thought the whole idea of prosecuting anyone under the circumstances was unfair. Half of the men, like Lt. (j.g.) Kallstrom, had been forced into the water, where they had behaved in a manner that probably deserved a medal, not a federal prison sentence. The captain also refused to acknowledge that there had been a breakdown in the chain of command that led to different interpretations of his original command to "transfer all wounded and evacuate all personnel not required to fight from the ship."

The Navy lawyer decided that the best strategy was to avoid a trial completely. He sent one of his subordinate officers, Lt. (j.g.) J. Randell Creel, a lawyer, down to the Officers' Club with instructions meant to stop the proceedings before they really got started. Creel was told to have a few drinks and engage other officers at the bar in conversations about the *Franklin*. In doing so, he was to let slip Wolf's proposed defense.

Creel confided to anyone who would listen that if Gehres and the Navy insisted on trying the junior officers, Wolf was going to make an issue of Admiral Davison and Bogan, along with their staffs, leaving the ship. "If the junior officers were charged with abandoning that floating hell, did they not have a lot of good company?" Creel quoted Wolf as saying, perhaps preparing his opening statement for court.

Having planted the seed, Creel left the Officers' Club. A few days later, all charges against the officers were dropped, as were all efforts to further punish the enlisted men. As Wolf anticipated, the government wasn't going to risk a messy trial that might hurt the public's perception of the Navy. After all, there were still war bonds to sell. The invasion of Okinawa had been bloodier than anticipated, and the analysts were estimating another million casualties to take the Japanese home islands. They could not afford to disenchant the public. Gehres was told to forget about it.

Instead, the Navy finally released the story of the *Franklin* epic to the media on May 17. The next morning, newspapers across the country carried stories and banner headlines about "The Ship That Wouldn't Die." There was no mention of charges of desertion or court-martials. Gehres was the courageous captain who refused to abandon his ship and laughed in the face of danger. A *Collier's* magazine article a month later would recount the exploits of Father O'Callahan and Lieutenant Gary under the headline: "Chaplain Courageous."

The most moving media account of the epic, however—one rife with inaccuracies but filled with emotion—was delivered the evening of May 17 by Gabriel Heater of the Mutual Broadcasting System. "This grim piece of news was made public just one minute ago . . ."

Ernest Scott had just walked into the kitchen of his friend Kenny Leland's parents, where he had first heard the news about Pearl Harbor, when Heater's impassioned voice caught his attention.

"It was on the morning of March nineteenth—many of the *Franklin*'s planes were on deck—loaded—preparing to take off—suddenly a Jap dive-bomber came out of a patch of clouds—he dropped two five-hundred-pound bombs. He was shot down one minute later, but within that minute tragedy had come to a great ship. The Japs said the carrier was sunk—they were sure of it—they had every reason to think so, for she seemed mortally wounded."

Scott shook his head; the last he heard, they were supposed to keep their mouths shut about the attack. *Guess the Navy changed its mind,* he thought. He and Eddie Carlisle had been home for two days on leave and all was right with the world as far as he was concerned. Vivian would be graduating from high school in June, and they planned to get married in July. She seemed to have missed him a whole lot and no longer had qualms about getting hitched.

Actually, Vivian's family was split on her getting married. Those against argued that there was a whole new world out there for women; she should have a career, see some of the world before settling down. But Vivian was ready to return to her little hometown. It was a good place to raise children, and with all that had gone on in the past four years, it felt safe. She figured she could do a whole lot worse than Ernest Scott. He certainly was persistent—there was something to be said for a boy who first proposed when he was eight years old and was still asking more than a dozen years later. *Besides,* she thought, *he's one of the better-looking ones, and if I don't grab him now someone else will.*

"'That ship is gone,' said Japan," Heater continued, his voice choked up. "'This ship will live,' said her gallant men. Back she came with her charred and battered hull. . . . Yet back she came—her flag high—her story an epic of raw courage."

Personally, Scott just looked forward to getting out of the Navy so he could settle down with Vivian, getting a job in the Woodland paper mill and starting a family. He had seen enough of the world, and the backwoods of Maine looked mighty good by comparison. It was going to take some doing to put the war out of his mind. He had witnessed more than a young man should have to, and there was a sadness that would not leave his heart for the friends and shipmates he had lost, like Chuck Berringer, who had had a premonition that the ship would be attacked and he wouldn't survive. Berringer was officially listed as missing in action, but they had never found his body.

"Every man onboard that ship saw the face of war that morning," Heater said. "Yet, there was no panic."

Scott nearly laughed at that. He remembered plenty of panic and plenty of fear—the important thing was that they had overcome it. He held nothing against the men who left the *Franklin;* he had considered jumping ship himself when the *Santa Fe* was alongside and the ammunition was going off behind him. He disagreed with the captain's attempt to court-martial or punish those other men.

"When the *Santa Fe* came alongside, there was a piece of seamanship men would never forget, for the *Santa Fe* came so close she damaged gun platforms on the carrier. But with that piece of daring, hundreds of wounded men were saved . . ."

Scott smiled now, remembering the courage of the men on the cruiser, who risked everything to help. He had to admit, Heater was really waxing poetic, the broadcaster's voice on the edge of tears.

Into New York harbor she came . . . her flag was high and the devotion of her brave and gallant men high enough to reach into the very heavens, where her dead were now in the tender embrace of God.

Within sixty miles of Japan's coastline she received what the Jap thought was her mortal wound—as he thought all ships he damaged at Pearl Harbor would never come back to claim their retribution. As he thought his treachery would find us weak and confused, only to find us now a little more than three hundred miles from his home islands . . .

Three hundred more tough and bloody miles, Scott thought and wondered how many of them he would have to cover once the *Franklin* was repaired.

. . . with the sky over those pagan islands blood red with flames of his war machine disappearing into smoke and rubble and ashes. He miscalculated everything, but more than anything else, he never knew these men who would man our ships or fight their way onto the beaches ...

All those foul little men in Japan or Germany who, not being free themselves, could never know the passion with which free men would fight back. Not believing in peace, how could they know the wrath with which men who wanted peace would fight for it? Knowing nothing of mercy or compassion, how would they ever know the heroism it would inspire in men who believed in mercy and compassion and would offer their lives for their comrades—for their country—for their ship.

The Lelands were looking at him with something akin to awe. Their Scotty had been on that ship? Why hadn't he said anything?

"One by one, the Jap cities will turn to ashes . . . one by one, each will feel the wrath and power of a free people . . . until the very last of Japan's suicide fanatics has made his last flight . . . until the Jap is forced to come in, as Germany's pirates came in, and lie about his fighting an honorable war but stand revealed . . . as a brute and a barbarian brought to his knees."

Scott now had tears in his eyes, remembering Berringer, and the men in the infirmary, and the hurried burials at sea. He hoped that what Heater said next would come to pass and knew that it would be up to his generation to see to it.

"And there will be peace on earth, and boys will be home again, and you and I and millions of Americans will say whether this sacrifice and death, and all this heroism is to be lost . . .

. . . or won and held fast and honored with the kind of world in which men will never again be asked to suffer all that these men on the great carrier *Franklin* endured . . . for us."

Heater's commentary on the *Franklin* was heard all over the country and became one of the most famous of the war. That one broadcast alone was said to have sold more than a million dollars in war bonds.

Scott was home four days later on May 21, 1945, when the largest mass award ceremony in Navy history took place on the charred deck of the *Franklin*. He didn't mind that he wasn't invited or recognized; he didn't consider himself brave or a hero, but he'd seen plenty of men who were.

Ninety-seven officers and enlisted men stood in ranks on the flight deck that morning waiting to be presented with their medals. A dozen more were missing, their medals delivered to their families along with the Secretary of the Navy's condolences.

Twenty men received the Navy Cross, including Captain Gehres, Cmdr. Joe Taylor, Cmdr. Stephen Jurika, Lt. Cmdr. James Fuelling, and Lt. Cmdr. George Fox, who received the award posthumously. All but three of the twenty—Ensign Fred Hall, Gunner's Mate Thomas M. Stoops, and Cpl. Stephen Nowak—were officers.

Nowak was somewhat amused by the entire affair, as he had gone from the captain's doghouse to the hero's pedestal in the course of a couple of days. On the way to Hawaii, he had fallen asleep in Gehres's easy chair, which had been moved to the foc'sle while the captain's quarters were restored. The captain caught him napping and was going to bring him up on charges until Nowak's commanding officer intervened. Two days later, he heard that he was going to be given a medal. It was no big deal to him, the medal and a quarter would buy him a cup of coffee. He had simply done what he had to do so that he could keep his promise to his young bride, Shirley, by coming home.

Twenty-three men received the Silver Star, which was spread a little more evenly between the officers, who received eight, and the enlisted men. Among those who got the award were the Protestant chaplain, Lt. Grimes Gatlin; Lt. (j.g.) Stanley S. Graham; as well as Lt. (j.g.) E. Robert Wassman and the five men he rescued from the steering room.

One hundred and nine men received the Bronze Medal, including Yeoman 2nd Class John Franklin Brown, who had given his life jacket to his best friend, Guido Cavallo. "Thus jeopardizing his own chance for survival . . . Brown's gallant conduct, courageous, self-sacrificing spirit, and loyal devotion to duty were in keeping with the highest traditions of the United States Naval Service."

Lt. (j.g.) Donald Kallstrom, who Gehres had wanted to court-martial, received the Bronze Medal instead. But there was some grumbling in the ranks when Private Wallace Klimkiewicz received the Bronze along with Gunner's Mate Ben Ricks and the other men who manned the 40-millimeter that turned away the Japanese Zero on March 20.

In talking to the press, Gehres had created a myth that his faithful orderly had demanded to help man the gun just before the attack, saying that as a Marine, "I can shoot anything, sir!" The way the captain made it sound,

Klimkiewicz practically took on the Zeke by himself. *He wasn't even there until afterwards,* Ricks thought to himself, angered that others who were on the gun, like Mike Gowden, received nothing at all.

Perhaps it was to be expected that there would be a number of injustices with the way the awards were handed out. The *Franklin* was truly a ship full of heroes. Still, the pilot on the fire hose with Matthew Little received the Silver Star. Little, who was troubled by nightmares ever since his labors to rescue the wounded and locate the dead, was given one of 230 Letters of Commendation. The letter gave him the right to pin an extra ribbon on his uniform.

There were numerous instances of men not receiving any sort of commendation who were in the same place, doing the same thing, at the same time, as men who were awarded medals. Of the dozen men who accompanied Lieutenant Gary to the fire room on the night of March 19, half of them received the Bronze Medal and the others were forgotten. Sam Rhodes didn't even receive a Letter of Commendation … and it was his Zippo that got the ship's heart beating.

When the ceremonies were finished, the men were shocked that two names were not called: Lt. Cmdr. Joseph O'Callahan and Lt. (j.g.) Donald Gary. But in this instance, at least, Gehres had done the right thing. In January 1946, President Harry S. Truman called O'Callahan and Gary to Washington, D.C., to present them with the Congressional Medal of Honor. "For conspicuous gallantry and intrepidity at the risk of his life above and beyond the call of duty . . ."

A few days later, columnist Drew Pearson of the *Washington Post* added a small sidelight to the story. According to Pearson's column, the Naval Awards Board did not want O'Callahan to receive the Medal of Honor unless Gehres also received it. However, Admiral King, who had been incensed at the captain's attempts to court-martial his officers, quashed the board's plan.

Gehres later told a freelance writer, Donald Davidson, that he was asked by the board if he thought that he should receive the Medal of Honor. "I said, 'No, it is the commanding officer's primary duty to save his ship, and I had done nothing beyond and above the call of duty.'"

The carrier and her crew never made it back to the war. Big Ben was mothballed, and in 1966 the ship that cost $63 million in war bonds to build was sold to a salvage company for $228,000. At the time, a film company was making a documentary about the *Franklin* and invited a small group of former crewmen and officers to the salvage yard. Many of them wept at the sight of the ship they'd worked so hard to save being torn apart.

CHAPTER TWENTY-SIX

The Bomb and the Lock of Hair

April 10, 1945
USS Santa Fe

When dawn broke all hands rushed topside to peer anxiously through the gray mist that obscured the California coastline. Al Mancini strained along with the rest of his shipmates, every man hoping to be the first to see the "good ol' USA" after fifteen months away.

When at last the call came, "Land ho!" they let out a cheer, but quickly went back to sprucing up both themselves and their ship in preparation for entering Los Angeles Harbor. Mancini inspected his dress blues uniform for flaws and shined his shoes for the millionth time.

It was hard to believe they were almost home. For a time after they pulled away from the *Franklin,* it looked like the Navy was doing everything it could to test the limits of the *Santa Fe's* vaunted luck. Once again, the Lucky Lady had been part of a "bait force," circling a wounded ship under tow as they crawled across the sea. They weren't even allowed to head for safety right away; instead, the Navy had the group sail west, toward Japan, hoping to lure more than the forty-five planes that had attacked the first night, or even trick the superbattleship *Yamato* out of hiding where it could be destroyed.

On March 20, the Zero had come within a hundred feet of finishing the *Franklin.* But other than the occasional submarine alert, the rest of the trip had been uneventful.

If there was anything good that came out of the disaster, it was that the *Santa Fe's* crew knew that there was no way another ship was going to get their yard duty this time. Their ship had a big gash in her hull just above the waterline that the ship's carpenter had stuffed with mattresses. Most of the guns on the port side also were damaged; if they were attacked now, they would be fighting with one hand tied behind their backs. They were a confident crew, but enough was enough, it was time to go home.

They felt sorry for the eight hundred-plus men they had taken off the *Franklin,* sharing their clothes, toiletries, and even giving up their bunks. One of the wounded men had died the first night with severe burns over most of his body, and the cruiser's crew had once again held a burial ceremony that wasn't for one of their own. Some of the survivors were in bad shape mentally—they wouldn't talk or give their names, every loud noise made them jump, and if they were belowdecks, sent them scrambling to get topside. The majority of the *Franklin* men, however, seemed to be okay, if saddened by what had happened to their ship, and just tried to stay out of the way.

Reaching Ulithi, most of the carrier's crew was transferred off the ship. The *Santa Fe* crew figured that it was just to await the return of their own ship later in the day. However, after the *Franklin* arrived, the cruiser's crew started hearing disturbing rumors that the carrier's captain wanted to punish the men who had left his ship.

The captain's anger was a surprise. Most of the cruiser's crew had been impressed with the job he had done to save his ship. In his daily "action report," Captain Fitz commended Gehres's performance as "heroic and highly efficient."

"No commanding officer could possibly be in a more difficult position for, until the fires had been brought under control aft, it was a touch and go proposition as to whether the ship should be abandoned. The crew of the *Franklin* remaining aboard followed the high example of the commanding officer in so far as was observed."

The crew of the *Santa Fe* didn't know what to make of the rumors. Thirty-eight of the men they had rescued were pulled in from the water where they had fled to save their lives. The cruiser's crew thought, as apparently the men from the *Franklin* had, that the rest were *supposed* to have left the ship; there had been officers on the flight deck watching the exodus, and none of them had said a word otherwise.

The more they heard about Gehres's reaction—that the junior officers were going to be charged with desertion and the rest of the crew was going to have to return to Pearl Harbor on other ships—the happier they were to be serving under Captain Fitz. If he didn't walk on water after the way he had handled the ship coming into the *Franklin,* they certainly thought he could work other miracles. Those who had seen the maneuver were asked to tell and retell the story until the legend had grown to where Fitz had pulled it off not once, but two or three times and at greater speeds each time.

Fitz was equally complimentary of his crew. "The performance of duty of all hands on this ship was at all times uniformly excellent," he wrote in the same action report in which he had lauded Gehres. "The officers and men were acutely aware of the hazards involved due to possible large explosions while alongside the *Franklin,* as the *Birmingham* had lost a large number of officers and men under similar circumstances when the *Princeton's* magazines blew up." The captain had submitted a list of thirty-four men he thought should receive medals and commendations, "though it was difficult to single out individuals. It was essentially a performance of the ship as a unit."

In Ulithi, the *Santa Fe's* crew anxiously waited while the *Franklin* was patched up enough to make the trip east. There seemed to be a lot of tension on that ship—one of the *Santa Fe's* chief warrant officers, Don Jackson, had gone over with a crew of his radar and radio repair men to offer assistance, but were turned away at the quarterdeck and told their services would not be needed.

As the *Santa Fe* waited, the pessimists voiced the opinion that there was still time for the Navy to add another "last operation." But finally the cruiser sailed out of the lagoon with its "homeward bound" pennant—a ribbon-like version of the American flag—streaming from the main mast, so long that its tail sometimes dipped in the ship's wake.

The *Franklin* was able to maintain a very respectable pace of twenty-five knots as it traveled with the *Santa Fe.* On March 28, the small group passed well to the north of the island-fortress of Truk, where the large Japanese garrison languished cut off from Japan, to avoid any unexpected danger.

The ships crossed the International Dateline on April 1, meaning the crew actually had two April Fools Days for practical jokes. No one thought it was a joke, however, when the radio operators reported that they had received a message from Admiral Nimitz saying their trip back to the States had been canceled. A groan went up from the crew when they were told that they would instead get temporary yard duty at Pearl Harbor, just long enough for a quick repair before being sent back to the front.

When they thought the crew had swallowed the "bad dope" long enough, the radio operators announced that it was just a joke—"April Fools, ha ha"— the ship was still going back to the States. Perhaps for their own protection from an irate crew, Fitz turned the tables on the comedians and had them thrown in the brig on a diet of bread and water. The punishment was especially meaningful as April 1, 1945, was also Easter Sunday, and they missed a good holiday meal.

Arriving at Pearl Harbor on April 3, the *Santa Fe* transferred the last of her *Franklin* "hitchhikers" and waited to hear which West Coast port the cruiser would be sent to. It wasn't long before they learned—Terminal Island at Long Beach—and left five days later.

As the ship drew nearer to California, the crew grew nervous. What would it be like? What had changed? They had been gone so long: There had been no extended leave since the ship left Philadelphia in March 1943; in fact, the last time most of them had been in the States was a couple days of liberty in January 1944, after Captain Wright assumed command. Otherwise, the only times they had even left the ship were a few days in Honolulu, or a few hours here and there with a warm beer and sand fleas on Mog Mog. They had been told that they would now all get thirty days leave, plus seven days travel time, once they got to Long Beach.

With no planes left onboard after the *Franklin* episode, Mancini had little else to do but get ready and imagine his homecoming when he got back to Greenwich, Connecticut. He had been a fifteen-year-old boy who had never even shaved when he left to join the Navy, and would be returning as a battle-tested veteran who smoked four packs of Camel cigarettes a day and had a fake identification card to get served in bars. He could imagine his mother's tears of joy as he manfully patted her shoulder and told her "it's all right, momma, I'm home."

Mancini had turned eighteen on April 1, though he wasn't quite sure if crossing the International Dateline on his birthday didn't make him nineteen. He had reflected that most of the guys his age back in Greenwich were just getting out of high school. While they had been studying and attending dances, he had fought his way across the Pacific—faced kamikazes and exploding aircraft carriers—right up to the very shores of Japan.

At last, the *Santa Fe* entered Los Angeles Harbor. *"Twooo-wheeeeet!"* The boson's mate piped the crew to attention as the ship nosed up to a Terminal Island receiving dock where most of them would disembark before the ship was moved to the Long Beach Naval Shipyard repair facility. For security reasons, they had not been allowed to tell anyone that they were coming home, so there were only a few women, a small Navy band, some officers, and the mooring party relaxing on the dock. However, one member of the welcoming party attracted all the crew's attention—the young blond woman who waved from a wooden stand spoke into the microphone, "Hi ya, fellas!"

The crew let out a roar, and then roared even louder when accompanied by the band, she broke into song. In a moment, they recognized the voice of the popular singer Dinah Shore. They didn't recognize the song—it was from a new musical they had never heard of called *Oklahoma*—but it was a perfect song as far as they were concerned.

> "Oh what a beautiful morning . . .
> Oh what a beautiful day
> I've got a wonderful feeling
> Everything's going my way."

Shore continued to sing as the mooring party tied the ship to the dock. More than one "old salt" was moved to tears when she asked the crew to join her in singing, "God Bless America." When the song was over, the crew cheered her, themselves, and their home, sweet home.

After the ship was secured, Fitz escorted Shore onboard where she was mobbed by the appreciative sailors, most of whom had not stood that close to a woman in a dress and lipstick in more than a year. Shore lived up to her reputation for graciousness and signed every scrap of paper or article of clothing they shoved at her; the most prized autograph, however, was the red lipstick imprint of a kiss she planted on their sailor's caps.

Mancini was in the first group to be granted leave and soon boarded a train with several shipmates bound for the East Coast. The train was halfway across the country on April 14 when the conductor entered the coach with tears streaming down his face. The president, he said, Franklin Delano Roosevelt, was dead. Mancini was stunned and saddened—he had been a schoolboy on December 7, 1941, and for once wasn't playing hooky the next day when those words came over the radio . . . *Yesterday, a day that will live in infamy* . . . and he had known then that as young as he was, he would find a way to fight for his country.

Yet life went on. When the train reached New York, Mancini and his pals went into Manhattan and spent some of their back pay to have new dress blue uniforms tailored for them. A couple of days later, looking sharp and several inches taller than when he left, he walked up the sidewalk to a small house in Greenwich.

His mother had remarried in July 1944 after writing to him and asking if he had any objections. Heck no, he had written back; she was still young and pretty, he just hoped that her new husband would take better care of her than his father, and it looked like his "stepdad" was doing that. It was a nice little home and he smiled to see the blue star in the window—his star.

Mancini had called his mother when he was partway across the country to let her know that he was coming. He looked up as the front door opened, and there she was, running to him. The last time he had seen her, she was crying at the kitchen table of their tiny little apartment as he walked out the back door into the rain. Just as he'd imagined, she started bawling now. "Hi, Momma, I'm home," he said and started crying, too.

The *Santa Fe* was moved to the repair yards while her crew dispersed to all parts of the country. Some less inclined to travel planned on staying in the Los Angeles area and seeing how many days out of thirty they could stay drunk before heading back to the war. A hotly debated topic was which two-year-old "lines" would still work on the girls.

Jim Hunter, who left the ship before the *Franklin* ordeal, was surprised to arrive in California to find that his old ship had beat him back after all. He wasn't the first from the Lucky Lady to hoist a cold beer.

Mike Hardy had every intention of pursuing his share of whiskey and women. But there was something he needed desperately before he could avail himself of either. Sleep. Locating a cheap hotel, he took a shower and crawled into bed, where he spent the first two days of his leave hibernating.

A number of men left the City of Angels knowing that they wouldn't be returning to the ship named after the City of Holy Faith. While in Pearl Harbor, Lt. Warren Harding received orders to report to Camp Peary in Williamsburg, Virginia, for temporary assignment. He was sad to leave the ship; she had been his home since 1943 and he felt blessed with a great crew, great captains, and great luck. But he was looking forward to shore duty and getting reacquainted with his wife, Jo; he had called her as soon as the ship got in and took the first train he could catch to San Francisco.

The fighting was probably over for him, although it might drag on for many months and even years the way the Japanese insisted on fighting to the last man. But he had been onboard ships on convoy duty since before the war "officially" started, and he would probably not get sea duty again, unless things took a turn for the worse. Sooner or later, the killing would end, and he would get out of the Navy and go into banking like his father. He and Jo would start a family, the war would fade and be forgotten, and everything would be as it had been before December 7, 1941.

The first inkling that it might not be as easy as all that was on the train that evening. He had entered the dining car to grab a bite to eat when two middle-aged businessmen noted the uniform and invited him to sit with them. They were interested in where he had been and what it had been like "out there." They were just friendly and inquisitive, and at first he had answered their questions as best he could without revealing those things they had been warned to keep secret. However, after a little while, he began to feel uncomfortable.

Harding realized that for two years he had been living in another world, a world the two men could never fathom. He didn't have the words that could make them understand the terror of watching a blazing kamikaze making a run at the ship. Or how the ocean could look more beautiful than he had ever seen it just a few hours after watching young Marines slaughtered on the beaches of Tarawa. Or how he felt watching the aircraft carrier *Chiyoda* sink and leaving all those men in the darkening ocean to die. Or the passions that would cause young Americans to want to shoot helpless sailors as they bobbed in the sea off Saipan, and feeling glad that it was Japanese sailors in the water and not the crew of the *Santa Fe*. There was no explaining these things, so he smiled and answered in generalities as best he could.

The feeling of being out of place continued after he was reunited with Jo, and they left to visit his folks in Walnut Creek. Jo's letters had always reflected a country united against the threat of Germany and Japan. Once, after the *Santa Fe* sailed and she had returned to the University of California–Berkeley to resume her studies, she told him how officials from some of the local fruit canneries in the South Bay area had showed up on campus begging students to help them get the pear harvest canned. The men who made up their usual workforce had gone into the service, and there was a danger that the harvest would rot. She and other students had loaded up on streetcars and rode to the canneries; yes, they were paid, but more than that, there was a feeling of being in it together, helping each other get through it.

After graduation, Jo had gone to work for a paint and asbestos manufacturing company. But every Saturday she volunteered with the Red Cross at a San Francisco hospital. All over the country, women had joined the workforce—Rosie the Riveter—building ships, planes, tanks. Sure it was a job, but they also knew that the harder they worked and the better they made the weapons of war, the sooner their men would come home. In their letters to their husbands, boyfriends, and sons, they tried to hide their fears and let them know that a home, and their love, would be waiting when they returned. There were plenty of "Dear John" letters, but more still from those girlfriends who promised to wait.

They collected metal and paper and had bake sales for the war effort; they rolled bandages and served coffee at the local USO facilities. Towns and cities competed to raise enough money in war bonds to "build an aircraft carrier." The people of the United States did not know it, but they were what Admiral Yamamoto had feared more than their weapons.

Jo often went to a theatre on Market Street in San Francisco that showed newsreels day and night of the fighting. The flickering black-and-white images from the Pacific were often accompanied by grim news, especially in the early days of the conflict. She would tell herself that if her husband had to be in a war, it was better that he was on a ship than some contested beach. The illusion of his safety was harder to maintain when the images of the kamikazes began hurtling across the screen—planes on fire, crashing down into ships as men ran for their lives, any one of whom could have been her husband. She was afraid, but she wrote to him about her job and the changing seasons around the bay, and about how much she missed him, and the life they would have again someday.

In Walnut Creek, Warren noticed that everyone talked about the shortages, and he realized again that there would never be a way to tell them about the real sacrifices young men were making a long way from home. There were no shortages of bullets or bombs in the western Pacific; the Japanese were said to be short of gasoline, but they seemed to have plenty to fill up the bellies of their suicide planes.

Yet, he also came to understand that when they talked about shortages, his wife and parents and friends weren't complaining. They were trying to tell him that they were doing their part, and doing it gladly, for him and the other young men. He knew that what he had been doing was important, and that he would probably never do anything as important again.

After his leave was up, Warren and Jo lived briefly in Virginia, and from there he was assigned to the University of New Mexico in Albuquerque, where he taught Navy ROTC. Life did seem to be returning to normal. They had rented a nice little home near the campus and they were even talking about starting a family.

One morning in July, just at dawn, he was walking to the men's dormitory to wake the cadets for their morning run when he happened to look to the south. In that instant, there was a flash of brilliant white light, more intense than the arrival of the sun. The only explanation he could think of was that a plane had gone down south of the town. The next day, Harding read a story in the Albuquerque newspaper that other people had reported seeing the flash too. A spokesman for the military attributed it to a plane crash.

The answer satisfied Harding, and he thought no more about it until he was reading another newspaper in August that spoke of a brilliant white light that rivaled the sun exploding over the southern Japanese city of Hiroshima.

Many years later, historical revisionists would argue that there was no need to drop atomic weapons on Japan; that the Japanese leaders, including the military leadership in de facto control, were prepared to surrender on the condition that the emperor retain his throne.

Nothing could be further from the truth. Ever since the loss of the Philippines, when it became clear that an invasion of the home islands was inevitable, the Japanese military had been preparing its forces, as well as the civilian population, for national suicide. This, they declared, was *Honto Kessen*, a holy war.

In the summer of 1945, there was a new war minister, but General Korechika Anami fiercely defended the need to continue fighting. The Japanese were still a formidable foe. The Imperial Japanese Army had 2,350,000 troops in the home islands, every one of them sworn to give his life for the Emperor. A similar number of soldiers were in China, waiting for a way to be devised to bring them home for the defense.

The generals boasted of having another army as well, 10 million strong. In July, the army decreed that there were no more civilians in Japan. Every man, woman, and child was a soldier of the emperor. Old men, cripples, women, boys and girls began training, usually with nothing more than sharpened sticks. They were told that they could strike a blow in the holy war by running into a group of American soldiers with a hand grenade, or strapping an explosive satchel to their bodies and throwing themselves beneath a tank. If they could each kill one American before dying, that would be enough. Or, better yet, stab one in the stomach so that another soldier would have to assist him, thus taking two out of the fight.

The Japanese fleet was no more. But if there was any doubt about the navy's intentions, Admiral Onishi, the creator of the kamikaze movement, was placed in charge of all naval air forces in Japan. As of July, there were nearly four hundred "special attack" squadrons, navy and army, based in Japan with four thousand planes and an industry still producing two thousand more a month. More than 6,000 pilots were ready to crash into ships and another 2,500 were in training.

The kamikazes were not just in the air. Six thousand small boats, powered by car engines and carrying two-ton explosive charges, were hidden all along the Japanese coast.

All the pilots, all of the boat crews, prepared to give their lives for the emperor.

Cpl. Fred "Andy" Anderson's return to the States started well and only got better. One day after leaving Pearl Harbor, he was told by a sergeant to take a few of the men and clean the warrant officers' quarters. He was down on his hands and knees in a corner, using a whisk broom to reach beneath a locker when a roll of cash popped out.

A twenty-dollar bill was wrapped around the outside, a ten was inside of that, and the rest was made up of two-dollar bills. The windfall totaled sixty-eight dollars, a fortune to a low-ranking Marine. The roll was covered with a couple years of dust and cobwebs and obviously forgotten by its owner, who had probably long since been transferred, but he still felt a little guilty sticking it in his pants pocket. After the ship arrived in Long Beach, he used the money to buy the dress blue uniform he had always wanted.

When his leave was up, Anderson returned to the ship only to learn that he had been reassigned to Saint Simon's Island, Georgia, as a guard at the naval air station there. He hated to leave the ship, but the good news was that he was being given another thirty days of leave, plus ten days traveling time, before he had to report.

Anderson went back to Tennessee with his friend "Whit" Whitby, who had recovered from his burns suffered when the suicide plane crashed, splashing flaming gasoline on him. While in Memphis, Anderson's friend Juanita invited him and Whitby to Hohenwald for a double-date. She was married, but she had another friend in mind for Whitby and thought Anderson might again enjoy the company of her first cousin, Leta Thompson. He remembered Leta as the young teenager he had met just before going into the service and from the letters she had written while he was away.

The idea sounded like fun and the two Marines were soon off to Hohenwald. When they arrived, they learned that Leta would be arriving on a bus from Nashville and went to wait for her at the corner drugstore where the bus would pull up.

Leta was now seventeen and had graduated from high school early. She worked for the Tennessee Department of Health as a secretary for an entomologist. Living in a country that was fighting a war was pretty much all she had known as a teenager. Paper drives to raise money for the war effort, double- and triple-dating because of gasoline rationing, and "doing without" were what was normal. The worst part was that all the "best" young men her age were gone; the only males left were too young, too elderly, or they were "unfit for military duty," and she figured that if the services didn't want them, neither did she. So a date with a real live Marine, even if he was a little old at twenty-five years, sounded like fun.

The bus arrived from Nashville, and Anderson walked out of the drugstore expecting to see the skinny teenager he remembered. Instead, a beautiful young lady stepped off the bus, and in that moment, he knew he had found the woman he wanted to marry. They dated for that month—she stayed with friends and relatives when she came to visit him in Memphis, including the first plane flight of her life, which cost the exorbitant amount of eleven dollars. Before he had to leave for Saint Simon's, he asked if she would marry him when the war was over and gave her an engagement ring.

Soon Anderson left for Georgia, and Leta stayed in Nashville. When he got to Saint Simon's he was glad they had waited to get married. Every day more Marines were being reassigned from Saint Simon's to the training base at New River, North Carolina. The scuttlebutt was that they were being prepared for the invasion of Japan, and the Corps was going to need every warm body it could get its hands on.

Some of the guys in the barracks reacted to their new orders by swearing they wouldn't go. Landing in Japan was going to be worse than Iwo Jima and Okinawa combined. It was suicide, they said. Soon word began filtering back to the men who remained at Saint Simon's that deserters were jumping off the trains on the way to North Carolina and going AWOL. They were going to need to be replaced, and Anderson figured that it was just a matter of time before he had to go.

There was no sense marrying Leta if all it meant was that in a few months she would be a widow. He had never told her about the worst aspects of the war; it wasn't something a young woman needed to hear.

Heck, he was a grown man, and he was still having trouble getting over one of the things he had seen the day after the *Franklin* was hit. The *Santa Fe* had circled around behind the carrier and was crossing its wake when he began to see bodies in the water. They wore the khaki uniforms of officers and the blue dungarees of sailors, their arms out stiffly to the side as they floated past like so many crucifixes on the water. He realized that they were the dead from the *Franklin* and were being dumped over the side of the ship without being sewn into weighted canvas bags. He guessed that there were probably too many for the crew to deal with; still, it disturbed him that they were not given a proper burial at sea.

It wasn't something he could tell Leta about, not with the prospect of him going away to die. But the more he thought about what might happen, the more he knew that if a few months was all he had left, then he wanted to spend them with her. He would ask, and if she accepted, they would take their chances.

Leta said yes and took a bus to Brunswick, the little town outside of the naval air station, arriving on the heels of stunning news. The United States had developed some sort of super bomb and had dropped two of them, each supposedly destroying an entire Japanese city.

Apparently, there was reason to hope that the Japanese would have finally had enough and the war would end. Leta Thompson might not have to be a seventeen-year-old widow after all. On August 11, 1945, five days after the obliteration of Hiroshima and Nagasaki, Cpl. Fred "Andy" Anderson, resplendent in his new uniform, and Leta Thompson, wearing a pretty blue suit, were married at a friend's house with the future still unsettled.

On July 30, the Japanese proved they were still capable of striking blows where the Americans did not expect them. That night, a Japanese submarine torpedoed and sank the heavy cruiser USS *Indianapolis* between the Marianas Islands and the Philippines. Three hundred men died in the initial explosion; nine hundred went into the water. The ship was not reported missing and the survivors were not spotted for almost five days; only 321 survived the sharks and the sea.

Before she crossed paths with the submarine, the *Indianapolis* had stopped off at the island of Tinian and delivered a top secret weapon—the atomic bomb—which was dropped on Hiroshima on August 6, killing 61,000 and injuring 19,000. Three days later, another atomic bomb was dropped on Nagasaki, killing 140,000.

But even the atomic bombs did not convince the Japanese military that it was time to give up. Three of the Japanese Supreme Council—Prime Minister Kantaro Suziki, Foreign Minister Shigemori Togo, and Admiral Mitsumasa Yonai—two of them civilians and therefore lacking any real power, favored peace at any cost. However, the other half of the council—the minister of war, General Anami; the army chief of staff, General Yoshijiro Umezu; and Admiral Soemu Toyoda, the navy chief of staff—wanted to fight on.

Japan, they said, was a fortress. A new Imperial Palace had been built in the mountains of northern Honshu. Food and weapons, even planes, were being secreted in caves. Aircraft from the manufacturing plants were being shipped to northern airfields, out of reach of the enemy. They could fight on for years until the Americans tired.

Those who favored war argued that the atomic weapons were no worse than anything else the Americans had been able to do. One bomb or a hundred bombs, what was the difference? The Japanese people could endure any hardship, and the Americans would have to invade to defeat them. But when they were within striking distance, the armies of Japan—soldiers and civilians—would rise up and aided by the kamikazes win the elusive decisive victory. The "soft" American public would clamor for peace.

The Japanese military could then negotiate the terms they would accept: The emperor would remain in power; Japan would conduct its own disarmament, leaving a defensive force intact, in which the admirals and generals would still retain their positions; any accusations of war crimes—such as the use of biological and chemical weapons against civilians in China, or the treatment of prisoners of war—would be weighed by Japanese courts; and any occupation by foreign troops would be short and perfunctory.

With the supreme council evenly split, they turned to Emperor Hirohito, who throughout the war was rarely consulted for his opinion. For one of the few times in his life, the emperor actually ruled and said it was time for the war to stop. With what they considered the ultimate arbiter having decided in their favor, the council members who favored peace notified the

Americans that they would surrender unconditionally, except for the matter of the emperor remaining on the throne.

But even then it was not over.

The crew's action during the *Franklin* rescue had earned them a Navy Unit Commendation "for exceptionally meritorious service," and there were a number of individual awards related to the event. Captain Fitz received the Navy Cross; Raymond Hilly, Joe Mosso, and Jack Kemp all received the Silver Star for diving into the water to rescue drowning or injured men; several Bronze Medals for valor were given, including one to the communications division officer, Lt. Norm Utecht.

Later, Lt. (j.g.) James R. Shannon, the ship's radio division officer under Utecht and one of Chief Warrant Officer Donald Jackson's direct superiors, told Charlotte Jackson that her new husband had been recommended for the Silver Star for his efforts in retrieving the transceiver that had been so instrumental in establishing ship-to-ship communications so that the *Franklin* could escape from Japanese waters. When she complained later to her husband that no medal had been awarded, he waved it off. "There were a lot of heroes that day, I wasn't one of them," he said. "I was just doing my job."

The way he looked at it, he'd received the only award he cared about back in April, when the letter from Charlotte Gates was waiting when the *Santa Fe* pulled into Pearl Harbor. Twenty-millimeter machine guns going off next to his bunk while he was sleeping wouldn't have made him as nervous as he was opening the V-mail.

He was reasonably sure that she cared for him, but he had no confidence that she would agree to get married with the war still going and his future uncertain. Still, it seemed to him that a precedent of sorts had been set. His best friend, Earl Watts, the fellow Iowan who had served on the battleship USS *Mississippi* prior to and at the beginning of the war with him, had married Charlotte's sister, Peggy, on the spur of the moment the previous August. Earl and Peggy had spent a quick wedding night in a motel, then he had to leave in the early morning hours to report back to his ship, which had deployed to the western Pacific.

Jackson reasoned that at least he would have time for a decent honeymoon when the *Santa Fe* got back to the States. Like the others, he would have thirty days leave, and the ship was scheduled to be undergoing repairs and overhaul for forty-five days. Still, as soon as the cruiser was ready, they'd be heading right back to the front for another two years, or however long it took to defeat Japan. A lot of time had passed since he last saw Charlotte in December 1943; they had seemed to care a lot for each other then, but things might have changed. Carefully, he opened the letter. *Dear Don* . . . uh-oh . . . *Of course, I'll marry you* . . . A whole squadron of kamikazes could not have dampened the rest of his day, though the trip to California seemed to last forever.

Jackson wasted little time once the *Santa Fe* docked at Terminal Island. There were a few things he had to do on the ship, as new radar was going to be added. But as soon as he was able, he rushed into Long Beach and for $125 picked up a diamond engagement ring and matching wedding band. Then he caught a plane to San Francisco, where Charlotte was a student in nurses' training at Saint Luke's Hospital.

Charlotte had had little time for dating. She was too busy working eight hours a day, six days a week, plus attending classes before and after her shifts. She was in the government's Nurse Cadet Corps—a program that paid for her schooling and gave her a small stipend in exchange for military service after she graduated.

She had never really been interested in anybody but Don Jackson. She remembered going into his room at her parent's home the night he had typed up the paper for her teacher so that she could go to the prom. She thought he was so cute then with his curly, dark hair and deep brown eyes. His letters were always warm and caring, though somewhat reserved, as he was uncomfortable with what he considered "private matters" being reviewed by the wartime censors. There was a stability and strength to his character.

When Charlotte wrote to Don and said she would marry him, she wasn't worried about what might happen in the future. The war had been a fact of life since she was in high school, it didn't mean she had to stop living. The only complaint she had about "doing without," was that some people did without more than others. As a nursing cadet she had to turn over her meat rations card to the hospital, which turned around and used them to make sure the male interns had plenty of steak. Smelling the aroma and hearing the sound of meat sizzling from the doctors' dining room—now *that* she and the other nurse cadets resented.

When Don Jackson wrote asking her if she would marry him, she wasn't really expecting the question. There might have been some subtle hints that it would be coming. He had told her that he always kept her ring on a chain around his neck, and he had given her the hope chest for Christmas. Once, before he had left to join the *Santa Fe* in 1943, he had mentioned that maybe when the war was over they might consider getting married. But he had never said a thing about it since . . . didn't matter, she loved him too, and she was happy he had asked.

Jackson arrived and took her for their engagement to the Saint Francis Hotel. They planned on celebrating with a bottle of champagne, but none was available on that day. The nation was in mourning, President Roosevelt had died.

The president's death shocked Jackson. He didn't know Roosevelt was in poor health. Thinking about the man and what he had meant to a frightened country brought back memories of December 8, 1941, and standing in the radio room aboard the *Mississippi,* listening to the president's speech as the battleship sailed from Iceland and headed west into the storm. It seemed so long ago, another lifetime really.

"Always will we remember the character of the onslaught against us. No matter how long it may take us to overcome this premeditated invasion, the American people in their righteous might will win through to absolute victory."

Ninety days and he would have been out of the Navy, preparing to pursue his dream of a college education, the first of a long line of farmers to aspire to such a thing. He had laid his life out like stepping stones across a river, but the rising tide of war had swept them under.

"I believe I interpret the will of the Congress and of the people when I assert that we will not only defend ourselves to the uttermost but will make very certain that this form of treachery shall never endanger us again."

Jackson recalled the anger and resolve in Roosevelt's voice, speaking for a nation that had been overwhelmingly opposed to going to war until the Japanese treachery persuaded them about the reality of the threat. It seemed now that Roosevelt had taken them to a hilltop where they could see the end of the road in the distance. But how deep and dark was the valley between was anybody's guess, and now other men would have to step forward.

It was a sad day, but also a happy one for Don and Charlotte. After all, their getting married at this point in time was an affirmation that they believed the valley would be crossed and they would find a life on the other side. So the young couple toasted their engagement that night with beer, and outside the hospital he slipped the engagement ring on her finger.

Eight days later, on April 22, 1945, Donald Clyde Jackson Jr. and Charlotte Grace Gates were married in the chapel at Stanford University. He was as handsome as any movie star in his Navy uniform, and there wasn't a woman on Earth more beautiful than she was in her white bridal gown. At lesat, that's how they saw each other.

They spent the first part of their honeymoon in Carmel-by-the-Sea and Monterrey, and then took a flight back to Iowa to see relatives. It was over all too soon. He had to return to his ship, and she to her training.

Time was such a precious commodity to a generation that had so little of it to spare. Fortunately, there was more time on weekends for young couples, especially when it was announced that the *Santa Fe* would not be leaving until mid-July. It was taking longer than anticipated to get her ready and with good reason. She had logged 221,750 miles and her tour had been the war's longest for any major naval unit. During that time, she had participated in forty-two air strikes, twelve shore bombardments, sunk seven ships, and officially knocked down seven planes, though there were plenty more sent to the sea in flames with holes from the *Santa Fe's* guns in them.

The ship's boilers were in sad shape and the big guns needed to have their barrels replaced. The biggest surprise, however, was when the ship was placed in drydock and the repair crews saw that the armor plating up near her bow had been partly buckled by a torpedo. The spot where the torpedo struck was just outside of the gunpowder magazines for the six-inch guns on the deck above. If the torpedo had detonated, the secondary blast would have torn the ship apart.

Part of the holdup of the ship returning to the fleet was due to yet another misadventure for Admiral William "Bull" Halsey. On June 5, 1945, he had once again ignored warnings that he was taking the Third Fleet into another typhoon.

This time only a dozen or so men lost their lives, but several carriers were damaged, and more planes were destroyed than in the December 1944 storm. Halsey said it was his aerographers' fault, but another court of inquiry placed the preponderance of blame on him and Task Force 38 commander, Admiral McCain. This second typhoon almost ruined Halsey's career, but again Admirals Nimitz and King felt that Halsey was still such a national hero that punishing him "would be contrary to the national interest."

One of the sidelights of the storm was that it ripped the bow off the heavy cruiser *Pittsburgh,* the ship that had towed the *Franklin* out of danger. The impact on the *Santa Fe* was that the shipyard workers were told to strengthen the bow of the light cruiser, adding to the time in the repair yards.

When the *Santa Fe* was at last ready to begin its sea trials before departing, the crew noticed the addition of more antiaircraft 40-millimeters, and those who were in the know, like Jackson, were also aware that improvements had been made to the radar. All of it inspired by the escalating danger from the kamikazes.

After the *Franklin* was hit, the American naval strategists wondered if the Japanese were changing tactics again, away from the suicide planes. During the five months preceding the attack on the *Franklin,* the Japanese had been increasingly relying on kamikazes; in fact, all known damage to U.S. ships during that period had been caused by planes crashing into them. But beginning with the plane that dropped the two bombs with such devastating results, and then the two subsequent attacks, each was a conventional attack. The carriers *Essex* and *Wasp* had also been struck by conventional attacks that night.

Any thought, however, that the Japanese had given up on the kamikaze attacks was dispelled with the invasion of Okinawa. In fact, the suicidal tactics reached new levels of ferocity.

On April 1, even as the *Santa Fe* and *Franklin* were sailing across the International Dateline toward Hawaii, an American armada of seventeen hundred ships containing more than five hundred thousand men arrived off Okinawa, a Japanese island 350 miles south of Kyushu. The Japanese strategy was simple—kill as many American soldiers, sailors, and Marines as possible before dying, and attack the Third Fleet with wave after wave of kamikazes. The whole premise was that the more American soldiers and sailors who died, and the more of their ships that were sunk, the fewer there would be to invade Japan.

As usual, Japanese losses were astronomical. Nearly all of the hundred-thousand-man garrison on Okinawa were killed, many in massed banzai charges. Some died on individual suicide missions, swimming out to the ships offshore and climbing up the anchor chains to attack the crews with swords and grenades.

The kamikaze attacks epitomized the insanity of the moment. Instead of attacking with a few planes, or even a dozen at a time, they swarmed by the hundreds to overwhelm the combat air patrols and ships' defenses. Before it was over, nearly twelve hundred kamikaze pilots had died.

Then on April 6, the Japanese high command came up with the grandest suicidal gesture of all; the battleship *Yamato* was sent on a one-way trip to Okinawa. The ship and her crew were supposed to blast their way through the American fleet and then ground the *Yamato* on a beach, where she would then become a land fortress. The idea was ridiculous. The ship and her accompanying destroyers and cruisers didn't make it halfway before they were set upon by approximately four hundred American planes. Less than two hours later, the most powerful ship ever built, and all but two of her escorts, were on the bottom of the ocean and more than four thousand Japanese officers and sailors were dead or soon would be. Except for its air corps and submarines, the Japanese Imperial Navy no longer existed.

The most horrifying of the casualties was the death of more than a hundred thousand Okinawan civilians. Some fell to American fire, including boys forced into the trenches by Japanese troops, but most either committed suicide or were killed by family members to prevent their falling into the hands of the Americans. The Japanese troops had assured them that Americans would torture any survivors and rape the women. The Japanese predilection toward suicide had taken a cynical twist.

Meanwhile, the Japanese strategy to inflict as much harm as possible on the Americans had succeeded. American ground forces suffered forty-eight thousand casualties, of which twelve thousand died. Out at sea, the kamikazes sank three light aircraft carriers and eighteen destroyers, damaging another sixty ships enough to put them out of the war for more than a month. Nearly two thousand officers and sailors were killed.

Although the details of the casualties at Okinawa were not yet public knowledge, the crew of the *Santa Fe* knew that the fight was a bloody one. This should have been a time of relief: Germany had surrendered in May and the entire Allied effort could now be focused on Japan. Indeed, troops were quickly being recalled from Europe to prepare for the Pacific. But those who had been fighting the Japanese for years, like the cruiser's crew, knew that the invasion of Japan would be far worse than anyone could imagine. At least the Germans surrendered when the fight was hopeless. Many of the letters the crew wrote home in the days leading to the ship's leaving Long Beach reflected the likelihood that this time they wouldn't be coming back.

Yet, they weren't jumping ship. The *Santa Fe* had thirteen battle stars— one for each major engagement, and there weren't many ships with more— and all without losing a man. If battle star number fourteen was going to be the hardest earned, then they owed it to each other and the Lucky Lady to see it through to the end.

The *Santa Fe* returned to Pearl Harbor on August 1, 1945 and was still in port when news broke of the "secret weapon" that had leveled two

Japanese cities. But there was no reason to believe that anything had changed; Tokyo had been burned to the ground in March and that hadn't stopped the fighting. On August 12, the cruiser sailed with the aircraft carrier USS *Antietam* and cruiser *Birmingham* to attack Wake Island. The poor *Birmingham* just couldn't stay out of trouble—she had just been undergoing repairs at Pearl Harbor after being hit for a third time, the latest by a kamikaze off Okinawa that had plunged through her weather deck and into her sick bay, killing a dozen more men.

Three days after sailing from the waters of Pearl Harbor, where fuel oil still leaked from the submerged hull of the *Arizona,* the men in Radio Two were the first on the *Santa Fe* to hear the stunning news. The Japanese had surrendered, the war was over. No one knew, not many people ever would, how close the Japanese military came to making sure the war would continue.

Hearing that the emperor had decided on surrender and planned to address the nation, certain factions within the Japanese army attempted to stage a coup with the tacit, and sometime outright, support of the pro-war members of the council and military. Some showed up at Prime Minister Kantaro Suziki's house, blasting it with machine guns and setting it on fire when they learned he had fled. A news release was given to the radio stations saying that the Imperial Army would continue to fight.

The most brazen act was an attempt by junior officers to capture the emperor and force him to reconsider. If they had captured or even killed Hirohito, the war would have go on. They came within a couple hundred feet of their objective before they were stopped by the Imperial Guard and forced to surrender.

One of the rebels was Lt. Col. Masahiko Takeshita, brother-in-law of war minister Anami, who would later write,

> It would be useless for the people to survive the war if the structure of the State itself were to be destroyed.
>
> Although a coup d' etat would mean temporary disobedience to the present Emperor . . . to act in compliance with the wishes of his Imperial Ancestors would constitute a wider and truer loyalty to the throne in the final analysis. Even if the whole Japanese race were all but wiped out, its determination to preserve the national policy would be forever recorded in the annals of history.

We decided that the peace faction should be overruled and a coup d'etat staged in order to prevail upon the Emperor to revoke his decision. The purpose of the project coup d'etat was to separate the Emperor from his peace-seeking advisers and persuade him to change his mind and continue the war. All we wanted was a military government with all political power concentrated in the hands of the war minister.

On August 15, 1945, the voice of the emperor was heard on radio for the first time. Even then, he never mentioned the word "surrender"; instead, the message was a confusing monologue about the war having taken a turn for the worse, and it was time for the Japanese people to accept "enduring the unendurable."

Not everyone accepted the emperor's decree. One admiral took off with eleven kamikaze pilots, saying he intended to dive on the American fleet at Okinawa. They were never seen nor heard from again.

That night, Admiral Onishi, who had sent so many others off to their deaths, took his sword and slit open his belly. He then tried to cut his own throat but was not successful. He wasn't discovered until the next morning, still alive but refusing assistance; he died that evening.

Onishi's legacy was 35 American ships sunk and another 368 damaged; four thousand nine hundred American officers and enlisted men were killed in the suicide attacks, and a similar number had been wounded. To accomplish this, three thousand kamikaze pilots had died.

Many more on both sides would have died than were killed at Hiroshima and Nagasaki if the war had continued. American strategists were predicting between five hundred thousand and one million U.S. and Allied casualties and ten times that number of Japanese, including civilians. An invasion of Japan would have been the greatest slaughter of human life in history.

On September 2, 1945, the Japanese officially surrendered aboard the USS *Missouri* in Tokyo Bay. Farther south, the *Santa Fe* and her sister ships in CruDiv13 were assigned to help land troops for the occupation of the huge Japanese naval base at Sasebo.

Four weeks later the ship left, bound for the island of Honshu, but a typhoon suddenly charged in from the South China Sea. It was too late for the divine winds to blow the barbarians to a watery grave, but it did force the *Santa Fe* to take refuge in another Japanese port. Nagasaki.

Since the ship was delayed in port for a couple of days until the storm passed, Captain Fitz arranged for those members of the crew who wanted to see the effects of "the bomb" to get a tour.

Chief Warrant Officer Don Jackson decided to go out of curiosity. All they had been told was that the bomb was the most powerful weapon ever designed, but nothing about radiation or how the bomb worked. At the pier the sightseeing crewmembers were loaded aboard Army trucks and told that under no circumstances were they to get down.

Nothing in his experience had prepared Jackson for the site of a city that was simply . . . missing. Few buildings were still standing, the rest looked like someone had come along with a giant broom and simply swept it all away. Steel girders were melted like sticks of butter on a stove, and everything looked as gray and lifeless as the surface of the moon.

He felt sorry for the people who had lived there. Those who had somehow survived walked about as if in a daze, their faces ravaged as though from some loathsome disease. They had been led down a ruinous path by their leaders—the sort of men who could put poorly trained teenagers into airplanes and convince them that killing themselves by crashing into ships would somehow get them into the Japanese version of heaven. Those leaders, of course, never led by example, at least not until it was all over and they cut themselves open or took poison, as Hitler was reputed to have done.

Still, Jackson had no regrets that the bombs had been dropped. Maybe he and many other Americans, and Japanese for that matter, were alive because of it. The Japanese had been the aggressor in the war—not just against the United States, but in China and throughout the Pacific.

What had happened to Nagasaki was horrible. But the people in the ruined city had no more right to live than had his cousin Robert Jackson, or friends Wilbur Ellis and Tommy Savin, all of them killed aboard the USS *Arizona* on December 7, 1941. Some might argue that the men killed at Pearl Harbor were a military target and the Japanese cities filled with only innocent civilians, but Robert, Wilbur, and Tommy weren't at war when they were killed without warning. They were members of a peacetime Navy, looking forward to a sleepy Sunday in Hawaii. And his friend Devere Knight had never hurt anyone in his life—never owned much of anything, except his dreams of a brighter future—but he had been killed by a sniper six thousand miles from the cornfields of Iowa.

War was hell. In Nagasaki it even looked like it. But maybe the sheer awesome horror of the ruined city would be enough to, as Roosevelt had once said, *"make very certain that this form of treachery shall never endanger us again."*

Jackson hoped so. He wanted to go back home and find that the waters of war had receded and that the stepping-stones across the river were rising above the tide again. Go to college, have a career, start a family with the woman he loved, and hope that his children never had to go through what his generation had endured.

That evening when he got back to the Lucky Lady, the memory of Nagasaki still fresh in his mind, Jackson opened the small safe in his compartment and took out an envelope. When the ship left Long Beach, his bride, Charlotte, couldn't get off work to see him leave. But the last night they were together, she gave him something to remember her by—a lock of hair about as thick as a finger and the color of clover honey. When he had moments alone as the ship crossed the ocean to what he had thought was going to be the final battle with Japan, he had taken the envelope's contents out to remember the feel of her hair and catch the scent of her perfume. Thus armed, he'd gone back to war.

Returning from the ruined city of Nagasaki, he lifted the lock of hair from the envelope and held it against his cheek with his eyes closed. He had been a lucky man. Lucky he wasn't granted his wish to be stationed in China before the war, or transferred to the *Arizona* or, later, to the *Indianapolis*—an assignment he'd coveted. Lucky his ship wasn't in Pearl Harbor. Lucky to have been on the Lucky Lady. Lucky that two bombs ended the war before the last battle. And lucky to have met Charlotte, an encounter he realized would have never happened had it not been for the war.

All things considered, he felt lucky just to be alive.

A FINAL NOTE TO READERS

September 11, 2002

A year ago, suicidal fanatics climbed aboard airplanes and crashed them into the World Trade Center buildings in New York City, the Pentagon and—thanks to the bravery of some fellow Americans— a field in western Pennsylvania. The killers were, of course, convinced by others that their acts of cold-blooded murder furthered some holy cause and would earn them a blissful afterlife.

The method of their criminal act was not lost on the men and and women with whom I sat in a hospitality room of a hotel in Norfolk, Virginia nine days later, on September 20, 2001, watching the television as President Bush addressed a frightened and grieving nation.

"Tonight we are a country awakened to danger and called to defend freedom. Our grief has turned to anger, and anger to resolution. Whether we bring our enemies to justice, or bring justice to our enemies, justice will be done."

I was attending the 55th annual reunion of the light cruiser USS *Santa Fe* with my father as part of my research for this book. On the morning of September 11, he had called when he learned that all airline flights had been grounded. He said he didn't know if planes would be flying when we were scheduled to leave for the reunion in a week, but if they were, "I'm going. Do you still want to go?" "Of course," I said. I already knew that he'd never allow cowards to dictate how he lived his life; how could I do any less?

"On September the eleventh, enemies of freedom committed an act of war against our country."

I looked for my father in the room as the president spoke and saw him surrounded by his former shipmates. Old men with not much in common really except that once, a long time ago, they were young men who gave up the flower of their youths to stop murderers and sociopaths who were determined to make the world believe and act as they wanted. I tried to judge the look on my father's face as he listened—there was certainly no fear, more a look of anger and resolve. I thought about how Bush's speech must be taking him back to that day so long ago in the radio room aboard the *Mississippi*.

*"Yesterday, December 7, 1941—a day that will live in infamy—the United
States of America was suddenly and deliberately attacked by naval and air forces
of the Empire of Japan."*

I thought, *We've seen this before. This is my generation's Pearl Harbor. But
will we be as up to the challenge as they were?* I wanted then to write this book
about the *Franklin* and *Santa Fe,* which had been started a year earlier, more
than ever. I wanted a book that said to my countrymen, "Have faith. Have
courage. There were once darker days than these, but we pulled together
as a people and came through them stronger than before. It will be all right."

*"Americans have known wars—but for the past 136 years, they have been wars
on foreign soil, except for one Sunday in 1941."*

I appreciated the president voicing the defiance and anger I felt that night,
as my father once appreciated Roosevelt speaking for him. Even more, I
appreciated how that morning at a memorial service aboard the old battleship USS *Wisconsin* for their shipmates who'd died in the past year, the men
of the *Santa Fe* and their wives, without prompting, began to sing. One voice
first, then another and another . . . *God Bless America, land that I love . . .*

Our unity in the face of a common threat is something our enemies have
never understood about us. They see the rancor of our politics, the parti-
san bickering, and the myriad beliefs of a diverse people and take it for weak-
ness, when in reality our differences are our source of strength.

They look at the affluence that hard work and inspiration have created,
and they believe us too attached to our creature comforts—that we are "soft."
It was a mistake the Japanese made on December 7, 1941; it was mistake
the terrorists made on September 11, 2001.

*"Americans have known the casualties of war—but not at the center of a great
city on a peaceful morning. Americans have known surprise attacks—but never
before on thousands of civilians. All of this was brought upon us in a single day—
and night fell on a different world, a world where freedom itself is under attack."*

The men and women in that room . . . they'd been labeled the Greatest
Generation. They were certainly one of the greatest, but they would get some
stiff competition from the generations of 1776 and 1862 and 1918. And
that's exactly the point: No matter how hard we fight, how much we sacrifice, there will always be evil in the world and each generation will be called
upon to stand up to it.

"I ask you to live your lives and hug your children. I know many citizens have fears tonight, and I ask you to be calm and resolute, even in the face of a continuing threat."

The World War II generation set a magnificent standard; it is up to us to try to live up to their steadfastness. However, we will also have to accept that there is only one way to wage war—with the same all-out determination that they fought theirs—and one acceptable result: unconditional surrender.

"I ask you to uphold the values of America, and remember why so many have come here. We are in a fight for our principles, and our first responsibility is to live by them."

If suicide bombers, the new kamikazes (the old at least had the courage to attack military targets capable of defending themselves) believe that the evil men who send them can then protect their families from repercussions, then we must send a message back: Nothing and no one you love is safe.

"The course of this conflict is not known, yet its outcome is certain. Freedom and fear, justice and cruelty, have always been at war, and we know that God is not neutral between them."

Those among us who argue that violence never solved anything, have never studied history: Sometimes violence is the only way to stop the violent. Shed our blood, consider us soft, believe that we do not have the stomach for the fight, and I would suggest to those who sponsor terrorists that they not only study the lessons of Tarawa, Saipan, and Iwo Jima, but also Tokyo, Hiroshima and Nagasaki. I would suggest that they recall the philosophy of George Santayana: "Those who do not learn from history are doomed to repeat it."

At the *Santa Fe* reunion, as I looked at those old faces and remembered what they did for us a half-century ago, I had one more thought for the men who planned the murders of September 11, 2001. It is the same truth Admiral Yamamoto realized even as he warned his comrades about our "terrible resolve." It is not our weapons the terrorists need to fear. It's the children and grandchildren of the men and women in that room.

"My fellow citizens we will meet violence with patient justice—assured of the rightness of our cause, and confident of the victories to come. In all that lies before us, may God grant us wisdom and may He watch over the United States of America."

Acknowledgments

I would like to express my heartfelt thanks to the men and women you've met on the pages of this book who shared their lives, memories, memoirs and diaries, dreams and nightmares with me: Mike Hardy. Al Mancini. Warren and Jo Harding. Jim Hunter. Fred and Leta Anderson. E. Robert Wassman. Ernest and Vivian Scott. Matthew Little. E. John Weil. Willard Gove. Edwin Garrison. Sam and Mimi Plonsky. Frank Turner. John Frajman. Stephen Nowak. Ben Ricks. Sam Rhodes. Without them, this book could not have been written.

However, my appreciation extends not only to those whose names and lives appear on these pages, but to many, many more who contributed in large or small part to the total picture. As lengthy as this book is, it could have been much longer if I had included every story of heroism and faith that I heard. Unfortunately, the constraints of time and space dictated that I had to pick and choose the stories I felt would well represent the backgrounds, experiences, and sacrifices of so many others.

Still, I would like to extend special thanks to a number of other heroes who contributed significantly to the book, but whose names don't appear, or but briefly, in the text. From the USS *Franklin:* Jim Erredge, James Stuart, John Blackwood, Robert Blanchard, Ed Driscoll, Robert Baines, Robert Tice, Gilbert Martin, Frances Maupin, John Vandegrift, Capt. Gary Schnurrpusch (ret). In particular, I wish to thank Robert St. Peters, the president of the *Franklin* association, and his compatriot Sgt. James Nilo (ret. USMC) for their assistance, memories, and permission to use their fine compilations in my research: *USS* Franklin *(CV-13): The Ship That Wouldn't Die* and *USS* Franklin *(CV-13) Original Documents 1943–1946*. I also wish to thank association board member Ray Bailey, for his memories, as well as assistance in securing U.S. Navy Archive photographs of two great fighting ships and the men who sailed them.

In 1987, a museum dedicated to the USS *Franklin*, CV-13, was established aboard the USS *Yorktown*, CV-10, which is permanently anchored in Charleston, South Carolina; the tattered battle flag hangs upon a bulkhead there. In truth, the men of the *Franklin* are still divided on their feelings toward Gehres and the 704 Club. To some, he is the captain who saved them and their ship, to others he is the ogre who unfairly branded them deserters and denied them what every sailor dreams of—sailing home aboard his ship.

However, the ties that bind those shipmates together are far stronger than old issues that once pulled them apart. They easily put aside their differences for a handshake and a hail fellow well met. As Matthew Little—who never did get to go to college, but he and his wife, Clara, made sure their three children did—told me at the 2001 *Franklin* reunion, "These men are my brothers."

I do have one disagreement with Ernest Scott, who tells schoolchildren that he was not a hero, but served on a ship full of them—Scotty, you belong in that pantheon of heroes as much as any man. Unfortunately, the war not only took lives, it stole years from some who did not have them to spare. Eddie Carlisle died of a heart attack at age twenty-five, leaving a wife and six-month-old son, who when he was an adult learned from Scotty that his father was "the best pal a guy ever had." In 1960, my uncle, Earl Watts, also died of a heart attack, leaving my aunt, Peggy, and his two young sons, Bob and Bill, and the best pal he ever had, my dad.

From the USS *Santa Fe* I wish to thank: John Shovlin, Dave Griffith, John Willis, Ken Harmet, Harold Hartmann, Jim Newgent, Richard Champagne, Frank Maye, Joe Flood, Edward McCorkle, George Lloyd, Bob Holden, Gerry Sultenfuss, and Jim and Adele Mitchell, who did the hard work of assembling the Action Reports and other documents pertinent to the *Santa Fe*.

To those named and unnamed on the pages of this book, I hope I have done you and your shipmates justice. Having met these men, it was no surprise to me—though I did not select them for this reason—that of those profiled in this book, all but one was married for at least fifty-five years. Neither was it a surprise to me that so many are still working, or in their retirement have devoted their energies to public service efforts.

One in particular, former fighter pilot Willard Gove, who retired in 1983 as a vice president at Honeywell, was honored in March 2002 by President Bush for his volunteer work that has ranged from helping the blind to providing housing for homeless refugees—those huddled masses, yearning for freedom.

"Will, I want to thank you for being someone who puts his heart and soul into making our community a better place," Bush told him at the start of a nationwide tour to promote volunteer service. "Someone who understands that you ought to love somebody just like you want to be loved yourself."

Gove said he does it out of gratitude that his life was spared during the war. He hasn't forgotten a promise he once made in a raft floating in the ocean, and still attends church every Sunday.

I am also deeply indebted to the "Sons of the Lucky Lady"—Arnold Harding and Bill Anderson, who read along behind me, offering invaluable observations, as well as editing. In that same light, I wish to thank Benilde Little, the author of the novel *Good Hair,* and James Shoemaker Jr. for insights regarding their fathers, as well as Jay O'Callahan, the nephew of "Father Joe" and a master storyteller whose fine works in the oral tradition include *Father Joe: A Hero's Journey,* for his own recollections, but also for the loan of his uncle's book.

This book does not exist without my publisher, Carroll &Graf. And I will never be able to repay executive editor Philip Turner and assistant editor Keith Wallman for their patience, enthusiasm for the book, and the quality of their work—all of which went beyond what any writer should expect.

As always, I am indebted to Michael Hamilburg, who is not only the best agent in the world but one of the truly nicest human beings I've ever met, and that goes as well for his consigliere, Joanie Kern. I also thank my lucky stars for the day I met my teacher Jon Franklin, who taught me the magic of non-fiction storytelling though it will irritate him to hear it described as magic.

I would be lost without the love and encouragement (and just enough flak to keep me honest) of my friends. Thanks for the mind-clearing beauty of Lake Powell and the companionship around campfires, thanks for Sunday afternoons at the football stadium, thanks for your music and dances, the mad potential, the "comfort food" on downer days, the emails and messages, the legal advice that was second to the friendship, thanks for the jujitsu, the laughs, even the tears—all usually when I needed them most.

My love and thanks to my brothers, Don, Todd, and John, and sisters, Carole, Mary, Dina, and Christa, my nephews, David, Robin and Michael, my niece, Jessica, as well as the other members of my extended family. A special thanks to my father-in-law Dick Torrisi and thanks to Pat Guiffra for the constancy of their love and support.

I would be worse than remiss not to acknowledge how very much my family and I have leaned on my mother-in-law Marie Torrisi. I believe the saying goes, "not blood of my blood, but certainly heart of my heart." We would have been lost without you.

Of course, those who had to put up with the worst of this process and yet were the most constant in their support of me were my wife, Carla, and daughters Mackenzie, Hannah, and Lillia. I am sorry that this book took so long and stole so much of our time, made daddy so stressed and crazy. You are proof that faith cannot only move mountains, it can also move an author past writer's block. To return to the sea imagery, you have been my sheltered harbor in the midst of the storm, and without you I would have foundered.

All this, of course brings me back to the two people I have most to thank for this book and my life: Don and Charlotte Jackson.

My father never got to pursue his dream of graduating from college; he stayed in the Navy for thirty years and took care of his family. I don't think he regretted it too much—with him it was always more about the knowledge, inspired by a toy electric motor he received as a child, than a diploma. Besides, the Navy let him play with some of the most sophisticated electronics ever devised; he retired in 1968 after his last transfer to Colorado Springs and the North American Air Defense Command.

Instead of college, Dad used part of the tuition money he'd been saving since 1937 to buy my mother, his lucky lady, a full-length ermine coat for their first wedding anniversary. As my mother mournfully points out, it is no longer politically correct to wear a fur coat, but it demonstrates the way his priorities have always been. His wife. His children. His country. He was complemented by the love of a woman who felt the same and sacrificed as much.

Like so many of their generation, my parents dreamed not for themselves, but for their children. The four children in my family knew from the day we first went to school that we would never have to worry about how to pay for a college education. In April, my parents celebrated their 57th wedding anniversary, and as my mother wrote to me while I was creating this book, "we are more in love today than we were 57 years ago, and will be more in love tomorrow than we are today. Love after this many years, is waking up in the night and knowing if he is not next to me in bed."

I was lucky to have two such wonderful people as my role models, though I fall woefully short of their standard. If I've said it once, and I have, I'll say it again: What I know of love, honor, truth, and sacrifice, I learned first from those two good people.

I wish all of you—my friends, my family, my countrymen—fair winds and a following sea.

Bibliography

In addition to hundreds of hours of conversations with the men of the
USS *Santa Fe* and the USS *Franklin,* as well as their wives, friends, and
associates, the author relied on the published and self-published works
of other authors both well-known and unknown while researching and writing this book.

The author is the first to acknowledge that *Lucky Lady* is purposely cen-
tered on what he terms "personal histories," some of which were written
down at the time and others penned nearly sixty years after the events they
describe, set against the backdrop of world history. At times, these personal
stories conflicted with one another or with the "official" account, or other
published histories of the war (though in several instances, the memoirs of
aged warriors were more accurate than either of the latter). The truth here
may not lie so much within the details as in the whole.

For a wider view of the last two years of naval warfare in the western
Pacific the author would refer his readers to the great works of Samuel Mor-
rison, Edwin P. Hoyt, Raymond Calhoun, and more recently David Kennedy.

Action Reports, Office of Naval Records and Library, Department of the Navy, Washington, D.C.

American Naval Fighting Ships, Naval History Division, Department of the Navy, Washington, D.C., 1976

Commodore Matthew Perry: American Black Ships in the Land of the Samurai by Rieko Shimizu, International English Center, University of Colorado-Boulder, July 2000

Danny Boy by Frederic Edward Weatherly, song, 1910.

Dictionary of American Naval Fighting Ships, Naval History Division, Department of the Navy, Washington, 1976

Divine Wind, The by Capt. Rihihei Inoguchi and Cmdr. Tadashi Nakajima with Roger Pineau, Greenwood Press Publishers, 88 Post Road West, Westport, CT 06881

Experiences of a Carrier Crewman, self-published by Jim Erredge, Zumbrota, Minnesota,

Father Joe: A Hero's Journey by Jay O'Callahan, audio tape, Artana Productions, P.O. Box 1054, Marshfield, MA 02050.

Freedom From Fear: The American People in Depression and War, 1929-1945 by David M. Kennedy, Oxford, May 2000.

I Was a Chaplain on the Franklin by Father Joseph T. O'Callahan, S.J., The Macmillan Company, New York, 1959

Kamikazes, The by Edwin P. Hoyt, Burford Books Inc., Short Hills, NJ 1983

History of United States Naval Operations in World War II by Samuel Eliot Morison, University of Illinois Press, 2001

Saving Seaman Stuart, The Story of a Boy and a Man Aboard the USS Franklin CV-13, self-published by Jim Stuart, Centerville, OH 45459.

Typhoon: The Other Enemy by Raymond Calhoun, U.S. Naval Institute Press, Annapolis, MD September 1981.

USS Franklin (CV-13) *Original Documents 1943-1946* compiled by Robert St. Peters and James Nilo, Turner Publishing Company, Paducah, Kentucky, 1996

USS Franklin (CV-13) *Original Documents 1943-1946*, The USS *Franklin CV-13* Museum Association Inc. and John Z. Kaczetow for the account of Cdr. Charles Howerton's experiences at Iwo Jima on July 4, 1944, Turner Publishing Company, Paducah, Kentucky, 1996.

USS Franklin (CV-13) *Original Documents 1943-1946, "Before the Colors Fade,"* by David Davidson, Turner Publishing Company, Paducah, Kentucky, 1996.

USS Franklin (CV-13) *The Ship That Wouldn't Die,* compiled by Robert St. Peters and James Nilo, Turner Publishing Company, Paducah, Kentucky, 1996

USS Santa Fe *Cruise Record: A Pictorial Record of a Light Cruiser During the War Years 1942-1945,* edited by Lt. (jg) Forrest W. Voss and Ensign Lewis A. Kremer, printed by Rogers Printing Company, Chicago and Dixon, Illinois.

World War II, published by SMITHMARK Publishers, a division of U.S. Media Holdings, Inc. 115 West 18th Street, New York, NY 10011

WEBSITES

CV-13 USS *Franklin,* www.NavyHistory.com

USS *Santa Fe* homepage, *http://santafe.paintrock.net*

Expansion in the Pacific, www.Smplanet.com

Commodore Matthew Perry: When We Landed in Japan, 1854, Modern History Sourcebook, compiled by Francis L. Hawks, www.Fordham.edu

Index